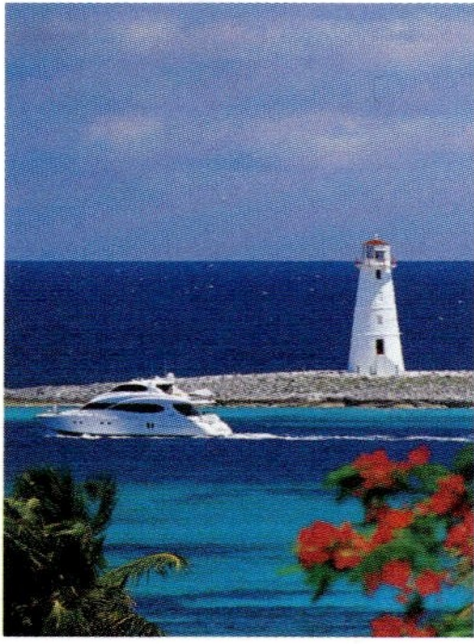

On the cover

A luxury yacht motors past the Paradise Island lighthouse at the entrance to Nassau Harbour. Photo by Roland Rose

Publisher
Etienne Dupuch Jr

Managing Editor
Dawn Lomer
Senior Editors
Ralph Deans, Gordon Lomer
Contributing Editor
Suzanne Twiston-Davies
Art Director
Jennifer O'Neill
Production Coordinator
Michelle Allen Ferguson

Etienne Dupuch Jr Publications Ltd
Oakes Field, PO Box N-7513, Nassau, The Bahamas
Tel (242) 323-5665 • Fax (242) 323-5728 • E-mail info@dupuch.com

ISBN 0-914755-80-3 (hardback)
ISBN 0-914755-79-x (softback)

ISSN 0067-2912

LINDA M HUBER/©DUPUCH

ISLANDS OF THE
Bahamas
UNITED STATES OF AMERICA
FLORIDA
Miami
Little Bahama Bank
Walker s Cay
Great Sale Cay
Cooper s Town
Rand Nature Centre
Lucayan National Park
McLean s Town
Green
West End
Treasure Cay
Eight Mile Rock
High Rock
Freeport
Lucaya
Peterson Cay National Park
ABACO
GRAND BAHAMA
MIAMI 105 miles
Moores Island
Gorda Cay (Castaway Cay)
Northwest Providence Channel
Sandy Point
Great Stirrup Cay
BIMINI
Great Harbour Cay
Alice Town
North Bimini
South Bimini
BERRY ISLANDS
Little Harbour Cay
MIAMI 185 miles
Cat Cay
Ocean Cay
Whale Cay
Chub Cay
Joulters Cays
Paradise Island
Nassau
Red Bays
Nicholl s Town
Lyford Cay
NEW PROVIDENCE
Great Bahama Bank
Fresh Creek
Andros Town
Cargill Creek
ANDROS
Moxey Town
Driggs Hill
Kemp s Bay
Tongue of the

N
North Atlantic Ocean
ELEUTHERA
Harbour Island
Gregory Town
Governor s Harbour
Tarpum Bay
Rock Sound
Deep Creek
Little San Salvador (Half Moon Cay)
Arthur s Town
CAT ISLAND
Smith s Bay
New Bight
Staniel Cay
Exuma Sound
Rudder Cut Cay
Rolleville
Moss Town
GREAT EXUMA
George Town
Little Exuma
Dixon Hill
Cockburn Town
SAN SALVADOR
CONCEPTION ISLAND
Conception Island National Park
RUM CAY
Port Nelson
Stella Maris
Simms
LONG ISLAND
Deadman s Cay
Clarence Town
SAMANA CAY
Jumentos Cays
RAGGED ISLAND
Duncan Town
Crooked Island Passage
CROOKED ISLAND
Colonel Hill
Chesters
Plana Cay
MAYAGUANA
Betsy Bay
Abraham s Bay
Delectable Bay
ACKLINS ISLAND
Mira-Por-Vos Passage
LITTLE INAGUA
Inagua National Park
Union Creek National Reserve
GREAT INAGUA
Matthew Town

8 LINDA M HUBER/©DUPUCH

contents

Photo gallery

8 **Bahamian scenes**
Colourful perspectives of the islands

Features

49 **Sir Sidney Poitier – son of the soil**
A troubled Out Island boy becomes a Hollywood legend

61 **Jewish community in The Bahamas**
Roots date back to the arrival of Christopher Columbus

73 **Bahamas conjures the muses**
Artists flock to these islands for inspiration

History

85 **An old town to be reinvented**
Downtown Nassau is undergoing a massive facelift

103 **A generation of cruise ships**
From cramped quarters and scurvy to luxury liners

121 **Residents and rulers of Parliament Street**
A short thoroughfare's contribution to Nassau's history

COURTESY DR D HEPBURN

59

Family Islands

141 **Cat Island: land of unfinished dreams**
Turbulent past, drowsy present and uncertain future

159 **Big boat racing – the glory days return**
Top sailors compete again in the Miami to Nassau race

175 **Abaco was ready for armed revolution**
Residents planned to break away from The Bahamas

Business

189 **Sol Kerzner – tycoon with a plan**
An eye for the unconventional helps him "blow away the customer"

213 **Bahamas targets speciality markets**
Travellers are looking for a purpose to visit and finding it here

235 **Hedge funds offer advantages**
Intriguing products for high-net worth investors

261 **Foundations Act – 1st in the Americas**
Progressive laws put The Bahamas ahead of the pack

283 **Construction projects on the rise**
New Providence and Paradise Island abuzz

291 **Out Island building: the pace quickens**
Projects in the works for every major island

299 **Real estate**
A selection of available properties

190 SARA MOSS/©DUPUCH

Bahamas Information

321 **Blue pages**
A-Z compendium on living, vacationing and investing in The Bahamas

COURTESY LADY HENRIETTA ST GEORGE

Freeport/Lucaya

517 **Freeport's Doug Silvera**
Low-key character with a high-profile life

535 **Lady Henrietta St George**
Extraordinary woman has helped hundreds of children

551 **Isle of Capri Casino to help the economy**
Slow start but new numbers spark optimism

563 **Big plans for Grand Bahama**
Major projects on the horizon could transform the island

Freeport/Lucaya Information

577 **More blue pages**
Handy facts and figures specific to Freeport/Lucaya

Government

610 **How government works**
611 **Governor General**
612 **Cabinet ministers & portfolios**
618 **Senators**
622 **House of Assembly**
633 **Parliamentarians' salaries; Parliamentary Secretaries**
634 **Permanent Secretaries; Commission chairpersons**
635 **Public service officials**
638 **Government offices**
640 **Resident diplomatic & consular representatives**
641 **Bahamas diplomatic & consular representatives**
645 **International organizations' representatives**
646 **Honorary consuls & representatives**
648 **Bahamas honorary consuls abroad**
649 **The Queen's New Year's Honours – 2004**

LINDA M HUBER/©DUPUCH

Classified Directories

310 **Nassau**
572 **Freeport/Lucaya**

Year in Review

651 **Aug 2003 through July 2004**

Indexes

658 **Advertisers in this book**
662 **Index**

BAHAMIAN
scenes
Bahamian flowers are bright and many
But few can match the frangipani

LINDA M HUBER/©DUPUCH

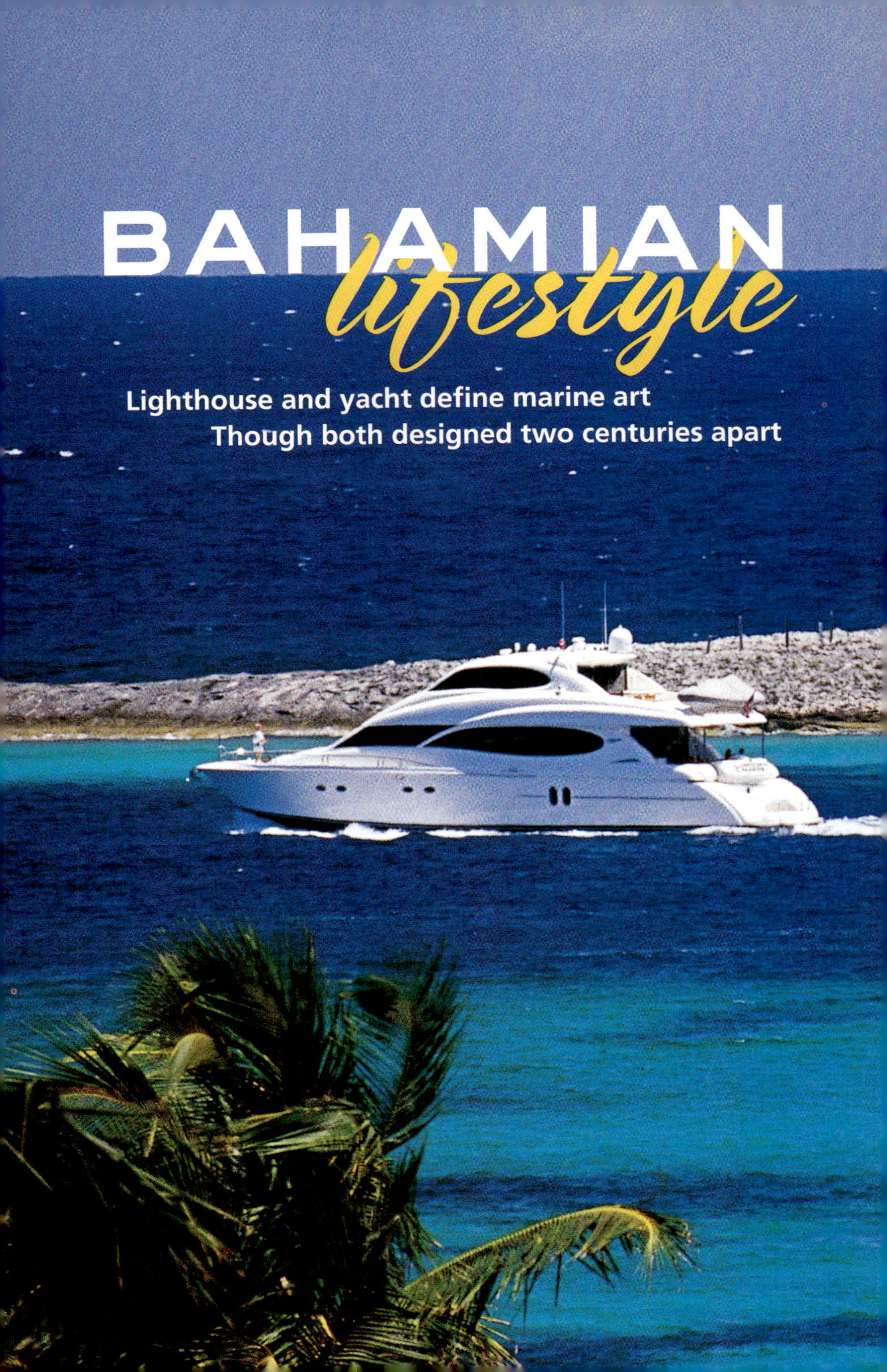
BAHAMIAN
lifestyle
Lighthouse and yacht define marine art
Though both designed two centuries apart

ROLAND ROSE/©DUPUCH

BAHAMIAN *faith*

**Faithful worshippers clad in white
Engage in baptism's holy rite**

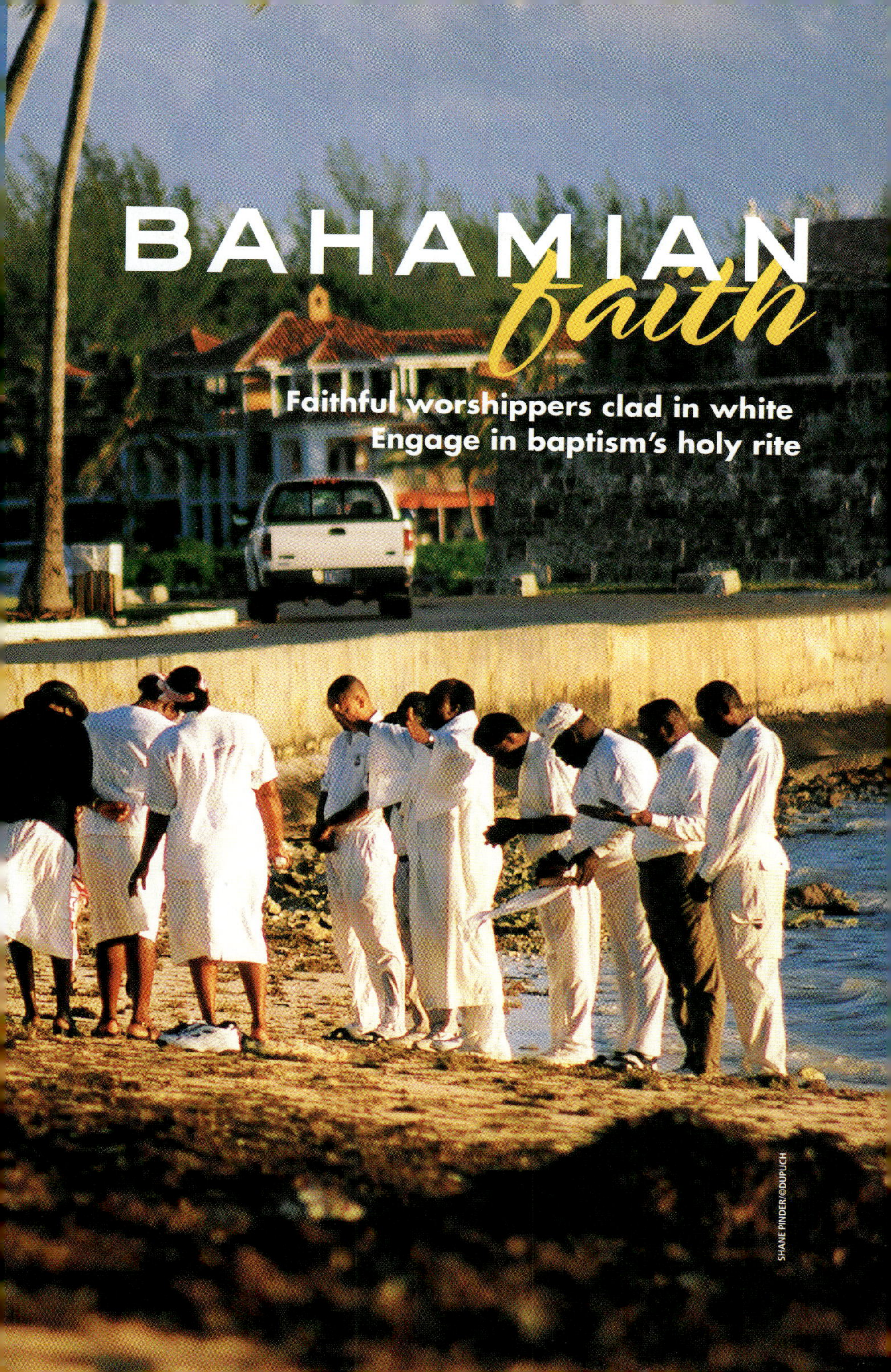

SHANE PINDER/©DUPUCH

JADE

BAHAMIAN *living*

A Hopetown house brings thoughts of boats
With gaily painted fishing floats

JENNIFER O'NEILL/©DUPUCH

ROLAND ROSE/©DUPUCH

BAHAMIAN *culture*

Art in watercolour, acrylic, oil
Adorn walls and halls of Villa Doyle

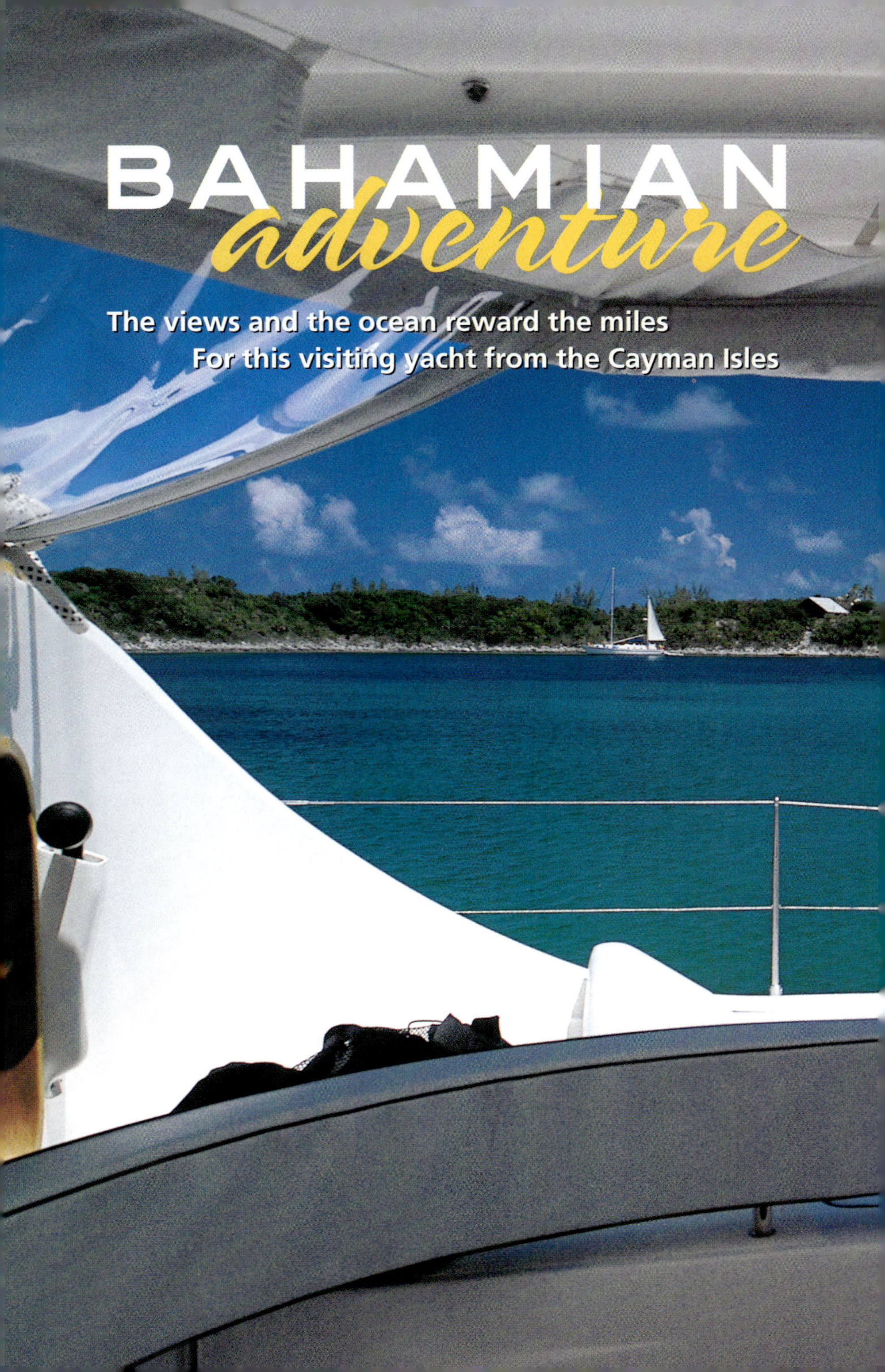

BAHAMIAN
adventure
The views and the ocean reward the miles
For this visiting yacht from the Cayman Isles

TIM VAN DER STEENE/©DUPUCH

ISLAND PICS/©DUPUCH

BAHAMIAN *attitude*

Tourists relax in the midday sun
Locals splash to
have their fun

LINDA M HUBER/©DUPUCH

BAHAMIAN *sights*

Painted Magna Carta improves the view
But can't disguise a two-hole loo

WATCHES • FINE JEWELLERY • LEATHER GOODS • PERFUMES • COSMETICS • CIGARS •

WATCHES • FINE JEWELLERY • LEATHER GOODS • PERFUMES • COSMETICS • PHOTOGRAPHIC EQUIPMENT • WRITING INSTRUMENTS • CIGARS •

A Tradition of Shopping Excellence since 1929

In 2004 **John Bull** celebrated its 75th Anniversary in The Bahamas.

In 1929 Asa Pritchard (later Sir Asa) opened an old English tobacco house in Nassau. He called it John Bull after a character in a 1712 British satire – a stout Englishman wearing a top hat, waistcoat, knickers and high boots. Despite the depression, Sir Asa's fledgling business prospered and continued to grow, quickly becoming a leading Bahamas retailer.

In the 1940s and '50s, Sir Asa's children completed their studies abroad and returned to Nassau with their families to join the business. The store expanded, first with a stationery department, started by the late Frank Hazlewood, that has grown into the foremost business centre in The Bahamas. In 1955, watches,

• GIFTS • WATCHES • FINE JEWELLERY • LEATHER GOODS • PERFUMES • COSMETICS •

WATCHES • FINE JEWELLERY • LEATHER GOODS • PERFUMES • COSMETICS • PHOTOGRAPHIC EQUIPMENT • WRITING INSTRUMENTS • CIGARS • GIFTS •

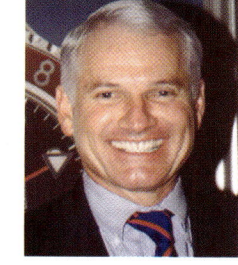

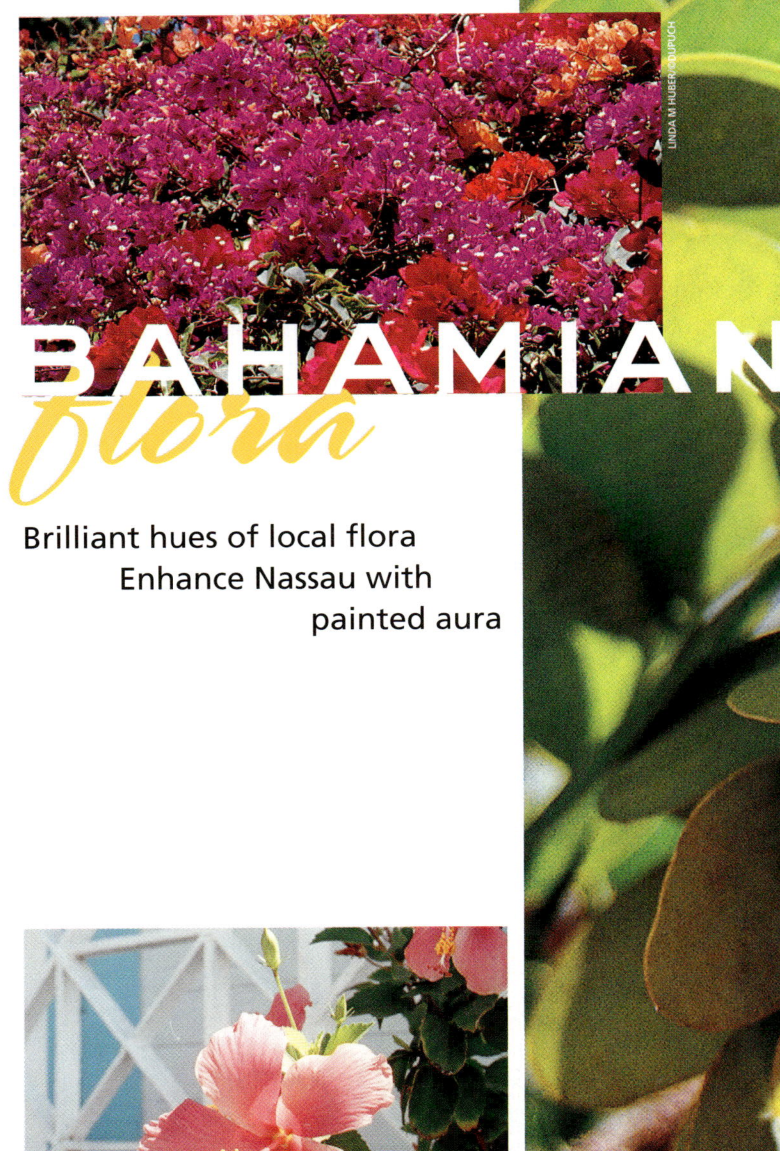

BAHAMIAN *flora*

Brilliant hues of local flora
Enhance Nassau with
painted aura

LINDA M HUBER/©DUPUCH

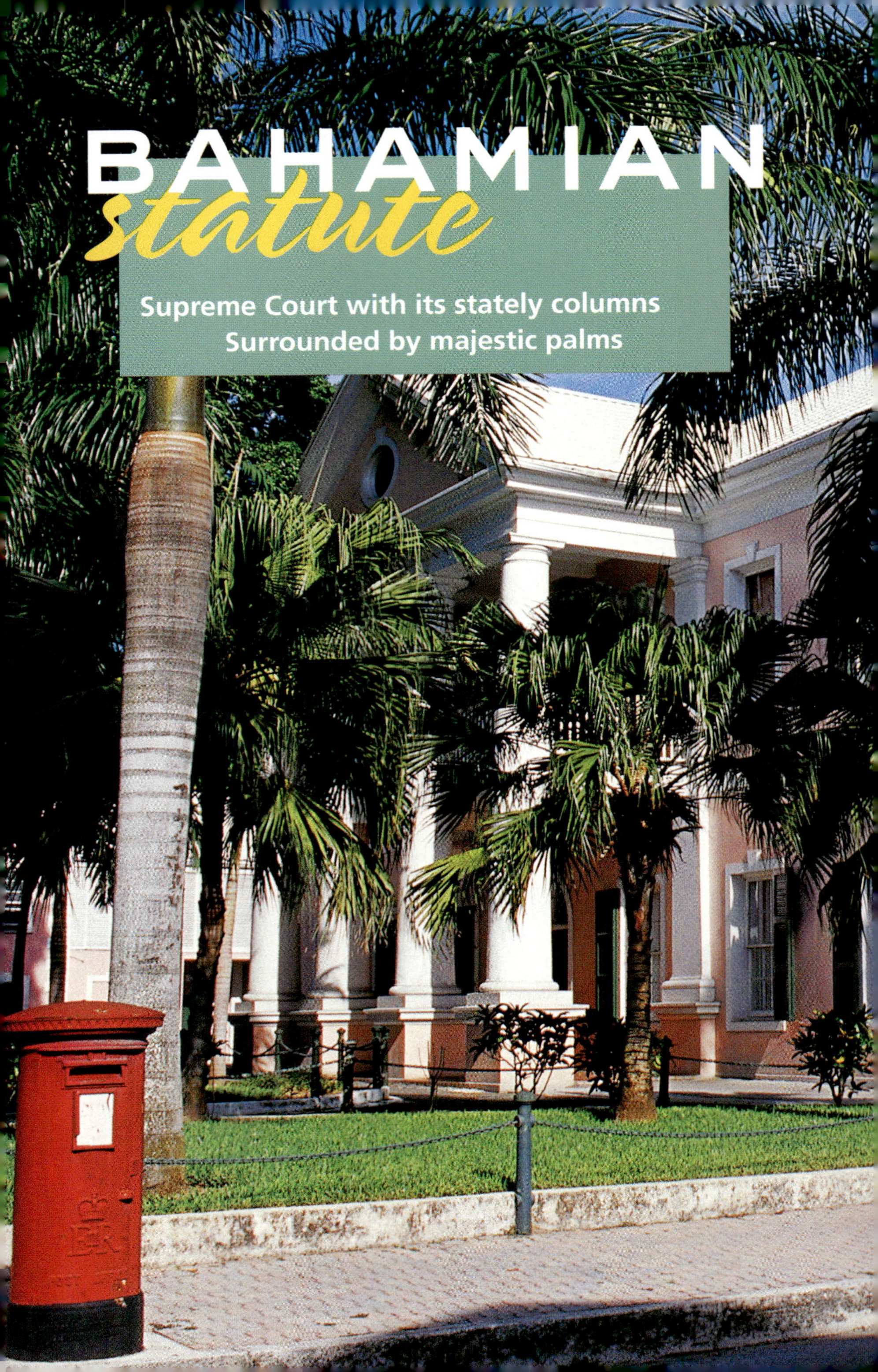
BAHAMIAN
statute
Supreme Court with its stately columns
Surrounded by majestic palms

LINDA M. HUBER ©DUPUCH

BAHAMIAN *tradition*

Royal Bahamas Police band marching to the top
Plays martial music, reggae, calypso, jazz and pop

LINDA M HUBER/©DUPUCH

ISLAND PICS/©DUPUCH

SHANE PINDER/©DUPUCH

BAHAMIAN *watersport*

Ocean blue to enjoy by boat
Or simply snorkelling afloat

SHANE PINDER/©DUPUCH

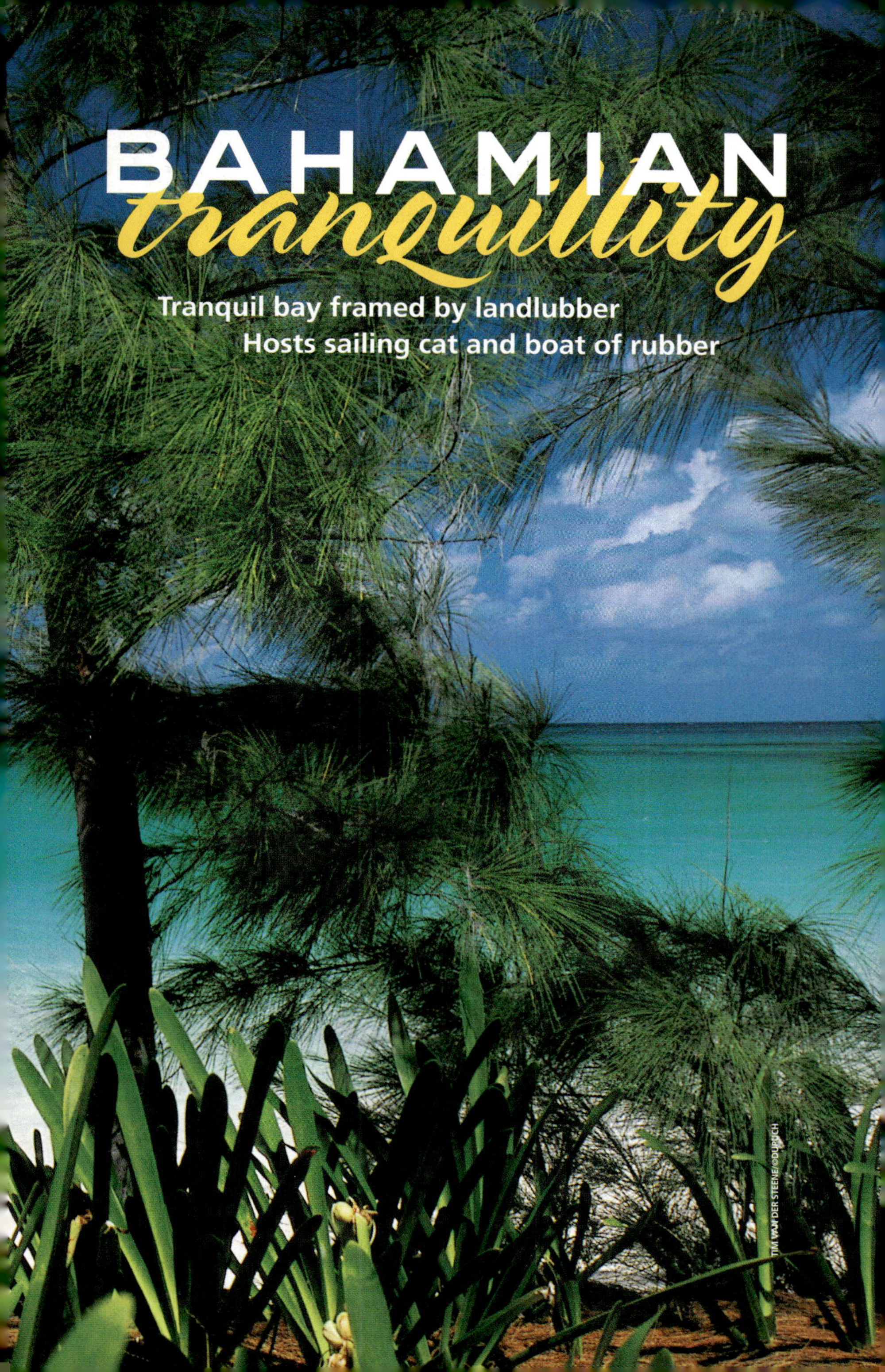

BAHAMIAN *tranquility*

Tranquil bay framed by landlubber
Hosts sailing cat and boat of rubber

LINDA M HUBER/©DUPUCH

BAHAMIAN *out island*

Tiny Bird Rock's silent light
Guides coastal shipping through the night

BAHAMIAN *underwater*

The underwater world teems with a plethora
Of interesting life like shark and remora

TIM VAN DER STEENE/©DUPUCH
TIM VAN DER STEENE/©DUPUCH
TIM VAN DER STEENE/©DUPUCH

BAHAMIAN *snoozing*

Pussycat, pussycat, where have you been?
Relaxing in Hopetown, where I won't be seen

The means of propulsion for warm ocean dippers
For fast you use motors,
for slower, use flippers

SHANE PINDER/©DUPUCH

COLUMBUS
HOTEL
NASSAU ARCADE
HOFFER BUILDING 1960

Features

AP/WIDE WORLD PHOTOS

Sir Sidney Poitier – son of the soil

A troubled Out Island boy becomes a Hollywood legend.

BY SHONALEE KING

Some remember him as the actor who smashed through Hollywood's rigid colour lines, becoming the first black to win an Academy Award for best actor for his role in *Lilies of the Field.* Others have come to know him as an articulate world leader, accepting graciously his status as an icon of film history. Bahamians know him as the man who grew up in the humility of a small settlement in Cat Island and went on to become a legend.

As the Ambassador of The Commonwealth of The Bahamas to Japan and the country's Permanent Ambassador to UNESCO, Sir Sidney Poitier, KBE has demonstrated a commitment to enhancing the image of The Bahamas on a global scale. He has used his celebrity status to attract attention to issues including health care and social reform and to enhance relationships between The Bahamas and other countries, such as Japan. Sir Sidney's most important cause continues to be creating educational opportunities for children, regardless of their life circumstances.

On a visit to Nassau, Sir Sidney met with the women of PACE (Providing Access to Continued Education). He encouraged the

Sir Sidney Poitier grew up in Cat Island.

Weighing less than three pounds at birth, Sidney Poitier came into the world fighting.

young mothers to pursue education. In 2003, when addressing a group of young men from YEAST (Youth Empowerment and Skills Training), he commended them for their participation in a programme that provides a positive outlet for at-risk young men.

Sir Sidney could truly sympathize with these teenagers. In his 2000 autobiography *The Measure of a Man*, he describes himself as a short-tempered young man dealing with issues of race and class, first in Nassau and later in the southern US where his parents sent him after he had a brush with the law.

Fighting injustice since his early days in Hollywood, Sir Sidney's social platforms have evolved over the years from confronting issues of race and discrimination on movie sets to human rights violations in East Asia. While his career and life work have taken him far from the remote settlement of Arthur's Town, Cat Island, where he grew up, Sir Sidney still remains connected to the values and life lessons learned in The Bahamas.

A shaky start

Weighing less than three pounds at birth, Sidney Poitier came into the world fighting. His parents, farmers Reginald and Evelyn Poitier, had left Cat Island in early 1927 on a mission to sell tomatoes at the

Sir Sidney speaks with school children during a visit to Cat Island.

©PETER RAMSAY

Sir Sidney greets a woman during a visit to Cat Island.

Miami Produce Exchange in Florida when their son's early arrival took them by surprise. Reginald was unsure that the frail baby would survive a few days, let alone a trip back to The Bahamas via boat. Distraught, he visited a local undertaker in Miami's black community and secured a shoebox just big enough to bury the baby. While Reginald prepared for the worst, his wife, desperate to find some hope in her situation, visited a local fortune teller in Miami who assured her that the tiny baby would survive and go on to do great things.

©PETER RAMSAY

Sir Sidney is an advocate for children.

"... poverty on Cat Island didn't preclude gorgeous beaches and a climate like heaven."

Sir Sidney's earliest and most vivid memories are of growing up in Arthur's Town, Cat Island. The man who would later become one of Hollywood's most esteemed actors started life in a small home where there was no electricity or indoor plumbing. His parents lived off the land and often bartered for goods and services, getting by on things provided by nature and the kindnesses of their neighbours.

"My father was a poor man, very poor in a British colonial possession where class and race were very important," Sir Sidney said in an interview with the Associated Press. "But my dad also was a remarkable man, a good person, a principled individual, a man of integrity. I decided in my life that I would do nothing that did not reflect positively on my father's life."

In recounting his life growing up in The Bahamas, Sir Sidney describes these moments as crucial in forming his character. "In a word, we were poor, but poverty was very different there," he writes in his autobiography. "It's not romanticizing the past to state that poverty on Cat Island didn't preclude gorgeous beaches and a climate like heaven."

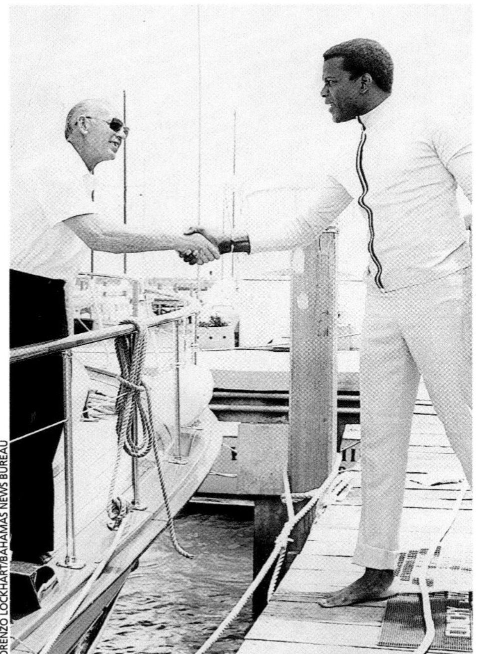
LORENZO LOCKHART/BAHAMAS NEWS BUREAU

Captain Albert Allusi extends a welcome greeting to Academy Award winner, Sidney Poitier, before sailing to Exuma for the Out Island Regatta.

Sir Sidney's life in Cat Island was filled with happy times with his parents and older siblings, who showered him with attention. The award-winning actor contends that it was the simplicity of growing up in an island paradise that shaped his character. Everyone around him in

LORENZO LOCKHART/BAHAMAS NEWS BUREAU

Sammy Davis Jr (left) shares a joke with composer Quincy Jones, Terrence McNeely and Sidney Poitier, aboard the yacht *Conchy Joe* in Nassau, before sailing to the Out Island Regatta in George Town, Exuma.

Cat Island lived on the same level and he never grew up feeling as though he was poor and lacking but rather had everything he needed all around him.

When he was almost 11, young Poitier's parents decided to move the family to Nassau where their children could go to school and have more opportunities than they would in Arthur's Town.

Nassau was a whole new world for the young boy. He had never seen an automobile or known anyone with indoor plumbing. The move to Nassau also brought new issues to the forefront – issues of class and colour. On Cat Island there were very few white people living in the community and those who were there did not hold powerful positions.

"There was one guy in Arthur's Town, a doctor, who was white and Damite Farrah, the shopkeeper, who was white. These guys were different-looking yes. But neither represented power," he recounts in his autobiography. "They were just there, and I never wondered why they were white and the rest of the people were black."

In Nassau, Poitier's life was very different. He attended Eastern Senior High School. On after-school adventures downtown and around the new city, Poitier encountered discrimination and racism,

Harlem was the hub for up-and-coming black actors such as Harry Belafonte, Ruby Dee and, later, Poitier himself.

memories that stayed with him long after he left The Bahamas. He recounts the anger and frustration he felt when he was walking downtown and an older white boy drove by on a bicycle and punched him in the face. Not being able to enter certain stores or restaurants in Nassau also frustrated the young man, who was used to the freedom of life on an Out Island.

Moving from a serene existence in Cat Island, where there were few class and race divisions, took its toll on Poitier. He began acting out his frustrations, becoming aggressive and angry at a moment's notice. By 13, he had dropped out of school and was working in construction.

While life in Nassau was difficult for the youngster, there were a few positive events that helped shape the course of his life. It was in Nassau that he saw his first feature film. The first time Poitier, his older brother and neighborhood friends pooled their small resources to buy tickets to the local theatre to see a cowboy film, he was overwhelmed by the experience. Movies became major events. He and his friends would rush home from the theatre and act out the parts they had seen on screen.

As he grew, Poitier's parents realized that their son, a young black high school dropout with a short temper, could easily get into trouble in Nassau. After a brush with the law, the Poitiers decided to send their son to live in Miami with his older brother.

The move to Miami proved even more challenging for the troubled young man. Living in a southern US state in the 1940s was not easy. The racism Poitier had experienced in Nassau paled in comparison to what he experienced living and working in Florida. He became a target of the Ku Klux Klan because of his temper and forthright attitude.

Poitier worked hard as a delivery boy and dishwasher, saved $80 and bought a ticket for a train heading north as far as his money could take him. He ended up in Harlem, New York, and enlisted in the US Army for a brief period, working as a psychotherapy aide.

A career begins

Moving to New York paved the way for Poitier's acting career. Harlem was the hub for up-and-coming black actors such as Harry Belafonte, Ruby Dee and, later, Poitier himself. He joined the

Poitier appears with Lilia Skala in a scene from the 1963 film *"Lilies of the Field."*

Poitier at the 36th annual Academy Awards in Santa Monica, CA, in 1964. He won best actor for his role in *"Lilies of the Field."*

American Negro Theater and worked as a stage hand in exchange for acting lessons in which he learned to subdue his distinctive island accent.

He soon landed roles in stage plays, working with all-black production companies, and found that acting came naturally to him. His first big break came as an understudy for Harry Belafonte in *Days of our Youth.* His performance marked him as an actor with enormous potential. No one at the Harlem-based theatre company could have predicted that the young man from The Bahamas would go on to become the only one among them to win Hollywood's top honour – an Oscar.

Poitier found a way to use his position as an actor to speak out against discrimination in Hollywood.

Perhaps his parents' proudest moment was when the family gathered in a theatre back in Nassau to watch their son in his movie debut in the 1950 film *No Way Out*.

Poitier found a way to use his position as an actor to speak out against discrimination in Hollywood. He turned down stereotypical roles given to black actors, refusing to play the butler, gardener or chauffeur, and instead opted to play the professor, the doctor or other educated characters.

"Almost all the job opportunities were reflective of the stereotypical perception of blacks that had infected the whole consciousness of the country," he recalls. "I came with an inability to do those things. It just wasn't in me. I had chosen to use my work as a reflection of my values."

There were times when Poitier did not have many choices but whenever there was a chance for him to voice his concerns regarding his roles, he spoke up.

He soon gained the respect of Hollywood's elite, working on projects with Katherine Hepburn and Spencer Tracey who

AP/WIDE WORLD PHOTOS

Sir Sidney arrives with his wife Joanna Shimkus and daughters Sydney, left, and Anika, far right, for the Academy Awards in 2002.

co-starred with Poitier in the film *Guess Who's Coming to Dinner.* In 1963, Poitier became the first black man to win the Academy Award for best actor in a film for his role in *Lilies of the Field.* Other noted works include *To Sir, with Love* and *In the Heat of the Night.* Poitier was knighted by the Queen in 1968 for his contributions to the arts and for his role in enhancing the image of The Bahamas. In 2002, the esteemed actor received an Honorary Academy Award celebrating his life's contributions to the world of cinema.

APWIDE WORLD PHOTOS

Sir Sidney poses with his honorary Oscar during the 2002 Academy Awards in Los Angeles.

A diplomatic assignment

In 1997, Sir Sidney took on a role of a different kind – Ambassador of The Commonwealth of The Bahamas to Japan. Since then, he has served as a diplomat, working closely with the Bahamian government to share common interests between the two countries. His more recent appointment as the permanent delegate for The Bahamas to UNESCO allows Sir Sidney to indulge his passion for learning and empowerment through education. Dr Davidson Hepburn, Chairman of the Bahamas National Commission for UNESCO, works closely with Sir Sidney on UNESCO projects.

"Sidney Poitier has a desire to serve. His vision for The Bahamas goes beyond his role as a Hollywood celebrity," says Hepburn. "He has a deep sense of where this country can go in terms of education. He has a genuine desire to enhance the world image of The Bahamas."

AP/WIDE WORLD PHOTOS

Sir Sidney arrives at the Imperial Palace in Tokyo. He formally became The Bahamas' Ambassador to Japan on April 16, 1997.

Both Hepburn and Sir Sidney represented The Bahamas at the UNESCO annual general conference in 2003 in Paris, France.

"UNESCO is focused on improving the world in fields of Science and Technology, Education and Culture. Sir Sidney Poitier has decided to focus on education as a way for Bahamians to take advantage of the opportunities presented to them. On his visits home, he takes every opportunity to speak with young people in general but in particular those participating in programmes like PACE for teenage mothers and YEAST for at-risk males, letting them know that they have been given an opportunity through education to redirect their lives," says Hepburn.

Through grants and educational projects, The Bahamas has already benefited from the work that Sir Sidney and his UNESCO team have done.

According to Minister of Education Alfred Sears, the work that Sir Sidney is doing with UNESCO will benefit The Bahamas now and into the future. "We are working to create a culture of excellence through a world-class education system that embraces innovation, creativity, critical thinking and communication, and that promotes the core values of equity, inclusiveness and excellence," said Minister Sears. "I am confident that, with the assistance of Sir Sidney Poitier, UNESCO will expand its assistance to The Bahamas."

COURTESY DR D HEPBURN

Sir Sidney Poitier and Dr Davidson Hepburn at a UNESCO conference in Paris

Sir Sidney's position as the permanent representative of The Bahamas to UNESCO will keep him busy working with the government of The Bahamas and other nations to assure that young people, and Bahamians in particular, are able to live up to their full potential.

Sir Sidney envisions a future for Bahamian children in which the issues of race and class that he faced as a child no longer apply to children growing up in Nassau and the Family Islands.

His official appointments in The Bahamas are a way for the famous actor to stay connected with the place where his core values were formed. The young boy from Arthur's Town, Cat Island, who pursued Hollywood dreams with little education and $80 in his pocket, went on to become the first black director to gross more than $100 million on a film. Sir Sidney Poitier continues to share a simple message with Bahamian children – with the opportunities available today, there are no limits.

ROLAND ROSE/©DUPUCH

Jewish community in The Bahamas

A small community with a huge impact traces its roots back to the arrival of Christopher Columbus.

BY SHONALEE KING

In fourteen hundred and ninety two
Columbus sailed the ocean blue
And in his crew there was a Jew
And his name was Luis De Torres.
Verse sung at Shabbat services at
Luis De Torres Synagogue, Grand Bahama

For such a small group of about 200 people in a country of 312,000, the Jewish community packs a powerful punch. They have been among the movers and shakers of the retail industry, owning and operating some of the leading businesses in The Bahamas. And their involvement in the community goes much further than the retail sector; they are lawyers, doctors, politicians and businessmen and women.

But while they comprise a small percentage of the population and, some may argue, their contributions may not be as noticeable as those made by larger groups, such as the Greeks, Chinese, and Lebanese, Jews in The Bahamas have had a great influence on the country's business and social landscape.

Harold Hoffer, head of the Jewish Congregation of New Providence

De Torres quickly became a Catholic to spare himself and was allowed to travel with Columbus as an interpreter.

Their story is centered around a handful of brave men and women who, despite isolation and anti-Semitism, made their lives and established businesses in The Bahamas. Family names such as Hoffer, Bott, Garfunkel, Yanowitz, Isaacs, Myers and Fienburg are represented among the first group of Jewish settlers.

1492 – the first Jew

Luis De Torres was the first documented Jewish person to set foot on Bahamian soil. In 1492 De Torres was among the crew sailing with Christopher Columbus on his inaugural voyage to the New World. An interpreter for Columbus, De Torres was a linguist hired by the Spanish monarchy for his fluency in Arabic, Spanish, Portuguese, French, Latin and Hebrew.

At the time when Columbus began his voyage, persecution of Jews was prevalent throughout Europe. On August 2, 1492, Spanish rulers Ferdinand and Isabella signed orders banning from the Iberian Peninsula all Jews who would not convert to Christianity. De Torres quickly became a Catholic to spare himself and was allowed to travel with Columbus as an interpreter. The synagogue in Grand Bahama, named in his honour, highlights his unique role in the history of the Jewish community in The Bahamas.

The majority of the country's first Jewish inhabitants settled in Nassau. During the 18th century, Moses Frank, an English Jew, was appointed Attorney General and Chief Justice of The Bahamas. Little is known about his time in office. Frank died in 1810. A slight peak in the Jewish population was observed shortly after the First World War, when families from Poland, the UK and Russia set up small communities in New Providence.

The Jewish business community

During the early 1900s, most West Indian islands saw a significant growth in the population of what was referred to then as "middleman minorities" – foreigners conducting businesses throughout the British, Spanish and French colonies. Merchants from as far away as Greece, Lebanon and the Orient were beginning to establish themselves as traders throughout the Caribbean.

While the rest of the British colonies, including Jamaica, were experiencing an increase in minority merchants, The Bahamas continued to impose laws limiting the trade opportunities available to the so-called minorities and prohibiting them from growing at the rate seen in other nations in the region.

Howard Johnson, author of *The Bahamas From Slavery to Servitude: 1783-1933,* describes the early twentieth century as a "merchant hegemony" noting that members of the House of Assembly enacted laws and policies that restricted the economic activities of minority groups. During the late 1920s and early 30s, a series of laws was enacted by the Bahamian Parliament making it illegal for aliens to "act as commission merchants unless registered." One such act "debarred any boat which was owned partly or wholly by an alien, or on which an alien was employed, from receiving a license."

According to Johnson, a 1928 act was designed to "limit economic competition for 'trading minorities'... Those immigrants who arrived in the colony in the late nineteenth and early twentieth centuries found a society controlled by the white merchant class, which exercised extensive political and economic control."

Principal among the opponents of foreign merchants was businessman R J Bowe, House of Assembly representative for the island of Exuma. Bowe's demands for restrictions paved the way for future limits to the growth of Jewish business in The Bahamas. In a

Left, Moses "Joe" Garfunkel. Above, the Garfunkel Shopping Centre in Palmdale was Nassau's first shopping plaza.

"In business and economics, American Loyalists, Chinese, Jews and Lebanese have had a profound influence in The Bahamas."

December 1926 issue of *The Nassau Guardian,* the politician outlined his concern regarding minority-owned businesses throughout the region:

"Is there any wonder that you have Jamaicans coming to this country in such large numbers? They are being pushed out of their own country by Celestials from the Far East and 'Jewestials' from the Near East."

Remarkably, and despite the objection of the legislature, many minority business owners went on to establish themselves as forces in the economy. A Department of Archives exhibition, *The Peoples of the Bahamas,* notes, "In business and economics, American Loyalists, Chinese, Jews and Lebanese have had a profound influence in The Bahamas."

Numbered among these was businessman, Moses "Joe" Garfunkel, who defied roadblocks set up by the legislature to become one of Nassau's leading Jewish businessmen. In 1923 Garfunkel opened the Home Furniture Company, an arm of a furniture franchise already established in Miami, FL. Because poor Bahamians frequented the store, Garfunkel and other minority businessmen were soon accused of undermining established Bahamian businesses. Historians Michael Craton and Dr Gail Saunders in their collaboration, *Islanders in the Stream,* compared the Jewish merchants to other foreign merchants: "Garfunkel and Jewish businessmen who came on his heels, though popular with their poorer customers, suffered even more severely from commercial opposition and personal criticism than did Armoury, Armaly, Moses or the Bakers, who were at least Christians."

Despite strong opposition from the business community, Garfunkel extended credit to civil servants and teachers and offered affordable furniture to Bahamians from low income homes. He endured a barrage of criticism, often being accused of trying to put other companies out of business. While Garfunkel was helping everyday Bahamians furnish their homes, he was also involved in the community. An avid sportsman, he built a playing field in the Palmdale area. The location was eventually turned into the Garfunkel Shopping Centre, the very first shopping plaza of its kind in Nassau. He was also a generous supporter of the Catholic Church, donating land and buildings.

The first surgeon

Dr Meyer Rassin and his wife Rosetta. Rassin founded Doctors Hospital in 1955. It was called Rassin Hospital.

Another monument to the tenacity of Jewish businessmen now stands at the intersection of Shirley Street and Collins Avenue. Doctors Hospital, formerly Rassin Hospital, was founded in 1955 by Dr Meyer Rassin of Latvia. Dr Rassin was posted to The Bahamas while in the Royal Air Force in the early 1940s, and eventually relocated his family to Nassau in '47. Because he was not Bahamian, an Act of Parliament was required before Rassin could be granted a medical license. The first surgeon in The Bahamas, Rassin had offices on Bay Street and Frederick Street before moving into the 22-bed Rassin Hospital.

Rassin's wife, Rosetta, was an English nurse who told stories of walking the streets of London after air raids to help those who had been injured and get them to safety. The couple had two sons – David, a PhD in Pharmacobiochemistry who resides in Texas, and Barry, current Chairman and CEO of Doctors Hospital Health System.

In addition to retail and health services, Jews who came to The Bahamas also found success in the legal profession. Ralph D Seligman, QC, formally of Dublin, Ireland, came to Nassau in 1957 after helping a client buy several acres of land from Sir Victor Sassoon, a prominent Jewish businessman living in Nassau. "I had no ties at the time, so I decided to relocate," says Seligman, who admits that the warm weather was another factor in his decision. He worked in a private trust company as magistrate and international legal consultant for ten years before being admitted to the Bahamas Bar in 1967. "These were the days before independence. I wasn't a

COURTESY RALPH SELIGMAN

Ralph D Seligman, QC, centre, serves as the Honorary Consul General for the State of Israel. Sons Arthur, left, and Edgar, right. Right, daughter, Helene Seligman.

COURTESY RALPH SELIGMAN

Bahamian," he recalls. "After ten years though, I was classified as a 'belonger,' and finally received a licence to practise law." Seligman serves as the Honorary Consul General for the State of Israel, a position he has held since 1974. His sons Arthur and Edgar are Bahamian lawyers, while daughter Helene lives in New York and is a member of the counter terrorism committee at the United Nations.

Austin Levy, a Jewish textile manufacturer from New England, was an early success story in the Out Islands. Levy visited The Bahamas on his honeymoon in 1915 and observed the lack of agricultural development. He also noted the country's dependency on its American neighbours for food imports. A man of vision, Levy saw the potential that the Out Islands had to produce goods on a large scale for local use and export. It took more than 20 years, but Levy was eventually able to buy property from the government – 2,000 acres in Hatchet Bay, Eleuthera – for a dairy farm and chicken hatchery. The farm had a workforce of about 200 and contributed to the island's economy and employment, but Levy was still greeted with some opposition. According to Craton and Saunders, Levy was "chided by the Governor, the Duke of Windsor, as setting a bad example," because he paid wages slightly higher than the Bahamian average. Like Levy, some Jewish immigrants opted to inhabit Out Islands, such as Eleuthera, Exuma and Cat Island, setting up small communities where they could trade on a much smaller scale.

"Historically, Jews have bypassed settling in The Bahamas in large numbers because of the economic limitations imposed by the ruling authority," says Janeen Isaacs, Chairwoman for the Sisterhood of the Nassau Jewish Congregation. Her great-grandfather Edward Isaacs, an American Jew, settled in Cat Island in the early 1900s. "He and his brother Louis Isaacs came from West Palm Beach. They ran a small operation moving produce and goods throughout the islands. He married a black Bahamian, Julia Campbell, and they settled in Cat Island."

COURTESY JANEEN ISAACS

Janeen Isaacs

One generation later, Edward's son, Sir Kendal G L Isaacs, QC, would become a member of the House of Assembly, serve as Attorney-General and president of the Bar Association, and go on to lead the official political opposition party – the Free National Movement.

Janeen, like most Jews living in The Bahamas, was raised in the Christian faith. "Many Jewish children are raised in the faith of their mother, and so my ancestors were raised under the faith of my Bahamian great-grandmother Julia Campbell."

It was not until she moved to Jamaica as a young girl that Isaacs discovered her Jewish heritage. She followed closely the teachings of the Old Testament and converted to Judaism at the age of 13. Since moving back to The Bahamas, Isaacs continues to be committed to preserving the Jewish faith here.

No vacancy

Despite their success in business, Jews living in the colony and those who visited during the 1930s found themselves facing discrimination. While The Bahamas continued to grow into a tourist hot spot, the anti-Semitic position of hoteliers and merchants persisted. Owner of the New Colonial Hotel, Allen Munson, refused to accept Jewish groups into his luxury hotel and pushed for their exclusion from all others. Craton and Saunders wrote, “the very few nonwhite tourists in the 1920s and 1930s were forced to find accommodations in the limited range of black-owned boarding houses, some of them Over the Hill.”

The Royal Victoria Hotel also discouraged travel agents from booking nonwhite guests. In a 1930s letter to a Miami travel agent, manager of the Royal Victoria Hotel, Lorraine Onderdont advised, “We are very much annoyed today when your party arrived in Nassau and I found that they were Jewish… It is up to agents to see that they keep at least one place a Christian resort.”

Jews were not accommodated at the Balmoral Hotel either, although the owner and operator, the late Sir Oliver Simmons, was himself a Jew.

The five families

Among notable Jewish business families was a group of Jewish-Bahamian merchants known as the “five families.” These included the Hoffers, Botts, Yanowitzes, Fienburgs and Garfunkels. In 1964, the descendants of these original families formed the Jewish Congregation of New Providence headed by Harold Hoffer, a prominent Bay Street merchant.

Hoffer was a year old when his parents migrated to The Bahamas from Poland in 1926. His family began Friemark and Hoffer as a dry goods store in the 1940s, just west of the present-day site of the HofferSport store on Bay Street.

ROLAND ROSE/©DUPUCH

HofferSport, on Bay Street, is just east of the original family business.

“My father followed his parents into the dry goods business. He along with his uncles, Jack and Rubin Bott, were all merchants,” says Norman Hoffer who, along with his brothers Edward and Steve, continue to run the family business. “We decided to get into business here after finishing school because things were booming at the time and we wanted to carry on

COURTESY HAROLD HOFFER

Rubin Bott's original merchant store, Rubin's, now thrives as a chain of clothing stores.

what our father started and improve the business further," Norman says.

Hoffer & Sons opened on Bay Street in 1956. Nearly fifty years later, under the direction of the Hoffer sons, the store underwent a major expansion, converting what was just a dry goods store on Bay Street into a modern, upscale sporting goods store.

ROLAND ROSE/©DUPUCH

Norman Hoffer

The Hoffer sons have continued their family business, but many more Jewish-Bahamians either moved away from The Bahamas, now practice other faiths, or are very unorthodox in their approach to religion. Members of Nassau's small Jewish community only meet during high holidays.

According to Geoffrey Hurst, president of the Freeport Jewish Congregation, the Nassau Congregation was

COURTESY DR WILLIAM PINTZOW

Rubin Bott, with daughter Cynthia Pintzow, left, and wife Dorothy.

COURTESY GEOFFREY HURST

Geoffrey Hurst, president of the Freeport Jewish Congregation

established as a way for local Jews to connect on a social and spiritual level. The founding families included brothers Jack and Rubin Bott (the latter established Rubin's Department Store); William Yanowitz, who operated William's Shoe Store in downtown Nassau between Elizabeth Avenue and Victoria Avenue; Joe Garfunkel, who owned the Home Furniture Company; and the Fienburg family, owners of the Fienburg Department Store. Steven Hoffer, son of founder Harold Hoffer is the current president of the Nassau Jewish Congregation.

A resting place for Jews

In the mid-19th century, a wealthy Jewish family purchased a portion of St Matthew's Cemetery in New Providence and designated it a Jewish burial ground. "The cemetery is presently administered by a trust set up by the late Eustace Myers, who emigrated to Nassau from Jamaica (where he had been the proprietor of the renowned Myers's Rum)," said Hurst. Myers, his wife and son were all buried in St Matthew's Cemetery. The Jewish portion of the cemetery, Section D, is located at the corner of Shirley Street and Lovers Lane. The oldest grave on record dates back to 1864; it is the tomb of Samuel Henry Benjamin who died at the age of 21.

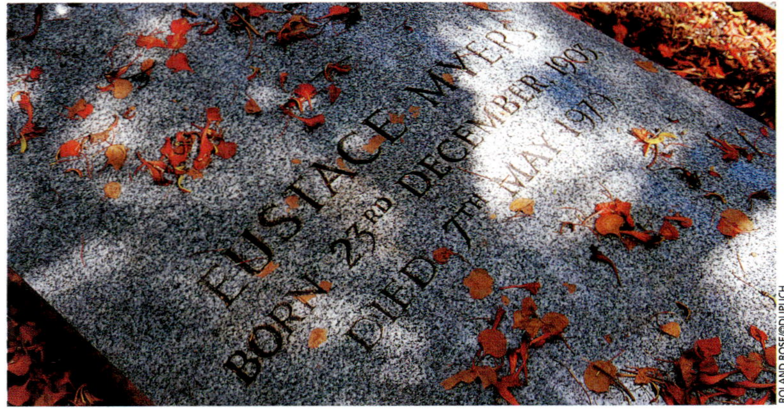

ROLAND ROSE/©DUPUCH

Final resting place of Eustace Myers in St Matthew's Cemetery in Nassau

COURTESY GEOFFREY HURST

Luis De Torres Synagogue is The Bahamas' only synagogue.

In Grand Bahama, the celebrated Luis De Torres Synagogue (the only synagogue in the country) is the meeting ground for Jews who live in and visit The Bahamas every year. Most religious activities centre around major holy days, such as Hanukkah and Yom Kippur.

"The synagogue was established in April 1973 and has been in existence for the past thirty-one years," says Anthony Gee, businessman and vice president of the Freeport congregation. "When we first opened, there was a large Jewish community of some 30 to 40 families with a lot of young children. We wanted to make sure that they had a sense of Jewish identity."

The Grand Bahama Port Authority donated the property for the synagogue and although it is a Jewish site, the congregation welcomes people of various faiths. To date there is no official rabbi.

"We're very open to all denominations; anyone can come and join in with the services. They are offered in both Hebrew and in English so that everyone can understand it as it goes along," Gee explains. The Freeport congregation is a member of the Union for Reform Judaism and the Commonwealth Jewish Council.

In 1996, Hurst became the first Jewish marriage officer in The Bahamas, making him qualified to perform the marriage ceremonies of Jewish residents and the many Jewish tourists visiting the country each year.

Today, unlike the early twentieth century, these visitors would not be turned away by any of the 296 hotels currently licensed to operate in The Bahamas. Perhaps one of the most prominent Jews living in The Bahamas is himself a hotelier – South African Jew Sol Kerzner, Chairman of Kerzner International and the Atlantis Resort and Casino, lives on Paradise Island.

PAMELA JONES

Bahamas conjures the muses

From rock stars to writers, artists have flocked to this tropical paradise for inspiration.

BY GORDON LOMER

Inspiration is a many-faced goddess. It takes divergent forms, the sources as varied as the Muses, the nine daughters of Zeus. Perhaps the crystal-clear ocean waters of The Bahamas provide the inspiration so many seek. Bahamian muses have inspired the creative juices of a broad array of artists. In many cases the Bahamian ambience serves to simply recharge the batteries of the creative before launching the next major project.

The list of artists who come to The Bahamas to be inspired is all-encompassing. They represent diverse art forms from lyric poetry, classic prose, drawing, painting and acting, to all types of music, including pop, heavy metal, rap, folk, classic rock, reggae and country.

Famous writers, composers and musicians who have lived, worked and been inspired in The Bahamas include the likes of John Steinbeck, Ernest Hemingway, Irving Berlin, Zane Grey, and more recently Lenny Kravitz, Julio Iglesias, Arthur Hailey, Sean Connery, Shania Twain and Celine Dion.

John Steinbeck lived in "The Pink-Un" on Bay Street, opposite the Nassau Harbour Club, in the 1950s and may have plotted or

Jimmy Buffett appreciates the changes in latitude that The Bahamas offers.

Hemingway drew much of his inspiration immersed in deep sea fishing at Bimini…

created some parts of *East of Eden* while living there. The book was written in New York City and on Nantucket Island. It was published in September 1952. Two months later *East of Eden* topped the fiction best-seller list. And 10 years later Steinbeck was awarded the Nobel Prize for Literature, largely on the strength of his masterpiece, *The Grapes of Wrath.*

Composer Irving Berlin lived at Jungle Cove, a house on the beach west of Nassau, in the late 1930s. It might have been where he wrote the musical comedy hit *Louisiana Purchase,* a spoof of sex and politics in New Orleans. It was Broadway's biggest hit in 1940 and was made into a movie by Paramount the next year, starring Bob Hope.

COURTESY JOHN F KENNEDY LIBRARY

Ernest Hemingway immortalized Bimini in his novel *Islands in the Stream.*

Fishing for inspiration

Bimini became famous as a piscatorial paradise after Ernest Hemingway published his prize-winning novels based on fishing in The Bahamas. Hemingway drew much of his inspiration immersed in deep-sea fishing at Bimini, where he lived, loved and cavorted off and on between 1936 and 1950. Out of that setting came his 1952 novella *The Old Man and the Sea,* and *Islands in the Stream,* published after his death in 1961. The latter novel immortalizes Bimini and the Compleat Angler Hotel where he bedded, boozed and brawled.

He found out about the legendary Bahama fishing from fellow writer, sportsman and Bimini fan, Zane Grey, better known as a writer of western stories. Grey, considered by many as the father of big game fishing, spent much of his recreational and inspirational time in Bimini. He set many rod and reel world records. His catches included a massive tuna and a great white shark and inspired some of his best writing. He was at one time the world's highest paid writer and the first American author to become a millionaire. Grey died in 1939, at 67.

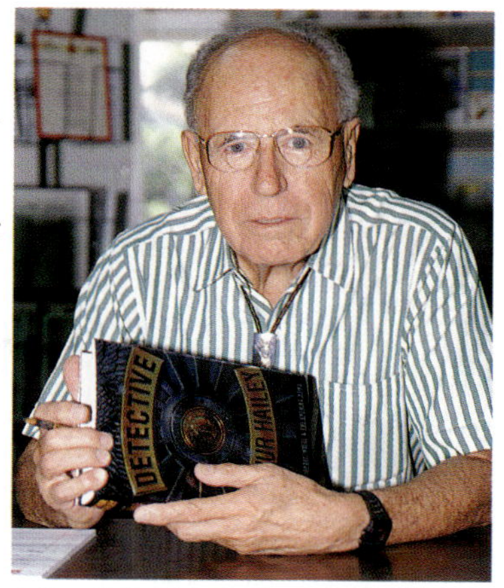

Arthur Hailey lives and writes at Lyford Cay, New Providence.

Author Arthur Hailey, who produced such classic best-sellers as *Wheels, Hotel* and *Airport,* still lives at Lyford Cay in western New Providence, where he continues to write. Born in Luton, England, Hailey moved to Canada after serving in the RAF from 1939 to 1945. But he eventually came to The Bahamas, induced not only by the weather and beautiful beaches but also by the absence of income taxes, which, at the time were approaching 90 per cent in the US and in Canada. His wife, Sheila is also inspired by the Bahamian muses and in 1978 wrote *I Married a Best-Seller.*

ROLAND ROSE/ ©DUPUCH

Sean Connery, Nassau's favourite secret agent, lives and golfs at Lyford Cay.

Sean Connery, 74, Edinburgh-born actor, also calls Lyford Cay home. Nassau's favourite secret agent set the standard for the James Bond genre of movies. He played the role of 007 six times, *Dr No* (1962), *From Russia with Love* (1963), *Goldfinger* (1964), *Thunderball*

Alice Simms penned Calypso Island *for pianist and singer Andre Toussaint, and* Lizzie Carry Basket on de Head.

(1965), *You Only Live Twice* (1967) and *Diamonds Are Forever* (1971) before breaking from the Bond image. He was later induced into returning to the role in *Never Say Never Again* (1983). He earned an Oscar as honest Chicago cop Jimmy Malone in the 1987 version of *The Untouchables.*

Connery and his wife, French artist Micheline Roquebrune Connery, had a place in Marbella, Spain, but sold it to escape to a more private life. He now considers The Bahamas home, where he relaxes, plays golf and enjoys a modicum of privacy, if not anonymity. He also works here and has recorded movie dialogues, TV documentaries and commercials at Compass Point Studios. He still prefers his martinis shaken, not stirred, unlike his audiences, which he would rather stir than shake.

Bahamian muses past and present

Winslow Homer, one of America's greatest artists who became famous for his intense seascapes, was a frequent visitor to Nassau. It was here that he derived much of his inspiration and perfected his watercolour technique. He experimented with applying transparent washes to create dramatic effects. He died in 1910.

Alice Simms, composer and singer, complemented the early Nassau tourist seasons collaborating with local artists Blind Blake, George Symonette and Freddie Munnings, among others. She penned *Calypso Island* for pianist and singer Andre Toussaint, and *Lizzie Carry Basket on de Head.*

Hoagy Carmichael (1899-1991) may have composed some of his most enduring songs at a home in Tower Heights, off Eastern Road. His younger brother Wayne, a musician in his own right, owned it. People in Nassau, including legendary drummer Berkely "Peanuts" Taylor, remember Wayne. Taylor played a few times with Hoagy, and knew Wayne as "a fair musician." Hoagy is remembered today as one of America's great composers of popular songs. Several of his tunes, such as *Star Dust, Georgia on My Mind, Up The Lazy River, Lazybones, Skylark* and *Heart and Soul* have become standards still widely played and enjoyed. Wayne's house was built in the late 1920s, about the same years Hoagy was at his writing peak.

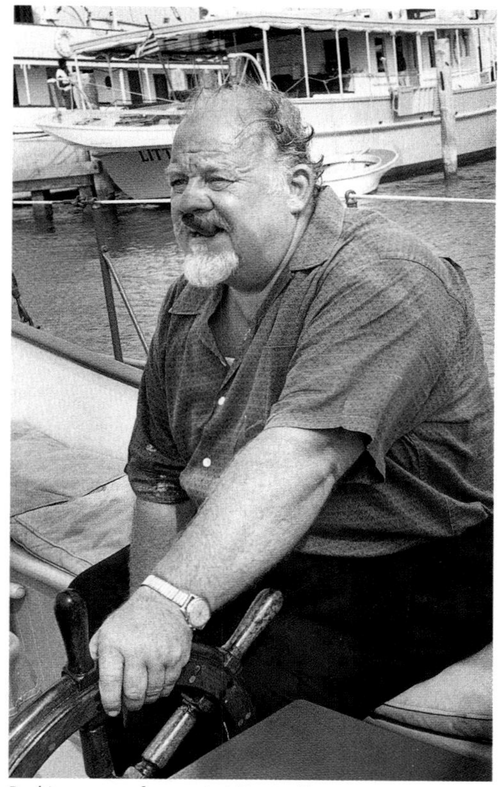
Burl Ives was a frequent visitor to Nassau.

Irish-born actor Richard Harris lived on Paradise Island off and on until his death in 2002. Harris cut as wide a swath off the stage as on it, and is remembered by many Nassauvians as a hard-living *bon vivant.* Despite his oft-repeated quote, "I hate movies. They're a waste of time," his stage and screen career spanned six decades, and included recent roles in *Harry Potter and the Sorcerer's Stone* and *Harry Potter and the Chamber of Secrets.*

Burl Ives, troubadour, balladeer, folk singer and purveyor of children's songs, was a frequent winter visitor. He came to Nassau to rejuvenate by sailing and fishing, his favourite recreational pursuits. He is possibly best remembered for his renditions of *Foggy Foggy Dew, Blue Tail Fly* and *Big Rock Candy Mountain.* In the 1960s he turned to country and released three major country/pop hits, *Funny Way of Laughing, A Little Bitty Tear* and *Call Me Mr In-Between.* He died in 1995 at 85.

Actor Sir Sidney Poitier, favourite native son, was born in Miami in 1927 but grew up on Cat Island in the southern Bahamas, where his father was a farmer. The family moved to Nassau when Sidney was almost 11 and he got his first taste of cinema. He moved to New York at age 16 and got menial jobs with the American Negro Theater in exchange for acting lessons. Poitier earned the role of understudy to Harry Belafonte in *Days of our Youth.* He made his debut filling in for Belafonte, which led to other roles. He continued theatre acting until 1950 when he made his film debut in *No Way Out*. The rest is history. Sir Sidney is now Ambassador of The Commonwealth of The Bahamas to Japan. (See also pg 49.)

State-of-the-art studio

Almost 30 years ago, music visionary Chris Blackwell was inspired by Bahamian muses. Blackwell, then owner of Island Records, built his state-of-the-art Compass Point Studios at Gambier, in northwestern New Providence, in 1977.

Jamaica's renowned reggae powerhouse, Bob Marley, was among the first of many artists who recorded at Compass Point Studios. Marley's promotion of brotherhood and peace complemented his musical brilliance. He produced international hits such as *Exodus* (1977), *Waiting In Vain* (1977), *Jammin'* (1977), and *Is This Love* (1978), and albums *Rastaman Vibration* and *Exodus*. On a European tour in 1977, Marley injured his foot playing soccer. Diagnosis showed cancerous cells, but he refused surgery. In 1980, he collapsed while jogging in New York's Central Park. The cancer had spread to his brain, lungs and liver. He died eight months later at age 36.

ADRIAN BOOT 1999

Bob Marley was one of the first artists to record at Compass Point.

Other artists who were part of the early Compass Point scene included Mick Jagger and The Rolling Stones, the longest-lived continuously active group in rock and roll history. Carly Simon emerged in the 1970s as a writer and singer of melancholy, romantic songs. Simon's film work included the hit,

Celine Dion has been a top-selling international artist since the early 1990s, and has recorded at Compass Point.

Nobody Does It Better, from the 1977 Bond frolic *The Spy Who Loved Me.* Soul diva Grace Jones, another Bond babe, played a spectacular role as the flat-topped villain who turned soft at the end of the 1985 film, *A View to a Kill,* with Roger Moore as 007. Jones is still best known for her 1982 classic *Pull Up To The Bumper* and her recent *Private Life: The Compass Point Sessions.*

Julio Iglesias lived at Capricorn, a house near the studios, while recording the album *Libra* in Spanish and Portuguese in 1985, the same year a star with his name was unveiled on the Hollywood Walk of Fame. The list of vocalists and instrumentalists who spent a little or a lot of time at Compass Point in its first decade also includes Eric Clapton, Judas Priest, U2, Dire Straits, The B-52s, Bad Company, Joe Cocker and many more.

In the late 1980s when Blackwell's other interests took him away from the studio and producer and studio manager Alex Sadkin died in a car crash, the studio deteriorated. Blackwell hired Terry and Sherrie Manning, both recording and video producers with impressive experience, connections and international business smarts, to run the studios. Since rebuilding and reopening in 1993, Compass Point Studios has regained its status, and the musicians are coming again.

Warmth inspires Canadians

Canadians have always been drawn to The Bahamas, partly for the obvious climate relief, and more recently for the state-of-the-art recording facilities.

Shania Twain, a native of Windsor, Ontario, grew up in Timmins where she was raised by her mother and stepfather, two singers, who were killed in an car accident when she was 21. *The Woman In Me* sold more than eight million copies, surpassing *Patsy Cline's Greatest Hits* as the best-selling country album of all time by a female artist. The album also won a Grammy in 1996 for Best Country Album.

Powerful French-Canadian chanteuse Celine Dion has been a top-selling international artist since the early 1990s, and has recorded at Compass Point. One of pop music history's brightest global stars, she is now halfway through a 600-performance gig at Caesar's Palace in Las Vegas, where she appears five nights a week in A New Day. The

Kravitz "would take the music tracks we had recorded, and play them in his Jeep while riding along the beach roads looking at the sun and the sea with the top down."

multi-media extravaganza was designed and orchestrated by Belgian entertainment impresario, Franco Dragone, of Cirque Du Soleil fame. Dion's contract at Caesar's runs through 2006.

Canadian Frank Mills, piano player and composer of *Music Box Dancer,* among others, is a former commodore of the Royal Nassau Sailing Club. Nowadays composer/arranger Mills spends much of his time creating music in his own computerized studio, surrounded by ocean and palm trees, at his home in Nassau, where he is a permanent resident. Mills still spends about three months a year on tour with his five-piece electronic band, doing about 60 shows.

Canada's Crash Test Dummies, a unique rock band formed in Winnipeg as a hobby by frontman Brad Roberts, an honours English and Philosophy graduate of the University of Manitoba, regularly recorded at Compass Point. They are best known for a song called *Mmm.*

International inspiration

The Aussie metallic rock group, AC/DC raised some decibels in The Bahamas while recording at Compass Point Studios after the death of their lead singer, Bon Scott. "They were in disarray and confusion," notes Terry Manning, "and had just hired a new singer. The result, once they were able to recover here, was the biggest selling hard rock album of all time, *Back in Black.*

Colombian Latin pop/rock singer Shakira is a superstar in Latin America and is emerging as a top international entertainer. Her female rocker style earned her the World Music Award for Latin Female Artist of the Year. Since her arrival on the music scene at age 14 in 1991, she has become the world's most famous Latin female artist. Her combination of Latin and rock music has moved critics to dub her a Hispanic Alanis Morissette.

Rocker Lenny Kravitz, whose music also includes elements of folk, gospel, blues, soul, jazz, classical and reggae, has done much of his recording at Compass Point, and has a loyal local following. His father was Russian Jewish TV producer, Syl Kravitz, and his mother was actress Roxie Roker, an American/Bahamian, who played Helen Willis in *The Jeffersons.* Kravitz recorded his biggest-ever album, *S,* at Compass Point. Kravitz "would take the music tracks we had

AP/WIDE WORLD PHOTOS
Lenny Kravitz has Bahamian roots and does much of his recording at Compass Point.

recorded, and play them in his Jeep while riding along the beach roads looking at the sun and the sea with the top down," says Manning. "This is how he wrote the words for his biggest single hit, *Fly Away.*"

Jimmy Buffett, the Florida cultural icon and troubadour, derives as much inspiration from The Bahamas as from his adopted home of Key West. He arranged financing to launch a road company of the revised *Don't Stop The Carnival,* (the musical adaptation of Herman Wouk's novel) that he and Wouk wrote together. The show played at Atlantis. He says Compass Point fits right into his lifestyle, as expressed in his trademark tunes, *Changes in Latitude, Changes in Attitude,* and *Margaritaville.*

Talented singer and songwriter Peter Frampton, a native of Kent, England, was at his creative best with his initial solo album, *Wind of Change,* which included friends Ringo Starr and Billy Preston. He wrote two of his finest songs, *Show me the Way* and *Baby I Love Your Way,* inspired by the sunset while sitting on the beach near what would become Compass Point Studios.

The Bahamian muses were working hard when Icelandic rock star and actress, Bjork, was recording her classic album *Post Live* at Compass Point. She was so inspired by the beauty of the sea, according to Manning, "that she decided to record her vocals while swimming in the ocean. We took the music tracks she had recorded, a generator, long cables, a microphone and headphones, and she recorded and sang while wading in the ocean at sunset…"

QUEEN OF NASSAU

History

COURTESY BAHAMAS NEWS BUREAU

An old town to be reinvented

Downtown Nassau is undergoing a massive facelift to better compete in world tourism.

BY RALPH DEANS AND SHONALEE KING

In what may turn out be his chief legacy to the Bahamian people, Prime Minister Perry Christie vows to turn downtown Nassau into "one of the most attractive harbour cities in this hemisphere."

Speaking of the redevelopment that got under way in mid-2004, prominent businessman Norman Solomon – a major player in the project – said that "the face of downtown Nassau will be totally altered forever."

With the help of local and international architects, urban planners and builders, Christie intends to turn the centuries-old town into "a city of romance… reflecting distinctive Bahamian charm, our rich history, culture… a world-class tourism destination."

The first step will be relocating four shipping yards from the north side of Bay Street, first to an interim location at Arawak Cay, then to a brand new port to be built on the south side of the island, near Coral Harbour. This will open up the spectacular vista of Nassau's waterfront, now hidden by buildings, fences and stacks of shipping containers.

It's hard to believe that this bustling street was once little more than a footpath, meandering along the open waterfront past a few shacks and coconut palms. More than three centuries ago, Nassau

Bay Street, circa 1950s

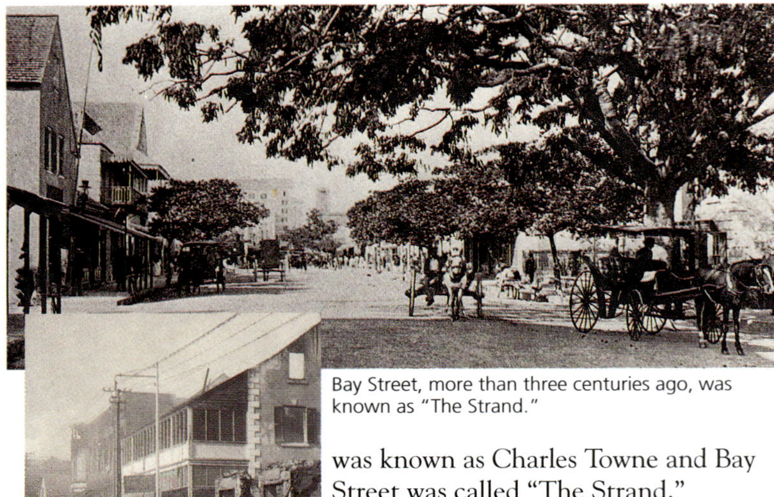

STANLEY TOOGOOD

Bay Street, more than three centuries ago, was known as "The Strand."

1942, the fire brigade fights a fire started by an arsonist.

was known as Charles Towne and Bay Street was called "The Strand."

The street has changed many times since 1695. Nassau had to be largely rebuilt after devastating hurricanes in 1861 and 1929. Reconstruction was required again in 1942 after the "Burma Road" riots, when workers protesting low wages smashed up stores on Bay Street. Later that same year, an arsonist set the city on fire, destroying many downtown buildings.

Despite these cataclysmic changes, Bay Street somehow retains its old-world charm. It remains the most famous street in the country, a showcase of Bahamian architecture and culture, as well as the nation's commercial and political heart.

Centuries of change

Pedestrians strolling Bay Street today are treading in ancient footsteps. The first British colonists and military officers who protected them walked up and down The Strand in the mid 1600s. Spanish, French and American invaders came and left. Pirates lived along the avenue in an era of lawlessness during the 17th and 18th centuries.

By 1728, the cut-throats had been mostly wiped out by Woodes Rogers, the nation's first Royal Governor. He once hanged eight of them at once on the beach in front of the British Colonial Hilton, where tourists now sunbathe by the sea. Rogers is also credited with paving the way for a representative assembly to draw up legislation, enforce it and govern the country.

Spanish conquistadors strode down Bay Street after they captured The Bahamas in 1782, but they didn't stay long. Andrew Deveaux, a British Empire Loyalist from South Carolina, put together a privately financed invasion and recaptured Nassau in 1783. Shortly thereafter the whole archipelago was restored to Britain by treaty.

Plantation owners and thousands of slaves – the forebears of 85 per cent of the Bahamian population today – began to arrive in Nassau from the Carolinas, Georgia and Florida, before, during and especially after the US War of Independence. Some stayed in New Providence, others left to set up plantations in the Out Islands.

COURTESY BAHAMAS MINISTRY OF TOURISM

Traders on Woodes Rogers Wharf

Later, traders made Nassau a trans-shipment point, sending out cargo of cotton, sisal, sponges and pineapples from the docks along Bay Street. Merchants began to set up shops along the thoroughfare.

Move ahead about 100 years and you would have found gunrunners striding up and down Bay Street, loading ships with munitions and supplies for the southern Confederacy in the US Civil War, which ended in 1862.

Another half century and Nassau was filled with pistol-packing bootleggers and rum-runners, sending illegal shipments of booze into a thirsty US during the Prohibition era.

Twenty-five years more, during the Second World War, and you might have seen the Duke of Windsor, the man who would not be

Slaves, the forebears of present-day Bahamians, "built some of our most beautiful homes," says Burnside.

king, strolling down Bay Street. By his side you might have seen his beloved Duchess, American divorcee Wallace Simpson, the woman he gave up the throne of England to marry.

Bay Street architecture

When urban planners and architects begin working in earnest on the redevelopment of downtown Nassau, they won't be working from scratch. Bay Street boasts many examples of what has become known as "distinctive" Bahamian architecture.

The major influence is Georgian, transplanted here by the Loyalists who abandoned grand plantation homes they had built in the Southern US.

Georgian details can be easily spotted up and down Bay Street today – louvred shutters, deep verandas with handrails, porticoes, balustrades, lattice work, and cornices. Many buildings display quoins, the outsized stones placed at the corners to strengthen the structures against hurricanes. You can see Bahamian shutters, which swing out at the bottom.

Jackson Burnside, a well-known artist and architect who heads up the Historical Nassau Renovation Committee, believes Bahamians have much to learn from these old buildings. As slaves, the forebears of present-day Bahamians, "built some of our most beautiful homes," says Burnside. They cut the stone with their own hands, "and for that reason we should be proud of these icons and what they represent."

Bahamas Development Board and Information Bureau is a prime example of typical Georgian architecture.

One building that is unlikely to be touched is the first building on the left as one walks east from the British Colonial, the Diocesan Building. Dating from 1893, it was once an Anglican church.

Even older is the nearby Vendue House, built circa 1784. Now the Pompey Museum of Slavery and Emancipation, it was once an open-air marketplace where, among other things, slaves were bought and sold.

Other distinctive buildings on Bay Street include the Royal Bank of Canada building, a stately grey stone structure that opened in 1919; the three-storey Masonic Temple, built in the late 1800s; and the ultra-smart Solomon's Mines store, located in a restored building from the late 19th or early 20th Century.

One part of the downtown area that is unlikely to change much when the cityscape is redrawn is the area where Rawson Square and Parliament Square face each other across Bay Street. This is the heart of downtown Nassau. It's a prime viewing area for the midnight-to-dawn Junkanoo parades, perhaps the best known icons of Bahamian culture, on Boxing Day and New Years Day.

This spot has a certain air of poignancy. A statue of Queen Victoria, surrounded on three sides by the pink Parliament Buildings, stares regally over the traffic to the bust of Sir Milo Butler, the first Bahamian-born Governor General, ensconced in a stand of magnificent tropical palms. A smiling Sir Milo looks back at the Queen, his arm half raised, seemingly in a friendly farewell to the days when Victoria ruled the world and The Bahamas was one of her colonies.

Diocesan Building

LINDA M HUBER/©DUPUCH

Vendue House, home of the Pompey Museum

LINDA M HUBER/©DUPUCH

Royal Bank of Canada

The Bahamian government commissioned the building of the Royal Victoria Hotel on Shirley Street… with lush gardens and room rates at a pricey $9 a night.

Rise of the merchant class

Two other events that affected the look of Bay Street were the abolition of slavery, finally accomplished in 1838, and the rise of the merchant class in Nassau when the thin soil of Bahamian plantations became exhausted.

By 1879, freed black women from nearby villages, such as Grant's Town, came downtown with straw trays on their heads with cakes, fruits, vegetables and peanuts to sell. They congregated in what was called the Public Market, separated into three sections where fisherman and farmers sold fresh fish, vegetables and meat products. Later, this became the Straw Market, another feature of the old Bay Street that is sure to endure.

In 1879, freed black women came downtown with wooden trays on their heads, selling candies, straw work and peanuts. They congregated at the Public Market, which became the Straw Market.

In the 1890s merchants, such as Anthony Baker Saadi of Lebanon, started successful businesses on Bay Street. The A Baker and Sons dry goods store, built on the corner of Frederick Street and Bay, was a well-known emporium.

In 1861, the Bahamian government commissioned the building of the Royal Victoria Hotel on Shirley Street, a block south of Bay Street, with lush gardens and room rates at a pricey $9 a night. It was used by Americans escaping the civil war and by tourists arriving by ship from New York.

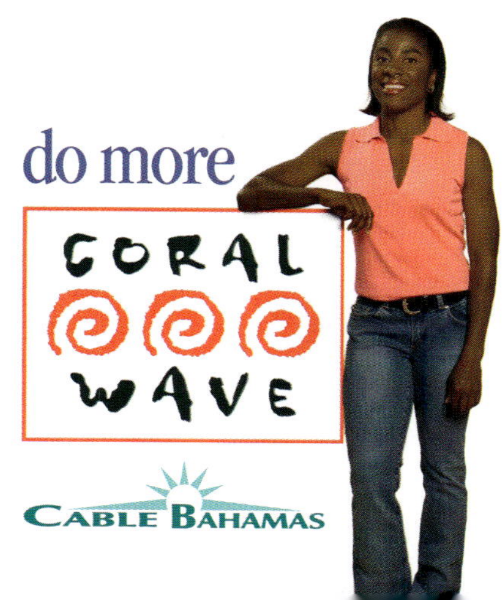

do more
CORAL
WAVE
CABLE BAHAMAS

The Bahamian economy was booming thanks to Prohibition, which lasted from 1919 to 1933.

This trade helped to alleviate an economic slump in the early 1900s that hit the Bay Street merchants hard. Some years later, though, the Bahamian economy was booming thanks to Prohibition, which lasted from 1919 to 1933. A *London Times* report in 1920 said outlawing alcohol in the US, "transformed the Bahamas government's financial position as if by magic from a deficit to a comparatively huge surplus, provided labour for large numbers of unemployed Bahamians and put more money into circulation in this little British colony than has been the case for many years."

More businesses sprang up on Bay Street, including the Bahamas Ironmongery, J P Sands' food store, William's Shoe Store, Mike's Shoe Store and Kelly's Hardware. Later, there were two jewellery stores, owned by R N Musgrove and Sir Joseph Brown. The high-end Nassau Shop was launched by the Saunders and Sands families.

John Bull Ltd was established by Asa H Pritchard, at one time Speaker in the House of Assembly. The Lofthouse family, headed by Harold Lofthouse, owned the Brick Store on George Street, famous for selling trendy Panama hats.

In 1908, the Solomon brothers, Eric and Cyril, opened the family's first retail store, the Pipe of Peace, a tobacco shop. It occupied a prime location on Bay Street across from the Royal Bank, where the present-day Solomon's Mines exists. After the Second World War,

LINDA M HUBER/©DUPUCH

John Bull main store on Bay Street

There's more to discover …
… Call us, let's make a deal

Nassau Intl Airport
377-9000

Paradise Island
363-3095

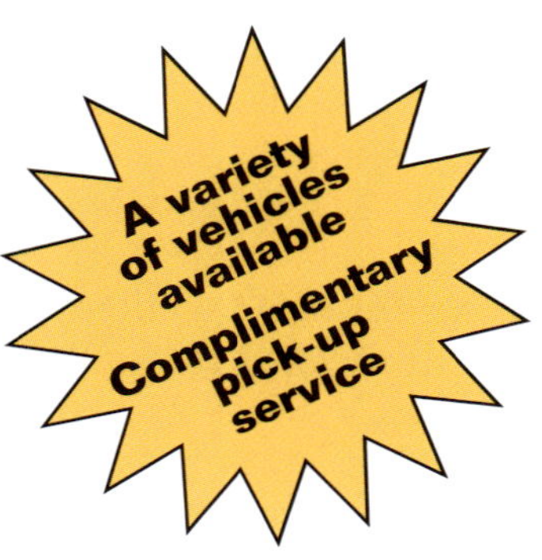

An Independent Budget System Licensee

A variety of vehicles available
Complimentary pick-up service

Julius Stafford and Mary Louise Solomon with their nine children. Eldest son, Percy, sits next to his parents. In front of them, left to right, are Eric, Kenneth, Vera, Minette and Cyril. At right are Winifred, Georgina, Roger Duncombe (Georgina's husband) and Neville. Eric's son, Roy Munro and Cyril's son, Fane, would ultimately preside over the growth of Solomon Bros Ltd, the countries largest wholesale and retail establishment.

Norman Solomon

the company expanded to include an insurance firm, along with wholesale and retail businesses.

Under the direction of President Norman Solomon, son of Eric, the Solomon Group of Companies now includes Mademoiselle, Wendy's restaurants and a zoo, Ardastra Gardens, Zoo and Conservation Centre. Solomon Bros Ltd, previously managed by Fane Solomon, son of Cyril, was bought by Burns House Ltd in 2004. It included Solomon's Mines and several luxury boutiques.

Nassau's wild nightclub era

The period 1945 to 1970 was another halcyon period for Nassau. Under the skilful and controversial direction of Sir Stafford Sands, Minister of Tourism in the ruling United Bahamian Party (UBP), The Bahamas was heavily promoted in the US as the best place in the world to relax and enjoy life.

Tourists came in droves, not only for sun, sea and sand but to enjoy such diversions as horse racing, LeMans-style car racing, big game fishing derbies, power and sail boat races and dusk to dawn partying.

COURTESY NASSAU DAILY TRIBUNE

LeMans-style racing was a large attraction for tourists.

Freddie Munnings Jr, whose father owned the famous Cat and Fiddle on Nassau Street in the heady days of the 1950s, recalls some of the big names who were frequent guest stars at the club, including Sam Cooke, Frank Sinatra, James Brown, Aretha Franklin and Nat King Cole.

Before 1949, hotels in Nassau were off limits to black Bahamians, even to black entertainers. But when the hotels shut down for the night, tourists and local whites would head to Bahamian night spots along Bay Street, and in the native quarter Over the Hill. There they would catch variety shows that included calypso, limbo and exciting fire-dancing acts, driven by pounding goatskin drums.

Bahamian performers who blossomed during this era include Freddie Munnings, Paul Meeres, dancing and drumming sensation Berkley "Peanuts" Taylor, guitarist and singer Eloise Lewis, Franklyn Ellis, better known as calypso performer Count Bernadino, composer and singer Blind Blake, crooner Richie Delamore, the still very popular Ronnie Butler and legendary goatskin drummer "Chippie"

ETIENNE DUPUCH JR/©DUPUCH

Clockwise from top left, George Symonnette, Alice Simms, Freddie Munnings Jr and Peanuts Taylor, at Blackbeard's on Bay Street.

The big downtown hotels that catered to the rich and famous of that era included the British Colonial, Royal Victoria, Prince George, Windsor and Carleton House.

Chipman, among many others. Ronnie Butler's Ronnie's Rebel Room on West Bay Street continued to operate into the early 1980s and Chipman still performs for cruise passengers on Nassau's Prince George Dock.

The big downtown hotels that catered to the rich and famous of that era included the British Colonial, Royal Victoria, Prince George, Windsor and Carleton House. There were many high-priced dining and entertainment spots on or near Bay Street, including Blackbeard's, Dirty Dick's, Big Bamboo and the Junkanoo Club.

Back to the future

While the renovation project cannot bring back the wild nightclub era, it does seek to recreate the sense of fun and abandon that marked that era.

With the shipping companies removed from the downtown area, the way will be clear to build an attractive pedestrian waterfront stroll from the landmark British Colonial Hilton hotel all the way to Potter's Cay, says Dr Keith Tinker, Director of the Antiquities, Monuments and Museums Corp (AMMC). Planners see a mile-long waterfront boardwalk lined with shops, sidewalk cafes, bars and night spots that offer dancing under the stars.

COURTESY DR KEITH TINKER

Dr Keith Tinker, director of AMMC

Coupled with the waterfront development will be a continuing effort to restore and spruce up many of Nassau's historic buildings, not only on Bay Street but on the quaint narrow streets that run down to it and the sea.

The initial revitalization exercise is concentrated in the area between East and Armstrong streets, where shipping companies are now located. Eventually, this industry will be moved to a location near the Royal Bahamas Defence Force Base in Coral Harbour, with the creation of a freight distribution terminal near Gladstone Road. This part of the project will cost an estimated $30 to $60 million. Scandinavian-

"Nassau is the only major city in the Caribbean area that does not use its downtown waterfront for tourism."

based COWI, a dock engineering firm that built the Freeport Container Port, has been awarded a lead role in this project.

Meanwhile, EDAW Inc, an internationally recognized urban planning firm, will be working with the Nassau Tourism and Development Board, and with local designers and architects on the overall Bay Street renovation project.

While the Bay Street renovation is driven partly by civic pride there is also an obvious and pressing need to keep Nassau competitive with other destinations in the Caribbean, all vying for the same tourism dollars. According to Tinker, "Nassau is the only major city in the Caribbean area that does not use its downtown waterfront for tourism."

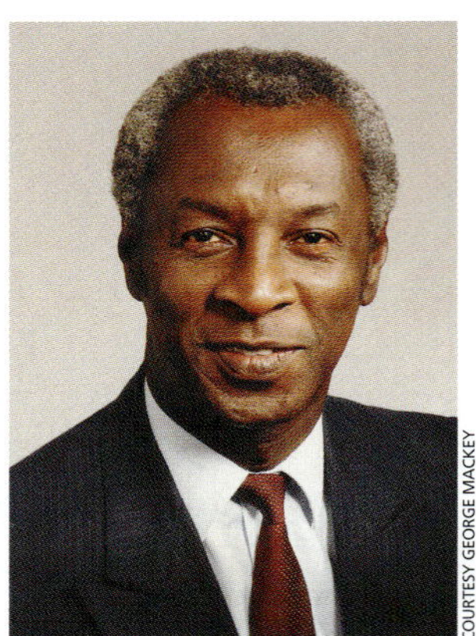
COURTESY GEORGE MACKEY

George Mackey, co-chairman of the AMMC

George Mackey, co-chairman with Norman Solomon of the Nassau Economic Development Commission, agrees. As Chairman of the AMMC, much involved with preservation and restoration of historic buildings, Mackey points to street renovations in Vancouver, BC, Canada; Melbourne, Australia; and Chattanooga, Boston, Cleveland and Baltimore in the US. As a result, those cities "have seen a tremendous boost in tourism," says Mackey.

ROLAND ROSE/©DUPUCH

Orjan Lindroth, developer

Orjan Lindroth, a Bahamian developer, points to first-class restoration work going on in Georgia and Florida as possible models for the Nassau renovation. "But we have an even more interesting tourism asset in Bay Street than either of those two. It's a tremendous asset," says Lindroth. "You have to look at Cuba. They are now restoring old Havana to a very high standard and it behooves us to offer travellers something equally as good." ⓓ

I want
to mix business
with pleasure.

WYNDHAM NASSAU RESORT℠
& CRYSTAL PALACE CASINO

A world of excitement!
A gracious charming property reflecting the colonial heritage of The Bahamas, located on a 3,000-ft-long section of Cable Beach. Ten acres of lush tropical gardens, two swimming pools, tennis courts, a fitness centre, full range of water sports, five restaurants, two bars and a nightclub, ensure you never have to leave the hotel complex. A golf course and casino are next door.
PO Box N-7756 • Cable Beach, Nassau, The Bahamas
Tel (242) 327-7711 • Toll free US & Canada 1-888-NASSAUB (627-7282)
Fax (242) 327-7615 or 327-8829
Email: reservations@nassaubeachhotel.com
www.nassaubeachhotel.com
NASSAU
BEACH
Hotel

COURTESY CARNIVAL CRUISE LINES

A generation of cruise ships

From cramped quarters and scurvy to luxury liners with gourmet dining

BY MELANIE HUTCHESON

The Bahamas' first tourists came by ship. With Rodrigo de Triana's momentous cry of "land ahoy," Christopher Columbus and his crew became the first visitors to The Bahamas and the New World. Centuries later, tourists sail in magnificent vessels to our shores in search of sun, sand and sea – a far cry from Columbus' cramped-quartered quest for new horizons.

The Bahamas cruise tourism industry began to take shape in the mid 1800s. Nassau, with its warm weather and proximity to the US, was known to a select few as a health resort. For a few months of the year – the tourist season – the island became a preferred call for cruise ships and transatlantic liners carrying wealthy travellers seeking respite from harsh winters. Historian T Seighbert Russell, author of *Nassau's Historic Buildings,* wrote that Edwin Charles Moseley, founder of *The Nassau Guardian,* was a driving force behind building a hotel for those looking for a suitable climate in which to "restore their health." Those who did not stay in second homes in New Providence vacationed at the fashionable Royal Victoria Hotel, Nassau's first hotel, which opened in 1861.

Carnival Miracle cruise ship visits Nassau.

ROLAND ROSE/BAHAMAS NEWS BUREAU

Queen of Nassau, docked in Nassau Harbour

The passage of the 1898 Hotel and Steam Service Act brought with it a ten-year contract between the Bahamian government and Florida oil magnate, and owner of the East Coast Railway, Henry Flagler, to buy and renovate the Royal Victoria Hotel. He also agreed to provide transportation between Nassau and Miami and incorporate Nassau into his system of hotels and railways in Florida. Dr D Gail Saunders, Director of The Department of Archives, wrote that this contract, together with the Act, "gave the colony a winter passenger service between Nassau and Miami and a high standard of hotel accommodation."

The Hotel Colonial, in its first incarnation (the resort would be sold, burned down and rebuilt in its 100-year-history) was opened in 1900. The Fort Montagu Beach Hotel followed in 1926.

By the early twentieth century, Nassau had three luxury hotels and began cruise tourism in earnest. *The Nassau Guardian,* in its customary activity report at the end of each tourist season, reported record arrival numbers (3,778) for the 1922 period, which began on December 27, 1921, when the *SS Miami* made its first trip and the

The cruise season brought excitement and employment to the small island.

Royal Victoria Hotel opened for the season, and ended on April 7, 1922, when the *SS Miami* made its last trip and the Hotel Colonial was scheduled to close.

A casual glance through early Bahamian newspapers reveals the sailing habits of Nassau residents. Formal articles announced the departure of certain families for visits to England and the US, and prominently placed ads offered sea passage for first, second, and "tourist" class trips to these countries aboard the luxury liners of the day.

ROLAND ROSE/BAHAMAS NEWS BUREAU

Fort Montagu Beach Hotel

High society cruise visitors

The cruise season brought excitement and employment to the small island. "This season's first English cruise will arrive here tomorrow, and on the following day the second and last English cruise of the season will call at Nassau," said a 1933 *Tribune* editorial. "Both ships are bringing men and women who occupy prominent positions in the social and political life of Great Britain. Last year English cruise passengers were very favourably impressed by Nassau and it is to be hoped that this year Nassau will again be in one of its typically bright, sunshiny moods. A satisfied customer is the best

COURTESY BJÖRN LARSSON/TIMETABLEIMAGES.COM

A Munson steamship

COURTESY BJÖRN LARSSON/TIMETABLEIMAGES.COM

Munson's *American Legion* travelled from New York to Nassau.

advertisement any resort could have, and thus no doubt accounts for the increased number of prominent English people who have already visited Nassau this season."

Most notable among the Nassau-bound steamships during this time was the Munson Line. Established in 1899 by sugar and molasses tycoon Walter D Munson, the ocean freight company began with three vessels to transport Munson's harvest to New York from fields in Cuba. With the decline of the sugar industry, Munson attempted to recover by starting cruises to The Bahamas. New York to Nassau trips were made by Munson's *American Legion,* the *Pan American,* and the *Munargo.* A common newspaper entry could read: "The *SS Munargo* sailed from New York for Nassau on Friday afternoon with 40 first class passengers, 14 second class passengers and 84 cruise passengers, and 90 bags of mail." The 432-foot ship was built in 1921 by the New

By the 1960s the number of visitors to the islands approached one million.

York Shipbuilding Corp. It weighed 7,100 tons, and travelled at a speed of 19 knots. In 1934, during the Great Depression, the Munson Line filed for bankruptcy. The ships were reportedly repossessed in 1938 and the company was dissolved by its shareholders in 1939. In 1941 the *Munargo* was acquired by the US military.

Cruise tourism takes off

In the 1950s, The Bahamas was making its name as a premier tourist destination, and breaking with its winter-tourist-season label for a year-round trade. By the 1960s the number of visitors to the islands approached one million. Popular ships for the New York-Nassau passage included the *Oceanic*, the *Homeric* and the *SS Nassau*. The transatlantic *Queen Elizabeth* began cruises from New York to Nassau in 1963, some 24 years after its original launch date. This ship registered a gross tonnage of 83,673 and could accommodate 2,283 passengers – 36 per cent of them in first class.

According to Sir Durward Knowles, the first Bahamian Olympic gold medallist and one of only three Bahamian harbour pilots of the time, ships in the 1960s were becoming larger and more grand. "The passengers were also a lot different than those we see today," he

WENDALL CLEARE/BAHAMAS NEWS BUREAU

Docking space at Prince George Wharf became a bit crowded as eight passenger cruise ships tossed their lines ashore. It was a record number of ships for 1977. The ships were: *Oceanic, Mardi Gras, Sunward II, Emerald Seas, Flavia, Dolphin, Daomacija* and *Aquarius.*

Before the Nassau Harbour was deepened the larger cruise ships would let their passengers out at Clifton Pier on the south-west side of the island, or anchor outside the harbour and transfer passengers to shore by tender.

recalls. "They were usually very wealthy people who stayed for a longer period of time, and spent much more money in the town."

The *Oceanic* made her maiden voyage to The Bahamas on Tuesday, April 20, 1965. The *Tribune* reported: "This 774 foot liner, seven years from planning to launching, boasts some of the most modern and artistic décor of the day. Among the many public rooms, there are two libraries, a cinema capable of seating 420 people, a permanent chapel for Catholics, beauty and barber shops, and even a shopping centre displaying many luxury items at bargain prices. There are closed circuit television sets strategically placed throughout the public rooms, giving the advantage of watching the liner's arrival and departure from port without the inconvenience of leaving the bar."

The ship also boasted 600 staterooms and eight penthouse apartments on the sun deck. It had a gross registered tonnage of 38,772, a passenger capacity of 1,898 and carried 565 crew members.

Sir Durward recalls that the *Oceanic* operated under subsidy from the government, which, he adds, also deepened and widened the harbour in 1967 to accommodate these larger ships. "Before they deepened the harbour, the large ships would discharge their passengers at Clifton Pier [at the south-western end of the island] and hire taxis to take the guests into town," he said. "Pilots like myself and Chris and Freddie Brown [now deceased] would set out in pilot boats to bring passengers ashore."

Oceanic ran seven-day cruises to Nassau from New York through the summer and longer trips to the Caribbean in the winter. She was

sold to Premier Cruises in 1986, and marketed as the Big Red Boat until Premier folded in 2000.

A tragedy at sea

In November of 1965, seven months after the successful maiden voyage of the *Oceanic,* tragedy struck one of the New York to Nassau vessels. The *Yarmouth Castle* caught fire and sank 60 miles north-west of Nassau. *The Nassau Guardian* reported that a fire started due to faulty wiring in a storage room of the 38-year-old ship at around 1am on November 13. The ship's manifest revealed that there were 550 aboard – 376 passengers, and 174 crew members.

According to survivors no alarm ever sounded, although this claim would be refuted later by *Yarmouth Castle* representatives. It was more than an hour before two other Nassau-bound ships – the US *Bahama Star* and the *Finnish Finnpulp* saw the ship and began a rescue operation.

Bahama Star captain Carl Brown described the ordeal for *Guardian* reporters, "Like the *Yarmouth Castle,* we were on our way to Nassau on one of our regular cruises. At about 10 miles north of Stirrup Cay, we saw the orange glow from the ship preceding us. I thought it was just the glow from the smoke stack, but as it began to shoot higher in the air I realized that a ship was on fire.

"It was about 2:20am when we saw the glow, we rushed to the scene and were there within half an hour. The first thing I saw was two life boats full of survivors leaving the scene of the fire. We called to them and told them to return with us to the scene.

At the end of the night, the number of passengers either dead or missing stood at 88.

"We lowered our life boats and began to rescue the survivors. My men had difficulty in getting some of the passengers to jump overboard... I saw the crew of the *Yarmouth Castle* breaking cabin doors to get the passengers out, many of them even gave away their life jackets."

Some of the lifeboats of the ill-fated ship were aflame and it was impossible to release many of them, which added to the disaster. The ship's captain of nine months, Byron Voutsinas, reportedly left the burning ship for safety aboard the *Bahama Star.* At the end of the night, the number of passengers either dead or missing stood at 88. The ship sank at 6:03am at 285 fathoms. US Consul General John L Banard praised the ship's crew for their heroic efforts.

It was charged that the fire was due to improper maintenance and neglect. A month later, on May 26, 1965, the fourth version of the International Maritime Organization's Safety of Life at Sea (SOLAS) Convention entered into force. Originally drafted in 1914 after the *Titanic* disaster, the new version represented the organization's progress in modernizing regulations and in keeping pace with technical developments in the shipping industry.

Most popular cruise line in the world

The 1970s was the era of "Fun Ships." In 1972, cofounder of the Norwegian Cruise Line, Israeli-born businessman Ted Arison, founded Carnival Cruise Lines. Its first vessel was the *Mardi Gras,* a refurbished former transatlantic liner. The company commissioned a number of other ships during the decade and into the 1980s for service to The Bahamas and the Caribbean, including 1978's *Tropicale,* described by *World of Cruising Magazine* as "the world's first large, purpose-built, mass-market ship and the largest new build since the QE2 in 1968." The 46,052-ton *Holiday* followed in 1985.

COURTESY CARNIVAL CRUISE LINES

Ted Arison, founder of Carnival Cruise Lines

Consistently adding new vessels to the fleet, the company soon began advertising itself as "The Most Popular Cruise Line in

it's just a click away

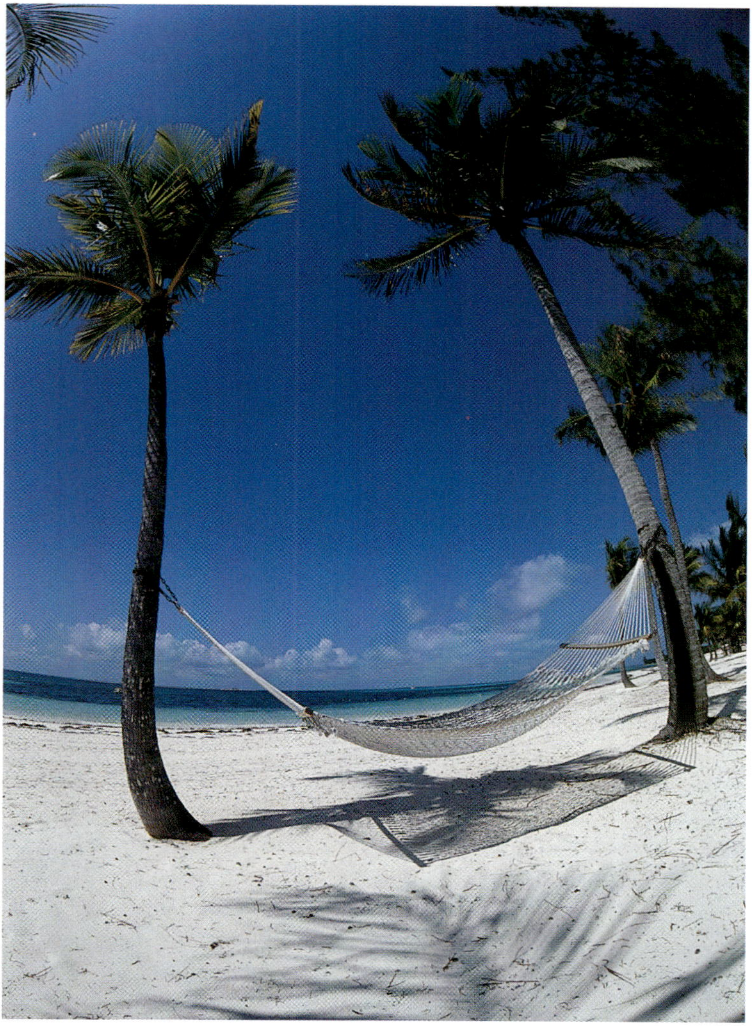

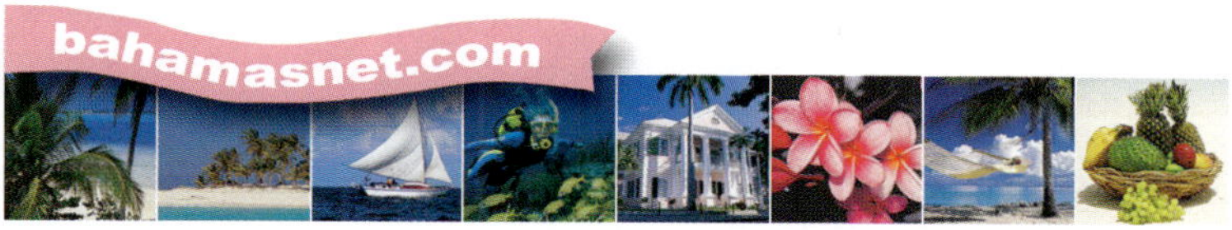

www.bahamasnet.com

LINDA M HUBER/©DUPUCH

Carnival *Glory* leaving Nassau Harbour

the World." The 1990s brought with it the demand for an increased number of rooms with private balconies and larger construction. Cruises on the 2,052-passenger *Fantasy* began in 1990. *Ecstasy* followed in 1991, *Sensation* in 1993, *Fascination* in 1994, *Imagination* in 1995. At 101,353 tons, the Carnival Line's *Destiny* became the first passenger vessel to exceed 100,000 tons when it entered service in 1996.

Disney entered the cruise vacation business in 1998 with the *Disney Magic*. The *Disney Wonder* followed in 1999. The luxury vessels have a gross tonnage of 83,000, are about 964 feet long and boast 875 staterooms each. The ships offer a seven-night Caribbean cruise vacation combined with the excitement of the Walt Disney World Resort. All cruises feature a day at Castaway Cay, Disney's private Bahamian island. The Norwegian Cruise Lines' fleet also calls on The Bahamas. Its newest ship, *Norwegian Dawn*, sails year-round from New York to The Bahamas, calling at Nassau and Great Stirrup Cay.

COURTESY DISNEY CRUISE LINE

Disney Wonder, built in 1999, features an all-day cruise to Disney's own private Bahamian island, Castaway Cay.

Cruise arrivals to The Bahamas have increased by more than one million over the past 10 years.

COURTESY ROYAL CARIBBEAN

Royal Caribbean *Navigator of the Seas*

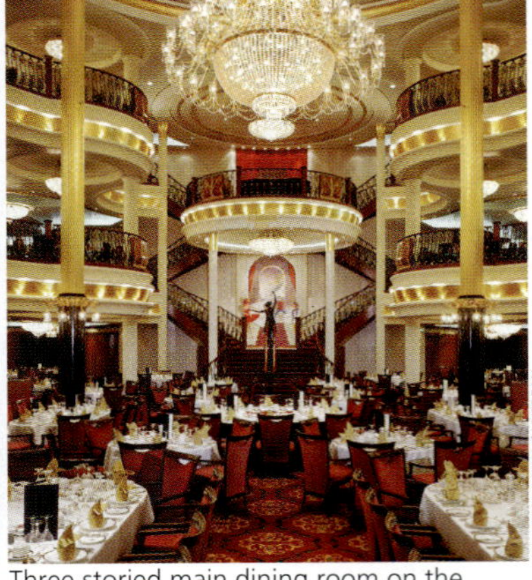

COURTESY ROYAL CARIBBEAN

Three storied main dining room on the *Navigator of the Seas*

According to Ministry of Tourism statistics The Bahamas is host to some 132 cruise ships. Friday, Saturday and Tuesday are the most active call days with as many as seven in port at a time. The most frequent visitors are *Disney Wonder, Enchantment, Explorer, Fantasy, Fascination, Majesty of the Seas, Millennium, Norwegian Majesty, Ocean Breeze* and *Sovereign of the Seas.*

Bigger, better and costlier

The Grand Bahama Port Authority (GBPA) is presently gearing itself for an expansion of maritime services, said President Willie Moss at the Bahamas Business Outlook conference in January 2004. The Grand Bahama Shipyard currently boasts two floating docks – including one of the largest in the world – with plans currently under way to construct a third.

Moss also reported that the GBPA plans a $10-million renovation of its cruise ship terminal to accommodate its 150 ship calls, a figure higher than last year's as a result of Carnival Cruises increasing its travel to Freeport by 100 per cent, as well as the addition of Royal Caribbean Cruises to the Freeport schedule.

Cruise arrivals to The Bahamas have increased by more than one million over the past 10 years. The Ministry of Tourism recorded

Many of the most respected international ship-owning companies and luxury vessels fly the Bahamian flag

2,114,096 visitors by sea alone in 1994; estimates for the same period in 2003 stood at 3,165,069. Eighty years before, *The Guardian's* cruise ship activity report boasted an unprecedented 3,778 visitors.

Enchantment of the Seas is a regular visitor to Nassau Harbour.

GARRY PORTER/©DUPUCH

Building costs also increased considerably over the years. The 1965 *Oceanic* was delivered at a cost of $40 million. In 1998 *Disney Wonder* cost builders $350 million. Carnival's *Legend* of 2002 cost the company $375 million.

Since the Merchant Shipping Act of 1976, more than 1,500 vessels representing over 25 million gross tons have chosen to register here. Many of the most respected international ship-owning companies and luxury vessels fly the Bahamian flag, including Exxon International, Maersk Line, Teekay Shipping, Chevron, Norwegian Cruise Line, Disney Cruise Line and Carnival Cruise Lines. The Bahamas' success as a marine centre is due to a number of factors – a favourable business climate, stable political structure, modern harbours in New Providence and Grand Bahama, and membership in the International Maritime Organization with adherence to principal safety conventions.

LINDA M HUBER©DUPUCH

Residents and rulers of Parliament Street

From ales to jails, this short thoroughfare has contributed much to Nassau's history.

BY GORDON LOMER

Parliament Street was an afterthought. The city plan for Nassau, as laid out in 1780 and revised in 1788, did not include Parliament Street. In fact there were no roads between East and Charlotte streets.

The street emerged between that 1788 map and 1813 as public buildings were erected between 1805 and 1813, creating the need for another thoroughfare. The buildings included what is now the House of Assembly, flanking the west side of Parliament Square. The Senate meets in the building facing Bay Street and the Treasury and other government offices occupy the building to the east.

At the time they were erected, the harbour came right up to Bay Street, with steps leading up to the square. Today's Parliament Street represents a pleasant stroll through the history of a developing, sometimes adventurous, sometimes benign, colonial city. Government buildings occupy the entire east side of the first block south of Bay Street. Behind the House of Assembly is the Garden of Remembrance and Cenotaph, commemorating Bahamian servicemen lost in two world wars.

Statue of Queen Victoria in Parliament Square

LINDA M HUBER/©DUPUCH

The Nassau Public Library used to be the city jail.

The Supreme Court stands regally facing the garden, and behind it on Shirley Street is the octagonal Nassau Public Library. It was built by Loyalist architect Joseph Eve in 1798-99 as the city gaol (British spelling of jail). The first two floors have central areas from which a single warden could see into eight pie-shaped cells.

In 1873, exactly 100 years before Bahamian independence, the building was converted to a library and museum. The cells are now lined with books and serve as cosy reading nooks. The building is modelled after a powder magazine in Williamsburg, VA. In 1802 architect Joseph Eve also built St Matthew's Church at Shirley and Church streets, with its octagonal spire. The similarities are obvious.

Across Shirley Street and up the hill to the south are the grounds where once stood a most magnificent structure, the Royal Victoria Hotel. The Royal Vic was built by government at a cost of £25,000, between 1859 and 1861. The western portion of the site had been occupied by a building used as King's College School, affiliated with King's College, London, and afterwards as a private residence.

The hotel opened in 1861 about the same time the Confederates were capturing Fort Sumter in Charleston, SC, triggering the American Civil War. The four-year war brought riches to southern plantation cotton growers and their Nassauvian clients. Both sides in the war were warmly welcomed in Nassau's first deluxe hotel.

The Royal Victoria overlooked the public buildings and the harbour. Its picturesque gardens were shaded by some of the oldest trees in the city, a couple of which are still standing. The building was almost entirely surrounded by wide verandas. This area of the town quickly became a Mecca for blockade runners, Confederate military officers and others sympathetic to the South.

Royal Victoria Hotel

The hotel was the magnet that attracted colourful characters of various nationalities, many of them profiteers who turned Nassau into a virtual boomtown. Among American proprietors, one was Lewis Cleveland, brother of US president Grover Cleveland (1885-89 and 1893-97). He was succeeded in the management by SS Morton, who leased it until it was purchased from the government in 1898 for £10,000 by Henry Flagler.

The hotel was then completely renovated, enlarged and fitted to take its place in the famous Florida East Coast Hotel system.

COURTESY THE H M FLAGLER MUSEUM

Henry Morrison Flagler

The Royal Vic continued to serve as an elegant hostelry until the late 1960s and changed ownership several times. However its deterioration reached the point of no return and it closed in 1971. The government bought the hotel the following year, but age and a 1990 fire finally put an end to the once elegant landmark. Some of the gardens remain, including the huge kapok tree in which a calypso trio used to entertain guests and passersby. A couple of the hotel's out buildings remain along Parliament Street.

Become a partner.
Help us keep The Bahamas
clean, green and pristine.

MINISTRY OF HEALTH
DEPARTMENT OF ENVIRONMENTAL HEALTH SERVICES
P.O. Box SS-19048 • Nassau, Bahamas
Tel: (242) 323-2296 • Fax: (242) 322-8118

In 1949 Lady Oakes, the widow of Sir Harry Oakes, acquired the property and left it to her daughter, Shirley Oakes…

Across the street is a huge flagstone courtyard guarding Jacaranda, a magnificent colonial structure. It was built at the top of Parliament Street in the 1840s by Chief Justice Sir George Johnson, the second Bahamian to be knighted. A load of ballast stones from Georgia went into the construction of Jacaranda, named after the fragrant tropical hardwood tree indigenous to The Bahamas and the Caribbean. The stately mansion, with its impressive yard and wrought iron gates, was subsequently owned by former Surveyor General William Miller, Sidney Farrington, and Capt Vyvian Drury, aide-de-camp to the Duke of Windsor.

In 1949 Lady Oakes, the widow of Sir Harry Oakes, acquired the property and left it to her daughter, Shirley Oakes, who bequeathed it to her sister, Nancy Von-Hoyningen Huene Oakes. The house has since been modernized and restored to its original grandeur and remains in the Oakes family as a private dwelling with a resident caretaker.

Next door, immediately to the north, is Green Shutters, constructed in the 1860s by shipwrights for Bruce Lockhart

1. The Diamond Shoppe
2. House of Assembly
3. Hansard building
4. Senate building
5. BayParl building
6. The Supreme Court
7. Parliament Hotel
8. Optique Shoppe
9. Magistrate's Court 13
10. Office building, formerly Bahamas National Trust headquarters
11. Magna Carta Court
12. Nassau Public Library
13. Rodney E Bain Building
14. Curry House
15. Green Shutters
16. Formerly part of the Royal Victoria Hotel
17. Jacaranda
18. Victoria Lodge, formerly part of the Royal Victoria Hotel
19. Formerly part of Royal Victoria Hotel

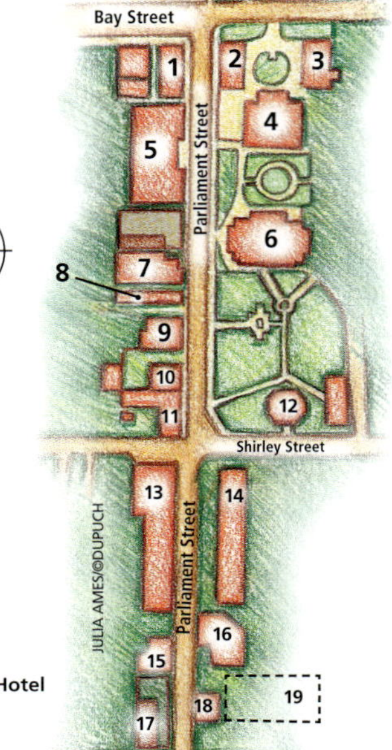

GORDON LOMER/©DUPUCH

Jacaranda

Burnside. In 1865 it was acquired by the Hon John Pinder, who bequeathed it to his daughter Virginia Ann a half century later. She sold it in 1947 and 15 years later it was bought by Charles Bennett Warry and his wife. As Ben Warry's Pub it became a hugely popular

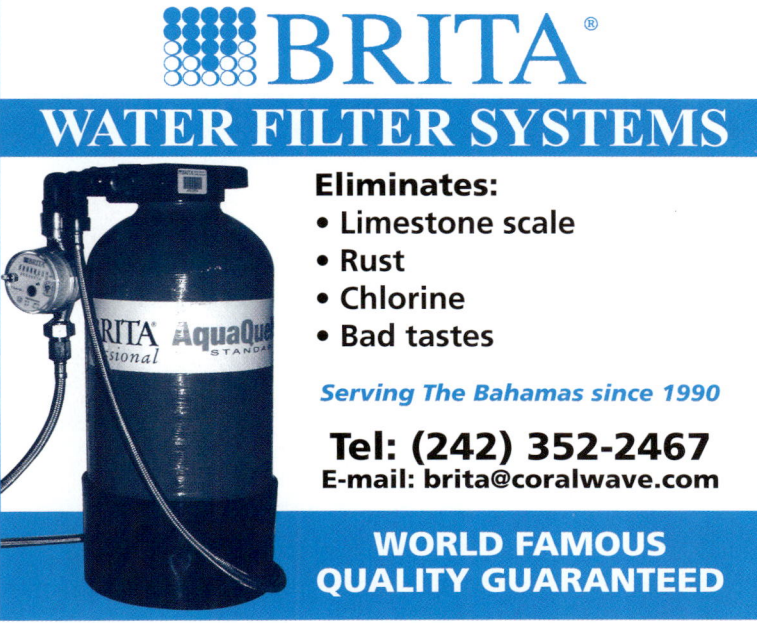

LINDA M HUBER/©DUPUCH

Green Shutters has operated as a pub for many years.

restaurant and hangout during the 1960s and '70s and is still fondly remembered by many Nassauvians and older residents. When Ben Warry, and later his wife, died in the mid 1970s it was purchased by Shirley Butler Oakes. It was renovated as a typically English pub and maintained its popularity for some years. From 1999 to early 2004 it was operated as the Green Shutters Restaurant and Pub by Sophie Wong and Michael Fowler. At press time, it was closed.

The Rodney Bain Building is the receptacle of records and documents pertaining to births, marriages and deaths, copyright, deeds and documents, industrial property, companies, business and company names, and the offices of the Registrar General. This four-storey edifice with glazed tile exterior on the ground floor, was built in the 1960s.

Magna Carta Court, certainly among the most attractive of Nassau's old buildings, was built of cut limestone and wood, probably in the late 1790s. Among its early owners were Loyalist merchant Robert Duncome, who sold it in early 1802 to settler and cabinet maker David Rogers for £460. Ten months later Rogers sold it for £1,000 to a Scotsman, Aaron Dixon, who had a business on Shirley Street. Dixon died seven years later and his will stipulated that the property be turned over to the parish of Christ Church, rented, and any profit be used to educate fatherless children.

The Vestry of Christ Church held the property until 1859. Dixon's will did not give the church the right to sell the property so an Act of the Legislature had to be passed to authorize the sale. It was sold at public auction at Vendue House, now the Pompey Museum on Bay Street, for £592.

The buyer was Sarah Elizabeth Sears Alday, a widow with six daughters. She died in 1885 and the daughters inherited Magna Carta Court. One of the daughters, Maria, who was married to Ernest Kingsbury Moore, bought out her five sisters 10 years later and the place became known as Moore House. Maria Moore operated a commercial bakery, and the remains of the oven exist in the reception room of the law office that now occupies the building.

In 1931 Maria Moore gave the property to her son, Walter K Moore (later Sir Walter), whose family, including

LINDA M HUBER/©DUPUCH

Rodney E Bain Building was built in the 1960s.

LINDA M HUBER/©DUPUCH

Magna Carta Court

two spinster sisters, occupied it until the last one died in 1975. It was rented as an antique shop until Walter K Moore Jr and his sister Winifred Moore Sands (onetime wife of Sir Stafford Sands) sold it. Current owner, attorney E Dawson Roberts, restored the building and it now serves as the offices of E Dawson Roberts and Company.

"When I bought the complex there was a carriage house in the back and a four-holer. It had been plastered over and it was an ugly brown colour," says Roberts. "Some of my friends awarded me the Ugly Ducking Trophy. Someone said to me: 'Why dress that lovely lady when she'd look so much better naked?' I wasn't sure if I had to get permission from the Historical Society or the government to change the outside. But I did take the plaster off and found this beautiful quarry stone underneath.

GORDON LOMER/©DUPUCH

E Dawson Roberts

"When we took the carriage house down I saved the stones to help repair the main building. I bought two chandeliers from the old British Colonial and installed them."

LINDA M HUBER/©DUPUCH

Magistrate's Court 13

The restoration job and change of name from Moore House to Magna Carta Court earned Roberts a Chamber of Commerce Award of the Month accolade in 1980. He painted the shutters a distinctive red and enclosed the west and north balconies with lattice. Throughout the building the original dark flooring has been restored.

Next to Magna Carta is a well preserved private home that is now an office. It served at one time as headquarters for the Bahamas National Trust, now located at The Retreat on Village Road. Stories abound that the area and next door were the old burial grounds for some horses that died in a cholera epidemic two centuries ago. One man involved in digging the excavation for one of the buildings was said to have contacted the disease and died. Hard evidence of this story is elusive.

Magistrate's Court 13 dates back to the early 1890s when the property was known as the "Old Livery Stables grounds," according to historian Dr D Gail Saunders. In 1893 the foundation was laid for the chapel of Salem Baptist Church and it opened the following year. The congregation eventually outgrew the modest chapel and was relocated to a larger edifice on Taylor Street. The original building remains and serves today as a magistrates' court.

All the property from the lane between the magistrate's court and Optique Shoppe down to Bay Street has been owned by one family

FREDDIE MAURA

The Parliament Hotel in its heyday

since 1882. It was bought that year by Abraham Turton Holmes. His brother, Dr Francis Holmes, was Speaker of the House of Assembly until he was succeeded in 1914 by the legendary Harcourt Malcolm (see *Bahamas Handbook*, 1975-76). Malcolm's father, Sir Osmond Malcolm, CBE, who owned Malcolm House on East Hill Street at the top of Parliament Street, was the first Bahamian Chief Justice of The Bahamas. That house is long gone, and the site is now occupied by the six storey main Post Office, which was completed in 1971. Abraham Turton Holmes died in 1908.

The Optique Shoppe was built about 1880 of limestone blocks with tile floors. Over the years it served as a sponge factory and as the home of *The Nassau Guardian*, which has been publishing since 1844. Now owned by Phillip Hillier, the building has been rented and occupied since 1979 by optometrist Randy Hall.

In front of the Optique Shoppe and further down the street stand two enormous sand box trees that some estimate to be 200 years old. During the season large wooden pods form. When ripe they pop audibly, showering seeds that ripple noisily through the leaves to the ground.

The Parliament Hotel was built in 1937 by Harry Prudden for Charles Eugene Albury, a grandson of Abraham Turton Holmes, on part of the Holmes property. In its heyday this 32-unit hotel was an oasis of gentility for winter residents. It offered fine dining on the

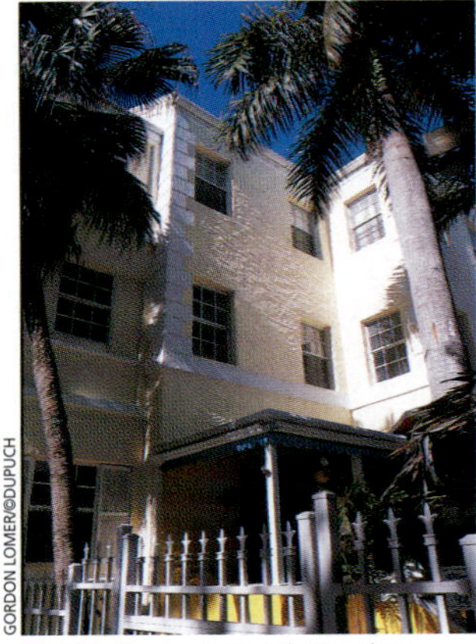

The Parliament Hotel now has offices and a restaurant.

porch and breakfast and afternoon tea for guests in the spacious lawn and gardens on the north side of the property. It has since gone through many reincarnations that have seen it through some trendy times and quieter days. It operated as a hotel until recent years and Steve Wrinkle, son of builder Skip Wrinkle and his wife Jean, remembers excavating for a new bar near the rear of the building and finding a huge cache of old wine and liquor bottles. The building now houses offices and the outside patio is a local bistro and lunch venue featuring Bahamian dishes.

On the property next to the Parliament Hotel a mansion believed to have been built about 1800, before the street was completed, became the Holmes home in 1882. Holmes' great granddaughter, Jean Wrinkle, who used to visit her great grandfather's home frequently, remembers the old estate manor with fondness. It was demolished in the mid 1950s and the BayParl Building was erected in 1957. Part of one of the original estate out buildings can be seen in the BayParl rear parking lot. The Holmes estate also included the land on which the first two office buildings along Bay Street to the west now stand.

With its wealth of mature shade trees, pleasant gardens and historical significance, Parliament Street represents one of Nassau's most rewarding strolls back through the ages. ㉒

BayParl Building

DHL
WE MOVE THE WORLD
Overnight Delivery • Air and Ocean Freight • Import Express
Domestic Delivery • World Mail • Brokerage and Custom Clearance
Nassau – Freeport – Abaco – Andros – Eleuthera – Exuma – Long Island
Island Traders Building, East Bay Street
PO Box N-3735 • Nassau, The Bahamas
Tel: 242-394-4040 • Fax: 242-393-8969

SHANE PINDER/©DUPUCH

Family Islands

D.O.M.
ET IN HONOREM
SANCTI FRANCISCI
HOC TEMPLUM SACRUM
CATHOLIC CHURCH

Cat Island: land of unfinished dreams

Gorgeous island with a turbulent past, a drowsy present and an uncertain future.

BY RALPH DEANS

Forty-eight miles long and four miles wide at the most, Cat Island is home to a dwindling population of about 1,600 breathing Bahamians and an unknown number of restless ghosts – they not being counted in the regular decennial censuses.

Whether ghosts and spirits inhabit the island's ancient graveyards and 16th century ruins or not – and Cat Islanders are famous for believing that they do – they cannot detract from the fact that Cat Island is one of the most exquisite places on the planet to stretch your mind, soothe your soul and kill some time.

"There's not a day goes by, rain or shine, I don't wake up and look at this place and be thrilled that I'm here," says Tony Armbrister, scion of an old Bahamian family and owner of Fernandez Bay Village, a superb boutique hotel on a mile-long, snow-white beach, which he operates with his wife Pam. "I am continually overwhelmed by the beauty of this place, and I've been here for 40 years," he says.

Some say the island was named after Arthur Catt, a sea-going desperado who hung around Cat Island with other cut-throats such as Henry Morgan and Blackbeard. Another story has it that the

Left, St Francis of Assisi Catholic Church, Cat Island, was built by Father Jerome.

COURTESY FERNANDEZ BAY RESORT

Fernandez Bay was once a collection of private beachfront homes.

island was named for feral cats left behind by Spanish settlers who supposedly abandoned the island in 1580. However, there is no historical record of such a settlement on Cat Island, nor have any artefacts been discovered. "The Spanish never made a permanent settlement in The Bahamas," says the authoritative *Catholic Encyclopedia*, "but shortly after the discovery they carried off many aborigines to the mines of Santo Domingo, and ere long the whole population, perhaps never very large, seems to have disappeared."

Originally known as San Salvador, the island was renamed in 1926 and the "San Salvador" moniker, bestowed by Christopher Columbus, was transferred to the now-famous smaller island, 45 miles to the southeast.

On the map, Cat Island looks like Italy on Slimfast, a slender boot that defines the mid-eastern limit of the Bahamian archipelago with the inexpressibly clear waters of Exuma Sound on one side and the equally clear, broad blue Atlantic on the other. According to a typically understated description in the *Yachtsman's Guide to The Bahamas*, Cat Island "offers some of the finest scenery and untrod beaches to be found in The Bahamas."

Indeed there are 60 miles of beaches here, white powder strands on the west coast and long pink beaches on the unpopulated eastern side, called "the north shore" by natives.

Today, it's an island of ruins, clearly visible in the bush along the main north-south road, the King's Highway, which hugs the western shoreline. Seemingly everywhere, one can see the tumbled down remains of some 40 great houses, slave barracks, churches, graveyards, storage sheds, cisterns, walls – the remnants of the plantation era that flourished in the late 1700s and began falling apart 170 years ago with the abolition of slavery.

A diverse population

Four thousand miles due east of New Bight, the administrative centre in southern Cat Island, is the bulge of Africa, home to the forebears of most of the island's present-day inhabitants.

Some of these are descendants of slaves who worked the great cotton, sisal and pineapple plantations, built by British Loyalists who fled to The Bahamas before and after the US War of Independence ended in 1783.

Later, slaves released by their masters on other Bahamian islands, principally Exuma, travelled to Cat Island to farm the land abandoned by the colonial plantation owners. They left when Britain finally ended slavery in 1838. The process of abolition actually began in 1808, when England outlawed any further taking and trading of slaves.

Still other residents are the descendents of "free slaves" – Africans who were rescued by British warships from Portuguese and Spanish slavers, before they could be sold into servitude in Cuba and South America. While some of these were returned to Africa via Liberia, colonial records show a total of about 6,500 free slaves arrived in The Bahamas between 1811 and 1838.

DAWN LOMER/©DUPUCH

Cat island is flanked by the Exuma Sound and the Atlantic Ocean.

LINDA M HUBER/©DUPUCH

The Deveaux plantation is one of the historic ruins that dot the Cat Island landscape.

They settled in communities throughout the chain, notably on New Providence, but also at Bennett's Harbour in north Cat Island. This picturesque cove, at the bottom of a hill festooned with bright red poinciana trees in spring and summer, was also once a pirate's hideout, according to Eris Moncur, Director of the Cat Island Historical Committee.

The Armbrister family

The Armbrister family has been a part of the history of Cat Island, since the late 1700s, when the patriarch, John Armbrister Jr, was forced to leave the continental US for The Bahamas after Britain had ceded Florida to Spain. Shortly before that, John Jr had fled South Carolina for Florida as a British Empire Loyalist after the War of Independence.

COURTESY PAMELA ARMBRISTER

Hon William E Armbrister

He settled in Nassau and was active in business and commerce, serving as a member of the general court. Around the turn of the century, he became interested in planting and chose Cat Island as his home. There he established a cotton plantation with slaves. He died there in 1828.

By 1834, with the ongoing abolition of slavery, cotton had been abandoned on Cat Island. "The red and chennile bugs, hurricane, blight and drought had wasted the already thin soil," according to The Armbristers, A short history, published in the *Journal of The Bahamas Historical Society*. W E Armbrister, John Jr's son, was a major figure of his day, representing Cat Island in the Executive Council and as president of the Legislative Council.

"He was a prime mover in setting up sisal plantations here in The Bahamas,' says Anthony, W E's grandson. "He put a huge area of Abaco, Grand Bahama, Andros and Cat Island into sisal," which was the raw material used in the manufacture of rope.

But after a few good years, the sisal plantations began to fail just as cotton had, due this time to competition from South America and Cuba. "Then came …the advent of synthetic rope, which destroyed the sisal business everywhere. The company went out of business in 1950 and my grandfather died in 1970 at the age of 90." Less than a month before he died, he was appointed Companion of the Most Distinguished Order of Saint Michael and Saint George.

W E's son by a second marriage, Cyril Edward, was born in Nassau in 1901, travelled to Canada with his mother and fought with the Canadian Militia in the First World War. Later, he worked as an actor, director and writer for theatre and radio in California, where he met and married the actress Francis Fintel who, according to the *Journal*, "coaxed Cyril to return to The Bahamas."

Anthony Armbrister was born in New York, visiting Cat Island for the first time when he was a 10-year-old. "I fell in love with the place immediately," he says. "I thought it was great; no electricity, mosquitoes, outhouses," he recalls. "I loved it." Armbrister returned after his first year of college to help his parents who were setting up a retirement home on the island. "One summer holiday ended up being a year, then two years and now it is going to be 40 years," he says with a laugh.

LINDA M HUBER/©DUPUCH

Visitors to Cat Island can see the ruins of the Armbrister plantation.

A room at Fernandez Bay

Armbrister rebuilt the family home after a fire destroyed the first one in 1971. Later, he began to finance and build beachfront homes for people who wanted vacation property on Cat Island.

"Everything was going great until the seventies when the world economy went soft and people could not make the payments on their houses. So most of it came back to me and that is how I started this hotel," Armbrister says. The hotel, now consisting of 15 oceanfront villas, was launched in 1980.

A pilot who frequently travels in his own plane to Florida, Armbrister began to fly his guests in and out to spend a restful or activity-filled holiday at Fernandez Bay.

High hills and tall tales

Cat Island is known today for many things. It's the highest island in The Bahamas, with bluffs, cliffs and hills rising up to 200 ft. Atop one of them, the highest point of all, now called Mount Alvernia, is the remarkable hand-built hermitage of a holy man, Englishman John Hawes, who converted from Anglicanism to Roman Catholicism and became known in the mid 1900s as Father Jerome, "the great heart of The Bahamas."

The island is also known for the comparative fertility of its soil, the unaffected friendliness of its natives and the stubborn insistence that Columbus made his famous landfall at what is now Port Howe, near the heel of the boot of Cat Island. In fact, the heel itself is called Columbus Point. The overwhelming weight of evidence, however, is that the great navigator dropped his anchor on October 12, 1492, into the waters of Long Bay on nearby San Salvador, formerly called Watlings Island.

As well, Cat Islanders are known for their enduring attachment to Obeah, an ancient form of African bush medicine and witchcraft. Although that attachment is perhaps not as strong as it was in times past, it continues into the present day, as islanders will readily confirm. Andros, Cat Island and Long Island are considered to be hotbeds of Obeah in The Bahamas.

Obeah is described as a form of "African sorcery medicine… the persistence of which fascinated, frightened, and confused the whites

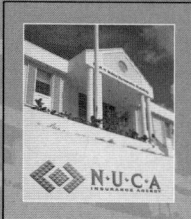

"People have been known to dig up their whole yard looking for a witch baby."

(in the late 1800s) in equal measure... (it is based on) the fundamental belief that all good as well as all evil – everything good or bad that happened to individuals – emanated from and was controlled by the spirit world and could be conjured, changed, or cured by the intervention of sorcery medicine or magic formulas." (Michael Craton and Gail Saunders, *Islanders in the Stream*).

Obeah is said to be related to voodoo as practiced in many places in the Caribbean area, especially Haiti. The rituals are unknown, there is no central deity, no communal services. The practice is said to be carried on by solitary individuals, Obeah men, who follow each other in a secret succession. Their practice is said to involve a knowledge of herbs and plants, deep introspection and connection in an unknown manner to a spirit world. Ghosts are harnessed to do the Obeah man's bidding through hexes, charms and curses. It has been called "a dark path" and "a crooked way," by those who study and write about such things.

Visitors may see signs that Obeah is alive and well in Cat Island. A bottle, filled with twigs, moss and sand, hanging from a tree warns thieves that it's charmed and anyone stealing from it will suffer. Kernels of dry corn may be arranged in a particular pattern on a doorstep, to ward off evil spirits.

When Bahamians talk about spirits and Obeah, they often do so with a smile, as though it's a bit of a joke, not to be taken too, too seriously. Many of the tales have a humourous twist.

Cat Islander Antoinette Seymour, now working at The College of The Bahamas in Nassau, says that anyone who had suffered a slight of some kind, might bury a "witch baby," similar to a voodoo doll, in the offenders yard, to "fix" the person. "People have been known to dig up their whole yard looking for a witch baby. If they find one, they have to burn it and it burns in a peculiar way; fizzes, sends out different colours," says Seymour with a laugh.

Obeah stories abound in Cat Island today: of zombies and ghosts being set by Obeah men to protect farm fields from theft, of a government official who was publically hexed to drown in two weeks, and did. One can sometimes see a bottle amid the stones of some broken-down graves on Cat Island, and this is thought to have an Obeah significance.

Armbrister, the hospitable and cosmopolitan hotel owner, who was a complete skeptic about Obeah in his youth, now says he has seen too many "coincidences" over the years to dismiss the belief system out of hand.

He recounts the story of a young woman, said by her mother to have been hexed to die so that another girl would win a competition for a government job. Discovering that her daughter was hexed, the mother travelled to Nassau to meet with a particularly powerful Obeah man. She paid him $400 (a princely sum to a Cat Islander in the 1970s) to remove a three-part hex.

"The witch doctor said a man would be on his way to deliver the final fatal dose of the hex when he would meet with an accident, would be laid up for several weeks (so the hex could not be completed). And I will be damned if that isn't exactly what happened to him," says Armbrister.

The Church and Obeah

Obeah has been the bane of officials and churchmen from the beginning of the colony. After a trip to Cat Island in 1887, Liston Diston Powles, a magistrate in the British colonial judiciary, wrote "The people here are very superstitious, and what is called 'obeah' is very common among them." (L D Powles, *The Pink Pearl*).

DIANA CAVILL/©DUPUCH

Harvest-time jamborees included singing and dancing.

Fifteen years later, Bishop Henry Churton, an Anglican priest, said that there had been "a bad outbreak of heathenish practices" around the islands in 1902, and commented, "The old African superstitions die very hard." (Quoted by Roscow Shedden, in his book *Ups and Downs in a West Indian Diocese*.)

"The old African superstitions die very hard."

Elgin Forsyth, a white commissioner, wrote eloquently about the superstitions of native Bahamians in his report to the colonial administration in 1930. Deep in the bush, they held harvest-time jamborees, with singing and dancing. "...the great stars look down, and eerie night noises lend wings to the imagination of an imaginative people who throng the woods with fearsome beings, among whom the yahoo, chanchilee, lusea (a flesh eating monster dwelling in blue holes, now spelled lusca) boccanice and chic sharney (now chickcharnie – a mythic, three-toed, owl-like creature said to have malign magical powers) hold high place."

One churchman who fought an unremitting battle against Obeah was the remarkable John Hawes, who began life as the pampered son of a well-to-do London barrister in 1877 and ended it 73 years later in 1956 as Father Jerome, the saintly hermit of Cat Island.

Three things seem to have driven Hawes's conflicted life: a wish to model himself on St Francis of Assisi, praying and meditating in solitude; his need to offer himself in service to the poor; and an extraordinary talent as an architect and builder.

Great heart of the Bahamas

On the brink of a certain career as a fashionable architect in his twenties, Hawes suddenly gave it all up and went tramping across England. He was once arrested for begging.

By the time he retired in 1939 he had been "an internationally known architect, philosopher, poet, essayist, fox-terrier breeder, sculptor and collector of archaeological treasures. (He had also been a Protestant minister, mule skinner on the Canadian Pacific Railroad, art expert, tramp, cowpuncher, Australian gold-rush priest and sailor," according to Bill Davidson, who interviewed him and wrote an article for *Collier's Magazine*, published on July 22, 1950.

Hawes converted from Anglicanism to Roman Catholicism when he was 35. He built churches for both faiths throughout The Bahamas, including St Augustine's Monastery and College at Fox Hill (1947-50) and the Convent and Chapel for the Sisters of Martin de Porres (1948-49) in New Providence, two churches in Long Island and four churches on Cat Island, between the years 1941 and 1945.

COURTESY MINISTRY OF TOURISM

The Hermitage, built by Father Jerome, is also his grave site.

But he is known today principally because of the jewel-like one-man monastery he built on Cat Island's Como Hill, which he bought in 1939 for £35 (an outrageous price at the time) and renamed Alvernia, after the hill in Tuscany that St Francis ascended to receive the wounds of the cross.

The Hermitage, as it is called, looks like something straight out of *Lord of the Rings*, J R Tolkien's classic story. As they climb Alvernia, passing Father Jerome's 12 sculpted stone stations of the cross, visitors can only marvel at the man's skill and the inner forces that lead him to come here to meditate and die. He is buried in a sealed cave under the chapel, a tomb where he sometimes slept on Ash Wednesdays, shooing away land crabs and snakes beforehand.

The complex includes a five-by-seven-ft cell, a five-by-eight-ft chapel, a five-by-seven-ft guest cell and a 12-ft high bell tower. Outside, there is an 18-ft wooden cross and a 900-gallon cistern. At one time a garden graced the hilltop but that is now long gone. The buildings, however, look as sturdy and new as they were when Father Jerome built them 65 years ago.

Davidson quotes Acting Bishop Bonaventure Hansen as saying in 1950; "He is our Christopher Wren. Tourists will be coming to look at his buildings a thousand years from now." The Cat Island commissioner of that time said, "He will be in the mythology of the

people for generations. Even now they call him The Great Heart of The Bahamas."

As for Obeah and the belief in ghosts, Father Jerome had a straightforward way of dealing with superstitions. If he heard that a ruin was haunted, he made a practice of sleeping there and emerging unscathed in the morning.

When a woman was said to be dying because she had eaten food from a garden that had been "fixed" by a hexed rotten banana tossed into it, Father Jerome reportedly ate something from every plant and, finding the banana, ate that too!

Father Jerome, in a letter to his bishop in 1948, said "I've rejoiced to rough things all my life and to rub shoulders amongst the people, but now I want a little rest and quiet." He wasn't to get it, however, because "people call to give you a look-in continually, they stay a long time talking about nothing and anxious to tell tales and lies about their neighbors or to borrow a dollar...," wrote Bishop Colman J Barry, OSB, in *Upon These Rocks*, a history of the Roman Catholic Church in The Bahamas up to 1972.

An uncertain future

Looking at Cat Island today, a believer might think that an Obeah man must have cursed the whole island, for its economic fortunes have been diminishing since the beginning of the 20th century.

At one time, more than 5,000 people lived on this paradisiacal island, workers mostly involved in agriculture. But as the young adults moved away for schooling and jobs, the population decreased until there were only 2,657 in 1970 and then 1,647 in 2000 a decline of more than 36 per cent in 30 years. And the slide is continuing, according to residents. The remaining population is getting both older and younger, as parents seek work in England, Canada, the

COURTESY FERNANDEZ BAY RESORT

Cat Island's peaceful beauty is not enough to keep islanders at home.

TREASURE CAY
HOTEL RESORT & MARINA
ABACO, BAHAMAS
A Full-Featured Resort, Marina & much more...
Prime Real Estate
Full Service Marina (150 slips)
Championship Golf Course
Hotel Rooms & Suites
Best Beach in the Bahamas!
U.S.: 1-800-327-1584 Bahamas: 242-365-8801
Real Estate Office: 242-365-8538
www.treasurecay.com e: info@treasurecay.com

"This is the land of unfinished dreams."

US and elsewhere in The Bahamas, leaving smaller children behind in the care of grandparents.

It seems inevitable to an outsider that Cat Island will one day become a major tourist destination. It's just too beautiful, too steeped in history, offering too many natural attractions, to go on being a sleepy backwater. Those attractions include not only the gorgeous beaches and reefs but blue holes, deep caves, bonefishing and mangrove flats, creeks and sea wrecks, with romantic ruins to explore and a warm, friendly population, all compressed into an area of about 200 square miles.

"There have been rumours of a big development here for years," says Armbrister. "I have been hearing them for 20 years." And while there have been several attempts to get a large development going, all of them have so far come to nothing.

One reason is the difficulty of getting clear title to the land. Much of northern Cat Island is "generational land" in which the buyer has to purchase it from each family member. "So the last guy in line, well, you have to buy him a jet and a condo in New York just to clear the title," says Armbrister.

Land of unfinished dreams

"My brother [Cyril Edward Armbrister, a US attorney] made an interesting comment when he was here, that 'this is the land of unfinished dreams.' So many times you see a project get started and it just never comes to completion. It dies. Typically [investors] underestimate the costs."

Meanwhile, interest in agriculture, once the island's mainstay, is diminishing among young Cat Islanders. "We are finding it more and more difficult to find the local produce that we like to buy.

"Our whole consumption of pineapples this year was three or four dozen. That is all we could get. There used to be some huge farms, and we'd start getting pineapples in May, right through regatta (a major event held in the first week of August). Now we get them for a few weeks.

"For agriculture to work there has to be an external market. Right now, we're the biggest employer and biggest consumer on the island,

and that's not saying much," says Armbrister.

What's the future then, for beautiful, sleepy Cat Island?

"I don't know," he says. "I think about it a lot and I don't know what the future holds for us. I envision a big project coming some day that will help boost the island, but we came as close last week to doing that [in July 2004] in 40 years and that fell through."

With its great climate and natural attractions, the island is an ideal location for soft industry; telecommunications firms, credit card and banking clearing houses, for example. But that would require a big improvement in the electronic infrastructure. Armbrister, who is forced to keep a booking and reservation office in Florida, says "you can't run a business from here if the phones don't work." However, he hopes to be able to transfer his reservations office to Cat Island within three years.

Cat Islanders remain optimistic. Raymond Rolle of Old Bight keeps his family going on an uncertain income from occasional work, a supply of vegetables from a garden in the back of his modest home on King's Highway, and fish caught in nearby Exuma Sound.

"We all'is get by somehow," says Rolle, sitting on a bench in the sun with two healthy, smiling daughters by his side.

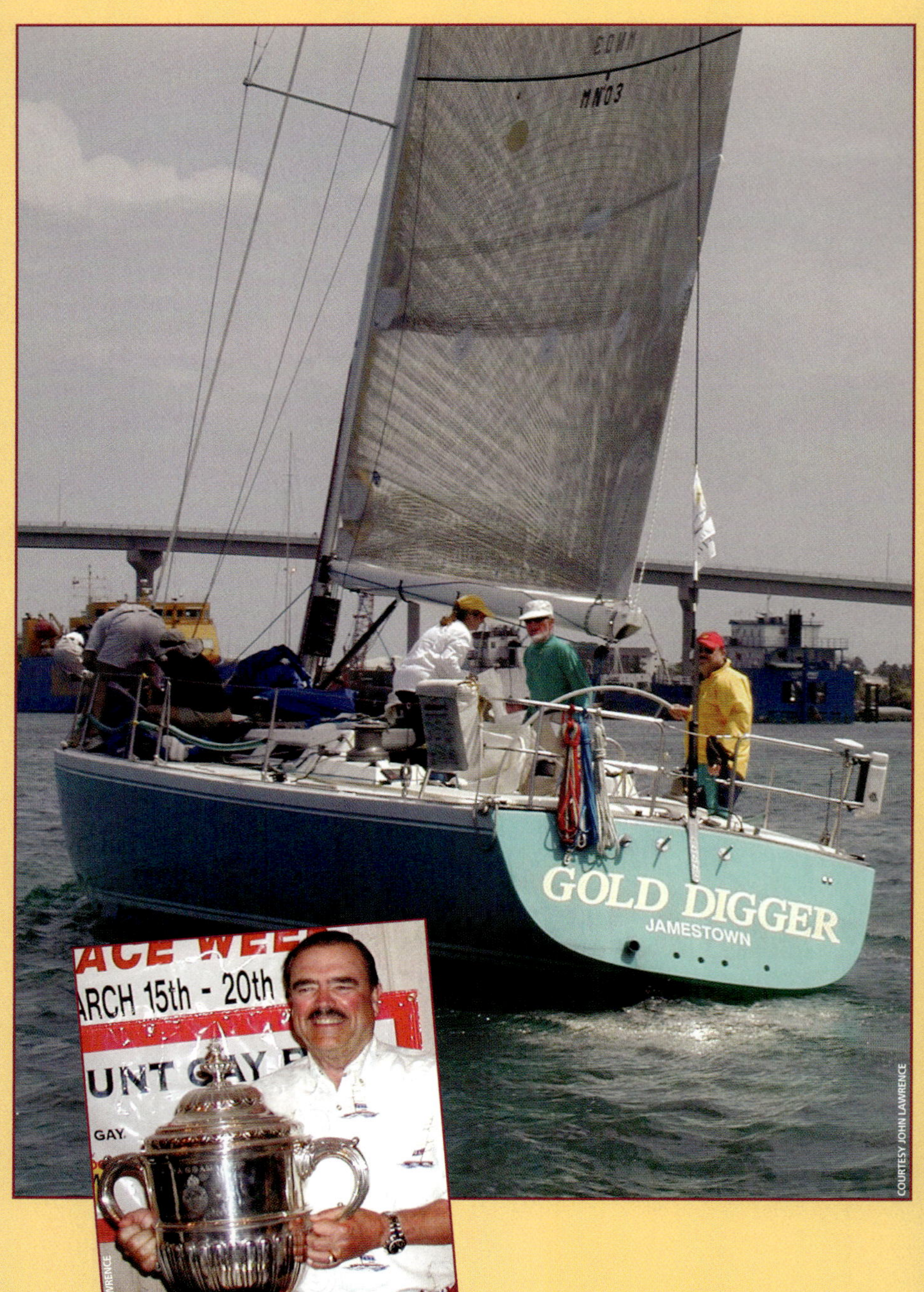

COURTESY JOHN LAWRENCE

COURTESY JOHN LAWRENCE

Big boat racing – glory days return

Top yachtsmen compete once again for the cherished Miami to Nassau Ocean Cup.

BY RALPH DEANS AND MACUSHLA DARVILLE

When mining magnate James Bishop piloted his J/44 class sailboat *Gold Digger* into Nassau Harbour on March 21, 2004, he joined a small group of yachtsmen who had won the famous Miami to Nassau Ocean Race in consecutive years. Bishop vows he'll make it three in a row in 2005.

No one has accomplished that (same skipper in the same boat for three years) since The Bahamas' first premier, Sir Roland Symonette, commissioned the Nassau Cup for the first Miami to Nassau Ocean Race back in in 1934. *Gold Digger's* 2004 victory was historic for another reason. It was the 71st anniversary of the first running. Twice suspended, the race was revived for the third time in 2003 and is now regaining the lustre that made it the most prestigious event in the Southern Ocean Racing Conference (SORC), drawing top skippers, designers, sailmakers, navigators and tacticians.

Only three boats finished that first race 71 years ago, eight others turned back in the face of a vicious storm. Not unexpectedly, the storied 72-ft trisail ketch *Vamarie* was first to arrive in Nassau

Left, Jim Bishop, inset, won the 2004 Miami to Nassau Ocean Race on his sailboat, *Gold Digger*.

©THE MARINERS' MUSEUM

Vadim Makaroff was the first of only three finishers in the premier Miami to Nassau Ocean Race.

Harbour. Owner and skipper Vadim Makaroff, a dashing émigré, son of a famous Russian admiral, had already sailed *Vamarie* to several trans-oceanic victories, winning nine major events between 1934 and 1936.

Memorable racers of yesterday

For the next eight years, the Miami to Nassau race brought excitement and challenge to the yachting scene, drawing the fastest boats and best skippers from yacht clubs up and down the Eastern Seaboard. One of the most renowned boats was *Stormy Weather,* a 53-ft, 11-in yawl, designed in New York by famed naval architect Olin Stevens when he was 25 years old. Another famous racer was the 72-ft *Tioga*, later renamed *Ticonderoga*.

Under three different owners *Stormy Weather* won five consecutive First Overalls in the Miami to Nassau Ocean Race, from 1937 to 1941. She continued to race and win through the decades. For example, she was First Overall winner in the 1997 Antigua Classic Yacht Regatta.

With the outbreak of war in 1942, the race was suspended until 1947. First winner of the re-established race was Harvey Conover,

Bobby Symonette

who sailed his 44-ft centerboard yawl *Revonoc II* (Conover spelled backwards) to victory. Conover, owner of the Conover-Mast Publishing Company, published several top notch magazines, including *Yachting* and *Aviation Age*. He won the Miami to Nassau Ocean Cup again in 1951.

Sir Roland Symonette's son, Bobby, a prominent Bahamian businessman and former Speaker of the House of Assembly, was an avid yachtsman and a strong supporter of the race. Symonette crewed aboard the *Finnistere*, which won the race in 1957 and 1958.

The 1947 race was a stormy and sad affair. Keith Taylor, writing in the SORC web pages says "...a gale-force southerly slammed the 14-boat fleet in the Miami to Nassau race, dismasting *Ticonderoga* and several other boats. Francisco Garcia, the professional aboard the cutter *Windy* was washed overboard and drowned. Altogether eight boats withdrew."

Conover and *Revonoc* were destined to become part of the Bermuda Triangle mystery. On Jan 1, 1958, Conover, his wife Dorothy, son Larry and a friend, Bill Fluegelman, left Key West for Miami. Neither they nor the boat were ever seen again.

A sailboat enters Nassau Harbour at the end of the race.

COURTESY TURNER BROADCASTING SYSTEM

Ted Turner won the Miami to Nassau Ocean Race twice, in 1970 and in '79.

From the late 1940s to the 80s, the Miami to Nassau race became a the top event in SORC. Back then, it was "a four-week-long regatta that included races in southern Florida, the Miami to Nassau race and then an around-the-buoy race in Nassau for the coveted Governor General's Cup," says John Lawrence of the Nassau Yacht Club, co-chairman of the 2004 race, along with Kenneth Benton of the Miami Yacht Club.

Long before he won the 1977 America's Cup in *Courageous*, a youthful Ted Turner, originator of CNN, won the 1970 Miami to Nassau Ocean Race with the 12-metre *American Eagle,* an older version of the famous America's Cup contender. Turner repeated in 1979, winning with the 61-ft *Tenacious*.

Taking a new tack

At its peak in the early 1980's, the Miami to Nassau race had Nassau Harbour buzzing with activity. Lawrence says more than 150 boats took part in the races back then and the crews enjoyed parties at the Nassau Yacht Club and at Hurricane Hole on Paradise Island, where many of the competitors docked their boats.

But as time went on, even millionaires couldn't afford to take a full month off for yacht racing. In 1988, the SORC was terminated, a victim of "the modern world's work requirements," says a press release issued by the Nassau Yacht Club, and the Miami to Nassau race ceased. The entire SORC was closed down in 1988 and was then revived in the early 90s consisting of "around the buoy" races off Miami Beach. But none of these events had the attraction and star-studded panache of the old Miami to Nassau race, with its many legendary winners.

ROLAND ROSE/MINISTRY OF TOURISM

Durward Knowles, left, and crewman, Cecil Cooke, celebrate their medals in 1964.

Modern-day skippers wanted to compete against the giants of bygone days and thus it was that the Miami Yacht Club and the Nassau Yacht Club revived the Miami to Nassau race. It was these two prestigious yacht clubs that had organized the first race back in 1934. Before relaunching the Miami to Nassau race in 2003, the Nassau Yacht Club had hosted Nassau Race Week, beginning in 1998, which consisted of three days of around-the-buoy races off New Providence.

This successful race week, which ran until 2002, has now been merged with the Miami to Nassau race to create what a press release calls "the ultimate in international sailing regattas."

Race organizers had support from many others, including sailing legend Sir Durward Knowles, 87. Knowles, the first Bahamian ever to win a gold medal at the Olympics, is quick to praise Lawrence and Benton. They're "doing a good job to get it going," he said. "This time around, I will do anything I can to make the Miami to Nassau race a success."

ROLAND ROSE/©DUPUCH

Sir Durward Knowles is a great supporter of the Miami to Nassau race.

Sir Durward competed in eight Olympic Games between

Tourism Minister Obie Wilchcombe calls the race "an event of the highest calibre."

ROLAND ROSE/©DUPUCH

John Lawrence, co-chairman of the 2004 Miami to Nassau race

1948 and 1988, winning gold in 1964 and bronze in 1956. He has also competed in 23 World Championships – once as crew for 12-time Star Continental Champion Ding Schoonmaker – winning a number of coveted races on his own. He is the oldest and longest-serving member of the International Star Class Yacht Racing Association.

Another supporter is Tourism Minister Obie Wilchcombe who calls the race "an event of the highest calibre, which explains the fact that it has survived for such a long time." Wilchcombe said the Ministry's support will continue, "as we renew our efforts to broaden the range of activities and attractions for our visitors." Other sponsors have included John Bull, Mount Gay Rum, Prime Bahamas, Calvert Sails, Sheraton Grand Hotel, Bahamas Food Services, Nassau Plastics and Seaboard Marine.

Only eight boats competed in 2003 but that tripled to 25 in 2004, with boats coming from as far away as Brazil. Lawrence estimates that if the event returns to the level of participation it enjoyed in the 1980s, it could mean the arrival of 2,250 people in Nassau for race week. "It's a type of tourism that we really want as a jurisdiction," said Lawrence. "it's that high-level, high-spending type of tourist that really differentiates them from the rest," he told *The Nassau Guardian*.

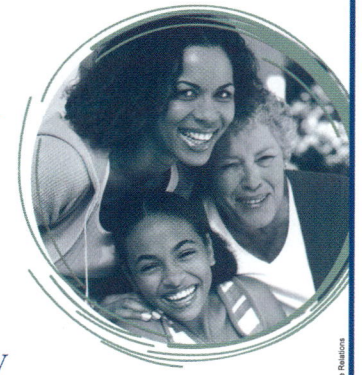

He said the successful running of the Miami to Nassau Ocean Race proves that, "We have the calibre of people who can run organized races," adding that the race brought people into The Bahamas who might otherwise have been racing in Florida or elsewhere in the Caribbean.

Chasing a record run

Pursued by so many famous yachtsmen, it's little wonder that the Miami to Nassau Ocean Cup has become one of the most coveted sailing trophies. Standing about 2½ ft tall and two ft across, the silver cup is engraved with the names of world-famous sailors: Lockwood Pirie, Carleton Mitchell, Bus Mosbacher, Dennis Conner, four-time winner of the America's Cup, and Ted Turner, along with Makaroff, Conover and many others.

©DANIEL FORSTER

Dennis Conner, of America's Cup fame, has also won the Miami to Nassau race.

The average race usually takes 24 to 30 hours but George Coumantaros shattered that record on the German Frers-designed 80-ft *Boomerang* in 1986. Blasting past the competition, Coumantaros peeled more than 10 hours off the estimated sailing time, clocking in a finishing time of 14 hours, 26 minutes and 39 seconds. On that day, recalls Lawrence, "everyone was flying."

©DANIEL FORSTER

Conner has won the America's Cup four times.

But it's a record that's not expected to last too long. "The technology of sailboats has improved dramatically since the course record was set… we will see an all-out assault on the record books in the coming years," predicts Lawrence.

Of the 24 boats registered in the 2004 competition, were three Bahamian vessels: *Woza*, skippered by Belgian Kristof Lingier, *Blue Moon*, skippered by Bahamian Oliver Liddell and *Balamena II*, skippered by another Bahamian, Peter Christie.

"These guys were some ways away from winning," Lawrence says. "The weather was pretty rough out there. The conditions may not have favoured them."

Said Lingier: "Competing was a big challenge because the winds were very strong.

ROLAND ROSE/©DUPUCH

Bahamian sailor Peter Christie has 50 years of racing experience.

COURTESY JOHN LAWRENCE

COURTESY JOHN LAWRENCE

Bahamian Oliver Liddell skippered the *Blue Moon* in the 2004 race.

We had winds of up to 30 knots and the seas in the Gulf Stream were up to 20 feet. It was definitely a challenge but we will do it again next year. I will do whatever is in my power to bring the cup home."

And although a Bahamian has yet to capture the prestigious trophy, it hasn't dampened their enthusiasm for the race. For all those hoping to snag next year's award, according to Lawrence, the boat competition is no easy feat. "You need to have experience in ocean racing," he advises.

COURTESY JOHN LAWRENCE

The crew of the *Woza*, one of the three Bahamian boats in the 2004 race.

ISLAND
QUEEN

BFS

SINCE 1978
CERTIFIED
ANGUS BEEF
BRAND

FROSTY
ACRES

Island Industries
(Bahamas) Ltd.

"It is rough water we're dealing with out there. Other competitors could be nowhere in sight for a long time..."

"It is rough water we're dealing with out there. Other competitors could be nowhere in sight for a long time and you need to know how exactly to deal with that situation. You also need to make sure that your boat is seaworthy for this type of competition, and that the crew is prepared as well."

Besides the Nassau Cup for best handicap time, other trophies include one for course record, first to finish multihull, first to finish monohull, first to third finishes for multihull and for monohull on handicap time and first to third for one-design classes.

For the Nassau around-the-buoy races, the coveted Governor General's Cup goes to best overall monohull. Other trophies are awarded for first to third place on handicap time for monohulls and also for multihulls, first to third for one design classes and first to third for cruising classes.

Faces of races past and present

Yacht *Vamarie* won nine ocean races between 1934 and 1936 with owner Vadim Makaroff at the helm.

©THE MARINERS' MUSEUM

Vadim Makaroff

COURTESY TURNER BROADCASTING SYSTEM

Ted Turner

Brash billionaire, 66-year-old Robert Edward Turner III, or as he is more commonly known, Ted Turner, became the world's best yachtsman, skippering his boat *Courageous* to win the coveted America's Cup in 1977. Founder of CNN, Turner masterminded the Goodwill Games in 1985, an international, world-class, multi-sport competition.

Ted Hood

Throughout the 1960s, Frederick E (Ted) Hood was known as the world's largest sail maker. He is also credited with building and designing yachts worldwide. The most famous of his vessels is the 60 ft, *American Promise*.

Dennis Conner is the winner of more than 100 America's Cup Trial races and won the main event in 1980, 1987 and 1988. Almost as impressive, Conner has been selected the United States Yachtsman of the Year three times and San Diego's Yachtsman of the Year seven times. In 1987, Conner launched Dennis Conner Sports, Inc.

Dennis Conner

Bobby Symonette

Bahamian Bobby Symonette competed several times in the development class of the 5.5m World Championship and won twice. Symonette also participated in the Miami to Nassau race on several occasions, serving as the main foredeckman on-board the yacht *Finnistere*. Symonette's team won the Miami to Nassau race in both 1957 and 1958.

After retiring from a 40-year legal career in 1992, Bahamian Peter Christie acquired H G Christie Ltd, a well-known real estate firm. Christie, who participated in the Miami to Nassau race in 2003, began sailboat racing 50 years ago in the Snipe class – a two-man dinghy race. He later began participating in the Squadrant – a race for bigger boats, 25 ft and over. From 1964-65, he served as Commodore of the Royal Nassau Sailing Club. The avid yachtsman has sailed in the Abaco Regatta every year for the past 25 years. He won that event in 1982. Christie now sails the yacht *Balamena II*.

ROLAND ROSE/©DUPUCH

Peter Christie

COURTESY JOHN LAWRENCE

Kristof Lingier

Bahamian resident Kristof Lingier is the manager of a local shipping company, Seaboard Marine. Born in Belgium, Lingier has lived in The Bahamas for three years. He started sailing at the age of 10 in an Optimist, a small sailboat designed for children. At 13, Lingier participated in a championship race in Holland and won in the open class. In 2003, he sailed aboard a friend's boat, the *Woza*, in the Miami to Nassau race. It was the first time Lingier had raced in 12 years. He participated again in 2004.

A keen yachtsman, Jim Bishop, steered his J/44 *Gold Digger* to victory in several world class races including the North American championships in 2002, and the biennial Block Island Race and the Miami to Nassau race in 2003 and 2004.

COURTESY JOHN LAWRENCE

Jim Bishop

BAHAMAS NEWS BUREAU

Abaco was ready for armed revolution

Residents planned to break away from The Bahamas in the 1970s and become independent.

BY RALPH DEANS

It may come as a surprise to younger Bahamians that not everyone was overjoyed when The Bahamas became an independent nation at the stroke of midnight on July 9, 1973. While most Bahamians celebrated far into the night, others were plotting to separate one island from the new nation, by force of arms if necessary.

Separatists had pleaded with Britain to permit Abaco to continue on as a colony if and when The Bahamas became independent. When Britain refused, some of the secessionists accepted defeat but others carried on, determined to turn Abaco into a sovereign nation.

Historian Michael Craton, in his 2002 biography of Prime Minister Lynden Pindling (later Sir Lynden), summed up their feelings this way: “If separatism were not possible by constitutional means and no aid or encouragement was forthcoming from Great Britain, so be it. They would accept help from wherever it was offered, and would resort to armed revolution if necessary.”

Left, Sir Roland Symonette, premier and leader of the United Bahamian Party

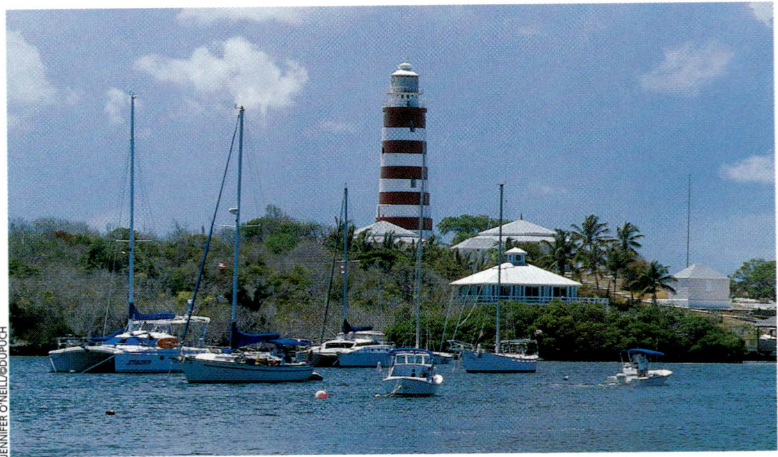
JENNIFER O'NEILL©DUPUCH

Hope Town's famous lighthouse became an emblem of Abaco's separatist movement.

In fact, there was a plan to declare Abaco's independence at the same time, or shortly after, The Bahamas did in Nassau. According to a reliable source close to the movement at that time, the plan fell apart because an avid American backer, a man named Mike Oliver of Carson City, NV, could not come up with the $200,000 needed to bring in British mercenaries. "Oliver gave much more than that over time, but he could not give us the money at that time in a lump sum," said the source.

Had the money been available, according to the now-aging revolutionaries, a "war plan" would have been put into effect, including a sketchy "operation ten plagues" in which a fifth column of supporters would disable Nassau by cutting off its water, electricity and communications systems.

Roots of the rebellion

The threat of separation was not new in The Bahamas, where the seat of power lies far away in Nassau. The Turks and Caicos had already broken away and there had been talk of separation in Long Island, Inagua, Mayaguana and the Ragged Island range.

Abaco's dissatisfaction took firm root when Pindling led the PLP to its first electoral victory in 1967, ending centuries of rule by the white minority. Many white Bahamians began to worry that the new black nationalist government might strip them of their wealth and land. Others, both black and white, who had opposed the PLP politically, feared "victimization" – being kicked out of government jobs, denied contracts and blocked in business affairs.

Still others, fiercely loyal to the British Crown and the social and economic stability it represented, wanted The Bahamas to remain a colony forever. "In 1973," said *The Tribune* on April 10, 2003, "the idea of a black racist government taking The Bahamas to nationhood, free of the colonial constraints which had kept the territory on track for three centuries, was repugnant to many white Abaconians. They felt chaos was bound to follow once London's role as benign and paternalistic overseer had come to an end."

BAHAMAS NEWS BUREAU

Sir Lynden Pindling led his party to power after three centuries of rule by the white minority.

A phalanx of zealots

John Marquis, then an aggressive young journalist for a British paper, recalls that when he arrived in Abaco on assignment in 1973, he was "confronted by a phalanx of earnest zealots who were ready to oil and prime their hog-hunting guns to protect a way of life they had cherished for 200 years."

Marquis, now managing editor of *The Tribune* in Nassau, met with Errington Washington Watkins, a leader of the separatist movement, "who talked of an armed rising, a full-scale rebellion with Abaconians fighting on the beaches, in the fields and presumably on the streets of Marsh Harbour in defense of a just cause."

Errington Watkins, a former senior policeman, became a key figure in the Abaco separatist movement.

Today, Watkins insists that, at least as far as he was concerned, the threat of an armed conflict was never more than a bluff. He says that violence was never an option but *threats* of violence were used "to intimidate and impress the powers that be of how serious we were." To that end, "we had chaps on the beach training with dummy rifles, wooden rifles... but they looked real." But he admits that others in Abaco were more than willing to use violence.

Watkins, a mixed race ex-policeman from Long Island, became a key and controversial figure early on in the insurrection story. He retired from a senior position in the Royal Bahamas Police Force in 1970 to protest the political appointments of persons he felt were unqualified. He was subsequently approached by the United Bahamian Party (UBP), which historically represented the interests of the white, mercantile minority. Watkins ran for the party's chairmanship and won in April, 1970.

He ran, Watkins says today, "because it was the only avenue I could find to combat victimization... Of course, for a black man to be a member of that party at that time, well, you were treated like a leper by your own people." While some of his former colleagues and opponents do not like Watkins to this day, they agree he was a fearless politician with "a hard mouth" – a man who spoke his mind.

Fight for separation

A few days after becoming chairman of the UBP, Watkins says he met with a delegation of Abaconians and agreed to lead a group called the Greater Abaco Council (GAC), which was seeking separation in the

"...we don't have a weak opposition, we have none at all. We have a junior branch of the Progressive Liberal Party!"

event of Bahamian independence. "I accepted because I saw that people were genuinely afraid. I thought at the time, 'I don't know if we can win but I'll try.'

In 1971,Watkins and other members of the GAC put together a petition to the Queen, asking that Abaco be separated if and when The Bahamas sought independence. It was refused.

While he fought for Abaconian interests, Watkins was also taking part in rough-and-tumble Bahamian politics. He ran and won as the member for Marsh Harbour for the newly formed Free National Movement (FNM). The FNM was made up of former UBP members and the "New PLP," also known as "The Dissident Eight" – defectors from the PLP. The first leader of the FNM was Cecil Wallace-Whitfield (later Sir Cecil).

When the PLP won 29 of the 38 seats in that election, it was taken as a mandate to seek independence. The PLP issued a white paper on it and the FNM leadership supported it. Watkins, who had been elected in Marsh Harbour, was furious. As reported in *The Nassau Guardian* on January 27, 1973, he shouted: "I am one who believes in independence never; Abaco believes in independence never." He also slammed his own party: "...we don't have a weak opposition, we have none at all. We have a junior branch of the Progressive Liberal Party!"

Shenanigans in London

Meanwhile, Leonard Thompson, co-chair of the GAC, had been encouraged to take their case directly to conservative members of the House of Commons and the House of Lords who would be voting on the independence bill.

Steve Dodge, Professor of History at Millikin University in Illinois, who lives in Abaco, has written a thorough and entertaining account of the entire Abaco secessionist story

ROLAND ROSE/BAHAMAS NEW BUREAU

Leonard Thompson led a delegation of Abaconian separatists to London.

in his scholarly *Abaco, The History of an Out Island and its Cays*. Dodge relates that Thompson, a much-respected businessman in Abaco and formerly a pilot with the Royal Canadian Air Force in the Second World War, was encouraged by two British MPs, Sir Frederick Bennett and Ronald Bell, to bring a delegation of Abaconians to England to put the separatist case directly to British parliamentarians. Among this group were Watkins and Chuck Hall, an ardent separatist.

COURTESY CHUCK HALL

FNM MP Cleophas Adderley (wearing tie) at a meeting of the Abaco Independence Movement

"At first," wrote Dodge, "they received encouragement but then their support eroded. The minister they were supposed to present their case to was sympathetic, but two days before the presentation was to be made, he was transferred and the man who replaced him was hostile to the Abaconians and their cause."

When Lord Balniel, a junior minister, told them their petition had no chance, Hall fell to his knees and cried "you've taken away my life." The final vote in the House of Commons was 50 to one in favour of independence for The Bahamas. Thompson returned to Abaco, quit politics, and the GAC fell apart.

While the debate was still going on in London, Watkins returned to Nassau and moved a motion in the

RALPH DEANS/©DUPUCH

Mike Lightbourn, now a prominent businessman in Nassau, supported self-determination for Abaco.

House of Assembly, asking for a United Nations-sanctioned referendum in Abaco on the issue of separation. The PLP allowed the motion but it was defeated as only four rebel FNM members voted for it: Watkins, Cleophas Adderley, Michael Lightbourn and former UBP Premier of The Bahamas, Sir Roland Symonette. All four were kicked out of the party, according to Lightbourn, but Adderley and Sir Roland were reinstated.

RALPH DEANS/©DUPUCH

Chuck Hall was the leader of the Abaco Independence Movement.

Still not ready to quit, Watkins and Hall formed a new group, the Council for a Free Abaco, which prepared yet another petition to the Queen. Like the others, it was turned down.

"It was a hard fight," says Watkins today. "I led the movement for three years. I took my fight to the United Nations, to Washington, the House of Commons and the House of Lords in London. And I lost. I lost my case everywhere."

A swing towards libertarianism

Still another separatist organization, The Abaco Independence Movement (AIM), was formed in late 1973 with firebrand Chuck Hall as chairman. Well organized, and funded by sympathizers in the

COURTESY CHUCK HALL

Dr John Hospers, leader of the US Libertarian party, addresses 1974 National Convention of the Abaco Independence Movement. Chuck Hall looks on.

HANS DODTHAGEN/©DUPUCH

Proposed flag for an independent Abaco shows the candy-striped lighthouse in Hope Town.

US, it created a mimeographed newsletter that evolved into well-written newspaper, the *Abaco Independent* edited by Englishman Adrian Day, a well-known right wing financial analyst.

In one of the founding documents of the proposed new nation, published for AIM's "National Convention" in 1974, an unknown scribe wrote: "We can choose to be dragged down with the Bahamian sinking ship, or we can become one of the freest and most prosperous little countries in the world."

The organizers designed a national flag and drafted a constitution which foresaw a limited republic, with no taxes of any kind, strong individual rights, a duty-free market system and "small" government with powers limited to the "prevention of force and fraud." The most controversial proposal was to redistribute all Crown lands to native-born Abaconians (from which they would earn $15,000 per year from lease income),

HANS DODTHAGEN/©DUPUCH

AIM proposed to distribute Crown land to native-born Abaconians, promising an income of $15,000 a year from lease agreements.

Philosophy professor, Dr John Hospers, speaks to Abaconians in 1974.

reserving 20 sq miles of land for investment. Ominously, the Atlas Development Company had already been set up in the Cayman Islands, to take control of this huge "Free Trade Zone" on Abaco.

The "Freedom Proposals," as they were called, could have been written into *Atlas Shrugged*, the classic novel by author Ayn Rand, without violating her "objectivist" theories. In fact, a principal speaker at AIM's national convention in 1974 was Dr John Hospers, close friend of Rand, and leader of the US Libertarian party. Hospers was a virtually unknown candidate in the presidential election won by Richard Nixon.

Enter the freebooters

Even before it was disbanded, the Council for a Free Abaco had been in touch with outsiders, mostly through Hall, who was even then exploring the possibility of taking a military stand in Abaco.

One of these contacts was Colin "Mad Mitch" Mitchell, a conservative MP for Dundee, Scotland, who had distinguished himself in Second World War, Palestine, Korea, Cyprus and Aden, as Lt Col of the 1st Battalion of the Argyll and Sutherland Highlanders. Mitchell considered helping the Abaco rebels but, after travelling to Abaco and looking at the situation, he withdrew.

Hall also established contact with Mitchell Livingston WerBell III, son of a cavalry colonel in the Russian Imperial Army. WerBell has been identified as a former guerrilla operative for the US Office of Strategic Services (OSS) and an international arms dealer with his own military training centre in Powder Springs, GA. Hall also met and dealt with WerBell's lawyer, Edwin Marger of Atlanta, GA.

Another key figure was Mike Oliver, a Lithuanian Jew who survived the Nazi concentration camps and then escaped from Stalinist Russia. He became a successful real estate developer in Carson City, NV, and an avid supporter of the Libertarian party. Oliver was a major fund raiser for the Abaco Independence Movement, collecting money from investors who saw opportunities for themselves in an independent and capitalistic Abaco.

COURTESY THE TRIBUNE

Abaconian "Spotty" Albury tells Lt Col Colin "Mad Mitch" Mitchell he is ready to "fight to the death."

A related group was the Friends of Abaco, a US foundation headed by Hank Phillips, a resident of Fort Walton Beach, FL. The FOA placed ads in various right wing publications, urging investors to support the Abaco rebels.

Not with a bang but a whimper

Dodge wrote that Oliver was "unable to produce funds in the amounts which were required at the time they were needed," adding that several other factors helped to head off the insurrection. Most importantly: "The organization was tied up with money men and military men – 'fuzzy libertarians' on the one hand, and 'cowboys' on the other – who threatened to take over the rebellion." At the same time, "there was a lack of coordination among groups on various islands and cays." Dodge quoted one observer as saying: "they couldn't decide whether to have it on Tuesday or a week from Wednesday." Another idea was simply that Hall "chickened out."

Hall disagrees with both assessments. "I didn't get cold feet at all, but support began to fade. At one time we were all agreed on when and how the action should begin," he says. "We just didn't have the money to pull it off."

Hall made a circuit of the US looking for support but, in the end, he decided there was just not enough of it. As well, he began to have problems with WerBell. "It got to the point where I knew that Mitch was not going to be appropriate," he said.

At one point, WerBell told a news conference that Abaco's independence day would be January 1, 1975, and that he and

"I believe that had Abaco remained a colony at that time it could have gone on to become another Switzerland..."

his mercenaries would be front and centre, ready to defend Abaco to the death.

According to Hall, the movement went on too long without any action and finally, interest sputtered out like a damp fuse.

Would a free Abaco have worked?

Could Abaco have made it as a separate country? Thirty years on, the question is moot.

ROLAND ROSE/©DUPUCH

Businessman Jack Albury believes an independent Abaco could have been an economic giant.

Despite her desire to see a libertarian outpost somewhere in the world, Lynn Kinski of *Reason* magazine asked some pertinent questions back in 1974: "are the people of Abaco prepared to actually live in a politically free society, open to extensive immigration by people with modern views? ...twenty years ago Abaco was a very clannish society and culturally and technically backward... today, an independent, *laissez-faire* Abaco would be in danger of sinking into the sea from the weight of all its visitors, new residents (and) new businesses."

Businessman Jack Albury, whose forebears were British Empire loyalists, says that while he is a staunch Bahamian nationalist today, "I believe that had Abaco remained a colony at that time it could have gone on to become another Switzerland, a financial mecca of the western hemisphere which would have developed an economy based on banking, financial services, insurance and tourism," he told *The Tribune*.

Watkins agrees with Albury. "I believe that had we succeeded, Abaco might not have been a Switzerland but certainly a Hong Kong of the west... If Abaco was allowed to keep the funds collected in revenue (rather than sending two-thirds to Nassau), its development would have, by far, surpassed that of New Providence."

Thirty years have come and gone since the Abaco rebellion that never was. Abaco is now one of the most economically vibrant islands in The Bahamas, still independently minded, but still firmly entrenched in the Bahamian Commonwealth. ⓓ

COURTESY KERZNER INTERNATIONAL

Business

COURTESY KERZNER INTERNATIONAL

Sol Kerzner – tycoon with a plan

An eye for the unconventional helps this colourful South African blow away customers all over the world.

BY DONN SELHORN

Whenever there is a slow news day in South Africa, journalists know there is always something that can be written about Sol Kerzner. He's the local boy from one of Johannesburg's poorest suburbs who went on to become a global developer of "theme" resorts – including Atlantis on Paradise Island – and one of the country's wealthiest and most controversial entrepreneurs.

He didn't disappoint his hometown scribes in November 2004, when *Hotels Magazine,* the bible of the worldwide hotel industry, named him "Hotelier of the World." It's hard to top this annual best-in-the-world honour, but Kerzner will probably come up with a suitable encore.

When he makes one of his periodic returns to South Africa to check on his holdings there, reporters clamour for interviews. Labelled the "Sun King" and "the Donald Trump of Africa" by his countrymen, Kerzner never seems to remain in a country long enough to enjoy all four seasons in any given year. "Sol Kerzner: Back With a Bang," is the way a Cape Town publication greeted one of his visits in early 2004. The purpose of his trip was to announce plans for the most expensive hotel development Africa has ever seen – a six-star resort in Cape

Left, South African tourism maverick, Sol Kerzner

"Love him or loathe him, there are few neutrals," claims London's Associated News Media.

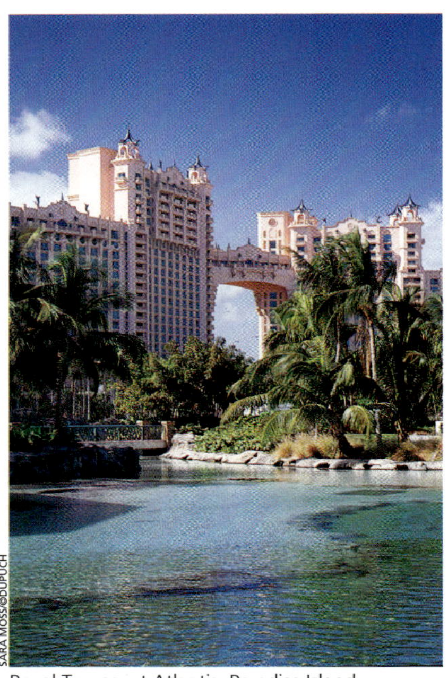
SARA MOSS/©DUPUCH

Royal Towers at Atlantis, Paradise Island

Town – to be built under his new One&Only line of luxury hotels, and due to open in 2006.

In the UK, Kerzner made a splash in the summer of 2004 when his company, Kerzner International (formerly Sun International Hotels Ltd), finalized an agreement to become the occupant of one of Britain's most desirous locales, the Millennium Dome, a redevelopment area along the Thames. To protect his $350-million investment, Kerzner made it clear that he wants Parliament to increase the number of slot machines allowed under Britain's law from 1,250.

Kerzner always thinks big or, as his official biography notes, he is "a visionary who has redefined the scope and scale of destination resort/casino development operation throughout much of the world." With that kind of success, it would be unusual if he didn't make a few enemies along the way. "Love him or loathe him, there are few neutrals," claims London's Associated News Media. In fact, a London court in 2002 ruled in favour of Kerzner by banning the publication of a book, *Kerzner Unauthorized*, about his past South African activities. According to the court, its decision was, "in the best interests of justice," that Kerzner get some closure on the issue.

Tough beginnings

Kerzner is not known for backing off from a fight, in business or otherwise. The youngest of four children born to Lithuanian Jewish parents who emigrated from Russia, he was no stranger to anti-Semitism. Growing up in a tough neighborhood, Kerzner became

adept at using his fists. "The fighting started in primary school," he once told a British reporter, adding that he was one of only two Jewish boys in the school. "The reason I started boxing was to defend myself when I was getting beaten up," he explained. "I began to love the sport." He later became welterweight boxing champion at Johannesburg's University of the Witwatersrand. Upon graduating in 1958, he immediately joined one of Durban's largest firms as a chartered accountant. By age 25 he was named a junior partner.

His father was a hawker who sold fruit before becoming a furniture mover. Kerzner remembers his parents working seven days a week, causing him to be raised mostly by an older sister. "We were a very close family," he says. Eventually the Kerzner finances improved and, by the time young Kerzner entered university, his father had bought a small kosher hotel in Durban. The Kerzner-hotel link had begun. Kerzner says his one thought was to get into business. The Witwatersrand alumnus persuaded his father to lease another hotel close to Durban, where Kerzner set out to "learn everything" about the business.

SARA MOSS/©DUPUCH

LINDA M HUBER/©DUPUCH

Seahorse and nautilus sculptures decorate balconies of Royal Towers at Atlantis.

So Kerzner's career in hospitality really began in 1960 with the purchase of Durban's Palace Hotel. Following the success of that and a second hotel, he bought and improved an underdeveloped site north of Durban, an area with unlikely appeal for tourists. This is one of the strategies behind his success – forging into mostly

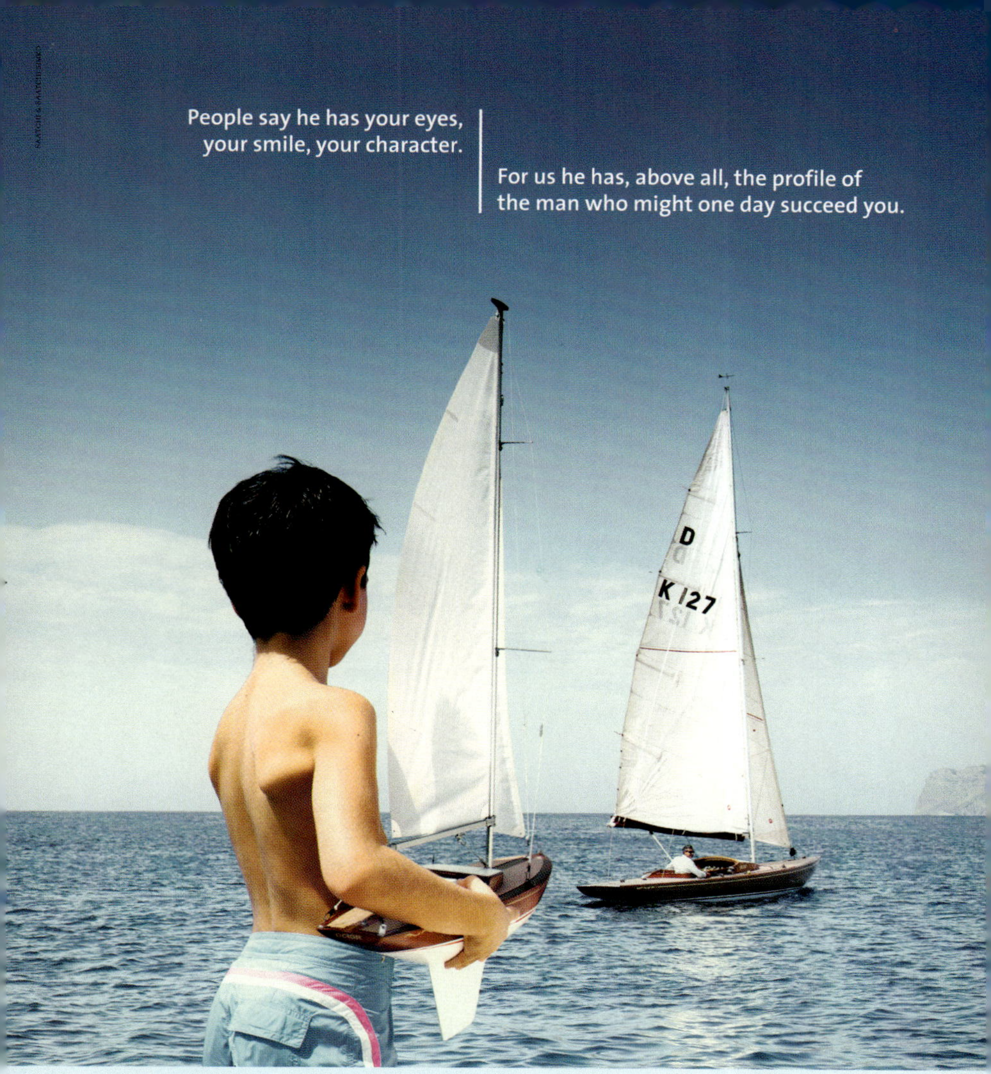
People say he has your eyes, your smile, your character.
For us he has, above all, the profile of the man who might one day succeed you.
D
K 127

Within a year, when he had just turned 30, Kerzner's endeavour was acclaimed as a premier resort for local and international tourists.

untapped territory where there's a strong possibility for growth. For example, prior to Sun City, the acreage was a virtual wilderness with no roads or infrastructure.

Contacts from his accounting days backed his revolutionary concept of a complete resort with entertainment and sporting facilities and a variety of speciality restaurants and bars. The result was the Beverly Hills Hotel, the first five-star hotel built in South Africa. Opened in 1964, it went up in a tiny fishing village north of Durban. Within a year, when he had just turned 30, Kerzner's endeavour was acclaimed as a premier resort for local and international tourists.

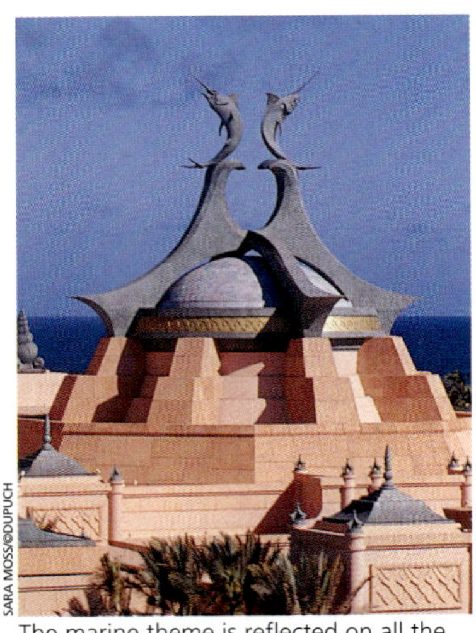
SARA MOSS/©DUPUCH

The marine theme is reflected on all the details at Atlantis.

After the Beverly Hills, he built the 450-room Elangeni, overlooking Durban's beachfront. And in 1969, in partnership with South African Breweries, he established a chain of Southern Sun Hotels, which eventually operated 30 luxury hotels with more than 5,000 rooms. In 1975 he opened his first international hotel, Le Saint Geran, on the Indian Ocean island of Mauritius.

If all this steady growth didn't shake up the world's hotel/casino industry, Kerzner's next bonanza, Sun City, certainly did. Built in 1979, it was the continent's most ambitious and glamorous resort ever. More importantly, it was considered a significant coup because he was able to legally conduct gambling there. Casino gambling was unlawful in South Africa proper, but Kerzner made a deal with the then-leader of Bophuthatswana, part of a so-called black independent homeland, for exclusive gambling rights. Bophuthatswana is a two-and-a-half hour drive from Johannesburg. The resort served as a blueprint for Kerzner's future works – showplaces that wow the public with superior service, lots of glitter, and the unexpected.

...the South African (Kerzner) "is more complex, more colourful, and has more edges to him than a Picasso painting."

Consisting of four hotels, Sun City included two golf courses, a 6,000-seat entertainment centre, a series of water rides, more than one million hand-painted trees and other attractions, as well as a casino that drew flocks of wealthy fun seekers.

A complex and colourful character

Trying to define what makes Kerzner tick is no easy task. Sighed David Cohen, a columnist for Britain's *The Evening Standard*, the South African "is more complex, more colourful, and has more edges to him than a Picasso painting." In retrospect, the thought of Kerzner, a college-trained accountant, pursuing a career of crunching numbers in a musty office is almost comical. A person doesn't achieve Kerzner's success by working nine to five. Said Wilf Rosenberg, who was a Sun City publicist, his boss "would be up at 6am, keep going until 2am, then end the day with a beautiful woman on his arm, a bottle of Scotch in his hand, and a gamble in his casino. The man never slept. He lived one of the fastest lives ever lived."

His executives soon learned he never suffered fools. "The way he ran meetings was unique," recalled Rosenberg. "He would keep us waiting, then swagger in dressed like a scruff, and kick off with an expletive, asking what was going on? "Then the suits had to talk fast.

COURTESY KERZNER INTERNATIONAL

Sun City was South Africa's most ambitious and glamourous resort.

Just the facts. He didn't want to hear your excuses. Try and con him and he'd rip you apart. You'd be out on your ear. There were no second chances." Yet Rosenberg believed his boss was like a porcupine, spiky on the outside but soft and generous on the inside.

Apparently Frank Sinatra liked Kerzner's style and the crooner agreed to perform at Sun City's opening. He was followed by the likes of Elton John and the rock group, Queen.

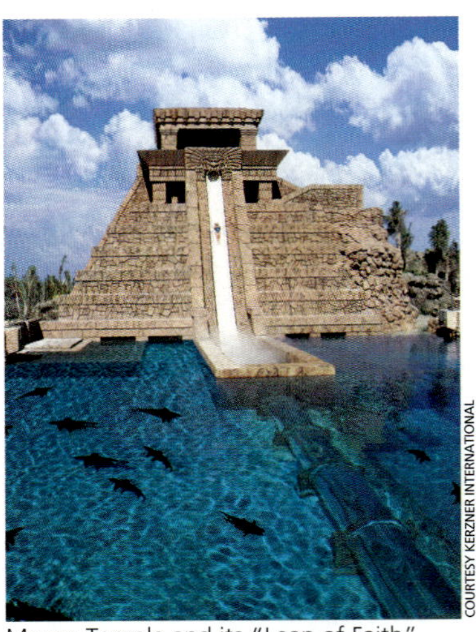

COURTESY KERZNER INTERNATIONAL

Mayan Temple and its "Leap of Faith" slide at Atlantis

Naturally, Sun City was a target of the anti-apartheid movement. Despite his best efforts, says Kerzner, he wasn't able to convince the South African Cabinet of the idiocy of apartheid. Today it still rankles him when critics say he supported the practice. Worth noting is that he received a warm welcome home in 2004 from Nelson Mandela. Believing that he should "give something back to his homeland," Kerzner and his 40-year-old son Butch (Kerzner International's CEO) made a sizeable donation towards the construction of a new hotel school in Johannesburg. Mandela labeled Kerzner "by far the greatest entrepreneur in the tourism industry" who was not interested only in his own enrichment.

Overcoming racial barriers

Kerzner insists that his coming from a country with a history of apartheid never affected his dealings in The Bahamas, where 85 per cent of the population is of African descent. "We have a great relationship, not only with the government, but with the community," he says. On a business level, he argues that it was only after Mandela was released from prison in 1990 that it was possible for a South African company to be accepted worldwide.

Apartheid ended in 1994 and The Bahamas officially recognized the South African state. A decade later, South African President Thabo Mbeki made an official state visit to The Bahamas. Minister of Financial Services and Investment Allyson Maynard Gibson

...he was tired of gossip columnists reminding readers that he was once married to South Africa's first Miss World...

announced that the jurisdiction is seeking to capitalize on closer investment links with that country.

As for Kerzner, he later erected Lost City in the same wilderness area that encompassed Sun City. It was a grandiose facility, including an artificial rainforest with waterfalls, a beach, a sea with waves, a golf course with live alligators, and the mandatory row upon row of slot machines.

Since he was operating on an international scale, Kerzner felt confined in his Johannesburg office, so he relocated to the UK in 1987. Besides, he was tired of gossip columnists reminding readers that he was once married to South Africa's first Miss World, labelling the couple "Sol and Doll." His five children all come from his first two marriages, though two of his children were left motherless when his second wife, Shirley, committed suicide in 1978. "A huge tragedy, probably the biggest setback I've ever experienced," he says of her death.

Being constantly on the go caught up to Kerzner in 1989, when he suffered a heart attack. His cardiologist laid down the law: no more cigarettes (he smoked three packs a day), cut the liquor, and reduce his daily intake of 20 cups of coffee a day. "I still like a drink now and

COURTESY KERZNER INTERNATIONAL

Royal Towers lobby at Atlantis

"In a word, they said I was nutty," he says, grinning. Before Kerzner arrived, The Bahamas tourism industry was in a slump, losing ground for five straight years…

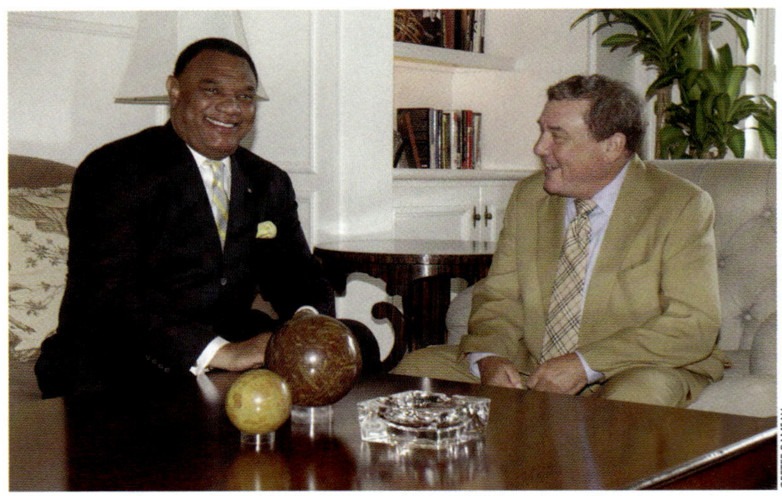
©PETER RAMSAY

Sol Kerzner, right, meeting with The Bahamas' Prime Minister Perry Christie

then," Kerzner admits. As a substitute for his smoking habit, he acquired a string of worry beads which he is now seldom without.

His business associates thought the worry beads were appropriate when Kerzner decided to buy a chunk of Paradise Island in 1994. "In a word, they said I was nutty," he says, grinning. Before Kerzner arrived, The Bahamas tourism industry was in a slump, losing ground for five straight years, according to the Ministry of Tourism. Making matters worse, travel agents in the US were steering tourists to other islands.

Hog Island to Paradise

Over the decades, more than one tycoon had tried to make something special out of Paradise Island, originally known as Hog Island. Perhaps the most publicized, at least in the US eastern seaboard media, was Huntington Hartford II, heir to the A&P grocery chain and a notorious playboy. He purchased four-fifths of the island in 1960 for $9.5 million from industrialist Axel Wenner-Gren. Hartford, always interested in art and architecture, hoped to create a retreat where the "architecture would be pristine, the talk smart and the beaches and women beautiful."

Casino at Atlantis

"Fine," Kerzner might have advised, "but how about the slots?" It's a given that Hartford and Kerzner would have been on different wavelengths. For example, Hartford was adamant that no building on Paradise Island would be taller than the island's tallest tree.

One Hartford idea might have tempted Kerzner. The American wanted to buy the chariots used in the movie *Ben Hur* and recreate a Roman spectacle of chariot races around the island. But no doubt Kerzner would have realized, as the insurance companies warned, that the horses would drop dead in the Bahama heat.

Things didn't go too well for Hartford's dream island and in 1966 he sold 75 percent of his holdings to the Mary Carter Paint Co, which opened a half-acre casino and put up a 650-seat cabaret theatre. The property continued to change hands until Kerzner came along in 1994 to buy nearly 70 percent of the island from Merv Griffin's Resorts International for some $125 million. The rest, as they say, is history.

Taking a page from famed psychic Edgar Cayce, who predicted in 1936 that the Lost Continent of Atlantis would be found in The Bahamas 32 years later, Kerzner began pouring hundreds of millions into building Atlantis, the largest island resort in the world. Judging by its massive and continuous marketing campaign, everyone in the English speaking world and beyond must now be familiar with the resort's attractions – from its cavernous marine habitat to its pools, beaches, fine dining, exquisite furnishings, spectacular slides and rides, and the huge casino that rivals anything Las Vegas has to offer.

Quest for the extraordinary

And Kerzner oversees every detail. Nothing can be "nice" or "good," it has to be close to mind-boggling. He strives to overwhelm his guests. Dale Chihuly, a master glass blower who is widely recognized as the world's premier contemporary glass artist, tells of his dealings with Kerzner, which illustrate the South African's quest for the extraordinary:

"I set about making an 18-ft-high Crystal Gate out of 3,100 handblown crystals."

"The most unusual aspect of the Atlantis project is that Sol Kerzner came to me asking if I would create the Temple of the Moon and the Temple of the Sun. I told him I would, even though I don't normally work with a theme. I knew I could create the sun very successfully," says Chihuly, "but the moon would somehow be blown and constructed in an entirely original way. I knew it would be difficult and force me to make something new."

Kerzner came to Chihuly's Seattle studio many times over the following nine months, and after viewing the beginning of the moon and the sun told the glass-blower about a crystal gate he planned at the entrance to the casino. He wanted to use real crystals, and the piece would be about six feet high. But then Kerzner decided that the scale wouldn't be monumental enough for the space, and he asked Chihuly how he might do the piece in glass.

"Of all the pieces for Atlantis, the Crystal Gate was the most challenging and difficult, Chihuly claims. "We redid it about five times before we could make glass and armature work together. Finally, I set about making an 18-ft-high Crystal Gate out of 3,100 handblown crystals."

SARA MOSS/©DUPUCH

SARA MOSS/©DUPUCH

Temple of the Sun and the Temple of the Moon sculptures by internationally acclaimed Seattle glass artist, Dale Chihuly

After they had installed the Temple of the Sun, the Temple of the Moon, and the Crystal Gate, Chihuly got a call from Kerzner asking him to fly immediately down to Atlantis and look at the high-limits area of the casino. "He was unhappy with how it looked and hoped I could come up with a solution and have it installed in time for the opening in three weeks! I flew down, we spent the afternoon working up some drawings, but he had to trust me since he wouldn't have time to fly to Seattle to approve the mock-up. He agreed, which was very hard for Sol because he likes to be hands-on.

SARA MOSS/©DUPUCH

Crystal Gate at the entrance to the Atlantis Casino

"I proceeded to blow and fabricate and install the Atlantis Chandelier by opening night. By the end of the day I had a 900-element sculpture, 12 by 10 ft, animated by sea life, and Sol loved it."

Continuing expansion

Atlantis is being built in phases. At the close of 2003, the company owned approximately 100 acres of undeveloped land that is available for future development. "Our plan is eventually to expand Atlantis to 4,000-5,000 rooms and to increase timeshare business from around 120 two-bedroom units to over 400 two-bedroom units," Kerzner and his son Butch (real name, Howard) noted in their 2003 annual report.

In 2004 Kerzner International announced plans for Phase 3, a $1-billion expansion development. This would bring its total investment in The Bahamas to an unprecedented $2 billion plus. Scheduled are a new 1,500-room hotel, a water theme park, a marina village with 22 retail stores, four new restaurants, and two additional phases at Harborside, the timeshare resort, as well as the largest ballroom in the Caribbean region.

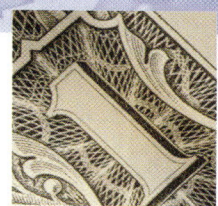

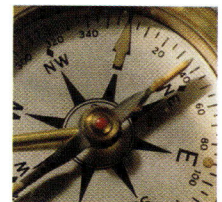

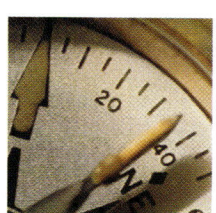

Howard "Butch" Kerzner is Sol Kerzner's son and CEO of Kerzner International.

Kerzner has also acquired the Club Med resort on Paradise Island, which is situated on 21 acres west of the Phase 3 site. This is where the company plans to build Phase 4.

All told, by 2006 Atlantis will be able to house 12,000 hotel guests and timeshare occupants on any given night, says Paul O'Neil, Atlantis' CEO. A veteran of the hospitality business, having held such posts as president and chief operating officer of Caesar's Palace in Las Vegas, O'Neil said in mid-2004 that in its 10-year reign on Paradise Island, Atlantis raised the occupancy level from 65 per cent to 82 per cent and more than doubled the daily room rate to $289. He credited the repositioning of the resort from a casino destination to a resort destination as one of the main reasons for the turnaround.

Atlantis also brings in motivational speakers to encourage employees to assume positive attitudes and share their joy with hotel guests. "We want to get repeat visitors," one speaker told his audience. "We want the person who stays here to go back to New York, Philly, Chicago, wherever, and say 'man, that Atlantis is something else.'" In fact, the Kerzner organization's core value, which is trademarked and even printed on their business cards, is "Blow away the customer."

Because of his Bahamas investments (making him the second largest employer next to The Bahamas government), Kerzner's request for permanent residency status was granted by the government in 2004. In the same year, exchange control regulations were waived to permit Kerzner International (KZL) to offer one million shares exclusively to Bahamians and permanent residents only. The offer came a few months after KZL announced its adjusted net income rose to $1.26 a share in the March quarter from $1.12 in the same quarter in 2003.

With enough projects on the drawing board to keep Kerzner busy for years, plus a stake in the Mohegan Sun Casino in Connecticut, why doesn't he slow down and smell the roses? "He could have retired a long time ago," says Butch, "but it's just not him."

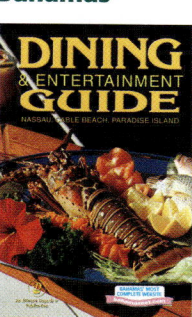

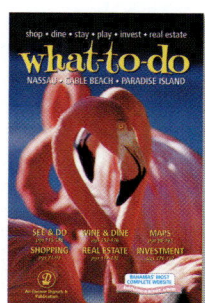

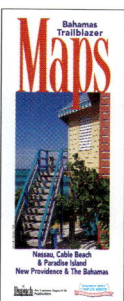

COURTESY MINISTRY OF TOURISM

Bahamas targets speciality markets

More and more travellers are looking for a purpose to visit and they are finding it here.

BY MELANIE HUTCHESON

Tourism and The Bahamas are a perfect fit. Miles of white sandy beaches, crystalline seas and a temperate climate make the country one of the region's premier destinations for travellers. But when Bahamas tourism was formally organized in the mid-1800s with the passing of the Tourism Encouragement Act (1851), it was recuperation, not recreation, that these visitors sought.

The elderly, frail and infirm comprised the first niche that the country attracted to its shores. Looking to convalesce in a sub-tropical paradise and restore colour to their wan cheeks, these travel pioneers made the annual trek to our shores on winter visits from New York and England.

Today The Bahamas' four million annual visitors are looking for something else. Taking their cues from the country's 50-year-old reputation as a year-round tourist playground, originally developed by the father of modern Bahamas tourism, Sir Stafford Sands, these visitors seek diversity and adventure. And what better choice than an archipelago? One that bills itself as a vacation within a vacation and offers a plan for every niche.

Left, visitors looking for adventure can find it in The Bahamas.

Niche markets usually attract a more discerning visitor, because those with a passion for a particular activity are generally willing to spend more in pursuit of it.

Simply put, a niche market – also called a vertical market – is a particular group with specific needs, explains Nalini Bethel, director of business development for the Ministry of Tourism. Compared with horizontal markets, which have a broad appeal and wide audience, vertical markets appeal to a narrow segment of the travelling public. "You can market directly to them because you know exactly who they are," Bethel says.

Market directors use opportunities such as trade shows, seminars, and specialized publications to grow and develop tourism's speciality markets. Led by Brigitte King, district marketing manager in the Ministry of Tourism's offices in Fort Lauderdale, FL, the Vertical Markets Unit positions each island as a haven for sports and aviation enthusiasts, eco-tourists, adventure seekers, sport fishermen, film makers, or those seeking to tie the knot in a warm and romantic place.

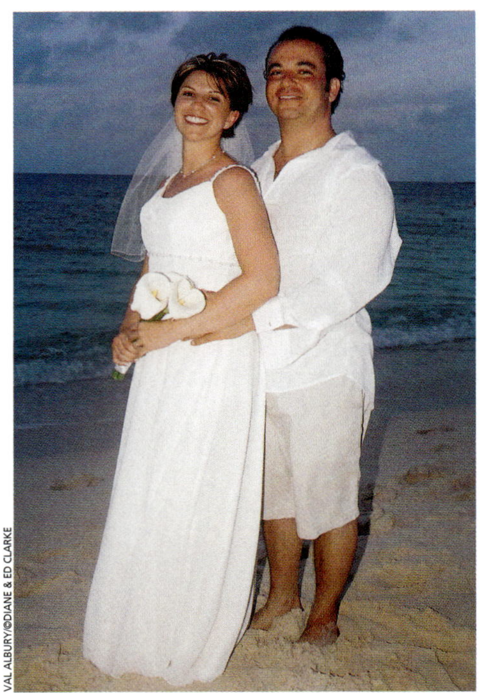
VAL ALBURY/©DIANE & ED CLARKE

Lovers flock to The Bahamas to get married on the beach.

Niche markets usually attract a more discerning visitor, King says, because those with a passion for a particular activity are generally willing to spend more in pursuit of it. They are often people with a higher disposable income, and their average expenditure while on vacation is critical to the distribution of income in the Out Islands and Grand Bahama. "The revenue generated from marriage licences and wedding services, fuel for boats and docking

COURTESY CRYSTAL PALACE CASINO

Gamblers represent a niche market with a huge potential.

fees, fishing fees and guide services, dive operation fees, and related travel costs, including hotels and restaurants, makes a significant contribution to overall tourism revenue," King says.

Private plane excursions

The Vertical Markets Unit is an integral part of The Bahamas tourism network and the units are staffed with qualified specialists in each field. Greg Rolle, district manager and aviation specialist, holds a pilot's licence and is the organizer of monthly fly-ins – three-day excursions for private pilots flying to the islands of The Bahamas. "It's important to have a licensed pilot leading this programme," Rolle says. "Some of our participants are wary of flying over large bodies of water alone. When I'm with them, they feel safe. And, when they realize that I'm using correct aviation lingo, and that I'm stressing safety above all else, they know that I'm authentic and trust me more."

Rolle and his associates attend about five trade shows per year to attract interested flyers. The Annual Airventure convention in Oshkosh, WI, one of North America's largest pilot shows, provides an opportunity to display literature and conduct registration for upcoming events. Additional efforts are directed toward trade magazines, associations including the Aircraft Owners and Pilots Association (AOPA), monthly e-mail distribution and word-of-mouth advertising. Once Rolle has a list of participants, they are

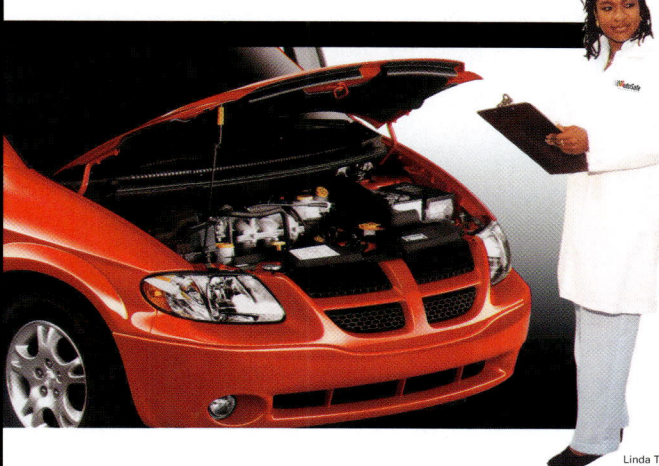

The private aviation niche is worth about $1 billion worldwide with the average income of private pilots estimated at about $100,000.

sent a pilot packet, comprising an itinerary, planning chart, navigation guide, and frequently asked questions about airport information and customs requirements.

Fly-ins take place during the first weekend of every month. Participants pilot themselves to the takeoff site – usually the FBO (fixed base operation) in Florida nearest to the Bahamian island to which the group is travelling – where Rolle assists with paperwork and reviews the flight plan. A common route from West Palm Beach to Grand Bahama Island takes only 30 minutes and on landing the group is greeted by an official from the Grand Bahama Island Tourist Board and led through immigration and customs.

The private aviation niche is worth about $1 billion worldwide, says Rolle, with the average income of private pilots estimated at about $100,000. The Bahamas has more than 60 airports around the country, and therefore the opportunity to attract a large number of these high-net worth individuals.

"One of our mandates is to provide economic benefits for all of the islands," says Rolle. The aviation industry is accomplishing this, he says, especially in the southern islands where the economic benefit is more concentrated. A fly-in can accommodate anywhere from eight to 50 planes, depending on the destination. A location like Staniel Cay, Exuma, because of its limited hotel rooms, will only allow for a minimal number of pilots. An Abaco or Grand Bahama fly-in, on the other hand, has room for more than 50 planes. A working relationship with hotels, attractions, and restaurants on the island ensures that guests are accommodated at group rates and can enjoy a fun-filled itinerary.

The movie market

Marketing strategies vary across niches, explains Bahamas Film Commissioner, Craig Woods. "We may use the same types of avenues to reach our markets – shows, magazines, and clubs, but the shows we attend are different, the magazines in which we appear are different, and the clubs at which we network are ones that suit our specific interests, and further the business of film making in The Bahamas."

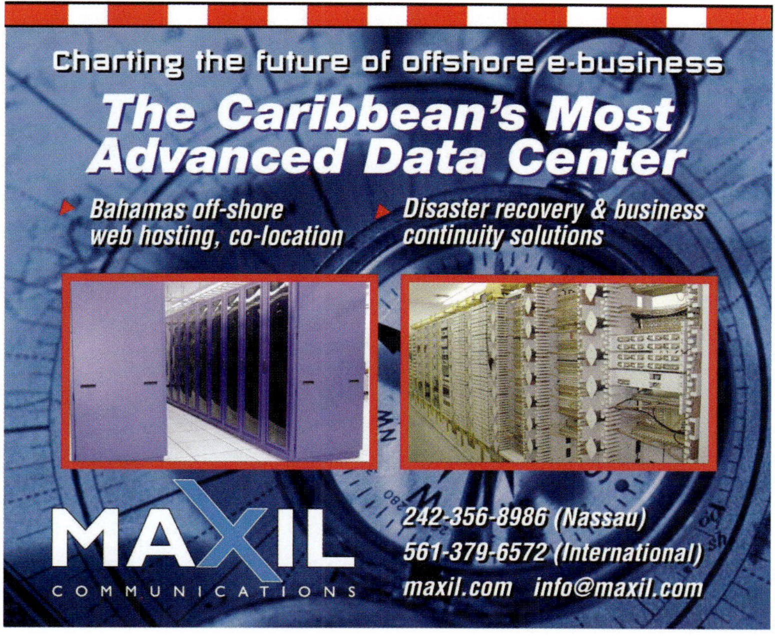
Charting the future of offshore e-business
The Caribbean's Most Advanced Data Center
Bahamas off-shore web hosting, co-location
Disaster recovery & business continuity solutions
MAXIL
COMMUNICATIONS
242-356-8986 (Nassau)
561-379-6572 (International)
maxil.com info@maxil.com

FIBER OPTIC GATEWAY – BAHAMAS
1,000 route kms of subsea fiber optic cable.
• International private line circuits
• Internet access
• Co-location
• Connectivity to US IP backbone providers
CARIBBEAN
CROSSINGS
Bahamas: 242-356-8986
U.S.: 561-379-6572
circuits@cablebahamas.com
www.caribbeancrossings.com

The film industry, Woods adds, is an important part of tourism because of its two main advantages. "First, it produces quick revenue," says Woods. "Film makers are also quick decision makers. They don't spend a lot of time debating a particular location. And in addition, it is an excellent way to display the imagery of the country to a large audience."

The Film Commission is aggressively attracting big Hollywood productions to The Bahamas, leading producers, directors and location managers to its website, www.bahamasfilm.com. The Commission is also repositioning the website to attract business from Europe, including the UK. A May 2004 trip to the London Broadcast Production Show in England is generating positive feedback for films, commercials, documentaries and docu-dramas, Woods reports.

In addition to tapping new markets, Woods is also strengthening his relationships with proven production companies who have projects on the front burner. "We are busy manning the telephones and e-mail to get the word out that The Bahamas as a film location is open for business. We are also checking the production charts with the Hollywood Reporter to see which films are in development that can use our immediate look. While some of this may not reap immediate dividends, we are planting the seed for future business."

COURTESY STUART COVE'S

The Bahamas is a top-notch film location.

Adding to blockbusters *Jaws*, *The Silence of The Lambs* and *My Father, the Hero*, which were shot on location on islands around the country, new films shot in The Bahamas still feature A-list Hollywood actors including Pierce Brosnan who filmed *After the Sunset* with Selma Hayek, Woody Harrelson, Naomie Harris and Don Cheadle in 2003. MGM spent 65 days from January to March 2004

The Bahamas International Film Festival was scheduled for December 2004 at the Atlantis Resort…

shooting *Into the Blue*, starring Paul Walker, Jessica Alba, Josh Brolin and Tyson Beckford, and Eleuthera hosted Billy Zane, Kelly Brook and Juan Pable DiPace for six weeks while they shot *Three.*

At press time the Film Commission was concluding plans to attend The Board Summit in New York City, known in the industry as the largest commercial show in the US. The Bahamas International Film Festival was scheduled for December 2004 at the Atlantis Resort; and The Bahamas film industry is to be represented at the Sundance Film Festival in Utah in January 2005, and at the Cannes Film Festival in Cannes, France in June.

Heritage tourism

Part of the appeal of on-location filming is the native backdrop. Yvonne Woods, Sr Manager of Family Island Heritage Events in the Ministry of Tourism, has observed a "heritage renaissance" in The Bahamas. "Bahamians are prouder than ever of who they are and are willing to share their cultural heritage with the world." Perhaps the most high profile exposé into Bahamian culture came at the Smithsonian Folklife Festival in July 1994 when the world got an in-depth look at Bahamian oral tradition, music, dance, art and craft, architecture and cuisine. This Smithsonian experience paved the way for the establishment in 1996 of the Heritage Tourism Unit led by Yvonne Woods. "We have been working feverishly with government ministries and events planning committees in Nassau and the Family Islands in an effort to encourage a greater awareness among our visitors and residents about what makes us truly Bahamian," she says.

One of the Unit's biggest successes was the Bahamas Heritage Festival, held at Arawak Cay in March 2004. The festival hosted more than 200 "tradition bearers" from 16 Bahamian islands and showcased the Bahamian art of Junkanoo, boat building, basket weaving and herbal medicine, among others.

Heritage Tourism organizers are now liaising with Out Island festival planners and committees to coordinate each island's "signature festival." In June 2004 Cat Island hosted the Cat Island Rake and Scrape Festival. Tourism's calendar for 2005 includes the

Exuma Out Island Regatta (April), the Abaco Island Roots Festival (May), the Eleuthera Pineapple Festival (June), the Central Andros Crabfest (June), the Berry Islands Lobster Festival (July) and the Bimini Native Fishing Tournament (Aug).

These festivals are attended by residents and an increasing number of visitors. Advertising takes place on the Ministry of Tourism's website, www.bahamas.com, and through overseas Bahamas Tourist Offices.

Eco-adventures for nature lovers

Visitors are also drawn to The Bahamas by activities that are not listed in the calendar. The diversity of the natural environment of The Bahamas lends itself to ecotourism, says Sheila Cox, general manager of ecotourism in the Ministry of Tourism. "In The Bahamas every island has its own character. Our islands possess rich forestry, water activities, birds, and a healthy population of animals that are sometimes endangered elsewhere in the world."

Cox defines ecotourism as responsible travel to natural areas that conserves the environment and well being of the local people. Cox works closely with the Bahamas National Trust and the Department of Environmental Health in preservation and conservation of the natural environment.

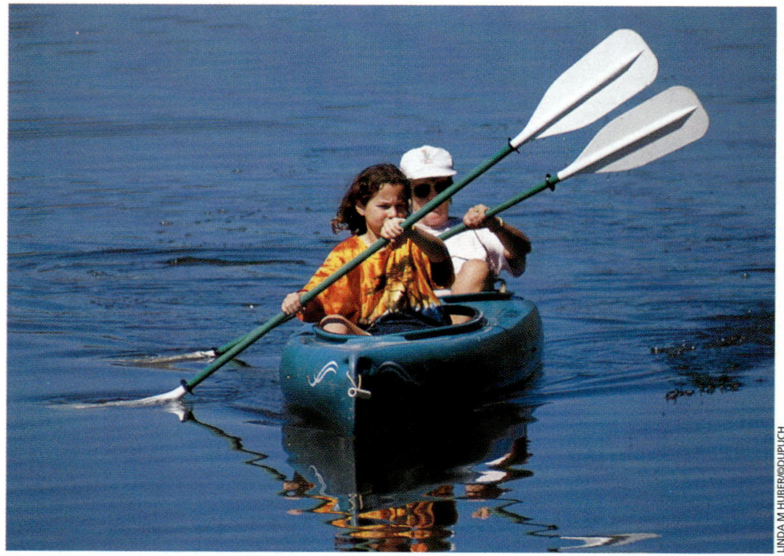

LINDA M HUBER/©DUPUCH

Nature lovers can go on kayak excursions in Grand Bahama and the Exumas.

The resort's "earth-kind resort practices" include being powered entirely by alternative energy…

"Ecotourists are special because they want to enjoy what we have to offer, but they are responsible visitors and want to protect the environment that they come into contact with. This is a class of tourist that we love!" Ecotourism activities include birdwatching, bonefishing, hiking, exploring nature trails, horseback riding, water sports, canoeing and kayaking. Erika Gates, operator of Kayak Nature Tours in Grand Bahama, trains professional nature guides to deepen their appreciation of the marine environment, and teaches them to share the wonders of the natural environment with visitors. Gates reported at the first Annual National Tourism Conference that her company worked with Disney Cruise Line for more than three years to create nature experiences for passengers of the *Disney Wonder* and the *Disney Magic* and started operating on Castaway Cay, Disney's private island in The Bahamas, in March 2003.

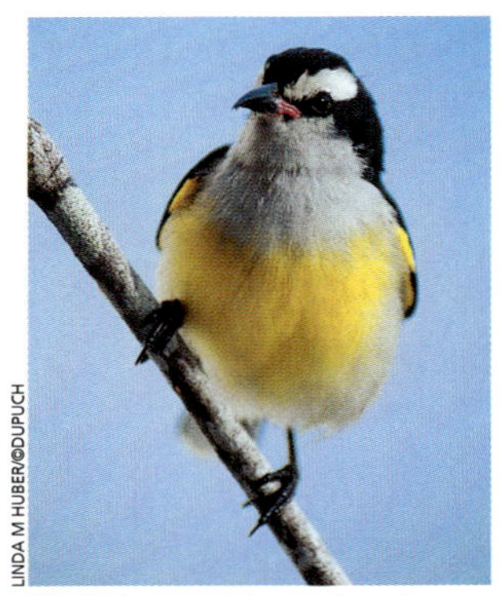
LINDA M HUBER/©DUPUCH

The Bahamas is home to a large variety of birds.

"Every niche in tourism should be ecotourism because in it you find elements of education and sustainability," says Cox. "We need to be an eco-nation." In addition to conservation centres such as the Bahamas National Trust and the Ardastra Gardens, Zoo and Conservation Centre in New Providence, the Garden of the Groves and Lucayan National Park in Grand Bahama, and other national parks throughout the archipelago, some hotels are attracting visitors because of their stance in conservation and protecting the environment.

In Andros, Tiamo Nature Resort recorded 65 to 70 per cent occupancy as early as its third year of operation. Tiamo targets a niche market so potential guests are educated on what they are buying into even before they reach Andros. The resort's "earth-kind resort practices" include being powered entirely by alternative energy via a solar electricity generating system and its use of low-flush composting toilets.

Bahamas' First Full Service Garden Depot
"Creativity Keeps Us On Top"
ML
MUNROE'S LANDSCAPING
SPECIALIZING IN:
Lawn care • Landscaping • Tree cutting • Garden Maintenance • Waterfalls
Irrigation • Indoor/outdoor plants • Fresh flower arrangements • and more...
Satisfied area clients include: Club Med, Paradise Island; Colina Financial Insurance; Central Bank; Old Fort Bay; Lyford Cay
MUNROE'S LANDSCAPING LTD.
Carmichael Road
PO Box CR-54261, Nassau, Bahamas
Tel: 242-341-2336/7 • Fax: 341-2337
Friendly, knowledgeable staff
Complete liability insurance - Fully licensed

COURTESY MOUNT TABOR FULL GOSPEL BAPTIST CHURCH

Five Days Ablaze brought worshippers to New Providence to see local and international evangelists.

Religious tourism

Besides recreation, international companies choose The Bahamas to host meetings, conventions and conferences. Ingrid Bartlett, general manager of groups and conferences for the Ministry of Tourism, says business travellers are divided into two groups – meetings and incentive groups. The Bahamas is an incentive destination, and trips here are used as rewards for outstanding employees, or for conventions where the group wants to conduct light business in a relaxing atmosphere. The Bahamas has hosted lawyers conventions, lodges, pharmaceutical companies, banks and fraternity groups. In marketing to meetings and incentive groups, niche market concepts still apply. One group that is easily identifiable and most welcome in the country is the religious tourist.

COURTESY MINISTRY OF TOURISM

Linda Thompson

The religious market is not new, says Linda Thompson, who is the manager of groups with responsibility for religious markets. "Organized religious groups have been coming to The Bahamas since the early 1960s with the arrival of the National Baptist Conventions under the leadership of Pastor Grace Cobbs. The Church of the Lord Jesus Christ of the Apostolic Faith has also been visiting since 1965," she says. More recently, religious tourism has been in the spotlight due to Prime Minister Perry Christie's relaunch of the market.

Visits by internationally renowned charismatic evangelists, Bishop T D Jakes and Pastor Benny Hinn of the US, and the popularity of Bahamian evangelists Pastor Miles Munroe and Bishop Neil Ellis, have boosted this market. An increase in meeting space and hotel rooms and the proximity to the US, make the country an obvious choice for religious meetings, Thompson says. "Religious groups are a wonderful market to work with because they are a varied market. Within this category there are also sporting groups, religious publishers, media, music, movies, gospel singers, film makers, and marriage clubs." The groups often travel in off periods, since their meetings are not confined to peak travel seasons, Thompson adds. Liaising with Bahamian evangelists who travel outside The Bahamas is also a part of Thompson's responsibilities. Clint Watson, director of Shaback, finds that his gospel choir is also seen as an ambassador for The Bahamas when travelling abroad.

Sports tourism

Golf, fishing and boating opportunities for sports enthusiasts abound in The Bahamas. In 2004 New Providence hosted a number of golf tournaments, including the Independence Golf Series, which kicked off in Florida on July 16 and continued on Bahamian golf courses in New Providence, Grand Bahama and Abaco.

Sports visitors also come to The Bahamas looking for a new and exotic place to race. The Conchman Triathlon in Grand Bahama draws participants from overseas each year as well as from other islands in The Bahamas. Cycling races and swim meets also bring athletes from abroad.

COURTESY THE LUCAYAN

Visitors are drawn to excellent golf courses, views and weather.

"The Bahamas has the largest flat areas and shallow waters in the world, and the largest tropical nursery system."

Soccer, baseball, tennis and basketball are popular sports in New Providence, but fishing rules supreme in the Out Islands, says Earl Miller, senior manager of sports tourism at the Bahamas Ministry of Tourism in Plantation, FL. "Fishing is huge in the Out Islands – they go hand in hand," Miller says.

The annual Wahoo Championship Series is a three-leg competition that takes place between November and February. The first and third legs are held at Port Lucaya Marina, Grand Bahama. The Bahamas Billfish Championship is a six-tournament series held throughout the Abacos between April and June. About 60 50-foot boats take part in each tournament which lasts four to five days. Miller estimates that while they are in the country, visitors on each boat spend about $30,000 on crew, dockage fees, fuel and accommodations. President of the Bahamas Sport Fishing and Conservation Association, Prescott Smith, reported that the fly fishing industry in The Bahamas is estimated at $500 million with about three per cent actually ending up in the hands of the Bahamian people or government. "The Bahamas has the largest flat areas and shallow waters in the world, and the largest tropical nursery system. We have the largest fishing ground of its kind in the world for recreational fishing," Smith said in a presentation at the inaugural National Tourism Conference in January 2004.

COURTESY UNEXSO

Divers flock to The Bahamas for spectacular scenery.

Boating, the third element in the Out Island sports offering, brings boaters to The Bahamas and takes Bahamians to the boats. Miller says marketing efforts require him to hold about 30 seminars per year at boating clubs in North America to inform interested boaters about the ease of boating in the Bahama islands. Miller also attends trade shows, including the Miami International Boat Show, and organizes regular boating flings – escorted flotillas from Florida to the islands of Grand Bahama, Bimini, Chub Cay, Andros and Abaco.

And then there are boat races, which attract a less-than-leisurely brand of boaters. The Miami to Nassau Ocean Race has been bringing crews of hardy sailors, including some famous names, to Bahamian shores off and on since 1934. (See *Big boat racing: the glory days return*, pg 158.)

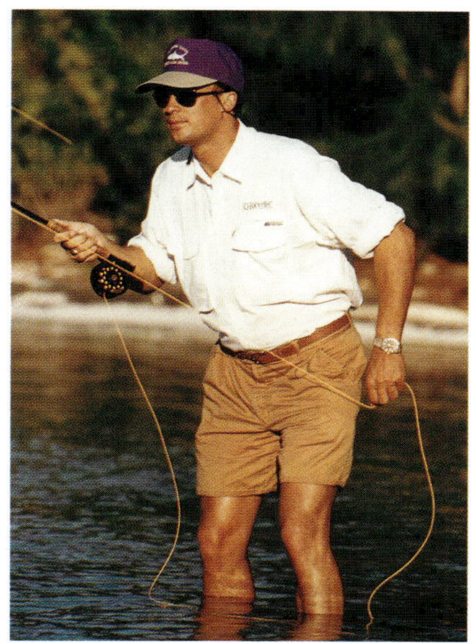

The fly fishing industry brings big dollars for Bahamians.

GORDON LOMER/©DUPUCH

Hedge funds offer advantages

The Bahamas provides intriguing products for high-net worth investors.

BY DONN SELHORN

Mutual funds or hedge funds? Investors debating which is the better option are really comparing apples and oranges.

First, a look at hedge funds. They have been around for more than 50 years but fell out of favour during Wall Street's bear markets of 1969 to '70 and '73 to '74. For the next dozen years hedge funds were barely visible in investment portfolios. Then, in 1986, a magazine article in *Institutional Investor* documented the performance of a hedge fund that produced an annual return of 43 per cent in its first six years of existence.

The article didn't start a stampede equal to the California Gold Rush, but it certainly gave the funds renewed respect. In subsequent years, and despite at least one highly publicized scandal, hedge funds worldwide have since grown into about 8,000 in number with an estimated $1 trillion in assets.

Today, a lot of hedge funds don't "hedge" in the strict sense of the term. So the label is a bit of a misnomer. In fact, a large number of the funds don't hedge against risk at all. Put simply, a hedge fund is a

Left, savvy investors look to The Bahamas for its wide range of financial services.

...in the past decade there's little doubt a growing number of hedge funds are calling The Bahamas home...

COURTESY KEITH SEYMOUR SR

Keith Seymour Sr

COURTESY MARK HOLOWESKO

Mark Holowesko

COURTESY DORIAN B FOYIL

Dorian B Foyil

COURTESY JANE SIEBELS

Jane Siebels

private investment partnership in which investors' assets are pooled for the purpose of investing in a variety of securities and derivatives. Many hedge funds look to take advantage of both up and down markets by both buying and shorting stocks. Hedge funds dominate in offshore sectors because of minimal regulations globally. They have a far more aggressive investment strategy.

At present, nearly 90 per cent of hedge funds are located in the US and tax-neutral jurisdictions including The Bahamas, Cayman Islands, British Virgin Islands and Bermuda. (London is Europe's leading centre for managers of hedge funds.)

Although it's been reported that more than 750 mutual funds do business in The Bahamas, hedge fund figures are more elusive. Keith Seymour Sr, manager of marketing surveillance for the Securities Commission, says the Commission in August 2004 didn't have a number but was tracking the funds and would use the data "for reporting purposes."

However, in the past decade there's little doubt a growing number of hedge funds are calling The Bahamas home, including three started by former Templeton funds alumni – Mark Holowesko, Dorian Foyil and Jane Siebels.

Investments for the wealthy

The Templeton funds were the work of Sir John Templeton, the financial guru and longtime Lyford Cay resident who created some of the world's largest and most successful international investment funds.

Investment managers "have reached a point where they are no longer interested in dealing with small sums such as $5 million, preferring $50 million or $100 million.

He sold his business in 1992 to the Franklin Group, and the new firm was renamed the Franklin Templeton Group.

COURTESY SIR JOHN TEMPLETON

Sir John Templeton

The Holowesko Global Fund, which is affiliated with Franklin Templeton, was founded in 2001 by Mark Holowesko and Gregory P Cleare. They currently manage $900 million for approximately 30 clients.

Hedge funds were a new venture for both men. Holowesko, the fund's president, is best known in financial circles for taking over the day-to-day management of Templeton funds (mostly mutual funds) upon Sir John's retirement. Holowesko had joined Templeton in 1985. Cleare, who is the chief operating officer, had previously been a partner at the accounting firm KPMG Bahamas Ltd.

ROLAND ROSE/©DUPUCH

Gregory P Cleare

Hedge funds are marketed to wealthy individuals and, increasingly, to institutions such as pension funds. The Bahamas Financial Services Board (BFSB) says that by dealing with high-net worth individuals and institutions through private placements, investment managers "have reached a point where they are no longer interested in dealing with small sums such as $5 million, preferring $50 million or $100 million

ROLAND ROSE/©DUPUCH

The Holowesko Global Fund is housed in the Templeton building at Lyford Cay.

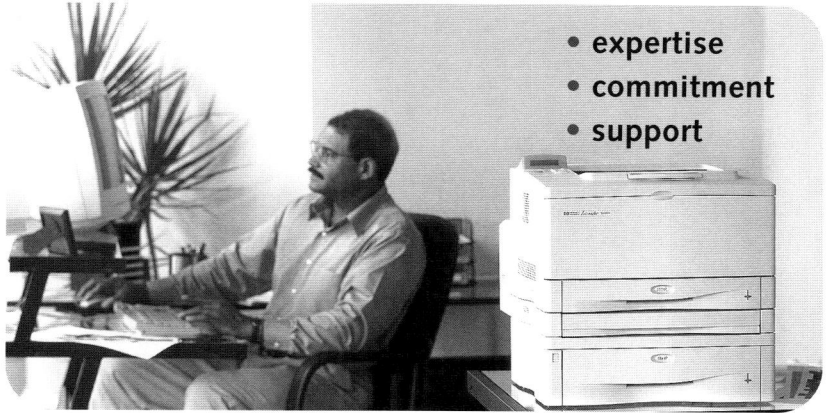

Offshore hedge funds are among the fastest growing investment alternatives to traditional equity and bond portfolios…

over a long period." On the other hand, the Holowesko Global Fund, headquartered at Lyford Cay, requires a minimum $3-million investment from individuals or institutions.

Foyil launched Foyil Asset Management in 1996. As president and chief investment officer, he oversees an independent, offshore fund management company that targets investment opportunities around the world. He certainly has the proper credentials. Prior to his five-year tenure at Templeton – where he had portfolio responsibility for some $800 million in global and emerging market mutual funds and institutional pension assets – he was a London-based analyst for UBS Securities and named as a top professional by Extel, an independent survey of the European investment community.

Offshore hedge funds are among the fastest growing investment alternatives to traditional equity and bond portfolios, says Foyil from his West Bay Street offices in Nassau. He emphasizes the importance of investors understanding the "style" of investment his/her hedge fund manager may prefer, specializing in currencies, futures, arbitrage, securities of distressed companies and so forth. Buzzwords seem endless. "More and more complicated measurement jargon creeps into the investment lingo each year," Foyil adds. "Terms like 'alpha,' 'beta,' 'sharpe ratios' and 'high water marks' are common."

HANS DODTHAGEN/©DUPUCH

Foyil Asset Management operates from offices at Caves Village in western New Providence.

The Bahamas enacted a new Investment Funds Act in 2003 designed to put the country on the cutting edge of modern investment administration.

First-time hedge fund investors should confer with their tax advisors before joining a fund, he urges, and they should learn a few basics as well.

Aggressive investment strategy

One reason hedge funds make money: "They are able to attract the best minds in the market," says Wendy Warren, the BFSB's CEO and executive director. She estimates that hedge funds provide up to 20 per cent of the profits to fund managers. Compared to mutual funds where the fees are largely based on assets under management, there are obviously strong incentives involved in hedge funds as managers are paid incentive fees based on the performance of the fund.

ROLAND ROSE/©DUPUCH

Wendy Warren, CEO and executive director, BFSB

Hedge funds, which are seldom advertised or publicly sold or purchased, are illiquid. They require a commitment of money for a minimum period of one year with exit privileges thereafter on a quarterly basis. The regulator of hedge funds in the US is the Securities and Exchange Control (SEC) and, in The Bahamas, the Securities Commission. In the US, the SEC requires that a majority of the investors in a hedge fund are "accredited," meaning they have a net worth of at least $1 million.

Hedge funds and transparency

The Bahamas enacted a new Investment Funds Act in 2003 designed to put the country on the cutting edge of modern investment administration. The Commission is now enforcing greater oversight. Like overseers in the Cayman Islands and some other offshore jurisdictions, the Commission can audit hedge funds.

The SEC announced in 2004 that the industry, which is mostly unregulated, should prepare itself for new disclosure rules, possibly by the end of the year. This would mean spot audits and more paperwork for fund managers but it is unlikely to root out fraud, complain many lawyers and managers.

The US Treasury made a similar proposal seeking more transparency in the hedge fund market in the late 1990s. At the time an irate Dion Friedman, chairman of the Bahamas-based hedge fund, Magnum, stated: "You can't go to the world and say you have to take down your underwear and expose every trade you make every day of the year and what your exposure is – because it doesn't work. You'd have so much bureaucracy that the whole system would come to a stop."

COURTESY JANE SIEBELS

Jane Siebels, Green Cay Asset Management

On the other side, and despite the extra record keeping, Holowesko says he would welcome the SEC plan. "I think the rules would be helpful. I'm all for full disclosure." The Holowesko Global Fund has been known to periodically issue up to 30-page reports to its clients. Also, in following the "Know Your Customer" trend in today's environment, Holowesko tells of hiring a private investigator to check out a prospective client.

Siebels, who manages $230 million as chief investment officer at Green Cay Asset Management in Lyford Cay, agrees. "Regulation of the industry is a good thing." However, she doubts the SEC will catch the people set on committing fraud by making them fill out more papers. According to her, the hedge fund fraternity is notoriously secretive. "Some traders don't want anyone to know their strategies," she says. "They're afraid that others would jump on the bandwagon and they wouldn't be able to execute their trades." But Green Cay is quite open in its dealings. "We give quarterly descriptions of the position of our funds, how long we are, how short we are," says Siebels "And the SEC doesn't even demand this."

cont on pg 248

Executive lifestyle – Bahamas style

With an income-tax-free environment, world-class financial services, a stable democracy, fast and easy access to the US, and a gorgeous subtropical climate, it's no wonder that people from other countries want to move to The Bahamas. But aside from the obvious business advantages, one other factor makes it sweeter than ever – the island lifestyle.

ROLAND ROSE/©DUPUCH

An executive living in The Bahamas probably has the funds to enjoy some of the very best things the country has to offer. There are generous options for fine dining. Top chefs work in the high-end restaurants here. The third-largest wine cellar in the world can be found at Graycliff in Nassau, an upscale boutique hotel with a five-star restaurant.

If you can afford to live on the ocean, the opportunities for watersports, entertainment and simply enjoying the view are limitless. Oceanfront and canalfront homes are in high demand, but there are still many available, either to buy or rent. Some have their own docks and many have pools and beautiful outdoor space for entertaining and just enjoying life in the sub-tropics.

If you have a boat, you'll have access to the 700 islands and cays on your doorstep, each with something unique to offer. A weekend away can include a trip to Harbour Island, home to top-notch hotels, fine restaurants, the most beautiful pink sand beach imaginable and quaint homes. Or you can zip down to the Exumas, an area described by astronauts as the most beautiful on earth. Fish for big game here, dive on pristine reefs and picnic on a tiny cay that you'll have all to yourself. Visit iguanas on their own turf and snorkel in Thunderball Cave, of James Bond fame.

GRAHAM DUPUCH/©DUPUCH

COURTESY OLD BAHAMA BAY

A weekend or a week in Abaco can include cruising, sailing, fishing, snorkelling, diving and even a pig roast on Guana Cay. Take time for a long walk along the beaches of the Abacos. Many are nearly deserted.

If you want to get away somewhere really remote, romantic and peaceful, you can always find a quiet Out Island hideaway. Cat Island, San Salvador, Andros, Long Island and Eleuthera are just a few of the many Out Islands offering peace and seclusion for those who don't want company.

ROLAND ROSE/©DUPUCH

Even the busy business centres of Nassau and Freeport offer the lifestyle every executive wants. Where else can you have it all without leaving home? Where else can you arise early to join the dozens of walkers and runners taking advantage of the cool early mornings year-round? Where else can you fit in a quick session of water-skiing after work, or dive into the sea from your back patio before dinner? Where else can you wake to the sounds of the warm Atlantic Ocean lapping the sand, or open your eyes to a golden-pink sunrise announcing the beginning of yet another easy, breezy day in paradise?

GRAHAM DUPUCH/©DUPUCH

One Green Cay policy that sets it apart from many funds is its interest in social responsibility.

cont from pg 244

Green Cay has been registered with the SEC since 1997, the year Siebels hung out her shingle. (At last count, about 40 per cent of hedge fund managers are SEC registered.)

One Green Cay policy that sets it apart from many funds is its interest in social responsibility. When picking companies in which to invest, Siebels often takes into account such things as a company's employee and community relations as well as environmental factors. "That kind of information isn't always easy to access," she explains, "but you can get it if you really dig."

The New American Foundation, a non-profit organization that researches cultural and environmental issues, praised Siebels' decision to get involved with a food company in Indonesia. One of her funds bought into Indofoods, a company that specializes in making noodles. The company always had trouble breaking into the Indonesian market because the country's traditional diet is based mostly on rice. Indofoods' big break, says Siebels, came during the Asian economic crisis when the company decided to sell its noodles below cost in order to help struggling Indonesians.

While other emerging market investors thought Indofoods' strategy was foolish, Green Cay decided that this approach would help the company's relationship with its customers and benefit the company

ROLAND ROSE/©DUPUCH

Many hedge funds are registered with the Securities Commission.

Mutual funds remunerate managers based on percentage of assets under management, while hedge funds remunerate on performance-related investment fees.

in the long run. "Sure enough," reported the New American Foundation, "when the crisis ended, people had acquired a taste for Indofoods' noodles and the company increased its market share."

Mutual funds more accessible

As for mutual funds, this sector was regulated in The Bahamas under the country's Mutual Funds Act 1995 and the Securities Board Act 1995, which led to a Securities Board operating on self-regulatory principles. In 1999 the Securities Board converted into the Securities Commission under the Securities Industry Act 1999.

The Mutual Funds Act divided investment funds into categories. These included exempt funds, which are exempt from licensing and have no more than 15 investors; authorized funds, having a minimum subscription level of $50,000 and listed on a recognized stock exchange; and other funds, which are required to be licensed.

Among the differences between mutual funds and hedge funds is the expected performance. The future performance of mutual funds is dependent more than hedge funds on the direction of equity markets. Mutual funds remunerate managers based on percentage of assets under management, while hedge funds remunerate on performance-related investment fees.

ROLAND ROSE/©DUPUCH

Many offshore banks, including Pictet, have headquarters in New Providence.

A stranger lugging a suitcase filled with cash into a bank must first satisfy the bank's curiosity before he can open an account.

Most mutual funds have restricted investment options, while hedge funds have flexibility in where and how they can invest. For instance, hedge funds can leverage (use borrowed money at a fixed interest rate to achieve a greater rate of return), sell securities short and invest across different asset classes. Because of the flexibility of leverage, hedge funds can potentially multiply their returns on the arbitrage opportunities in the market.

Some mutual funds require an investment of less than $1,000. So deciding whether to become a player in a hedge depends mostly on how deep a person's pockets are.

Hedging on bank confidentiality

If any hedge fund manager fits the traditional image as a secretive operator, he or she may be using a strategy that is believed to provide a competitive but legitimate advantage. In essence, as Siebels indicated, they don't want others to know what horses they're betting on.

In banking, "privacy" and "confidentiality" are the preferred terms. Mention "secret" and regulators materialize quickly.

A stranger lugging a suitcase filled with cash into a bank must first satisfy the bank's curiosity before he can open an account. The prospective customer's identity and the source of his large cash stash must be verified. Also, if he says he expects to establish a company in The Bahamas, he must spell out the kind of company and other specific details. If he's a genuine businessman and/or investor, there is no problem. Otherwise he will be turned down.

Offshore company managers and banks have adopted "Know Your Customer" principles following the worldwide introduction of anti-money laundering legislation and other measures that focused on "tax havens," such as The Bahamas, Cayman Islands and Bermuda. With its Money Laundering (Proceeds of Crime) Act of 1996, The Bahamas was one of the first offshore jurisdictions to make money laundering a crime. How much information about its clients banks should be required to surrender to agencies like the Internal Revenue Service in the US is a controversial question among offshore jurisdictions. Some jurisdictions complain that tax information exchange treaties

"Any permitted disclosure of relevant information is strictly circumscribed and monitored,"

between countries have now eroded confidentiality to the extent that it is unrealistic to believe that it exists at all.

Balance of privacy and responsibility

Banking is the crown of The Bahamas financial service offerings. So keeping a client's interest in strict confidentiality from other countries or entities is considered vital.

In early 2004, The Bahamas government passed legislation to exchange tax information with the US Treasury Department. "A few years ago, that type of activity would have been regarded as something representing treason," says Minister of State for Finance James Smith. Still, Allyson Maynard Gibson, Minister of Financial Services and Investments, insists The Bahamas keeps a tight rein on shared information. "Any permitted disclosure of relevant information is strictly circumscribed and monitored," she says.

Some Bahamas bankers claim their privacy policies have not been changed too noticeably by recent legislation. One is Ross McDonald, the Royal Bank of Canada's (RBC's) senior vice-president of The Bahamas and the Caribbean. The RBC was established on Nassau's Bay Street in 1908, when the population of the entire colony was 55,000. It served as the islands' only bank from 1910 until the Second World War.

McDonald points to the bank's "Ten Privacy

SARA MOSS/©DUPUCH

Ansbacher House is home to offshore banks.

Customer information will be shielded with policies "that are appropriate to the sensitivity level of the information."

Principles" as evidence of its commitment to protecting customer information. The first principle is accountability. In part, the rule states that each RBC company is "responsible for maintaining and protecting the customer information under its control." Another principle, safeguarding customer information, assures that customer information will be shielded with policies "that are appropriate to the sensitivity level of the information."

Were the principles drafted in response to the OECD and other watchdog organizations? "Not at all," says McDonald. "They've been part of the bank's policy ever since I can remember – and I've been here 28 years."

For the record, RBC's presence in The Bahamas is pervasive. Aside from its scores of branch offices throughout New Providence and the Out Islands, its many companies include the Royal Trust Corporation of Canada and Royal Mutual Funds Inc, among others.

A final note on bank confidentiality. Sometimes it could be a matter of life and death. Recalls one Bahamas banker, "Many of my Latin American clients desire an offshore account so that guerrilla groups and other armed bands can't access bank records, find out their net worth, and then kidnap and ransom them." Ⓓ

ETIENNE DUPUCH JR/©DUPUCH

Royal Bank of Canada was Nassau's only bank from 1910 until the Second World War.

Flying The Bahamas Flag at Sea

Kamanna Valluri, managing director, Dockendale Shipping Co Ltd

World shipping companies looking for a place to locate their headquarters can't ignore The Bahamas, says Leslie J Fernandes, retired president and CEO of Nassau-based Dockendale Shipping Co Ltd.

"You can locate your office anywhere, you only need good communication service and access to travel," says Fernandes. "The Bahamas has both of those things. It also has good weather, which makes for nice working conditions for the staff."

His sentiments are echoed by Kamanna Valluri, Fernandes' successor and Dockendale's managing director. He points to other advantages: a stable government; a British legal system, which has very straightforward laws when it comes to shipping; conducting business in the English language and the discount that companies receive when registering more than one ship with the Bahamian flag.

According to The Bahamas Maritime Authority, The Bahamas today is the world's third-largest ship registry, and ranks as number one in cruise and passenger ships.

In 1978 there were just 60 vessels in The Bahamas register. By 2003, there were 1,600 vessels totalling 34 million gross tons.

Dockendale's security measures and reputation as a world-class organization helped it land a sensitive and crucial contract with the US in 2003. The company supplied ships to transport arms, ammunition and helicopters to American troops in Iraq preparing for war with Saddam Hussein.

The company's founder, George T R Campbell, a legendary Scottish naval architect, started the firm in Halifax, Nova Scotia, before relocating in 1950 to Japan, where he almost single-handedly rebuilt Japan's post-Second World War shipbuilding industry to become the largest in the world. He constructed almost 600 oceangoing dry-cargo merchant vessels in every major Japanese shipyard during his 43 years in that country.

When the Japanese yen strengthened in the 1980s, Japanese shipbuilders could no longer be competitive on the world market and Dockendale moved its offices to Nassau. From 1989 onwards, the company's fleet increased to 14 ships. A significant joint venture in 1993 with Clipper Shipping Company, headquartered in Copenhagen, more than doubled the total.

"Dockendale has 36 ships sailing today in virtually every part of the world," says Valluri, who joined the company in 1980. "Fifteen are owned by us and the other 21 are Clipper ships."

The company has few of its vessels built in Japan (still too expensive, Valluri notes), opting instead for ships produced in Korea and China.

The Bahamas Ship Owners Association is a "who's who" of the world's most prominent shipping names. Among these, Exxon, Texaco, Chevron, Teekay, Cunard, Maersk, Carnival, and Holland-America all have a significant number of their ships registered in The Bahamas.

Of course, yachts also get their due from the Bahamas Maritime Authority. Yacht registration in The Bahamas is a favourite for individuals with crafts ranging from 40 ft to well over 100 ft. For the record, a yacht is defined by the BMA as a vessel that doesn't carry more than 12 passengers, is not operated for any commercial purpose at any time and never carries cargo.

Apparently Dockendale's home is permanent. It recently built Dockendale House, a four-storey, $5-million corporate headquarters in Nassau, dedicated to the memory of the man who started it all, George Campbell. ⓓ

SHANE PINDER/©DUPUCH

Dockendale House, home of Dockendale Shipping Co Ltd

LINDA M HUBER/©DUPUCH

Foundations Act – 1st in the Americas

Progressive trust and foundations laws put The Bahamas ahead of the pack.

BY DONN SELHORN

It would be a tough act to follow. At least that was the opinion of Allyson Maynard Gibson, Minister of Financial Services and Investments.

She was referring to The Bahamas Parliament's approval in early 2004 of the Foundations Act. "A milestone for the local financial services industry," she announced. "A landmark legislation… probably the most important bill the House will pass this year."

Allyson Maynard Gibson

With this act, The Bahamas becomes the first common law jurisdiction with legal provisions for foundations. "We'll now be able to attract new business from high-net worth individuals from Europe and South and Central America," the minister said. "The Bahamas will be in the forefront of the [financial] sector rather than having to play catch-up."

Talk to virtually any Bahamas executive or government official and the consensus is the same: the Foundations Act will grab the

Left, Montague Sterling Centre houses private banks and investment and accounting firms.

...it has made The Bahamas the only jurisdiction in the world able to cater to clients with business interests in both the North American and South American markets.

attention of Continental clients and stimulate access to a new market.

Andrew Law, former chairman of the Association of International Banks and Trust Companies (AIBT) in The Bahamas, says his organization is a firm supporter of the Act, because it has made The Bahamas the only jurisdiction in the world able to cater to clients with business interests in both the North American and South American markets. "We won't have a competitor," he told an audience of the Caribbean Society of Trust and Estate Practitioners shortly before the Act went into effect.

ROLAND ROSE/©DUPUCH

Andrew Law

Even the opposition party, the Free National Movement (FNM), lauded the Act. "When it comes to what's in the best interest of The Bahamas, there can be no divergence on purely partisan lines," said an FNM statement.

Foundations offer more control

Sean McWeeney, one of the nation's leading trust attorneys, says the Act permits the use of European foundation trust structures in The Bahamas. "Foundations take the civil law foundation that applies throughout continental Europe and reapplies that same concept within an English jurisprudential context." The high levels of accountability and liability required in an English trust can be a disincentive for clients from other countries, who aren't used to relinquishing that much control, he explains.

On the other hand, the foundation offers the "settlor" more effective control of the assets. One of the disadvantages of a trust is that there remains a need to convince somebody to

COURTESY SEAN MCWEENEY

Sean McWeeney

give up his money to somebody he doesn't know, to trust his trustees. "That can be psychologically quite discomforting for some clients," McWeeney says. "A foundation enables you, to a large extent, to get the best of both worlds. You have a structure which reserves anonymity and at the same time gives you a larger measure of control than you have under a conventional trust." This is very important to clients from Latin America and continental Europe, the primary markets for offshore trusts in The Bahamas.

When Maynard Gibson presented the foundations bill in the House of Assembly, she pointed out that it was vital to the continued growth of the financial services sector. "We expect that having the most progressive trust laws and foundations law will seal The Bahamas' reputation as the first choice for clients seeking international estate and inheritance planning solutions." Like the country's Trustee Act, which has a global reputation as being the primary choice of many settlors, the new Act is expected to be the first choice for a foundation, the minister said. She predicted that Bahamas-domiciled foundations would probably be used mainly for holding and managing assets.

Simpler, cheaper and safer

Maynard Gibson said that foundations represent an expansion of The Bahamas' ability to service a new client base and shows a commitment to remain relevant to potential clients domiciled in civil-law countries. "Product features and advantages include the benefits of greater… simplicity for clients and reduced cost to clients vis-à-vis the trust, and… avoidance of issues related to sham trusts and perpetuity issues."

ROLAND ROSE/©DUPUCH

Wendy Warren

The Bahamas Financial Services Board's CEO and executive director, Wendy Warren, said, "There is a constant need to upgrade and enhance a jurisdiction's product offerings. Without question, we're out to reassert preeminence in a highly competitive marketplace."

The foundation concept has been used in Latin/civil law countries for centuries. It is a legal entity separate from its creditors, constituted through

Trusts were frequently misunderstood because complete legal ownership has to be surrendered to the trustee.

one donation, or several donations, that form an independent and autonomous estate for a single purpose. Investors in civil-law jurisdictions were more comfortable with foundations as opposed to trusts, which operate in common-law jurisdictions such as The Bahamas. Trusts were frequently misunderstood and not always acceptable, mainly because, unlike foundations, complete legal ownership has to be surrendered to the trustee. However, as Maynard Gibson says, foundations have now become well known and acceptable in many civil law jurisdictions, especially in Europe and Latin America.

Put another way, the difference between common law and civil law is that the former is based on common knowledge, therefore subject to diverse court interpretations and rulings, while the latter is based on legal codes and written documents. Civil law is said to be less flexible than common law.

After a marketing trip to Europe in the spring of 2004, Maynard Gibson and members of the AIBT and Bahamas Financial Services Board (BFSB) scheduled a similar tour later in the year to South America, where the Foundations Act, in particular, was expected to draw considerable interest.

SARA MOSS/©DUPUCH

Goodman's Bay Corporate Centre on West Bay Street is home to the Bahamas Financial Services Board and private banks.

"Charities have a place in the offshore similar to that of investment funds and other products. Offshore provides greater flexibility in a tax neutral environment."

Carefully drafted law

There was initial concern locally and internationally about the Act, since it merged the common law of the jurisdiction with the civil law observed in other countries. "But extreme care was taken in drafting the innovative law," says Maynard Gibson. "We were very meticulous in our approach" and consulted with global experts in writing the more complex aspects of the Act.

Liechtenstein popularized the use of foundations for asset protection, tax and estate planning purposes, with legislation dating back to 1926. Panama followed suit with a much less expensive and rather more flexible version in 1995. Not wanting to miss out on the opportunity to boost its government revenues, The Bahamas has now come on board.

When promoting the foundations bill in the House of Assembly, one would think Maynard Gibson was addressing a room full of potential investors. She announced that, with the introduction of foundations, The Bahamas would reinforce its position as a high-end legal jurisdiction and attract quality clients who are comforted by the nation's stringent "Know Your Customer" regime. "For the high-net worth person, setting up a foundation can provide unique opportunities for both tax mitigation and dynastic control... Charities have a place in the offshore similar to that of investment funds and other products. Offshore provides greater flexibility in a tax neutral environment."

Flexible, confidential, responsible

In essence a foundation is a legal entity designed to manage funds on behalf of others. While the popularity of modern foundations developed in civil law jurisdictions in the early part of the twentieth century as a result of upheavals then underway in Europe, some form of foundations existed in Roman times. In that period, foundations were created to let the wealthy (such as Roman army officers going off to battle) leave their assets in the hands of administrators for the benefit of their families, the beneficiaries.

Σ SIGMA
Management
BAHAMAS

Confidentiality has its limits. Foundations will have an obligation to keep accounts (as stipulated in the legislation).

GORDON LOMER/©DUPUCH

Registrar General's office

As noted, foundations are highly flexible. They can be formed for public or private goals, including:

- charitable and philanthropic purposes;
- international estate and inheritance planning;
- tax planning, including mitigation of estate and gift taxes;
- creditor protection;
- holding direct investments, such as stocks, bonds and bank accounts; and
- holding interest in companies, including controlling interests.

There are obligations of confidentiality imposed on officials dealing with foundations. Among them:

- the foundation must be resident and domiciled in The Bahamas;
- it is able to sue and be sued in its own name; and
- it has tax-free status.

Confidentiality has its limits. Foundations will have an obligation to keep accounts (as stipulated in the legislation). The Act requires certain information to be provided when lawfully required or permitted by any court of competent jurisdiction within The Bahamas or under any provisions of any law of The Bahamas.

Whatever the outlook for foundations business, The Bahamas can't linger, warned the FNM. "The Act is comparable to foundations laws in other jurisdictions. We will have to distinguish ourselves with quality service and the length of time it takes to create such an entity. This means the Registrar General's Department must have the necessary resources to expedite matters."

No problem, assured Maynard Gibson, whose ministry anticipated such concerns. To improve the efficiency and effectiveness of the Registrar General's office, her ministry and other government officials formed what she called "swat teams." Their mission is to assist in clearing up a backlog of documents found in almost every section of the registry.

A series of legislative acts has strengthened trustee safeguards in The Bahamas.

Trusts vs foundations

Foundations and trusts are two of the main vehicles for asset protection and estate planning. Both of them allow the endowment of an estate to be administered according to the wishes of a settlor or founder, and in favour of appointed beneficiaries. In addition, a trust or foundation is able to operate in a tax-free environment.

Foundations differ from ordinary trusts in that there is often not a particular specified beneficiary, but rather a specific purpose for which the foundation is established to promote – although many jurisdictions, including The Bahamas, now allow the establishment of "purpose trusts," which are somewhat similar to foundations.

In sum, a trust involves a unique relationship. It allows an individual or a legal entity (the "settlor") to transfer assets – which may be of almost any type – to a third party (the "trustee"). The assets are then administered for the benefit of persons chosen by the settlor (the "beneficiaries") in accordance with the provisions of a document (the "trust deed").

A series of legislative acts has strengthened trustee safeguards in The Bahamas. For example, the Perpetuities Act, 1995, and 2004 amendments, modernized existing law relating to

LINDA M HUBER /©DUPUCH

The Bahamas Financial Centre is home to international banks.

Since 1983
Micronet
BUSINESS TECHNOLOGY

DELL

hp
invent

TOSHIBA
Don't copy. Lead.

Microsoft
CERTIFIED
Partner

COMPAQ

"...this new regulatory requirement and other measures that have enhanced our regulatory environment have also attracted new trust companies and banks to our shores."

perpetuities by allowing families to plan for five generations. A standard-setting statute – the Trustees Act, 1998 – placed The Bahamas at the forefront of international jurisdictions in terms of premier trust legislation.

The 1998 Act, widely circulated and discussed by practitioners in the field, was the principal act in this area. The Act clarifies the role of trust settlers and the rights of beneficiaries to information about trusts, as well as the rights and duties of professionals, while enhancing the use of trusts as an investment vehicle.

"It addresses several problems which had been the bane of practitioners worldwide," says Maynard Gibson. "In particular, it permits a settlor to retain certain discretionary powers without invalidating the trust. More important, it recognizes the concept of a protector of trusts – the protection of assets against potential creditors, indemnities for trustees, and avoidance of forced heirship laws."

Trusts – a cornerstone of the industry

"Today, we're one of the foremost trust jurisdictions in the world," says the BFSB's Warren. Trusts in The Bahamas remain a strong and growing business and one of the cornerstones of the country's broad ranging financial services industry." She reported in early 2004 that more than 270 trust companies and banks were still operating in The Bahamas, a decline from a peak of 415 in 2000. "The decline can be largely attributed to the decision in 1999 to phase out managed banks in The Bahamas," she explained. "But this new regulatory requirement and other measures that have enhanced our regulatory environment have also attracted new trust companies and banks to our shores." She estimated that approximately two-thirds of the institutions licensed by The Central Bank of The Bahamas have a trust license and many are connected to a global institution.

Another attraction is the fact that trust and company service providers in The Bahamas have had to be licensed since 1965, nearly 40 years before the Channel Islands and the Isle of Man made their licenses compulsory.

"They can also help avoid family squabbles that often follow a death, such as protecting assets from spendthrift family members."

"We've made a conscious decision to focus on the private client market," Warren emphasized. "For many years we have looked after private clients and understand that wealth management requires special attention and expertise. Through the institutions, accountants and lawyers based here, we definitely can deliver 'best in class' service."

In Maynard Gibson's opinion, The Bahamas is able to maintain its competitive edge because, while its trusts have many advantages, the fees charged by companies, banks and attorneys to establish and manage trusts are comparable to those charged globally. Fees are negotiable and may be chargeable either on a lump sum basis or on a percentage of the value of the trust company. Formation fees vary and, to a large extent, depend on how simple or complex the terms of the trust are.

It isn't unusual for individuals who have built significant wealth to have personal or business interests outside their home country. This creates both opportunities and challenges for financial and estate planning.

"There are many reasons to establish a trust," says John Lawrence, director of Windermere Corporate Management in Nassau. "Asset protection, estate planning and tax efficient holding of assets, to name a few. They can also help avoid family squabbles that often follow a death, such as protecting assets from spendthrift family members." He added that an offshore trust could be a good tax planning tool and, if correctly structured, will produce savings in income tax, capital gains tax, inheritance tax and stamp duty.

ROLAND ROSE/©DUPUCH

John Lawrence

While the tax benefits of setting up a trust in The Bahamas may be limited for Americans, many are using the vehicle for protecting assets, transferring assets to non-US beneficiaries, holding foreign securities that cannot be offered in the US, holding foreign property, or holding assets of a non-resident grantor during his or her lifetime for ultimate distribution to US beneficiaries.

Alyson I Yule

With the trust business growing in The Bahamas, some say that more trust officers are needed to handle the increase. Lawrence agrees, and he is among those doing something about it. In mid-2004 he completed a term as chairman of The Bahamas' branch of the Society of Trust and Estate Practitioners (STEP). STEP is a professional organization for private wealth management, especially in the field of trusts and estates – and it seeks new members to learn the profession of trusts and estate planning.

Formed in the UK, STEP has more than 10,000 members and 125 branches worldwide. The Bahamas and its 375 members ranks fifth in size. Among its many activities is the education and training of potential professionals in trusts and estate practice. The training is divided into four six-month modules with scholarships for Bahamian students offered in each of the modules. Lawrence's successor in heading STEP is Alyson I Yule, managing director of Banca del Sempione (Overseas) Ltd.

Yule is optimistic about the future for foundations. In the past, when clients inquired about setting up a foundation, "This meant we had to work with a jurisdiction outside The Bahamas," she says. "But the Foundations Act will be changing all that."

Benefits of trusts for private individuals and families include:

- Legitimate mitigation of taxation;
- deferral of taxation;
- avoidance of forced heirship provisions in the domestic jurisdiction;
- succession planning for family-owned companies;
- protection of assets from spendthrift family members;
- significant mitigation of probate complexities for international estates; and
- consolidation of widely dispersed assets.

Why invest in The Bahamas?

- Ideal climate
- Ideal lifestyle
- 50 miles off the coast of the biggest economy in the world
- Same time zone as New York
- An investment-friendly government
- Consultative approach
- A top corps of professionals in key government ministries
- A Ministry of Financial Services and Investments that facilitates a world-class, blue chip financial services centre
- Compliant legislation
- Red carpet treatment
- Top professionals offering keen oversight of the entire investment process
- Educated workforce
- A peaceful and stable democracy since 1729
- Many islands and cays to choose from

SHANE PINDER/©DUPUCH

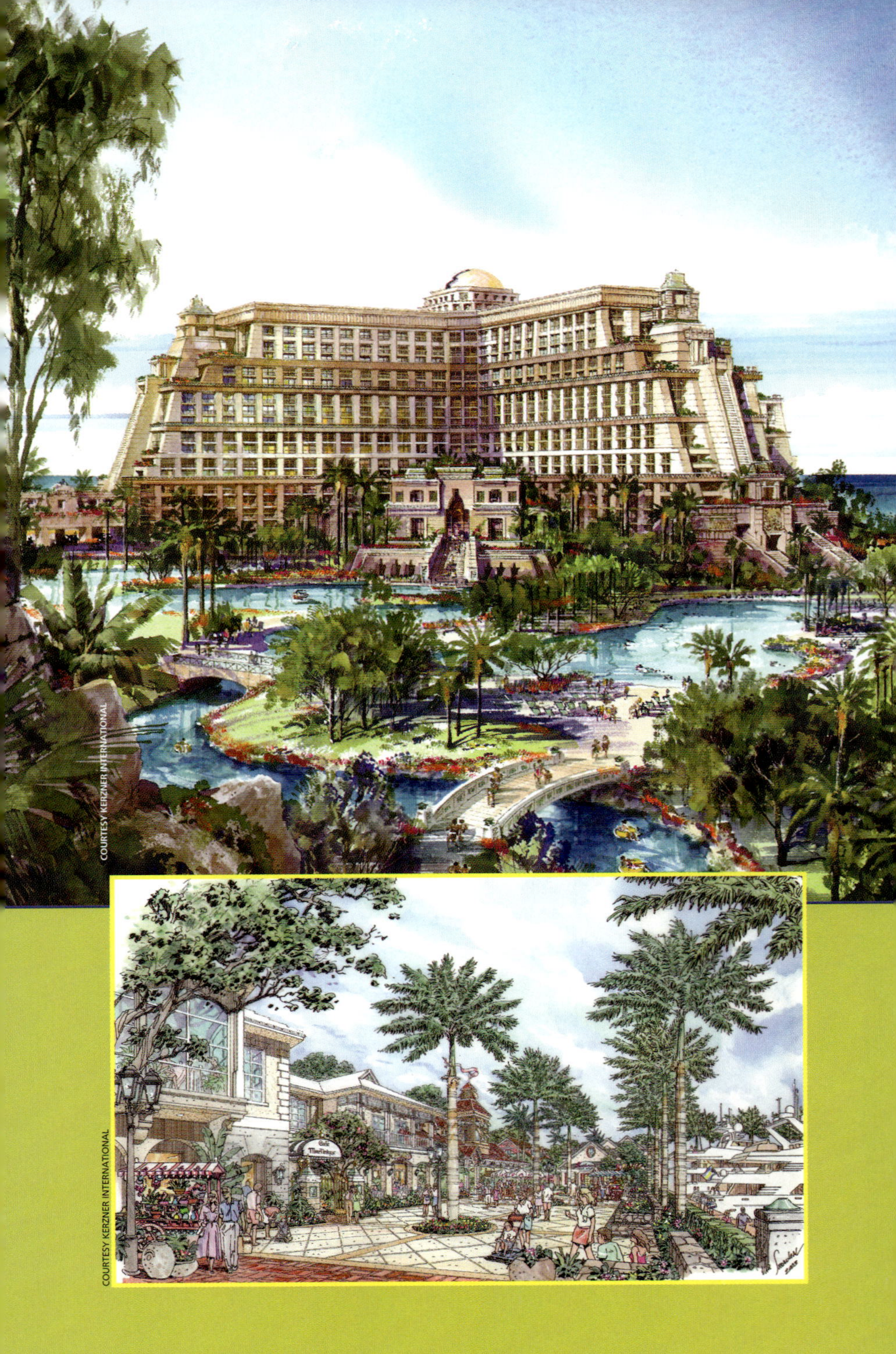

COURTESY KERZNER INTERNATIONAL

COURTESY KERZNER INTERNATIONAL

Construction projects on the rise

New Providence and Paradise Island abuzz with new developments and upgrades.

BY GILLIAN BECKETT

While construction activity remained sluggish in 2003, still recovering from the recession that followed terrorist attacks in the US in September 2001, the outlook was considerably brighter for the future, according to The Central Bank of The Bahamas.

"Activity is expected to strengthen in 2004, as significant new foreign investment projects commence in the hotel sector," said the Central Bank in its annual report for 2003, released in April 2004.

The most significant development was the decision by Kerzner International to proceed with its Phase 3 addition to the Atlantis resort property on Paradise Island.

"This $1-billion investment will bring Kerzner's investment to over $2 billion in The Bahamas and we will be creating the largest single resort outside of Las Vegas," said CEO Butch Kerzner at the announcement in May 2004. It will be the single largest tourism development in The Bahamas. Included in the project is a new 1,500-room hotel resembling a giant Mayan temple. The development will also include a water theme park including a river ride, water slides and

Left artist's concepts of Kerzner International's proposed $1-billion dollar investment – Phase 3 of the Atlantis development, on Paradise Island; below, Marina Village will feature shops and restaurants.

A proposal to redevelop Cable Beach into a Las Vegas-style attraction strip and luxury resort set The Bahamas hotel industry abuzz.

a dolphin encounter attraction as well as a $120-million two-phase development at Harborside at Atlantis, adding approximately 320 suites and a 200,000-sq-ft convention centre. A new complex called Marina Village will feature 22 retail stores and four restaurants, including a recreation of the upscale Café Martinique that graced Paradise Island in its heyday.

As part of the $1-billion development at Atlantis, it was announced that the One&Only Ocean Club would also be expanded. Included in the plan was the construction of three new luxury villas, a links-style 18-hole golf course on Athol Island, east of Paradise Island, a new retail shop, executive boardroom, expanded fitness centre and family pool.

Construction of Phase 3 began in May 2004, creating more than 2,000 jobs. In total, approximately 4,500 permanent jobs will be established for the daily operation of the new complex. Once completed in 2006, there will be a total of 3,800 rooms and suites at Atlantis.

Hotels respond

With construction of Phase 3 at Atlantis well under way, there were additional proposals to improve and expand existing hotels and resorts in New Providence and Paradise Island.

In June, 2004, work was under way to transform the former Sheraton Grand Resort on Cabbage Beach, Paradise Island. Spanish hotel operator RIU Hotels & Resorts purchased the 340-room property, which was built in 1982. Renovations were expected to upgrade the resort to five-star status. The hotel was due to re-open in December 2004.

A proposal to redevelop Cable Beach into a Las Vegas-style attraction strip and luxury resort set The Bahamas hotel industry abuzz. Bids to develop the Radisson Cable Beach and Golf Resort, began to come in early 2004, initiated by Lyford Cay billionaire Dikran Izmirlian. California-based Calstar Properties also offered a bid of approximately $280 million to redevelop the site. Included in Calstar's proposal were plans to construct an amusement park, event centre and parking lot – upon acquiring the Radisson, the golf course and land opposite the resort, including the grass median on the Cable Beach strip. At press time, negotiations for bid proposals were still ongoing between potential developers and the government.

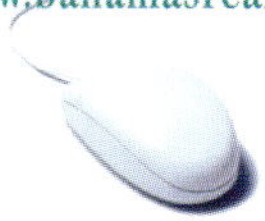

COURTESY EVES

The new Eves development at Cable Beach will contain14 villas and condominiums.

Residential developments

Just as the hotel industry was planning grand-scale developments to attract more tourists to The Bahamas, the residential construction market was gearing up to make more homes available to foreign and domestic buyers.

According to The Central Bank of The Bahamas' *Quarterly Economic Review* for December 2003, an expected increase in future investments resulted in a "5.1 per cent rise in the number of mortgage commitments for new construction and repairs on residential and commercial structures."

However, the Central Bank also said, "while the outlook for construction was favoured by approved investment projects and increased commitments under domestic mortgage financing, the quarter's output was weaker than in 2002."

Nevertheless, there were several high-end developments scheduled for completion in 2004 and 2005, particularly in western New Providence.

"There's a small construction boom going on," says Carmen Massoni, realtor and marketing broker with Coldwell Banker. "Compared to the last two years, a lot more people's confidence in the economy has turned around. The Atlantis project has given (that confidence) a boost."

On Cable Beach, the new Eves development continues to take shape with the construction of 14 villas and condominiums. Set in a gated, oceanview setting, the property will also feature a pool and access to a private beach. The units are 3,000 sq ft or more and include full emergency generator power and two-car garages. The property will

Included in development plans for Old Fort Bay is a proposed 18-hole golf course...

also include a 4,200-sq-ft penthouse. The villas start at $795,000, condos start at $1.25 million and the penthouse is $2.395 million. According to developers, construction on the condominium building was set to begin in early fall 2004 with completion set for January 2006.

Further west and nearly completed is Love Beach Walk, a development that will feature two luxury beachfront buildings in a gated community. Phase 1 was completed in the spring of 2004 and features 18 units, each approximately 1,740 sq ft. Construction on Phase 2 began in summer 2004 and was scheduled to be completed by 2005. Prices are from $550,000 to $1.8 million for the penthouse.

GILLIAN BECKETT/©DUPUCH

Love Beach Walk

Near prestigious Lyford Cay is the Old Fort Bay development. The site of a former 17th century fort will feature a variety of beachfront properties, club villas, and canalfront residences within a gated community. Lots range from $300,000 to more than $2 million. Included in development plans for Old Fort Bay is a proposed 18-hole golf course which would be built on existing land adjacent to the property. At press time, the project was being negotiated by developers and the government.

On Paradise Island, construction commenced in July 2004 on a $120-million addition to Harborside Resort at Atlantis. The construction on this phase of the timeshare resort will add 116 luxury villas, resulting in a total of 198 villas.

Government initiatives

While the tourism industry in The Bahamas is set to boom with the new construction at Atlantis and the proposed Cable Beach development, there are a number of projects which will also benefit New Providence's residents.

During late summer of 2004, construction was to begin on four low-cost housing projects. According to Wade Russell, assistant architect with the Department of Housing, development began on 88 houses in Golden Isles, 60 houses at Farm Road and Bain Town, 64 houses in the Jubilee Gardens subdivision and six houses in Yellow Elder near Oakes Field. Russell explained that each year the government develops a certain number of low-cost housing projects.

"We will (make) every effort to meet (that number)," says Russell. In addition, plans were under way to refurbish and expand health care facilities on the island. This includes extensive renovations at the Eloise Penn Ward at Sandilands Rehabilitation Centre, adding up to 26 more beds.

During the 2003/04 fiscal year, the maternity ward at Princess Margaret Hospital underwent an extensive renovation, including the construction of new delivery and labour suites and an operating theatre. Ron Pinder, parliamentary secretary in the Ministry of Health, announced in June 2004 that the 2004/05 capital budget will see the continuation of upgrades to public health facilities in New Providence.

Other projects included the construction of a new court building in Fox Hill and plans to build a state-of-the-art, 5,000-sq-ft medical waste treatment plant at Gladstone Road. This $750,000-facility, the first of its kind in The Bahamas, was due to be completed in December 2004 by Bahamas Waste Management.

Airports and seaports

A much-anticipated road improvement project began in 2004. Upgrades to Harrold Road began in March and developers plan to expand the road to four lanes, from East Street to Bethel Avenue. According to a spokesman from the Ministry of Works and Utilities, construction on the road is to be finished in 2005 at a cost of $6.3 million. The government also embarked on a $50-million road upgrade programme in other parts of Nassau. A new road link was constructed in Sea Breeze; Sir Milo Butler Highway was widened and Gladstone Road was upgraded. It is expected that 16 more roads will be improved across New Providence.

Another highly anticipated venture is an upgrade to Nassau International Airport. In May 2004, the government signed a $34-million contract with construction firm Lagan Holdings International to repair the airport's main runway. Minister of

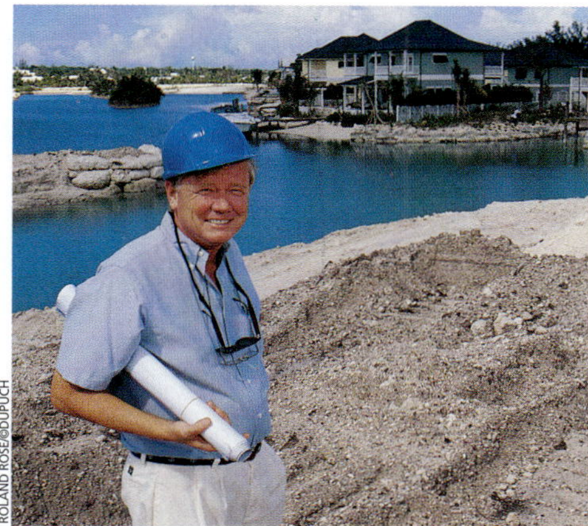
ROLAND ROSE©DUPUCH
Orjan Lindroth, developer of Old Fort Bay property

Transport and Aviation Glenys Hanna Martin announced in July 2004 that repairs to the 11,500-ft runway are part of Phase 1 of the overall refurbishment of the airport, which will also include realignment of taxi ways, insertion of high-speed exits and upgrades to lighting, drainage and landscaping. Phase 2, worth about $200 million, will include renovations to the terminal building. When renovations are complete, Nassau International Airport is slated to be renamed Sir Lynden Pindling International Airport.

Over the next few years, Prince George Dock will be upgraded at a cost of about $10 million. Modern mooring fenders have already been installed and access bridges to the dock are due to be repaired at a cost of $400,000.

On the drawing board

Continuing from the end of 2003 and into 2004 were plans to redevelop Nassau's Bay Street, downtown area and the waterfront. In June 2004, Prime Minister Perry Christie noted the proposed development would cost up to $60 million. Plans call for refurbishment of cultural and historic sites on Bay Street and downtown as well as beautification of the waterfront and improvements to make it accessible to the public. Also included are plans to reorganize the bus system and develop additional public parking. A master design plan for the project was scheduled to be completed by Jan 2005.

In western New Providence, plans for the development of a heritage theme park at the 600-acre Clifton Plantation site are in the works. The site holds historically important artefacts and buildings from the days of slavery. At press time, no deadline had been set for the project, expected to become a World Heritage Site.

COURTESY EMERALD BAY

Out Island building: the pace quickens

Projects in the works for every major island in the archipelago.

BY RALPH DEANS

At press time, 2004 was shaping up to be a very good year for the construction industry in the Out Islands. Firms were building, renovating or repairing major hotels, homes, public buildings, hospitals and clinics, airports and roads throughout the archipelago.

Indeed, there were so many big resort projects on the go, ready to go and under consideration – reportedly worth a total of $4 billion – that there was concern about whether there were enough skilled construction workers in The Bahamas to handle the load. Prime Minister Perry Christie has stipulated that every heads of agreement for a new resort will require the developer to provide training for Bahamian workers.

Two other government priorities also augur well for increased Out Island construction: a promise by the government to seek an anchor resort or a major commercial project for every populated island in the chain and a vow by Tourism Minister Obie Wilchcombe to strongly boost tourism to the Out Islands. The government continued a $5-million promotional campaign in 2004, called "Island Hopping," to reposition The Bahamas as a more competitive destination in the Caribbean area.

Left, Emerald Bay golf course, Exuma

Visits to the Out Islands totalled more than 1.3 million during 2003, according to figures released by the Ministry of Tourism in mid 2004. This was an increase of nearly 12 per cent over the previous year.

It was announced late in 2003 that the government wanted to upgrade airports throughout the Out Islands to enable scheduled flights from points in the US as well as from Nassau and Freeport. Subsequently, the US Federal Aviation Administration approved airports in Exuma and San Salvador for night flights and Continental Connection instituted three flights weekly from Fort Lauderdale into Cat Island, making a stopover at Governor's Harbour, Eleuthera.

Abaco

All but finished in 2004 was the exclusive $160-million Abaco Club resort in Winding Bay near the fishing village of Cherokee Sound, built by well-known British tycoon Peter de Savary. Among many other amenities, Abaco Club features the world's first tropical links-type golf course, capable of attracting international tournaments, beachfront and ocean ridge houses, Bahamian-style cottages, bedroom suites and an elegant plantation-style clubhouse.

Construction of first and second homes continued at an uninterrupted pace throughout the Abacos over the past year.

In February, Deputy Prime Minister Cynthia A Pratt opened a new police station on Moore's Island, an isolated cay off mainland Abaco, once used by drug traffickers. The opening was part of the government's announced programme to bring the full protection of the law to every community.

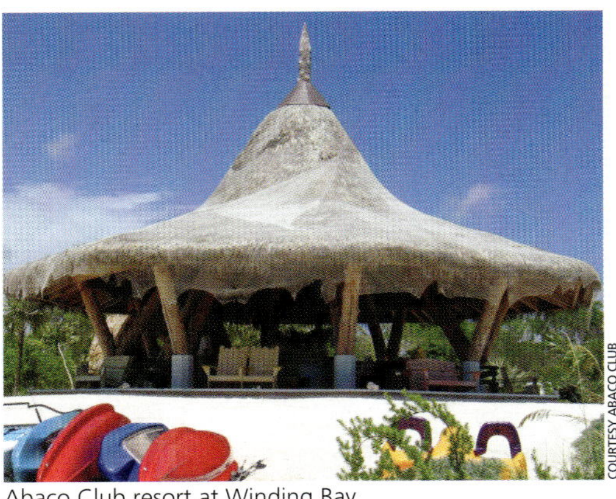
COURTESY ABACO CLUB

Abaco Club resort at Winding Bay

In June 2004, The Ministry of Public Works and Utilities began a $500,000 project repairing roads on Elbow Cay and worked on another $500,000 project begun the previous November to repair roads at Sandy Point.

Andros

In January, 2003, the Ministry of Public Works and Utilities began a much needed $3.2-million project to upgrade roads and the Congo Town Airport on South Andros.

A community health centre, built 10 years ago in Johnson's Bay but never properly equipped or furnished, was finally opened, unofficially, in September 2003. Prime Minister Perry Christie and several Cabinet ministers were on hand in February 2004 to officially commission the centre.

Bimini

The big news in Bimini in 2004 was the signing of an amended heads of agreement to develop the $70-million, five-star Bimini Bay Resort by Florida developer Geraldo Capo. The original agreement, signed in 1997, ran into environmental problems so severe the project had to be shut down.

The new agreement calls for a reduction in the number of residential units from 5,041 to 2,130. Under the terms of the agreement, the government is committed to upgrading the South Bimini airport, bringing it into line with the Federal Aviation Administration regulations and standards, and repairing roads to facilitate development of the 700-acre project.

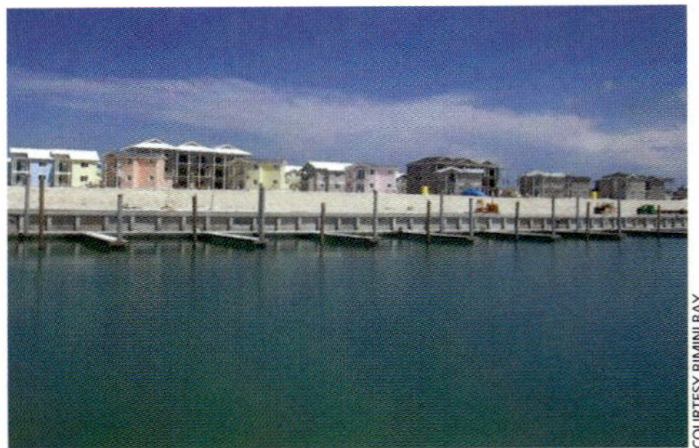
COURTESY BIMINI BAY

Bimini Bay is under construction.

Plans include the construction of a 410-room hotel, condominiums, casino, restaurants, fitness centre, marina, docking facilities, and other amenities. In June 2004 Works and Utilities Minister Bradley Roberts committed the government to dredging the harbour.

Another significant project was the acquisition and re-development of the famous Bimini Big Game Fishing Club by new owners. They plan to construct 52 more hotel rooms at the Club, along with additional marina facilities. Construction was to be completed by the summer of 2005.

Cat Island

In Cat Island, the Ministry of Works and Utilities continued work on the sea wall and roads at Arthur's Town in the north, valued at about $300,000. Another $1.4 million was expended on the repair of main roads, begun in September 2003, throughout the island.

A 100-cottage, $19.7-million resort, health club and spa has been proposed for Lucky Mount, and a $5- to $10-million expansion is set to begin at Hawk's Nest, including the construction of more rooms, a spa, marina, cottages and a reverse osmosis water plant.

Eleuthera

The $2.5-million Aqua Design Eleuthera Desalination Facility was opened in Waterford in June 2004. The plant, capable of producing 180,000 gallons of potable water a day, will serve Deep Creek, Green Castle, Wemyss Bight, Waterford, Fox Bay and Cotton Bay.

On scenic Harbour Island, construction continued at the popular Valentine's Resort & Marina, with the opening of the waterfront bar in December 2003, following the earlier opening of the marina and dive shop. Newly constructed condos were expected to be available by the winter of 2004. The $25-million project is expected to be completed in 2005

In Governor's Harbour, Philadelphia businessman Eddie Lauth III plans to build a $40-million development, including a spa, villas, condos, restaurants, marina and resort, on property that once held a Club Med operation. At press time, Lauth's firm, Governor's Harbour Resort and Marina Ltd, had demolished the old buildings, clearing the way for construction to begin in late 2004.

Exuma

The Grand Isle Villas, an $84-million development within the Four Seasons Resort property at Emerald Bay, was launched late in 2003. Phase 1 of the three-phase project, a total of 16 buildings of four villas each, was completed in 2004 and work continued on phases 2 and 3. Ownership of the villas includes membership in Emerald Bay's Greg Norman-designed golf course, spa, and other amenities. The $300-million Emerald Bay development opened its 219 rooms in 2004.

Also in the Exuma islands, the government signed a heads of agreement with Holmes Company Ltd for the development of a $243-million eco-sensitive resort on Crab Cay and Little Crab Cay near George Town. Prime Minister Perry Christie said the company would work "hand in hand" with the Bahamas Environment, Science and Technology (BEST) Commission to preserve the legendary beauty of the Exumas for future generations of Bahamians.

Minister of Housing and National Insurance Shane Gibson was on hand to break ground early in December, 2003, for the construction of 24 homes ranging in price from $60,000 to $85,000 – part of the government's programme to build affordable housing throughout The Bahamas. Many of these homes were expected to be bought by workers at the resorts at Emerald Bay and Crab Cay.

Grand Bahama

An exciting new development is in the works for west Grand Bahama – a $2.5-billion proposal by the Ginn Development Company of Orlando, Florida, in partnership with DEVCO, the Grand Bahama Port Authority's real estate arm. The partners plan to develop a 2,150-acre property over 18 years. It will include resorts, condominiums, golf courses and residential and yachting communities, says DEVCO president and CEO, Graham Torode.

The Ginn Company was in negotiations with the principals of the Old Bahama Bay resort in West End to develop the large tract of land between the resort and Bootle Bay, along what is called the Settlement Point shoreline.

Meanwhile, construction continued on the Old Bahama Bay resort in West End. This hotel is expanding its hotel property to 48 units with plans to increase the marina from 72 to 125 slips.

Grand Bahama Port Authority president Willie Moss revealed in 2004 that the Port Authority was negotiating for a third dock, the largest in the world, capable of handling the planet's biggest ships. Meanwhile, Grand Bahama's new $30-million terminal is capable of handling 800 passengers an hour, four times the airport's previous capacity.

Gold Rock Creek Enterprises Ltd, a US firm, is proposing to build a multi-million-dollar, state-of-the-art film studio and entertainment complex in east Grand Bahama. The 3,500-acre compound will include

GORDON LOMER/©DUPUCH

Old Bahama Bay

a film and television production and post-production facility, a music recording studio, a movie theme park, water park, restaurants, retail stores and a historic Bahamian village. The first sound studio will be constructed within an existing building on the site, which a spokesman for Gold Rock Creek said would be finished in mid 2005.

Early in 2004, Deputy Prime Minister Cynthia A Pratt officially opened the new Gerald Bartlett Police Headquarters on The Mall Drive in the Northern District of Freeport. Named for the late Commissioner of Police, this $9.2-million complex was funded by National Insurance.

The most ambitious proposal ever presented for the Out Islands was revealed in a July 30, 2004, press release. Michael R Henderson, chairman of RJH Holdings, announced that the company had entered into a Memorandum of Understanding with The Grand Bahama Port Authority to build Moon Bahamas off the north shore of the island. It was expected that Moon Bahamas would be completed in 2010 at an estimated cost of US$4.5 billion, excluding the real estate component. Estimated revenue from timeshare and real estate sales was US$33 billion. The project is to comprise five man made islands which will house the world's largest casino, a 12,000-suite hotel, ten cruise ship terminals, 50 restaurants, the worlds largest resort wine cellar, the worlds largest mega yacht marina, aquatic centre, 22,000 condominiums, huge convention centre and four golf courses.

Rum Cay

Montana Holdings Ltd, a company based in the UK, is approved to build two separate resorts on tiny Rum Cay, midway between San Salvador and Long Island in the southern Bahamas. The $90-million Rum Cay Club & Villas project includes a 190-room hotel, another 60-room hotel, an 18-hole golf course, villas, timeshares, retail outlets, a dive club and a 50-berth marina. The resort is expected to provide 75 construction jobs and 300 permanent jobs when it is completed in 2007.

This project will be in three phases, the first to begin in June of 2004, the second in February 2005 and the third in April 2006. The entire project is expected to be completed in 2011.

During 2003 and 2004, the Ministry of Public Works and Utilities spent $2.5 million on a new airport and 3.5 miles of roads on Rum Cay. The Port Nelson Airport, replacing a private airstrip, was officially opened on February 27, 2004.

COURTESY SHORELINE

Real Estate

Following is a selection of properties available in The Bahamas at press time.

COURTESY DAMIANOS REALTY

Luxury oceanfront living at Caves Point

NEW PROVIDENCE

CAVES POINT: Oceanfront luxury three-bdrm, three-bath apartments in a 24-hour secure gated community of 67 apartments with gymnasium, three swimming pools and beach, with upscale shopping complex across the street. Available units include: beautifully furnished fourth floor unit with large seaside balcony for $699,000 (Internet ref #1781); furnished second floor unit with spacious balcony and great sea views for $665,000 (Internet ref #923); and an unfurnished second floor unit with covered terrace and ocean views for $625,000 (Internet ref #2117). Contact George Damianos, Damianos Realty Co Ltd, PO Box N-732, Nassau, tel (242) 322-2305, fax (242) 322-2033, e-mail sales@damianos.com, or visit www.damianos.com.

CAVES POINT: Exquisite four-bdrm, four-bath penthouse apartment occupies an entire floor at Caves Point, an exclusive gated community in the western district of New Providence. The location commands panoramic ocean views. Its unique design includes a formal entrance through double arched mahogany doors, an oceanside veranda that runs the full length of the penthouse with large sliding glass doors accessed from the kitchen, living room, dining room and master bedroom, and all modern appointments. The floors are a combination of coral sandstone tiles and marble. The bathrooms have marble floors and countertops. $2.15 million. Contact Bahamas Realty Ltd, PO Box N-1132, Nassau, tel (242) 393-8618, fax (242) 393-0326, e-mail lroberts@bahamasrealty.bs, or visit www.bahamasrealty.bs.

COURTESY BAHAMAS REALTY

Caves Point offers panoramic views.

Left, Shoreline, a private beachfront community in Grand Bahama

COURTESY BAHAMAS REALTY

EASTERN ROAD: Oceanfront living at its best. Recently remodelled four-bdrm, 3½-bath home features large open rooms, a modern kitchen, large closets, vaulted ceilings trimmed with Abaco pine, a two-car garage, swimming pool with fountain, a cabana with built-in bar, a brick fireplace and large patio areas that are great for entertaining. Additional features include 20,000-gallon rainwater tank and a standby generator. $750,000. Contact Bahamas Realty Ltd, PO Box N-1132, Nassau, tel (242) 393-8618, fax (242) 393-0326, e-mail lroberts@bahamasrealty.bs, or visit www.bahamasrealty.bs.

LYFORD CAY: Top of the Cay. Elegant 8,400-sq-ft luxury residence perched atop the highest elevation in Lyford Cay. Exquisite 2.4-acre estate with grand Port Cochere entrance features formal living room with wet bar and separate dining and family room, all open to covered terraces. Italian stone flooring throughout and kitchen with granite countertops. Top floor master suite with panoramic sea views. Three guest bdrms, swimming pool and cabana with full bath, maid's quarters, two-car garage and much more. $5.5 million (Internet ref #895). Contact George Damianos, Damianos Realty Co Ltd, PO Box N-732, Nassau, tel (242) 322-2305, fax (242) 322-2033, e-mail sales@damianos.com, or visit www.damianos.com.

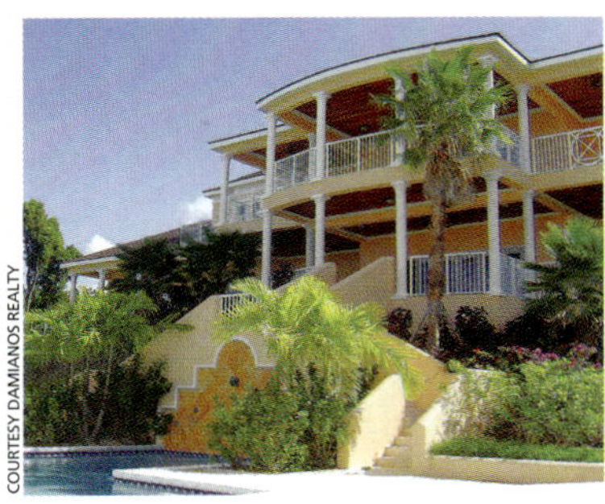
COURTESY DAMIANOS REALTY

LYFORD CAY: Villa Contenta. Tranquil and timeless beachfront retreat reflects a mix of classic detail and Caribbean informality. Manicured grounds with gated entry, 195 ft of sandy beach. This charming two storey five-bdrm, 5½-bath residence, with views of the sea from all major rooms, features a formal living room with fireplace, formal dining room, and a sitting room with a bar – ideal for entertaining. Swimming pool and oceanfront patio. There is also an office that can be converted into a staff bed and bath. $5.6 million (Internet ref #206). Contact George Damianos, Damianos Realty Co Ltd, PO Box N-732, Nassau, tel (242) 322-2305, fax (242) 322-2033, e-mail sales@damianos.com, or visit www.damianos.com.

COURTESY DAMIANOS REALTY

OLD FORT BAY: Beautiful colonial with sun-drenched verandas sits nestled in the upscale gated community of Old Fort Bay. This four-bdrm, 4½-bath, 4,855-sq-ft home features a spacious one-bdrm office/apartment that offers a breathtaking view. The ground-level patio deck surrounds a heated swimming pool. Lushly landscaped 10,000-sq-ft grounds with canal frontage and docking facilities. $2.35 million (Internet ref #2160). Contact George Damianos, Damianos Realty Co Ltd, PO Box N-732, Nassau, tel (242) 322-2305, fax (242) 322-2033, e-mail sales@damianos.com, or visit www.damianos.com.

PORT NEW PROVIDENCE: Stately Georgian-style villa with six bdrms, 6½ baths, stands amidst 5.12 acres of manicured tropical gardens with an infinity-edge swimming pool facing the turquoise ocean. Features include limestone floors, 12-ft ceilings, mahogany millwork, central air, two-bdrm guest cottage, cabana and lots of state-of-the-art amenities. $6 million. Contact Bahamas Realty Ltd, PO Box N-1132, Nassau, tel (242) 393-8618, fax (242) 393-0326, e-mail lroberts@bahamasrealty.bs, or visit www.bahamasrealty.bs.

PORT NEW PROVIDENCE: Beautifully designed three-bdrm, 3½-bath home on the front of a wide canal with 135 ft of frontage and a private dock. Features include pine v-joint ceilings, tiled floors throughout, 40,000-gallon water tank, tiled two-car garage, 30kW soundproofed Kohler generator, hurricane-proof glass, swimming pool with fountain, large shaded patio and landscaped grounds. $1.4 million. Contact Bahamas Realty Ltd, PO Box N-1132, Nassau, tel (242) 393-8618, fax (242) 393-0326, e-mail lroberts@bahamasrealty.bs, or visit www.bahamasrealty.bs.

ROSE ISLAND BEACH & HARBOUR CLUB: Private and secluded residential home sites on a popular private island located east of Paradise Island and just a short ferry ride from the conveniences of downtown Nassau. This developing community offers waterfront, beachfront and sheltered harbourfront lots in addition to white, sandy beaches, woodland areas and high bluffs. Amenities will include a nature reserve, private marina and restaurant. Starting at $500,000 (Internet ref #3349). Contact H G Christie Ltd, PO Box N-8164, Nassau, tel (242) 322-1041, fax (242) 326-5642, e-mail sales@hgchristie.com, or visit www.hgchristie.com.

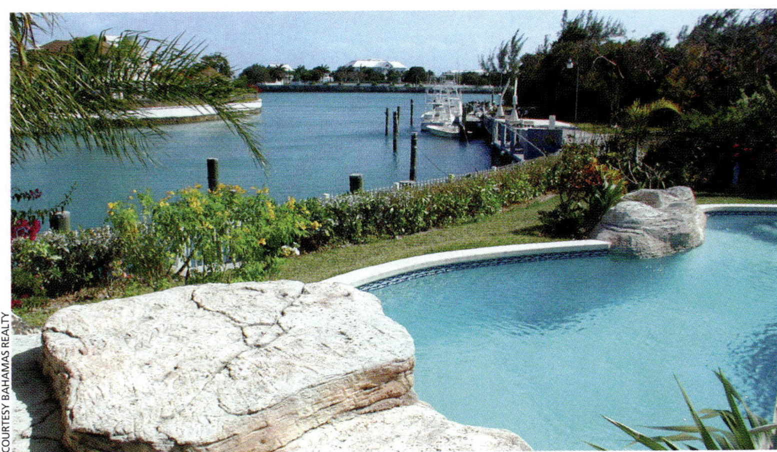
COURTESY BAHAMAS REALTY

Port New Providence canalfront home and grounds with private dock

The Bahamas' Oldest
& Most Extensive
Real Estate Service
Grand Bahama 351-8501
Abaco
Marsh Harbour 367-5454
Hope Town 366-0700
Green Turtle Cay 365-4052
Man-O-War Cay 365-6156
Treasure Cay 365-8467
Exumas 336-2274
Long Island 338-8820
Eleuthera
Governors Harbour 332-3404
Harbour Island 333-3375
Windermere Island 334-2298
Exclusive Affiliate of
CHRISTIE'S
GREAT ESTATES
HGC
Since 1922
H. G. CHRISTIE LTD
Providing Elegant Lifestyles In The Islands
Millars Court, East and Shirley Sts
PO Box N-8164, Nassau
Tel: 242 322-1041. Fax: 242 326-5642
Email: sales@hgchristie.com
www.HGChristie.com

LOWES REALTY
Est. 1967
We Cut The Red Tape in Owning
a Piece of Paradise!
A safe place for you and your money!
Tel: (242) 322-1741 - Fax: (242) 322-7600 - info@lowesrealty.com
www.bahamasrealestate.com
Paradise Island - Nassau - Abaco - Berry Islands - Exuma - Eleuthera - Grand Bahama

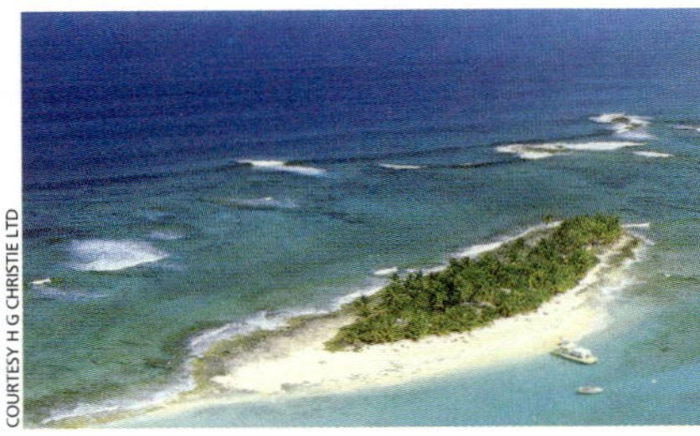
COURTESY H G CHRISTIE LTD

SANDY CAY: This 2.956-acre private island gem is the most photographed island in the world. The island features two native stone cottages, long sandbar, picnic tables, lavatories and showers, unspoiled sea gardens, requisite palm groves and two 10,000-gallon rain water tanks. Two rustic cottages suitable for camping are also on the island. A coveted and personal isle with natural beauty. Ideal financial investment. $1.842 million (Internet ref #282). Contact H G Christie Ltd, PO Box N-8164, Nassau, tel (242) 322-1041, fax (242) 326-5642, e-mail sales@hgchristie.com, or visit www.hgchristie.com.

SANDYPORT: Two-storey, four-bdrm, three-bath home situated on one of the largest lots in one of Nassau's most popular gated communities. Private swimming pool, screened-in porch, decks, fully enclosed yard, large dock and jet ski davit for outdoor living. Features include an automatic standby generator, hurricane shutters, surround sound system, zoned sprinkler system, zoned central air, timbered ceilings, R/O water system, Jacuzzi tub, oak staircase, two-car garage and more. $989,000. Contact Bahamas Realty Ltd, PO Box N-1132, Nassau, tel (242) 393-8618, fax (242) 393-0326, e-mail lroberts@bahamasrealty.bs, or visit www.bahamasrealty.bs.

COURTESY BAHAMAS REALTY

SANDYPORT: Brand new four-bdrm, four-bath partly furnished three-storey town house with its own private dock in a secure gated family community. $540,000. Contact Jason McCarroll or Alex Alexiou, Lowes Realty, PO Box N-3371, Nassau, tel (242) 322-1741, fax (242) 322-7600, e-mail info@lowesrealty.com, or visit www.bahamasrealestate.com.

WINTON: Located on a hilltop in the eastern district of Nassau this solidly built four-bdrm house, with fantastic ocean views, sits on more than one acre of prime real estate. The property has a mature garden with swimming pool, solar panels, gas heater and central air-conditioning. $695,000. Contact Jason McCarroll or Alex Alexiou, Lowes Realty, PO Box N-3371, Nassau, tel (242) 322-1741, fax (242) 322-7600, e-mail info@lowesrealty.com, or visit www.bahamasrealestate.com.

PARADISE ISLAND

Harbour view ground floor two-bdrm, two-bath unit in a small attractive condominium community. $465,000. Contact Jason McCarroll or Alex Alexiou, Lowes Realty, PO Box N-3371, Nassau, tel (242) 322-1741, fax (242) 322-7600, e-mail info@lowesrealty.com, or visit www.bahamasrealestate.com.

COURTESY H G CHRISTIE LTD

Exclusive Ocean Club Estates, Paradise Island

OCEAN CLUB ESTATES: Luxury four-bdrm, 4½-bath, 5,332-sq-ft residence. Luxury finishes including marble, limestone or granite flooring throughout most rooms, granite or marble countertops. Master bath with jetted tub, oversized shower and much more. Resident amenities include beaches, a world-renowned golf course and club, and all amenities at the One&Only Ocean Club and the Atlantis resort. $3.5 million (Internet ref #1995). Contact George Damianos, Damianos Realty Co Ltd, PO Box N-732, Nassau, tel (242) 322-2305, fax (242) 322-2033, e-mail sales@damianos.com, or visit www.damianos.com.

OCEAN CLUB ESTATES: Exclusive, gated development of harbour, golf course and beachfront lots overlooking the Atlantic Ocean on world renowned Paradise Island. Owner benefits include a social and tennis membership at the One&Only Ocean Club including access to dining, tennis, swimming and spa amenities, access to the facilities at Atlantis resort and optional golf membership. From $1.03 million. Contact H G Christie Ltd, PO Box N-8164, Nassau, tel (242) 322-1041, fax (242) 326-5642, e-mail sales@hgchristie.com, or visit www.hgchristie.com.

GRAND BAHAMA

BELL CHANNEL CLUB & MARINA: Beachfront community of two-bdrm, two-bath suites and a three-bdrm, three-bath penthouse, includes private patios, ocean and channel views, central air, designer interiors, cable TV, whirlpool tubs, security gate, 25-slip marina, pool and tennis court. Prices on application. Contact Megeve Investments Ltd, PO Box F-44053, Freeport, tel (242) 373-2673 or 373-3801, fax (242) 373-3802, e-mail bellchan@batelnet.bs, or visit www.bellchannelclub.com.

FORTUNE CAY: Located on almost two acres of tropical landscaping within a prestigious, gated community, this exquisite property boasts over 180 ft of pristine ocean frontage and provides the ultimate in luxurious beachfront living. With more than 10,000 sq ft of living space, this immaculate and beautifully designed two-storey home comprises two ensuite guest bdrms and a media room on the ground floor, guest bdrm, master suite with spacious boudoir and a gym on the second floor. Other features include a grand entrance foyer with 50-ft ceilings, separate formal living and dining areas, full kitchen, office, wraparound balconies and central air. This amazing showpiece enjoys picturesque views of the ocean and is highlighted by a three-car garage with overhead staff quarters and an office in addition to swimming pool and gazebo overlooking sparkling crystalline waters and miles of unspoiled beach. $3.35 million (Internet ref #GB1448). Contact H G Christie, PO Box F-42498/#360, Freeport, Grand Bahama, tel (242) 351-850, fax (242) 351-7491, e-mail grandbahama@hgchristie.com, or visit www.hgchristie.com.

LUCAYAN MARINA VILLAGE: Midshipman Rd, 10 minutes from Grand Bahama International Airport. Private waterfront residential community of luxury homes with unobstructed views of the marina and Bell Channel. Amenities include a swimming pool, 125-slip full-service marina, restaurants and 24-hr security. Private water shuttle ferries residents and guests to Port Lucaya Marketplace. Contact New Hope Holdings Co Ltd, PO Box F-43234, Freeport, tel (242) 373-7616, fax (242) 373-7630, e-mail newhope@coralwave.com, or visit www.lucayanmarinavillage.com.

OLD BAHAMA BAY: A small luxury hotel property that is the ultimate getaway for tranquillity, relaxation and pampered service. This 150-acre resort, marina and residential community lies just 56 miles off the coast of Florida. Home sites on Pine Island available with 145 ft of ocean frontage and 145 ft of channel dockage. Also available are beachfront condominiums. Old Bahama Bay features all beachfront suites, three restaurants, a full-service deep-water marina with customs and immigration services and a public-use helipad. Contact Old Bahama Bay, PO Box F-42546, West End, tel (242) 350-3500, fax (242) 346-6546, or visit www.oldbahamabay.com.

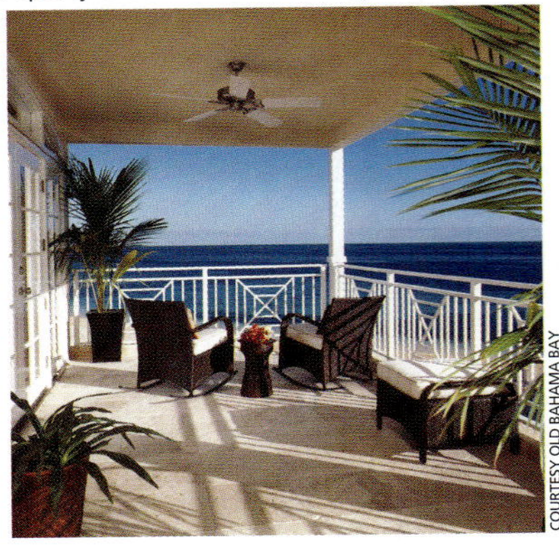
COURTESY OLD BAHAMA BAY

PRINCESS ISLE, THE SEAVIEW ESTATE: This Mediterranean-style beachfront estate boasts a six-bdrm, seven-bath home set on more than an acre of lush, manicured grounds in a premiere, gated community. The interior is accented by 22-ft ceilings, a large family room and marble floors. Highlights include covered patios, a three-car garage and a swimming pool. An adjacent ⅓-acre lot offers 100 ft of canal frontage ideal for yacht dockage, and a guest house. $3.3 million (Internet ref #GB1184). Contact H G Christie, PO Box F-42498/#360, Freeport, tel (242) 351-850, fax (242) 351-7491, e-mail grandbahama@hgchristie.com, or visit www.hgchristie.com.

SHORELINE: A stunning private community situated on its own idyllic beach amid beautifully landscaped gardens, Shoreline comprises 76 luxuriously appointed beachfront properties. The spacious homes are constructed to hurricane-resistant standards and are fully insulated throughout. Large balconies and verandas provide an ideal area for entertaining and relaxation. Oceanfront homes available. Those not directly on the ocean are a short stroll to the miles-long, white-sand beach. Other amenities include seven swimming pools and barbecue areas, a pool bar with fully equipped kitchen, a club house with gym facilities and three tennis courts. Interior features of all homes include vaulted ceilings, marble and wood floors, marble bathrooms, granite countertops and vanity units, and hardwood kitchen cabinets. All models have covered verandas and porches as well as an uncovered patio deck.

Some models have garages. At $2.325 million, the Camellia or Casuarina has four bdrms, four baths and a study. At $2.45 million, the Bauhinia or Bougainvillea also has four bdrms, four baths and a study. The Juniper or Jasmine has three bdrms, two baths plus loft for $650,000. For $710,000 the Azalea or Acacia offers three bdrms and three baths. The Palmetto or Poinciana, at $720,000, has four bdrms and three baths. Contact Michelle Hanson, Shoreline Properties, PO Box F-44958, Freeport, tel (242) 374-2496, fax (242) 374-2493, e-mail shoreline@coralwave.com, or visit www.shorelinebahamas.com.

COURTESY SHORELINE

Shoreline's Azalea offers three bedrooms and three bathrooms.

ABACO

CORNISH CAY: Island kingdom comprising 38 acres, a mile of pink sand beaches, elevations to 50 ft, over two miles of pathways and commanding views. The island features a hilltop residence with two bdrms, two baths and large wraparound deck. Highlighted by two separate guest houses, a caretaker's cottage, a workshop, tennis court, garden house, boat harbour, covered electric boat lift and a beach cabana. $4.9 million (Internet ref #AB119). Contact H G Christie Ltd, PO Box N-8164, Nassau, tel (242) 322-1041, fax (242) 326-5642, e-mail sales@hgchristie.com, or visit www.hgchristie.com.

COURTESY H G CHRISTIE LTD

GREAT GUANA CAY: Magnificent waterfront property located on the south end of the cay. This one-of-a-kind, well-elevated property contains 5.19 acres with fabulous views of the Sea of Abaco and the Atlantic Ocean and lots of palm trees and flowering trees. The property boasts 395 ft of oceanfront and 160 ft on the Sea of Abaco in addition to 245+ ft of well-protected, semi-private boat basin frontage. $2.95 million (Internet ref #AB5176). Contact H G Christie, PO Box AB-20777, Bay St, Marsh Harbour, tel (242) 367-4608, fax (242) 367-5452, e-mail abaco@hgchristie.com, or visit www.hgchristie.com.

COURTESY DAMIANOS REALTY

HOPE TOWN/ELBOW CAY: Bali Hai on Tahiti Beach is a sophisticated, yet comfortable 5,900-sq-ft waterfront estate overlooking one of the most sought-after beaches on the island. This turnkey property is ideal for entertaining with open floor plan, commercial kitchen, 12-seat dining, four bdrms with private baths, grand master suite with his and hers baths. Private dock can accommodate up to an 80-ft vessel. $2.9 million (Internet ref #2041). Contact George Damianos, Damianos Realty Co Ltd, PO Box N-732, Nassau, tel (242) 322-2305, fax (242) 322-2033, e-mail sales@damianos.com, or visit www.damianos.com.

HOPE TOWN/ELBOW CAY: Twin Dolphin Point is a private 1.6-acre property consisting of two turnkey elevated waterfront island homes in a lush tropical setting with picturesque sea views. One furnished home has three bdrms, three baths, office and two kitchens and is divided into two rental units. The second furnished home has five bdrms, four baths and two kitchens and is also divided into two rental units. Good rental income history. $2.3 million (Internet ref #2072). Contact George Damianos, Damianos Realty Co Ltd, PO Box N-732, Nassau, tel (242) 322-2305, fax (242) 322-2033, e-mail sales@damianos.com, or visit www.damianos.com.

TREASURE CAY: Prime beachfront, multi-family property and designated high rise lots are available at this 1,400-acre resort with 3½ miles of beach. Lots have water, sewer, electricity, telephone and cable television hook-up. Amenities at the resort include a par-72, Dick Wilson-designed golf course, 150-slip marina, dive shop and hotel with beach villas. Jet airport nearby with daily flights from Florida. More than seven miles of sea wall protects home sites on the canal/marina, golf course and beachfront. Hotel sites available. Contact Anne Albury or Marcellus Roberts, Treasure Cay Ltd, Real Estate Division, tel (242) 365-8538, fax (242) 365-8587, or e-mail tcrealestate@oii.net.

BERRY ISLANDS

FROZEN & ALDER CAYS: A rare private island paradise of endless possibilities. 83+ unspoiled acres are rimmed with pristine white sand beaches and unparalleled sport-fishing waters. Well appointed, air-conditioned accommodations include six-bdrm residence, manager's cottage, staff housing and fishing guide camp. Self sufficient systems, heated swimming pool, state-of-the-art marina and two docking facilities. Splendidly secluded, it is accessible only by boat or sea plane and is just 35 miles from Nassau. $8.5 million. Contact Bahamas Realty Ltd, PO Box N-1132, Nassau, tel (242) 393-8618, fax (242) 393-0326, e-mail lroberts@bahamasrealty.bs, or visit www.bahamasrealty.bs.

CAT ISLAND

BUTLER TRACT: Stretching across 1,200 ft of first class beach on Fine Bay, this spectacular 50.37-acre tract is situated between a pond and the Atlantic Ocean and just 20 minutes from the New Bight Airport. Enjoy a combination of powdery, pink sand beach, turquoise waters, sunny skies and prevailing breezes from the Exuma Sound. Ideal for a small hotel, a group of cottages, development of custom lots or a private estate. Offered at $1.5 million (Internet ref #294). Contact H G Christie Ltd, PO Box N-8164, Nassau, tel (242) 322-1041, fax (242) 326-5642, e-mail sales@hgchristie.com, or visit www.hgchristie.com.

ELEUTHERA

GOVERNOR'S HARBOUR: Oyster Harbour is an extraordinary waterfront property with approximately 448 acres extending from prime beach on the Atlantic to the banks. Glorious vistas abound from high bluffs and rolling hills reaching up to 100 ft. Total water frontage exceeds four miles. The property's deepwater lake offers an exceptional opportunity to develop a safe harbour and marine community. Starting at $10 million (Internet ref #549). Contact H G Christie Ltd, PO Box EL25, Governors Harbour, Eleuthera, tel (242) 332-3404 or 332-2503, fax (242) 332-3406, e-mail eleuthera@hgchristie.com, or visit www.hgchristie.com.

WINDERMERE ISLAND: An exceptional enclave for those who treasure privacy, aquamarine waters and endless pink-sand beach. These superb residential lots are ready to build on and include all utilities. Located on a secure, private island subdivision connected to Eleuthera by a bridge offering 24-hour security and dramatic views of Savannah Sound. The members only club at Windermere offers dining, tennis and a heated swimming pool. Starting at $108,000 (Internet ref #286). Contact H G Christie Ltd, PO Box EL25, Governors Harbour, Eleuthera, tel (242) 332-3404 or 332-2503, fax (242) 332-3406, e-mail eleuthera@hgchristie.com, or visit www.hgchristie.com.

NEWBERRY HOUSE: Picturesque Double Bay beachfront property just under nine acres with 570 ft of pristine pink sand beach. Idyllic and private. House on property is 2,500 sq ft with four bdrms, 3½ baths with large living and dining rooms opening to seaside deck with great ocean views. Ideal for development, with open zoning. $1.4 million (Internet ref #1810). Contact George Damianos, Damianos Realty Co Ltd, PO Box N-732, Nassau, tel (242) 322-2305, fax (242) 322-2033, e-mail sales@damianos.com, or visit www.damianos.com.

COURTESY DAMIANOS REALTY

EXUMA

BAHAMA HIGHLANDS: Perched on a hilltop with elevations to 80 ft, these island lots comprise 11,000 sq ft to 14,000 sq ft. Two lots front the main road and two have private road access. Utilities are available from the main road and there is access to a public beach at the bottom of the hill. The properties are conveniently centered between the Four Seasons Resort and George Town and just minutes from the airport. Offered at $200,000 (Internet ref #EX2). Contact H G Christie Ltd, PO Box EX-29178, George Town, Exuma, tel/fax (242) 336-2274, e-mail exuma@hgchristie.com, or visit www.hgchristie.com.

JIMMY HILL: This exceptional, turnkey home is a showcase of custom craftsmanship accented by Bahamian face stones. Set on a half acre of landscaped grounds with fruit trees with views of the surrounding cays, this unique, 2,400-sq-ft home features two bdrms, two baths, a storage room ideal for a third bdrm with separate entrance, and a one-car garage. A private beach with deeded access is just minutes away. $530,000 (Internet ref #5062). Contact H G Christie Ltd, PO Box EX-29178, George Town, Exuma, tel/fax (242) 336-2274, e-mail exuma@hgchristie.com, or visit www.hgchristie.com.

Bahamas classified directory

See also Freeport/Lucaya classified directory, pgs 572-576

ACCOUNTANTS/ACCOUNTING FIRMS

BDO Mann Judd 229
Ernst & Young 269
Galanis & Co 231
KPMG 223
PricewaterhouseCoopers 277
Sigma Management Bahamas 269
See also **Audit & related services.**

AIR CARGO/FREIGHT

Bahamasair 533
DHL Worldwide Express 137
Tropical Brokerage Services Ltd 165
See also **Courier service, Import & export services, Movers – packing & crating, Shipping companies** and **Trucking.**

AIRLINES

Bahamasair 533

ALUMINUM BUILDING SUPPLIES – MANUFACTURE

Commonwealth Building Supplies Ltd 131

ARCHITECTS

The Architectural Studio 227
Island Industries (Bah) Ltd 169

ATTORNEYS/NOTARIES PUBLIC

See **Law Firms.**

AUDIO/VIDEO SYSTEMS

Satellite Bahamas 173

AUDIT & RELATED SERVICES

Galanis & Co 231
PricewaterhouseCoopers 277
Sigma Management Bahamas 269
Sovereign (Bah) Ltd 223
See also **Accountants/Accounting firms.**

AUTOMOBILE LEASING

NMC Leasing 271
See also **Car rental companies.**

BANKS, FINANCIAL HOUSES & TRUST COMPANIES

Accuvest Ltd 271
Accuvest Fund Services Ltd 271
Ansbacher (Bah) Ltd 201
ATC Trustees (Bah) Ltd 265
Atlantic Asset Mgmt Ltd (AAM) 253
Banca del Gottardo 256
Bank deGroof Group 245
Bank of The Bahamas Intl 254
The Bank of Nova Scotia Trust Co (Bah) Ltd 237
Banque Privée Edmond de Rothschild Ltd 207
Banque SCS Alliance (Nas) Ltd 249
Bearbull Intl Ltd 245
BSI Overseas (Bah) Ltd 205
Butterfield Bank 263
Cardinal Intl 209
The Central Bank of The Bahamas 105
Credit Suisse (Bah) Ltd 203
Dartley Bank & Trust Ltd 279
Derivatives Portfolio Mgmt (Bah) Ltd (DPM) 267
Experta Trust Co (Bah) Ltd 275
Ferrier Lullin Bank & Trust (Bah) Ltd 199
RBC Finco ....Back cover
J P Morgan Trust Co (Bah) Ltd 279
Lombard Odier Darier Hentsch Private Bank & Trust Ltd 193
Montaque Securities Intl 267
Pictet Bank & Trust Ltd 195
The Private Trust Corp Ltd 273
RBC Dominion Securities (Global) Ltd ....Back cover
RBC Finco ....Back cover
RBC Royal Bank of Canada ....17, Back cover
RBC Royal Bank of Canada Global Private Banking 17
RBC Royal Bank of Canada Trust Co (Bah) Ltd ....17, Back cover
Scotia Private Banking Services 237
Scotiabank (Bah) Ltd 237
Scotiatrust 237
Sentinel Bank & Trust 265

Sovereign (Bah) Ltd 223
UBS (Bah) Ltd 191
United European Bank & Trust
(Nas) Ltd (UEB) 231

BATTERIES – AUTOMOTIVE, HEAVY EQUIPMENT & MARINE
Machinery & Energy Ltd 157

BEEPERS/PAGERS
Bahamas Telecommunications
Co (BTC)/BaTelCo 109

BOOKS & MAGAZINES
Bahamas Trailblazer Maps 173, 211, 608
Dining & Entertainment Guide 211, 608
Etienne Dupuch Jr Publications Ltd 173, 211, 318, 529, 575, 607, 608
Welcome Bahamas 211, 529, 608
What-to-do 211, 608
See also **Newspapers.**

BROADCASTING
See **Communications & broadcasting.**

BROKERAGE SERVICES
Accuvest Ltd 271
Accuvest Fund Services Ltd 271
Berkeley (Bah) Ltd 241

BUILDING CONTRACTORS/ CONSTRUCTION
Bahamas Marine Construction 293
Island Industries (Bah) Ltd 169
Mosko's Group of Building Cos 293
Mosko's United Construction 293

BUILDING/CONSTRUCTION EQUIPMENT & SUPPLIES
Commonwealth Building
Supplies Ltd 131
Island Industries (Bah) Ltd 169
JBR Building Supplies Ltd 149
Machinery & Energy Ltd 157
NP Building Supplies 293
Tops Lumber & Plumbing 149
See also **Hardware, Hurricane shutters, Paint supplies, Plumbing supplies** and **Tiles & supplies.**

BUSINESS ADVISORY SERVICES
BDO Mann Judd 229
Centre for Entrepreneurship 97
The College of The Bahamas 97
Ernst & Young 269
Halsbury Chambers 275
IBM 233
KPMG 223
PricewaterhouseCoopers 277
Veritas Consultants Ltd 95
See also **Accountants/accounting firms; Banks, financial houses & trust companies; Corporate finance, management & advisory services; Investment advisory/asset management services** and **Law firms.**

BUSINESS SYSTEMS CONSULTING, MANAGEMENT, TROUBLESHOOTING
Custom Computers Ltd 239
IBM 233
KPMG 223
Micronet Business Technology 273

CABINETRY
Mosko's Furniture 293

CABLE COMPANIES
Cable Bahamas 91

CAPTIVE INSURANCE
Britannia Consulting Group 225
See also **Insurance.**

CAR RENTAL COMPANIES
Avis 381
Budget 93

CASINOS
Crystal Palace Casino 101

CATERING/CONVENTION SERVICES
See **Hotels.**

CELLULAR PHONES/SERVICE
Bahamas Telecommunications
Co (BTC)/BaTelCo 109

CHARTERED ACCOUNTANTS
See **Accountants/accounting firms** and **Audit & related services.**

COMMUNICATIONS & BROADCASTING
Bahamas Telecommunications
Co (BTC)/BaTelCo 109
Cable Bahamas 91

Satellite Bahamas 173
See also **Books & magazines, Internet services** and **Newspapers.**

COMMODITIES

Berkeley (Bah) Ltd 241

COMPANY INCORPORATION & MANAGEMENT

ATC Trustees (Bah) Ltd 265
Atlantic Asset Mgmt Ltd (AAM) 253
Bahamas Incorporation Services Ltd 253
Bank deGroof Group 245
Bank of Nova Scotia Trust Co (Bah) Ltd 237
BDO Mann Judd 229
Bearbull Intl Ltd 245
Britannia Consulting Group 225
Butterfield Bank 263
Dartley Bank & Trust Ltd 279
Davis & Co 221
Experta Trust Co (Bah) Ltd 275
Fitzgerald & Fitzgerald 241
FTP Corporate Services Ltd 241
Halsbury Chambers 275
J P Morgan Trust Co (Bah) Ltd 279
Jerome E Pyfrom & Co 253
KPMG 223
McKinney, Bancroft & Hughes 229
Miriam J Curling & Co 173
Montaque Securities Intl 267
PricewaterhouseCoopers 277
The Private Trust Corp Ltd 273
Scotia Private Banking Services 237
Scotiabank (Bah) Ltd 237
Scotiatrust 237
Sentinel Bank & Trust 265
Sigma Management Bahamas 269
Sovereign (Bah) Ltd 223
United European Bank & Trust (Nas) Ltd (UEB) 231
See also **Accountants/accounting firms; Banks, financial houses & trust companies; Corporate finance, management & advisory services; Investment advisory/asset management services** and **Law firms.**

COMPUTERS – SALES, SERVICE & SUPPLIES

Custom Computers Ltd 239
IBM 233
Micronet Business Technology 273

CONCRETE – READY-MIXED

NP Building Supplies 293

CONSTRUCTION COMPANIES

See **Building contractors/construction.**

CONSTRUCTION MANAGEMENT

The Architectural Studio 227
Veritas Consultants Ltd 95

COPIERS – SALES, SUPPLIES & SERVICE

Custom Computers Ltd 239
Micronet Business Technology 273

CORPORATE FINANCE, MANAGEMENT & ADVISORY SERVICES

Accuvest Ltd 271
Accuvest Fund Services 271
Ansbacher (Bah) Ltd 201
ATC Trustees (Bah) Ltd 265
Atlantic Asset Mgmt Ltd (AAM) 253
Bahamas Incorporation Services Ltd 253
Banca del Gottardo 256
Bank deGroof Group 245
The Bank of Nova Scotia Trust Co (Bah) Ltd 237
Banque Privée Edmond de Rothschild Ltd 207
Banque SCS Alliance (Nas) Ltd 249
BDO Mann Judd 229
Bearbull Intl Ltd 245
Britannia Consulting Group 225
BSI Overseas (Bah) Ltd 205
Butterfield Bank 263
Cardinal Intl 209
Credit Suisse (Bah) Ltd 203
Dartley Bank & Trust Ltd 279
Ernst & Young 269
Experta Trust Co (Bah) Ltd 275
Ferrier Lullin Bank & Trust (Bah) Ltd 199
FTP Corporate Services Ltd 241
Galanis & Co 231
J P Morgan Trust Co (Bah) Ltd 279
KPMG 223
Lombard Odier Darier Hentsch Private Bank & Trust Ltd 193
Montaque Securities Intl 267
Pictet Bank & Trust Ltd 195
PricewaterhouseCoopers 277
The Private Trust Corp Ltd 273
RBC Dominion Securities (Global) Ltd ....Back cover
RBC Royal Bank of Canada ....17, Back cover

RBC Royal Bank of Canada Global Private Banking 17
RBC Royal Bank of Canada Trust Co (Bah) Ltd ....17, Back cover
Scotia Private Banking Services 237
Scotiatrust 237
Scotiabank (Bah) Ltd 237
Sentinel Bank & Trust 265
Sovereign (Bah) Ltd 223
UBS (Bah) Ltd 191
United European Bank & Trust (Nas) Ltd (UEB) 231
See also **Law firms.**

COURIER SERVICE
DHL 137

CREDIT CARDS
Bahamas Incorporation Services Ltd 253
Sovereign (Bah) Ltd 223
See also **Banks, financial houses & trust companies.**

CUSTOMS BROKERS
DHL 137
Tropical Brokerage Services Ltd 165

DATA CENTRE
Maxil Communications 219

DIVE SHOP & SUPPLIES
Treasure Cay Hotel Resort & Marina (Abaco) 155

DOCUMENT MANAGEMENT
Custom Computers Ltd 239
IBM 233
Micronet Business Technology 273

DRY CLEANING & LAUNDRY SERVICES
New Oriental Cleaners 315

EDUCATION
Centre for Entrepreneurship 97
The College of The Bahamas 97, 115
IBM 233
See also **Schools.**

ELECTRICITY COMPANIES
Bahamas Electricity Corp (BEC) 251

ELECTRONIC/ELECTRICAL EQUIPMENT – SUPPLIES & REPAIRS
Satellite Bahamas 173

EMPLOYEE TRAINING/MOTIVATION
Strategic Marketing Corporate Services 271

EMPLOYMENT AGENCIES
Strategic Marketing Corporate Services 271

ENGINEERS
Island Industries (Bah) Ltd 169
Mosko's Group of Building Cos 293
Mosko's United Construction Co Ltd 293

ENVIRONMENTAL SERVICES
Dept of Environmental Health Services 125

FINANCIAL FUTURES
Berkeley (Bah) Ltd 241

FINANCIAL SERVICES
Bahamas Financial Services Board 197
Ministry of Financial Services & Investments 215
The Central Bank of The Bahamas 105
Securities Commission of The Bahamas ..243
See also **Banks, financial houses & trust companies; Corporate finance, management & advisory services** and **Investment advisory/asset management services.**

FOREIGN EXCHANGE BROKERS
Berkeley (Bah) Ltd 241

FREIGHT SERVICES – Air & Ocean
DHL 137
Tropical Brokerage Services Ltd 165

FURNITURE
Mosko's Furniture 293
See also **Office equipment, furniture & supplies.**

GARDEN CENTRE
Fox Hill Nursery 149
Munroe's Landscaping Ltd 227

GENERATORS
Machinery & Energy Ltd 157

GOLF COURSE
Treasure Cay Hotel Resort
& Marina (Abaco) 155

GROCERIES – WHOLESALE & RETAIL
Bahamas Food Services 169

HARDWARE
Commonwealth Building Supplies Ltd 131
JBR Building Supplies Ltd 149
Tops Lumber & Plumbing 149

HEAVY EQUIPMENT SALES & SERVICE
Machinery & Energy Ltd 157

HOTEL & RESTAURANT SUPPLIES
Bahamas Food Services 169

HOSPITALS & CLINICS
Geriatric Hospital 133
Princess Margaret Hospital 133
Sandilands Rehabilitation Centre 133

HOTELS
British Colonial Hilton 95
Nassau Beach Hotel 101
Treasure Cay Hotel Resort
& Marina (Abaco) 155
Wyndham Nassau Resort &
Crystal Palace Casino 101

HUMAN RESOURCES CONSULTING/ MANAGEMENT
BDO Mann Judd 229
Strategic Marketing Corporate Services ..271

HURRICANE SHUTTERS – MANUFACTURE & SALES
Commonwealth Building Supplies Ltd 131

IMMIGRATION
Sovereign (Bah) Ltd 223

IMPORT & EXPORT SERVICES
DHL 137
Tropical Brokerage Services Ltd 165
See also **Freight services – air & ocean, Courier service, Movers, Shipping companies** and **Trucking.**

INFORMATION TECHNOLOGY SERVICES
Custom Computers Ltd 239
Galanis & Co 231
IBM 233
Integrated Business Solutions Ltd 231
KPMG 223
Micronet Business Technology 273

INSURANCE
Bahamas First General Insurance
Co Ltd 217
Britannia Consulting Group 225
Cole Insurance 249
DMG Intl Marine Services Agency 155
Lampkin & Co 165
The National Insurance Board 135
NUCA Insurance Agency 147
WAM Co Ltd 155
See also **Captive insurance.**

INTERIOR DESIGN SERVICES
The Architectural Studio 227

INTERNET SERVICES
Bahamas Telecommunications Co
(BTC)/BaTelCo 109
Cable Bahamas 91
Caribbean Crossings 219
CoralWave 91
Satellite Bahamas 173

INVESTMENT ADVISORY/ASSET MANAGEMENT SERVICES
Accuvest Ltd 271
Accuvest Fund Services Ltd 271
Ansbacher (Bah) Ltd 201
ATC Trustees (Bah) Ltd 265
Atlantic Asset Mgmt Ltd (AAM) 253
Bahamas Incorporation Services Ltd 253
Banca del Gottardo 256
Bank of deGroof Group 245
The Bank of Nova Scotia
Trust Co (Bah) Ltd 237
Banque Privée
Edmond de Rothschild Ltd 207
Banque SCS Alliance (Nas) Ltd 249
BDO Mann Judd 229
Bearbull Intl Ltd 245
Britannia Consulting Group 225
BSI Overseas (Bah) Ltd 205
Butterfield Bank 263
Cardinal Intl 209
Credit Suisse (Bah) Ltd 203
Dartley Bank & Trust Ltd 279
Experta Trust Co (Bah) Ltd 275
Ferrier Lullin Bank & Trust (Bah) Ltd 199

Fitzgerald & Fitzgerald 241
FTP Corp Services Ltd 241
Galanis & Co 231
J P Morgan Trust Co (Bah) Ltd 279
KPMG 223
Lombard Odier Darier Hentsch Private Bank & Trust Ltd 193
Montaque Securities Intl 267
Pictet Bank & Trust Ltd 195
PricewaterhouseCoopers 277
The Private Trust Corp Ltd 273
RBC Dominion Securities (Global) Ltd ....Back cover
RBC Royal Bank of Canada ....17, Back cover
RBC Royal Bank of Canada Global Private Banking 17
RBC Royal Bank of Canada Trust Co (Bah) Ltd ....17, Back cover
Scotia Private Banking Services 237
Scotiabank (Bah) Ltd 237
Scotiatrust 237
Sentinel Bank & Trust 265
Sigma Management Bahamas 269
Sovereign (Bah) Ltd 223
UBS (Bah) Ltd 191
United European Bank & Trust (Nas) Ltd (UEB) 231
See also **Law firms.**

INVESTMENT OPPORTUNITIES

Ministry of Financial Services & Investments 215
See **Insurance, Investment advisory/asset management services** and **Real estate.**

LANDSCAPING CONTRACTORS

Munroe's Landscaping Ltd 227

LAW FIRMS

Davis & Co 221
Fitzgerald & Fitzgerald 241
Halsbury Chambers 275
Holowesko & Co 137
Jerome E Pyfrom & Co 253
Kendolyn V Cartwright-Robinson 318
McKinney, Bancroft & Hughes 229
Miriam J Curling & Co 173

LAWN & GARDEN EQUIPMENT & SUPPLIES

Munroe's Landscaping 227

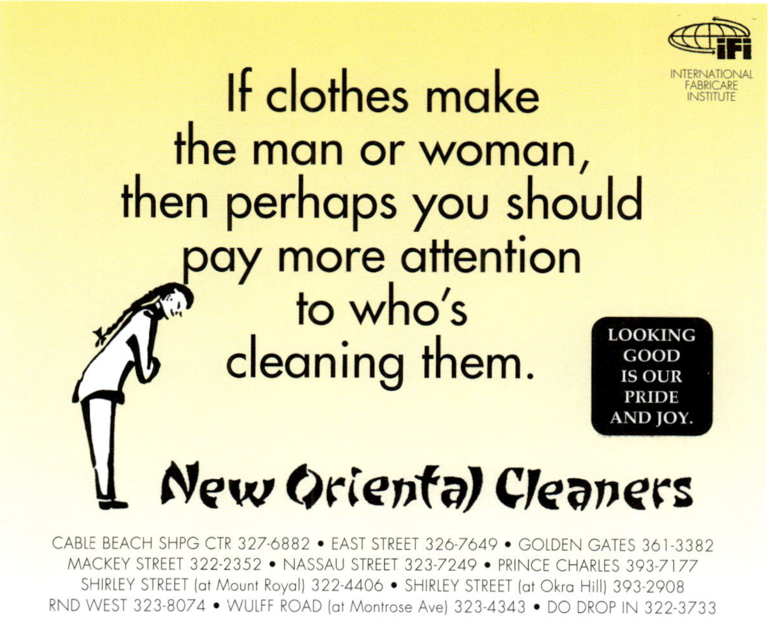

LIGHTING FIXTURES
Tops Lumber & Plumbing 149

MAGNETIC RESONANCE THERAPY
Magnetic Resonance Therapy (Bah) Ltd ..119

MANAGEMENT CONSULTING
BDO Mann Judd 229
KPMG 223
PricewaterhouseCoopers 277

MARINAS
Treasure Cay Hotel Resort
& Marina (Abaco) 155

MARINE CONTRACTORS/CONSTRUCTION
Bahamas Marine 293
Mosko's Group of Building Cos 293
Mosko's United Construction Co Ltd 293

MARINE SERVICES
DMG Intl Marine Services Agency 155
WAM Co Ltd 155

MEDIA
See **Books & magazines, Communications & broadcasting** and **Newspapers.**

MEDICAL SERVICES
Magnetic Resonance Therapy (Bah) Ltd 119
See also **Hospitals & Clinics.**

MOVERS – PACKING & CRATING
Tropical Brokerage Services Ltd 165
See also **Air cargo/freight, Import & export services, Shipping companies** and **Trucking.**

MUTUAL FUNDS
Accuvest Ltd 271
Accuvest Fund Services Ltd 271
Atlantic Asset Mgmt Ltd (AMM) 253
Derivatives Portfolio Mgmt
(Bah) Ltd (DPM)................................267
The Private Trust Corp Ltd 273
See also **Banks, financial houses & trust companies; Corporate finance, management & advisory services** and **Investment advisory/asset management services.**

NETWORK PLANNING
Custom Computers Ltd 239
IBM 233
Micronet Business Technology 273

NEUROLOGICAL DISORDERS (TREATMENT)
Magnetic Resonance Therapy (Bah) Ltd 119

NEWSPAPERS
The Nassau Guardian.............................117

NURSERY
Fox Hill Nursery 149
Munroe's Landscaping 227

OFFICE EQUIPMENT, FURNITURE & SUPPLIES – SALES, INSTALLATION & SERVICE
Bahamas Telecommunications
Co (BTC)/BaTelCo 109
Custom Computers Ltd 239
Executive Printers of The Bahamas, Ltd 123
IBM 233
Micronet Business Technology 273
Satellite Bahamas 173
See also **Furniture.**

ONLINE BANKING
Bank of The Bahamas Intl 254

ONLINE TRADING PLATFORMS
Berkeley (Bah) Ltd 241

PAIN MANAGEMENT
Magnetic Resonance Therapy (Bah) Ltd ..119

PAINT SUPPLIES
JBR Building Supplies Ltd 149
Tops Lumber & Plumbing 149

PHOTOCOPY SERVICE
Wongs' Rubber Stamp
& Printing Co Ltd 119

POULTRY & LIVESTOCK
Bahamas Food Services 169

PLUMBING SUPPLIES
Commonwealth Building Supplies Ltd 131
JBR Building Supplies Ltd 149
Tops Lumber & Plumbing 149

PRECIOUS METALS BROKER
Berkeley (Bah) Ltd 241

PRINTING
Executive Printers
of The Bahamas, Ltd 123
The Nassau Guardian..............................117
Wongs' Rubber Stamp
& Printing Co Ltd 119

PROPERTY MANAGEMENT
Bahamas Realty 285
H G Christie Ltd 303

PUBLISHERS
Etienne Dupuch Jr Publications Ltd........38, 173, 211, 318, 319, 529, 575, 607, 608
Dupuch Publications 38, 173, 211, 318, 319, 529, 575, 607, 608

REAL ESTATE – APPRAISALS, DEVELOPMENTS, RENTALS & SALES
Bahamas Realty 285
Damianos Realty 301
H G Christie Ltd.....................................303
Lowes Realty 303
Lyford Cay Sales and Rentals 301
Treasure Cay Hotel Resort
& Marina (Abaco) 155

RESTAURANTS
British Colonial Hilton 95
Nassau Beach Hotel 101
Treasure Cay Hotel Resort
& Marina (Abaco) 155
Wyndham Nassau Resort
& Crystal Palace Casino 101

RETAILER – LUXURY GOODS
John Bull 23-25

RUBBER STAMPS
Wongs' Rubber Stamp & Printing
Co Ltd 119

SALVAGE & TOWING
DMG Intl Marine Service Agency 155
WAM Co Ltd 155

SATELLITE SYSTEMS & SERVICE
Satellite Bahamas 173

SCHOOLS
The College of The Bahamas 115

SEAFOOD – WHOLESALE & RETAIL
Bahamas Food Services 169

SEWER SERVICE
Water and Sewerage Corp 153

SHIP REGISTRATION
Miriam J Curling & Co 173
Sovereign (Bah) Ltd 223
See also **Law firms.**

SHIP SERVICES/CHANDLERS
DMG Intl Marine Service Agency 155
WAM Co Ltd 155

SHIPPING COMPANIES
DHL 137
Tropical Brokerage Services Ltd 165
See also **Freight services – air & ocean, Courier service, Import & export services, Movers** and **Trucking.**

SPACE PLANNING
The Architectural Studio 227

SPORTS INJURIES
Magnetic Resonance Therapy (Bah) Ltd 119

STAMPS (COMMEMORATIVE)
Bahamas Post Office Philatelic Bureau 99

STEAM PRESSING
New Oriental Cleaners 315

STEEL BUILDINGS
Island Industries (Bah) Ltd 169

STOREFRONT SYSTEMS
Commonwealth Building Supplies Ltd 131

SURVEYORS – MARINE
DMG Intl Marine Services Agency 155
WAM Co Ltd 155

TAX PLANNING
Montaque Securities Intl 267
Sovereign (Bah) Ltd 223
See also **Captive insurance, Corporate finance, management and advisory services, Investment advisory/asset management services** and **Law firms.**

TELECOMMUNICATIONS
Bahamas Telecommunications Co (BTC)/BaTelCo 109
Cable Bahamas 91
Caribbean Crossings 219

TILES & SUPPLIES
Commonwealth Building Supplies Ltd 131
JBR Building Supplies Ltd 149

TOOLS – BUILDING/CONSTRUCTION
Commonwealth Building Supplies Ltd 131
JBR Building Supplies Ltd 149
Tops Lumber & Building Supplies 149

TOURISM INFORMATION
Bahamas Ministry of Tourism 32

TRAVEL
Bahamas Ministry of Tourism 32
Bahamasair 533
See also **Hotels.**

TRUCKING
Tropical Brokerage Services Ltd 165
See also **Air cargo/freight, Import & export services, Movers** and **Shipping companies.**

TRUSTS & ESTATE PLANNING
See **Accountants/accounting firms, Banks, financial houses & trust companies; Corporate finance, management & advisory services; Investment advisory/asset management services** and **Law firms.**

WAREHOUSE STORAGE
Tropical Brokerage Services Ltd 165

WATER FILTER SYSTEMS
Brita Water Filter Systems 127

WATER SERVICE
Water and Sewerage Corp 153

WATER HEATERS
Tops Lumber & Plumbing 149

WEB HOSTING
Maxil Communications 219

WEBSITES
bahamasnet.com 113, 513
BankBahamasOnline.com 254
caribbean.com 38, 319
See also **Internet services.**

New Providence

Measurements at widest points, 21 x 7 miles

Bahamas Information

Blue page index, this section

Accommodations
Accounting firms
Agriculture
AIDS/HIV
Air service
Airports
Ambulance/air ambulance services
Animals
Antiquities, Monuments and Museums Corp (AMMC)
Arawak Cay
Architectural firms
Archives
Art galleries
Asset Protection Trusts
Atlantic Undersea Test & Evaluation Centre (AUTEC)
Awards
Bahamahost
Bahamas Agricultural & Industrial Corp (BAIC)
Bahamas Air Sea Rescue Assoc (BASRA)
Bahamas Development Bank (BDB)
Bahamas Family Planning Assoc (BFPA)
Bahamas Financial Services Board (BFSB)
Bahamas Historical Society
Bahamas Humane Society (BHS)
Bahamas International Securities Exchange (BISX)
Bahamas Investment Authority (BIA)
Bahamas National Trust (BNT)
Bahamas Red Cross
Balance of payments
Banking
Banks
Birds
Boating
Broadcasting
Budget
Building contractors
Building costs
Building permits
Business licence fee
Business name registration
Cable television
Captive Insurance
Car rental companies
Caribbean Basin Initiative (CBI)
Caribbean Community
CARIBCAN
CARICOM
Casinos
Censorship (films, plays & printed material)
Chamber of Commerce
Churches
Cinemas
Citizenship
Climate
Community organizations & service clubs
Company formation
Constitution
Consumer protection
Copyright laws
Cost of living
Cotonou Agreement
Courier services
Crime
Cruise ships
Cruising facilities
Culture & cultural activities
Currency
Customs
Defence Force
Dentists
Departure tax
Diving
Divorce
Doctors
Driver's licence & vehicle information
Drugs
Economy
Education
Electricity
Emergency numbers
Employers' organizations
Engineering companies
Entertainment
Environment
Exchange control
Export
Export entry
Extradition
Fire services
Fishing
Fitness
Flora & fauna
Forts
Free Trade Area of the Americas (FTAA)
Freight services
Gambling
Geography
Golf courses
Government

Governors
Gross domestic
& gross national product
Gun permits
Harbour control
Health care
Health/medical services
History
Holidays
Hospitals & clinics
Hotels
Hotels encouragement
Hunting
Hurricanes
Immigration
Immovable Property Act
Import & export statistics
Import entry
Industrial relations
Industrial Tribunal
Industries encouragement
Industry
Inflation
Insurance
International Business Company (IBC)
International Persons Landholding Act
Internet
Investing
Judicial system
Junkanoo
Labour relations
Law firms
Libraries
Liquor Laws
Lomé IV Convention
Lotteries
Mailboats
Manufacturing
Marinas & cruising facilities
Marine parks & exhibits
Marine research
Marriage licences
Motor vehicle insurance
Museums
Mutual funds
National anthem
National Insurance
National parks, reserves
& protected areas
National symbols
Nature centres
Newspapers
North American Free
Trade Agreement (NAFTA)
Organization of American States (OAS)
Paradise Island
Passports
People-To-People
Pharmacies
Police force
Population
Ports of entry
Postal information
Potter's Cay
Property tax
Property transactions
Public finance
Public health
Radio stations
Real estate companies
Religion
Royal Bahamas Defence Force
Royal Bahamas Police Force
Schools
Securities Commission of The Bahamas
Ship registration
Shipping
Shopping
Small business loans
Social services
Sports
Statistics
Straw markets
Tax benefits for Canadians
by *Guy Masson*
Tax benefits for Europeans
by Howard M Liebman
Tax benefits for US citizens & companies
by Arthur J Lynch
Telecommunications
Television
Theatre & performing arts
Time
Time-sharing
Tourism
Trade agreements
Trade unions
Transportation
Trusts
Vaccination requirements
Veterinarians
Visas for Bahamians
Voting
Wages
Water supply and rates
Water-skiing
Weather
Weights & measures
Wildlife Preserves
World Trade Organization (WTO)
Yachts
YWCA
ZNS
Zoo

ACCOMMODATIONS

Accommodations in New Providence, Paradise Island, Grand Bahama and the Out, or Family, Islands include something for everyone and every budget. In Nassau and Paradise Island, 62 hotels (8,222 rooms) include opulent suites, guest houses and cottages with ocean views available throughout the year. According to the Hotel Licensing Unit of the Ministry of Tourism, as of June 2004, Grand Bahama offered 31 hotels with 3,867 rooms; the Out Islands, 200 hotels with 3,163 rooms.

Most resorts and hotels are either on or near the ocean. Larger facilities offer access to world-class golf courses, tennis courts, spectacular beaches, watersports, snorkelling and scuba diving, swimming pools, parasailing and nightclubs. Contact the concierge to make further arrangements at nearby facilities.

During high season,* double room rates average $170 per day in Nassau and $300 on Paradise Island.

Special package rates offered by tour operators in North America and Europe include air fare, accommodations, sightseeing and transfers. A typical package advertised in *The New York Times* in August 2004 offered four-night packages starting from $439 for hotels in Nassau and $625 for hotels on Paradise Island. In the same month, *The Miami Herald* carried advertisements offering packages to Nassau, including flight, airport/hotel transfers, standard room accommodations, hotel taxes and gratuities for three nights at $399 per person, double occupancy. Packages to Grand Bahama were also advertised at $529 per person, double occupancy, for five nights.

Modified American Plan (room, breakfast and dinner) and European Plan (room only) are available at most hotels. Guest houses in downtown Nassau are often less expensive. While many are room only, restaurants in the area are plentiful and conveniently located.

Guests in the Out Islands enjoy a relaxed, casual atmosphere in many small hotels. During high season, double room rates average $80 per day. Larger resorts, comparable to those in Nassau, are found on several of the islands with double room rates averaging $139 per day. Dining facilities outside Out Island hotels are often limited. Modified American and European Plans are available at most hotels.

* *High season rates are applicable Dec 19, 2004-Apr 23, 2005. Summer rates, Apr 24-Dec 17, 2005, are slightly lower. There is a room occupancy tax, which includes a 6% government tax and a 6% tax added by member hotels of the Nassau/Paradise Island Promotion Board and Paradise Island/Cable Beach Tourism Development Assoc to fund joint promotional and advertising budgets. Most major hotels add another 2% tax, and a maid tax of $3 per person per night. Some hotels also add an energy tax of $3 per person per night.*

See also **Hotels** and **Freeport/Lucaya information, Accommodations.**

ACCOUNTING FIRMS

Following is a selection of accounting firms operating in New Providence:

Alan E H Bates & Co 322-8464
BDO Mann Judd 325-6591
Beneby & Co.....................341-5475
* Deloitte & Touche 302-4800
Ernst & Young 502-6000
F A Hepburn & Co 322-6000
Ferguson & Co..................326-1288
Galanis & Co.....................328-4540
Gomez Partners & Co (Horwath Intl).................356-4114
Graham Cooper & Co 322-2504
Grant Thornton Intl...........322-7516
Ingraham & Co 394-7880
* KPMG...............................393-2007
L Sydney Saunders 327-4950
M E Lockhart Accounting ..325-6616
* Michael Hepburn & Co 322-8814
Moore, Stephens, Butler & Taylor..............393-0224
* Pannell Kerr Forster...........322-8560
* PricewaterhouseCoopers....302-5300
Richard C Demeritte & Co....327-5729
Ronald Atkinson & Co.......325-7355

* *Freeport office also.*

AGRICULTURE

Approx 90% of agricultural land available in The Bahamas is owned by the government. Under the Ministry of Agriculture (Incorporation) Act, 1993, the Prime Minister has leased 65,887 acres of prime agricultural land to the Minister of Agriculture for 50 years, enabling him to hold and lease the land to Bahamian farmers for a max of two consecutive 21-year terms.

Lands made available were 1,800 acres in New Providence, 13,869 acres in Andros, 39,676 acres in Abaco and 10,542 acres in Grand Bahama.

The value of the agricultural sector in 2003 was estimated at approx $51.78 million, a decrease of 5% from the 2002 estimate of $54.08 million. Lower broiler (chicken) meat production was primarily responsible for this decline.

A Plant and Animal Health Unit monitors the importation of fruit, vegetables and ornamentals into The Bahamas. All commercial importers of fresh produce, ornamentals, meat, milk, eggs and poultry must obtain permission from the Dept of Agriculture prior to importation.

Subsidies are available for Bahamian farmers in the form of interest-free credit on purchase of supplies from the Ministry's Fish & Farm Store on Potter's Cay Dock.

In 1994, a census of agriculture was conducted for the first time since '78, providing important baseline data on the agricultural sector. The report on findings is available from the Ministry of Agriculture at a price of $10 per copy.

Agricultural Manufactories Act

The Agricultural Manufactories Act, 1965, offers exemptions from customs duty on all machinery, fixtures, supplies, farm trucks and a wide range of production, building and processing material imported for the construction or alteration of an agricultural factory.

Crops

Crop production for export is concentrated on four islands: Abaco, Andros, Grand Bahama and New Providence. Agricultural exports for 2003 amounted to an estimated 25,530 short tons valued at $14.6 million. Exports consist mainly of citrus fruits (red and white grapefruits, lemons, and oranges) which are sent to the US.

Packing house produce purchases for 2003 were $1.63 million, an increase of 37% from 2002 ($1.19 million).

Some crops are marketed on their respective islands, however the bulk of produce is shipped to New Providence and sold at the Produce Exchange at Potter's Cay.

At press time, damage to the agricultural sector sustained from hurricanes Frances and Jeanne of Sept 2004 was being assessed. Preliminary estimates exceed the $36 million in damage caused by Hurricane Floyd in 1999.

For the past few years, farmers on Grand Bahama and Abaco have diversified their crops by introducing red leaf, romaine, green leaf and iceberg lettuce, plum, cherry and roma tomatoes, zucchini, squash, parsley, basil, red and green kale, chayote, chives, different varieties of cabbage and sage, to name a few.

Farmers market their produce directly to wholesalers, hotels and retailers and earned more than $10 million in 2003.

Poultry

Chicken is the most popular meat for Bahamians who consume nearly 100 lbs per person per year – among the highest per capita rate in the world. Broiler statistics revealed production decreased by 50% in 2003 ($8.61 million) due to the closing of Gladstone Farms in Nov 2002. Value of production in 2002 was estimated at $17.06 million.

Egg production in 2003 was 6.44 million dozen, an increase of 0.31 million dozen or 5%, over the 2002 figure of 6.13 million dozen. The Bahamas is 99% self-sufficient in egg production.

Livestock

One of the areas of emphasis in the agricultural policy is livestock production, and the aim is to make each island self-sufficient in poultry and pork production. Establishment of a modern meat processing plant is a top priority. The Dept of Agriculture is developing a national swine production programme, targeted at small farmers in the central and southern Bahamas. The programme aims to improve incomes of livestock and crop farmers throughout the country.

Total red and white meat production in 2003 is estimated at $0.84 million, a decrease of 22% from 2002 figures of $1.06 million. This was attributed to a drop in production on Grand Bahama caused by contaminated feed.

AIDS/HIV

According to the Dept of Public Health, AIDS is the leading cause of death among Bahamian men and women aged 15-44.

From 1983 to Dec 31, 2003, a total of 4,549 AIDS cases had been reported in The Bahamas. A further 5,215 individuals were reported to be HIV positive, without symptoms of the disease.

Between 1985 and 2003, 3,320 (73%) persons with AIDS had died. The number of persons dying of AIDS decreased between 1997 and 2003 due to antiretroviral (AIDS/HIV) medication and is expected to decrease further. Almost 40% of all HIV positive persons in The Bahamas are on antiretroviral medication. However, the fastest growing group infected with HIV is young people ages 15-29, with females in this age group outnumbering males 2:1.

The Bahamas has had some success with the HIV/AIDS programme in mother to child HIV transmission. Prior to 1995, 30% of infants born to HIV-infected women were born with the virus. In one year following treatment, it dropped to 10% and was 3% at the end of 2001. As of Dec 2002, mother to child transmission rate was 6.6%.

The disease occurs in The Bahamas primarily among heterosexuals, with an overall male to female ratio of 1.1:1.

Worldwide statistics revealed that as of Dec 2003, 38 million people were living with HIV/AIDS. Approximately five million children and adults were newly infected in 2003, including 630,000 children under 15 yrs. An estimated 2.9 million adults and children died from AIDS in 2003.

The Bahamas has stringent reporting procedures not adopted by some countries. The National HIV/AIDS Programme enforces a vigilant follow-up of new HIV/AIDS cases, advising them to adopt safer sex practices to help prevent the spread of HIV/AIDS.

The government allocated $500,000 of its 2003/04 budget towards testing, clinical management, cure and support for HIV and AIDS.

AIDS Foundation of The Bahamas

This non-profit, non-governmental organization was founded on World AIDS Day, Dec 1, 1992, and is the largest voluntary agency in the fight against HIV/AIDS.

Main objectives are:

1. Providing a facility for counselling people with HIV/AIDS.
2. Informing and educating the public about all aspects of HIV/AIDS, including prevention.
3. Cooperating with organizations which have similar objectives.
4. Raising and distributing funds in line with stated objectives.

This work includes care and support of persons with HIV/AIDS and their families. The Foundation also aims to promote and sustain continuing research on the local HIV/AIDS problem. It is maintained by donations and annual subscriptions. Membership applications are available from the AIDS Foundation of The Bahamas, PO Box CB-12003, Nassau, tel 325-9326/7, fax 325-9327, or visit www.aids.org.bs.

HIV/AIDS Centre

The AIDS Secretariat was founded in 1989. It is the central organizing body in the Ministry of Health to coordinate and implement strategies and projects in the national programme on HIV/AIDS and has recently expanded to become the HIV/AIDS Centre.

The new centre comprises five operational units: HIV prevention education; clinical care management, support/ treatment; HIV/AIDS clinical research; Caribbean HIV/AIDS regional training (CHART); and HIV laboratory diagnosis.

The Centre also addresses psychological and social issues of persons with HIV/AIDS and their families.

Contact the HIV/AIDS Centre (formerly the AIDS Secretariat), Royal Victoria Gardens, Shirley and Parliament Sts, PO Box N-3729, Nassau, tel 328-2260/1 or 323-6363, fax 322-6610, or e-mail medicineid@batelnet.bs.

The Samaritan Ministry

This programme of caring ministry was established in The Bahamas in 1988 by the Catholic Diocese of Nassau to help people suffering in any way as a result of HIV/AIDS – the afflicted, their families and friends. A Freeport ministry was commissioned in 1999. The Salvation Army group was certified in May 2002.

Trained volunteers are known as Samaritans. Training involves 2½-hour sessions once a week for 10 weeks, with presentations on the art of listening effectively and compassionately; dealing with feelings; and ministering to people experiencing sickness, depression and hospitalization, as well as people dying of HIV/AIDS.

The Samaritan Ministry is also active in educational programmes for youth and church groups and service organizations. It operates the counselling ministry which gives support and guidance to persons with HIV/AIDS, tel 325-9326/7.

Contact Sister Clare Rolle, OSB, St Martin's Monastery, PO Box N-940, Nassau, tel 323-5517, fax 325-1377.

See also **Public health services.**

AIR SERVICE

The following direct flights are scheduled but are subject to change. Connections to other cities are available via the major cities listed.

Between Nassau and

US destinations: Atlanta, Charlotte, Cincinnati, Ft Lauderdale, Houston, Miami, New York, Orlando, Philadelphia, Tampa and West Palm Beach. Other international destinations: Cuba, Grand Cayman, Kingston, London, Milan, Montego Bay, Turks & Caicos Islands and Toronto.

Between Paradise Island and

Ft Lauderdale

Freeport flights

See **Freeport/Lucaya information, Air service**

Out (Family) Island flights

Bahamasair, the national airline, has scheduled flights linking Out Islands with Nassau, Grand Bahama and the US.

Abaco Air operates two daily flights between Nassau and Marsh Harbour one flight on Sun; and Marsh Harbour to North Eleuthera Fri and Sun.

American Eagle travels to Miami from Marsh Harbour and George Town.

Cat Island Air has daily flights between Nassau and Great Harbour Cay, New Bight and Sandy Point.

Chalk's Ocean Airways operates daily Ft Lauderdale-Bimini, Paradise Island-Ft Lauderdale and two flights weekly between Ft Lauderdale and Walker's Cay.

Gulfstream International flies to Miami and Ft Lauderdale from Marsh Harbour, North Eleuthera and Treasure Cay; and West Palm Beach from Marsh Harbour.

Sky Unlimited flies daily from Nassau to Bimini and George Town, Exuma.

Southern Air provides regular service to Governor's Harbour, North Eleuthera, Treasure Cay, Marsh Harbour, Chub Cay and Arthur's Town.

Services are also provided between Marsh Harbour and Toronto, Treasure Cay and New York, Freeport and Milan, and Eleuthera and Milan.

US Airways travels from Marsh Harbour and Treasure Cay, as well as North Eleuthera to Ft Lauderdale.

Charters are available in Nassau through a number of companies including Abaco Air, Bahamasair, Congo Air, Le-Air, Sky Unlimited and Southern Air.

Some charter operations are based in Grand Bahama and Out Islands such as Andros and Abaco.

Airline offices

Air Canada
Reservations 1-888-247-2262

Air Jamaica
Reservations 1-800-523-5585

American Airlines/American Eagle
Reservations 1-800-433-7300

Bahamasair
Nassau Intl Airport 377-7377
or 377-8222
Reservations......................377-5505
or 1-880-222-4262

British Airways
Nassau Intl Airport 377-2338
Reservations 1-800-247-9297

Chalk's Ocean Airways
Paradise Island 363-3114
Reservations 1-800-424-2557

Continental Connection /Gulfstream Intl
Nassau Intl Airport 377-4314
Reservations 394-6019

Delta/Comair
Reservations 1-800-221-1212

US Airways
Nassau Intl Airport ....377-8886(to 8)
Reservations 1-800-622-1015

AIRPORTS

Fig 1.0 is a Civil Aviation Dept list of civil airports and airstrips with runway specifications and GPS coordinates, size of the facilities and whether they are designated as ports of entry for international flights.

Heliports

There are two heliports in the vicinity of New Providence, with emergency airlift/air ambulance service provided by Paradise Island Helicopters on Paradise Island. The heliports are privately owned and leased to the operators. They are not ports of entry.

The Paradise Island Heliport, owned by Kerzner International, is on the south side of the island, west of Paradise Island Western Bridge. Approx dimensions are 173.2 ft x 173.2 ft, 30,000 sq ft at coordinates 250489N, 771951W.

The heliport on Blue Lagoon Island (Salt Cay) measures 60 ft x 60 ft, 3,600 sq ft at coordinates 250580N, 771647W.

The frequency 130.75 MHz CTAF* is monitored. Nassau Harbour Traffic monitors frequency 128.82 MHz CTAF. Call ahead for clearance.

* *CTAF: Common Traffic Advisory Frequency.*

Airport parking

The parking lot at Nassau International Airport is operated by the Airport Authority. Long-term parking is $3 for the first hour or part thereof and $1 for each additional hour. Daily max is $8 for the first day and $3 for each additional day or part thereof for up to seven days, at which time the rate structure starts over. Lost tickets incur a penalty of $15.

Parking meters are available for a max period of 20 mins of continuous parking. Each 10-min period costs 50¢. Bahamian or US 25¢ coins may be used.

Vehicles parked in no-parking zones may be towed to the Airport Authority holding compound. A fine of $50 must be paid to have the vehicle released.

AMBULANCE/AIR AMBULANCE SERVICES

Air ambulance

American Jets
1-880-ABLE JET (225-3538)
1-800-526-1071
Collect (772) 465-0893

Advanced Air Ambulance (AAA)
1-800-633-3590
Collect (305) 232-7700

Aero Jet Intl
1-880-443-8042 or (954) 730-9300

Air Ambulance Network
1-800-522-3467
Collect (727) 934-3999

Air Ambulance Professionals Inc (AAPI)
1-800-752-4195
Collect (954) 491-0555

Air Ambulance Services Ltd
362-1606 or 457-3149 (mobile)

LifeFlight (paediatrics)
1-881-LIFEFLT (543-3358)
or (305) 663-6859

Air/ground ambulance

Doctors Hospital Health System ETS
302-4747

Med-Evac Ambulance Service
322-2881 or 323-8919

Medical Air Services Assoc, Bahamas
393-5048 (for members)

Ground ambulance

Princess Margaret Hospital
919, 911, 323-2597 or 323-2586

See also **Doctors** and **Hospitals & clinics.**

FIG 1.0

CIVIL AVIATION DEPT LIST OF CIVIL AIRPORTS

ISLAND/AIRPORT LOCATION ON ISLAND	GPS COORDINATES[2]		PORT OF ENTRY	DIMENSIONS
Abaco				
Gorda Cay (Castaway Cay) SW (Pvt)	260501.31797	773158.56909	x	2,400 x 60
Marsh Harbour C (Gov)	263101.27725	770458.48613	√	5,000 x 100
Moores Island S (Gov)	261901.29324	773358.59204	x	3,010 x 100
Sandy Point[1] S (Gov)	260001.32750	772358.53030	√	4,500 x 100
Scotland Cay CE (Pvt)	263801.26550	770358.48919	x	3,300 x 100
Spanish Cay NE (Pvt)	265701.22655	773158.61808	x	5,000 x 80
Treasure Cay NC (Gov)	264501.24934	772358.57630	√	7,000 x 150
Walker's Cay[1] N (Pvt)	271601.18084	782358.82658	√	2,800 x 80
Acklins				
Spring Point C (Gov)	222701.64025	735757.32372	x	5,000 x 150
Andros				
Andros Town C (Gov)	244201.45695	774758.51655	√	4,000 x 100
C A Bain Airport SE (Gov)	241701.49417	774058.43550	√	5,000 x 75
Congo Town SE (Gov)	240901.50505	773458.39180	√	5,300 x 100
San Andros N (Gov)	250301.42430	780258.61853	√	5,000 x 100
Berry Islands				
Big Whale Cay S (Pvt)	252401.38801	774658.58128	x	2,600 x 60
Chub Cay SE (Pvt)	252501.38642	775258.60840	√	5,000 x 100
Great Harbour Cay N (Gov)	254501.35169	775158.63235	√	4,500 x 100
				5,000 x 100
Little Whale Cay S (Pvt)	252701.38291	774558.58130	x	2,000 x 50
Bimini				
Cat Cay S (Pvt)	253600.00000	791600.00000	√	1,300 x 75
Ocean Cay S (Pvt)	253001.38379	790958.94305	x	1,650 x 60
				1,600 x 60
South Bimini C (Gov)	254201.36025	791558.97843	√	5,430 x 100
Cat Island				
Arthur's Town NW (Gov)	243801.46444	753957.96888	x	7,000 x 150
Cutlass Bay SW (Pvt)	240901.50548	752357.84943	x	2,450 x 60
Hawks Nest CW (Pvt)	240901.50481	753057.87678	x	3,000 x 100
New Bight W (Gov)	241901.49182	752657.88097	√	5,000 x 100
Cay Sal				
Cay Sal (Pvt)	234201.58639	802458.99985	x	2,000 x 100
Crooked Island				
Colonel Hill C (Gov)	224501.61800	740857.39943	x	3,500 x 60
Pitts Town N (Pvt)	225001.61046	742057.45091	x	2,240 x 60

ISLAND/AIRPORT LOCATION ON ISLAND	GPS COORDINATES[2]		PORT OF ENTRY	DIMENSIONS
Eleuthera				
Governor's Harbour C (Gov)	251701.40354	761958.20097	√	7,950 x 150
North Eleuthera N (Gov)	252901.38283	764058.30771	√	6,000 x 100
Rock Sound S (Gov)	245401.43879	760958.12034	√	7,200 x 150
Exuma				
Black Point C (Gov)	240510.00000	762450.00000	x	2,700 x 60
Darby Island C (Pvt)	235101.52639	761358.01085	x	1,500 x 100
Exuma Intl (Moss Town) S (Gov)	233341.54945	755225.88572	√	7,000 x 150
Farmer's Cay NW (Gov)	235601.51971	761858.04241	x	2,500 x 60
Fowl Cay C (Pvt)	241600.00000	763300.00000	x	1,300 x 40
Hog Cay SE (Pvt)	232401.56114	762758.00443	x	2,500 x 100
Lee Stocking Isl S (Pvt)	234701.53188	760557.96973	x	3,000 x 75
Little Darby Isl C (Pvt)	235201.52510	761258.00902	x	2,000 x 50
Norman's Cay N (Gov)	243601.46346	764858.25080	x	3,000 x 70
Rudder Cut Cay C (Pvt)	235301.52372	761458.01933	x	2,700 x 100
Sampson Cay C (Pvt)	241301.49646	762858.11387	x	2,400 x 60
Staniel Cay C (Gov)	241001.50058	762858.11387	x	3,030 x 75
Grand Bahama				
Deep Water Cay[1] E (Pvt)	263801.25587	775658.70135	√	2,000 x 100
Grand Bahama Intl W (Pvt)	263301.25958	784158.87326	√	11,000 x 150
Inagua				
Matthew Town W (Gov)	205701.74103	733957.06422	√	8,000 x 100
Long Island				
Deadman's Cay C (Gov)	231044.00000	750539.00000	x	4,000 x 100
Hog Cay N (Pvt)	233601.54846	751957.76504	x	1,800 x 50
Stella Maris N (Pvt)	232301.56495	751557.72124	√	3,700 x 60
Mayaguana				
Mayaguana C (Gov)	222301.65484	730157.13935	√	7,700 x 150
New Providence				
Nassau Intl W (Gov)	250225.48	772813.79	√	8,240 x 150
				11,000 x 150
Ragged Island				
Duncan Town S (Gov)	221101.64675	754357.64796	x	3,800 x 75
Rum Cay				
Port Nelson C (Gov)	233901.54759	745057.66262	x	4,500 x 100
San Salvador				
Cockburn Town NW (Gov)	240401.51858	743057.63918	√	8,000 x 150

1 Sufferance port – Customs by request.
2 Coordinates conform to NAD 83 standards.

N=North S=South E=East W=West C=Central Pvt=Private Gov=Government

ANIMALS

A valid import permit ($10) is required to import any animal into The Bahamas. Unless otherwise indicated, a permit can only be used once and only during the period specified on the permit. Dogs and cats imported from countries with rabies must be six months or older. To apply for an import permit, phone 325-7502/9, or write to the Director of Agriculture, PO Box N-3028, Nassau. State your name and address, the type, age and number of animals you wish to import, the country of export and origin, the purpose for importing the animal(s), as well as anticipated date of arrival and destination in The Bahamas.

Main provisions of the import permit as it applies to dogs and cats are:

1. Dogs and cats must be accompanied by a veterinary health certificate issued within 48 hours of embarkation, and a valid certificate of rabies vaccination for either the one-year or three-year duration.
2. The one-year-duration vaccine must have been administered within not more than 10 months and not less than one month prior to arrival in The Bahamas.
3. The three-year-duration vaccine must have been administered within not more than 34 months and not less than one month prior to arrival in The Bahamas.
4. The conditions specified on a permit depend on the disease status of the originating country and available technology. Conditions for entry are subject to change but will be reflected in the permit.

Dogs and cats from any rabies-free country may enter without a rabies vaccination if accompanied by a valid import permit, veterinary health certificate and certificate stating there have been no cases of rabies in that country of origin for the two years immediately prior to date of embarkation and that the animal has been in that country for six months, or if it is less than six months of age, since birth.

Animals not meeting these conditions are not allowed to enter the country.

A duty for permanent entry of all animals into The Bahamas is levied, based on the cost/insurance/freight value of the animal plus 2% stamp duty.

Entry duties

Dogs and cats 10%
Horses 15%
Sheep and goats 10%
Cattle 15%
Pigs 10%

Fees for dog licences

Male or spayed female $2
Female $6

Fee schedule for services provided by Dept of Agriculture

Import permits for cattle, sheep, goats, pigs, horses, dogs, cats and other large animals $10
Inspection of horses and other large animals for export............. $100
Duty-free permits $5
Import permits for plants, fruit and vegetables .... $2 per page
Import permits for tropical fish, bees and other invertebrates $10

Where possible, permits should be paid via international or postal money orders.

The Bahamas is a party to the Convention on International Trade in Endangered Species (CITES). Import or export of any specimen listed must comply with the requirements of CITES. To obtain a list of animals authorized for export, contact the management authority within the Dept of Agriculture or the scientific authority in the Dept of Fisheries, or visit the CITES website at www.cites.org/eng/append/index.shtml.

For other information on animals, see **Bahamas Humane Society, Flora & fauna, Veterinarians** and **Wildlife preserves.**

ANTIQUITIES, MONUMENTS AND MUSEUMS CORP (AMMC)

The National Museum of The Bahamas, Antiquities, Monuments and Museums Corporation (AMMC) is an autonomous government corporation established on July 1, 1999, as the principal heritage conservation agency in The Bahamas. It has responsibility for the preservation, conservation, restoration and promotion of historical sites, national monuments and other artefacts of inestimable archaeological and cultural value. The corporation, established by the Antiquities, Monuments and Museum Act, 1998, operates The Pompey Museum of Slavery and Emancipation; the Long Island Museum; the San Salvador Museum; the Balcony House Museum; Forts Charlotte, Montagu and Fincastle and other military fortifications.

The AMMC is responsible for establishment and operation of the national museum system. It also organizes national historic preservation programmes, national aquatic and terrestrial archaeological programmes and is the guardian of the National Register of Historic Resources of The Bahamas.

The AMMC opened a state-of-the-art conservation laboratory in June 2003. Located in the Advance Guard House at Fort Charlotte, the laboratory is used by scientists to preserve Bahamian artefacts.

Contact Dr Keith L Tinker, Director, The National Museum of The Bahamas, Antiquities, Monuments and Museums Corporation, 36 Sears Rd, PO Box EE-15082, Nassau, tel 326-2566, 356-3977 or 356-3981, fax 326-2568, e-mail pompey@batelnet.bs. See also **Archives, Bahamas Historical Society, Forts** and **Museums.**

ARAWAK CAY

Heritage Village at Arawak Cay, off West Bay St, across from Fort Charlotte's Clifford Park, is part of the Ministry of Tourism's vision to develop an authentic Out Island village atmosphere for Bahamians and visitors.

A lively fish and conch vendor's area with a colourful mix of eateries offers fresh Bahamian seafood prepared to order, such as fried fish, conch salad, conch fritters, crack' conch and crack' lobster.

The site also has a police station, a story-telling porch, a rock oven and an extensive "village green" where festivals, cultural events and concerts are held.

ARCHITECTURAL FIRMS

For a complete listing of architectural firms staffed by architects licensed with the Professional Architects Board, in accordance with the Professional Architects Act, 1994, contact the Professional Architects Board, PO Box CB-13040, Nassau, tel 326-3114, fax 322-8100.

ARCHIVES

The Dept of Archives, Mackey St, Nassau, serves as the repository for records and archives of the government as well as private deposits, including archives of the Anglican Church, the Methodist Church and St Andrew's Presbyterian Church.

The Dept of Archives has a microfilm collection of historical documents, including newspapers, dating back as far as 1700, a photograph collection, oral history collection and a number of maps, plans, prints and artefacts including ceremonial duhos (carved wooden stools) used by chiefs or religious leaders of the Lucayans. Hand-paper repair of documents and book-binding are carried out in the repair-bindery section. A small photographic laboratory was established. In May 2001, the National Records Centre officially opened. This repository and central administration for non-current government records is located at the rear of the National Archives building.

Publications available at the Dept of Archives are the *Guide to the Records of The Bahamas, Supplement to the Guide to the Records of The Bahamas* and booklets on past exhibitions, as follows:

The Lucayans
Columbus and the Encounter 1492
Highlights in Bahamian History 1492-1983

The Bahamas in the Age of Revolution 1775-1848
The Loyalist Bi-Centennial
Aspects of Slavery
Aspects of Slavery II
The Bahamas in the Mid-Nineteenth Century 1850-1869
The Bahamas in the Late Nineteenth Century 1870-1899
The Bahamas in the Early Twentieth Century 1900-1914
The Bahamas During the World Wars 1914-1918 and 1939-1945
The Bahamas 10 Years After Independence 1973-1983
The Bahamian-American Connection
The Boat-Building Industry of The Bahamas
Constitutional Development in The Bahamas
A Selection of Historical Buildings of The Bahamas
Junkanoo
The Pineapple Industry of The Bahamas
The Salt Industry of The Bahamas
Settlements in New Providence
The Peoples of The Bahamas
The Sponging Industry
The Tricentenary of Nassau: The Development of the Metropolis of The Bahamas up to the Early Twentieth Century
Highlights in the History of Communication in The Bahamas 1784-1956

Booklets containing transcripts from St Matthew's Cemetery and Christ Church Cathedral Cemetery have been printed, as well as:

The Life and Times of The Lucayans, The First Bahamians
A Guide to African Villages in New Providence
A Guide to Selected Sources for the History of the Seminole Settlements at Red Bays, Andros 1817-1980
Loyalists, Slavery, Emancipation and Junkanoo
Official Reports on the Out Islands of The Bahamas, Thomas Harvey
Colonial Secretary Papers: Report on The Bahamas 1861-1876
Important Facts About The Bahamas
Bahamian History Through Archaeology
Some Personalities in Bahamian Education
A User's Guide to the Records Centre
Looking Back: A Guide to Genealogical Research in the Dept of Archives
Preservum: The Journal of the National Archives, Vol 1, #1, Sept 1996
Preservum: The Journal of the National Archives, Vol 2, #1, Dec 1998
Preservum The Journal of the National Archives, Vol 3, #1, Dec 2000

Published annual reports for 1971-2000 are available, along with the booklet *The First Ten Years 1969-1979 – A History of the Bahamian Archives* and *The Dept of Archives 25th Anniversary Booklet, Sept 1996.*

The Dept of Archives is open 10am-4:45pm weekdays except holidays. Contact Dr D Gail Saunders, Director of Archives or M Elaine Toote, Deputy Director, Dept of Archives, Mackey St, PO Box SS-6341, Nassau, tel 393-2175, fax 393-2855, e-mail archives@batelnet.bs, or visit www.bahamasnationalarchives.bs.

ART GALLERIES

Andrew Aitken Frame Art Gallery, Madeira St, Palmdale. Wide selection of Bahamian artists in a variety of styles. Lithographs and prints are the most popular items. Mon-Sat 8:30am-5:30pm. Tel 328-7065.

The Central Bank of The Bahamas, Market St, operates a gallery and hosts frequent local cultural art exhibitions featuring Bahamian artists. Mon-Fri 9:30am-4:30pm. Tel 322-2193.

Chan Pratt's Art Gallery, Bonney Way, off Johnson Rd. Renowned Bahamian artist Pratt specializes in Bahamian landscapes and old Bahamian homes. Pratt also does commissioned paintings in oils and watercolours. Mon-Sat 9am-5pm (call for appointment). Tel 364-4047.

The Kennedy Gallery, Parliament St, in the Bayparl Bldg, features a wide variety of watercolours, oils, acrylics and pencil drawings including originals and limited edition prints, photographs, sculptures, bronzes, glass work and more. Mon-Sat 9am-5pm. Tel 325-7662.

Chambers House and Garden, Lyford Cay Shopping Centre, carries a wide selection of oils, watercolours, prints and sculptures by international artists. Mon-Sat 9am-5pm. Tel 362-4034.

Nassau Art Gallery, East Bay Shopping Centre, near the Paradise Island Bridge, features the work of Elyse Wasile, including hand-painted, limited-edition porcelain collector's plates. Mon-Fri 9am-4pm. Tel 393-1482.

Nassau Glass Company, Mackey St, has a large selection of Bahamian art, including oils, watercolours, prints and posters. Mon-Fri 8am-4:30pm, Sat 8am-4:30pm. Tel 393-8165.

National Art Gallery of The Bahamas (NAGB), West Hill St. The stately 1860s Villa Doyle was restored to house the National Art Gallery of The Bahamas. The project was overseen by archivist and historian Dr D Gail Saunders and architect Anthony Jervis. The gallery is now a part of the national museum system. National collection of paintings, sculpture, textiles, ceramics, photography and other mixed-media works. Open Tues-Sat 11am-4pm. Tel 328-5800.

Paradise Tees, Hurricane Hole Plaza, Paradise Island, has a selection of souvenirs and clothing as well as an art gallery which highlights original oils and watercolours and the work of Bahamian artists. Mon-Sun (incl holidays) 9am-9pm. Tel 363-2609.

Princess Street Gallery, Lyford Cay Shopping Centre, is a branch of the Princess Street Gallery, Harbour Island. The gallery specializes in local and international fine art and museum-quality originals. Also available are antique maps and prints, copper plate etchings, limited edition reproductions, sculpture and custom framing. Mon-Fri 10am-4pm. Tel 362-5557.

ASSET PROTECTION TRUSTS

See **Investing.**

ATLANTIC UNDERSEA TEST AND EVALUATION CENTER (AUTEC)

The US Navy's Atlantic Undersea Test and Evaluation Center (AUTEC) is based at Andros, largest Bahamian island and site of the mile-deep Tongue of the Ocean. The four-station centre was formally dedicated in 1966 as part of the Naval Undersea Warfare Center to research submarine and anti-submarine warfare.

Andros was chosen because the immense ocean drop-off to some 6,000 ft was so close to shore that the US Navy could use relatively short cables to connect underwater detectors to read-out facilities at the base.

The base, the world's largest laboratory of its kind, is run by a maintenance and operations contractor employing approx 415 US personnel and 200 Bahamians. US Navy personnel are headed by an officer-in-charge.

AWARDS

Several awards have been established to give Bahamian achievers due recognition. They include the Cacique Awards, Caribbean Gospel Music Marlin Awards, Dundas Annual National Seasons Awards (DANSA), Governor General's Youth Award and Order of Merit.

Cacique Awards

The Cacique Awards were created by the Ministry of Tourism in 1995 to recognize individuals who have made valuable contributions to the growth and development of the tourism industry. Categories include lifetime achievement, minister's award, transportation, human resources development, nature tourism, sports and leisure, creative arts-handicraft, special award and people's choice.

Caribbean Gospel Music Marlin Awards

The Marlin Awards were introduced in 1996 to recognize Bahamian gospel music. In 2000, the awards were renamed the Caribbean Gospel Music

Marlin Awards. They are presented in more than 30 categories including outstanding album of the year and outstanding song of the year. The awards are produced by Harris Communications Group. Tel 325-1615, fax 325-1616, e-mail info@marlinawards.com or visit www.marlinawards.com.

DANSA Awards

The DANSA Awards give credit to the talented contributions of Bahamians and residents to plays, musicals and revues staged at the Dundas Centre for the Performing Arts and other venues. Categories include production, choreography, special effects, costume and make-up, sound, set design, best actor/actress and best director. Awards ceremonies are held in Jan.

See also **Theatre & performing arts.**

Governor General's Youth Award (GGYA)

The Governor General's Youth Award provides a programme of practical, cultural and adventurous activities to develop self-reliance, confidence, initiative and social awareness in young Bahamians. Participants work, from units based primarily in schools and youth groups, towards bronze, silver or gold medals by completing activities over one to three years in four categories: skills, physical recreation, expeditions and community service. There are approx 1,000 participants working from 31 units in New Providence and nine in the Out Islands. The national director is Denise Mortimer and the national patron is the Governor General of The Bahamas.

Order of Merit

This award was established in 1996 to recognize Bahamian "heroes" who achieve excellence in three specific nation-building categories: business, civics and arts and education.

Nominees must show evidence of advancement in the goals of their particular category, and exhibit excellence and achievement; provide consistent and significant contributions and have a positive impact on national development.

BAHAMAHOST

Bahamahost is a lecture series and self-improvement training programme designed in 1978 by the Ministry of Tourism to upgrade quality of service and attitudes in the hospitality industry. The programme's goals are to help individuals develop personal growth, self-esteem and confidence. Participants are familiarized with the country's history, geography, civics, culture, economics and places of interest. In addition, they receive training in customer service, interpersonal relationships and how to develop positive attitudes.

More than 23,000 people are qualified Bahamahosts, including public service drivers, hotel and restaurant employees and straw vendors.

The Bahamahost programme is coordinated by the Industry Training Unit, the education and training arm of the Ministry of Tourism for The Bahamas' hospitality industry. The Unit also offers a variety of other programmes to the Bahamian community, such as customer services seminars, adventures in attitudes and a Tourism Education Awareness Module (TEAM) in primary and secondary schools.

Contact the Ministry of Tourism, Industry Training Unit, Norfolk House, 1st Floor North, Frederick St, PO Box N-3701, Nassau, tel 326-5179 or 326-6184, fax 325-3412, e-mail tourism@bahamas.com.

BAHAMAS AGRICULTURAL & INDUSTRIAL CORP (BAIC)

The Bahamas Agricultural and Industrial Corp (BAIC) is a government agency that promotes, encourages and facilitates business development in The Bahamas. It provides technical assistance, advice and guidance to Bahamian entrepreneurs.

BAIC is structured to meet the government's goal of economic diversification, trade competitiveness and job creation through the development of business enterprises in The Bahamas. BAIC performs its function through its primary business units – business services division, property and office administration, handicraft development and human resources. Services offered by BAIC include:

1. Identifying investment/business opportunities and developing project profiles on viable businesses.
2. Preparing business proposals for submission to financial institutions for funding consideration.
3. Advising and assisting potential and existing entrepreneurs with the development, establishment or expansion of businesses.
4. Providing factory space for processing and manufacturing activities in the Industrial Park, Old Trail Rd, at subsidized rates, as well as land for processing, farming and other business ventures.
5. Conducting entrepreneurial development training workshops and seminars.
6. Coordinating and liaising with other government agencies for receipt, processing and implementation of business inquiries.
7. Providing avenues for market testing of Bahamian-made products at local and international trade shows.
8. Providing public relations assistance to spotlight new manufacturers and entrepreneurs.

BAIC works closely with the Bahamas Development Bank, the Centre for Entrepreneurship, the Bahamas Technical & Vocational Institute (BTVI) and the Broadcasting Corporation of The Bahamas to facilitate business projects.

Contact BAIC corporate office, Levy Bldg, East Bay St, PO Box N-4940, tel 322-3740 (to 3), fax 322-2123. BAIC also has offices in Grand Bahama, Eleuthera, Abaco and Andros.

See also **Bahamas Development Bank.**

BAHAMAS AIR SEA RESCUE ASSOC (BASRA)

BASRA, a volunteer organization supported by donations from the public, is the official search and rescue organization of The Bahamas.

Its headquarters are manned by one full-time employee during the day and volunteers after hours with assistance from the police answering service. VHF, SSB and aircraft radios are monitored seven days a week.

BASRA owns two vessels, a self-righting 38-ft Lochin and a 25-ft Boston Whaler, both of which are specially designed and equipped for rescue work. Nassau Flying Club aircraft are also used. The US Coast Guard is called upon for emergency night searches.

Contact BASRA, East Bay St, PO Box SS-6247, Nassau, tel 325-8864, fax 325-2737, e-mail co@basra.org, or visit www.basra.org.

BAHAMAS DEVELOPMENT BANK (BDB)

The Bahamas Development Bank (BDB) was established by an Act of Parliament on Oct 8, 1974, and opened its doors to the public on July 21, '78.

The BDB finances self-employed individuals, cooperatives and small businesses for development enterprises which contribute to the economic growth and well-being of the country.

These enterprises should create new employment opportunities; use local materials and resources; reduce imports or increase exports; introduce new technology and skills; and place new wealth into new hands, particularly in the Out Islands. The BDB finances short-term loans (six months to one year), medium-term loans (one year to five years) and long-term loans (five years to 20 years).

The major sectors financed by the BDB include tourism and ancillary services; industrial enterprises; agro-based industrial enterprises; farming; fishing; marine and land transportation and small businesses.

During its years of business, the BDB's operations have grown to $40.9 million, with funding affecting 22 Bahamian islands and cays. Total assets of the BDB at Dec 31, 2002, were $45.9 million (latest figures available at press time).

BDB headquarters are in Cable Beach, Nassau, with branches in Freeport, Grand Bahama, and Marsh Harbour, Abaco. Banking hours are Mon-Fri 9:30am-4:30pm. Contact the BDB, Cable Beach, PO Box N-3034, Nassau, tel 327-5780 (to 6), fax 327-5047, or visit www.bahamasdevelopmentbank.com.

See also **Bahamas Agricultural & Industrial Corp (BAIC), Industries encouragement** and **Manufacturing.**

BAHAMAS FAMILY PLANNING ASSOC (BFPA)

This private, non-profit organization is approved and supported by the Ministries of Health and Social Development, although it is not government funded.

BFPA is an affiliate of Caribbean Family Planning Affiliation Ltd. It has operated a clinic on East Ave, Centreville, since 1988, and is staffed by a full time registered nurse and a licensed child and adolescent psychologist.

Obstetricians and gynaecologists hold regular visiting hours at the clinic three days per week.

BFPA has expanded its services to include a comprehensive information, education and counselling unit, serving all members of the family, referred to as the Health and Family Life Resource Centre.

BFPA is governed by a board of directors. Daily activities are supervised by a full-time, salaried executive director. Funding is provided by modest charges for client services, members' annual dues, fund-raisers and private donations.

Contact Valerie Knowles, Centre Manager, Bahamas Family Planning Assoc, 37 East Ave, PO Box N-9071, Nassau, tel 325-1663, fax 325-4886, e-mail bahfpa@batelnet.bs.

BAHAMAS FINANCIAL SERVICES BOARD (BFSB)

The Bahamas Financial Services Board (BFSB) was established in Apr 1998 to market and develop the country's financial services sector. BFSB is a joint venture between the private sector and The Bahamas government.

BFSB is a multi-disciplinary organization, drawing on expertise and contacts in every field involved in the country's financial services industry. Members include organizations and companies involved in banking, trust, corporate services, insurance, investment fund administration, public accountancy, legal services, e-commerce, and investment advisory services. Others who have an interest in the financial services industry can join BFSB as associate members.

Contact Wendy C Warren, CEO and Executive Director, Bahamas Financial Services Board, Goodman's Bay Corporate Centre, PO Box N-1764, Nassau, tel (242) 326-7001, fax (242) 326-7007, e-mail info@bfsb-bahamas.com, or visit www.bfsb-bahamas.com.

BAHAMAS HISTORICAL SOCIETY

The Bahamas Historical Society, Shirley St and Elizabeth Ave, Nassau, is a non-profit cultural and educational organization dedicated to stimulating interest in Bahamian history and to collecting and preserving related material. The society operates a small museum at its headquarters with historical, anthropological and archaeological artefacts spanning more than 500 years of Bahamian history.

The museum is usually open Mon-Fri 10am-4pm and Sat 10am-12 noon. Visitors should call to verify times. The society holds monthly talks and publishes an annual journal.

Contact the president, PO Box SS-6833, Nassau, tel 322-4231, e-mail bahistsoc@coralwave.com, or visit www.bahamashistoricalsociety.com.

See also **Archives, Art galleries, Forts, History** and **Museums.**

BAHAMAS HUMANE SOCIETY (BHS)

The Bahamas Humane Society (BHS) is the oldest charity in The Bahamas. It was founded in 1924 by the wife of a former colonial secretary and was originally called the "Dumb Friends League."

BHS is affiliated with numerous international organizations including the World Society for the Protection of Animals (WSPA). Since 1989, BHS has been given membership in the Standards of Excellence Programme sponsored by The American Humane Assoc. BHS is the only humane organization in the Caribbean to qualify for membership.

BHS employs three full-time veterinarians and maintains an animal hospital and shelter. It offers 24-hr emergency ambulance service and provides care for sick, injured and abandoned animals. BHS also conducts an education programme for schools and youth groups and provides tours of the animal shelter. Animal cruelty investigations are carried out by trained BHS inspectors.

BHS employs a staff of 14 as well as a number of volunteers. The board of directors consists of 12 people. While the clinic generates some funds, it depends mainly on donations and fund-raising events.

BHS is not responsible for collection of stray or dead animals. This falls under jurisdiction of the Dept of Agriculture and the Dept of Environmental Health Services, respectively.

Application forms are required for adopting dogs and puppies. Approval usually takes two to three days. The fee is $40 for dogs and $30 for puppies. Adoption of cats and kittens may be approved immediately upon completion of an interview. The fee is $25 for cats and $20 for kittens. Adoptive owners must agree to bring puppies and kittens back to be spayed or neutered (included in the fee). No mature animal may be adopted unless it has been spayed or neutered. Tel 323-5138 or 325-6742, fax 356-2659, e-mail info@bahamashumanesociety.com, or visit www.bahamashumanesociety.com.

See also **Animals.**

BAHAMAS INTERNATIONAL SECURITIES EXCHANGE (BISX)

The Bahamas International Securities Exchange (BISX) was incorporated in Sept 1999 as a private company and began trading in May 2000. Following its preliminary registration, the Securities Commission officially registered the company as a securities exchange on Jan 30, 2001.

BISX provides trading and settlement facilities for its broker-dealer members and listing facilities for issuers and mutual funds. BISX operates on a commercial basis, charging fees for access and use of its facilities. BISX also exercises regulatory functions delegated to it by the Securities Commission of The Bahamas. The Chief Executive Officer and the executive staff of the exchange manage the day-to-day operations of BISX and execute and enforce the regulatory requirements set out in the BISX rules. Members or issuers who are admitted to membership and listing are required to meet certain criteria: a high level of transparency, due diligence, full disclosure and continuing obligations on the part of all market participants subject to the BISX rules.

At Aug 11, 2004, there were 18 listed issuers trading with a market capitalization of $1.8 billion. At June 30, 2004, there were 10 listed mutual funds with net assets of more than $155 million under management.

Contact BISX, 4th Floor, British Colonial Centre of Commerce, No 1 Bay St, PO Box EE-15672, Nassau, tel 323-2330, fax 323-2320, e-mail info@bisxbahamas.com, or visit www.bisxbahamas.com.

See also **Securities Commission.**

BAHAMAS INVESTMENT AUTHORITY (BIA)

The Bahamas Investment Authority (BIA), established in 1993, is a one-stop investment facilitator under the umbrella of the Ministry of Financial Services and

Investments. It is the government agency responsible for investment policy formulation, international promotion of investment opportunities in The Bahamas as well as review and evaluation of foreign direct investment proposals. The role of the BIA includes:

1. Administering the National Investment Policy of The Bahamas.
2. Assisting international investors during implementation of approved investment projects.
3. Coordinating investment matters with other government agencies.
4. Ensuring effective administration of the range of incentives available under all investment and business encouragement legislation.

The National Economic Council (NEC) is the approval body for foreign direct investments in The Bahamas. The NEC meets regularly to consider investment proposals.

Contact the Bahamas Investment Authority (BIA), Ministry of Financial Services and Investments, Goodman's Bay Corporate Centre, West Bay St, PO Box N-7770, Nassau, The Bahamas, tel (242) 356-5956-9, fax (242) 356-5990, e-mail info@investbahamas.org, or visit www.investbahamas.org.

See also **Investing, National Investment Policy.**

BAHAMAS NATIONAL TRUST (BNT)

Since its creation in 1959, the Bahamas National Trust (BNT) has been dedicated to conservation of the natural and historic resources of The Bahamas and has won national and international recognition for its achievements.

One of the most celebrated of BNT accomplishments is the saving of the nearly extinct West Indian flamingo, national bird of The Bahamas. As a result of the BNT's conservation efforts, there are 50,000 flamingos in Great Inagua. Equally important are BNT programmes to prevent extinction of the green turtle, white-crowned pigeon, Bahama parrot and the hutia.

The BNT administers the country's entire national parks system comprising more than 644,600 acres in 22 parks and protected areas.

The 112,640-acre Exuma Cays Land and Sea Park was the first land and sea park in the world. The first marine fishery reserve in the wider Caribbean has been set aside within the park.

BNT maintains close ties with major scientific organizations in the US, including the US National Park Service, New York Zoological Society, Smithsonian Institution, National Audubon Society, American Museum of Natural History and Rosenstiel School of Marine Sciences at the Univ of Miami, all of which are represented on the BNT Council.

BNT headquarters are at The Retreat, an 11-acre Nassau property with one of the finest private collections of palms in the western hemisphere. Self-guided tours can be taken from 9:30am-4:30pm Mon-Fri. Guided tours can be arranged by appointment and cost $5 per person. Group rates are available.

BNT is maintained by annual subscriptions of BNT members, donations, a small annual grant from the government and an endowment fund. Dues and fees paid by US citizens are tax deductible when paid in US dollars to the Environmental Systems Protection Fund. Membership in this non-profit, non-governmental organization is an annual subscription of $30. Presently, there are more than 4,000 members. Membership applications are available from the Bahamas National Trust, The Retreat, Village Rd, PO Box N-4105, Nassau, tel 393-1317, fax 393-4978, e-mail bnt@batelnet.bs.

See also **Nature centres** and **Wildlife preserves.**

BAHAMAS RED CROSS

Established in 1939, The Bahamas branch of the International Red Cross is a non-profit organization with approx 1,000 members – 300 youths and 700 adults.

The society provides a number of programmes and services throughout

The Bahamas, including social welfare to the aged and housebound, youth development, training, education of the deaf, Out Island development, service to refugees, meals-on-wheels and disaster and emergency relief.

It has an annual operating budget of approx $500,000 financed by fund-raising, donations, membership subscriptions and a government grant.

Contact the Bahamas Red Cross Society headquarters, John F Kennedy Dr, PO Box N-8331, Nassau, tel 323-7370, fax 323-7404.

BALANCE OF PAYMENTS

See **Fig 1.1.**

BANKING

On Dec 31, 2003, there were 284 institutions licensed to carry on banking and/or trust business under The Banks and Trust Companies Regulation Act, either within or from the Commonwealth of The Bahamas. Of these, 169 were permitted to deal with the public, and 115 had restricted and non-active licences.

Of the 169 public institutions, 24 were designated by the Exchange Control Dept to deal in Bahamian and foreign currencies and gold. Of these 24, 15 trust companies were designated authorized agents to deal in foreign securities, seven were authorized dealers in gold, foreign currency and Bahamian dollars, and two were authorized agents/dealers operating in Bahamian and foreign currency and securities and in gold and foreign currencies. Of the remaining 145 public institutions, there were 42 Eurocurrency branches of foreign banks and trusts based in the US, Canada, UK, South America, Central America, Asia and Europe. Of the remaining 103, 81 were subsidiaries of banks or other institutions based outside The Bahamas and the remaining 22 were Bahamian-based banks and/or trust companies.

Interest rates

The average interest rates on deposits, as of Dec 31, 2003, were 2.66% for savings deposits, and 3.81% (lower maturity) to 4.59% (higher maturity) for fixed deposits.

Average rate charged for consumer loans was 13.83%, other local loans 8.65%, 8.90% for residential, and 9.04% for commercial mortgages.*

* *In Apr 1980, legislation was enacted to exempt banks and trust companies from the provision of the Rate of Interest Act which prohibits interest rates in excess of 20% per annum. This amendment facilitated the worldwide dealings of licensed financial institutions in The Bahamas in case of changing international monetary conditions. The 20% ceiling still applies to non-licensed lending institutions and individuals.*

Banking hours

Banks are open Mon-Thurs 9:30am-3pm and Fri 9:30am-4pm. Commonwealth Bank is open Mon-Thurs 9am-3:30pm and Fri 9:30am-4:30pm. British American Bank and Finco open Mon-Fri 9:30am-4pm.

Central Bank

The central financial institution in The Bahamas is The Central Bank of The Bahamas. It was established in June 1974 by an Act of Parliament as successor to The Bahamas Monetary Authority. Its responsibilities include:

1. Safeguarding the value of the Bahamian dollar.
2. Credit regulation, note issue.
3. Administration of Exchange Control regulations.
4. Administration of banks and trusts legislation.
5. Compilation of financial statistics.

The Central Bank of The Bahamas, like most other central banks, does not accept deposits from, nor make loans to, the public but acts as a banker to banks and to the government.

For queries on banking in The Bahamas, contact The Central Bank of The Bahamas' Bank Supervision Dept, Frederick St, PO Box N-4868, Nassau, The Bahamas, tel (242) 322-2193, fax (242) 322-4321.

See also **Investing** and **Exchange control.**

FIG 1.1

BALANCE OF PAYMENTS

	B$ millions			
	2002 (provisional)		2003 (provisional)	
	Credit	Debit	Credit	Debit
Current Account	**2,537.8**	**2,877.0**	**2,500.9**	**2,927.5**
Goods & services	2,427.7	2,598.6	2,403.9	2,706.1
Goods	446.2	1,597.5	424.7	1,628.3
Merchandise	322.4	1,594.3	338.5	1,625.1
Oil trade (local consumption)	0.0	290.2	0.0	284.3
Non-oil merchandise	322.4	1,304.1	338.5	1,340.8
Goods procured in port by carrier	123.9	3.2	86.2	3.2
Services	1,981.4	1,001.1	1,979.3	1,077.8
Transportation	57.5	222.8	55.6	230.9
Passenger services	12.9	93.9	13.0	98.0
Air & sea freight services	0.0	117.5	0.0	120.1
Port & airport charges	44.5	11.4	42.6	12.8
Travel	1,762.1	243.9	1,782.0	304.7
Insurance services	0.0	91.2	0.0	104.4
Freight insurance	0.0	13.1	0.0	13.3
Non-merchandise insurance	0.0	78.1	0.0	91.0
Construction services	0.0	55.2	0.0	37.8
Royalty and licence fees	0.0	13.7	0.0	14.6
Offshore companies' local expenses	126.3	0.0	106.0	0.0
Other services	9.2	287.3	9.2	301.7
Government services	26.3	87.1	26.5	83.8
Resident government	3.0	87.1	3.2	83.8
Foreign government	23.3	0.0	23.3	0.0
Income	54.7	265.4	48.2	211.4
Compensation of employees	0.0	49.8	0.0	56.3
Labour Income	0.0	49.8	0.0	56.3
Investment income	54.7	215.5	48.2	155.1
Direct investment	0.0	0.0	0.0	0.0
Official transactions	16.5	7.8	16.4	10.7
Central Bank investment income	16.5	0.0	16.4	0.0
Interest on government transactions	0.0	7.8	0.0	10.7
Other private interest & dividends	38.3	207.7	31.7	144.5
Commercial banks	36.9	97.0	30.3	59.1
Other companies	1.4	110.8	1.4	85.4
Current transfers	55.4	13.0	48.8	10.0
General government	54.2	5.2	47.6	3.5
Other sectors	1.2	7.8	1.2	6.4
Workers' remittances	0.0	7.8	0.0	6.4
Other transfers	1.2	0.0	1.2	0.0
Capital and Financial Account	**497.3**	**116.8**	**700.3**	**492.3**
Capital Account	0.0	24.5	0.0	37.4
Capital Transfers	0.0	24.5	0.0	37.4
Migrants' Transfers	0.0	24.5	0.0	37.4
Financial account	497.3	92.3	700.3	454.9
Direct investment	180.9	28.1	190.7	45.7
Equity	105.3	3.7	76.9	16.3
Land purchases/sales	75.6	24.4	113.8	29.5
Other investments	316.4	64.1	509.6	409.2
Central government	11.6	33.2	205.0	9.0
Other public sector capital	5.7	19.2	1.9	139.6
Domestic banks	183.6	0.0	118.1	234.8
Other private	115.5	11.7	184.7	25.8
Net errors & omissions	**19.5**	**0.0**	**329.6**	**0.0**
Overall Balance	**60.8**	**0.0**	**110.8**	**0.0**
Financing	**0.0**	**60.8**	**0.0**	**110.9**
Change in SDR holdings	0.0	0.0	0.1	0.0
Change in Reserve Position with the Fund	0.0	0.6	0.0	0.8
Change in External Foreign Assets (increase = debit)	0.0	60.1	0.0	110.2

Figures are supplied by The Central Bank of The Bahamas and are subject to subsequent updating.

Private banking

Financial services, the second industry in The Bahamas behind tourism, accounts for approx 15% of the country's Gross Domestic Product (GDP). Nassau, the capital, ranks in the Top 10 offshore jurisdictions worldwide and is arguably the leading offshore banking centre in North and South America.

The 284 banks and trust companies licensed to do business in The Bahamas represent premier institutions of the global financial industry. Most banks are engaged in private banking – personalized management of assets for high net-worth individuals. This includes investment counselling and financial analysis, stock trading in currencies and precious metals, and management of trusts, mutual funds and pension fund assets.

One of the greatest advantages of private banking is that a host of services is offered under one roof. Personal attention is also crucial.

The political stability of the Bahamian government and absence of taxes are factors in The Bahamas' attractiveness as an offshore jurisdiction. Sound fiscal and economic policies have ensured the Bahamian dollar remains on par with the US dollar (since 1966) and there is an experienced combination of both local and international staff officers.

Banking laws

On Dec 29, 2000, government enacted an updated series of banking laws:

Banks and Trust Companies Regulation Act, 2000, increased the level of reporting requirements for banks and trust companies to allow cross-border supervision and made reporting an administrative function, enforceable by law. Banks must now have manuals and procedures on such things as suspicious transactions and money laundering. The bank is liable for breaches, inadvertent or not.

The act expands the role of regulators, specifically the governor of the Central Bank and the inspector of banks and trust companies. It also allows a foreign supervisory authority that is responsible for regulating a bank or trust company with a branch or subsidiary in The Bahamas, to conduct limited inspection of books and accounts in The Bahamas with the approval of the inspector and on condition of confidentiality.

Central Bank of The Bahamas Act, 2000, expands the functions of the Central Bank. The Central Bank may require any financial institution or trust company to provide documents and information which it considers necessary to carry out its functions, and may provide this information to an overseas regulatory authority for conducting investigations and enforcing laws, regulations and rules administered by that authority. The Central Bank may choose not to disclose the information if it is not satisfied with the purpose for which the information is to be used.

Penalties for not complying with Central Bank's requests for information or documents include fines and imprisonment.

Criminal Justice (International Cooperation) Act, 2000, allows government to assist foreign courts and tribunals in obtaining evidence in The Bahamas relating to offences that fall under the Proceeds of Crime Act, 2000.

Dangerous Drugs Act, 2000, incorporates relevant provisions of the Vienna Convention Against the Illicit Traffic in Narcotic Drugs and Psychotropic Substances and makes new provisions for the forfeiture of personal property used while committing offences.

Financial and Corporate Service Providers Act, 2000, requires that International Business Companies and Exempted Limited Partnerships be registered only by a licensed bank or trust company, or a person authorized by the new Financial and Corporate Service Providers Act, 2000.

Corporate service providers must follow strict "know your client" requirements and maintain records on the identity of IBC owners and partners in Exempted Limited Partnerships.

This Act created the office of Inspector of Financial and Corporate Services, which maintains a general overview of financial and corporate services in The Bahamas. The inspector also monitors corporate service providers' compliance with new banking legislation and other laws. The inspector has the power to suspend licences without a court order for up to 30 days or revoke a licence under certain circumstances.

There are fines up to $100,000 for offences contravening the Act.

Financial Intelligence Unit Act, 2000, creates an investigative body, the Financial Intelligence Unit (FIU), to find, analyse and report information-related offences outlined under the Proceeds of Crime Act, 2000, and the Financial Transactions Reporting Act, 2000, such as money laundering, drug trafficking, bribery and other indictable offences.

The FIU can demand information relevant to its investigation (except information subject to the legal professional privilege) and can share information with a foreign FIU. It can, without a court order, prevent the completion of a transaction for up to 72 hours and can freeze a bank account for up to five days on the request of a foreign FIU or a law enforcement authority.

Failure to comply with FIU regulations can result in fines up to $100,000.

Financial Transactions Reporting Act, 2000, makes it an offence for financial institutions to engage in business without first verifying the identity of the customer through set procedures, including customers making transactions over $10,000 without an account at the institution. Specific details for each account holder are to be kept on file for at least five years following a transaction.

A financial institution is obligated to report any transactions deemed suspicious as defined in the Proceeds of Crime Act, 2000. It is an offence to tip off any unauthorized person that a suspicious transactions report has been or will be filed.

A compliance commission has been established to regulate compliance by financial institutions.

International Business Companies Act, 2000, requires that all persons incorporating IBCs are registered under the Financial and Corporate Service Providers Act, 2000. All Memorandums and Articles of Association of IBCs must be filed with the Registrar of Companies. IBCs must have at least two directors and an annual general meeting for its members. A register of officers and directors must be maintained and open to public inspection.

IBCs may own interest in lease or real property located in The Bahamas and do business with people resident in The Bahamas, subject to exchange control approval.

IBCs can no longer deal or trade in securities, act as an agent for securities or render securities advice. The issuance of bearer shares is prohibited.

Proceeds of Crime Act, 2000, provides a statutory definition of money laundering. The Act makes provisions for the confiscation of proceeds of crimes, particularly drug trafficking and money laundering, into a newly created fund, the assets of which may be used for limited purposes.

BANKS

Banking and financial services offered in The Bahamas include asset protection, private and commercial banking, captive insurance, portfolio management, foreign exchange transactions, administration and establishment of trusts, company formation, securities transactions and mutual funds.

Definition of terms

Authorized dealer: A bank authorized by the Central Bank to deal in gold and all foreign currencies. It may open and maintain accounts in such currencies within limits issued in exchange control notices by the Central Bank. Under authority delegated by the Central Bank, an authorized dealer may approve certain applications for foreign currency within specified currencies and limits.

Authorized agent: A bank or trust company authorized by the Central Bank to deal in Bahamian and foreign currency securities and to receive securities into deposits (ie, to act as custodians) in accordance with terms of the Exchange Control Regulations Act and exchange control notices issued by the Central Bank.

Public licensee: A restricted bank and/or trust company that is permitted to carry on banking and/or trust business with the public. The institution's exchange control designation determines whether the licensee is resident or non-resident.

Resident: Resident status allows a bank or trust company to deal only in Bahamian dollars; operations in foreign currencies require exchange control authorization. This does not apply to an authorized agent or authorized dealer that is designated resident.

Non-resident: A non-resident designation permits a bank and/or trust company to operate freely in foreign currencies. Exchange control approval is necessary to operate a Bahamian dollar account to pay local expenses.

Restricted: A restricted bank and/or trust company is one allowed to carry on business for certain specified persons usually named in the licence.

Non-active: A non-active company is either in voluntary liquidation or wishes to keep the word bank or trust in the company's name even though it is not carrying on banking or trust business (not included in the list following).

Nominee: A nominee company is one which holds securities and other assets in its name on behalf of clients of its parent bank or trust company and carries on no other trust business (not included in the list following).

These public banking (B) and trust (T) companies were licensed in The Bahamas as of June 30, 2004. Current information can be obtained from the Central Bank, tel 322-2193 or 302-2600.

Authorized dealers & agents

Barclays Bank, plc ....B & T
Royal Bank of Canada ....B

Authorized dealers

Bank of The Bahamas Ltd ....B & T
British American Bank
(1993) Ltd ....B
Citibank, NA ....B
Commonwealth Bank Ltd ....B
Finance Corp of Bahamas Ltd ......B & T
FirstCaribbean Intl Bank
(Bah) Ltd ....B & T
Scotiabank (Bah) Ltd ....B

Authorized agents

Ansbacher (Bah) Ltd ....B & T
Bank of Butterfield (Bah) ....B & T
Bank of Nova Scotia
Trust Co (Bah) Ltd ....B & T
Bank of The Bahamas Trust Ltd ....T
CIBC Trust Co (Bah) Ltd...............B & T
Cititrust (Bah) Ltd ....B & T
Fidelity Merchant Bank
& Trust Ltd ....B & T
ITK Trust Co Ltd ....B & T
J P Morgan Trust Co (Bah) Ltd......B & T
Latin American Investment
Bank Bahamas Ltd.........................B
Leadenhall Bank & Trust
Co Ltd......................................B & T
Pictet Overseas Trust Corp Ltd ....T
Royal Bank of Canada
Trust Co (Bah) Ltd ....B & T
SG Hambros Bank & Trust
(Bah) Ltd (resident branch) ......B & T
UBS Trustees (Bah) Ltd ....T

Other public licensees

Andbanc (Bah) Ltd ....B & T
Arner Bank & Trust (Bah) Ltd........B & T
ATC Trustees (Bah) Ltd ....T
Austrobank (Overseas) Ltd ....B & T
BAC Bahamas Bank Ltd................B & T

BBA – Creditanstalt Bank Ltd........B & T
BBM Bank Ltd ....B & T
BGP Banca di Gestione
Patrimoniale, SA ....B
BSI AG ....B
BSI Overseas (Bah) Ltd..................B & T
BSI Trust Corp (Bah) Ltd....................T
Bamont Trust Co Ltd ....T
Banca del Gottardo ....B & T
Banca del Sempione
(Overseas) Ltd ....B & T
Banca Serfin, SA ....B
Banco Atlantico (Bah)
Bank & Trust Ltd ....B & T
Banco BBA Creditanstalt, SA ....B
Banco BBM, SA ....B
Banco Bilbao Vizcaya
Argentaria Brasil, SA ....B
Banco Bilbao Vizcaya Argentaria, SA ....B
Banco Boavista InterAtlantico, SA ......B
Banco Cacique, SA ....B
Banco de Bogota (Nass) Ltd................B
Banco del Istmo (Bah) Ltd ....B & T
Banco del Pichincha Ltd ....B & T
Banco Espirito Santo, SA ....B
Banco Fibra, SA.................................B
Banco Ita BBA, SA ....B
Banco Nacional de Mexico, SA ....B & T
Banco Popular Intl Ltd ....B & T
Banco Santander Bahamas
Intl Ltd ....B
Banco Santander Central
Hispano, SA ....B
Banco Santander Portugal, SA............B
Banco Votorantim, SA........................B
Banistmo Intl (Bah) Ltd ....B & T
Bank Hofmann (Overseas) Ltd ....B
Bank Leu Ltd ....B
Bank of Baroda ....B
Bank of Hawaii ....T
The Bank of Nova Scotia ....B
Bank of Nova Scotia Intl Ltd ....B
The Bank of Tokyo-Mitsubishi
Trust Co ....B & T
Bank Boston Banco Multiplo SA ....B
BankBoston, NA ....B
BankBoston Trust Co Ltd.............B & T
Banque Privee
Edmond de Rothschild Ltd........B & T
Banque SCS Alliance (Nass) Ltd......B & T
Barrington Bank Intl Ltd ....B & T
BluBank Ltd.................................B & T
Boavista Banking Ltd ....B

Cayside Trust Co Ltd ....T
Citco Bank & Trust Co
(Bah) Ltd ....B & T
Citicorp Banking Corp ....B
Cofivalle Finance (Bah) Ltd ....B
Coral Credit Bank Ltd ....B
Corner Bank (Overseas) Ltd ....B & T
Credit Lyonnais ....B
Credit Lyonnais Management
Services (Bah) Ltd..........................T
Credit Lyonnais Suisse (Bah) Ltd..........B
Credit Suisse (Bah) Ltd ....B & T
Credit Suisse First Boston ....B
Credit Suisse First Boston
(Bah) Ltd ....B & T
Credit Suisse Trust Ltd ....T
Credit Suisse
Wealth Management Ltd ....B & T
Cuscatlan Intl Bank &
Trust Ltd ....B & T
Dartley Bank & Trust Ltd ....B & T
Deltec Bank & Trust Ltd...............B & T
Deutsche Bank Trust
Co Americas ....B & T
Eni Intl Bank Ltd ....B & T
Eurobanco Bank Ltd ....B & T
Euro-Dutch Trust Co (Bah) Ltd ....T
Experta Trust Co (Bah) Ltd ....T
Ferrier Lullin Bank &
Trust (Bah) Ltd ....B & T
Ferrier Lullin Trust Co (Bah) Ltd ....T
Finter Bank & Trust (Bah) Ltd ....B & T
First Overseas Bank Ltd ....B
First Trust Bank Ltd ....B & T
FirstCaribbean Intl Finance
Corp (Bah) Ltd...............................B
Franklin Templeton Fiduciary
Bank & Trust Ltd ....B & T
Gonet Bank & Trust Ltd ....B
Gottardo Trust Co Ltd ....B & T
Guaranty Trust Bank Ltd ....B & T
HSBC Asset Management
(Bah) Ltd ....T
HSBC Bank Bah Ltd ....B
HSBC Investments (Bah) Ltd ....B & T
HSBC Private Bank (Suisse) SA ....B
Habib Banking Corp Ltd ....B & T
Hang Seng Bank (Bah) Ltd ....B
Hang Seng Bank Trustee
(Bah) Ltd ....T
Hang Seng Bank Trustee Intl Ltd ....T
Harris Trust & Savings Bank ....B

The HongKong & Shanghai Banking Corp Ltd ....B
Hottinger Bank & Trust Ltd ....B & T
Intercredit Bank & Trust Ltd..........B & T
Istituto Bancario San Paolo di Torino – Istituto Mobiliare Italiano SPA (San Paolo IMI SPA)..................B & T
J Safra Bank (Bah) Ltd ....B & T
J P Morgan Chase Bank................B & T
Lombard Odier Darier Hentsch Private Bank & Trust Ltd ....B & T
MMG Bank & Trust Ltd ....B & T
MeesPierson (Bah) Ltd..................B & T
Metropolitan Bank (Bah) Ltd ....B
Mizuho Corporate Bank (USA) ......B & T
National Bank of Canada ....B
National Bank of Canada (Intl) Ltd ....B & T
Occidental Bank & Trust Intl Ltd ....B & T
Oceanic Bank & Trust Ltd ....B & T
PIB Trust Co Ltd..................................T
PNC Bank, NA ....B
POBT Bank & Trust Ltd. ....B & T
Pasche Bank & Trust Ltd ....B & T
Pictet Bank & Trust Ltd ....B & T
Pribanco Internacional Ltd............B & T
Private Investment Bank Ltd ....B & T
The Private Trust Corp Ltd............B & T
Riggs Bank, NA ....B
The Royal Bank of Scotland (Nass) Ltd ....B & T
Rural Intl Bank Ltd..............................B
SG Hambros Bank & Trust (Bah) Ltd ....B & T
Safra Intl Bank & Trust Ltd............B & T
Santander Bank & Trust (Bah) Ltd....B & T
Santander Investment Bank Ltd ....B
Santander Merchant Bank Ltd ....B
Sentinel Bank & Trust Ltd ....B & T
The St James Bank & Trust Co Ltd..........................B & T
Standard Chartered Bank ....B
State Bank of India ....B
Sud Bank & Trust Co Ltd ....B & T
Syz & Co Bank & Trust Ltd............B & T
Transamerica Bank & Trust Co Ltd ....B & T
UBP Intl Trust Ltd..................................T
UBS (Bah) Ltd ....B & T
Unibanco – União de Bancos Brasileiros, SA ....B & T
Union Bancaire Privée ....B & T
Union Bancaire Privée (Bah) Ltd ....B
United European Bank & Trust (Nass) Ltd ....B & T
Votorantim Bank Ltd ....B
Westrust Bank (Intl) Ltd ....B & T
The Winterbotham Trust Co Ltd ....B & T

BIRDS

The birds of The Bahamas are from the US, Cuba and the Caribbean. Approx 300 species of birds have been recorded in The Bahamas – 109 of which breed in the islands and are either permanent residents or summer visitors. The rest are either migrants or vagrants passing through. Only a few are endemic to The Bahamas. These include the Bahama woodstar hummingbird, the Bahama swallow and Bahama yellowthroat. The Bahama parrot is an endemic sub-species closely related to the Cuban parrot and Cayman parrot.

Other birds seen in The Bahamas of interest to birdwatchers are the West Indian woodpecker, Bahama mockingbird, red-legged thrush, great lizard cuckoo, loggerhead kingbird, black-cowled oriole and Greater Antillean bullfinch.

Birdwatchers can participate in tours with accredited guides through the Bahamas National Trust (BNT) Ornithology Group. Tel 393-1317, BNT or 362-1574, Carolyn Wardle.

Abaco has the most Bahamian speciality birds with 22 different species, while Grand Bahama has more migrants and a larger total number of species. Inagua is a birdwatcher's paradise, with a rookery of approx 50,000 West Indian flamingos, roseate spoonbills and a large proportion of the world population of reddish egrets. The Bahama parrot is also found in Inagua. These birds are under the protection of the BNT, which administers the 287-sq-mile Inagua National Park.

The lagoons and mangrove swamps of The Bahamas attract a variety of herons and egrets. Seabirds and waders abound on the coasts and hummingbirds are common. At the other extreme of size is the magnificent frigatebird, which pilots have encountered at 8,000 ft. There are many North American migrants.

The Wild Birds Protection Act is designed to ensure the survival of all bird species throughout The Bahamas. Hunters should obtain a copy of the Act from Government Publications, the Old Lighthouse Bldg, Bay St, Nassau.

*1. **Closed season Mar 1-Sept 15 on the following birds:** Eurasian-collared (ring-necked) dove and mourning (Florida) dove.

*2. **Closed season Apr 1-Sept 28:** Bobwhite quail, chukar partridge, Wilson's snipe, coot, and all wild geese and ducks.

*3. **Closed season Mar 1-Sept 28:** White-crowned pigeon and zenaida dove. It is illegal to kill or capture a white-crowned pigeon or zenaida dove from a boat, vessel, vehicle or aircraft in or over water.

4. **Totally protected species:** The West Indian whistling duck, white-cheeked pintail (Bahama duck), and ruddy duck are protected year-round as well as all birds not listed in (1), (2) and (3). They may not be shot, killed or caught at any time.
5. **Status of hunters:** Only Bahamian citizens, permanent residents and licensed foreigners, or those who have resided in The Bahamas for a continuous 90-day period, may hunt here.
6. **Bag limits:** At present, 50 wild birds may be taken by one person per day. The possession limit is 200 birds at any one time.
7. **Wild bird reserves:** It is an offence to hunt, kill or capture any wild bird in certain areas. A list of these places, condensed following, may be obtained from the Dept of Agriculture, Nassau.

   New Providence area: Paradise Island, Cable Beach golf course, the caves, Lakeview, Red Sound, Twin Lakes, Westward Villas, Lake Cunningham, Waterloo, Adelaide Creek, Goulding Cay, Prospect Ridge, Prospect Waterworks and Skyline Heights.

   The Abacos: Pelican Cays Land & Sea Park and Black Sound Cay Reserve.

   Andros: High Cay, Grassy Creek Cays and Rocks, North Rocks and Small Rocks, Washerwoman's Cut Cays including Dolly Cay, Sister Rocks, Pigeon Cay and Joulter Cays, Big Green Cay and Little Green Cay.

   Berry Islands: Crab Cay and Mamma Rhoda Cay.

   Eleuthera: Wood Cay, Water Cay and Schooner Cays, Bottle Cay, Cedar Cay and Finley Cay.

   Exuma: Big Galliot Cay, Channel Cays, Flat Cay, Big Darby Island, Little Darby Island, Guana Cay, Goat Cay, Betty Cay, Pigeon Cay, Cistern Cay, Harvey Cay and Rocks in vicinity of Leaf Cay, Exuma Cays Land and Sea Park area.

   Grand Bahama: Peterson Cay and Lucayan National Park.

   Inagua: BNT areas have by-laws which are in force.

   Little San Salvador: Little Island or Little San Salvador and Goat Cay.
8. **Penalties:** Any person who commits an offence against the Act is liable to a fine of up to $500 or one-month imprisonment. The gun, ammunition, car, boat or plane and all equipment used on the hunting expedition are liable to be forfeited and auctioned. If the car, boat or plane is used by another person who commits an offence, the owner could still lose his property by forfeiture unless he proves he did not commit an offence and had reported the incident to police or game wardens.
9. The Act provides a reward of $500 or one-half the proceeds of the sale of forfeited articles, whichever is the greater, to persons who give information leading to conviction of the offender.

* *During closed season on these birds, it is an offence to kill, capture or have in possession any such bird unless it can be proved the bird was taken in season.*

See also **Flora & fauna** and **Wildlife preserves.**

BOATING

The Bahamas is a boater's paradise with some 700 islands and cays stretching over 100,000 miles of virtually pollution-free ocean. Chartering a yacht, bareboating, deep-sea fishing or day or dinner cruises are aqua-adventure possibilities. Out Islands such as the Abacos and Exumas are considered among the finest boating destinations in the world.

Motor boating

It is forbidden to drive a motor boat or jet ski in the 200-ft zone of water directly offshore any Bahama island – unless the boat is approaching or leaving a marina, jetty, dock, etc, at a speed not exceeding three knots.

It is illegal to drive a boat or jet ski in a reckless manner, or while under the influence of drugs or alcohol.

It is illegal for anyone under 18 yrs of age to drive a motor boat with an engine of more than 10 hp, unless aged 17 and supervised by someone 18 or over.

Water-skiing

Water-skiing within the 200-ft zone is prohibited, unless the skier is being towed within a lane clearly marked with buoys or ropes. Water-skiers are required to wear an efficient flotation device. In the towing boat there must be a look-out (in addition to the driver) aged 18 or over. Skiing is forbidden in hours of darkness.

Boat registration

The Water-skiing and Motor Boat Control (Amendment) Act, 1989, requires annual registration of Bahamian motor boats with an engine rated over 10 hp. Jet skis for commercial use must also be registered. Any person wishing to use such boats in Bahamian waters must apply to the port controller in Nassau or administrator in the Out Islands. Initial registration fees are:

Motor boats–private:

15 ft in length or less $10
15 ft or longer,
but less than 30 ft......................$20
30 ft or longer,
but less than 50 ft....................$100
50 ft or longer,
but less than 100 ft..................$200
100 ft or longer $400
Fishing boats primarily designed
to navigate under sail, with an
auxiliary engine of less
than 10 hp ....nil

Commercial

The Boat Registration Act (Amendment to schedule) Order 2003, requires annual registration and inspection of all boats plying for hire in the waters of The Bahamas.

Registration fees:

15 ft in length or less $30
15 ft or longer, but less than 25 ft ..$50
25 ft or longer,
but less than 50 ft....................$100
50 ft or longer,
but less than 100 ft..................$200
100 ft or longer $400
each transfer of registration $10
duplicate certificate of registration ..$10

Inspection fees:

15 ft in length or less $30
15 ft or longer, but less than 25 ft $30
25 ft or longer, but less than 50 ft $40
50 ft or longer, but less than 100 ft ..$60
100 ft or longer $80

The Boat Registration (Yacht) Amendment Rules, 2003, requires all foreign registered yachts (foreign yacht charters) desiring to conduct charters in The Bahamas to be registered and inspected annually.

Application for annual or
temporary permit $50
Annual permit for a boat:
Up to 35 ft $625
Up to 50 ft $875
Up to 65 ft...............................$1,250
66 ft up to 100 ft......................$1,875
101 ft up to 150 ft....................$2,500
151 ft and longer......................$3,750
Temporary permit $437

Masters' (captain's) licence fees:

Fees in respect of masters operating vessels in the waters of The Bahamas are subject to an annual licence fee:

'A' class $50
'B' class...$30
Duplicate licence fee $10
Examination fee $30

The port controller or administrator where the boat is registered must be notified of any change of ownership or the fitting of a new engine to the registered boat. The registration number must clearly show on both sides of the boat's bow. Failure to comply may result in a fine up to $75.

Any person using an unregistered motor boat to which the Act applies is liable to a fine up to $75 plus an additional fine equal to twice the appropriate registration fee.

Duty on boats

Customs and stamp duty are not payable on foreign-registered/foreign-owned pleasure boats that remain in The Bahamas up to one year after having been imported initially under their own power and subject to specified conditions. Thereafter, written application for an extension of a cruising permit must be made to the Comptroller of Customs and once approved, a $500 fee (for one year) is applicable. The vessel may then remain in The Bahamas provided it is not used for commercial purposes or hire. The max period a vessel may remain in The Bahamas under this provision is three years, thereafter full customs duties must be paid. Vessels temporarily imported, otherwise than under their own power, must be re-exported within 12 months of arrival, or full customs duties must be paid.

Bahamians or others employed here more than six months pay customs duty and stamp duty on importation of pleasure craft. Customs duty depends on length of craft and gross tonnage. Customs duty for a pleasure craft 30 ft or longer and less than 150 gross tons is 5%, stamp duty is 1%. Duty on a pleasure craft less than 30 ft and less than 150 gross tons is 20%, stamp duty is 7%.

There is a $150 charge for each foreign pleasure vessel under 30 ft and a $300 charge for vessels more than 30 ft, containing up to four passengers, entering The Bahamas. (If a foreign pleasure boat departs The Bahamas and returns within a 90-day period, it is exempted from these charges.) There is a charge of $15 for each additional passenger. These charges cover customs and immigration services as well as fishing and cruising permits.

See also **Marinas & cruising facilities.**

BROADCASTING

Radio stations (government-owned)

The Broadcasting Corp of The Bahamas is a government-owned corporation operating out of studios at Third Terrace (East), Centreville, Nassau, and at the Bahamas Government Office Complex, The Mall, Freeport, Grand Bahama.

ZNS-1: Radio Bahamas, ZNS-1, transmits on 50,000 watts and is received throughout The Bahamas 24 hours a day. Programming is adult contemporary/talk shows.

ZNS-2: ZNS-2 is powered by 1,000 watts. Programming, which is religious, is simulcast on FM at 107.1 MHz, and 107.9 MHz in the southeastern Bahamas. ZNS-2 operates 6am-12 midnight at 1240 AM on the dial.

ZNS-FM: Power 104.5 FM went on the air in Nassau July 10, 1988, at frequency 104.5 MHz. It operates 24 hours with a contemporary urban format and has a transmitting power of 5,000 watts.

ZNS-3: Radio Bahamas Northern Service was established in May 1973, and transmits on a frequency of 810 kHz with 10,000 watts. It broadcasts from Freeport, Grand Bahama, throughout the northern Bahamas and to a small section of South Florida. Its programming parallels that of ZNS-1.

Radio stations (private)

In 1993, legislation was passed to allow private broadcasting.

100 JAMZ, the first private radio station in The Bahamas, was established Oct 10, 1993, transmitting on a frequency of 100.3 FM with 5,000 watts. The station, on Shirley and Deveaux Sts, Nassau, is owned by The Tribune Radio

Ltd and operates 24 hours. 100 JAMZ is received in New Providence, Grand Bahama, Abaco and Eleuthera, with plans to expand to Exuma. Format is island and urban music.

MORE 94.9 FM: This station on Carmichael Rd first aired in Dec 1995. With a strong community-minded philosophy it broadcasts a variety of musical genres including reggae, soca, hip hop, R & B, alternative rock and AC rhythmic tunes. It is the only FM station in The Bahamas that devotes the entire day on Sun to gospel programming. Frequency is 94.9 FM in New Providence and 94.1 FM in Grand Bahama. The station plans to expand to the rest of the country. MORE 94.9 is owned by the Saunders Group of Companies.

LOVE 97 & Love 97 FM-North: Operational since Sept 24, 1994. Frequency is 97.5 FM with 5,000 watts, operating 24 hours with an adult/ contemporary format. Owned by Jones Communications Ltd, the station is on East St in Nassau and in the Regency Centre in Freeport.

ISLAND FM: This station, began airing on Aug 1, 2001, on a frequency of 102.9 with 5,000 watts. The format includes predominantly Bahamian and island music with a mix of World, Latin and Caribbean music. The station is located on Dowdeswell St and is owned by Carter Broadcasting Bahamas Ltd.

JOY FM: The newest radio station and the only 24-hour FM gospel station in The Bahamas began transmitting on a frequency of 101.9 FM with 5,000 watts in June 2003. The studios are located on the second floor of the Librery Bldg on Dowdeswell St opp School Ln.

Radio licences

On Mar 25, 2000, the Public Utilities Commission (PUC) took over responsibility from the Bahamas Telecommunications Co.

The PUC provides application forms for licences which are renewable annually. At press time licence fees per year were:

Fixed private stations $150
Amateur (ham) operators $25
Fixed base unit $250
Marine radios: pleasure boats $30
Ocean-going work vessels:
over 1,600 tons $150
under 1,600 tons $75

Citizens band equipment, which requires no licence, is limited to five watts and 23 channels max.

Contact PUC, PO Box N-4860, Nassau, tel 322-4437.

See also **Cable television** and **Television.**

BUDGET

See **Public finance.**

BUILDING CONTRACTORS

A selection of New Providence construction companies:

Carl G Treco Contractors Ltd
Tel 393-8725, fax 393-0732
Cavalier Construction Co Ltd
Tel 323-5171, fax 325-5244
Gilles Deal
Tel 324-3596
M & T Construction
Tel 326-8424 (to 6), fax 323-5029
Mosko's United Construction Co Ltd
Tel 322-2825, fax 325-2571
Osprey Developers Building Contractors
Tel 322-2429, fax 356-9086
Sunco Builders & Developers Ltd
Tel 323-4966, fax 323-7656

BUILDING COSTS

See **Cost of living** and **Building permits.**

BUILDING PERMITS

Bahamas building permits issued by the Ministry of Public Works

Year	Permits issued	Estimated value (B$)
1999	3,206	646,539,358
2000	3,208	536,586,121
2001	3,087	759,005,434
2002	3,063	533,048,670
2003	2,846	332,103,849

Rates for commercial and residential properties

Floor area	Cost of permit
Up to 500 sq ft	$10
501-1,000 sq ft	$8/100 sq ft
1,001-1,500 sq ft	$10/100 sq ft
1,501-5,000 sq ft	$15/100 sq ft
5,001-10,000 sq ft	$20/100 sq ft
More than 10,000 sq ft	$25/100 sq ft

Other charges

To build a wall, fence or any boundary structure ....$8/100 linear ft
Removal of sheds, garages and other structures (non-demolition) ....$25 minimum
Reclamation of land............$5/100 sq ft
Building of small private docks and any size swimming pool.............$5/sq ft

Renewals

Where gross area of floor space is:

Up to 1,000 sq ft	$10
1,001-1,500 sq ft	$25
1,501-5,000 sq ft	$45
5,001-10,000 sq ft	$60
More than 10,000 sq ft	$100

Deposits

Up to 500 sq ft	$5
501–1,000 sq ft	$10
1,001–1,500 sq ft	$25
More than 1,500 sq ft	10% of total fee

Building permit rates were being revised at press time.

Other projects

Approval from the Dept of Physical Planning is required for land excavations and removal of protected trees.

Approval from the Docks Committee, Port Dept, is required for the building of docks and marinas.

BUSINESS LICENCE FEE

The Business Licence Act, 1980, made it mandatory for anyone operating a business aimed at obtaining a turnover to apply for and obtain a licence.

Annual licence renewal applications and payments are due every Jan-Apr, and expire on Dec 31. Fees are based, for most businesses, on their annual gross receipts less the direct cost of producing the turnover. They range from zero for a petty business to 1½% of turnover or $500,000 (whichever is greater) for a very large business with a high profit. See **Fig 1.2.**

Companies designated non-resident under the Exchange Control Regulations Act pay an annual fee of $100.

Companies licensed under The Banks and Trust Companies Regulation Act, 2000 (which imposes separate fees), do not pay for a business licence. Gas stations pay a fixed fee of 1/5 of 1% of turnover (a business with a turnover of $250,000 per year or more).

The Act's definition of "business" includes all types of manufacturing and commercial undertakings, and covers professions such as law, accounting and medicine. Where a business consists of separate and distinct undertakings, a separate licence must be obtained for each.

A Bahamian or Bahamian company (ie, one with 100% Bahamian ownership) wishing to start a new business may commence operations as soon as the application for a licence is submitted, and prior to determination of the application, if the company has complied with requirements of all other government agencies. A copy of the applicant's passport, National Insurance number (or the business number for a self-employed person) and $10 fee are submitted with Form A and a receipt is issued. The licence is ready within 24 hours (if other statutory requirements have been met). A non-Bahamian or a company not 100% Bahamian-owned must first obtain approval from the National Economic Council and then wait for the licence application to be approved.

The Act provides for automatic annual renewal for Bahamian businesses (if other statutory requirements have been met, including payment of applicable fees), however, the licensee must still complete and submit Form B to renew the business licence. Renewal of a non-Bahamian business licence is at the discretion of the Minister of Finance.

Business licence fee schedule
See **Fig 1.2.**

Highlights of amendments to Business Licence Act
Businesses with a turnover less than $50,000 (based on the gross income derived from the selling of goods or services) are not required to pay a fee. They are, however, required to register under the Act.

Following are further amendments to the Business Licence Act:

1. Gross profit is defined as turnover less allowable cost, which is defined in the Act.
2. Business licences may be suspended if fees are not paid.
3. Where a business operates out of the owner's premises, no business licence will be granted unless real property taxes are up to date.
4. Medium, large and very large businesses require a certificate from a qualified, professional accountant verifying accuracy of the amount of turnover and gross profits. If turnover is $500,000 or above, certification by a Bahamas Institute of Chartered Accountants member must accompany the application.
5. The Ministry of Finance's secretary for revenue has power to have the books of a licensee audited at least once a year. Books are to be maintained for at least two years.
6. Businesses importing goods must provide a current business licence for customs inspection when requested.

See also **Company formation, Investing** and **National Insurance.**

BUSINESS NAME REGISTRATION

Before a company is incorporated, its proposed name must be approved – by phone if one wishes – by the Registrar General as meeting requirements laid down in the Companies Act, 1992, International Business Companies Act, 2000, The Business Names Act, The Banks and Trust Companies Regulation Act, and The Insurance Act.

The Business Names Act is not administered by the Companies Section but by a separate section of the Registrar General's Dept.

See also **Company formation.**

CABLE TELEVISION

In 1994, The Bahamas government issued a 15-year licence to Cable Bahamas Ltd for the construction and operation of a cable television system to service The Bahamas.

In June 1995, the company's initial share offering generated approx 3,000 Bahamian shareholders. Non-Bahamian ownership, which began at 49% with the initial share offering, has now been reduced to 29.8%. Seventy percent ownership is shared between the Bahamas government and Bahamians. In 1995, Cable Bahamas also purchased Grand Bahama CATV, which had been providing cable services since 1965. This purchase gave Cable Bahamas a franchise for cable television services in Freeport, Grand Bahama.

Cable television services are available to 96% of Bahamian households and are provided to 16 Bahamian islands. As of July 2004, Cable Bahamas had approx 65,000 subscribers. Cable Bahamas installs, free of charge, cable service and broadband Internet access in government-operated schools and libraries. Government ministries charitable organizations and church-operated schools are also granted free installation of cable services. In addition Cable Bahamas operates a community channel and carries a parliamentary channel, which transmits live broadcasts of parliamentary proceedings from The House of Assembly.

In 2000, Cable Bahamas was granted an Internet Service Providers licence from the Public Utilities Commission. This licence permits Cable Bahamas to provide leased circuits and

FIG 1.2

BUSINESS LICENCE FEE SCHEDULE

Profit (gross)	Petty under 50,000	V small 50,000-100,000	Small 100,000-250,000	Medium 250,000-1,000,000	Large 1,000,000-28,000,000	V large 28,000,000 plus
			Turnover (Sales) $			
Low (under 25%)	–	$250	$500	0.5% of turnover	0.5% of turnover	½ of 1% of turnover or $140,000 (the greater)
Medium (25-50%)	–	$500	$750	1.00%	1.00%	1% of turnover or $280,000 (the greater)
High (50-75%)	–	$700	$1,000	1.50%	1.50%	1½% of turnover or $420,000 (the greater)
Very high (over 75%)	–	$800	$1,250	1.50%	1.50%	1½% of turnover or $500,000 (the greater)

Internet services to the public over its high-speed hybrid fibre-rich broadband network. As of July 2004, Cable Bahamas had approx 22,500 broadband Internet subscribers.

On Aug 5, 2004, Cable Bahamas acquired Internet Bahamas, a subscription base of Bahamas Online.

Cable Internet access is currently available on the islands of New Providence, Grand Bahama, Eleuthera and Abaco.

See also **Internet** and **Television.**

CAPTIVE INSURANCE

See **Insurance.**

CAR RENTAL COMPANIES

Avis, downtown....................326-6380
or 322-2889
- Nassau Intl Airport............377-7121
- Paradise Island..................363-2061

Budget Rent A Car
- Nassau Intl Airport............377-9000 or 377-7405
- Paradise Island....................363-3095

Davis Car Rental....................364-5042

Dollar Rent A Car
- Nassau Intl Airport............377-7231 or 377-8300
- Downtown 325-3716

Hertz
- Nassau Intl Airport............377-8684 or 377-6321
- East Bay St.........................393-2326 or 394-1269

Orange Creek Rentals 323-4967

Teglo Car Rentals..................362-4361

Virgo Car Rental
- East West Hwy..................394-2122
- Kemp Rd & Shirley St........393-7900

Wallace's U-Drive-It Cars 393-8559

See also **Driver's licence & vehicle information, Motor vehicle insurance** and **Transportation.**

CARIBBEAN BASIN INITIATIVE (CBI)

The Caribbean Basin Initiative (CBI) was established by the US in 1982 to promote growth in the Caribbean region, including The Bahamas, by stimulating investment in non-traditional industries producing goods for the US market. CBI permits duty-free import of most products shipped from the Caribbean.

The duty-free provisions were made permanent in 1990 and other enhancements to CBI were added. If a product is not entirely grown, produced or manufactured in one or more CBI countries, certain minimum value-added and substantial transformation requirements are imposed.

Products eligible for duty-free importation into the US include:

1. electronic and electro-mechanical assembly
2. ethnic and regional foods (eg, spices, jams, liqueurs and confectioneries)
3. fresh and frozen seafood
4. handicrafts, giftware and decorative accessories
5. hand-loomed, handmade and folklore items
6. knit apparel (excluding socks) conforming to CBI specifications, in limited quantities.
7. medical and surgical supplies
8. ornamental horticulture
9. recreational items, such as sporting goods and toys
10. textiles and apparel using US fabric and yarn
11. textile luggage conforming to CBI specifications
12. tropical fruit products
13. T-shirts (excluding underwear) in limited quantities
14. winter vegetables
15. wood products, including furniture and building materials

The CBI law excludes the following articles from duty-free entry status:

1. certain leather, rubber and plastic gloves
2. certain leather apparel
3. luggage, handbags and flat goods (except certain textile luggage)
4. textiles and apparel (not using US fabric and yarn)

Bahamian exports currently benefiting from CBI regulations include chemicals, seafood and pharmaceuticals. In 2003, the US imported from The Bahamas a total of $479.3 million worth of products, representing an increase of $29.6 million over 2002 trade figures.

CARIBBEAN COMMUNITY

The Caribbean Community, including the CARICOM Single Market and Economy (CSME) became a reality in July 2001, with the signing of the Revised Treaty of Chaguaramas. The Revised Treaty, is the successor treaty to the original Treaty of Chaguaramas which was signed on July 4, 1973, to establish the Caribbean Community and Common Market (CARICOM).

The original treaty was signed by four independent countries of the Caribbean: Barbados, Jamaica, Guyana and Trinidad and Tobago.

The Caribbean Community, including the CSME, is a successor to the West Indian Federation of 1958-62. The failure of the Federation led to the establishment of the Caribbean Free Trade Association (CARIFTA), which was transformed into CARICOM.

CARICOM aims to create a single economic space to improve standards of living, coordinate foreign economic policies, and enhance functional cooperation in health, education, transportation, telecommunications and culture.

CARICOM heads of government meet twice yearly in July and Feb. They met in Nassau July 3-6, 2001 and in Georgetown, Guyana July 3-5, 2002. The Bahamas became the 13th member state of CARICOM on July 4, 1983, but is not a member of the common market. The other CARICOM members include Antigua and Barbuda, Barbados, Belize, Dominica, Grenada, Guyana, Haiti, Jamaica, Montserrat, St Kitts and Nevis, St Lucia, St Vincent and the Grenadines, Suriname and Trinidad and Tobago. Anguilla, Bermuda, the British Virgin Islands, Cayman Islands and Turks and Caicos Islands are associate members of the Caribbean Community.

The CARICOM Secretariat has headquarters at Liliendaal, East Coast Demerara, Guyana, PO Box 10827, tel (011) 592-226-2980/9, fax (011) 592-226-7816, or visit www.caricom.org.

CARIBCAN

In 1986, the Canadian government established CARIBCAN, a programme to encourage trade, investment and industrial cooperation with the Commonwealth Caribbean region.

There are 18 countries or dependent territories eligible to receive benefits of the duty-free provisions of CARIBCAN. These are: Anguilla, Antigua and Barbuda, The Bahamas, Barbados, Belize, Bermuda, the British Virgin Islands, the Cayman Islands, Dominica, Grenada, Guyana, Jamaica, Montserrat, St Kitts and Nevis, St Lucia, St Vincent and the Grenadines, Trinidad and Tobago, and the Turks and Caicos Islands.

The programme's basic objectives are to expand Canadian and Commonwealth Caribbean trade and promote new investment opportunities in the region.

CARIBCAN's main feature is duty-free access to the Canadian market for most exports from the Commonwealth Caribbean countries. There are some notable exclusions, such as textiles, clothing and footwear, which continue to be subject to the General Preferential Tariff.

Goods may qualify for CARIBCAN treatment if at least 60% of the ex-factory price to Canada is made up of materials, parts or produce of CARIBCAN countries. The exporter must submit a completed standard international certificate of origin or an exporter's statement of origin to the Canadian importer for the goods to enter Canada duty free.

Canadian imports from CARIBCAN countries are fairly diversified. The most important are alumina from Jamaica, iron and steel from Trinidad and Tobago, seafood and organic chemicals from The Bahamas and food and beverages from many other Caribbean territories. In 2003, goods imported into Canada from The Bahamas totalled CDN$48.15 million (US$37.04 million). Canadian exports to The Bahamas over the same period were CDN$32.77 million (US$25.21 million). These figures do not reflect the growing bilateral trade in services.

The CARIBCAN programme contains measures to encourage Canadian investment and industrial cooperation with the region. Canadian high commissions and trade commissioners can assist business people from the Commonwealth Caribbean.

Another Canadian organization that can assist Caribbean exporters with the CARIBCAN programme is the Trade Facilitation Office Canada (TFOC), which provides practical assistance for promotion of Caribbean exports to Canada by helping producers in trade fair participation, bringing business visitors to Canada, preparing practical market information papers and maintaining a database matching importers and exporters.

Contact the Business Development Office, Canadian High Commission, 3 West Kings House Rd, PO Box 1500, Kingston 10, Jamaica, WI, tel (876) 926-1500, fax (876) 511-3491, e-mail kngtn-td@dfait-maeci.gc.ca, or visit www.infoexport.gc.ca.

CARICOM

See **Caribbean Community.**

CASINOS

See **Entertainment** and **Gambling.**

CENSORSHIP (FILMS, PLAYS & PRINTED MATERIAL)

The Bahamas Plays and Films Control Board reviews films, synopses of films and stage plays intended for public showing, classifying the material as:

A: Suitable for universal exhibition or performance (US: **G**).

B: Suitable for adults and persons under 18 when accompanied by a parent or other responsible adult (US: **PG 13** and **PG**).

T: Suitable for any person over 15 (US: **PG 13**).

C: For adults only, with persons under 18 not admitted whether accompanied by an adult or not (US: **R**).

D: Unapproved films or plays, although the board may change the classification if portions of the work it deems "undesirable in the public interest" are excised.

The board is appointed for a one-year period.

A max fine of $2,000 and/or imprisonment for a term not exceeding six months is the penalty for any public performance or exhibition given without authorization by The Bahamas Plays and Films Control Board. Any persons concerned in the organization or management of that performance or exhibition; and any other person who, knowing or having reasonable cause to suspect the contravention, allows premises to be used or made available for the performance or exhibition, will be held liable.

If an obscene play or film is exhibited in public or private, any person responsible for presenting or directing that showing (whether for gain or not) will be liable, on summary conviction, to a fine not exceeding $2,000 or to imprisonment for a term not exceeding six months; or, on conviction on information, to a fine not exceeding $5,000 and/or to imprisonment for a term not exceeding three years.

In addition, if the Governor General considers a publication to be contrary to the public interest, he/she may prohibit its importation, including future issues. Any person who imports, publishes, sells, offers for sale, distributes, reproduces, or possesses any publication which has been prohibited is subject to imprisonment for one year or a fine of $500 or both for a first offence. A person is liable to two years' imprisonment if he or she publishes, sells, or offers for sale any blasphemous or obscene book, writing, or representation.

CHAMBER OF COMMERCE

The Bahamas Chamber of Commerce is a non-profit, non-political corporate body of businesses and professionals. Its primary interest is promoting, fostering and protecting Bahamian commerce and industry. It also provides government with a responsible vehicle for dialogue with the private sector.

Since the Chamber is concerned with all phases of the Bahamian economy, it maintains active standing committees which parallel the areas of responsibility of most government ministries. These committees meet at least monthly. Routine business includes recommendations to government and requests from government for private sector cooperation on projects such as Free Trade Area of the Americas (FTAA).

Members of the Bahamas Chamber of Commerce include representatives from every business sector. Offices are located on the corner of Shirley St and Collins Ave, PO Box N-665, Nassau, The Bahamas, tel (242) 322-2145, fax (242) 322-4649 or 326-3366, e-mail info@bahamaschamber.org, or visit www.bahamaschamber.org.

CHURCHES

See **Religion.**

CINEMAS

Nassau has two spacious multiplex cinemas operated by Galleria Cinemas offering first-run movies, concession stands and parking.

Galleria Cinemas 11, an 11-screen theatre at the Mall at Marathon, features wall-to-wall screens with Dolby Digital Stereo and Surround Sound. Matinee seats cost $6 for adults and $2.50 for children. Evening seats (after 6pm) cost $7 for adults and $3.50 for children. Call 380-FLIX (3549) for movies and show times.

Galleria 6 is a six-screen multiplex theatre in the RND Plaza on John F Kennedy Dr with the latest projection equipment and Dolby Digital Stereo and DTS Digital Sound. Matinee seats cost $6 for adults and $2.50 for children (under 12). Evening seats (after 6pm) cost $7 for adults and $3.50 for children. Call 380-FLIX (3549) for movies and show times.

CITIZENSHIP

The Constitution of The Bahamas contains detailed provisions of who is, or who can become, a citizen. Other provisions affecting the acquisition or loss of citizenship are contained in The Bahamas Nationality Act, 1973.

1. Under the Constitution, those who became or were eligible to become citizens on the date of independence – July 10, 1973 – include:
   a. A person born in The Bahamas who was, on July 9, 1973, a citizen of the UK and colonies.
   b. A person born outside The Bahamas if his father did, or would have before his death, become a citizen of The Bahamas, provided this person is or was a citizen of the UK and colonies on July 9, 1973.
   c. A person who was registered as a citizen of the UK and colonies under the British Nationality Act, 1948, by virtue of having been registered in the former colony of the Bahama Islands under that Act. Excepted from this provision are those persons registered under the British Nationality Act, 1948, and who were not resident in The Bahamas on Dec 31, '72; or who were registered on or after Jan 1, '73, or who on July 9, '73, possessed the nationality of some other country.
2. Other sections of the Constitution relate to those persons born after July 9, 1973. They provide that:
   a. A person born in The Bahamas after that date shall be a citizen if either of his parents was a citizen of The Bahamas.
   b. A person born in The Bahamas, neither of whose parents is a citizen, shall be entitled to be registered as a citizen of The Bahamas, subject to exceptions or qualifications prescribed in the interests of national security or public policy, by making application within 12 months after his 18th birthday. Such persons, if they are citizens of another country, will be required to renounce that citizenship, take an oath of allegiance, and make a declaration of intent concerning residence.
   c. A person born outside The Bahamas after July 9, 1973, whose father is Bahamian by birth and the parents are married, is a citizen regardless of the mother's nationality. If the child is illegitimate and the mother is not Bahamian, or if legitimate and the father was also born outside The Bahamas, though of Bahamian parents, he is not Bahamian.
   d. A person born legitimately outside The Bahamas after July 9, 1973, if his mother is a citizen of The Bahamas, is entitled to make application between the ages of 18 and 21 to be registered as a citizen, subject to national security and public policy considerations. He is required to renounce any other citizenship, take an oath of allegiance and make a declaration of intent concerning residence. If his mother registers him as a minor prior to his 18th birthday and it is approved, renunciation would not be necessary and dual nationality would result.
   e. If a child is born illegitimately abroad and the mother is Bahamian, he is a Bahamian citizen by birth.
   f. Any woman who, after July 9, 1973, is married to a person who is or becomes a citizen of The Bahamas is entitled upon making application to be registered as a citizen, provided she is still married to that person and subject to national security and public policy considerations. Once approved, she does not have to renounce her previous nationality.

In all cases (with the exception of 1a, 1b and 1c), registration as a citizen is subject to exceptions or qualifications prescribed in the interests of national security or public policy.

Prior to independence, the designation "Bahamian status" was given to some British subjects who met certain qualifications, including at least five years' residence in The Bahamas, and to others who automatically acquired Bahamian status by marriage. Bahamian status conferred on them equal rights with Bahamians with regard to employment and business.

Foreigners who were not British subjects qualified for Bahamian status by becoming British subjects naturalized in The Bahamas.

Aliens who are not entitled to be registered or naturalized by virtue of an existing status are nevertheless able to apply for citizenship in The Bahamas under the Nationality Act. Qualifications include:

1. Seven years' lawful residence of the 10 years immediately preceding, and inclusive of, date of application, ie, work permit, residency permit or permanent residence certificate.
2. Knowledge of the English language.
3. Intent to continue residing in and making The Bahamas their permanent home.

See also **Immigration.**

CLIMATE

The Bahamas has a tropical maritime climate with winter incursions of modified polar air and generally experiences neither frost, snow, sleet nor extreme temperatures. An exception occurred on Jan 19, 1977, when parts of the northern Bahamas experienced a brief flurry of light snow. The lowest recorded temperature was 41.4°F on Jan 20, 1981. See **Fig 1.3.**

In centrally-situated New Providence, winter temperatures seldom fall much below 60°F and usually reach about 75°F in the afternoon. In summer, temperatures usually fall to 78°F or less at night and seldom rise above 90°F during the day. Winter temperatures are lower in more northerly islands than in New Providence, and about five degrees higher in the south. In summer, temperatures tend to be similar all over The Bahamas. Sea surface temperatures normally vary between 74°F in Feb and 83°F in Aug.

Humidity

Humidity is fairly high, especially in summer months. Winds are predominantly easterly throughout the year but have a tendency to become northeasterly from Oct-Apr and southeasterly from May-Sept. Wind speeds are, on average, below 10 knots; in winter months, periods of a day or two of north and northeast winds of about 25 knots may occur.

There are more than seven hours of bright sunshine per day in Nassau on average, though periods of a day or two of cloudy weather can occur at any time of year. Daylight hours vary from 10 hours, 35 mins in late Dec to 13 hours, 41 mins in late June.

Rain showers occur any time of year, but the rainy months are May-Oct; for example, in Nassau, rainfall averages two ins a month from Nov-Apr and six ins a month from May-Oct. In the northern islands, it is up to 20% more. The southern islands normally receive only half the Nassau total. Rainfall is mainly in the form of heavy showers or thundershowers, which clear quickly.

See also **Hurricanes.**

COMMUNITY ORGANIZATIONS & SERVICE CLUBS

Organizations and clubs in The Bahamas provide a range of services.

Abilities Unlimited 325-2150
AIDS Secretariat 325-5120/1
American Men's Club of The Bahamas (William Whitaker)............322-8663
American Women's Club (Jayne Holland) 362-4431
Bahamas Air Sea Rescue Assoc (BASRA) 325-8864
Bahamas Assoc for the Mentally Retarded (Lowell Mortimer)..............356-9777
Bahamas Assoc for the Physically Disabled 322-2393
Bahamas Assoc for Social Health (BASH) 356-2274

FIG 1.3

CLIMATOLOGICAL MEANS & EXTREME VALUES FOR NEW PROVIDENCE 1971-2000*

	JAN	FEB	MAR	APR	MAY	JUN	JUL	AUG	SEP	OCT	NOV	DEC
TEMPERATURE (°F)												
Highest temperatures	86.9	88.7	88.5	91.4	94.3	97.7	95.4	95.0	95.2	93.2	92.1	86.9
Mean of daily max temperatures	77.7	77.9	79.9	82.2	85.4	87.8	89.6	89.7	88.8	85.9	82.0	79.2
Mean daily temperatures	70.8	70.6	72.3	74.7	77.9	80.8	83.2	82.3	81.5	78.9	75.7	71.8
Mean of daily minimum temperatures	63.2	63.2	64.3	67.2	70.6	73.9	75.2	75.2	74.7	72.5	69.1	65.0
Lowest temperatures	41.4	45.8	46.0	48.6	55.5	59.0	64.2	64.4	59.5	56.0	51.0	41.5
HUMIDITY												
Mean relative humidity (%)	78	77	76	74	77	80	78	80	81	80	79	78
Mean dew point (°F)	62.8	62.2	63.4	65.4	68.7	70.0	75.0	75.3	75.0	72.0	68.5	64.7
WIND												
Mean wind speed (knots)	8.1	8.3	8.8	8.3	7.7	6.9	6.9	6.5	6.2	7.2	8.2	8.1
SUNSHINE												
Mean daily sunshine (hours)	7.4	8.0	8.2	9.3	9.0	7.9	8.7	8.5	7.4	7.4	7.3	6.9
RAINFALL												
Total monthly rainfall (inches)	1.55	1.95	2.14	2.73	4.17	8.59	6.33	9.28	6.46	6.37	3.17	1.96

**The Dept of Meteorology updates these tables every 10 years.*

Bahamas Council on Alcoholism (David Knowles) ....322-1685 or 558-0517
Bahamas Family Planning & Resource Centre 325-1663
Bahamas Girl Guides Assoc (Louise Barry) 322-4342
Bahamas Heart Assoc (Linda LaFleur) 327-0806
Bahamas Historical Society....322-4231
Bahamas Humane Society (BHS) 323-5138
Bahamas National Pride Assoc................................326-3330
Bahamas National Trust (BNT) 393-1317
Bahamas Red Cross............323-7370/3
Bahamas Sickle Cell Assoc (Dr Patrick Roberts) 328-8085
Business & Professional Women's Club of NP (Sheila Stubbs) ....393-2224 or 502-6620
Canadian Men's Club (Thomas Muir)..................324-4495 or 323-1048/9
Canadian Women's Club (Carolyn Merk) 324-0377
Cancer Society of The Bahamas 323-4482
Crippled Children's Committee........................328-6147
The Crisis Centre 328-0922
Drugs & AIDS Hotline 322-2308/9

Hispanic Women's Club
(Hellen Norat-Crespo) 327-5619
Innerwheel Club of
East Nassau
(Sandra Kemp)..................393-6729
Innerwheel Club of Nassau
(Flora Sawyer) 322-8210
or 326-0937
(Cindy Wilde)....................322-4782
Jugs Inc
(Lana Deal) 341-2462
Kidney Foundation of
The Bahamas
(Dr Ada Thompson) 322-4281
Kiwanis Clubs of:
Cable Beach; Fort Montagu;
Nassau; Nassau, AM;
New Providence;
Over-the-Hill
(Roy Davis)........................394-4354
Lions Club
(Mike Martinborough) 324-5158
Nassau Amateur Operatic
Society
(Amanda Meyers) 364-0677
Nassau Chapter of
Links Inc
(Dorothy Philips) 323-4880
Nassau Music Society
(Patrick Thomson) 327-7668
National Drug Council........325-4633/4
National Pan-Hellenic
Council, Inc
(Cindy Williams) 322-6209
Pilot Club of Nassau
(Marjorie "Sue" Munroe)....364-0463
Rotary Clubs of:
East Nassau, Nassau,
Southeast Nassau,
West Nassau
(Rotary recorded info line) ..325-5906
Samaritan Ministry
(Sis Clare Rolle) 323-5517
Scout Assoc of The Bahamas
(Winston Newton) 325-2757
Teen Challenge 341-0829
or 341-0613
Toastmasters Intl
(Roderick Colebrook) 363-2000
ext 65613
or 457-4157
Training Centre for
the Disabled......................323-3808
Women's Corona Society
in The Bahamas
(Carmelita Hall) 327-5053
Young Women's Christian
Assoc (YWCA) 323-3149
or (Lady Fawkes) 328-3777
Zonta Club of Nassau
(Tonya Galanis) 326-8507

Many of these phone numbers are office numbers of volunteer individuals and are subject to change.

COMPANY FORMATION

In order to incorporate a company in The Bahamas, a copy of the Memorandum of Association must be filed with the Registrar General.

The Memorandum should be signed by a minimum of two subscribers and witnessed by an additional person. The witness will have to sign and swear to an affidavit stating that the two subscribers signed the Memorandum in his presence.

A subscriber who is not a resident of The Bahamas, or his nominee, must get permission from the controller of exchange. Such permission is usually not difficult to obtain.

There is a filing fee of $300 for each Memorandum of Association. The Memorandum gives the company name and its authorized capital (if limited by shares). It must also state the part of The Bahamas in which the registered office is proposed to be situated.

Articles of association may be filed with the Memorandum of the company at the time of incorporation, or within six months thereof, for a fee of $30. The incorporators may adopt the "ready-made" articles embodied in the first schedule of the Companies Act. If no articles are submitted within the six-month period, those listed in the first schedule are adopted. The articles should be signed by a minimum of two subscribers and witnessed by an additional person.

Before a company is incorporated, its proposed name must be approved – by phone if one wishes – by the Registrar General as meeting requirements laid down in the Companies Act, 1992, The Business Names Act, The Banks and Trust Companies Regulation Act, and The Insurance Act.

Stamp duty is payable on authorized capital and any further increases. For every Memorandum of Association of a company where the capital is up to and including $5,000, duty is $60. For every additional $1,000, or fraction thereof, the duty is $3.

If the authorized capital is increased after incorporation, additional fees are payable to the Treasury on filing the resolutions. An increase of $6 is payable for every $1,000 increase or fraction thereof.

An annual licence fee of $350 is payable for a registered company in which Bahamians beneficially own 60% or more of the shares. If Bahamians beneficially own less than 60% of the shares, the company must pay an annual fee of $1,000. The fee should be paid by Jan 1 of each year but payment may be up to 30 days later in some cases.

Non-profit companies under the provisions of section 14 of the Companies Act, 1992, do not have to pay an annual fee and their stamp duty is reduced to $5.

Foreign or overseas companies

To be registered under the provisions of the Companies Act, 1992, a company must have been incorporated outside The Bahamas and must deposit with the Registrar General particulars about the company and a copy of documents of incorporation certified and authenticated under public seal of the country under whose laws it has been incorporated.

Stamp duty for a foreign company is $600 and the registration fee is $50. All foreign companies registered under this section must pay an annual fee of $1,000.

Requirements for all companies

All companies must file with the Registrar General copies of the names of all company officers, directors and managers and a registered office address. In the case of banks, proper records must be kept and annual statements showing the bank's true financial position must be published in *The Gazette*.

Every company which has its capital divided into shares must file an annual return at the Registry, containing the following information:

1. A list of company members stating the names, addresses and occupations of all members mentioned and the number of shares held by each.
2. Amount of the company's capital and number of shares into which it is divided.
3. Number of shares taken from the formation of the company up to the date of summary.
4. Amount of calls made on shares.
5. Amount of calls received.
6. Amount of calls unpaid.
7. Amount of shares forfeited.
8. Names, addresses and occupations of persons who have ceased to be members since the last list was compiled and number of shares held by each.
9. The registered number of the company.

Companies, except those registered under section 14 of the Companies Act, 1992 (non-profit companies), must send the Registrar General a list of the names, addresses and occupations of its directors or managers and must give any subsequent changes which take place in such officers and directors.

Every company registered under the Companies Act, 1992, must forward to the Registrar General, before Jan 1 in each year after the year in which the company first commenced business, a return declaring whether or not 60% of its shares are beneficially owned by Bahamians.

Companies may be public or private. Public companies are those in which shares are to be offered to the general public. These companies are governed by the Securities Industry Act, 1998. Such companies must submit a prospectus or statement containing specific information as required by the Act in relation to the company's operations. All other companies are private. Companies must hold a statutory meeting every year, and one must be held within three months from the date the company is incorporated. Meetings may be held outside The Bahamas.

The Central Bank may allow a company to be incorporated with its capital expressed in a foreign currency and to conduct its affairs in that currency. However, the Bahamian dollar equivalent must be expressed in the Memorandum of Association. Application for such approval should be submitted to the Central Bank, PO Box N-4868, Nassau, The Bahamas, tel (242) 322-2193, fax (242) 322-4321.

International Business Company (IBC)

An IBC may be incorporated in The Bahamas within 24 hours from the time the proper documents arrive at the Registrar General's Dept. In urgent cases, it may be incorporated within 20 mins while waiting. Electronic incorporation of IBCs was introduced in Feb 2003, and is available through licensed financial and corporate service providers. Register an IBC name by:

1. Visiting the Registry of Companies, Shirley House, Shirley St, Mon-Fri 9:30am-4:30pm, or
2. Telephoning the company name reservation service, Mon-Fri 9:30am-4:30pm. Tel (242) 322-7147 or 322-7160, fax (242) 322-5553, or
3. Writing to Registrar General's Dept, PO Box N-532, Nassau, The Bahamas.

Approval will be given immediately if the name is available. Confirmation within New Providence is faxed and confirmed by mail and e-mail; confirmation overseas and in Freeport is by mail. Documents of incorporation should then be submitted for registration with the incorporation fee. IBC fees are $330 (Memorandum of Association $300 and Articles of Association $30) where the authorized capital is less than $50,000, and $1,000 when authorized capital exceeds $50,000. Incorporation documents must include the memorandum of association and the articles of association.

Documents of incorporation are then inspected. If approved, a certificate of incorporation will be issued within 24 hours from the time the documents arrive at the Registry. If urgent, it may be issued within 20 mins.

Where an IBC is registered by Dec 31 of any year, an annual licence fee must be paid to the Registrar General by Apr 30 of the following year.

A company incorporated under the Companies Act, 1992, or incorporated outside of The Bahamas may apply to continue in The Bahamas as a company incorporated under the IBC Act if it meets the Act's provisions. Contact the Registrar General's Dept, Registry of Companies, PO Box N-532, Nassau, The Bahamas, tel (242) 322-8038, fax (242) 322-5553.

IBCs are exempt from exchange control regulations in The Bahamas if operations are intended to be exclusively overseas. For an IBC to do business in The Bahamas with Bahamians, Exchange Control approval must be obtained from the Central Bank. Other advantages are:

1. No minimum capital required.
2. Only two shareholders.
3. Shares may be issued with and without par value.
4. Director or directors or registered agent may be individuals or corporations, banks or trust companies. The registered agent must be based in The Bahamas.
5. An IBC may transfer assets in trust for the benefit of its creditors, shareholders or other persons having an interest.
6. IBCs may be limited by shares or guarantee, or "unlimited."

See also **Banking, International Business Companies Act, 2000.**

Limited Duration Company (LDC)

The Limited Duration Company (LDC), a hybrid of the IBC, is basically structured like the IBC except that the "life" of the company is limited to 30 years or less. The company name must also state its LDC status. The transfer of a share or interest of a member requires the unanimous resolution of all other members if stipulated in the articles of the company. The articles may also provide for certain members to manage the company based on their share or other ownership interest. Properly structured, the LDC can have the characteristics of a partnership and be treated as such for tax purposes in the US.

Exempted Limited Partnership (ELP)

The ELP allows the character of a normal partnership to be structured to provide more flexibility in transacting business. Like the IBC, the ELP is free to carry on every lawful business anywhere in the world except that it cannot transact business with the public in The Bahamas. However, this does not specifically preclude doing business with IBCs or foreign companies registered in The Bahamas under the Companies Act, 1992.

An ELP must have one or more general partners who assume responsibility for all debts and obligations of the partnership in the event the assets of the partnership are inadequate, and at least one limited partner. A general partner may also have an interest as a limited partner. Partners may be from anywhere, although at least one general partner must be a Bahamas resident or incorporated under the IBC Act, 2000, or Companies Act, 1992, of The Bahamas. Under the Exempted Limited Partnership Act, 1995, every ELP must have a registered office in The Bahamas and must be registered with the Registrar of Companies.

Certain disclosures must be made as to the general nature of business of the ELP (eg, investments) and the names and addresses of general partners. Certain subsequent changes in the nature of the partnership must be filed with the Registrar.

An ELP is exempt for 50 years from the issuance of the certificate of registration from any business licence fee, stamp duty, income tax, capital gains tax or any other tax on income or distributions. It is also exempt from provisions of the Exchange Control Regulations Act, except where a partner is a resident of The Bahamas for exchange control purposes. Partners, their executors or administrators, are also exempt from any estate, inheritance, succession or gift tax on any interest in the partnership.

Copies of the legislation referred to in this article may be obtained for a small fee from Government Publications, PO Box N-7147, Nassau, The Bahamas, tel (242) 322-2410.

See also **Business licence fee, Business name registration, Exchange control** and **Investing.**

CONSTITUTION

When independence from the UK was achieved on July 10, 1973, a constitution representing the supreme law of the land went into effect for the Commonwealth of The Bahamas.

The constitution proclaims The Bahamas as a sovereign democratic state, establishes requirements for citizenship and guarantees fundamental human rights such as freedom of conscience, expression and assembly. It also protects the privacy of the home and prohibits deprivation of property without compensation and/or due process of law.

The Bahamas retains its ties with the Commonwealth of Nations and also retains the British monarch as its head of state. The Queen is represented in The Bahamas by a Governor General who is appointed and serves at Her Majesty's pleasure.

There is a bicameral Parliament consisting of a Senate and a House of Assembly. The Senate has 16 members, nine appointed by the Governor General on the advice of the prime minister, four on the advice of the leader of the opposition and three on the advice of the prime minister after consultation with the leader of the opposition. This arrangement provides for the opposition to have no less than four members in the Senate and to claim up to three more based on its numerical strength in the House of Assembly.

The House of Assembly must have at least 38 elected members. This number may be increased on the recommendation of the Constituencies Commission, which is charged with reviewing electoral boundaries at least every five years. Present membership is 40.

The executive branch consists of a Cabinet of at least nine members, including the prime minister and the Attorney-General. All ministers must be Members of Parliament and the prime minister and the Minister of Finance must be members of the House of Assembly. Up to three ministers can be appointed from among the Senators.

An independent judiciary, including a Supreme Court and a Court of Appeal is provided for, along with the right of appeal to Her Majesty's Privy Council.

Also provided under the constitution are a Public Service Commission, Public Service Board of Appeal, a Judicial and Legal Service Commission and a Police Service Commission.

The constitution can be amended by an Act of Parliament but there are two categories of provisions – entrenched and specially entrenched – which can be amended only by prescribed voting formulas and with approval by the electorate in a referendum.

The entrenched provisions include those relating to establishment of the public service and qualifications for Members of Parliament. These provisions can be amended only by a two-thirds majority vote in both houses of Parliament and by referendum.

The specially entrenched provisions relate to citizenship, fundamental rights, establishment and powers of Parliament, the Cabinet and the judiciary. These can be amended only by a three-quarters majority vote in Parliament and by referendum.

The first referendum for Bahamian constitutional reform was held on Feb 27, 2002. The five proposed amendments to the 1973 constitution, which were passed by the House of Assembly and the Senate, sought to: remove all forms of discrimination against Bahamian women with regard to their ability to pass nationality to their children and spouses; entrench in the constitution a Teaching Service Commission; entrench in the constitution the position of an Independent Parliamentary Commissioner; create an independent Boundaries Commission; and increase the retirement ages of judges of the Supreme Court and Court of Appeal. All proposals were rejected.

A constitution review commission has been established to review and amend the constitution.

CONSUMER PROTECTION

The Dept of Consumer Welfare, within the Ministry of Trade and Industry, is committed to protecting consumers from exploitation and ensuring controls and standards are enforced.

The three main areas for consumer protection are availability, price and quality, with the government responsible for providing the legislative and environmental framework under which adequate and effective competition is encouraged.

Government efforts to ensure a wide range of choice for goods and services are considered more effective than legislative price control, as the consumer becomes the regulator.

The government has initiated consumer protection programmes with the main thrust on competition and consumer choice and awareness. However, as long as price control remains in force as a mechanism of consumer protection, it will be enforced and any infractions prosecuted. Deliberate overpricing of goods may result in:

1. A fine not exceeding $5,000 or imprisonment for a term not exceeding 12 months.
2. Seizure of overpriced goods for donation to charity.

A significant aspect of consumer protection is the development of a national system of standards, quality control and quality assurance involving relevant government agencies.

The Consumer Action Line deals with complaints involving all aspects of consumer rights such as price control, faulty goods, and problems with rents and utility corporations. Mediation and moral persuasion are used to reach a mutually acceptable solution.

The Consumer Advocacy Group publishes *Consumerism Today*, a monthly education booklet. Speaker's Corner is a programme administered by the Dept of Consumer Welfare through schools, service clubs and church groups to educate the public on their rights as consumers.

COPYRIGHT LAWS

The Copyright Act, 1998, was enacted on Jan 4, 2000. It repeals the Copyright Act, 1956, on which it is based. The new Act introduces a Copyright Royalty Tribunal which advises on royalty rates and receives and disburses payments. A Copyright Registry, overseen by a registrar of copyright, receives applications, registers claims and issues certificates of registration. However, copyright is not dependent on registration.

Creative works must be classified under one of five categories in order to be protected. They are: non-dramatic literary works, works of the performing arts, works of visual arts, sound and recordings, and serial works including periodicals, newspapers, journals and proceedings. Under the Act, only the author, other copyright claimants, the owner of exclusive rights or their authorized agents may reproduce, distribute, prepare derivatives of, perform, or display copyrighted works.

The new Act adheres to the international standard for copyright duration – life plus 70 years. It imposes fines and allows copyright owners to sue unauthorized users of their work.

Although previous copyright laws in The Bahamas contained the ingredients for general copyright protection, they did not cover modern concerns such as computer-generated work and digital transmissions. The new Act brings The Bahamas to world standards and is an important concern in the signing of future international agreements.

COST OF LIVING

Food, autos and some items of clothing are comparatively expensive in Nassau because of freight and customs duties.

Residents are billed monthly for electricity charges and quarterly for water charges. Telephone rental is on a monthly basis. The average deposit for electrical service varies with home size and location, ranging from $200 to more than $1,500, with about $300 as average. Telephone deposits range from $50-$500 for landlords, and $150-$1,000 for tenants. A $55 water deposit is required for buildings with one water closet or bathroom and $115 for those with two or more.

Virtually all homes and apartments for rent or sale are basically furnished. Rents vary according to location and season. Summer is the best time for apartment hunting.

In general, an efficiency apartment rents monthly on a one-year lease for $500-$1,000; one bdrm, $500 and up; two bdrms, $700-$6,000. A two-bdrm detached house can rent for $1,200-$5,000. A three-bdrm detached house or condo rents for $2,500-$8,000 per month depending upon location. Short-term leases usually include utilities. Rent is higher for short-term leases.

Building costs for an average three-bdrm house – living room, dining room, kitchen, bath and patio – are a minimum of $110 per sq ft, which comes to $165,000 for a 1,500 sq ft home. The price varies according to materials used, building standards and area. According to a Nassau builder, Lyford Cay building costs range from $250-$450 and higher per sq ft.

Medical care and dentistry can be less costly than in the US. An out-patient clinic at Princess Margaret Hospital in Nassau is available at $10 per visit for residents and $30 for non-residents – but you may wait several hours for treatment. Specialists' office calls average $150-$350. At Princess Margaret Hospital a bed on the public ward is $30 a day, plus expenses. Private rooms are $80 with a bathroom, and $70 without, per day. Semi-private rooms are $65 and $70 with a bathroom, per day. At Doctors Hospital rooms are $570 private and $495 semi-private, per day. Round-the-clock nurses are included in the cost at Doctors Hospital.

New Providence has well-stocked supermarkets carrying US brands as well as a range of name brands from other countries.

New Providence prices (August 2004)
Grocery items

½ gal Fieldcrest milk....................$2.99
1 doz extra large eggs $1.55
6 oz Starkist chunk white tuna
  in spring water........................$0.79
4 lbs (1.8 kg) Evercane sugar $1.57
5 lbs Robin Hood
  all purpose flour......................$2.39
Dial antibacterial
  deodorant soap (3 bar pack) $2.47
16 oz Oscar Mayer sliced bacon $5.79
1 lb ground beef $3.32
1 lb Barilla spaghetti....................$1.69
8 oz Nescafé classic $4.49
8 oz Nescafé decaf......................$4.49
100 Lipton Yellow Label tea bags....$6.50
32 oz Kraft mayonnaise $3.05
5 lbs potatoes $3.99
1 head Romaine lettuce $3.99
1 lb premium tomatoes $2.39
½ gal Haagen Dazs ice cream $18.69
1 lb Fleischmann's
  soft margarine $1.78
8 oz Axelrod
  plain low-fat yogurt $0.99
1 loaf Roman Meal
  whole wheat bread $2.85
1 gal Aquapure water $1.25
1 case Coca-Cola sodas $11.59
10 lbs Uncle Ben's rice $5.45
87 oz Tide (with bleach)...........$10.19
8 oz Kraft salad dressing $2.19
64 oz Tropicana orange juice
  not from concentrate $5.49
14½ oz Carnation
  evaporated milk $0.74
½ lb Fern Leaf butter $0.77
1 lb onions.................................$1.39
18 oz Kellogg's Corn Flakes $4.39
8 oz Kraft cheddar cheese (sharp)..$2.59

Other items & services

1 pack filter cigarettes ......$2.20-$4.25
The New York Times (Sun) $8.00
1 litre (33.8 oz)
  Tanqueray gin $17.95
1 litre Bacardi rum $8.95
1 litre Drambuie........................$31.95
1 litre Absolut vodka $13.95
1 case beer (Kalik) $36.80
1 case beer
  (Coors & Coors light) $38.10
1 case premium beer
  (Heineken) $42.55
Shampoo and set* $25
Manicure*....................................$25
Men's haircut* $25
Women's haircut* ....$25-$30
1 US gal Esso Optima IV gasoline
  (premium unleaded)................$3.28
Dry cleaning:
  1 dress $8.50
  1 men's suit $8.50

** Prices may vary*

COTONOU AGREEMENT

With the expiration of Lomé IV, a new partnership was successfully concluded between the European Union (EU) and African Caribbean Pacific (ACP) States. The new 20-year pact, the Cotonou Agreement, was signed on June 23, 2000, in Cotonou, Benin, and comes into force after ratification by two-thirds of the ACP countries. The countries of the EU had not completed the process at press time. The new agreement was to take effect by Jan 1, 2008, unless earlier dates are agreed upon between partners. It combines politics, trade and development, based on five interdependent pillars:

1. A comprehensive political dimension to address all issues of mutual concern and to ensure consistency and increased impact of development cooperation.
2. The promotion of participation to ensure the involvement of civil society and the economic and social players.
3. A strengthened focus on poverty reduction that will guide development strategies tailored to

the situation of each ACP country.

4. The setting up of a new framework for economic and trade cooperation to promote the smooth and gradual integration of ACP economies into the world economy and enhance cooperation in all areas of trade.
5. A reform of financial cooperation in which the allocation of funds will be assessed not only on each country's need, but also on its policy performance.

The Bahamas has completed its internal process and on Feb 6, 2003 signed both the National Indicative Programme and the Bahamas Support Strategy Paper. The EU was represented by HE Jerd Jarchow and Adelayo Babijide of the European Commission in Kingston, Jamaica.

Contact the Ministry of Trade and Industry, Manx Corporate Centre, West Bay St, PO Box N-4849, Nassau, tel 328-2700 (to 5), fax 328-1324.

COURIER SERVICES

Four major international courier companies and several smaller ones serve New Providence and the Out Islands.

DHL Worldwide Express 394-4040
Federal Express ....322-5656 (to 8)
GWS 322-8907
UPS 393-3795

It costs $10-$15.37 to send a package under 2 lbs to Freeport, $18-$24.13 to Miami, $26.50-$32.86 to New York, and $36.50-$43.22 to London, England.

See also **Postal information.**

CRIME

The Royal Bahamas Police Force is employed throughout The Bahamas for maintenance of law and order, preservation of peace, prevention and detection of crime, apprehension of offenders and enforcement of all laws with which it is charged. The government has undertaken to improve police performance with a number of measures which include increasing the vehicle fleet, improving communications and boosting numbers in the ranks by implementing ongoing recruitment programmes. The strength of the Royal Bahamas Police Force at Dec 2003 stood at 3,352.

In Jan 2001, the police force began a division-wide community policing programme in New Providence to improve services through communication among neighbours and between the general public and the police.

A consultative board, made up of residents and local business owners, focuses on crime prevention methods and community safety issues. These representatives act as the liaison between the community and the police. Since its inception, relationships between the police and communities have improved, crime level has decreased and significant flow of intelligence has resulted in the arrests of a number of fugitives.

In 2002 the Farm Road Safe Community Project was launched. The police, assisted by government agencies, surveyed all residents to identify their social, economic and environmental needs. Buildings in dilapidated condition were demolished, derelict vehicles carried away and overgrown lots cleared, resulting in a reduction in crime. Because of the programme's success, it has been adopted by several neighbouring communities and was introduced at the 18th annual conference of the Association of Caribbean Commissioners, held in Bermuda in May 2003. The project received an award from Motorola and other regions in the Caribbean are now implementing similar programmes.

The government has provided funds to fully integrate the criminal justice system, provide secure communications, and computerize the police control room and patrol cars to help in the fight against crime. The government has entered into an agreement with CDR International of London to establish a permanent detective training school as part of the existing police college to better train and equip detectives and the police force as a whole. As part of the devolution process, Divisional Detective units are being established to provide more effective police services.

In Sept 2000, a policy geared to the prevention, detection and treatment of corruption, dishonesty and unethical behaviour was publicly launched. It is intended to reduce the incidence of unethical and corrupt behaviour in the police force.

The statute laws of The Bahamas provide for the execution of convicted murderers by hanging. There are currently 32 inmates on death row. In 1996, The Bahamas witnessed its first hanging in 12 years. At press time the latest hanging was on Thurs, Jan 6, 2000.

The homicide rate decreased by 4% in 2003. There were 50 recorded homicides compared to 52 in 2002. Of the 50, 34 were solved, demonstrating a detection rate of 68%, a decrease from 2002. In 2003, 24% of homicides were domestic, a decrease of 60% from 2002. Firearms accounted for 46% of weapons used.

During 2003, 194 firearms and other illegal devices, including imitation weapons and 1,320 rounds of ammunition were confiscated from the streets of The Bahamas.

While dangerous drugs transiting The Bahamas are not reflected on the streets of the nation, hard-core users of cocaine, crack and marijuana are responsible for a disproportionate number of crimes, particularly robberies, burglaries, thefts and house and shop break-ins.

The Bahamas enjoys diplomatic relationships with many countries and the Royal Bahamas Police Force cooperates with law enforcement agencies of these countries and is a member of INTERPOL. The Bahamas also has extradition treaties with many countries.

See also **Drugs, Extradition, Judicial system** and **Royal Bahamas Police Force.**

CRUISE SHIPS

The cruise ship industry plays a vital role in bringing visitors to The Bahamas. They bring more than a million people, mostly Americans and Europeans, to Nassau alone each year.

Some modern cruise ships can carry more than 3,000 passengers.

Fri, Sat, Mon and Tues are the busiest days for cruise ship arrivals in the port of Nassau, with some seven ships in port on Sat alone.

Cruise ships that call most frequently at the port of Nassau are *Disney Wonder, Enchantment of The Seas, Explorer of The Seas, Fantasy, Fascination, Majesty of The Seas, Millennium, Norwegian Majesty, Regal Empress* and *Sovereign of the Seas.*

See also **Ports of entry.**

Cruise ship incentives

In 1995, Parliament passed the Cruise Ship (Overnighting Incentives) Act, granting concessions to encourage tourism in The Bahamas. The Act allows cruise ships docked at Prince George Dock for at least 18 hours, or travelling to or from Bahamian designated ports, to operate casinos, shops and sell liquor, 7pm-3am.

The Act also provides discounts on port tax. Cruise ship lines transporting up to 400,000 passengers per year to The Bahamas are charged the regular fee of $15 per person. For every passenger over this 400,000 quota, not exceeding 500,000, the cruise line pays $10 per person. For every passenger exceeding 500,000 in the course of a year, the cruise line pays $5 per person.

See also **Customs, Departure tax, Gambling, Hotels encouragement** and **Shopping.**

CRUISING FACILITIES

See **Marinas & cruising facilities** and **Freeport/Lucaya information, Marinas.**

CULTURE & CULTURAL ACTIVITIES

See **Art galleries, Entertainment, Junkanoo, Museums, National anthem, National symbols** and **Theatre & performing arts.**

CURRENCY

Legal currency of The Bahamas is the Bahamian dollar, although the US dollar is accepted throughout the islands. The Bahamian dollar is on par with the US dollar.

The Canadian dollar was worth approx B$0.7493 and the pound sterling approx B$1.8224 on Aug 27, 2004.

CUSTOMS

Generally, the *ad valorem* (of the value) tariff for imported goods is 35%, clothing 25%, and underwear 15%.

For customs purposes the value includes the cost of the goods, ocean or air freight, insurance – cost/insurance/freight (cif) – and all other charges incidental to their importation.

Some items have a higher tariff, such as fine cut tobacco 160%, pool tables 100%, automobiles 45-75%, car parts and accessories 50%, cigarettes containing tobacco 210%. A 7% stamp duty is also payable on these goods.

Some staple food items have a low duty tariff, including cheese 10%, pasta 10% and potatoes nil. In addition to duty, there is a 2% stamp duty on food.

There are no customs duties on the most popular tourist items: china, crystal, fine jewellery, leather, crocheted linens and tablecloths, liquor, perfume and cologne, photographic equipment and accessories, sweaters and watches. However, variable stamp duty is applicable to those duty-free products imported to The Bahamas, as follows:

Duty-free goods stamp duty (% of value)

China, crystal, cameras, sweaters (wool, cashmere or Angora) and photographic accessories ..8%
Wristwatches and clocks with watch movements 10%
Fine jewellery and fine jewellery incorporating pearls, precious and semi-precious stones........10%
Crocheted table linens and table linens 10%
Leather goods 20%
Perfume, cologne and toilet waters 20%
Still and sparkling wines............50%
* Brandy, gin, rum, vodka and whiskey.............$10 per Imperial gal
* Cordials, liqueurs and other spirits ....$10 per Imperial gal

* *If goods being imported are for processes carried on at any Bahamas distillery or brewery, 7% (stamp duty) of the value of the goods is paid.*

Customs duty on vehicles varies – according to value and intended use – from 45-75% of the cif value of the vehicle. Duty on new and used motor vehicles valued at less than $10,000 is 45%, more than $10,000 and less than $20,000 is 50%, more than $20,000 and less than $25,000 is 65%. New and used motor vehicles valued at more than $25,000 carry a rate of duty of 75%. Motor vehicles for the transport of 10 or more persons, including the driver, carry a 45% rate of duty and golf carts, 20%.

See also **Boating, Duty on Boats.**

Stamp duty

There is usually a 7% stamp duty of the cif value of imported goods requiring an entry (with the exception of those items previously indicated).

There is also a $10 stamp duty on exports. An additional fee is added for the export of crawfish.

Duty exemptions

Certain items may be imported exempt from customs duty, including:

1. All goods imported with the prior approval of the Minister of Finance by a charitable organization to be used exclusively for charitable purposes.
2. Models, teaching aids, sound recordings, scientific apparatus and materials to be used exclusively for the purpose of scientific or cultural institutions, if approved by the Minister of Finance.
3. Certain church goods, including musical equipment, service supplies and adornments, upon submission and approval of an application to the Comptroller of Customs.

Additional information on customs duty and exemptions may be found in the Tariff Act, 1996. Copies may be obtained from Government Publications, Old Lighthouse Bldg, Bay St, PO Box N-7147, Nassau, The Bahamas, tel (242) 322-2410.

Duty-free importation

Certain items are customs duty free, but a 7% stamp duty is charged on the cif value. These include:

1. Orthopaedic appliances, surgical belts, trusses etc; splints and other fracture appliances; artificial limbs, eyes, teeth and other artificial body parts; hearing aids and other appliances worn, carried or implanted to compensate for a defect or disability.
2. Paintings, drawings and pastels executed entirely by hand other than industrial drawings or hand-printed manufactured articles.
3. Antiques over 100 years. Proof of age from a recognized antique association required.
4. Television cameras, still image recorders, video camera recorders and computers, parts and accessories.

Temporary importation

Certain goods may be imported on a temporary basis against a security bond or deposit, equal to the prescribed duty on the goods, which is refunded when the items are exported. In addition to payment of the prescribed fees, an import duty of 7% and stamp duty of 4%, which are not refundable on re-exportation, are also paid. Prior approval for this must be obtained from the Ministry of Finance for which an application should be made to the Comptroller of Customs, Customs House, Thompson Blvd, PO Box N-155, Nassau, The Bahamas, tel (242) 326-4401. Temporary items can include:

1. Any fine jewellery, approved as such by the Comptroller of Customs, imported on consignment for a period of six months.
2. Goods for business meetings or conventions for a period up to one month after the meeting or convention is over.
3. Travelling salesman's samples, approved by the Comptroller of Customs, for up to three months. The salesperson must have a valid Immigration permit.
4. Automobiles or motorcycles brought into the country by a *bona fide* visitor for not more than six months, provided the vehicle will not be used for commercial purposes while in The Bahamas. Only one permit per family may be issued during any calendar year.
5. Photographic and cinematographic equipment belonging to members of the foreign press, radio, TV or motion picture services, as well as clothes and props belonging to actors and actresses accompanying these services, for up to 90 days upon approval of the Ministry of Tourism and Ministry of Finance. Application for an extension of temporary importation may be made to the Minister of Finance.
6. Any goods such as special tools for repair work or testing equipment.

Import & export entry requirements

For clearance of commercial imports via air and sea cargo/freight, a completed entry (four copies) is required. Imports by sea are released to the importer on presentation of forms processed at Customs House, Thompson Blvd. For goods by air, entry forms are presented to the customs officer in the Air Express building at Nassau International Airport. Similar facilities also exist at Out Island ports of entry. A formal entry is required for clearance of commercial shipments imported via parcel post, air or sea. Commercial goods imported by parcel post with a value of less than $500 require no entry.

Goods may be cleared through Customs without proper invoices by provisional entry. The importer leaves a deposit sufficient to cover duty (usually double the estimated duty of the imports), with the understanding that when the invoices arrive, the provisional entry must be adjusted. The residue of the deposit made is refunded after payment of the proper duty amount. Payment in a foreign currency for goods imported to The Bahamas may be arranged by a Bahamas bank after presentation of approval by Exchange Control.

There is a 7% stamp duty on the value of imported goods, except inexpensive gifts (up to $100) arriving by post. See **Export entry.**

Importing possessions

A person settling in The Bahamas as a resident pays duty on household effects, eg, furniture, china and appliances. Most personal effects such as clothing and articles of personal adornment already in use and possession are not dutiable if imported as accompanied passenger baggage.

Duty-free quotas for visitors to The Bahamas

Visitors may bring in certain items free of customs and stamp duty. They include:

1. Apparel, toilet articles and similar personal effects.
2. One qt of alcoholic beverage; one qt of wine; one lb in weight of tobacco or 200 cigarettes or 50 cigars (adults only).
3. Any other articles up to the value of $100.

Duty-free quotas for returning Bahamians and residents

A Bahamian through birth or naturalization, or a person granted permission by the Immigration Dept to reside in The Bahamas and who has been in residence for over one year, may return from two trips abroad annually with duty-free goods worth up to $300 (does not apply to children under age 12). A resident who has been abroad for more than one year may bring in $500 worth of goods duty free. No stamp duty is payable in either situation.

Duty-free quotas for Bahamas residents going abroad

US: Bahamians and Bahamas residents visiting the US are entitled to bring in up to $200 worth of merchandise duty free for personal or household use. This exemption may include 200 cigarettes, 50 cigars (Cuban cigars are prohibited), 150ml of perfume containing alcohol, and if the person is 21 years or over, one litre of alcohol (of any origin other than Cuba).

As well as the $200 personal exemption, visitors may bring in to the US, once every six months, duty-free gifts worth up to $100. These gifts may not include alcoholic beverages, but may include 100 cigars (Cuban cigars are prohibited). To take advantage of this $100 gift exemption, the visitor must remain in the US at least 72 hours. Family members may not combine their gift exemptions.

Canada: Bahamians or Bahamas residents may take with them on a visit to Canada duty free, apart from personal effects, any number of gifts valued up to CDN$40 provided these gifts are not advertising matter. For personal use, persons 16 or older may take in 200 cigarettes, 50 cigars and 7oz of tobacco. Up to 40 oz of liquor may be brought in for personal use provided the individual meets the age requirement of the province or territory through which he enters Canada.

UK: Those visiting the UK from The Bahamas (or from outside the EU) may take in, free of duty and tax, 200 cigarettes or 100 cigarillos or 50 cigars or 250g of tobacco. Alcohol and alcoholic beverage allowance:

Still table wine........................two litres

and

Spirits or strong liqueurs over 22% alcohol by volume................one litre

or

Fortified or sparkling wine, and other liqueurs..............two litres

These allowances are not for persons under 17. The allowance for perfume is 60ml toilet water, 250ml and £145 sterling worth of other goods including gifts and souvenirs.

All other goods
Goods brought into the UK worth more than £145 sterling will have duty charged on the full value, not just on the value over £145 sterling. Rates of duty and tax are complicated and change from time to time so it is advisable to check with your airline or travel agent for current regulations when making reservations.

Duty-free quotas for visitors leaving The Bahamas

US residents: Each US resident (including a minor) may take home duty-free purchases up to US$600 in retail value if he or she has been outside the US more than 48 hours and has not taken the exemption in 30 days. The exemption may include up to two litres (67.6 oz) of liquor per person 21 or older, provided one litre is manufactured in The Bahamas or another CBI (Caribbean Basin Initiative) country; 200 cigarettes; and 100 cigars (Cuban cigars not allowed) per person 18 or older. A single household family travelling together may pool exemptions, ie, a family of four may take home US$2,400 worth of goods.

Articles up to US$1,000 value accompanying the traveller, in excess of the US$600 duty-free allowance, are assessed at a flat rate of 3%. For example, a family of four would prepare a joint declaration for goods purchased for US$4,500. Each family member would be eligible for a US$600 exemption, for a total of US$2,400. The remaining US$2,100 would be assessed at a duty rate of 3%. Thus, total duty for the purchases from this trip would be US$63. You may not apply the flat rate more than once every 30 days.

If the returning US resident is not entitled to the US$600 duty exemption due to the 30-day or 48-hour minimum limitations, he or she may still import, duty free, US$200 worth of personal or household items. This exemption may not be pooled.

Articles purchased in US duty-free shops and brought back into the US may not be included in your exemption and are dutiable.

One person, on one day, may receive a shipment of goods purchased in The Bahamas and sent to an address in the US so long as the value does not exceed US$200. The shipment will be passed free of duty by US Customs, unless there is reason to believe the shipment is one of several lots of a single order. Supporting documents are required.

Antiques, food, trade marks, US money

Antiques are admitted to the US duty free provided they are over 100 years old. The Bahamas store selling an antique should provide the buyer with a form indicating the value and age of the object. The buyer must present this form to US Customs.

Importation of fruit, plants, meat, poultry and dairy products is generally prohibited. There are, however, exceptions. Contact the Customs and Border Protection (CBP), Nassau International Airport, tel 377-7127.

More than $10,000 in US or foreign coin, currency, traveller's cheques, money orders and negotiable instruments or investment securities in bearer form must be reported to Customs. It is not illegal to transport or cause to be transported any amount into or out of the US, but more than $10,000 must be reported on Customs Form 4790, available at all US ports of entry.

Certain items carrying a trade mark or trade name may be brought into the US in specified amounts only, or not at all. Importation of Bahamian tortoise or turtle shell goods is prohibited. Many medicines sold over the counter in The Bahamas are not allowed entry.

For a copy of *Know Before You Go,* contact CBP, Nassau International Airport, tel 377-7126. Or contact the CBP, 1300 Pennsylvania Ave NW, Washington, DC 20229.

Canadian residents: A Canadian may take advantage of one of three categories of duty-free exemptions. If he or she has been out of Canada for 24 hours, he may make a verbal declaration to claim a CDN$50 duty-free allowance any number of times per year, which would not include alcohol or tobacco. If he or she has been out of the country for 48 hours any number of times per year, a written declaration must be made; he may claim a CDN$200 allowance which could include up to 200 cigarettes, 50 cigars and two lbs tobacco, and 40 oz alcohol.

Anyone who has been out of Canada seven days or more, any number of times per year, may make a written declaration and claim the CDN$750 exemption, including the amounts of alcohol and tobacco indicated for the CDN$200 allowance.

In general, the goods brought in under personal exemption must be for personal or household use, as souvenirs of the trip or as gifts for friends or relatives. Goods brought in for commercial use, or on behalf of another person, do not qualify and will be subject to full duties. Goods declared in a child's name must be for his or her use only.

For the importation of tobacco, the claimant must be over 16. In the case of liquor, wine or beer, the person must have attained the age prescribed by the provincial or territorial authority at the point of entry.

Goods acquired in The Bahamas or elsewhere outside continental North America may be shipped or mailed separately if declared at the first port of entry.

UK residents: Same allowances as Bahamian residents visiting the UK. See **Duty-free quotas for Bahamas residents going abroad, UK.**

Sending gifts from The Bahamas

To the US: Any number of gifts may be sent to the US from The Bahamas. The recipient pays no US duty if the gift received is worth US$100 or less. If the gift is worth more than US$100, he or she pays duty on the full value. According to US regulations, the duty-free status applies under the following conditions:

1. Only US$100 worth of gifts may be received by the US addressee in one day.
2. Value of the gifts must be clearly written on the package, as well as the words "unsolicited gift."
3. No cigars, cigarettes or liquor may be sent as gifts. Perfumes valued at more than US$5 may not be sent.
4. Persons in the US are not permitted to send money to The Bahamas for gifts to be shipped to them duty free. Gifts must be unsolicited.
5. Shops and commercial firms may wrap and mail the duty-free gifts for customers who pay for them personally in The Bahamas.
6. Persons may not mail a gift addressed to themselves.

To Canada: Bona fide unsolicited gifts may be sent to Canada duty free as long as they are valued under CDN$40 and do not contain any alcoholic beverages, tobacco products or advertising matter. If the gift is valued at more than CDN$40, the receiver will have to pay regular duty and tax on the excess amount.

To the UK: Bona fide gifts sent to the UK are subject to duty and Value-Added Tax (VAT) unless they comply with the following rules:

1. The value of the goods must not exceed £36 sterling (45 Euro).
2. They must be private gifts; this means they must be addressed to a private person in the UK and sent by a private person abroad.
3. The gifts must not be for commercial or trade use, but only for personal or family use.
4. They must not be paid for by the recipient, either directly or indirectly.
5. Any tobacco products, alcoholic beverages, perfumes or toilet waters sent at one time must be within the allowances mentioned. Anything over these allowances is liable to charges.
6. They must be of an occasional nature only.

DEFENCE FORCE

See **Royal Bahamas Defence Force.**

DENTISTS

Nassau

Dr Kay Sweeting Bain
Dr Owen Bastian
Dr Dante Bazard
Dr Sythela Cambridge
Dr Antoine Clark
Dr Desiree Clarke
Dr Vaughan Conliffe
Dr Norman Cove
Dr Artherine Coverley-Aranha
Dr Ricardo Crawford
Dr Brasil Cumberbatch
Dr Mark Davies
Dr Anthony P Davis
Dr Cleveland W Eneas Jr
Dr Sparkman Ferguson
Dr Charles Forbes
Dr Emmanuel Francis
Dr Fiona Fritschi (orthodontist)
Dr Gill I Gibson
Dr John A Godet
Dr Melanie G Halkitis
Dr Karen Johnson
Dr Kirk Lewis
Dr Nigel Lewis
Dr H Mitchell Lockhart
Dr John H Louis Jr
Dr John V Louis (periodontist)
Dr Leo Lundy III
Dr Michelle Mackey
Dr Kendal Major (periodontist)
Dr Michelle Major
Dr Cyd McCartney
Dr Kareem McIver
Dr Veronica McIver
Dr Curtis McMillan
Dr Tanya Mortemore
Dr Derwin Munroe
Dr Kenworth Newbold
Dr Sheguel Pearce
Dr Renée Peet-Iferenta
Dr Joyous Pickstock
Dr Munir Rashad (oral surgeon)
Dr Kimberley Richardson (child and adolescent dentistry)
Dr Osmond W A Richardson (oral surgeon)
Dr L Barry Russell (orthodontist)
Dr Marlene Sawyer
Dr Tavette Scavella
Dr Copline Seymour
Dr Sonia Shepherd
Dr Rosemund Smith-Erskine
Dr E Strachan-Moxey
Dr Wendy Stuart
Dr Sidney Sweeting
Dr Julius Theophilus
Dr Woodley Thompson (orthodontist)
Dr Therese Thompson-Bonamy
Dr Todd Tilberg
Dr Cyril O Vanderpool
Dr Christopher Varga
Dr Annette Warren
Dr Adra Gibson Washington
Dr James Washington Jr
Dr Marsha Williams-Bethel
Dr Cynthia Wood

Out Islands

Abaco, Dr Jacolin Archer, Dr V McWeeney, Dr James Newman,* Dr Howard Spencer,* Dr Therese Thompson-Bonamy*
Berry Islands, Dr Michael Ryan (oral and maxillofacial surgery)
Eleuthera, Dr Olga Bacchus, Dr Mark Davies,* Dr Hadassah Knowles, Dr Roy Schatzley
Exuma, Dr William Lee

* *Visiting dentists.*

See also **Freeport/Lucaya information, Dentists.**

DEPARTURE TAX

Air

A $15 government departure tax is included in the cost of most airline tickets for passengers leaving The Bahamas. Children under six are exempt. There is an additional $10 security fee for international passengers departing Freeport, Grand Bahama.

Sea

Departure tax for passengers travelling by cruise ship, known as port tax, is payable by the cruise ship line and is usually included in the price of the ticket. Children under six are exempt. See also **Cruise ships, Cruise ship incentives.**

Ticket tax

There is a $7 Bahamas government tax and a minimum travel agency service fee of $6 (domestic), $12 (international) or more on the price of each airline or cruise ship ticket purchased in The Bahamas. This is included in the price of the ticket and should not be confused with the departure tax. Additional ticket taxes apply, depending on destination.

DIVING

See **Sports.**

DIVORCE

In The Bahamas, a husband or wife may petition for divorce on grounds of adultery, cruelty, sodomy, desertion, separation, homosexuality, bestiality, and, in the case of a wife, if her husband has been found guilty of rape during the course of the marriage. A petition for divorce may be filed after two years from the date of the celebration of the marriage, unless permission is gained from the court to petition earlier.

Three months after a *decree nisi* is granted, the divorce may become final and a *decree absolute* issued provided that, where appropriate, a judge is satisfied with arrangements made for the welfare of children. In special cases, this period may be reduced to six weeks. Marriages not consummated may be annulled.

A couple of any nationality may obtain a divorce in The Bahamas if it can be established that the husband is domiciled here. Otherwise, the wife may petition if she can establish that:

1. She and her husband have lived three years of their married life here and these years directly preceded commencement of the suit.
2. Her husband has deserted her and has gone abroad.

In 2003, 438 divorces were granted in The Bahamas compared with 461 in 2002.

A divorce obtained abroad will be recognized in The Bahamas if the court is satisfied the party obtaining the divorce had a real, substantial connection with the country in which the divorce was obtained.

DOCTORS

New Providence

Some doctors listed have a general practice in addition to specialization:

Anaesthesiology

Dr S Bascom-Bruney
Dr G Beneby
Dr G de Castro
Dr P de Souza
Dr R Francis
Dr B McCartney
Dr R Neymour
Dr G Pennerman
Dr S Pierre
Dr A Regis
Dr M Weech

Cardiology

Dr C Brown
Dr P Cargill
Dr H Coleman
Dr F Eugenio
Dr D Sands (cardiac thoracic surgery)
Dr C D Tseretopoulos

Dept of Public Health

Dr R Ajero
Dr T Augustin
Dr A Begum
Dr M Bhargavi
Dr M Brooks
Dr J Carter
Dr M Catala Rodriques
Dr J Cunningham
Dr M Imana
Dr G Kshatriya
Dr E McPhee
Dr M Moxey
Dr M Oshodi
Dr C Payos
Dr S Sandadi-Reddy
Dr L Sands
Dr L Quiling
Dr E Yirenkyi

Dermatology

Dr C Gooding
Dr J Hepburn
Dr R Ingraham
Dr H Orlander
Dr Q M S Richmond
Dr B E Sears

Ear, Nose & Throat (ENT)
Dr W Campbell
Dr W Gibson
Dr C Johnson
Dr R Ramsingh

Emergency Medicine
Dr T Burke
Dr C Burnett
Dr J Iferenta
Dr S Friday
Dr A Hanna

Endocrinology
Dr S Peter

Gastroenterology
Dr H Munnings
Dr L Nembhard

General practitioners
Dr G Ageeb
Dr A Alingu
Dr P Armbrister
Dr T Bartlett
Dr C Basden
Dr G Carey
Dr R E Crawford
Dr K R Culmer
Dr L W Culmer
Dr D Donaldson
Dr E L Donaldson
Dr A Eneas-Carey
Dr P Forte
Dr N Fox
Dr E Fung Chung
Dr N R Gay
Dr M Gerassimos
Dr R Gorospe
Dr E Gray
Dr G Holder
Dr M Ingraham
Dr T P Jupp
Dr I Kelly
Dr L J McCarroll
Dr M Moxey
Dr T Pinder
Dr M Poitier
Dr B E A Rolle
Dr H Simmons
Dr C Strachan
Dr A D Thompson
Dr J Wavell Thompson
Dr B Tynes
Dr R Van Tooren
Dr F W Walkine
Dr D Williams
Dr G White
Dr P Whitfield
Dr A Zervos

Internal medicine
Dr S Antonio
Dr C W M Bethel
Dr C Chin-Chea
Dr J A Constantakis
Dr J Eneas
Dr P Gomez
Dr C Hanna-Hennis
Dr J A Johnson
Dr J A Lunn
Dr K Moss (pulmonology)
Dr V Nwosa (rheumatology)
Dr A Sawyer
Dr A M Thompson-Hepburn

Nephrology
Dr J Eneas
Dr I Grant-Taylor
Dr J Johnson
Dr R Knowles
Dr A Sawyer

Neurosurgery/neurology
Dr E Demeritte (paediatrics)
Dr M Ekedede
Dr C Munnings
Dr E Newry
Dr C Rahming

Obstetrics & gynaecology
Dr H Bloomfield
Dr R Butler (oncology)
Dr A Carey
Dr B Carey
Dr R Carey
Dr A Davis
Dr A Donaldson
Dr F Leon
Dr M Hall-Watson
Dr J Johnson
Dr Lyons
Dr F Mackay
Dr H Minnis
Dr B Nottage
Dr R Patterson

Dr M Sawyer
Dr G Sherman
Dr H Simmons
Dr J Stewart
Dr S Thompson
Dr P Ward

Oncology & haematology
Dr J Lunn
Dr T Turnquest

Ophthalmology
Dr K W Knowles
Dr R McKinney
Dr S Mikhael
Dr K J A Rodgers
Dr G Sweeting

Orthopaedics
Dr D Barnett
Dr R L Gibson
Dr M Hestmo
Dr W Philips
Dr W Thompson

Paediatrics
Dr G Bethel
Dr M Carey
Dr T Cartwright
Dr J Colaco
Dr J Cunningham
Dr J Davis-Dorsett
Dr P Forte
Dr C Hanna-Hennis
Dr P Hennis (paediatric cardiology)
Dr P Hunt (allergy-immunology)
Dr J Lightbourne (paediatric cardiology)
Dr S Lochan (neonatology)
Dr G E McDeigan (neonatology)
Dr P McNeil (ICU)
Dr P B Roberts
Dr P D Roberts
Dr D Sands
Dr Y Skeffrey
Dr C Thomas (neonatology)
Dr J Wilson
Dr C Sin Quee-Brown (haemotology & oncology)

Pathology
Dr A Brathwaite
Dr G Bruney
Dr A Hanna
Dr G Raju

Physiatry/rehab
Dr K de Souza

Psychiatry
Dr D Allen
Dr T Barrett
Dr N Clarke
Dr S Fairclough
Dr B Humblestone
Dr I Kishore
Dr M Neville
Dr A Nizamudeen

Radiology
Dr L Carroll
Dr E Darville
Dr C De
Dr I Major
Dr S Payne-Fielding

Surgery
Dr O Case
Dr W Chea
Dr C Diggiss
Dr I E Farrington
Dr N Hepburn
Dr J McCartney
Dr L Munroe
Dr G Neil (plastic)
Dr M Rashad (oral)
Dr O Richardson

Urology
Dr J Evans
Dr R Roberts

Private practitioners, Out Islands
ABACO
Marsh Harbour: Dr F Boyce, Dr J S Fifer, Dr M Gerassimos (weekends), Dr E Lundy
Treasure Cay: Dr J Hull, Dr R Wilson

ELEUTHERA
Governor's Harbour: Dr D Sands (available every two weeks)
South Eleuthera: Dr Smith
Spanish Wells: Dr S Bailey

LONG ISLAND
Deadman's Cay: Dr B Almira

Medical officers,
Out Islands (government)
ABACO
Cooper's Town: Dr D Mukerjee
Marsh Harbour: Dr B Swarna,
Dr S Swarna
Sandy Point: Dr M Consulta

ACKLINS & CROOKED ISLAND
Spring Point: Dr In Pa Kim

ANDROS
Fresh Creek: Dr U Chavan
Kemp's Bay/Mangrove Cay:
Dr A Swamy
Nicholl's Town: Dr R Ajero

BERRY ISLANDS
Bullock's Harbour: (vacant at press time)

BIMINI
Alice Town: Dr K Rao

CAT ISLAND
Smith's Bay: Dr J Neely-Bartlett

ELEUTHERA
Governor's Harbour: Dr F Hoover
Harbour Island: Dr J Mensah
Rock Sound: Dr S Smith

EXUMA
George Town: Dr A Rabasto
Steventon: Dr M Poitier

GRAND BAHAMA
See **Freeport information, Doctors.**

INAGUA/MAYAGUANA
Matthew Town: Dr P Panday

LONG ISLAND
Deadman's Cay: Dr H Ameeral
Simms: Dr K Malshe

SAN SALVADOR
Cockburn Town: (vacant at press time)

Penal/prison service
Dr D Donaldson

See also **Ambulance/air ambulance services, Health care** and **Hospitals & clinics.**

DRIVER'S LICENCE & VEHICLE INFORMATION

The Bahamas follows the British system of driving on the left-hand side of the road. As most cars are generally imported from the US, they have the steering wheel on the left.

The speed limit downtown and in congested areas is 25 mph. Everywhere else in The Bahamas, it is 30 mph. Cars travelling west of the Ministry of Works building on John F Kennedy Dr (towards the airport), on Independence Dr and Harrold Rd, may travel at 45 mph.

There are three types of driver's licences in The Bahamas, which cover the following vehicles:

1. Motor vehicles with standard shift or automatic transmission.
2. Two-wheel vehicles (motorcycles, scooters, etc).
3. Commercial and public service vehicles.

The Road Traffic Dept is located in the Clarence A Bain Bldg, Thompson Blvd and Moss Rd. All applications for driving permits and licences are processed there.

Driver's licences carry the bearer's photograph and personal information such as date of birth, gender and height, with a valid passport or voter's card being presented at the time of application. Drivers are required by law to have licences in their possession at all times.

See **Fig 1.4** for information on the number of drivers licensed and vehicles registered in New Providence and Grand Bahama.

Driver's licence requirements

Applicants must be at least 17 to qualify to drive a motor car, motorcycle or motor-assisted cycle equipped with pedals. First-time applicants must obtain a learner's permit for $10 and then take an oral/written test and a road test when they are ready to drive unaccompanied. Each test costs $10. The fee is not refunded for cancellations less than 24 hours prior to the test.

The oral/written test concerns highway code (traffic regulations). Upon successful completion of the oral/written test, the

FIG 1.4

LICENSED DRIVERS & VEHICLES REGISTERED	2004*	2004†
Licensed drivers	**New Providence**	**Grand Bahama**
Private	134,944	15,224
Provisional (learner's permit)	6,300	2,174
Public service	649	682
International	189	44
Total	**142,082**	**18,124**
Vehicles registered	**New Providence**	**Grand Bahama**
Private cars	72,770	18,561
Government-owned cars	700	146
Private trucks	13,260	3,105
Government-owned trucks	380	7
Private motorcycles	311	102
Government-owned motorcycles	108	16
Government-owned miscellaneous vehicles	63	8
Private miscellaneous vehicles	1,520	520
Taxicabs	972	487
Jitney & Public Schedule	500	–
Self-drive cars	963	904
Self-drive scooters	166	127
Tour cars	96	–
Private Buses	435	257
Government-owned buses	60	9
Livery cars	84	–
CD	41	–
Bonded Vehicles	29	–
HCC	32	–
Total	**92,490**	**24,249**

** As of Sept 2004 †June 2003-June '04*

applicant may take the road test.

A period of one hour is allowed for the road test. Latecomers are rescheduled for a later date – possibly as much as three months later.

A driver's licence costs $20 and is renewable by the end of the driver's month of birth on an annual basis for $20, or for three years at a cost of $50.

Bahamian driver's licences are issued only to Bahamians or persons who have Bahamian status, residency, or permission to work in The Bahamas. It is recognized internationally.

Drivers holding a valid licence issued outside The Bahamas may apply to the Road Traffic Dept for a Bahamian licence. The licence is issued upon presentation of the driver's current valid licence at a fee of $20 per annum, renewable by the end of the driver's month of birth.

A separate application must be made to receive a public service licence. There is an additional fee of $50 to drive a tour car, $40 to drive a taxi and $75 to drive an omnibus. The applicant must be a Bahamian citizen, present current police and traffic records, three passport-sized photos, and successfully complete a road test and written examination.

Visitors or persons staying, but not working, in The Bahamas may drive on their foreign licence for up to three months. Expatriate employees must have a valid Bahamian driver's licence once they start work. Periods of settling in are not considered. The licence is necessary only when employment actually begins.

Motorcyclists (drivers and passengers) are required by law to wear a protective helmet. Laws on use of seat belts and child restraint seats went into effect on June 1, 2002, however, at press time, they were under review.

International driver's licence

The Road Traffic Dept issues an international licence at a cost of $50, valid for one year. This licence is issued only to legal residents and work permit holders, and can be used in any country except the country of issue. Applicants must be at least 18 years old and must hold a valid Bahamian driver's licence in order to qualify for an international driver's licence.

Vehicle inspection

All vehicles must be taken to the Road Traffic Dept for inspection before being licensed to operate on the streets. The fee is $25. The controller of road traffic and the police are empowered to demand a further examination of any vehicle they consider to be of questionable roadworthiness.

Privately owned vehicles are inspected annually by the end of the owner's month of birth. Public service vehicles are inspected twice annually, usually in May and Oct. Company and government-owned vehicles are inspected in Mar.

Inspectors examine hand and foot brakes; tires; headlights and dip switch; parking, signal, brake and reverse lights; windshield; muffler; bodywork and mirrors. In public service vehicles further inspections are made of seats, floors, other interior, body, trunk, tires, windows and doors.

Vehicle ownership (licensing)

A vehicle ownership fee is paid annually by the end of the owner's month of birth. The fee is $75-$360, depending on size of the vehicle. The owner must produce proof that the vehicle is covered by minimum road act insurance.

There is a fee of $10 for transfer of a vehicle already licensed. The new owner must also present a bill of sale with a 25¢ postage stamp affixed, and the registration card with his name entered in the space provided.

Owners of newly imported vehicles must present a certificate of ownership issued by the Dept of Customs.

Owners of omnibuses and self-drive cars must present a receipt of payment for all outstanding fees owed to the Road Traffic Dept.

Licence plates

There are different coloured plates for private cars, public service vehicles, trucks, motorcycles, parliamentary, government and diplomatic vehicles. Private car, truck and motorcycle licence plates have a blue background with yellow numbers and/or letters. Bonded vehicles have orange backgrounds with black numbers and the words "bonded vehicle" embossed at the top. Trade or OT plates are black with orange letters preceded by OT.

Public service vehicles have either a yellow, white, black, green or orange background, as follows:

1. **Taxicabs:** Yellow background with black letters and numbers.
2. **Tour cars:** White background with red letters preceded by TC.
3. **Self-drive (rental) cars and scooters:** White background with green numbers preceded by SD.
4. **Livery plates:** Black background with yellow numbers and letters.
5. **Public schedule buses:** Green background with yellow numbers and letters.
6. **Private schedule buses:** Green background with white letters and numbers.
7. **Privately chartered buses:** Green background with black letters and numbers.
8. **Miscellaneous:** Orange background with white letters and numbers.

A duplicate plate (ie, to replace one that was lost) costs $5, or $10 for the pair.

Importing an automobile

Cars imported to The Bahamas should be insured before leaving the dock. All cars from right-hand drive countries

must have their headlights adjusted to dip left. The car should be driven directly to the Road Traffic Dept for inspection and registration.

For import duty, see **Customs.**

See also **Motor vehicle insurance.**

DRUGS

The Dangerous Drugs Act, 2000, makes it an offence for an unauthorized person to import, export or be in possession of Indian hemp (marijuana), cocaine, morphine, opium, or lysergic acid (LSD) in The Bahamas. The only exception is for a qualified person (registered medical practitioner, registered dentist, licensed veterinary surgeon or licensed pharmacist) to whom special permission is granted for medical or scientific purposes.

The provisions of the Act are stringently enforced and visitors from countries where drug laws are less strict should be aware of this Bahamian law. The Act, provides the following penalties for contravention of its provisions:

1. On conviction of an indictable charge of possession with intent to supply, a fine of up to $500,000 or imprisonment for up to 30 years or both such fine and imprisonment.
2. On summary conviction, a fine of up to $250,000 or to imprisonment for five years, or both such fine and imprisonment.

The Proceeds of Crime Act, 2000, created new offences for drug trafficking and the ancillary offence of facilitating a drug trafficking offence. Any person convicted of such offences or who can be shown after conviction to have benefited from drug trafficking, is liable to the increased fine and confiscation of the proceeds of drug trafficking without compensation.

The Act also allows authorities to investigate these offences, or to trace the proceeds of them, on the basis of either knowledge or suspicion that a person had trafficked, facilitated and/or benefited from a drug trafficking offence.

The confiscation may take the form of a monetary fine on the assessed value of the proceeds of drug trafficking. For this purpose, a receiver may be appointed to take possession of the proceeds and sell them to qualified people, for medical or scientific purposes, to realize the fine.

In 2003, the Drug Enforcement Unit confiscated 9,609 lbs of cocaine, 0.6 lbs of heroine, 14,512 lbs of marijuana, 14,112 marijuana plants, 5 lbs of methamphetamine (ecstasy) and made 1,596 arrests. In 2002, 5,450 lbs of cocaine, 25,333 lbs of marijuana and 110 marijuana plants were seized, and 1,896 arrests were made.

See also **Crime.**

ECONOMY

According to *The Central Bank of The Bahamas Annual Report,* 2003, "After stabilizing in the aftermath of the 2001 setback to tourism, the Bahamian economy grew mildly in 2003. Amid the lacklustre recovery in US households' travel expenditure, tourism gains stalled during the middle of the year, but resumed at a healthier pace in the final quarter, on account of mildly appreciated stopover pricing and continued growth in cruise arrivals. Construction output slowed as both commercial and residential investments weakened, although the outlook for 2004 is favoured by the impending start of foreign investment projects concentrated in the hotel sector. Fiscal sector developments were underscored by an enlarged deficit for the first six months of fiscal year 2003/04, explained by the combined effect of elevated expenditures, partly linked to unplanned salary increases and reduced revenue intake from tourism and trade related sources. In the context of Central Bank's credit restraint policy and improved foreign currency inflows, the financial sector featured stronger money growth relative to credit expansion. As a consequence, the system's net foreign liabilities were reduced, and liquidity conditions were markedly more buoyant. On the prices front, domestic inflation firmed during the year, owing both to increased internal and external cost pressures. In the external sector, net invisible outflows and higher import demand extended the deficit on the current account, while a reversal in short-term flows through the banking system caused a reduction in net capital and financial receipts. The net private foreign investment component, however, was slightly increased."

Gross domestic product (GDP)

The gross domestic product (GDP) is the sum of the remuneration of Bahamian labour, capital and land employed in the creation of The Bahamas economy. When indirect taxes are included in the total, it is known as GDP at market prices. When they are not included, it is known as GDP at factor cost.

Based on estimates in the International Monetary Fund, *World Economic Outlook* (Apr 2004), real GDP in The Bahamas increased by 0.9% in 2003 compared to 0.7% in 2002. GDP at market prices was estimated at approx $5.2 billion in 2003, compared to about $5.1 billion in 2002. Using these figures, the GDP per capita was $16,400 compared to $16,218 the previous year.

The Bahamian economy is based mostly on tourism and offshore banking. The agricultural and industrial sectors are comparatively small.

The Bahamas is the leading Caribbean region tourist destination, and the tourism sector has long been the engine of the Bahamian economy. Tourism generates about 50% of the total GDP and directly or indirectly employs about 50,000 people, roughly half the total workforce.

According to the Ministry of Tourism, tourist arrivals to The Bahamas rose by 4.3% to 4.6 million in 2003, extending the 2002 increase of 5.3% and surpassing the 2000 mark by 9.3%. After consecutive declines in the previous two years, air traffic rebounded by 1.9% to 1.4 million, which remained some 3.5% below 2000. Sea arrivals (cruise visitors) at 3.2 million continued to dominate the mix.

The banking and finance sector is the second pillar of the Bahamian economy, accounting for roughly 15% of GDP. According to The Central Bank of The Bahamas' 2003 survey, the sector employs 4,253 persons, 93.8% of whom are Bahamians; total salaries and wages paid are estimated to be in the region of $196.5 million per year.

The majority of banks and trust companies are engaged in the management of assets for wealthy individuals. They are generally non-resident or offshore companies that generate no Bahamian dollar earnings and cover all their expenses for administrative cost, utilities, maintenance and other local overhead by bringing in foreign exchange. Including salaries, total expenditure for these items by the banks is more than $396 million per year.

Commercial fishing is reserved exclusively for Bahamians. However, several foreign investors are involved in aquaculture projects.

Foreign investors enjoy complete freedom of repatriation on their investments and profits. Among major foreign investments in The Bahamas are the Grand Bahama container port by Hong Kong's Hutchison Port Holdings (HPH); Our Lucaya by Hutchison Lucaya Ltd; The Royal Oasis (Crowne Plaza) by Driftwood Bahamas Ltd; the Atlantis, Paradise Island, mega resort by Kerzner International Ltd; the Wyndham Nassau Resort and Crystal Palace Casino and Convention Centre, by the Ruffin Hotel Group, which also owns Coral Island and the Nassau Beach Hotel; the multimillion-dollar fantasy island Castaway Cay, Abaco, by Disney Cruise Line; Sandals Royal Bahamian Resort & Spa, by Sandals Resorts; SuperClubs Breezes Bahamas, by SuperClubs SuperInclusive Resorts; the British Colonial Hilton Nassau, by RHK Capital; and Emerald Bay Resort in Exuma, by EBR Ltd.

Gross national product (GNP)

The gross national product (GNP) either at market prices or factor cost differs from GDP by including the income of Bahamian capital earned abroad, and by excluding the contribution of foreign capital to the Bahamian economy. Such contributions are represented by interest, dividend receipts and payments from and to abroad.

According to the Dept of Statistics, the current GNP was not approved for release to the public at press time. The latest figures available from the Dept of Statistics are from 1995, when the net property and entrepreneurial income received from abroad totalled $97 million, which put the GNP at market prices at an estimated $2.972 billion.

National debt

According to The Central Bank of The Bahamas, in 2003, the country had accrued a debt of $2.37 billion, a further increase of 7.3% after increasing by 12.5% in 2002. Of this amount, direct liabilities of the government rose by 7.4% to $1.94 billion, as compared to an increase of 12.7% ($202.9 million) in 2002. Government guaranteed debt of the public corporations rose by $27.5 million to $429.2 million.

Inflation

Inflation, as mentioned by changes in the average retail price index, rose to 3% from 2.2% in 2002. This mainly reflected accelerated price increases for recreation & entertainment services (9.8%), medical care & health (9.8%), furniture & household operations (3.85%), transport & communication (1.82%), housing costs (0.74%) as well as other non-disaggregated goods and services (12.04%). Conversely, the increase in average education costs abated sharply to 1.1% from the 12.9% tuition-fee-led hike during 2002; was tempered for food & beverages (0.5%), while average clothing & footwear costs decreased slightly (0.1%).

EDUCATION

Education in The Bahamas comes under the jurisdiction of the Ministry of Education.

There are currently 191 schools in The Bahamas. Of these, 147 (77%) are fully maintained by the government and 44 (23%) independent. In New Providence, 40 are government-owned and 21 independent. In the Out Islands, 107 are government-owned and 23 independent.

See **Fig 1.5** for a breakdown of the school population.

Schools in The Bahamas are categorized as follows:

Preschool ....ages 3-5
Primary ....ages 5-11
Secondary ....ages 11-16+
All-age................................ages 5-16+
Special education......................all ages
(for exceptional students or those with severe learning disabilities)

Free education is available in government schools throughout The Bahamas. Students must attend school until age 16.

The Ministry of Education, in consultation with the University of Cambridge Local Examinations Syndicate, introduced The Bahamas General Certificate of Secondary Education (BGCSE) in 1993. Twenty-five subjects covering academic, technical and vocational areas are offered. Grades are on a seven-point scale, A-G. It is based on the UK General Certificate of Secondary Education (GCSE), and is targeted to a wider range of abilities than the former GCE O levels. The Bahamas Junior Certificate (BJC) is taken by grade 9 students in 10 subjects. Grades are on a seven-point scale, A-G. A diagnostic test, the Grade Level Assessment Test (GLAT), is administered to grades 3 and 6. It is used to identify weaknesses and strengths in language arts and mathematics programmes in schools. Social studies and science are added at grade 6. The grade 6 test is also used as a placement examination for pupils entering grade 7 in government high schools.

Independent schools provide primary and secondary education. The term "college" connotes a fee-paying

FIG 1.5

SCHOOL POPULATION 2002-03

	Government	Independent	Total
Primary			
New Providence	17,395	3,022	20,417
Out Islands	8,090	1,778	9,868
All-age			
New Providence	–	8,671	8,671
Out Islands	3,025	904	3,929
Secondary			
New Providence	13,638	1,411	15,049
Out Islands	7,883	1,992	9,875
Special schools			
New Providence	334	–	334
Out Islands	117	–	117
Preschools/Nursery			
New Providence	436	860	1,296
Out Islands	376	1,962	2,338
Totals	**51,294**	**20,600**	**71,894**

Figures are supplied by the Ministry of Education.

school rather than a university.

Several private schools of continuing education offer secretarial and academic courses. The government-operated Princess Margaret Hospital offers a nursing course through the School of Nursing, at the College of The Bahamas' Oakes Field Campus.

Literacy

In 1998 the United Nations Educational Scientific and Cultural Organization (UNESCO) reported that 79% of Bahamians are literate. Other reports document the number closer to 95%. Literacy is based on the number of students completing sixth grade. While more than 95% of Bahamians complete sixth grade, they are not all functionally literate. The National Literacy Services was established in 1999 and has expanded to include family literacy and adult literacy. To become a National Literacy Services volunteer or to register as an adult student contact Ministry of Education, tel 356-7643, fax 356-7644.

Higher education

The College of The Bahamas and the Bahamas Technical and Vocational Institute (BTVI) are publicly financed institutions offering higher education. The University of the West Indies (UWI) maintains a presence in The Bahamas offering degrees in Hotel and Tourism Management. Medical students enrolled in the Bachelor of Medicine and Bachelor of Surgery (MB BS) programme at UWI campuses in Jamaica and Trinidad can complete the clinical years (comprising the 4th and 5th years) at Princess Margaret Hospital.

There has been a marked increase in private institutions offering tertiary level education and degrees. Every school must be registered with the Ministry of Education, although prospective students should check each one to determine accreditation.

In addition, some US schools offer degree programmes in The Bahamas. Examples are Univ of Miami, Kent State Univ, Sojourner-Douglass College and Nova Southeastern Univ. Classes are usually offered on weekends and at night.

NEW PROVIDENCE SCHOOLS

A selection of schools in New Providence follows. For a complete list, including the Out Islands, contact the Ministry of Education, PO Box N-3913, Nassau, The Bahamas, tel (242) 502-2704 or (242) 322-8410, fax (242) 328-8970 or e-mail info@bahamaseducation.com.

Nursery schools & kindergarten

Infant Education Centre Ltd: East Ct, Centreville. For children 2-5 yrs. Four terms, $300 per term. 7:30am-4pm. After school care until 6pm (extra). Tel 325-8567, or e-mail glendawallace03@hotmail.com. **Nursery division,** 9th Terr East, Centreville. For children 6 wks-2 yrs. hand-fed infants $50 weekly, others $45 weekly. 7:30am-6pm. PO Box N-10576, tel 326-5855, or e-mail glendawallace@hotmail.com.

Munro School: Williams Ct off William St. For children 2-6 yrs. Four terms, $650 per term. 8:30am-1pm. Afternoon care available. Nursery and kindergarten classes, including grade 1 preparation, specializing in art. Ministry of Education approved curriculum. Qualified teachers. Sylvia Munro, PO Box N-134, tel 393-2957, fax 393-1847.

Strawberry Patch Pre-School: West Bay St, opp Saunders Beach. For children 18 months (verbal)-5 yrs. Three terms, $650 per term. 8am-4pm. After-school care until 6pm (extra). PO Box N-10576, tel 322-5074, or e-mail glendawallace03@hotmail.com.

Wee Wisdom School: Collins Ave, Centreville. For children 2½-5 yrs. Three terms. K2 (2-3 yrs) $485 per term, $1,350 per year; K3-K5 (3-5 yrs) $575 per term, $1,650 per year. 9am-2:30pm. A division of Nassau Christian Schools. Baptist International Missions Inc, PO Box N-3923, tel 322-1586 or 393-2641.

Private primary schools

Xavier's Lower School: West Bay St. Roman Catholic. Kindergarten (4½ yrs)-grade 6. Three terms, $2,022 per year plus $120 book fee, $5 PTA and $20 insurance fee, all for first term only. Approx 410 pupils, 26 lay teachers, two teacher's aides, one priest, one nurse and one guidance counsellor. Cynthia Moss, headmistress, Xavier's Lower School, PO Box N-7076, tel 322-3077 or 323-3649, fax 325-1571, or e-mail xaviers@batelnet.bs.

Private primary-secondary schools

Christian Heritage School: Dean's Ln at Fort Charlotte. Kindergarten-grade 9. Three terms $725-$825 per term. Books and supplies not included. Curriculum includes computers and Spanish. Approx 160 pupils. Principal/administrator Carol Harrison, PO Box N-3939, tel 322-4271/4, fax 322-4273.

Jordan-Prince Williams Baptist School: Cowpen Rd. Baptist. For students 4-18 yrs. Three terms: primary section $650 per term; secondary section $750 per term. Incidentals: uniforms and text books. Secondary section students may take BJC, BGCSE and Pitman exams. Commercial subjects and computer courses also offered. Approx 1,200 pupils, 70 teachers. Principal, Eugene Bonamy, PO Box GT-2198, tel 361-4046 or 361-4847/9, fax 361-1193.

Kingsway Academy: Bernard Rd. Inter-denominational, Christian school. Kindergarten-grade 12. Three terms, $700-$1,035 per term depending on grade level; $86-$239 book fee for kindergarten-grade 6; grades 7-12 purchase books locally. Classes: kindergarten-grade 6, 8:15am-2:45pm (2pm on Fri); grades 7-12, 8:15am-2:55pm (2pm on Fri). Curriculum for all grades includes computer and Spanish. High school grades offer auto mechanics, carpentry & joinery and technical drawing. Students take BJC, BGCSE, PSAT and SAT exams. Approx 850 pupils. PO Box N-4378, tel 324-6269 or 324-6887, fax 393-6917, e-mail khamilton@kingswayacademy.com.

Lyford Cay School: Lyford Cay. International school for students

3-18 yrs. Accredited by the European Council of Intl Schools and the New England Assoc of Schools and Colleges. Also a member of the Council of International Schools. Two semesters. Early learning centre (nursery & pre-kindergarten), $4,100 per semester; kindergarten, $4,250 per semester; elementary school (grades 1-5), $4,875 per semester; middle school (grades 6-10), $5,400 per semester; high school (grades 11 & 12), $5,975 per semester. Lyford Cay School implements and is approved to run the middle years and diploma programmes of the International Baccalaureate. Application and testing fee of $250. Non-refundable development fund fee $1,100 per student for Bahamian families, or $3,000 per student for non-Bahamian families (max $9,000 per family). Principal, PO Box N-7776, tel 362-4774 or 362-4269, fax 362-5198, e-mail admin@lyfordcayschool.net, or visit www.lyfordcayschool.net.

Queen's College: Village Rd. Methodist. For students 3½-5½ yrs (early learning centre), 5½-11½ yrs (primary school) and 11½-17½ yrs (high school). Three terms: early learning centre, $850; primary school, $1,045; high school, $1,155. Incidental fees include technology fees (grades 1-12), locker fees (grades 7-12), uniforms, annual magazine, materials for practical subjects and selected textbooks and workbooks. Students may sit PSAT, SAT I, SAT II, Microsoft Office Specialist, Advanced Subsidiary Level, Advanced Placement, BJC and BGCSE exams. Academic and special interest classes are held for adults through the evening institute – The Centre for Further Education. Approx 1,300 pupils, 85 teachers. Principal Andrea Gibson, PO Box N-7127; tel 393-2153, 393-1666 or 393-2646; fax 393-3248, e-mail info@qchenceforth.com or visit www.qchenceforth.com.

St Andrew's School, The International School of The Bahamas: Yamacraw Rd. Independent, International Baccalaureate (IB) school. Students 2½-18 yrs. Three terms, $1,335-$3,350 per term depending on class. Students take BJC, BGCSE, SSAT, PSAT, SAT and IB diploma exams. Approx 760 pupils and 68 teachers. Principal, PO Box EE-17340, tel 324-2621, fax 324-0816, e-mail svarani-jones@st-andrews.com, or visit www.st-andrews.com.

St Anne's School: Fox Hill. Anglican. Students 4½-18 yrs. Three terms: primary, $885 per term plus $125 books first term only; secondary, $1,000 per term. Incidental fees: insurance $20 per year, lab fees $25 per term, uniforms, books and equipment. Students take BJC, BGCSE, Pitman, PSAT and SAT exams. Admission by exam. Approx 750 pupils and 62 teachers. Cynthia Wells, principal; Clayton Newbold, vice-principal of the secondary dept, Sonia Johnson, vice-principal of the primary dept. PO Box SS-6256; tel 324-1203, 324-1226 or 324-1481; fax 324-0805.

St John's College: Bethel Ave. Anglican. Established in 1947. Students 4-17 yrs. Three terms: preparatory dept, $885 per term, plus $137.75 book fee, first term only; secondary dept $1,000 per term, plus $25 lab fee and $20 insurance fee. Books additional. BJC, BGCSE, PSAT, Pitman and SAT exams. Admission to secondary dept is by examination. Approx 865 pupils, 45 full-time teachers in secondary dept and 32 full-time in preparatory dept. Cleomie Woods, principal, PO Box N-4858, tel 322-3249.

Tambearly School: Sandyport, Cable Beach. International student body 3-15 yrs. Prepares students for integration into schools abroad. All students use the computer and take French or Spanish. Grades 6-9 take Latin. Three terms. Infants $1,785; kindergarten-grade 6, $2,445 per term; grades 7-9, $2,555 per term. Accommodates up to 16 students per class. Approx 150 pupils, 12 full-time and 4 part-time teachers. Alice Langford, principal, PO Box N-4284, tel 327-5965, fax 327-5963, e-mail tambearly@coralwave.com, or visit www.tambearly.com.

Westminster College: Blake Rd & R E Cooper Blvd. Christian. Grades 1-12. Students are prepared for GLAT, BJC and BGCSE examinations and for entrance to colleges both locally and abroad. Only school to offer the Bahamas GED certificate. Dr R E Cooper Jr, President, PO Box N-8572, tel 327-3622, fax 327-4588.

Private secondary schools

Aquinas College: Madeira St. Roman Catholic. Three terms. Grades 7-12. Prepares candidates for BJC, BGCSE and American College Board exams. Tuition: $2,046 per year. Registration: $50 (non-refundable). Uniforms. Approx 500 pupils, 36 teachers. Elizabeth Miller, principal, PO Box N-7540, tel 322-8933/4, fax 323-1620.

St Augustine's College: Bernard Rd. Roman Catholic. Grades 7-12. Students 11-18 yrs. Education equivalent to British comprehensive schools, incorporating elements of American junior and senior prep school along with computer science. Three terms, $2,775 per year plus a $200 seat fee. Students sit BJC, BGCSE, PSAT and SAT exams, and 75% of graduating students receive a minimum of five subject passes with grade C or better. Entrance exams are held in Jan of each year. Approx 950 pupils and 55 teachers. PO Box N-3940, tel 324-1511.

Special education

Blairwood Academy: Village Rd, south of Queen's College. Kindergarten-grade 12. Three terms. Blairwood Academy is an alternative school, dedicated to average to bright students who benefit from a small structured environment. Special programmes for students with learning disabilities, language deficits or attention deficits. There is a full-day school programme, after-school tutoring and summer school. Testing and evaluations can be done to diagnose learning strengths and weaknesses. The school maintains contact with an extensive network of related professionals and can provide referrals to other services as needed. PO Box N-524, tel 393-1303 or 394-3329, fax 393-6952, or e-mail blairwood_mls@yahoo.com.

Hopedale Centre: Highbury Park, immediately west of Holy Cross Church off Soldier Rd. For students 5-21 yrs who have not been successful in traditional classroom settings. Approx 35 pupils with eight to a class, or one-on-one if necessary. Eight teachers. Structured, supportive classroom environment and basic skills curriculum. Ungraded programme allows students to work at their own pace. An Individual Education Plan (IEP) for each student is based on assessed learning needs. Life skills, vocational and career training are part of the curriculum. Arlene Davis, director, PO Box N-8883, tel 393-8924, fax 394-4792.

Tertiary education

Bahamas Baptist Community College: Jean St off Prince Charles Dr. Baptist. Established in 1995, it is the first community college in The Bahamas. Full-time and part-time programmes, including Associates of Arts degrees in accounting, biology, computer science, economics, mathematics, teacher education and law and criminal justice. Associate of Arts degree programmes are also offered in Eleuthera. Short certificate courses and programmes include basic accounting, word processing, public administration, marketing management and secretarial studies. The college operates on a semester system, Sept-Dec, Jan-April, with two summer sessions, May-June and July-Aug. Approx 750 full- and part-time students and 29 full- and part-time lecturers. Tuition is $85 per credit. Institute of Theology offers diploma/certificate courses. Courses are also offered through the continuing education division in conjunction with the University of the West Indies. President Dr Brendamae C Cleare, PO Box N-4830, tel 364-0695, fax 364-3209.

Bahamas Technical & Vocational Institute (BTVI): Nassau and Freeport. The mission of BTVI is to produce highly skilled individuals with a strong work ethic through market-driven career and technical education and training, enabling them to achieve national or international credentials and participation in national development.

Programmes are structured on the semester system, with two 15-week semesters and a four-week job internship period. Programmes include construction, mechanical, service, automotive and electrical trades and souvenir manufacturing. BTVI also offers six-week professional and personal development courses. There are approx 1,600 students at the Nassau campus and 350 in Grand Bahama. PO Box N-4934, tel 393-2804, fax 393-4005.

The College of The Bahamas (COB): Established in 1974, the college has three campuses: Oakes Field and Grosvenor Close in New Providence, and Freeport, Grand Bahama. Associate and Bachelor degree courses are also offered in Exuma, Abaco and Eleuthera. The college offers a range of programmes leading to the bachelor and associate degrees. The instructional programme is administered through three faculties and nine schools. The Faculty of Education and Liberal Arts comprises the schools of Education, Communication and Creative Arts, English Studies and Social Sciences. Included in the Faculty of Business, Hospitality and Tourism Studies are the Schools of Business and Administrative Studies, Hospitality and Tourism Studies and The Centre for Entrepreneurship. The schools of Natural Sciences and Environmental Studies, Nursing and Allied Health Sciences and Technology make up the Faculty of Pure and Applied Sciences.

Bachelor's degrees can be obtained in accounting, administrative office management, banking and finance (also available with a foreign language), computer information systems, economics and finance, finance, general business, law (in conjunction with the Univ of The West Indies), management, marketing, nursing, public administration, social work and teacher education (primary and secondary levels) and physical education.

Through outreach programmes, the Centre for Continuing Education and Extension Services (CEES) offers courses in personal and professional development and academic upgrading.

The college is associated with two field stations in Andros and San Salvador where various research projects are conducted.

The Centre for Entrepreneurship was launched in Oct 1997 to encourage entrepreneurship in The Bahamas by providing assistance and services to emerging businesses. Modelled after the Dingman Centre for Entrepreneurship at the Univ of Maryland, the centre is located on Clayton Rd, Nassau.

The former Bahamas Hotel Training College was amalgamated into COB as the School of Hospitality and Tourism Studies in Aug 2000.

COB operates on a semester system, Aug-Dec and Jan-Apr, with two summer sessions, May-June and June-July. Tuition is $100 per credit hour for Bahamians for courses at 100 and 200 level, and $150 per credit hour for courses at 300 and 400 level. Fees for non-Bahamians are double. Approx 4,000 full- and part-time students. Admissions Office, College of The Bahamas, PO Box N-4912, Nassau, tel 302-4377 or 302-4499, fax 302-4586, admissions e-mail vcollie@cob.edu.bs, general information e-mail dclarke@cob.edu.bs, or visit www.cob.edu.bs.

Eugene Dupuch Law School: This law school operated by the Council of Legal Education is conducting classes from temporary quarters at the College of The Bahamas' School of Hospitality and Tourism Studies. The school is named in honour of the late Eugene A P Dupuch, QC. The law library is temporarily located opposite the Clarence A Bain Bldg on Thompson Blvd. The administration dept is located on Farrington Rd and the Legal Aid Clinic is housed in the VBM Building on

Horseshoe Dr, Oakes Field. The Law School building, when constructed, will be located on JFK Drive next to the St John's College playground.

Graduates of Eugene Dupuch Law School receive a Legal Education Certificate, a professional qualification enabling the holder to be admitted to practice in the Caribbean territories. The two-year programme includes civil procedure and practice I; civil procedure and practice II; conveyancing and registration of title; criminal practice and procedure; evidence and forensic medicine; landlord and tenant; legal drafting and interpretation; law office management, accounting and technology; remedies; ethics, rights and obligations of the legal profession; and succession.

A six-month programme is also offered for common law professionally trained persons. Graduates are eligible to be admitted to practice in the Commonwealth Caribbean. Administration, PO Box SS-6394, Nassau, tel 326-8507/8, fax 326-8504, or e-mail admin@edls.edu.bs.

Grosvenor Academy: A division of International Language Resources (ILR), 64 Grosvenor Close, Shirley St. Variety of courses for all age groups, preschool to adult. Language courses predominate, but general interest courses are also offered, along with enrichment/remedial courses for children. A full-time English as a Foreign Language (EFL) programme started in June 1998.

ILR also serves The Bahamas business community with translation and interpreting, as well as on-site language courses tailored to the needs of a particular business or industry. Dr John Knowles, PO Box SS-19823, tel 323-2078, fax 323-6914.

Sojourner-Douglass College: Gold Circle House, East Bay St. Branch campus of Sojourner-Douglass, Baltimore, MD. The college is committed to providing mature Bahamians access to higher education. It allows adults to pursue full-time undergraduate studies without disrupting their jobs or leaving home. The average student is 36 yrs old. The college offers specialized training geared to government employment, banking, criminology and industry specific needs. Provides teacher training for The Bahamas' primary and secondary school system and continuing education and master's degree programmes as of fall 2003. There are approx 33 full- and part-time faculty and staff. PO Box SS-5630, tel 394-8570, fax 394-8623.

Success Training College: Bernard Rd. The nation's first private college was established in Nassau in 1982 and expanded to Freeport in 1998. The college offers a wide array of associate degree programmes in business, accounting, hospitality, medical assisting, dental assisting, early childhood education, journalism, electronic technology, computer engineering technology, network administration, Internet communication and others. Day, evening and weekend classes are available. The college conducts a self-contained weekend programme that permits working persons to complete an associate degree programme in computer information systems, business administration, accounting or public administration by attending classes on Sat only.

The college also offers a large number of certification courses and programmes including PC Technician, Internet Technician, Microsoft Certified System Engineer and Microsoft Office User Specialist. Bachelor of Science degree programmes in business are also available for external students through the Univ of London. Preparation for the Bachelor of Law degree is offered in conjunction with Holborn College in England. Admission into all programmes is year-round and anyone with passes in BGCSE English and mathematics, plus a high school diploma may apply. A college preparatory course is available for students without admission qualifications. Office of Admissions, PO Box FH-14161, tel 324-7770/1, fax 324-0119, or visit www.successbahamas.com.

University of The West Indies (UWI): The Bahamas has been affiliated with the University of the West Indies since Jan 1964. It is regional, serving most of the English-speaking Caribbean, and has three campuses on the islands of Jamaica, Trinidad and Barbados. It maintains a UWI Centre and full-time resident tutor in Nassau through whom Bahamian students may seek admission to any of the campuses. The office also coordinates distance education programmes of the university in areas such as agriculture, business and public administration, education, and counselling.

Degree programmes are also offered at the Centre for Hotel and Tourism Management, a dept of the Faculty of Social Sciences of the university. The final two years of the these programmes are completed in Nassau at the Tourism Training Centre, Thompson Blvd.

At Princess Margaret Hospital, UWI offers Part II of the medical degree programme (MB BS). Students completed Part I at UWI campuses in Jamaica or Trinidad prior to coming to The Bahamas.

A UWI bachelor degree in law (LLB) is offered as a joint programme with The College of The Bahamas. UWI Centre, School of Continuing Studies, PO Box N-1184, tel 323-6593, fax 328-0622, or e-mail uwibahamas48@hotmail.com.

Schools for the handicapped

Bahamas Red Cross Centre for Deaf Children: Horseshoe Dr. Government-assisted. Preschool-18 yrs, with some students integrated in special classes in government primary and high schools. Help is also given to hearing-impaired children in ordinary classes. No tuition fees. General studies with the help of modern hearing-aid equipment. Classes 9am-3pm. Approx 60 students, 13 specialist teachers. Also parental guidance, comprehensive audiological testing facilities, and counselling for deaf people of all ages. Tessa Nottage, principal, Bahamas Red Cross Centre for Deaf Children, PO Box N-91, tel 323-6767.

The Salvation Army Erin Harrison Gilmour School for the Blind & Visually Impaired Children and May & Stanley Smith Resource Centre: 33 Mackey St. Coed for school-aged blind and partially sighted students. Although the school follows curriculum guidelines of the Ministry of Education, adaptations are made for individual students in motor development, mobility training (using a cane) and daily living skills. Special media are used to teach blind and partially sighted students, including Braille machines, large-print material, writing guides, talking calculators and abacus equipment. Blind students may take computer classes with talking computers. A library is available to visually impaired people with books in Braille, talking books and giant-print books. Blind and partially sighted students are encouraged to study for and sit the BGCSE. Divisional Commander, PO Box N-205, tel 394-3197 or 393-2745.

Stapledon School: Dolphin Dr. Government-owned. For the educable and trainable mentally and physically handicapped. The curriculum includes computer studies, ceramics, crafts and a programme that teaches basic farming skills. Speech therapy and counselling are provided. Approx 140 students on site, 20 physically handicapped at the Bahamas Association for Physically Disabled, 17 teachers. Tuition free. Classes 9am-3pm. Apply to headmistress, Stapledon School, or Special Services Division, PO Box N-3913, tel 323-4669 or 323-6000.

ELECTRICITY

In New Providence, electricity is generated by the Bahamas Electricity Corp (BEC) at Clifton Pier and Blue Hills Power Stations. Eight diesel-driven alternators are used at Clifton Pier, and eight single cycle gas turbines at Blue Hills.

In the Out Islands, BEC generates and distributes electricity in Bimini; North, Central and South Andros;

Abaco and cays; Black Point, Farmer's Cay and Staniel Cay in the Exuma Cays; Exuma; San Salvador; Great Harbour Cay; Eleuthera; Cat Island; Long Island; Ragged Island; Mayaguana; Rum Cay; Acklins; Crooked Island and Long Cay. Total electricity consumers connected by BEC in New Providence, Paradise Island and the Out Islands as of Sept 30, 2003, amounted to 87,063.

For principal rates in New Providence, Paradise Island and designated Out Islands, see **Fig 1.6.**

New Providence, Paradise Island & Out Islands
Total annual units* (kWh) generated by BEC

1998-99 1,184,599,322
1999-00 1,281,089,827
2000-01 1,330,300,000
2001-02 1,383,584,897
2002-03 1,503,014,649

** Each year's figure refers to the 12-month period ending Sept 30, ie, the 1998-99 figure reflects Oct 1, '98-Sept 30, '99.*

Total installed capacity...........423 MW
Max demand 2003.............204.5 MW
(New Providence only)

Supply voltages & frequency
3 phase, 4 wire, 208/120 volts, 60 cycles.
1 phase, 3 wire, 240/120 volts, 60 cycles.

Fuel surcharge provisions
Basic rates and charges shall be increased by a surcharge of $0.0001 for each unit of electricity consumed.

The surcharge of $0.0001 is increased or decreased as follows:

1. By $0.001029 per unit for every $1 per barrel increase/decrease in the price of automotive diesel oil above or below $30 per barrel.
2. By $0.000859 per unit for every $1 per barrel increase/decrease in the price of Bunker "C" fuel oil above or below $20 per barrel.

A "true up" adjustment to yearly fuel surcharge begins with bills rendered on Nov 1 of each year, by adding or subtracting an amount equal to the difference between actual fuel cost and fuel cost recovered during the 12 months from Oct 1, divided by the estimated number of units to be sold during the ensuing year from Nov 1.

Other charges

1. Special reading, check reading, fuse replacement.....................$5
2. Meter test minimum $10
3. Visit with intent to disconnect:
   residential $10
   commercial $15
4. Reconnection fees $20

EMERGENCY NUMBERS

Police ....919, 911 or 322-4444
Fire ....919, 911 or 302-8404
Ambulances
Princess Margaret Hosp.............919
Med-Evac (ambulance/emergency airlift services) 322-2881
Doctors Hospital Health Systems EMT – (ambulance/emergency airlift services) 302-4747
Hospitals
Doctors (DHHS) ....322-8411 or 302-4600
Princess Margaret 322-2861
Lyford Cay 362-4025
Airport Crash, Fire & Rescue 377-7077
Bahamas Air Sea Rescue Assoc (BASRA) 325-8864
Bahamas Electricity Corp (BEC) ....323-5561 (to 4)
The Crisis Centre ....328-0922 or 322-4999
Stat Care Medical & Emergency Centre....328-5596 (to 7)

EMPLOYERS' ORGANIZATIONS

The following organizations are located in Nassau:

Assoc of Tertiary Institutions in The Bahamas (ATIB), PO Box N-4912
Bahamas Assoc of Land Surveyors, PO Box N-7782
Bahamas Assoc of Social Workers, PO Box GT-2699

FIG 1.6

PRINCIPAL ELECTRICITY RATES IN NEW PROVIDENCE/PARADISE ISLAND & DESIGNATED OUT ISLANDS, OCT 1, 2003

	B$
Tariff A – residential	
For electricity supplied to premises used as private residence:	
1. For each unit up to 800 units per month	0.1500
2. For each unit in excess of 800 units per month	0.1841
3. Min charge per month	3.00
Tariff B – commercial	
1. Electricity supplied to commercial installations, max demand of which does not exceed 10 kVA:	
a. Each unit of electricity	0.1828
b. Min charge per month	6.40
2. Electricity supplied to commercial installations, max demand of which exceeds 10 kVA:	
a. Max demand charges per kVA per annum	123.96
b. Unit charges – for each unit of electricity	0.1285
c. Min charge per month kVA demand	10.33
Tariff C – churches, open-air cinemas, floodlit sports arenas with max demand of 10 kVA or more	
1. Max demand charges per kVA per annum	46.56
2. Each unit of electricity	0.1351
3. Min charge per month kVA demand	3.88
Tariff D – temporary service*	
1. Each unit of electricity consumed	0.2012
2. Connection fee	10.00
3. Meter rental per month	7.00
4. Cost of installing connection	–
Special tariff – street lighting	
Electricity supplied per unit consumed	0.1351

* *Service will be disconnected if used to supply any part of a permanent electrical installation not inspected and passed by a BEC inspector, or if the premises are being used for residential or commercial purposes.*

Bahamas Boatmen's Assoc, PO Box N-552
Bahamas Chemical Manufacturing Assoc, PO Box N-1534
Bahamas Contractors' Assoc, PO Box N-4632
Bahamas Employers' Confederation, PO Box N-166
Bahamas Glass-Bottom Boat Assoc, PO Box N-552
Bahamas Hotel Employers' Assoc, PO Box N-7799
Bahamas Inst of Professional Engineers, PO Box N-7869
Bahamas Manufacturers Agents & Wholesalers' Assoc, PO Box N-272
Bahamas Mechanical Contractors' Assoc, PO Box FH-14316
Bahamas Motor Dealers' Assoc, PO Box N-4177
Bahamas Real Estate Dealers' Assoc, PO Box N-4051
Bahamas Soft Drink Bottlers' Assoc, PO Box N-272
Bahamas Supermarket Operators' Assoc, PO Box N-4206
Bahamas Used Tyres & Commodities Assoc, PO Box N-3308 or N-1979
Bahamas Welding Contractors' Assoc, PO Box N-1283
Corp of Accountants & Auditors, PO Box N-1669
Nassau Assoc of Shipping Agents, PO Box N-1451
Natl Consumer Assoc, PO Box CB-11671
Professional Photographers of The Bahamas, PO Box N-8162
Restaurant Owners Assoc of The Bahamas, PO Box N-7799

ENGINEERING COMPANIES

Following is a list of firms approved by the Ministry of Works.

CSB Consultants Ltd 325-7869
Caribbean Civil Group...........327-6479
Engineering & Technical
Services............................394-3219
The Engineering Group 326-3467
George V Cox & Co Ltd 322-3121
Integrated Building Service....324-5445
Larry A Treco Consulting
Engineering 393-4996
McAce Technical Services......394-3720
Paul E Hanna & Assoc 323-7592
Quantum Technologies.........326-1619
Rowlands Engineering Ltd.....328-7681

Two private organizations register/license engineers in The Bahamas: the Bahamas Institution of Professional Engineers, tel 322-3356, and the Bahamas Society of Engineers, tel 328-1858 or visit www.bahamasengineers.org.

ENTERTAINMENT

A number of native shows, bands and cabaret acts are staged at hotels, clubs and restaurants throughout the Bahama Islands. Junkanoo and rake 'n scrape are indigenous music styles that can be heard throughout the islands. Traditional gospel music is also popular and takes place in churches and at frequent concerts.

Café Johnny Canoe at Nassau Beach Hotel hosts a Fri night Junkanoo rush-out, where visitors experience the colour, rhythm and excitement of Bahamian culture in action. The Living Room, also at Nassau Beach Hotel, features live bands Fri and Sat nights. At the British Colonial Hilton, Just Friends performs Thurs-Sat nights and the Blue Note Lounge offers live jazz and classic R&B Fri and Sat nights. A calypso band performs at the Blue Marlin on Paradise Island. The evening also includes a flaming limbo act and contest, fire dancer and a Junkanoo rush-out. The Energizers keep patrons entertained in the Oasis Lounge at Club Land'Or Tues-Sun nights. Catch live piano music at Chez Willie on Sat nights. The piano bar at Villaggio, on West Bay St at Caves Point, offers even more jazz, Thurs-Sat nights. Dream Quest plays a mix of reggae, soca and Junkanoo Tues-Sun nights at the Stage Lounge at the Wyndham Nassau Resort. The King and Knights at Cable Beach also offers a native show. See also **Junkanoo.**

Atlantis, Paradise Island's Entertainment Complex, offers dancing, gambling, shopping and dining. The Jokers Wild Comedy Club features top comics from the US and Canada.

The Rainforest Theatre in the Crystal Palace Casino and the Atlantis Theatre at Atlantis, Paradise Island, host various performances.

Gaming

New Providence offers two internationally renowned casinos – the 35,000-sq-ft Crystal Palace Casino and the 50,000-sq-ft Casino at Atlantis. Both are open 24 hours and offer craps, roulette, blackjack, baccarat, big six wheels, Caribbean stud poker and let-it-ride poker. The Crystal Palace Casino has paigow poker, sports betting and pari-mutuel betting. The Pegasus Race & Sports Book opened at the Casino at Atlantis in early 2004 and features wagering on all major sporting events. By law, Bahamas residents are prohibited from gambling.

Nightclubs

There is a thriving night life in New Providence with many clubs open until 4am or later. Nightclubs include The Zoo, West Bay St; Club Waterloo, East Bay St; Club Eclipse, Bay St; Dragons, Atlantis Entertainment Complex; Fluid Lounge, Bay St; Cocktails & Dreams, West Bay St; Señor Frogs, Navy Lion Rd on the water; the Drop Off, Bay St; Bahama Boom Beach Club, Elizabeth Ave; and Hurricanes Disco at SuperClubs Breezes.

See also **Cinemas, Gambling** and **Theatre & performing arts.**

ENVIRONMENT

The government of The Bahamas is committed to environmental protection and conservation.

The Bahamas Environment Science and Technology Commission (BEST) was established in 1994 as a policy-building agency of the government to coordinate its action supporting environmental sustainability.

In 1995 an Ambassador for the Environment was appointed and in '98 an Environmental Court was established.

HE Keod Smith is the Chairman of the Board, BEST Commission, and Ambassador for the Environment. BEST is located at Nassau Ct, off Marlborough St, PO Box CB-10980, tel 322-2576, fax 326-3509, or visit www.best.bs.

Environmental conventions

The Bahamas is signatory to a number of international environmental conventions.

The Convention on Biological Diversity (CBD) calls for the conservation of biodiversity, sustainable use of its components and fair and equitable sharing of the benefits arising out of the use of genetic resources. Visit www.biodiv.org.

In response, The Bahamas developed the Bahamas Biodiversity Data Management (BDM) Plan in 1997 and the Bahamas National Biodiversity Strategy and Action Plan (NBSAP) in '98.

The Bahamas' 22 national parks, four of which are marine protected areas (MPAs), constitute the present system of protected areas called for under the CBD.

The Cartegena Protocol on Biosafety resulted from the CBD's requirement to develop procedures for the safe transfer, handling and use of genetically modified plants, such as crops enhanced for disease resistance, and animals.

The United Nations Framework Convention on Climate Change (UNFCCC) aims to stabilize atmospheric greenhouse gas concentrations at a level that would prevent dangerous human-induced interference with the climate system. The National Climate Change Committee, part of the BEST Commission, was created to respond to the UNFCCC. Visit www.unfccc.int.

The Bahamas' first national communication to the UNFCCC, and the national inventory of greenhouse gases for the period of 1990-94, was submitted and accepted in April 2001.

The Vienna Convention for the Protection of the Ozone Layer, along with the subsequent Montreal Protocol on Substances that Deplete the Ozone Layer, calls for the phasing out of all ozone-depleting substances. The Bahamas has agreed to do so by 2010. Visit www.unep.org/ozone/index.shtml.

The Convention on International Trade in Endangered Species of Wild Fauna and Flora (CITES) requires parties to this convention to ban commercial international trade of specified endangered species. CITES also requires the regulating and monitoring of trade in other species that may become endangered. Visit www.cites.org.

The Ramsar Convention on Wetlands of International Importance Especially as Waterfowl Habitat strives for sustainable development of wetlands throughout the world. The Bahamas responded by adding Lake Windsor in Inagua National Park to the List of International Importance in 1997. Visit www.ramsar.org.

The Basel Convention on the Control of Transboundary Movements of Hazardous Wastes and Their Disposal strictly regulates the movements of hazardous wastes. Under this convention, The Bahamas must ensure that such wastes are managed and disposed of in an environmentally sound manner. Visit www.basel.int.

The United Nations Convention on the Law of the Sea governs all aspects of ocean space, such as boundary determination, marine scientific research, environmental control, economic and commercial activities, transfer of technology and the settlement of disputes relating to ocean matters. Visit www.un.org/Depts/los/index.htm.

The International Convention for the Prevention of Pollution from Ships (Marpol 73/78) seeks to prevent intentional and minimize accidental pollution of the marine environment by oil and other harmful substances. Visit www.imo.org.

Other conventions The Bahamas is party to include: The United Nations Convention to Combat Desertification promotes sustainable management of dryland ecosystems. Visit www.unccd.int. The World Heritage Convention encourages protection of the world's cultural and natural heritage. Visit www.unesco.org/whc.

Environmental organizations

Bahamas Reef Environment Educational Foundation (BREEF), Sir Nicholas Nuttall/Casuarina McKinney, tel 362-6477, fax 362-6478, e-mail breef@breef.org, www.breef.org

Bahamas National Trust (BNT), tel 393-1317, fax 393-4978, e-mail bnt@batelnet.bs

BEST Commission, tel 322-4546, fax 326-3509

Department of Environmental Health Services, tel 322-8048 or 322-8037, fax 322-8118, www.dehs.bs

Dolphin Encounters – Project BEACH (The Bahamas Education Association for Cetacean Health), Annette Dempsey, tel 394-2200, fax 394-2244, e-mail education@dolphinencounters.com, www.dolphinencounters.com

Friends of the Environment, tel (242) 367-2721, fax (242) 367-5177, e-mail info@friendsoftheenvironment.org, www.friendsoftheenvironment.org

Island Expedition, Dragan & Nicolas Popov, tel/fax 327-8659, e-mail orders@islandexpedition.com or nicholas@islandexpedition.com, www.islandexpedition.com

Oceanwatch Bahamas, Stuart Cove/Sally Varani, tel 362-4171, e-mail stuart@stuartcove.com

Re-Earth, Sam Duncombe, tel/fax 393-7604, e-mail reearth@batelnet.bs

See also **Bahamas National Trust; Birds; Fishing; Flora & fauna; Marine research; Nature centres; Public health, Public health services** and **Wildlife preserves.**

EXCHANGE CONTROL

Exchange control is a country's imposition of rules and regulations on transactions to conserve its foreign currency resources. In The Bahamas, exchange control is administered by The Central Bank of The Bahamas. The Central Bank is, therefore, responsible for the control and regulation of gold and foreign currency under the Exchange Control Act, 1952, and the Exchange Control Regulations, 1956.

The Bahamian dollar is legal tender in The Bahamas; all other currencies are foreign, although the US$ is accepted and is on par with the B$.

For exchange control purposes, the world has been divided into two categories: The Bahamas and the rest of the world. The Central Bank has the authority to determine residential status of all persons (including legal entities). Resident individuals are either citizens of The Bahamas or citizens of other countries who have been so designated by the Central Bank. Residents are subject to many, although liberal, exchange control regulations. Residents in The Bahamas may not purchase foreign currency, maintain foreign currency accounts or remit foreign currency abroad without permission from the Central Bank.

Non-resident individuals are citizens of a country outside The Bahamas who may reside in but are not gainfully employed in The Bahamas. These persons are subject to minimal currency regulations. Foreign currency deposits held by non-residents are exempt from exchange control regulations.

Foreign citizens who are gainfully employed within The Bahamas for one year or longer are regarded as "temporary residents." Such persons may be eligible for certain exemptions which permit them to retain all existing non-Bahamian assets, to operate foreign currency accounts and to repatriate Bahamian assets on leaving The Bahamas.

Investment currency: This is a pool of foreign currency available for capital investment abroad by residents. Central Bank permission is required for its acquisition and disposition. Investment currency changes hands at a premium determined by the demand and supply for the foreign currency.

Authorized agents/dealers: The Central Bank appoints authorized agents for the purpose of dealing in Bahamian and foreign currency securities and receiving securities into deposit. Authorized dealers are banks permitted to deal in all foreign currencies, and are also appointed by the Central Bank to approve certain exchange control applications under delegated authority as laid out in exchange control notices. Presently, there are 18 authorized agents, eight authorized dealers and two authorized agents/dealers.

Direct investment: This works two ways – by non-residents inward and residents outward.

1. Permission of the Investments Board is required for a non-Bahamian to invest in property in The Bahamas in excess of five acres or property for commercial use. If the non-resident investment in The Bahamas is made with foreign currency which is converted to Bahamian dollars, it is accorded "approved status," allowing the investor to repatriate income and capital gains accruing from the investment.
2. Permission for resident-owned companies in The Bahamas to extend their business outside The Bahamas depends largely on the probability of a good return to The Bahamas via increased income of foreign currency and/or increased exports. Direct investment outside The Bahamas must be an extension of an existing business within The Bahamas.

   Foreign currency to finance direct outward investments is normally purchased through the investment currency market. However, as of Sept 2002, special criterion investments were allowed an increased limit of $1 million per person or entity at the official rate, with an overall limit of $5 million per transaction, accessible once every three years.

Purchase of property outside The Bahamas: Residents of The Bahamas may purchase one piece of property outside The Bahamas for use by the family. If the application is approved by the Central Bank, the foreign currency necessary to acquire the property must be purchased through the investment currency market conducted by the banking department of The Central Bank of The Bahamas.

Loans: Resident companies wholly owned by residents require Central Bank permission to borrow foreign currency.

Personal allowance cards (dollar cards): Residents may submit application to the Central Bank for a dollar card, which permits the resident to purchase foreign currency drafts of up to $25,000 per card for credit card bills, and $10,000 for gifts to non-residents. It is renewable on presentation of the used dollar card, but a new one must be picked up for each calendar year.

Payment for imports: Permission from the Central Bank is required to purchase foreign currency for payment of non-oil imports in excess of $500,000. This requirement applies in New Providence and Grand Bahama. Authorized dealers in the Out Islands (excluding Grand Bahama) can sell foreign currency for imports without prior Central Bank permission. Application for purchase of foreign currency to pay for imports must be accompanied by a relevant invoice.

Allowances: Citizens and permanent residents of The Bahamas may convert $10,000 into foreign cash/traveller's cheques per person per trip for personal and holiday travel purposes. Commercial banks (authorized dealers) may issue and approve payments without exchange control permission. Supporting documents (ie, passport and airline ticket) and completion of Delegated Authority Exchange Form (E1) are required.

Business travel limit: $50,000 in cash or traveller's cheques per resident per annum.

Medical: Authorized dealers may sell up to $10,000 per person per trip in cash/traveller's cheques. There are no limits on amounts being paid directly to hospitals/clinics abroad by way of draft or wire transfer, where supported by appropriate invoices.

Educational: Authorized dealers may sell up to $10,000 cash/traveller's cheques per person per trip. There are no limits on amounts being paid directly to schools abroad by way of draft or wire transfer, where supported by appropriate invoices.

Emigration: A resident leaving The Bahamas must apply to the Central Bank to convert his Bahamian assets. Currently, he is permitted to convert up to B$125,000 to foreign currency at the official rate of exchange. Applications for amounts exceeding this limit are reviewed on a case-by-case basis. Temporary residents are permitted to repatriate all of their Bahamian dollar balances on leaving The Bahamas.

Exchange control liberalization

Since the 2001 amendment to limits on current and capital account transactions, the authorities continue to consider further adjustments to exchange control laws that would promote increased efficiency and benefit the economy.

See also **Bahamas International Securities Exchange; Banking,** Central Bank; **Import entry; Investment;** and **Property transactions,** Intl Persons Landholding Act.

EXPORT

See **Bahamas Investment Authority,. Import & export statistics, Industries encouragement** and **Manufacturing.**

EXPORT ENTRY

An export entry form is required for goods being exported from The Bahamas. The goods normally are subject to $10 stamp duty. Forms are available at several Nassau book shops and office supply stores. Completed forms should be taken to Bahamas Customs, Thompson Blvd, Oakes Field, Nassau.

Ordinary parcels, clothing, gifts, tourist items, etc, to be sent through post offices or parcel post do not incur the $10 stamp duty as they do not require an export entry form.

See also **Customs.**

EXTRADITION

In 1990, an Extradition Treaty was signed between The Bahamas and US in response to drug trafficking and other crimes. The agreement established more effective cooperation between the two countries and allowed for extradition of persons accused or convicted of extraditable crimes.

The Extradition Act, 1994, allows for persons accused or convicted of certain offences to be extradited to and from Commonwealth countries and foreign states. Extradition requests must be made through diplomatic channels. Persons against whom extradition is sought must have their case heard in a Bahamian court, which must find that there is a case to answer. Before the order may be issued, the treaty state must satisfy the Bahamian court that it has information against the accused that would constitute a crime in The Bahamas. The Bahamian court is not concerned with the guilt or innocence of the fugitive.

FIRE SERVICES

Royal Bahamas Police Force Fire Services operates under provisions of the Fire Services Act, which gives the director of fire services overall responsibility for fire defence policies, as well as the commissioner of police as the fire authority. Presently, Superintendent Alexander Roberts is director of fire services.

New Providence
Fire Services consists of 106 trained fire suppression/extrication technicians, including managers, supervisors and line staff. Officers are stationed in New Providence and deployed between five stations strategically positioned throughout the island. The administration section consists of director of fire services, chief fire officer, administrator, training officer, a fire prevention unit, arson investigation unit, mechanical repair workshop, and maintenance and water supplies. The operations division is responsible for all emergency responses, and is divided into three dutied guards – blue, green and red. The fire control room within each guard receives fire reports, as well as the police control room.

Out Islands
Grand Bahama Fire Services' structure is similar to New Providence's but with two stations and 34 officers. Inspector Walter V Evans is the chief fire officer for Grand Bahama and the Northern Bahamas.

There are four trained fire suppression/extrication officers in Eleuthera, strategically placed throughout the island.

One trained driver/pump operator, fire suppression/extrication technician is stationed in both Abaco and Cat Island.

Training
Enlistees in Fire Services undergo a 16-week training programme in various subjects including law, traffic, and policies. An additional eight-week programme in the art of fire science follows. This programme includes instruction in chemistry, physics, fire conditions and behavioural practices. This is complemented with practical fire-fighting training. At the completion of entry-level training, officers are posted on operational guards for further hands-on experience. Local training is supplemented with studies in the US and UK.

On June 18, 2003, 29 recruits enlisted, including five female direct-entry fire officers. Volunteer training targets small communities which may not have fire brigade officers.

In 2003, the brigade responded to approx 1,714 structural, vehicle, vessel and rubbish fires, bomb threats and vehicular accidents in New Providence. Total damages were estimated at $10,147,850.

Nine islands have fire-fighting equipment.

New Providence: Two KME pumpers, one KME 100-ft aerial ladder truck, one 2003 freightliner, two Navistar Pierce pumpers, two MS 200 Mack pumpers, and a 1500 GPM trailer-mounted Hale pump.

Abaco: Cherokee Sound, Green Turtle Cay and Sandy Point each have a portable pump. Marsh Harbour has five pumper trucks.

Andros: Nicholl's Town has one 1965 Mack truck.

Berry Islands: Bullocks Harbour has one Hale portable pump.

Bimini: One Toyota pick-up pump truck.

Cat Island: Arthur's Town has one 1976 Howe International pumper truck.

Crooked Island: Colonel Hill has one Hale portable pump.

Eleuthera: Spanish Wells has one Hale portable pump. Harbour Island has one 1976 Dodge International pumper truck. Governor's Harbour has one 1965 GMC pumper truck. Rock Sound has one 1969 Ford pumper truck.

Grand Bahama: One 2000 KME pumper, one 2003 freightliner, one MS 200 pumper.

In the event of a fire dial 911 or the district police or fire station.

FISHING

Bahamian waters produce a variety of game and food fish. Anglers from all parts of the world come to test their skill. World record (line) game fish caught in The Bahamas include: amberjack, one; bonefish, six (four line; two fly rod); dolphin (mahi-mahi), two; wahoo, six. Modern facilities to accommodate sport fishermen are available throughout The Bahamas.

Following is a list of some of the game species found in Bahamian waters, with a guide to seasons and locations where they can be caught.

Allison tuna: On and off throughout the year but best months are June, July and Aug. All deep-water areas.

Amberjack: Nov-May. Near all reef areas and around old wrecks.

Barracuda: Year-round. Found throughout The Bahamas, especially near reefs. Also in shallow water and occasionally offshore.

Blackfin tuna: May-Sept. Plentiful in vicinity of Nassau.

Bluefin (giant) tuna: May 7-June 15. Bimini, Cat Cay and West End, Grand Bahama.

Blue marlin: Off and on throughout the year but best months are June and July. Found all along the western side of The Bahamas, from Bimini and Cat Cay to Walker's Cay; off Andros, at the Berry Islands near Chub Cay; both sides of Exuma Sound and in the Atlantic Ocean from North Eleuthera to Green Turtle Cay, Abaco.

Bonefish: Year-round. This king of the shallow waters can be found in quantity throughout the islands.

Dolphin (mahi-mahi): Winter and spring. All deep-water areas.

Grouper: Year-round, except Dec and Jan, when harvesting of grouper is illegal. All reefs throughout The Bahamas.

Kingfish: May-July. Good fishing all over, but Berry Islands and western Abaco among the best spots.

Sailfish: Summer and fall. Berry Islands, Chub Cay, Bimini, Cat Cay, West End, Walker's Cay and Exuma Sound.

Tarpon: Year-round. Best bets are Andros and Bimini.

Wahoo: Nov-Apr, best months Jan and Feb. Most plentiful in Exuma Sound around the cays and at the lower end of Eleuthera. Other good areas: Northeast Providence Channel from Nassau to Spanish Wells and in the Northwest Providence Channel around the Berry Islands and off Sandy Point, Abaco.

White marlin: Winter and spring. Bimini east to Eleuthera, and Walker's Cay south to Exuma Sound in the ocean, or nearby deep channels.

Marine patrol craft

In 2001, the Dept of Fisheries purchased two, 26-ft Paramount patrol craft to assist in enforcement efforts. The vessels are clearly marked "Department of Fisheries, Marine Patrol." One is stationed in New Providence and the other in Abaco.

No-take zones

The Dept of Fisheries is in the process of designating five areas, including North Bimini, Berry Islands, South Eleuthera, Exuma Cays and North Abaco Cays, as no-take zones, where fishing will be prohibited.

At press time the boundaries of these no-take zones were not defined, although the dept was conducting community outreach and baseline data surveys for each area. Long-term plans call for the establishment of more marine fishery reserves. To protect the Nassau grouper, seasonal no-take periods have been designated during the peak spawning season.

The Bahamas National Trust (BNT) manages 22 parks, reserves and protected areas, most of which are no-take zones, the most notable being the Exuma Cays Land and Sea Park.

Fishing laws

Following is a summary of the Fisheries Resources (Jurisdiction and Conservation) Regulations, 1986:

Underwater fishing (spear fishing)

It is illegal:

1. To use underwater breathing apparatus (except a snorkel) to capture any fish or marine product. The use of an air compressor is restricted to the commercial fishing sector with a permit issued by the Dept of Fisheries. Visitors to The Bahamas may use an air compressor for observation purposes only and may not harvest any resources while using it. See **Licences** following.
2. To use any device other than a pole spear or a Hawaiian sling for the

discharge of a missile underwater. (The Hawaiian sling is a device – usually made of wood or plastic – for discharging a missile by the force of a rubber spring.)

Licences

Foreign vessels intending to engage in sport fishing must have a permit. Several rules apply under this permit:

1. Fishing gear is restricted to hook and line unless otherwise authorized. Only six lines are allowed in the water at one time, unless otherwise authorized. Cost of the permit is $20 per trip or $150 annually. (Note: If more than six reels are allowed on a party fishing boat, for instance, the permit is $10,000 annually.)
2. The bag limit for kingfish, dolphin and wahoo is a max combined total of six fish per person on the vessel, comprising any combination of these species.
3. Vessel bag limits for other marine products are 20 lbs of scale fish, 10 conch and six crawfish per person at any time. The possession of turtle is prohibited. The above amounts may be exported by the vessel upon leaving The Bahamas.

A $50 permit is required to conduct foreign fishing for scientific or research purposes. A licence is required to engage in foreign fishing – fishing by a non-Bahamian vessel – for commercial purposes. Such permission can be issued only to foreign states that have a fishery treaty with The Bahamas.

Bahamian commercial fishing vessels 20 ft in length or greater must have a valid fishing permit. "Bahamian," in relation to a fishing vessel, is one owned by a citizen of The Bahamas resident in The Bahamas; or a company registered in The Bahamas under the Companies Act, in which all the shares are beneficially owned by citizens of The Bahamas resident in The Bahamas.

A $10 permit is required for the use of an air compressor (hookah) in fishing. Permits are issued to Bahamians only, and use is restricted to Aug 1-Mar 31. Applicants must provide proof of dive competency. Divers are limited to a depth of 30-60 ft.

It is illegal to export any marine product for commercial purposes unless:

1. The person involved has an export licence for the product he wishes to export.
2. The product is inspected by a fisheries inspector at the time of export.
3. The export duty on the product, if any, is paid.

Prohibitions

It is illegal to:

1. Use bleach or other noxious or poisonous substances for fishing or have such substances on a fishing vessel without written approval from the Minister.
2. Use firearms or explosives for fishing.
3. Spearfish within one mile off the coast of New Providence; one mile off the southern coast of Freeport, Grand Bahama; 200 yds off the coast of all other Out Islands.
4. Use fishing nets with a minimum mesh gauge of less than two ins. Exceptions are nets used for catching goggle-eyes and pilchards.
5. Use a scale fish trap which does not have a self-destruct panel and minimum mesh sizes less than one by two ins for rectangular wire mesh traps and 1½ ins (greatest length of mesh) for hexagonal wire mesh traps.
6. Take coral.
7. Build artificial reefs without permission from the Minister.
8. Sell fish in New Providence without a permit from the Minister. Exceptions are those with a peddler's permit or shop licence.

Crawfish (spiny lobster): Closed season for crawfish is Apr 1-July 31.

The minimum size limit for crawfish is a carapace length of 3¼ ins from the base of the horns to the end of the jacket, or 5½ ins tail length. A $10 permit is required to trap crawfish.

Crawfish traps, unless otherwise approved, should be wooden slat traps not more than three ft in length, two ft in width and two ft in height with slats not less than one in apart. It is illegal to possess an egg-bearing crawfish or to

remove eggs from a female crawfish.
Conch: It is illegal to catch or possess conch with a shell that does not have a well-formed lip.
Turtles: Closed season for turtles is Apr 1-July 31. It is illegal to capture or possess a hawksbill turtle. Minimum size limit for a green turtle is 24 ins back length and for a loggerhead turtle, 30 ins back length. All turtles captured must be landed whole. Taking or possessing turtle eggs is prohibited.
Scale fish: It is illegal to:

1. Capture bonefish by nets.
2. Buy or sell bonefish.
3. Catch grouper and rockfish weighing less than three lbs.
4. Export live rock or small reef fish for commercial purposes.
5. Export hermit crabs.

Stone crab: Closed season is June 1-Oct 15. Minimum harvestable claw length is four ins. It is illegal to catch female stone crabs.
Marine mammals: It is illegal to capture, export or molest marine mammals. People who wish to capture such mammals for scientific, educational or exhibition purposes must apply to the Minister for permission.
Sponge: The minimum size limit is 5½ ins for wool and grass sponge and one in for hard-head and reef sponge.

Long-line fishing

Long-line fishing is defined by the Fisheries Resources (Jurisdiction and Conservation) Act, 1993, as the use of 10 or more baited fish hooks connected to a main line or cable capable of extending beyond 20 yds from the point where it is cast.

Under the Act long-line fishing is illegal without a permit. It stipulates that no person shall:

1. Have in his possession on a fishing vessel any apparatus intended for use in long-line fishing.*
2. Use for fishing within the exclusive economic zone (as defined by the Act) any apparatus for long-line fishing.*

** Unless written permission is provided by the Governor General. This is given only where it would not endanger elements essential to sustainable fishery development or prejudice the development and expansion of ecotourism.*

Any person who contravenes the Act is guilty of an offence and liable on summary conviction, subject to provisions of the Act, to a fine of not less than $50,000 or to imprisonment for a term of one year, or to both such fine and imprisonment.

Applications for permits and licences may be obtained from the Dept of Fisheries, East Bay St, PO Box N-3028, tel 393-1014/5.

See also **Bahamas National Trust** and **Wildlife preserves.**

FITNESS

Running, jogging and walking are popular fitness pursuits. Venues include the median along the Cable Beach strip, the bridges leading to and from Paradise Island, and the many long white sand beaches on the islands.

Fitness centres in New Providence include: Gold's Gym, corner of Mackey and East Bay sts, tel 394-4653; The Fitness Centre, Wyndham Nassau Resort, Cable Beach, tel 327-6200; Better Bodies, Shirley St Shopping Plaza, tel 394-5900; Bally Total Fitness, Sandyport, tel 327-2685; Mystical Fitness & Health Spa on Madeira St, tel 322-3814; Curves, Cable Beach Shoppers Haven, tel 327-3226, Harbour Bay Shopping Centre, tel 394-5518, and Faith Ave. Smaller fitness facilities are scattered throughout the island. Some hotels also offer fitness facilities for guests.

The Nassau Hash House Harriers is a social club for runners and walkers. Weekly runs are set in various locations around the island. Contact Brian Crick, tel 325-2831 (w) or 477-4624 (cell), or visit www.nassauhash.com.

Local organizations stage fun runs and walks throughout the year.

The Sivananda Yoga Retreat on Paradise Island offers daily asana (or posture) classes on harbourfront and beachfront decks. Non-guests can participate for a fee. Tel 363-2902, e-mail nassau@sivananda.org, or visit www.sivananda.org.

See also **Sports.**

FLORA & FAUNA

Fauna

The Bahamas, being a chain of islands with limited large open space, is unable to support animals of great size. However, the fauna remains diverse and unique.

Invertebrates

There is an abundance of invertebrates, including many species of ants and spiders, paper wasps, honey bees, land crabs, some 90 species of butterflies and the giant bat moth. Marine invertebrates include the conch, crawfish, the chalice sponge and numerous other species that depend on coral reefs for support.

Reefs & marine life

There are some 900 sq miles of reefs in The Bahamas, including the third-longest barrier reef in the world off the east coast of Andros. The reefs are rich with a diversity of marine life including green moray eels, cinnamon clownfish, queen angelfish, barracudas, the Nassau grouper, the placid nurse shark and inflatable porcupine fish. Reefs, like rainforests, are important as they help to reduce atmospheric carbon dioxide levels implicated in global warming.

Amphibians

There are six species of amphibians including the Cuban treefrog and the free-toed frog.

Reptiles

Some 44 species of reptiles are found in The Bahamas. These include the Cat Island freshwater turtle, Inagua freshwater turtles, green, loggerhead and hawksbill sea turtles, and the occasional leatherback turtle. Several turtle species are now endangered. There are also 10 species of snake, including the Bahamian boa constrictor, pygmy boa and blind worm snake. There are no poisonous snakes in The Bahamas. There are 29 species of lizard, including iguanas and curly tailed lizards. Several iguana species are now rare and endangered.

Birds

About 230 species of birds migrate to or live in the Bahama islands. Some are rare or endangered. They include the Bahama parrot, now found only in Abaco and Great Inagua, Bahama woodstar hummingbird, Bahama swallow, osprey, Kirtland's warbler, red-bellied woodpecker, West Indian flamingo and West Indian tree duck. Other interesting birds include the great blue heron, barn owl, peregrine falcon and Bahama duck. The Bahamas is also home to many species of seabirds, with many found nesting on cays throughout the archipelago.

Mammals

It is believed 13 species of mammals are native to The Bahamas, of which 12 are bats. The other is the hutia, a rodent-like creature once nearly extinct. It was rediscovered on East Plana Cay where it is now thriving and has been translocated to two cays in the Exuma Cays Land and Sea Park. Several species of whales and dolphins, including the humpback and blue whales and spotted dolphin, are found in seas around the Bahama islands as they migrate to and from their breeding grounds. Populations of sheep, goats and pigs are reared for agricultural purposes. There are also populations of wild pigs, donkeys, goats, racoons and Abaco wild horses that co-exist with local fauna with limited adverse effects.

Invasive fauna

A few introduced or exotic species have become pests in The Bahamas. The ring-necked dove, introduced in 1975, has displaced some native birds.

Extinct species

Extinct species include the New Providence iguana, Caribbean monk seal, paleoprovidence tortoise, chickcharnie owl and Bahamian population of American crocodiles.

Poisonous fauna

The **black widow spider** or bottle spider is possibly the most venomous species in The Bahamas. Its small, jet-black body is characterized by a red hourglass-shaped marking on its underside. The venom of the black widow is a powerful neurotoxin, capable of killing a human but more likely to cause severe pain followed by weakness, tremors, cramps and aches.

The **centipede,** a caterpillar-like creature that can grow to eight ins long, injects a potent venom into its victim.

The **Cuban tree frog** is covered with an irritating mucus which causes local inflammation and itching when rubbed into a cut or abrasion, and can cause excruciating pain, swelling and temporary blindness when brought into contact with the eyes.

Three species of stingray live in Bahamian waters, the **eagle ray, southern stingray** and **yellow stingray.** Some stingrays have tail barbs with venom glands. The most common injury results from stepping on barbs of a stingray half-buried in the sand.

The **Portuguese man-of-war** is a coelenterate that appears as a translucent blue float on the ocean surface with hanging tentacles as long as 80 ft. Poisons discharged by the tentacles can be lethal to humans.

Flora

Vegetation in The Bahamas is similar to that of Florida and Cuba. However, factors such as rainfall, temperature and our limestone substrate effect differences in appearance. Of the more than 1,200 species of plants, 9% are endemic.

Native species

Of all the species of plants found in The Bahamas, 120 are not found anywhere else in the world.

Trees: The following important native species are protected by law under the Conservation & Protection of the Physical Landscape of The Bahamas Act: Lignum vitae *(Guaiacum sanctum),* Horseflesh *(Lysiloma sabicu),* Mahogany *(Swietenia mahagoni),* Caribbean pine *(Pinus caribaea var bahamensis),* Red cedar *(Juniperus bermudiana),* Brasiletto *(Caesalpinia vesicaria),* Candlewood *(Gochnatia ilicifolia),* Rauwolfia *(Ravwolfia nitida),* Beefwood *(Guapira discolor),* Bullwood *(Pera bumelifolia),* Silk cotton *(Ceiba pentandra)* included for historical reasons.

Other important native trees include: Gumelemi *(Bursera simaruba),* Cancer tree *(Jacaranda coerulea),* Five finger *(Tabebuia bahamensis),* Cinnecord *(Acacia choriophylla),* Paradise tree *(Simarouba glauca),* Ram's horn *(Pithecellobium keyenses),* Princewood *(Exostema caribaeum),* Geiger tree *(Cordia sebestena),* Pigeon plum *(Coccoloba diversifolia),* Mastic *(Mastichodendron foetidissimum)*

Shrubs: Cascarilla *(Croton eleuteria),* Strong back *(Bourreria ovata),* Yellow elder *(Tecoma stans),* Golden dew drop *(Duranta repens),* Coco plum *(Chrysobalanus icaco)*

Mangroves: Black mangrove *(Avicennia germinas),* White mangrove *(Laguncularia racemosa),* Red mangrove *(Rhizophora mangle),* Buttonwood *(Conocarpus erectus)*

Palms: Hog cabbage palm *(Pseudophoenix sargentii),* Silver top palm *(Coccothinax argentata),* Pond top palm *(Sabal palmetto),* Buffalo top palm *(Thrinax morrisii)*

Exotic species

Naturalized: Royal Poinciana *(Delonix regia),* African tulip *(Spathodoea campanulata),* Poor man's orchid *(Buhinia purpurea)*

Invasive species: Brazilian pepper *(Schinus terebinthifolius),* Australian pine *(Casuarina equisetifolia),* Bottlebrush *(Melaleuca quinquervia),* Ink berry *(Scaevola plumieri)*

Fruit trees

Native edible wild fruits: Governor's plum *(Flacourtia indica),* Darling plum *(Reynosia septentrionalis),* Pigeon plum *(Coccoloba diversifolia),* Coco plum *(Chrysobalanus icaco),* Sea grape *(Coccoloba uvifera),* Tamarind *(Tamarindus indica),* Sapodilla *(Manilkara zapota),* Sugar apple *(Annona squamosa),* Custard apple *(Annona reticulata),* Mamey *(Mammea americana),* Mamey sapote *(Pouteria campechiana),* Soursop *(Anona muricata),* Guava (Andros) *(Psidium androsianum),* Guana berry *(Brsonima lucida),* Saffron *(Chrysophyllum oliviforme)*

Cultivated backyard fruits: Mango *(Mangifera indica),* Banana *(Musa sp),* Avocado *(Persea americana),* Juju

(Zizyphus mauritiana), Guinep *(Melicoccus bijugatus)*, Paw paw *(Carica papaya)*, Breadfruit *(Artocarpus communis)*, Hog plum *(Spondias purpurea)*, Scarlet plum *(Spondias purpurea var lutea)*, Gooseberry *(Phyllanthus acidus)*

Poisonous flora

Poisonwood is a member of the sumac family, which includes mango, cashew and pistachio. Poisonwood contains the poison urushiol, which causes a rash, and in cases of smoke inhalation, lung damage. Most people do not have a reaction to urushiol on first exposure, but most do on further contact.

Manchineel is a highly dangerous tree because of its poisonous green fruit and toxic latex. Rain water or dew from these trees can cause temporary blindness if brought into contact with the eyes.

Protection of flora & fauna

The Bahamas is a signatory to the Convention on Trade in Endangered Species (CITES), the Convention on Biological Diversity, Ramsar Convention on Wetlands, and the UN Climate Change Convention. Several acts directly or indirectly protect native species and ecosystems. These include:

1. Agriculture and Fisheries Act
2. Wild Bird Protection Act
3. Wild Animal Protection Act
4. Fisheries Resources (Jurisdiction and Conservation) Act
5. Plant Protection Act
6. Bahamas National Trust Act
7. Conservation and Protection of the Physical Landscape of The Bahamas Act

An extensive network of protected areas has been designated. This includes wild bird reserves managed by the Dept of Agriculture, national parks managed by the Bahamas National Trust (BNT) and marine reserves managed by Dept of Fisheries.

BNT plays an integral role in protecting Bahamian plants and animals primarily through its involvement in protecting threatened habitats. BNT manages a large national park in Inagua which supports the largest breeding colony of West Indian flamingos in the western hemisphere. This colourful and unusual bird is the Bahamian national bird.

See also **Animals, Bahamas Humane Society, Birds, Fishing, National Symbols, Nature Centres** and **Wildlife preserves.**

FORTS

Fort Charlotte, West Bay St, overlooking Clifford Park. Completed in 1789, this fort was built to guard the western entrance to Nassau Harbour. Fort Charlotte comprises three separate forts – Fort Charlotte, Fort Stanley and Fort D'Arcy. Visitors may tour the fort, moat, drawbridge, which features the original dungeons, and mounted cannons. Escorted and self-guided tours daily 8am-4pm, tel 325-9186.

Fort Fincastle, off East St, south of downtown Nassau. Completed in 1793, this ship-shaped structure with mounted cannons, atop Bennett's Hill protected Nassau town and harbour, the Battery at Paradise Island and the eastern territory. It is near the 126-ft water tower built in 1928 as a water supply reservoir. The water tower provides a superb view of the harbour and Nassau.

Fort Montagu, East Bay St. Completed in 1742 on the western point of Montagu foreshore, this fort was built to guard the eastern entrance to Nassau Harbour. The oldest standing fort in The Bahamas, it has mounted cannons and defended the harbour during skirmishes with Spaniards and Americans.

Fort Nassau. Built in 1697 on the site now occupied by the British Colonial Hilton Nassau, Fort Nassau was destroyed within six years by a Spanish-French invasion. It was reconditioned in 1744, and finally razed in 1837 to make way for military barracks.

Remains of fortifications can be seen at Winton, Blue Hills, South West Bay Rd, Old Fort, Potter's Cay and Paradise Island.

See also **Antiquities, Monuments and Museums Corp.**

FREE TRADE AREA OF THE AMERICAS (FTAA)

At the Summit of The Americas in Dec 1994, Heads of State of the 34 nations of the western hemisphere, signed a Declaration of Principles affirming commitment to the negotiation of a proposed Free Trade Area of the Americas (FTAA). The free trade zone would stretch from Alaska to Argentina.

Principle objectives are promotion of prosperity through economic integration and establishment of a free trade area in which barriers to trade in goods and services and investment will be progressively eliminated. The Bahamas has reduced the number of tariff items from more than 100 to 29, to simplify the process and further encourage investment. More than 50% of government revenues are derived from import duties.

The Bahamas Trade Commission was established in Dec 2002 to review the Bahamian taxation system, with particular reference to possible membership in regional (FTAA) and international trade agreements (WTO). The Commission comprises 28 members from the private and public sectors.

The two major economic sectors in The Bahamas are services – tourism and finance – although there are exports of rum, pharmaceuticals, salt, aragonite and crawfish. The government has pledged to negotiate an agreement based on the interests of The Bahamas, and seeks to secure adjustment periods which are fair and equitable for small economies in order for them to become fully integrated in the global economy.

Contact the Ministry of Trade and Industry, Dockendale House, 3rd Floor, West Bay St, PO Box N-4849, Nassau, tel 328-2700, or visit www.ftaa-alca.org or www.wto.org.

See also **Trade agreements.**

FREIGHT SERVICES

Goods to be sent as air freight from New Providence should be taken to Nassau International Airport for handling by the airline that will transport them or to a forwarding agent. International goods being exported require an export entry form.

Goods to be sent via ship should be taken to the shipping company or the dock, depending on company policy, or handled by a forwarding agent.

See **Export Entry** and **Shipping, Cargo shipping** and **Shipping agencies.**

Incoming freight

Freight not claimed at the dock or air cargo section within five working days is sent to the Queen's Warehouse, John F Kennedy Dr. Storage rates are based on size. There is a charge for transporting goods to the warehouse. Goods not claimed within three months may be put up for auction.

GAMBLING

Casino gambling is legal in The Bahamas for non-residents 18 and older. Bahamas residents are prohibited from gambling in the casinos under a max penalty of a $500 fine or six months' imprisonment. There are casinos at Cable Beach and Paradise Island, and in Freeport, Grand Bahama.

The Crystal Palace Casino is operated by Ruffin Leisure Industries. The Paradise Island casino is operated by Paradise Enterprises Ltd, a subsidiary of Kerzner International Ltd. The Royal Oasis Casino (also called The Casino at Bahamia) in Freeport is part of the Royal Oasis Golf Resort owned by Driftwood Bahamas Ltd. The Isle of Capri Casino at Our Lucaya Beach & Golf Resort in Freeport opened on Dec 15, 2003.

Sports betting

An Act to make provision for sports betting in The Bahamas was passed by Parliament in Oct 1995. The Act, amending the Lotteries and Gaming Act, allows for placing bets on any athletic game or sport other than horse racing that takes place within or outside The Bahamas.

Sports betting cannot, however, be conducted by telephone or other telecommunication device, or on behalf of another person.

The Bahamas offers four full-service Las Vegas-style sports books, at the Crystal

Palace Casino in Cable Beach, New Providence, tel 327-6200 ext 6882; at the Atlantis Paradise Island Casino, tel 363-2000; and in Grand Bahama at the Royal Oasis Casino, tel (242) 350-7000, and the Isle of Capri Casino at Our Lucaya, tel (242) 373-1333.

Pari-mutuel wagering

An act to make provision for pari-mutuel wagering was passed in Parliament in Oct 2002. The amendment to the Lotteries and Gaming Act allows casinos to offer pari-mutuel wagering, provided there is simultaneous transmission of pictures of the horse, harness or dog races.

Pari-mutuel wagering cannot be conducted by telephone or other telecommunications device, or on behalf of another person. It is currently offered at the Crystal Palace Casino and the Atlantis Paradise Island Casino.

Cruise ship gaming

The Cruise Ships (Overnighting Incentives) Act, 1995, allows approved cruise ships docked at the Prince George Dock for at least 18 hours, or travelling to or from Bahamian designated ports, to operate casinos 7pm-3am. The ship must have made no less than 20 voyages a year from outside the country to one of the designated ports – Great Harbour Cay, Rock Sound or Nassau – and must arrive at the Prince George Dock no later than 11am and depart no earlier than 3am the following day.

Bahamian residents or anyone gainfully employed in The Bahamas may not participate in cruise ship gaming unless employed by the licensee or operator of the casino, and gaming is within the course of their employment.

See also **Entertainment** and **Lotteries.**

GEOGRAPHY

The Bahamas is a 100,000-sq-mile archipelago that extends over 500 miles between southeast Florida and northern Hispaniola; between longitudes 72°35'W and 80°30'W and latitudes 20°50'N and 27°30'N.

The waters surrounding The Bahamas are virtually free of pollution and silt, making them among the clearest and most colourful in the world. Bordered on the west by the great "ocean river" known as the Gulf Stream, the islands have a near-perfect climate. Highest land elevation is 206 ft.

Some of the deepest water in the world is in the Tongue of the Ocean east of Andros, and flanked by the world's third-longest barrier reef. More than one mile deep, these waters are used for oceanographic research by the Atlantic Undersea Test and Evaluation Centre (AUTEC), a multimillion-dollar US Navy research base. See **Atlantic Undersea Test & Evaluation Center (AUTEC).**

The estimated land area of The Bahamas has been listed as 5,382 sq miles by the Dept of Lands and Surveys. Grand total for all land, including small uninhabited rocks and islets, is approx 5,400 sq miles. Figures are subject to change as more accurate surveys and maps are completed.

Modern mapping techniques are allowing advances in remeasuring the islands, some of which have suffered considerable loss of coastline due to erosion and man-made features, while there is some accretion to others. See **Fig 1.7** for land area of each island and its highest point.

GOLF COURSES

See **Sports** and **Freeport/Lucaya information, Golf courses.**

GOVERNMENT

See **Government section.**

GOVERNORS

Proprietary Governors

1670	Hugh Wentworth
1671	John Wentworth
1676	Charles Chillingsworth
1677	Capt Robert Clarke
1682	Robert Lilburne
1687	Thomas Bridges
1688	Lieut Governor Stede
1689	Cadwallader Jones

FIG 1.7

LAND AREA OF EACH ISLAND & ITS HIGHEST POINT

Island	Highest point (ft)	Area (sq miles)
Abaco	120	649
Acklins	142	150
Andros	102	2,300
Berry Isl	80	12
Bimini	20	9
Cat Isl	206	150
Cay Sal Bank	10	2
Conception Isl	66	4
Crooked Isl	155	92
Eleuthera	168	200
Exuma (Gt & Lt)	125	72
Exuma Cays	130	40
Grand Bahama	68	530
Inagua (Gt)	120	596
Inagua (Lt)	99	49
Little San Salvador (Half Moon Cay)	93	8
Long Cay	108	9
Long Isl	178	173
Mayaguana	131	110
New Providence	123	80
Plana Cays	63	6
Ragged Isl	116	9
Rum Cay	130	30
Samana Cay	80	15
San Salvador	123	63
Other cays	–	24
	Total sq miles:	**5,382**

1693 Nicholas Trott
1696 Nicholas Webb
1699 Read Elding
1700 Elias Hasket
1701 Ellis Lightfoot
1703 Edward Birch
1716 Roger Mosteyn

Royal Governors

1717 Woodes Rogers
1721 George Phenny
1728 Woodes Rogers
1733 Richard Fitzwilliam
1738 John Tinker
1759 Maj-Gen William Shirley
1767 Gen Sir Thomas Shirley, Bt
1774 Montfort Browne
1779 John Maxwell
1787 Earl of Dunmore
1797 William Dowdeswell
1801 John Halkett
1804 Charles Cameron
1820 Gen Sir Lewis Grant
1829 Sir J C Smyth
1835 Lieut Col W M G Colebrook
1837 Sir F Cockburn
1844 George B Matthew
1849 John Gregory
1854 Sir A Bannerman
1857 Charles John Bayley, CB
1864 Sir Rawson W Rawson, CB
1869 Sir James Walker, KCMG, CB
1871 Sir G C Strachan, RA, KCMG
1873 Sir John Pope-Hennessy, KCMG
1874 Sir W Robinson, KCMG
1880 T F Callaghan, CMG
1882 Sir C C Lees, KCMG
1884 Sir H A Blake, KCMG
1887 Sir Ambrose Shea, KCMG
1895 Sir William F Haynes-Smith, KCMG
1898 Sir G T Carter, KCMG
1904 Sir William Grey-Wilson, KCMG
1912 Sir George Haddon-Smith, KCMG
1914 Sir William L Allardyce, KCMG
1920 Maj Sir Harry Cordeaux, KCMG, CB
1926 Sir C W J Orr, KCMG
1932 The Hon Sir Bede Clifford, KCMG, CB, MVO
1936 The Hon Sir Charles Dundas, KCMG, OBE
1940 HRH The Duke of Windsor, KG, Kt, KP, GCB, GCSI, GCMG, GCIE, GCVO, GBE, ISO, MC
1945 Sir William L Murphy, KCMG
1950 Sir George Sandford, KBE, CMG
1951 Maj-Gen Sir Robert A R Neville, KCMG, CBE, RM
1953 Rt Hon Earl of Ranfurly, KCMG
1957 Sir Raynor Arthur, KCMG, CVO
1960 Sir Robert Stapledon Stapledon, KCMG, CBE
1964 Sir Ralph Grey (later Lord Grey of Naunton), GCMG, KCVO, OBE
1968 Sir Francis Cumming-Bruce (later Lord Thurlow), KCMG
1972 Sir John Warburton Paul, GCMG, OBE, MC (to July 9, 1973)

Governors General from independence – July 10, 1973
See **Government section.**

Decorations

Bt	Baronet
CB	Companion of the Bath
CBE	Commander of the British Empire
CMG	Companion of St Michael and St George
CVO	Commander of the Royal Victorian Order
GBE	Knight (or Dame) Grand Cross of the British Empire
GCB	Knight Grand Cross of the Bath
GCIE	Knight Grand Commander of the Indian Empire
GCMG	Knight Grand Cross of St Michael and St George
GCSI	Knight Grand Commander of the Star of India
GCVO	Knight Grand Cross of the (Royal) Victorian Order
ISO	Imperial Service Order
JP	Justice of the Peace
KBE	Knight Commander of the British Empire
KCMG	Knight Commander of St Michael and St George
KCVO	Knight Commander of the Royal Victorian Order
KG	Knight of the Garter
KP	Knight of St Patrick
Kt	Knight
MC	Military Cross
MVO	Member of the Royal Victorian Order
OBE	Officer of the British Empire
QC	Queen's Counsel
RA	Royal Army
RM	Royal Marine

GROSS DOMESTIC & GROSS NATIONAL PRODUCTS (GDP/GNP)
See **Economy.**

GUN PERMITS
The Firearms Act, 1969, and amendments set out government policy on firearms, establish comprehensive procedures for controlling possession by private individuals, and state fees payable.

Under the Act, there are three licence categories: revolvers, rifles and guns. Revolvers include all handguns including magazine-fed self-loaders, commonly called automatics, and cylinder-fed revolvers. Rifles apply to rim-fire and centre-fire shoulder arms. Guns mean smooth bore guns such as shotguns with barrels not less than 20 ins in length. Air guns and air rifles are prohibited weapons.

Completely forbidden are tear-gas pens, military arms such as artillery, flame-throwers, machine guns and automatic carbines. Exempt from any licensing requirements are toy guns, dummy firearms and spear guns designed for underwater use.

Revolvers
A special licence, granted sparingly, is issued by the commissioner of police. A person wishing to import or possess a revolver must fill out an application form. A reason considered acceptable by police must be given for possession of a handgun and must be verified by police investigation before the special licence is issued. The licence is then carried to customs or parcel post if the revolver is being imported, or to the dealer if it is being purchased locally. Revolvers or pistols being imported are subject to a customs charge of 65% of their value.

Rifles, other firearms & ammunition
An application form for the issue of a firearm certificate must be completed and submitted to the commissioner of police. A separate application must be made for each firearm and each quantity of ammunition. Presentation of the certificate and payment of duty, if an import, will bring the rifle, firearm or ammunition into possession. Rifles and ammunition being imported are subject to a customs charge of 100% of their value.

Guns
An application for a gun licence is made to the commissioner of police in New Providence, or to the administrator in the

Family Islands. A separate application must be made for each gun. Presentation of the gun licence and payment of duty, if an import, will bring the gun into possession.

Fees

Gun licences issued under the Act cost $50. Rifle licences cost $100. A revolver requires a special licence costing $250. All must be renewed annually. A $250 dealer's licence expires on the yearly anniversary of the date of issue. Replacement of a lost certificate, special licence or licence costs $5.

Temporary importation

Temporary importation of guns (excluding handguns) must be authorized by the police commissioner.

Exemption

Non-residents of The Bahamas visiting aboard a foreign vessel are not required to obtain permits or pay any fees or duty on firearms during the visit. This exemption is limited to three months following the arrival of the vessel at its first port of call. Once registered, the three-month period may be extended to one year. Conditions are:

1. Possession of firearms aboard the vessel must be declared to a Customs officer or an administrator within 48 hours of arrival.
2. The firearms are not used in the territorial waters of The Bahamas.
3. They are not brought ashore.

A note of caution

Any person introducing a revolver into The Bahamas or found in possession of a revolver in contravention of the Act is liable to a $1,000 fine and:

1. On conviction on information to imprisonment for a term of not less than three years.
2. On summary conviction before a Stipendiary and Circuit Magistrate to imprisonment for a term of not less than two years.

Any person introducing a firearm into The Bahamas in contravention of the Customs Act is liable to a fine of $5,000 and possible imprisonment for three years. Similarly strict measures are applied to persons found with any other firearms or ammunition without a licence as detailed under the Act.

Although not a provision of the law, it is recommended that firearm applicants ensure there is a safe place to deposit firearms and ammunition.

HARBOUR CONTROL

Nassau Harbour Control regulates and gives clearance to all ships entering and leaving Nassau Harbour. Harbour pilotage is compulsory for foreign vessels of 30 gross tons and above. Permission must be obtained from Harbour Control prior to anchoring in the harbour area and for the movement from one berth to another while in the harbour. Dumping of garbage, sewage, oil and other discharges is prohibited in the harbour area. The office operates 24 hours.

Operators of small fishing boats or small pleasure craft should telephone Harbour Control at 322-1596 before leaving the harbour so their locations can be determined if overdue.

The VHF radio frequencies of Harbour Control are: Channels 06, 09, 12, 14, 16, 20, 65, 66, 68, 73, 74 and 79. The Bahamas Telecommunications Co (BTC) maintains a constant watch on VHF Channel 16, the emergency frequency. For commercial traffic, VHF Channel 27 should be used through the Nassau marine operator.

AM radio ship-to-ship frequencies are 2182, 2638 and 2738 kHz, however, 2638 and 2738 have been phased out and cannot be re-licensed. They should be used only in emergencies. The international emergency frequency, 2182 kHz, is controlled by BTC. For commercial traffic, AM frequency 2198 should be used. Single side band frequencies are 3300.0, 4139.5, 5057.0 and 8100.0.

All vessels arriving from foreign destinations must clear customs and immigration prior to landing. Vessels travelling from The Bahamas to foreign destinations must clear customs prior to departure. Vessels must clear at first port of call.

See **Customs.**

HEALTH CARE

There are two government-operated hospitals in New Providence and one in Grand Bahama. Government clinics are available throughout New Providence, Grand Bahama and the Out Islands. Bahamians who can demonstrate legitimate need pay nominal fees at government clinics and hospitals.

Health insurance is available through local and international insurance companies. Group plans are available where employers arrange a health insurance plan on behalf of their employees. Benefits vary according to the plan.

See also **Hospital & clinics, Public health** and **Freeport/Lucaya information Hospital & clinics.**

HEALTH/MEDICAL SERVICES

See **AIDS/HIV, Ambulance/air ambulance services, Bahamas Family Planning Assoc, Dentists, Doctors, Health care, Hospitals & clinics, Public health** and **Vaccination requirements.**

HISTORY

Before recorded history, what was to become The Bahamas was inhabited by Aborigines of Mongol descent. Their roots dated to the first great migration from the Old World to the New.

During the last Ice Age up to 100,000 years ago, ancestors of the original Bahamians came to the Americas by way of a land bridge that once linked Alaska with Siberia.

Lucayans, the Amerindians here when Columbus arrived on Oct 12, 1492, were part of what is called the Neolithic Revolution. The word *Lucayan* comes from *Lukku-Cairi*, or *Island People*. They were excellent farmers, good potters, weavers of cotton fibres, expert divers and skilled navigators in dugout canoes of their own invention. Only recently have their community sites been excavated and their artefacts retrieved from caves sometimes used as sacred burial vaults.

Important dates in the past 512 years of Bahamian history are:

1492: New World discoverer Christopher Columbus landed first at a Bahamian island called Guanahani. He renamed it San Salvador, Castilian for Holy Saviour.

1625: French settlers made an unsuccessful effort to colonize what was created as a Barony of the Bahamas. When a supply ship arrived from France, no trace of the first colony could be found.

1628: A treasure-laden Spanish galleon believed to have been captured by Dutch freebooter Piet Heyn sank just off Lucaya, Grand Bahama. In 1964, an estimated $2.8 million in treasure was recovered from the ancient wreck.

1647: The Company of Eleutherian Adventurers, a Pilgrim group, founded the first republic in the New World. Its purpose was to colonize the depopulated Bahama Islands and claim them for Great Britain. The colonists arrived in 1648 and took over an island the Amerindians called Cigatoo. It was renamed Eleuthera, after the Greek word for freedom.

1656: A Spanish galleon with treasure estimated to be worth more than $2 billion sank in the Little Bahama Bank. Captain Herbert Humphreys began salvaging the *Nuestra Señora de las Maravillas* in the late 1980s and announced his most recent find in '91.

1670: Six Lords Proprietors of South Carolina were granted the Bahama Islands by King Charles II of England.

1695: Lords Proprietors authorized construction of a fort and city on the island of New Providence. The city, called Charles Towne in honour of King Charles II, was renamed Nassau. The new name honoured King William III, formerly Prince of Orange-Nassau.

1697: Fort Nassau was completed on the site now occupied by the British Colonial Hilton Nassau. Artefacts are on display at the resort.

1717: Captain Woodes Rogers was named first Royal Governor of the Bahama Islands. He restored order by ending the rule of pirates and paved the way for a representative Assembly.

1729: The Bahamas House of Assembly first officially convened. The House has met in the west building of

Parliament on Bay St since 1805.

1741: Construction of Fort Montagu began at the eastern entrance to Nassau Harbour. Completed in 1742, it still stands as a tourist site.

1776: Eight American Colonial warships captured Fort Montagu and Fort Nassau for a short period. This is believed to be the first foreign occupation by the US. In 1778, Americans again invaded.

1782: Spaniards, irked by pirate and privateer raids on their shipping, re-captured the Bahama islands.

1783: The Bahama islands were restored to Great Britain by treaty. Andrew Deveaux, a Loyalist from South Carolina who was unaware of the agreement, seized the islands in the name of the Crown.

The immigration of American Loyalists began. Many brought their slaves and set up a plantation economy. A cotton blight was later to wipe out this lifestyle. Ruins of old plantation homes dot the Bahama Islands to this day.

1789: Completion of the main portion of Fort Charlotte overlooking the western entrance to Nassau Harbour. This major tourist attraction was restored in the early 1990s at a cost of $1 million.

1793: Fort Fincastle, shaped like a paddle-wheel steamer, was built at one of New Providence's highest points. Today, a water tower nearby serves as a favourite lookout for visitors and residents.

1838: Slavery was fully abolished. Agriculture declined. Wrecking, controlled by licences, flourished until the Imperial Board of Trade dotted the islands with lighthouses. Some are still in operation, with Abaco's candy-striped Hope Town lighthouse the most revered and photographed.

1861-65: The American Civil War brought great wealth to Nassau, a major supply base for the Confederacy. Nassau's first resort hotel, the Royal Victoria, was built.

1892: The first Florida to Nassau telegraph submarine cable was laid and began operations. It came ashore at what is now called Cable Beach.

1898: Nassau was officially developed as a fashionable winter season resort with the Hotel and Steam Ship Service Act.

1914: John Ernest Williamson shot the first undersea motion picture in history. Since then, many films have used Bahamian locations, including the James Bond classic, *Thunderball, My Father the Hero, Zeus and Roxanne, Flipper* and *Speed 2, Cruise Control*.

1920: US prohibition of alcoholic beverages brought a boom to the Bahama Islands, where liquor was legal and plentiful.

1930s: Famous writers came to live and work in The Bahamas, among them Ernest Hemingway, Zane Grey and John Steinbeck.

1940: A destroyers-for-bases agreement between the US and UK led to establishment of bases at Grand Bahama, Eleuthera, San Salvador and Mayaguana. They were to play a major role in the early days of the Space Age when missile tracking stations were set up on Bahamian bases.

1942-45: Nassau became a Royal Air Force Training Base and western bastion of an "air bridge" which ferried aircraft to World War II war zones.

1950: Nassau, aided and abetted by the 1940s governorship of the fashionable Duke of Windsor, joined the front rank of year-round resorts.

1955: Signing of the Hawksbill Creek Agreement, which paved the way to establish Freeport/Lucaya as the second-largest city in the country.

1962: Universal adult suffrage granted; Bahamian women voted for the first time.

1964: The Colony gained internal self-government. Sir Roland Symonette was named premier. Leader of the opposition was Lynden O Pindling, head of the Progressive Liberal Party (PLP).

1966: The first bridge connecting New Providence to Paradise Island was built. Another was completed in Dec 1998.

1967: The PLP won the majority of House of Assembly seats and Pindling became the new premier.

1969: Constitution revised. The Colony of the Bahama Islands became a Commonwealth; Pindling became prime minister.

1973: The Bahama Islands became the free and sovereign Commonwealth of The Bahamas on July 10, ending 325 years of British rule.

1990: The $300-million Crystal Palace Resort and Casino, Cable Beach, formally opened, launching a new era of mega-resorts in The Bahamas.

The International Business Companies (IBC) Act became law, crystallizing The Bahamas' reputation as a top international financial centre.

1992: The opposition Free National Movement (FNM) was voted in as the new government Aug 19, ending the PLP's 25-year rule. The Rt Hon Hubert A Ingraham became prime minister.

The Bahamas celebrated the 500th anniversary of the landing of Columbus at Guanahani/San Salvador.

1994: Official fifth Bahamas tour of Her Majesty, Queen Elizabeth II, constitutional Bahamas head of state represented by the Governor General. While in The Bahamas, the Queen officially opened the Bahamas Tourism Training Centre, Nassau, and the Garnet Levarity Justice Centre, Freeport.

1995: Tricentennial of the city of Nassau, officially named on Apr 12, 1695.

Sun International Hotels Ltd (later Kerzner Intl), of South Africa, opened the Atlantis, Paradise Island, resort and casino, complete with a legendary waterscape featuring the world's largest man-made marine habitat.

1996: At the Atlanta Centennial Olympics, The Bahamas track and field team won the silver medal in the women's 4x100m relay.

The Bahamas' first execution in 12 years took place with the hanging of Thomas Reckley, 44.

1997: The Free National Movement (FNM) was voted in for a second term on Mar 14.

The first female speaker of the House, The Hon Rome Italia Johnson, was appointed.

The $78-million Freeport Container Port was officially opened, transforming Freeport into a major world trans-shipment centre.

1998: Royal Towers at Atlantis, including 1,202 new rooms, the Marina at Atlantis, a 100,000-sq-ft entertainment complex, and additional water features and convention space, opened. The new bridge linking Nassau and Paradise Island was completed.

1999: Bahamas Telecommunications Corporation downsized in preparation for privatization.

The Securities Industry Act, 1999, came into effect, paving the way for the creation of the Bahamas International Securities Exchange (BISX).

Hurricane Floyd, a strong Category 4 storm, raged through The Bahamas in Sept, causing severe damage.

2000: Sir Randol Fawkes, father of the labour movement, and Sir Lynden Pindling, the country's first and longest-serving prime minister, died.

A census was taken, the first since 1990.

The women's 4x100m relay team won gold at the 2000 Olympic Games in Sydney, Australia.

Nine new financial laws were passed in response to Bahamas blacklisting by the Financial Action Task Force (FATF).

2001: US Internal Revenue Service approved The Bahamas as a qualified jurisdiction for trade in US securities.

Former prime minister Lynden Pindling replaced the Queen on the $1 bill.

The Bahamas was removed from the FATF blacklist.

2002: Bahamians voted on five amendments to the Constitution on Feb 28, in the first national referendum since independence. All proposals were rejected.

After ten years as the official opposition, the Progressive Liberal Party (PLP) was voted in as the new government on May 2. The Rt Hon Perry G Christie became the nation's third prime minister.

The first female deputy prime minister, the Hon Cynthia Pratt, was appointed.

2003: Sir Gerald Cash, second and longest-serving Bahamian Governor General, died at 85.

The Bahamas went on full alert in March as the US invaded Iraq, beginning a months-long Gulf war.

Kerzner International announced plans for a $600-million Phase 3 addition to Atlantis. Isle of Capri Casino in Freeport was completed.

The Bahamas' first National Art Gallery opened in the restored Villa Doyle on West Hill St.

2004: Kerzner International announced the start of its $1-billion Phase 3 development at Atlantis. Plans include construction of a 1,200-room hotel, retail complex, water-themed attractions, additional timeshare units and a golf course to be built on Athol Island.

Dr Rodney Smith was named new president of The College of The Bahamas taking over from former president Dr Leon Higgs.

Renowned Bahamian artist Brent Malone died at the age of 63.

Former MP and Free National Movement party adviser Jimmy Shepherd died at the age of 85.

Sir Gordon Bryce, last Supreme Court Chief Justice of a non-independent Bahamas, died at the age of 90.

John D Rood, of Jacksonville, Florida, became the eleventh US Ambassador to The Bahamas.

Prime Minister Perry Christie officially opened the new 19,000-sq-ft Isle of Capri Casino in Grand Bahama.

Bahamian sprinter Tonique Williams-Darling won the gold medal in the women's 400-metre final at the 2004 Olympic Games held in Athens, Greece. Debbie Ferguson won bronze in the women's 200-metre final.

Hurricane Frances and Hurricane Jeanne hit The Bahamas in Sept causing considerable damage, especially to San Salvador, Cat Island, Abaco, Eleuthera and Grand Bahama.

See also **Archives** and **Bahamas Historical Society.**

HOLIDAYS

The following public holidays are observed in The Bahamas:

- New Year's Day
- Good Friday
- Easter Monday
- Whit Monday (seven weeks after Easter)
- Labour Day (first Fri in June)
- Independence Day (July 10)
- Emancipation Day (first Mon in Aug)
- Discovery Day/Heroes' Day (Oct 12)
- Christmas Day (Dec 25)
- Boxing Day (Dec 26)

Holidays which fall on Sat or Sun are usually observed on the previous Fri or following Mon as dictated by the Public Holidays Act. Stores in New Providence and most Out Islands are closed on holidays.

HOSPITALS & CLINICS

High-quality health care is available throughout The Bahamas, through government and privately operated hospitals and walk-in clinics.

The Public Hospitals Authority (PHA) is a government corporation established July 1, 1999. Governed by a chairman and 11 board members, it has direct responsibility for the on-going development and management of the government-owned hospitals (Princess Margaret Hospital, Sandilands Rehabilitation Centre and Rand Memorial Hospital) Grand Bahama Public Health Services and National Emergency Medical Services. The PHA is headed by managing director Herbert Brown.

Princess Margaret Hospital: Shirley St. Government operated, 436-bed acute-care hospital with private wards. Specialist services include: family medicine; internal medicine; anaesthesiology; cardiology; cardiovascular surgery; dentistry; dermatology; ear, nose and throat; gastroenterology; general surgery; oral maxillofacial surgery; plastic surgery; endocrinology; pulmonary medicine; podiatry; rheumatology; paediatrics; obstetrics and gynaecology; oncology; neurology; urology; nephrology; ophthalmology; radiology; psychiatry; intensive care unit; critical care services; neonatal intensive care and special care baby unit; dietetics; speciality clinics; dialysis unit; burns unit; neurodevelopment and pharmacy services.

Rehabilitative services include physio, occupational, audiology and speech therapies.

Diagnostics and other allied health services include: stat lab; general laboratory; biochemistry and microbiology labs; blood bank; radiology with mammography; diagnostic imaging; CT scan; EKG and ECHO. Chief hospital administrator, Coralie Adderley, tel 325-0048.

Doctors Hospital: Corner of Shirley St and Collins Ave. Acute care, privately operated hospital with 72 patient beds. Medical specialities include, but are not limited to, emergency medicine; ear, nose and throat; general surgery; orthopaedic surgery; obstetrics and gynaecology; ophthalmology; neonatology; pulmonology; internal medicine; family medicine; gastroenterology; urology; cardiology; cardiovascular surgery, neurosurgery, plastic surgery, psychiatry and paediatrics. There are three operating rooms, one with laminar flow; intensive care unit with eight beds; level 3 nursery and maternity suite with 14 beds. Emergency doctors are on the premises 24 hours a day, seven days a week. All emergency room staff is ACLS (Advanced Cardiac Life Support) certified. Ancillary depts: clinical laboratory, blood bank, imaging (tele-radiology, X-ray, ultrasound, mammography, bone densitometry, nuclear medicine, MRI and spiral CAT scans), pharmacy, EEG/ECG, diet and nutrition counselling, cardiac catheterization and rehabilitation (physiotherapy, occupational therapy, speech language pathology, ergonomics and physiatry). The medical staff comprises over 130 hospital physicians and physicians in private practice. Tel 302-4600.

Doctors Hospital Health System (DHHS) accepts most major insurance plans. DHHS offers emergency services with ambulances. Chief executive officer, Barry Rassin, FACHE, tel 302-4701.

Sandilands Rehabilitation Centre: Fox Hill Rd. Government-owned. Comprises the 352-bed **Sandilands Psychiatric Hospital** and the 128-bed **Geriatric Hospital.** The hospitals are staffed by consultants, medical officers, podiatrists, qualified dentists, a team of nurses, psychologists, social workers and other allied health workers. The centre is managed by an executive management committee headed by the hospital administrator, Catherine Weech, tel 324-6881 or 324-1553.

An outpatient community counselling and assessment centre, located on Market St, provides services for mental disorders, stress, substance abuse and depression. Tel 323-3295/3 or e-mail rehabcentre@juno.com.

Sandilands Psychiatric Hospital: Built in 1956 to accommodate, treat and rehabilitate patients with mental illnesses and substance abuse related problems so they may return to their respective communities. The hospital includes a max security unit, acute psychiatric male and female wards, Timothy O McCartney child and adolescent unit, Lignum Vitae (drug) unit, detox and evaluation unit, Brian Humblestone (alcoholic unit) and day hospital facilities. Services for rehabilitation include special education, recreational therapy, occupational therapy, physical therapy, psychological evaluation and social services.

The hospital also provides a child guidance day care programme and a half-way house for long-stay patients.

Geriatric Hospital: Established in 1965 to provide comprehensive medical and nursing care to elderly patients who are chronically ill and unable to be cared for at home or in any other community facility.

An outpatient gerontology clinic for ambulatory elderly community residents is located at the Ann's Town clinic.

Lyford Cay Hospital/Bahamas Heart Institute: Lyford Cay, six in-hospital beds, including four-bed coronary care unit and two-bed telemetry unit. There is also an operating theatre, X-ray and laboratory as well as an emergency room with a doctor on call 24 hours. Specialist treatment is offered in cardiology, internal medicine and family practice. Echocardiography, stress echocardiography, transtelephonic ECG, peripheral vascular ultrasound, holter monitoring, exercise stress testing, enhanced extracorporeal counter pulsation (EECP) and recompression chamber/hyperbaric oxygen therapy are also available. The full-time cardiologist is also on the staff of the Cleveland Clinic, Ft Lauderdale, FL; Duke Medical Center, Durham, NC, and the Miami Heart Institute, Miami Beach, FL. The hospital is affiliated with all three institutions. Tel 362-4400.

Stat Care Medical & Emergency Centre: Nassau and Delancy Sts. A free-standing health care facility designed to provide outpatient healthcare services. The centre offers on-site consultation with board-certified speciality physicians.

Open Mon-Sat 8am-8pm, Sun and holidays 12 noon-8pm, tel 328-5596/8, fax 328-6391.

Out Island clinics

The Ministry of Health operates 116 clinics of varying size, complexity and scope of services. In cases where more medical assistance is needed, patients are flown to Princess Margaret Hospital in Nassau. Visitors needing medical assistance in the northern Bahamas may receive coverage from the Rand Memorial Hospital, Grand Bahama.

Other services

Community and environmental health services are offered throughout The Bahamas. Bachelor's and associate's degree programmes in nursing are offered through The College of The Bahamas. There is also a basic course in clinical or practical nursing and six post-basic courses. A nursing cadet programme was implemented by the Ministry of Health in 1996. A Faculty of Medicine in conjunction with the University of the West Indies was founded in Apr 1997.

See also **Ambulance/Air Ambulance.**

HOTELS

See **Fig 1.8** for hotel listings. Only hotels with 20 rooms or more are listed for New Providence, Paradise Island and Grand Bahama, although smaller hotels and guest houses are available. Generally, Out Island hotels listed here have 15 rooms or more. Hotels with fewer rooms are available at:

Abaco: Casuarinas Point, Elbow Cay, Grand Cay, Green Turtle Cay, Guana Cay, Hope Town, Man-O-War Cay, Marsh Harbour, Sandy Point, Spanish Cay, White Sound, Wood Cay.
Acklins: Spring Point.
Andros: Behring Point, Blanket Sound, Cargill Creek, Driggs Hill, Fresh Creek, Johnson Bay, Kemps Bay, Lisbon Creek, Mangrove Cay, Nicholl's Town, North Andros, Staniard Creek.
Berry Islands: Great Harbour Cay.
Bimini: Alice Town, Bailey Town, South Bimini.
Cat Island: Fernandez Bay, New Bight, Orange Creek, Pigeon Cay, Port Howe.
Crooked Island: Cabbage Hill, Colonel Hill, Landrail Point.
Eleuthera: Dunmore Town, Governor's Harbour, Gregory Town, Harbour Island, Hatchet Bay, Palmetto Point, Rock Sound, Spanish Wells, Tarpum Bay, Upper Bogue.
Exuma: George Town, Staniel Cay.
Grand Bahama: Deep Water Cay, West End.
Inagua: Matthew Town.
Long Island: Clarence Town.
Mayaguana: Abraham's Bay.

Contact the Ministry of Tourism, Nassau, tel 322-7500, or the Bahama Out Islands Promotion Board, tel (305) 931-6612.

See also **Accommodations.**

HOTELS ENCOURAGEMENT

The Bahamas, with tourism as its No 1 industry, gives special encouragement to private capital for building hotels and resorts throughout the country.

The Hotels Encouragement Act provides customs duty exemptions on materials imported to construct and equip hotels, as well as tax guarantees and concessions for improvement of guest facilities.

Investors must apply in writing to the Ministry of Financial Services and Investments, citing details of the proposed hotel or residential club, amenities, estimated cost and proposed plans for location and building(s). A project application form and plans must be filed with the Dept of Physical Planning for land use approval. Plans must also be approved by the Dept of Public Health and the Dept of Public Works.

The government then may enter into an agreement with the investor to be exempt from customs duties on materials imported to construct, extend, equip, furnish or complete the hotel.

Upon approval, the investor may also import duty free the construction plant to construct, extend and complete the new facility. The exemption active dates are decided by government.

cont on pg 425

FIG 1.8

HOTELS

Hotel/location	No of rooms	Beach/ water-front	Pool	Tennis	Golf course	Dive resort	Tel (242)	Fax (242)
New Providence								
British Colonial Hilton Nassau, No 1 Bay St	291	√	√	x	x	x	322-3301	302-9009
Buena Vista Hotel, Delancy St	5	x	x	x	x	x	322-2811	322-5881
Casuarinas, Cable Beach	78	√	√	√	x	x	327-7921	327-8152
Club Crystal Hotel Taylor St, Nassau Village	20	x	x	x	x	x	393-4442	394-0943
Colony Club Resort, St Albans Dr	104	x	√	x	x	x	325-4824	325-1240
The Corner Hotel, Carmichael Rd & Faith Ave	53	x	x	x	x	x	361-7445	361-7448
El Greco Hotel, Augusta & West Bay Sts	27	x	√	x	x	x	325-1121	325-1124
Grand Central Hotel, Charlotte St	35	x	x	x	x	x	322-8356	325-2018
Graycliff Hotel, West Hill Street	20	x	√	x	x	x	322-2796	326-6188
Harbour Moon Hotel, Bay & Deveaux Sts	30	x	x	x	x	x	323-7330	328-0374
Holiday Inn Nassau, Nassau & West Bay Sts	185	x	√	x	x	x	356-0000	323-1408
Island Outpost, Compass Point, Love Beach	*cottages* 18	√	√	x	x	x	327-4500	327-3299
Lyford Cay Club, Lyford Cay	*clubhouses* 47 *cottages* 20	√	√	√	√	x	362-4271	362-4528
Mondingo Hotel, Nassau Village	26	x	x	x	x	x	393-0333	393-9461
The Montagu Beach Inn, Village Rd & Shirley St	33	x	x	x	x	x	393-0475	393-6061
Nassau Beach Hotel, Cable Beach	400	√	√	√	x	x	327-7711	327-8829
Nassau Harbour Club, East Bay St	50	√	√	√	x	x	393-0771	393-5393

Hotel/location	No of rooms	Beach/ water-front	Pool	Tennis	Golf course	Dive resort	Tel (242)	Fax (242)
Orange Hill Beach Inn, West Bay St	30	x	√	x	x	x	327-7157	327-5186
The Orchard Hotel, Village Rd	32	x	√	x	x	x	393-1297	394-3562
Park Manor Hotel, 45 Market St north	35	x	√	x	x	x	356-5471	325-3554
Poinciana Inn, Bernard Rd	52	x	√	x	x	x	393-1897	394-1030
Quality Inn Junkanoo Beach, West Bay & Nassau Sts	63	√	√	x	x	√	322-1515	322-1514
Radisson Cable Beach & Golf Resort, Cable Beach	700	√	√	√	√	x	327-6000	327-6987
Red Carpet Inn, East Bay St	40	x	√	x	x	x	393-7981	393-9055
Sandals Royal Bahamian, Cable Beach	403	√	√	√	x	√	327-6400	327-3971
Sir Charles Hotel East St south & Malcolm Rd	20	x	x	x	x	x	322-5641	361-5887
South Ocean Golf & Beach Resort, Adelaide Rd (also timeshare)		*closed for renovations*					362-4391	362-4810
Sun Fun Resorts, West Bay St	40	x	√	x	x	x	327-8827	327-8802
SuperClubs Breezes, Cable Beach	391	√	√	√	x	x	327-5356	327-5155
Towne Hotel, George St	46	x	√	x	x	x	322-8450	328-1512
West Bay Hotel, West Bay St	40	x	x	x	x	x	323-1000	326-5251
Wyndham Nassau Resort, Cable Beach	850	√	√	x	x	x	327-6200	327-5227
New Providence timeshare (no of villas not rooms)								
Guanahani Village, Cable Beach	35	√	√	√	x	x	327-0688	327-0731
Sandyport Beaches Resort, West Bay St	72	√	√	√	x	x	327-4279	327-1109
South Ocean Golf & Beach Resort, Adelaide Rd		*closed for renovations*					362-4391	362-4810
Westwind I Club, Cable Beach	21	√	√	x	x	x	327-7680	327-7251
Westwind II Club, Cable Beach	54	√	√	√	x	x	327-7211	327-7529

Hotel/location	No of rooms	Beach/ water-front	Pool	Tennis	Golf course	Dive resort	Tel (242)	Fax (242)
Paradise Island								
Atlantis, Paradise Island	2,317	√	√	√	√	x	363-3000	363-3524
Beach Tower, Casino Dr	423	√	√	√	√	x	363-3000	363-3724
Coral Towers, Casino Dr	693	√	√	√	√	x	363-3000	363-3524
One&Only Ocean Club, Paradise Island Dr	106	√	√	√	√	x	363-3000	363-6464
Royal Towers, Casino Dr	1,201	√	√	√	√	x	363-3000	363-6309
Best Western Bay View Suites, Bay View Dr	30	x	√	√	x	x	363-2555	363-2370
Club Land'Or, Paradise Beach Dr (also timeshare)	72	√	√	x	x	x	363-2400	363-3403
Comfort Suites, Paradise Island Dr	228	x	√	x	x	x	363-3680	363-2588
Holiday Inn SunSpree, Harbour Rd	245	√	√	√	x	x	363-2561	363-3803
Sheraton Grand Resort Paradise Island, Casino Dr	*closed for renovations*						363-2011	363-3193
Sivananda Yoga Retreat	54	√	x	x	x	x	363-2902	363-3783
Sunrise Beach Club & Villas, Casino Dr (also timeshare)	22	√	√	x	x	x	363-2234	363-3739
Sunshine Paradise Suites, Paradise Island Dr	24	x	√	x	x	x	363-3955	363-3840
Paradise Island timeshare (no of villas not rooms)								
Harborside Resort at Atlantis, Marina Dr	164	√	√	x	x	√	363-7500	363-6810
Paradise Harbour Club & Marina, Paradise Island Dr	22	√	√	x	x	x	363-2992	363-2840
Paradise Island Beach Club, Ocean Ridge Dr	44	√	√	x	x	x	363-2814	363-2130
Grand Bahama								
Bell Channel Inn, King's Rd	31	√	√	x	x	√	373-1053	373-2886
Best Western Castaways Resort & Suites, The Mall & Intl Bazaar	118	x	√	x	x	x	352-6682	352-5087

Hotel/location	No of rooms	Beach/ water-front	Pool	Tennis	Golf course	Dive resort	Tel (242)	Fax (242)
Crowne Plaza Golf Resort & Casino at the Royal Oasis, The Mall & W Sunrise Hwy	965	x	√	√	√	x	350-7000	350-7002
Crowne Plaza Tower	400	x	√	√	√	x	350-7000	350-7002
Crowne Plaza Country Club	565	x	√	√	√	x	350-7000	350-7001
Flamingo Bay Hotel & Marina, Jolly Roger Dr	67	√	√	√	x	x	373-5640	373-4421
Freeport Resort & Club, Rum Cay Dr (also timeshare)	50	x	√	√	x	x	352-5371	352-8425
Island Palm Resort, The Mall	143	x	√	x	x	x	352-6648	352-6640
Island Seas Resort 123 Silver Point Dr	177	√	√	√	x	√	373-1271	373-1275
New Victoria Inn, Midshipman Rd & Victoria Pl	40	x	√	x	x	x	373-3040	373-3874
Ocean Reef Resort & Yacht Club, 48-60 Bahama Reef Blvd	63	√	√	√	√	x	373-4661	373-8261
Old Bahama Bay, West End	47	√	√	√	x	x	350-6500	346-6546
Pelican Bay at Lucaya, Royal Palm Way	90 *suites* 96	√	√	x	x	x	373-9550	373-9551
Port Lucaya Resort & Yacht Club, Bell Channel Bay Rd	160	√	√	x	x	x	373-6618	373-6652
Redwood Motel, Bell Channel Rd & Royal Palm Way	28	√	√	x	x	x	373-7881	373-6154
Ritz Beach Resort, Jolly Roger Dr	109	√	√	√	x	x	373-9354	373-4421
Royal Islander, The Mall	100	x	√	x	x	x	351-6000	351-3546
Royal Palm Resort, East Mall & Settlers Way	47	x	√	√	x	x	352-3462	352-5759
Viva Fortuna Beach, Doubloon Rd & Churchill Dr (also timeshare)	276	√	√	√	x	√	373-4000	373-5555
The Westin and Sheraton at Our Lucaya Beach & Golf Resort, Royal Palm Way	1,260	√	√	√	√	x	373-1333	373-5151
Westin at Breaker's Cay	526	√	√	√	√	x	373-1333	373-5151
Westin at Lighthouse Pt	223	√	√	√	√	x	373-1333	373-5151
Sheraton at Our Lucaya	511	√	√	√	√	x	373-1333	373-4056
Xanadu Beach Resort & Marina, Sunken Treasure Dr (also timeshare)	168	√	√	√	x	√	352-6782	352-5799

Hotel/location	No of rooms	Beach/ waterfront	Pool	Tennis	Golf course	Dive resort	Tel (242)	Fax (242)
Grand Bahama timeshare (no of villas not rooms)								
Vacation Club at Bahamia The Mall & W Sunrise Hwy	98	x	√	√	√	x	350-7000 ext 4541	350-7085
Viva Fortuna Beach, Doubloon Rd & Churchill Dr	55	√	√	√	x	√	373-4000	373-8591
Taino Beach Resort Vacation Club, Jolly Roger Dr	38	√	√	√	x	x	373-4677	373-4421
Abaco								
Abaco Beach Resort & Boat Harbour, Queen Elizabeth Dr, Marsh Harbour	82	√	√	√	x	√	367-2158	367-4154
Abaco Inn, Hope Town	22	√	√	x	x	x	366-0133	366-0113
Bahama Beach Club, Treasure Cay	44	√	√	x	x	x	365-8950	365-8501
Banyan Beach Club, Treasure Cay	22	√	√	x	x	x	365-8111	365-8112
Bluff House Beach Hotel, Green Turtle Cay	41	√	√	√	x	x	365-4247	365-4248
Crystal Villas & Waters, Resort, Hopetown	*info not available at press time*						366-0522	
Different of Abaco/ Great Abaco Bonefish Lodge, Casuarina Point	28	√	√	x	x	x	366-2150	327-8152
Dolphin Beach Resort, Great Guana Cay	21	√	√	x	x	√	365-5137	365-5163
Green Turtle Club & Marina, Green Turtle Cay	34	√	√	x	x	x	365-4271	365-4272
Guana Cay Seaside Village, Great Guana Cay	*rooms* 8 *cottages* 7	√	√	x	x	x	365-5106	365-5146
Hope Town Harbour Lodge, Hope Town	25	√	√	x	x	x	366-0095	366-0286
Island Bay Front Hotel, Grand Cay (off Walker's Cay)	*info not available at press time*						353-1200	353-1202
Ocean Frontier Hideaway, Great Guana Cay	18	√	x	x	x	√	(519) 389-4846	(519) 389-3027
Spanish Cay Resort , & Marina, Spanish Cay	18	√	√	√	x	x	365-0083	365-0453

Hotel/location	No of rooms	Beach/ water-front	Pool	Tennis	Golf course	Dive resort	Tel (242)	Fax (242)
Treasure Cay Hotel Resort & Marina, Treasure Cay	102	√	√	√	√	√	365-8535	365-8847
Walker's Cay Hotel & Marina, Walker's Cay	68	√	√	√	x	√	353-1252	353-1339
Abaco timeshare								
Regattas of Abaco, Marsh Harbour	32	√	√	√	x	x	367-2227	367-3927
Andros								
Andros Lighthouse Yacht Club, Fresh Creek	20	√	√	√	x	x	368-2305	368-2300
Creekside Lodge, Cargill Creek	19	√	√	x	x	√	368-5395	368-5397
Emerald Palms of South Andros, Driggs Hill	20 *cottages* 22	√	√	x	x	x	369-2661	369-2711
Kamalame Cay Resort, Staniard Creek	19	√	√	√	x	x	368-6281	368-6279
Mangrove Cay Inn, Mangrove Cay	12	√	x	x	x	x	369-0069	369-0014
Pineville Motel, Nicoll's Town	16	x	x	x	x	x	329-2788	329-2788
Small Hope Bay Lodge, Fresh Creek	21	√	x	x	x	√	368-2013	368-2015
Westside Fishing Resort, Nicoll's town	14	x	x	x	x	x	329-4200	329-4200
White Sand Beach Hotel, Mangrove Cay	13	√	x	x	x	x	369-0159	369-0774
Berry Islands								
Chub Cay Club, Chub Cay	31	√	√	√	x	x	325-1490	322-5199
Tropical Diversions, Great Harbour Cay	21	√	x	x	√	x	367-8838	367-8115
Bimini								
Bimini Big Game Fishing Club, Alice Town	35 *cottages* 12	√	√	x	x	√	347-3391	347-3392
Bimini Blue Water, Alice Town	12	√	√	x	x	x	347-3166	347-3293
Bimini Sands Beach Club, South Bimini	38	√	√	x	√	x	347-4500	347-3501
Bimini Sands Condominiums, South Bimini	41	√	√	√	√	x	347-3500	347-3501

Hotel/location	No of rooms	Beach/ water-front	Pool	Tennis	Golf course	Dive resort	Tel (242)	Fax (242)
Cat Island								
Boggie Pond Lodge, Roker's	16	x	x	x	x	x	354-2215	354-2074
Fernandez Bay Village, Fernandez Bay, New Bight	*houses* 6 *cottages* 9	√	x	x	x	x	342-3043	342-3051
Greenwood Beach Resort, Port Howe	20	√	√	x	x	√	342-3053	342-3053
Orange Creek Inn, Orange Creek	16	√	x	x	x	x	354-4110	354-4042
Sea Spray Hotel, Orange Creek	15	√	x	x	x	x	354-4116	354-4161
Crooked Island								
Pittstown Point Landings, Landrail Point	12	√	x	x	x	√	344-2507	344-2507
Eleuthera/Harbour Island								
Adventurer's Resort, Harbour Island	19	√	x	x	x	x	333-4883	333-5073
Cambridge Villas, Gregory Town	14 *apartments* 4	x	√	x	x	x	335-5080	335-5308
Coral Sands Hotel, Harbour Island	35	√	√	√	x	x	333-2350	333-2368
The Cove Eleuthera Hotel, Gregory Town	28 *suites* 4	√	√	√	x	x	335-5142	335-5338
Dunmore Beach Club, Harbour Island	14	√	x	√	x	x	333-2200	333-2429
Ethel's Cottages, Tarpum Bay	16	√	x	x	x	x	334-4233	334-4233
Ingraham's Beach Inn, Tarpum Bay	16	√	x	x	x	x	334-4066	334-2257
Palmetto Shores Vacation Villas, Palmetto Point	15	√	x	x	x	x	332-1403	332-1305
Pink Sands, Harbour Island	25	√	√	√	x	x	333-2030	333-2060
Quality Inn Cigatoo Resort, Harbour Island	22	x	√	√	x	x	332-3060	332-3061
Romora Bay Club, Harbour Island	22	√	√	√	x	x	333-2325	333-2500
Royal Palm Hotel, Harbour Island	30	x	x	x	x	x	333-2738	333-3333
Tingum Village Hotel, Harbour Island	18	x	x	x	x	x	333-2161	333-2161

Hotel/location	No of rooms	Beach/ water-front	Pool	Tennis	Golf course	Dive resort	Tel (242)	Fax (242)
Unique Village Hotel & Villas, North Palmetto Point	16	√	x	x	x	x	332-1830	332-1838
Valentine's Resort & Marina, Harbour Island	9	√	√	√	x	√	333-2142	333-2135
Exuma								
Club Peace & Plenty, George Town	32	√	√	x	x	√	336-2551	336-2093
February Point Resort George Town	18	√	√	√	x	x	336-2661	336-2660
Four Seasons Resort at Emerald Bay, Farmer's Hill	219	√	√	√	√	x	336-6800	336-6801
Grand Caribbean Resort, Emerald Bay, Farmer's Hill	16	√	√	x	√	x	358-4400	358-4401
Mount Pleasant Hotel Old Hoopers Bay	26	x	√	x	x	x	336-2960	336-2964
Palm Bay Beach Club, George Town	*cottages* 27	√	√	x	x	x	336-2787	336-2770
The Palms at Three Sisters, Mount Thompson	12	√	x	√	x	x	358-4040	358-4043
Peace & Plenty Beach Inn, George Town	18	√	√	x	x	√	336-2250	336-2253
Two Turtles Inn, George Town	12	x	x	x	x	x	336-2545	336-2528
Long Island								
Cape Santa Maria Beach Resort, Cape Santa Maria	*villas* 10	√	x	x	x	√	338-5273	338-6013
Gems at Paradise, Clarence Town	16	√	x	x	x	√	337-3016	337-3037
Greenwich Creek Lodge, Cartwrights	*suites* 12	√	√	x	x	x	337-6278	337-6282
Stella Maris Resort, Stella Maris	29	√	√	√	x	√	338-2051	338-2052
Mayaguana								
Baycaneer Beach Resort, West Bay St	*info not available at press time*						339-3605	339-3605
San Salvador								
Club Med, Columbus Isle	271	√	√	x	x	√	331-2000	331-2458
Riding Rock Inn, Cockburn Town	42	√	√	√	x	√	331-2631	331-2020

cont from pg 416

The new facility is exempt from real property taxes and other taxes hereafter imposed on real property for 10 years from the date the new hotel opens. There is further exemption from real property taxes in excess of $20 for every bedroom in the hotel for the second 10 years of operation.

Real property tax exemption may be granted for further periods of up to 10 years, provided the hotel property is well maintained and refurbished. In this case exemption is $250 for every bedroom for hotels in New Providence and $100 for every bedroom for hotels in the Out Islands.

Hotel earnings, or rental paid for lease or sub-lease, are exempt from direct taxation for 20 years from the opening date. If the investor or operator is a company, there is an exemption from direct tax "on or against dividends declared in respect of its indebtedness" for the same 20-year period. However, this does not include exemption from business licence fees.

Existing hotels and new hotels may be rehabilitated, remodelled, air-conditioned or extended, and exemption from payment of customs duty may be obtained on materials imported for such alterations by applying in writing to the Permanent Secretary, Ministry of Financial Services and Investments, stating the nature, extent, and estimated cost of the alterations in order to obtain approval in principle from government. This approval in principle must be obtained prior to purchases if the investor wishes to receive exemption from payment of customs duty.

To obtain these concessions, a new hotel in New Providence or Paradise Island must have at least 10 bedrooms and suitable public rooms for the accommodation and entertainment of guests. A new hotel in the Out Islands must have at least four bedrooms.

These concessions apply to all amenities offered in conjunction with the hotel: golf courses, marinas, harbours, roads, airfields, etc.

Contact the Ministry of Financial Services and Investments,
PO Box N-7770, Nassau, The Bahamas,
tel (242) 356-5970, fax (242) 356-5990.

See also **Customs** and **Investing.**

HUNTING

See **Birds.**

HURRICANES

The Bahamas receives weather forecasting from the forecast section of The Bahamas Dept of Meteorology at Nassau Intl Airport.

The Dept's warning time is 24 hours in advance of a storm. A five-day coastal weather forecast is available to boaters. This is essential in the Out Islands where materials for surviving severe storms are less readily available.

The Doppler radar network covers portions of The Bahamas, as do satellites positioned in geosynchronous orbit above North America.

Improved satellite reporting, a new generation of Doppler radar, better reports from hurricane-hunting aircraft and greater understanding of expanded information from inside a storm will lead to upgraded predictions of storm track and future direction as well as greater knowledge of a storm's internal dynamics.

The GOES-8 satellite gives forecasters more information about wind speed and storm direction as well as forces within the storm and location of the precise centre of cyclone winds. Rain bands, wind shear factors and other elements – even severe thunderstorms – are tracked with the same accuracy. Member countries of Region IV, comprising North and Central America and the Caribbean, have agreed that fixed coordinates of tropical cyclones be provided by the United States Tropical Prediction Center to aid in the issuance of warnings.

Hurricane-hunter aircraft continue to fly higher and faster so scientists can sample greater areas and provide more data from tropical ocean environments.

Weather forecasting is a relatively new science. Techniques and results are being steadily upgraded. Hurricane specialist Dr Edward Rappaport, of the US National Hurricane Center, Coral Gables, FL, estimates the 12- to 72-hour forecast of a storm's track and intensity has improved by about 0.5% per year – representing an improvement of 10% over the past 20 years.

Only in May 1994 did aircraft begin to regularly penetrate hurricanes and report findings. But hurricanes are unpredictable. They have swept full circle, reversed course, even dissipated, only to reconstitute themselves and deliver a devastating punch to unsuspecting areas.

Hurricane season

Nassau can be affected by hurricanes or tropical storms between June 1 and Nov 30, the greatest risk being in Aug, Sept and Oct.

Hurricane Frances of Sept 2-5, 2004, was the first hurricane to affect the entire archipelago of The Bahamas. Islands directly hit by the eye of Frances included San Salvador, Cat Island, Eleuthera, Abaco and Grand Bahama. The deadliest hurricane in years resulted in two fatalities.

Hurricane Jeanne struck later the same month, causing additional damage in Abaco and Grand Bahama.

Hurricane Michelle of Nov 4-6, 2001, packed winds from 74-95 mph. Michelle was the only hurricane in more than 35 years to make direct landfall on the island of New Providence. The last hurricane to do so was Betsy in 1965.

Based on figures compiled for the past 90-year period, Nassau may expect to experience hurricane conditions an average of once every nine years. An efficient warning system gives ample notice for necessary precautions to be taken.

See also **Climate.**

IMMIGRATION

Renowned as one of the most politically stable countries in the western hemisphere, The Bahamas has enjoyed uninterrupted parliamentary democracy for 276 years since its introduction in 1729.

The Bahamas, a former British colony, gained its independence on July 10, 1973. It is located just 60 miles from Miami at its nearest island, Bimini, and around 480 miles from Haiti in the south. At some points, Cuba, which borders the southwest perimeters, is less than 25 miles from Bahamian cays. As a result, The Bahamas contends with a serious immigration situation.

The government is committed to an amicable solution, and as such, its immigration policy is aimed at ensuring the reasonable security, well-being and economic progress of The Bahamas and its people.

The government gives consideration to citizenship, permanent residency and work permits for non-Bahamians provided there is compliance with the immigration laws of The Bahamas and policies of the government. Accelerated consideration is given to applications for annual or permanent residence by major international investors and to "fit and proper" owners of residences valued in excess of $500,000.

As The Bahamas is a major tourist resort, every effort is made to keep visitors' immigration formalities to a minimum. Non-Commonwealth citizens should inquire at the Ministry of Tourism for entry requirements, as they vary from country to country.

Each person entering The Bahamas must fill out, upon entry, an embarkation-disembarkation card. In the case of non-residents, the designated portion is retained and must be surrendered upon departure from the country.

Visitors must be in possession of a return ticket to their homeland or to some other country where they would be accepted. As a part of the admittance process, visitors may be required to produce evidence that they are able to sustain themselves while in The Bahamas.

Visitors may visit The Bahamas for a max of eight months, provided they can indicate means of financial support for this period. Visitors are not allowed to engage in any form of gainful occupation while in The Bahamas.

Anyone found guilty of smuggling or assisting in the smuggling of illegal immigrants may be fined $3,000 and sentenced to a max of two years in prison and confiscation of any aircraft or boat used in the act.

Passports

Passports are required by all persons except:

1. Citizens of the UK and colonies, and Canadian citizens on visits not exceeding three weeks. However, passports are

required for re-entry into the UK. British visitors' passports are accepted.

2. Citizens of the US entering The Bahamas as visitors for a period not exceeding eight months who are in possession of proof of nationality, ie, birth certificate, naturalization certificate etc and government-issued photo identification or photo drivers licence for adults.

Visas

Visas are required by all persons entering The Bahamas except:

1. British Commonwealth citizens and landed immigrants of Canada, for visits not exceeding 30 days if in possession of Form 100.
2. US citizens entering as visitors for a stay not exceeding eight months.
3. Alien residents of the US who, upon arrival, are in possession of their national passports and US alien registration cards and work or residence permits for visits not exceeding 30 days.
4. Nationals of the following countries for visits not exceeding 14 days: Argentina, Bolivia, Brazil, Chile, Costa Rica, Ecuador, El Salvador, Guatemala, Honduras, Mexico, Nicaragua, Panama, Paraguay, Peru, Suriname, Uruguay and Venezuela.
5. Nationals of the following countries for visits not exceeding three months: Austria, Denmark, Finland, France, Germany, Israel, Japan, Republic of Ireland, South Africa and Sweden.
6. Nationals of the following countries: Belgium, Greece, Iceland, Italy, Liechtenstein, Luxembourg, The Netherlands, Norway, San Marino, Spain, Switzerland and Turkey.
7. Persons in possession of a valid residence or work permit issued by the Director of Immigration.
8. Persons in transit, including stateless persons in possession of a valid refugee or stateless person's travel document, provided they are in possession of valid passports and tickets to some destination outside The Bahamas and that their stay, while awaiting onward passage on the first available ship or aircraft, does not exceed three days.

   This exemption does not apply to nationals of Haiti and the Dominican Republic who must always possess visas even in direct transit by air.

Applications for visas from persons in the following categories must be referred to the nearest Bahamian Consular Office:

1. Nationals of the Dominican Republic.
2. Nationals of Haiti.
3. Nationals of Colombia.
4. Nationals of Asian countries, ie nationals of China, including nationals resident in Hong Kong; North and South Korea, Vietnam, Thailand, Myanmar (formerly Burma).

Visas for persons in the following categories may be granted without prior reference:

1. Nationals of countries not mentioned in the previous paragraph provided that the visit is only intended for a period not exceeding three months.
2. Stateless persons who must be in possession of a document permitting re-entry into their country of residence and whose visit is only intended for a period not to exceed three months.

There are a number of ports of entry at which one may lawfully enter The Bahamas from foreign countries. See **Ports of entry** and **Airports.**

Procedure for obtaining an annual residence permit

Persons wishing to reside in The Bahamas on an annual basis may qualify under one of four categories:

1. Spouse or dependent of a citizen of The Bahamas.
2. Spouse or dependent of a permit holder.
3. Independent economic resident.
4. Resident home owner, or seasonal resident home owner.

The following documents are required:

Category 1

a. Immigration Form 1, Section B, completed and notarized with $4 in Bahamian postage stamps affixed thereon.

b. A covering letter from the supporting applicant stating relationship and accepting financial responsibility for the subject of the application.

c. Birth, marriage and/or any certificate evidencing dependence of the subject of the application.
d. The applicant's birth certificate.
e. Medical certificate dated not more than 30 days prior to submission.
f. Police certificate issued less than six months earlier.
g. Two passport-size photographs.
h. A processing fee of $25.

If an applicant is married to a Bahamian citizen, a resident spouse permit may be issued, provided the marriage has existed for less than five years. The resident spouse permit is issued for a max period of five years. A one-time fee of $250 is charged to cover the permit, regardless of the amount of time remaining in the five-year period. An application is made for permanent residence or citizenship after five years or more of marriage. See this section, **Permanent residence.**

Category 2

a. Items (a) through (h) of category (1).
b. A copy of the sponsor's work permit, permit to reside, certificate of permanent residence or other lawful authority to reside in The Bahamas.

Category 3

a. Items (a) through (h) of category (1), except item (c).
b. Financial reference from a reputable bank verifying economic worth, ie, citing a figure range.
c. Two written character references.

For an annual residence permit, a head-of-household pays $1,000 and each dependent, $25.

Category 4

Under this category, non-Bahamians who own second homes in The Bahamas may apply to the Director of Immigration for an annual home owner's residence card. This card is renewable annually and entitles the owner, spouse and any minor child/children endorsed on the owner's card when travelling with the owner, to enter and remain in The Bahamas for the validity of the card. The fee is $500 per year, and is intended to facilitate entry into The Bahamas with minimal formalities by:

1. Obviating the need for return tickets.
2. Obviating provision of proof of maintenance ability upon entering the country.
3. Entitling the holder to visit for a stay of up to one year.

Requirements for qualifying under this category are:

1. Letter of request.
2. Two passport-size photographs of applicant.
3. Application form.
4. Proof of property ownership in The Bahamas.
5. Proof of existence of a home (house) on property.
6. Processing fee of $25.

Successful applicants in any of these categories are not permitted to engage in employment.

Procedures for obtaining a work permit

An inflexible principle of The Bahamas government is that no expatriate may be offered a position that a suitably qualified Bahamian is available to fill.

Employers with vacant posts are required to advertise locally and consult The Bahamas Employment Exchange. If unsuccessful in fulfilling their requirements by these methods, they may apply to the Dept of Immigration for permission to recruit outside The Bahamas.

The following documentation will then need to be submitted:

1. Application Form 1, Section A, completed and notarized with $4 in Bahamian postage stamps affixed.
2. A covering letter from the prospective employer stating reasons for the application, the position, and the period of time needed.
3. Two passport-size photographs with signature on reverse of prints.
4. Police certificate covering a period of five years' residence immediately preceding the application or a sworn affidavit in lieu of same.
5. Medical certificate dated not more than 30 days prior to submission.
6. Written references from previous employer(s).

7. Copies of exam certificates referred to in the application.
8. Copies of local newspaper advertisements with replies thereto and results of interviews, if held.
9. Certificate from the Dept of Labour (Employment Exchange) indicating that a Bahamian is not available to fill the position.
10. A processing fee of $25.

Normally an application will not be processed if the prospective employee is already in The Bahamas, having entered as a visitor.

Work permit fees range from $350 to $10,000 per year depending on the category. The Bahamas Immigration Bahamianization Policy, which is critical to the granting of work permits, provides that:

1. Whenever there is a position which a Bahamian is qualified to fill, he should be given the position in preference to anyone else.
2. The Bahamian must be given that job on the same terms and conditions as his expatriate counterpart.
3. Where the company has a career structure, whether here or abroad, the Bahamian employee must be given the same opportunities for advancement as would be afforded other employees.
4. The Bahamian must be helped whenever possible to broaden his skills in his chosen field of endeavour by constant exposure to further training at home and abroad.

Where work permits have been granted, each employer will be required to identify a suitable Bahamian to understudy the expatriate so that the Bahamian trainee will fill the expatriate's position within a reasonable time frame.

Genuine investors usually have little difficulty in complying with these requirements.

Employers may obtain permits for longer periods than the standard one-year period in respect to certain key personnel on contract. Such contracts should indicate their renewal would be subject to obtaining the necessary immigration permission, and they may be endorsed to the effect that the employee is expected to train or be replaced by a suitable Bahamian within a stipulated period.

Each permit issued by the Immigration Board relates to a specific post. Permits are not altered by the Director of Immigration to reflect change of employment or residence. However, a person holding a work permit may make application for a new one (his new employer having been unsuccessful in recruiting a qualified Bahamian to fill the post) without having to leave the islands.

The renewal of a permit on expiration is not automatic. Generally, no expatriate may be continually employed in the country in any capacity for more than five years. However, there are likely to be cases where hardship will be caused by rigid implementation of this policy; according to government, this factor will be kept in mind in applying the regulations.

An employer must inform the Dept of Immigration within 30 days that a non-Bahamian employee is no longer employed or be liable to a fine not exceeding $150.

A non-Bahamian who ceases to be employed must take his permit to the Dept of Immigration for cancellation within seven days of ceasing to be employed. The permit shall be deemed cancelled with effect from expiration of that seven-day period. An employee failing to comply with this regulation is liable to prosecution and may, if convicted, be liable to a fine not exceeding $100.

Bonding

A bond is required for each person granted a work permit, if necessary, to repatriate the employee and his dependents and to pay any public charges, including medical expenses, incurred by the employee.

Travelling salesman's permit

Travelling salesmen planning to do business in The Bahamas must obtain work permits from the Dept of Immigration, and a licence from the Licensing Authority. The requirements for such a permit are:

1. Completed Immigration Dept Form I (notarized, with $4 in stamps), with two passport-size photographs signed on the reverse, and a police certificate.

2. Two letters of character reference.
3. Passport or other travel document.
4. A letter from salesman's company stating he is travelling to The Bahamas to sell on its behalf. Letter should be addressed to: Director of Immigration, PO Box N-831, Nassau, The Bahamas.
5. Two letters sponsoring him as a salesman from two sponsors in The Bahamas in the type of business on which he plans to call.
6. A complete list of accounts on which he will call.
7. Payment of an annual fee of $4,000 (a permit may be obtained for any period up to six months at a prorated fee).

The licence is issued when the approved work permit is presented at the Licensing Authority office.

Permanent residence

Applicants for this status of residency must be of good character and prepared to show evidence of financial support. Such an applicant must also state that he intends to reside permanently in The Bahamas.

Persons may apply for permanent residence in any of the following categories provided they satisfy statutory requirements of The Bahamas:

1. As the spouse of a citizen of The Bahamas, and in the case of a male, he must have been married for not less than five years.
2. As an economic applicant; that is, one who seeks to permanently reside in The Bahamas because of:
   a. Investment – business or home.
   b. Established roots through family ties.

Persons who held valid certificates of permanent residence prior to the Immigration Act, 1975, continue to hold such status automatically.

To initiate an application in either of the above categories, the requisite application form should be completed in duplicate, notarized and submitted along with the following documents to the Ministry of Labour and Immigration:

Category 1
(Application Form IV A)

a. Two passport photographs.
b. A police certificate of not more than six months' issue, covering five years' residence immediately prior to the date of application, or where these are not issued, a sworn affidavit in lieu of same.
c. Birth certificate.
d. Spouse's birth certificate.
e. Marriage certificate.
f. Proof of immigration status in The Bahamas.
g. Processing fee of $25.

Spouses of Bahamians may be issued a certificate of permanent residence with the right to engage in gainful employment. In the case of a male, such application may only be made after five years of marriage to the Bahamian wife. Women married to Bahamians may apply at any time after marriage.

Category 2
(Application Form IV)

a. Items (a) through (g) in category (1).
b. Financial reference from a reputable bank verifying economic worth.
c. Two written character references.
d. A medical certificate dated not more than 30 days prior to submission of the application.
e. Proof of ownership of property and/or investment in The Bahamas in the form of copies of conveyances, deeds or mortgage contracts, etc.

A person holding a certificate of permanent residence who wishes to include his wife, or dependent child under the age of 18 and ordinarily resident in his household, may have them endorsed on the certificate at the time of his original application or at a subsequent date, subject to such conditions as might be laid down by the Immigration Board.

Cost of a permanent residence certificate varies according to status. A person who has resided in The Bahamas at least 10 years and less than 20 years and who holds a work permit may pay anything from $1,000-$5,000.

A person who has resided in the country at least 20 years and who holds a work permit may pay anything from $500-$2,500. The spouse of a Bahamian citizen pays $250. A person without a work permit, or holding a work permit in one of the top professional categories, and who has resided in The Bahamas for less than 10 years, not married to a Bahamian citizen, pays up to $10,000.

Persons who held valid certificates of permanent residence prior to the Immigration Act, 1975, continue to hold such status automatically.

Persons who formerly possessed Bahamian status (belongers) whose applications for citizenship were not determined by Aug 1, 1976, should have also applied for permanent residence. Belongers who failed to apply prior to Aug 1, 1976, lost their immigration status. Persons in this category, on acquiring a permanent residence certificate, would continue to enjoy the same rights and privileges they had known under the old Bahamian status, with the exception of the right to vote in a parliamentary election.

Permanent residents who were formerly belongers enjoy the new status for life. The certificate is free and contains no restriction regarding the right of the holder to engage in gainful employment.

A certificate of permanent residence may be revoked if the person holding the certificate:

1. Has been ordinarily resident outside The Bahamas continuously for a period of three years.
2. Is or was imprisoned for a criminal offence for one year or more.
3. Has so conducted himself that in the opinion of the Immigration Board it is not in the public interest that he should continue to enjoy the privileges conferred by the certificate.
4. Being the wife of a holder of a permanent residence certificate, she becomes legally separated from her husband or the marriage is dissolved or annulled.

Temporary annual residence permit

A person attending an institution of higher education in The Bahamas on a full-time basis or as a trainee pays $25 a year.

Business investors

A business-sensitive legal framework and investor-friendly climate encourages non-Bahamian investments, supported by the Bahamas Investment Authority (BIA), Ministry of Financial Services and Investments, PO Box N-7770, Nassau, The Bahamas, tel (242) 327-5970 (to 4), fax (242) 327-5907.

Although an investor is granted a licence by the Licensing Authority, he must still apply for a work permit if he is to be resident and an employee of/or operating the business himself.

Contact the Director of Immigration, Ministry of Labour and Immigration, Post Office Bldg, East Hill St, PO Box N-831, Nassau, The Bahamas, tel (242) 322-7530.

See also **Citizenship** and **Investing.**

IMMOVABLE PROPERTY ACT

See **Property Transactions, Intl Persons Landholding Act.**

IMPORT & EXPORT STATISTICS

Commodity classifications, from the Dept of Statistics, are based on the Standard Intl Trade Classifications (SITC). See **Fig 1.9** for the latest available information.

IMPORT ENTRY

Commercial banks may approve and issue payment for goods imported into The Bahamas, on behalf of the Exchange Control Dept of The Central Bank of The Bahamas, Frederick and Market Sts, Nassau.

The Import Entry Form (1) must be completed in quadruplicate and taken to the bank with supporting invoice(s) and payment. However, the form must first be approved by the Exchange Control Dept if value of the goods (non-oil imports only) is more than $100,000.

See also **Exchange control.**

INDUSTRIAL RELATIONS

See **Labour relations, Industrial Tribunal** and **Trade unions.**

FIG 1.9

IMPORT & EXPORT STATISTICS

Value of 2001 domestic exports & re-exports

	Section (totals rounded off)	B$
1	Live animals; animal products	73,998,718
2	Vegetable products	8,947,288
3	Animal or vegetable fats and oils and their cleavage products; prepared edible fats; animal or vegetable waxes	515
4	Prepared foodstuffs: beverages, spirits and vinegar; tobacco and manufactured tobacco substitutes	41,521,246
5	Mineral products	90,064,636
6	Products of the chemical or allied industries	26,343,156
7	Plastics and articles thereof; rubber and articles thereof	72,180,866
8	Rawhides and skin, leather, fur skins and articles thereof; saddlery and harness. Travel goods, handbags and similar containers; articles of animal gut (other than silk-worm gut)	94,432
9	Wood and articles of wood; wood charcoal; cork and articles of cork; manufactured straw, esparto or other plaiting materials; basketware and wickerwork	352,137
10	Pulp of wood or of other fibrous cellulosic material; recovered (waste and scrap) paper or paperboard; paper and paperboard and articles thereof	947,840
11	Textile and textile articles	4,102,154
12	Footwear, headgear, umbrellas, sun umbrellas, walking-sticks, seat-sticks, whips, riding-crops and parts thereof; prepared feathers and articles made therewith; artificial flowers; articles of human hair	54,302
13	Articles of stone, plaster, cement, asbestos, mica or similar materials; ceramic products; glass and glassware	999,018
14	Natural or cultured pearls, precious or semi-precious stones, precious metals, metal clad with precious metals and articles thereof; imitation jewellery; coin	147,437
15	Base metal and articles of base metal	7,033,008
16	Machinery and mechanical appliances; electrical equipment; parts thereof; sound recorders and reproducers, and parts and accessories of such articles	30,590,781
17	Vehicles, aircraft, vessels and associated transport equipment	14,466,769
18	Optical photographic, cinematographic, measuring, checking, precision, medical or surgical instruments and apparatus; clocks and watches, musical instruments, parts and accessories thereof	2,819,049
19	Arms and ammunition, parts and accessories thereof	215
20	Miscellaneous manufactured articles	1,007,168
21	Works of art, collectors' pieces and antiques	210,460
		$375,881,195

Exports of commodities to principal trading areas	
Trading areas	**B$**
Canada	5,943,764
Caribbean Commonwealth Countries	2,478,331
EU *(excluding the UK)*	42,044,820
OPEC	48,827
UK	12,032,729
USA	288,773,120
Other countries	24,559,604
	$375,881,195

Value of 2001 imports		
Section (totals rounded off)		**B$**
1	Live animals; animal products	85,946,885
2	Vegetable products	66,061,181
3	Animal or vegetable fats and oils and their cleavage products; prepared edible fats, animal or vegetable waxes	5,584,703
4	Prepared foodstuffs: beverages, spirits and vinegar; tobacco and manufactured tobacco substitutes	190,884,081
5	Mineral products	311,829,608
6	Products of the chemical or allied industries	135,229,051
7	Plastics and articles thereof; rubber and articles thereof	63,402,423
8	Rawhides and skin, leather, fur skins and articles thereof; saddlery and harness. Travel goods, handbags and similar containers; articles of animal gut (other than silk-worm gut)	7,623,219
9	Wood and articles of wood; wood charcoal; cork and articles of cork; manufactured straw, esparto or other plaiting materials; basketware and wickerwork	63,423,834
10	Pulp of wood or of other fibrous cellulosic material; recovered (waste and scrap) paper or paperboard; paper and paperboard and articles thereof	60,349,636
11	Textile and textile articles	72,141,927
12	Footwear, headgear, umbrellas, sun umbrellas, walking-sticks, seat-sticks, whips, riding-crops and parts thereof; prepared feathers and articles made therewith; artificial flowers; articles of human hair	19,014,790
13	Articles of stone, plaster, cement, asbestos, mica or similar materials; ceramic products; glass and glassware	56,532,224
14	Natural or cultured pearls, precious or semi-precious stones, precious metals, metals clad with precious metals and articles thereof; imitation jewellery; coin	11,608,864
15	Base metals and articles of base metal	114,737,909
16	Machinery and mechanical appliances; electrical equipment; parts thereof; sound recorders and reproducers, and parts and accessories of such articles	313,817,652
17	Vehicles, aircraft, vessels and associated transport equipment	202,732,825
18	Optical photographic, cinematographic, measuring, checking, precision, medical or surgical instruments and apparatus; clocks and watches, musical instruments, parts and accessories thereof	35,707,980

Value of 2001 imports (cont)		
Section (totals rounded off)		**B$**
19	Arms and ammunition, parts and accessories thereof	211,750
20	Miscellaneous manufactured articles	82,793,159
21	Works of art, collectors' pieces and antiques	29,115,960
		$1,928,749,661

Imports of commodities from principal trading areas	
Trading areas	**B$**
Canada	19,900,806
Caribbean Commonwealth Countries	17,851,764
EU *(excluding the UK)*	25,731,047
OPEC	108,347,457
UK	9,870,968
USA	1,602,436,789
Other countries	144,610,830
	$1,928,749,661

INDUSTRIAL TRIBUNAL

The Bahamas Industrial Tribunal was established by the government in Apr 1997, with wide powers to resolve conflict in the workplace, including power to order reinstatement and levy damages. The Tribunal hears disputes in both essential and non-essential services. Hearings are held in public, at the Nassau headquarters on Thompson Blvd, and at the regional office in Freeport.

The Tribunal consists of a president at the Nassau headquarters and two vice-presidents, one in Nassau, and one at the regional office in Freeport. The Tribunal is assisted by two panels, of six persons each, representing workers and employers. Panelists are recommended by their union or employer association and appointed by the Director of Labour for a three-year term.

Tribunal hearings are informal and follow normal court practice, with evidence followed by cross-examination. The service is free, and parties may represent themselves.

Industrial Tribunal, Monument Bldg, Nassau, tel 325-6923, 325-6954 or 325-6942; fax 325-7614. Regional Office, Freeport, tel (242) 352-3797.

See also **Labour relations** and **Trade unions.**

INDUSTRIES ENCOURAGEMENT

To broaden the base of the Bahamian economy, the government has a policy of diversification which means encouragement of industries other than tourism. In 1970, the Industries Encouragement Act was passed to provide incentives for manufacturers of approved products. These incentives include duty-free importation of machinery and raw materials.

The Ministry of Trade and Industry is responsible for administration of the Act. The minister, designated by the Act, may declare a manufactured product an approved product if it is in the public interest and the product would benefit The Bahamas, "both economic and social considerations being taken into account." Every approved manufacturer can import into The Bahamas duty free:

1. Machinery and raw material necessary to manufacture the approved product.
2. Any scheduled article for the purpose of constructing, reconstructing, altering or extending, but not repairing, the factory premises. Scheduled articles include all building materials, tools, plant equipment, pipes, pumps, conveyor belts or other materials or appliances necessary. In New Providence, this excludes equipment used to

manufacture wooden door frames, moulding, cement tiles or cement blocks. The manufacturer is guaranteed no export taxes on the approved product, no income tax in respect of any profits or gains from the product's manufacture.

An amendment to the Industries Encouragement Act requires payment of a 7% stamp duty on imports by persons registered thereunder.

Application for registration under the Industries Encouragement Act, 1970, must be addressed to the Permanent Secretary, Ministry of Trade and Industry, PO Box N-4849, Nassau, The Bahamas, tel (242) 328-2700, fax (242) 328-1324.

The Tariff Act

Three items in the fourth schedule of the Tariff Act provide for duty exemptions on specified raw materials, supplies and equipment for agriculture, floriculture, horticulture, fisheries, forestry, cottage and light industries, and commercial printing. A schedule for each item lists raw material exempt from duty. A business registered under one of the three items with the minister responsible for agriculture and fisheries, trade or industry, may apply for a 10% reduction of duty on material, supplies and equipment not listed in the schedule.

Application for concessions under the Act is made to the ministry under which the business is registered.

See also **Bahamas Agricultural Industrial Corp (BAIC), Bahamas Investment Authority (BIA), Bahamas Development Bank (BDB), Caribbean Basin Initiative (CBI), Caribbean Community, CARIBCAN, Exchange control, Import and export statistics** and **Manufacturing.**

INDUSTRY

Tourism, which annually attracts more than four million visitors to The Bahamas, continues to be the linchpin of the Bahamian economy, representing 50% of the Gross Domestic Product (GDP). In 2003, visitors to The Bahamas spent $1.756 billion. See also **Tourism.**

Banking/finance is the No 2 industry, representing 15% of the GDP. There are 284 licensed banks and trust companies. At the end of 2003, the banking industry employed 4,253 persons. See also **Banking** and **Economy.**

The construction boom continues to play a major role in the economy. In 2003, 3,060 construction permits were issued at a value of $451 million.

Domestic exports include crawfish, other seafood, fruit and vegetables, rum and crude salt.

At press time, export figures for 2003 were not available. Totals from the Dept of Statistics for 2001 showed exports of rum valued at $39.6 million.

During 2001, The Bahamas exported 1,215,362 net tons of crude salt, valued at $13.507 million, to the US, Canada, Jamaica, Iceland and Mexico.

The lobster industry exported $95.8 million worth of spiny lobster in 2002.

The Bahamas Maritime Authority's ship registry is a burgeoning industry. The Bahamas had the world's third-largest fleet in mid 2003, with a gross tonnage of 35.4 million.

Film and television production is an emerging industry in The Bahamas and generated revenue in excess of $20 million between Jul 2003 and May 2004. In 2004, plans were under way to develop Gold Rock Creek Enterprises film studios in Grand Bahama. Located on approx 3,800 acres on the site of a de-commissioned US Navy base at East End, the $78-million studios will feature sound stages, a shooting tank for underwater filming and an 8,000 ft runway.

Industries in Freeport include manufacturing of chemicals, polystyrene and fragrances, as well as ship repair, agriculture, limestone processing and oil-related industries.

Oil is not refined in The Bahamas. The Bahamas Oil Refining Company (BORCO), in Grand Bahama, operates as a terminal which trans-ships, stores and blends oil. South Riding Point Holding also trans-ships and stores oil.

See also **Freeport/Lucaya Information, Agriculture** and **Industry.**

Petroleum

Under the Petroleum Act, 1971, and the Petroleum Regulations, 1978 (as amended), foreign enterprises may apply for a permit, licence or lease for petroleum exploration in The Bahamas. A permit gives the non-exclusive right to carry out geophysical or geological studies but does not guarantee the granting of a lease or licence.

A licence gives the sole right to enter the licensed area and search for hydrocarbons. According to Petroleum Regulations, companies holding petroleum exploration licences are entitled to a renewal after expiry of the initial licence term, but must drill an exploratory well in the first year of the renewal period.

There are currently three companies exploring for oil in The Bahamas. Liberty Oil has three licenses to undertake oil exploration in The Bahamas, while nine licenses have been granted to Kerr McGee and Atlantic Petroleum Company, a subsidiary of Kerr McGee.

The AES Corporation has submitted a proposal to construct, own and operate an LNG facility at Ocean Cay, Bimini. Discussions between the Ministry of Trade and Industry and representatives from AES Corporation, to finalize the Heads of Agreement, are ongoing. At press time the draft agreement was being considered by the Office of the Attorney General. If approved, the centre will include a liquified natural gas (LNG) terminal, utility plant, and an undersea gas pipeline to South Florida (if it meets environmental standards demonstrated in an environmental impact assessment study and is approved by US Federal and State of Florida agencies).

Contact the Permanent Secretary, Office of the Prime Minister, PO Box CB-10980, Nassau, The Bahamas, tel (242) 327-5826, fax (242) 327-5806.

See also **Agriculture, Manufacturing** and **Freeport/ Lucaya information, Industry.**

INFLATION

See **Economy.**

INSURANCE

Responsibility for the prudential regulation of insurance activity in or through The Bahamas rests with the Office of the Registrar of Insurance Companies, a unit of the Ministry of Financial Services and Investments. It is concerned with the ongoing monitoring and control of insurers, agents, brokers, salesmen, and, internationally, underwriting managers and external insurers.

All local insurance operations (as distinct from offshore, or captive, insurance) are covered by the Insurance Act, 1969. Registered insurers writing local business pay a premium tax of 3% of gross premiums collected each quarter.

As of Mar 2004, 55 insurers were licensed to write local business, eight indigenous companies and 47 foreign companies writing through local offices. In support of this activity, there are 20 agents, 38 brokers who also act as agents, and six brokers.

Domestic insurance companies, agents and brokers dealing with general insurance business are members of The Bahamas General Insurance Assoc. Those insurers handling life and health business belong to The Bahamas Assoc of Life and Health Insurers.

The Bahamas is a member of the following regulatory bodies:

- Caribbean Assoc of Insurance Regulators (CAIR)
- Offshore Group of Insurance Supervisors (OGIS)
- International Assoc of Insurance Supervisors (IAIS)

The Bahamas has relations with:

- Insurance Assoc of the Caribbean (IAC)
- Life Insurance Marketing and Research Assoc (LIMRA)
- National Assoc of Insurance Commissioners, USA (NAIC)
- United National Conference on Trade and Development

Offshore insurance

An offshore insurer is an insurance company that is either incorporated in The Bahamas under the Companies Act, 1992, or incorporated elsewhere but registered under The Bahamas Foreign Companies Act and:

1. Is registered under the insurance laws of The Bahamas.
2. Insures only risks located outside The Bahamas.
3. Manages its business from within The Bahamas.

The Bahamas offers a convenient and professionally administered location for such operations. There is a well-equipped and capable regulatory office (the office of the Registrar of Insurance Companies) and an adequate professional infrastructure to support such business as may materialize.

The activity of offshore insurance companies is regulated by the External Insurance Act, 1983.

Registrar's requirements

Before an offshore company may be registered, the Registrar of Insurance Companies must be satisfied with:

1. Fitness of key parties to engage in the proposed operation.
2. Business ethics involved.
3. Feasibility of the planned business.
4. Security of outward reinsurance.

This process may be facilitated by introductory meetings between the applicant and the Registrar.

Both insurance laws lay down the minimum capital and surplus requirements with requirements for external insurers based on the nature and scope of business presented. The Registrar would not expect to see an initial capitalization of less than US$250,000, which would normally be in cash and adequate to support the proposed volume of business.

Once licensed, the insurer is subject to minimal but important ongoing reporting requirements consisting basically of filing an annual audited financial statement. In addition, the External Insurance Act calls for submission of certain statutory statements indicating compliance with the terms of registration.

All offshore insurers incorporated in The Bahamas are expected to operate through one of the registered underwriting managers. There are currently eight such management companies registered, all of which operate out of Nassau. Offshore insurers and underwriting managers are members of the Bahamas International Insurance Association (BIIA).

As of Mar 2004, 27 companies were registered under the External Insurance Act, 1983. This Act was amended on Dec 24, 1996.

For copies of insurance laws and regulations, contact Government Publications, PO Box N-7147, Nassau, The Bahamas, tel (242) 322-2410, or visit www.bahamas.gov.bs/oric.

Captive insurance

The captive insurance industry is governed in The Bahamas by the External Insurance Act, 1983. The Act allows companies to underwrite business from outside The Bahamas, confers advantageous solvency margins and allows captives to trade in any currency (except Bahamian).

Other provisions of the Act include a confidentiality clause to protect the policy holder, and tax exemptions for a period of 15 years from the date of first registration.

Captive insurance companies – alternative providers of protection against the risk of damage or loss and third party liabilities – differ from traditional firms in the nature of risks they underwrite or reinsure. They minimize the cost of risk management and may substantially reduce, or even avoid, other expenses such as administration and settlement of claims, loss control expenses, brokerage commissions and other acquisition costs and consulting fees.

Captives also allow self-insurance of a company with a better loss history than its industry average, plus centralization and tailoring of a company's risk management programmes to improve loss control efficiency. They offer cash flow benefits; access to the reinsurance market; wider cover than the conventional market – such as providing coverage for a new or potentially hazardous product – and the chance to diversify into open market insurance services and generate profits from outside or unrelated business.

Annual fees payable by captive insurance companies in The Bahamas:
External insurer $2,500
Underwriting manager $650

Contact the office of the Registrar of Insurance Companies, Ministry of Financial Services and Investments, PO Box N-7770, Nassau, The Bahamas, tel (242) 328-1068, fax (242) 328-1070.

See also **Investing.**

INTERNATIONAL BUSINESS COMPANY (IBC)

See **Company formation** and **Investing.**

INTERNATIONAL PERSONS LANDHOLDING ACT

See **Property transactions.**

INTERNET

Internet access is readily available through local service providers.

Internet service providers

Fibre-optic submarine cables link The Bahamas with the US, providing state-of-the-art telecommunications.

The Bahamas offers high-speed Internet connection through a variety of independent service providers, using dial-up, DSL, wireless broadband and cable connections.

The number of companies providing Internet connections from New Providence is growing rapidly. Major providers include:

Bahamas On-Line, tel 325-1000, 325-0011 or 502-8950, fax 325-0226, e-mail info@bahamas.net.bs, or visit www.bahamas.net.bs.

BaTelNet, tel 394-7NET, 300-2638, fax 394-7655, e-mail info@batelnet.bs, or visit www.batelnet.bs.

Coralwave/Coralwave Pro, tel 356-6780 or 356-2200, e-mail info@coralwave.com, or visit www.coralwave.com or www.cablebahamas.com.

INVESTING

The Bahamas is a tax-free financial centre with close proximity to the US, good communications and infrastructure and sound investment-oriented legislation. There are 284 banks and trust companies, as well as reputable, well-known law and accounting firms, and an established, experienced and highly qualified financial community.

Non-Bahamians wishing to open a business or local branch are assured of an investor-friendly climate with a business-sensitive legal framework and government committed to building free enterprise with minimal red tape. To this end, the government has established the Bahamas Investment Authority (BIA), a "one-stop-shop" for investors.

The prospective investor should submit to the BIA a project proposal with supporting documents. See **National Investment Policy,** this section.

See also **Bahamas Investment Authority (BIA)** and **Immigration, Business investors.**

Asset Protection Trusts (APTs)

In an increasingly litigious society, professionals, companies and high net worth individuals are seeking legitimate ways to protect their assets against possible future creditors.

The Fraudulent Dispositions Act, introduced as law in The Bahamas on Apr 15, 1991, protects assets from all litigation started more than two years after the assets were placed in the trust. Under the Act, foreign judgements are not recognized. The creditor must institute independent proceedings in the Bahamian courts and must prove intent to defraud.

An APT offers a high degree of safety and confidentiality. It involves the settlor giving legal title to property to a trustee to hold and use for the benefit of a beneficiary. It is most often used as part of a traditional estate plan and typically formed along with an International Business Company (IBC). Because the assets legally belong to the trustee rather than the settlor, they cannot be seized by creditors.

Trustees may be individuals or a trust corporation. If a Bahamian company acts as trustee, it must have a trust licence issued by The Central Bank of The Bahamas under the Banks and Trust Companies Regulation

Act. Individual trustees do not need to be licensed. To establish a Bahamian trust under the Trusts (Choice of Governing Law) Act, at least one of the trustees must be resident in The Bahamas, and the trust must be governed by the laws of The Bahamas although none of the assets, nor the settlor nor beneficiaries, need be resident or located in The Bahamas.

The highest degree of asset protection is afforded those assets which can be physically located offshore. As long as physical assets remain outside The Bahamas, a judge may assert jurisdiction over them on behalf of a successful plaintiff.

The objective of the APT is to avoid litigation altogether by using a package involving prudent use of professional advice and foreign legislation. It is not intended to protect crooked or incompetent individuals against possible creditors.

International Business Company (IBC)

See **Company formation, International Business Company (IBC).**

Trustees Act, 1998

The Trustees Act, passed by Parliament in 1998, replaces the Trustee Act, 1893, and several other pieces of trust legislation. Some provisions of the Act are:

1. Recognizing the existence of "protectors" of trusts.
2. Giving legal weight to trusts designed to protect beneficiaries from creditors, under certain circumstances.
3. Providing a legal basis to create a trust for a purpose that is not charitable, under certain circumstances.
4. Eliminating payment of income tax, capital gains tax, estate tax, inheritance tax, succession tax, gift tax, and other charges and duties by a beneficiary who is treated as a non-resident for exchange control purposes. Note: These provisions would not affect a situation where the asset in question is real property located in The Bahamas, even if the beneficiaries are non-resident for exchange control purposes. Stamp duty is payable if the trust owns property in The Bahamas conveyed to a beneficiary or third party.
5. Clarifying what beneficiaries are and are not entitled to know about the existence and details of a trust and trustee's deliberations.

The Act provides the flexibility necessary to sustain The Bahamas as a top-level offshore trust jurisdiction.

NATIONAL INVESTMENT POLICY

In 1994, the government introduced a National Investment Policy to support an investment friendly climate and foster economic growth and development of The Bahamas. An edited version of the policy document follows:

The investment environment

To support the National Investment Policy the government will provide:

1. A politically stable environment conducive to private investment.
2. An atmosphere where investments are safe and the expropriation of investment capital is not considered.
3. A legal environment based on a long tradition of parliamentary democracy, the rule of constitutional and statute laws and where security of life and personal property are guaranteed.
4. A stable macro-economic environment bolstered by a prudent fiscal policy, a stable exchange rate, flexible exchange control rules and free trade.
5. An environment in which freedom from capital gains, inheritance, withholding, profit remittance, corporate, royalty, sales, personal income, dividends, payroll and interest taxes is ensured.
6. Essential public services, a well-equipped police constabulary, modern health and education facilities and other social services.
7. Dependable public utilities.
8. Essential public infrastructure, such as roads, ports and airports.

The government is also committed to enhancing the image of The Bahamas as an international financial centre. To this end the government will:

1. Maintain The Bahamas as a leading financial services centre.
2. Monitor all developments in the international financial markets and amend any rules, regulations or legislation that would preserve and enhance the competitiveness of the financial services sector of the Bahamian economy.
3. Ensure the operation of a clean financial centre with specific rules and regulations to prevent laundering of criminally derived assets.
4. Support The Central Bank of The Bahamas in its commitment to bank supervision and promoting high standards of conduct and sound banking practices.
5. Support the self regulatory measures of the Assoc of International Bank and Trust Companies (AIBT), particularly the established code of conduct for banks and trust companies.
6. Continue enforcement of bank secrecy laws.

Investment incentives

Investment incentives under the following Acts include exemption from the payment of customs duties* on building materials, equipment and approved raw materials and real property taxes for periods up to 30 years.

- Export Manufacturing Industries Encouragement Act
- Industries Encouragement Act
- Agricultural Manufactories Act
- Tariff Act
- Hotels Encouragement Act
- Spirits and Beer Manufacture Act
- Family Island Development Encouragement Act
- Free Trade Zone Act

** Customs duty exemptions do not apply to personal consumables.*

The following trade arrangements are also in effect:

- Cotonou Agreement
- CARIBCAN
- Caribbean Basin Initiative (CBI)

Other incentives include investors acquiring publicly owned lands for approved developments on concessionary terms.

Administration of policy

The National Economic Council (NEC), headed by the Prime Minister, is responsible for executive management of the investment policy. Operational activities are the responsibility of the Bahamas Investment Authority (BIA).

Project proposal

An international investor seeking to do business in The Bahamas should submit to BIA a project proposal containing:

1. Name and address, including telephone/fax.
2. Executive summary of project.
3. Type of business – whether share company, partnership, individual or joint venture.
4. Principals – investors, major beneficial shareholders, including their dates and places of birth, as well as passport or social security numbers.
5. Proposed location.
6. Land requirements.
7. Start-up date.
8. Employment projections – number of Bahamian and non-Bahamian employees.
9. Management/personnel requirement – years of experience, training and work permits* for key personnel.
10. Financial arrangements for project, including bank reference.
11. Environmental impact – toxic waste, disposal procedures, toxic input.
12. Total capital investment in project with a breakdown of items and start-up cost. Minimum investment is $250,000.

** Necessary work permits for key personnel will be granted. Businesses requiring permits for persons other than key personnel are encouraged to consult BIA in advance.*

Areas targeted for overseas investors

Following is a list of certain investment areas especially targeted for international investors. However, the list is not exhaustive, and investors interested in areas not included should consult BIA. Joint ventures with

Bahamian partners are encouraged, with the choice of partner being at the discretion of the investor.

1. Touristic resorts.
2. Upscale condominium, timeshare and second home development.
3. Marinas.
4. Information/data processing.
5. Assembly industries.
6. Hi-tech services.
7. Ship registration, repair and other ship services.
8. Light manufacturing for export.
9. Agro-industries.
10. Food processing.
11. Mariculture.
12. Banking and other financial services.
13. Captive insurance.
14. Aircraft services.
15. Pharmaceutical manufacture.
16. Offshore medical centres.

Areas reserved for Bahamians

1. Wholesale and retail operations.*
2. Commission agencies engaged in the import/export trade.
3. Real estate and domestic property management agencies.
4. Domestic newspaper and magazine publications.
5. Domestic advertising and public relations firms.
6. Nightclubs and restaurants, except speciality, gourmet and ethnic restaurants, and restaurants operating in a hotel, resort complex or tourist attraction.
7. Security services.
8. Domestic distribution of building supplies.
9. Construction companies, except for special structures for which international expertise is required.
10. Personal cosmetic/beauty establishments.
11. Shallow water scale fish, crustacea, mollusk and sponge-fishing operations.
12. Auto and appliance service operations.
13. Public transportation.

* *International investors may engage in the wholesale distribution of any product they produce locally.*

Access to credit facilities

The Bahamas Development Bank (BDB) was created to help Bahamians establish new businesses or expand existing ones through concessionary funding and technical assistance, for projects that generate jobs and contribute to economic growth and development.

Contact the Bahamas Development Bank, Cable Beach, PO Box N-3034, Nassau, tel 327-5780 (to 6), fax 327-5047, e-mail dev.bank@batelnet.bs, or visit www.bahamasdevelopmentbank.com.

See also **Bahamas Development Bank (BDB), Bahamas Financial Services Board (BFSB), Bahamas International Securities Exchange (BISX), Bahamas Investment Authority (BIA), Banks, Business licence fee, Company formation, Hotels encouragement, Industries encouragement, Property transactions, Securities Commission of The Bahamas** and **Trade agreements.**

JUDICIAL SYSTEM

English common law is the basis of the Bahamian judicial system, although there is a large volume of Bahamian statute law. The highest tribunal in the country is the Court of Appeal, which sits on a full-time basis throughout the year. Five judges are appointed by the Governor General, including the residing president, three resident judges and one non-resident judge. Generally, three judges sit to conduct hearings. In practice, they are usually leading judges of Commonwealth countries, and they need have no former ties with The Bahamas.

The chief justice or one of the other ten justices who are appointed by the Governor General presides in the Supreme Court, which has general, civil and criminal jurisdiction. In addition there is a Supreme Court and two resident justices in Freeport, Grand Bahama, dealing with the northern region of The Bahamas, which includes Bimini, Abaco and Grand Bahama. The Supreme Court hears civil and criminal matters throughout the year, beginning on the second Wed in Jan.

New Providence has 14 magistrates' courts (including one drug court, one firearms court, one coroner's court, one night civil court and two night traffic courts). Grand Bahama has four magistrates' courts (three in Freeport and one in Eight Mile Rock). These courts are presided over by stipendiary and circuit magistrates, including the chief magistrate, a deputy chief magistrate who sits in Freeport and two senior magistrates, who exercise summary jurisdiction in criminal matters and in civil matters involving amounts not exceeding $5,000. Abaco has one magistrate.

In addition, all Out Island administrators exercise summary jurisdiction in criminal matters of a less serious nature and in civil matters involving amounts not exceeding $400.

An appeal from a decision of a Family Island administrator acting in his capacity as a magistrate goes to the stipendiary and circuit magistrate, and an appeal from a decision by a stipendiary and circuit magistrate exercising original jurisdiction goes to the Supreme Court and in some instances, directly to the Court of Appeal. An appeal from a Supreme Court decision goes to The Bahamas Court of Appeal, and an appeal from The Bahamas Court of Appeal goes to the judicial committee of the Privy Council in England.

Queen's Counsel

There are currently five members of Her Majesty's Counsel, or Queen's Counsel (QCs), for the Commonwealth of The Bahamas.

These "appointments of silk" are conferred on the most outstanding counsel of the country, and mark the pinnacle of achievement for an attorney-at-law. Eminent lawyers who are senior at the Bar may apply to the Attorney-General, who consults with the chief justice, president of the Bar Council and anyone else he sees fit. The Attorney-General recommends appointment to the prime minister, who may advise the Governor General to appoint the applicant a QC. Successful applicants are appointed to the Inner Bar and represent the Crown.

The five members are Sir Orville Turnquest, J Henry Bostwick, Harvey Tynes, Ralph D Seligman and Thomas Evans.

JUNKANOO

Junkanoo is the quintessential Bahamian celebration, a parade – or "rush-out" – characterized by colourful costumes, goatskin drums, cowbells, horns and a brass section.

Junkanoo is one of the few examples of uniquely Bahamian culture. The stunning crêpe-paper and cardboard costumes of Caribbean colours are worked on most of the year. When the celebrations are over, most of them – some of them art masterpieces – are thrown away, although the Junkanoo Expo now preserves the best pieces for exhibit.

Junkanoo, which has been compared to Mardi Gras in New Orleans and Carnival in Rio, is staged in the early hours of Dec 26, Boxing Day, and again in the early hours of Jan 1, New Year's Day. If either date falls on a Sun, the celebrations are held Mon morning. The parade moves clockwise downtown through Bay St, Elizabeth Ave, Shirley St, Frederick St, King St and George St.

Teamed with hypnotic music conducive to uninhibited dancing, Junkanoo is a never-to-be-forgotten festival of fun and frivolity.

No one knows for certain where it came from or how its name came to be. Some credit it to John Canoe, a legendary West African chieftain. Others say it comes from the French phrase *gens inconnus*, unknown, or masked, people.

Regular groups in Junkanoo contests in Nassau include the Valley Boys, Saxons, One Family, Vikings, Music Makers, Roots, Fancy Dancers, Z-Bandits, Barrabas and the Tribe, Colours, The Prodigal Sons, and the PIGS (Progress through Integrity, Guts and Strength).

There is a mini-Junkanoo, or "rush-out," staged somewhere in Nassau and Freeport every week.

LABOUR RELATIONS

Industrial Relations Chapter 321 Statute Laws of The Bahamas, as amended in 2000, makes it unlawful for a trade union to operate in The Bahamas – or for any person to take part in its activities – unless the union is registered.

Applications to register a trade union should be made to the registrar of trade unions at the Labour Dept.

The registrar shall refuse to register a trade union if the union's principal objects are unlawful or contrary to statutory objects, or if its name is misleading or so similar to an existing name as to deceive the public, or if there is failure to comply to specified balloting procedures.

Upon registration, the trade union is issued a certificate as evidence of that registration. Every trade union is required to have a registered office. Unions may own or lease land, but all real and personal property is vested in the trustees of the union.

No person under age 16 may be a member of a trade union. A union may not have foreign connections without a proper licence in writing from the minister responsible for labour.

An employer is required to recognize a union as bargaining agent if more than 50% of the employees are members. An employer has 14 days to accept or reject a union claim for recognition. No employee can be dismissed or adversely treated as a result of his union involvement.

All industrial agreements between employer and union must be sent in writing to both the Industrial Tribunal and the minister responsible for labour. The minister has 14 days to make comments to the tribunal. After taking these comments into consideration, the tribunal may register the agreement if found to contain no illegalities. Properly registered industrial agreements are considered binding.

Any strike is illegal that has a purpose other than the furtherance of a trade dispute, or if designed to coerce the government. The same applies to a lockout. A picket must be able to produce on his person written authorization by a trade union official, and he must picket peacefully near a place or building where a party to the dispute works, with no more than 14 other pickets.

In 2002, government enacted a series of new labour laws. The Employment Act, 2001, the Minimum Wage Act, 2001, and Health and the Safety at Work Act, 2002, established minimum standards for employment and improved settlement of trade disputes.

Contact the Labour Dept, PO Box N-1586, Nassau, tel 502-1052 or 502-1047.

See also **Industrial Tribunal** and **Trade unions.**

LAW FIRMS

For information on lawyers and law firms in The Bahamas, contact the Bahamas Bar Association, PO Box N-4632, Nassau, tel (242) 326-3276, fax (242) 328-4615.

LIBRARIES

Carmichael Public Library, Carmichael Rd, Mon-Fri 10am-7pm and every first and third Sat 10am-3pm. Tel 341-8256.

Coconut Grove Community Library, Acklins St, Coconut Grove, Mon-Fri 10am-6pm. Tel 323-4310.

College of The Bahamas Library, Poinciana Dr, Mon-Thurs 8am-9pm, Fri 9:30am-6pm, Sat 9am-5pm, Sun 1pm-5pm (Sept-June). Call for summer hours. Tel 302-4552 or 302-4517.

Eastern Public Library, Mackey St, Mon-Fri 10am-9pm, Sat 10am-5pm July-Sept: Mon-Fri 9am-8pm, Sat 10am-4pm. Tel 393-2196.

Fox Hill Public Library, Bernard Rd, Mon-Fri 10am-8pm, Sat 10am-1pm. Tel 324-1458.

G K Symonette Library, Yellow Elder, Mon-Fri 9am-5:30pm. Tel 322-5303.

Kemp Rd Community Library, Kemp Rd, Mon-Fri 9am-5pm. Tel 393-1541.

Learning Resources Library, Mackey St, Mon-Fri 9am-5:30pm. Tel 393-5379.

Lillian G W Coakley Library, Baillou Hill Rd north, Mon-Fri 10am-9pm, Sat 10am-2pm (Sept-June); Mon-Fri 10am-6pm, Sat 10am-2pm (July-Aug). Tel 322-1056.

Nassau Public Library, Shirley St (main library), Mon-Thurs 10am-8pm, Fri 10am-

5pm, Sat 10am-4pm. Tel 322-4907.

South Beach Library, East St south, Mon-Thurs 10am-8pm, Fri 10am-5pm, Sat 10am-3pm. Call for summer and holiday hours. Tel 392-1156.

LIQUOR LAWS

The legal drinking age in The Bahamas is 18. Liquor licence applicants must be over 21. It is illegal to sell intoxicating liquor in The Bahamas without a licence. Under the Act Relating to the Sale of Intoxicating Liquors, this includes spirits, wines, ale, beer, porter, stout, cider, perry and other malt liquor, and any fermented or distilled liquor. A licence is not necessary for:

1. Intoxicating liquor sold by virtue of legal process or law which authorizes the sale.
2. Intoxicating liquor that is pure alcohol and sold in the drug store of a licensed chemist or pharmacist, or is in medicinal form and sold by a qualified medical practitioner or licensed chemist or pharmacist.
3. Intoxicating liquor which forms part of the estate of a deceased person and the Licensing Authority authorizes sale thereof, or where the liquor is sold by a licensed auctioneer under conditions set by the Licensing Authority.
4. Intoxicating liquor sold at premises duly registered as a members' club.
5. Intoxicating liquor sold on board any ship calling at The Bahamas and lying outside the limits of any port, to be consumed aboard ship.
6. Intoxicating liquor sold to passengers aboard any ship calling at The Bahamas and lying within the limits of any harbour for a period not exceeding 72 hours, to be consumed aboard ship.

There are six types of liquor licences: general, wholesale, proprietary club, hotel, restaurant and bar, and occasional. The occasional licence is granted for the sale of intoxicating liquors for consumption at a stated place and time not exceeding three days at any one time. In New Providence, an occasional licence may be granted by the chairman of the Licensing Authority.

Issuing, cancelling or transferring of a liquor licence is at the discretion of the Licensing Authority. No general licence will be granted in districts where a prohibitive order is in force.

Once a liquor licence has been granted the applicant pays the fee to the Public Treasury in New Providence or in the case of the Out Islands, to the local administration. Liquor licences expire on Dec 31 each year.

According to the Act, no licensee other than the holder of a hotel, proprietary club or restaurant licence shall sell, expose for sale or dispose of intoxicating liquor on Sun, holidays, during polling hours on election day, and before 9am or after 9pm on any weekday, unless otherwise authorized by the Licensing Authority.

Contact the Business Licence and Licensing Authority, Nassau, tel 322-5200, or the Financial Secretary, Ministry of Finance, PO Box N-3107, Nassau, tel 327-1530.

LOTTERIES

Under provisions of The Lotteries and Gaming Act, it is unlawful for any person to be involved in a lottery promoted or proposed to be promoted, without the prior approval of the minister with responsibility for gaming. This includes printing of tickets, distribution, advertisements, listing of prize winners and connection with a lottery in any manner. Offenders will be subject to a fine or imprisonment.

However, lotteries (raffles) are permitted when they are incidental to certain entertainment. This includes bazaars, sales of work, dinners, dances and other similar functions, which must be previously approved, in writing, by the minister with responsibility for gaming.

The following conditions apply:

1. The whole proceeds of the entertainment (including the lottery), after deductions, must be devoted to purposes other than private gain.

2. None of the lottery prizes shall be money.
3. Participating in lotteries cannot be the only substantial inducement to attend the entertainment.

A private lottery is permitted. This is a lottery in which sale of tickets or chances by the promoters is confined to:

1. Members of one society (clubs, institutions, organizations, etc) established and conducted for purposes not connected with gaming, betting or lotteries.
2. Persons who work or live on the same premises.

Private lotteries must adhere to several regulations, details of which are available through the ministry with responsibility for gaming.

Any three or more residents of The Bahamas may organize a lottery for the purpose of fund-raising for religious, educational or charitable purposes, promotion of athletic games or cultural activities, or for promotion of the welfare of the community.

Organizers of such lotteries must:

1. Obtain prior approval, in writing, from the minister with responsibility for gaming.
2. Declare the purposes for which the lottery is being held.
3. Enter into a bond with the Treasurer for payment of 15% of gross receipts of the lottery (duty payable on the lottery).
4. Pay this duty within 14 days of the lottery, along with an accountant's statement verifying the amount. The Minister of Finance may waive or refund duty payable on the lottery.

In New Providence, contact the ministry with responsibility for gaming, PO Box N-3701, tel 322-7500. In Freeport, contact the senior administrator, Dept of Local Government, PO Box F-40001, tel (242) 352-6332. In the Out Islands, contact the administrator on that island.

MAILBOATS

See **Transportation.**

MANUFACTURING

According to latest figures from the Dept of Statistics, 1997 manufacturing output in The Bahamas totalled $230,813,420. The leading manufactured products are beverages and pharmaceuticals – particularly rum and liqueurs, which have been among leading manufactured items since 1961, when Bacardi shareholders reconstituted their Cuban company in The Bahamas. Today, Bacardi & Co Ltd employs 151 persons on a permanent basis, and another 30 indirectly. Bacardi, one of the world's leading distilled-spirit manufacturers, has invested more than $100 million in its Nassau facility. This includes a distillery, a rum blending/processing plant, a bottling plant, an international quality-control laboratory and seven ageing warehouses – each with a storage capacity of more than 50,000 barrels. Products produced locally for the European market include Bacardi 8, Carta Blanca and several other Bacardi dark premium rums. Bacardi also exports the rum spirits for Bacardi Limón and low-proof Breezer. The company also produces the above products for the local market, as well as Castillo silver and gold rums, Nassau Royale liqueur, Natasha Vodka and flavoured rums, including coconut, pineapple and banana flavours. More than 95% of Bacardi products are exported to Europe.

Commonwealth Brewery Ltd (CBL), Clifton Pier, represents an investment of more than $30 million in The Bahamas. The partners comprise international and Bahamian interests: Heineken International and Associated Bahamian Distillers and Brewers (ABDAB). The company has a brewing capacity of 2.25 million cases per annum.

In 2001, a $5-million refurbishment and upgrade of the brewery facility with automated production processes and systems significantly increased packaging speed and quality. In 2002 and 2003, CBL invested an additional $2 million in technical modifications at the brewery to achieve optimal production efficiency.

The first two products in CBL's locally produced portfolio were Heineken and

Guinness. Then came Vita Malt and the Bahamian beer Kalik – named for the "kalik-kalik" sound of cowbells during Junkanoo – which is the No 1 selling beer in The Bahamas. CBL has launched two product extensions from Kalik, Kalik Gold and Kalik Light. Heineken and Kalik have won international gold medal awards. In Aug 1997, CBL began selling Kalik to Royal Caribbean Intl's *Sovereign of the Seas.* CBL currently exports Kalik to the US and Canada.

At Bahamian trade shows, locally manufactured goods on display include shell crafts, art, wood carvings, straw work, ceramics, condiments, beverages, Bahamian cassettes and CDs.

Bahamian factories include Imperial Mattress, Scottdale Bedding Co Ltd, Simmons Manufacturing Co Ltd (shoe manufacturer), Bahamas Extruders & Investment Co Ltd (PVC pipes manufacturer), and Graycliff Cigar Factory.

Other manufactured goods are Androsia batik fabrics, bleach, soaps, detergents, polystyrene beads, medical devices (stents), pharmaceuticals, soft drinks, handcrafted boats, paint and paper items, bottled water, dolls, gold and shell jewellery, handcrafted furniture and fragrances.

The government has removed many cumbersome manufacturing requirements and introduced incentives to diversify the country's tourism-based economy and encourage a stronger manufacturing sector.

See also **Industry, Trade agreements, Import & export statistics** and **Freeport/Lucaya information, Industry.**

MARINAS & CRUISING FACILITIES

Listings for marinas and cruising facilities indicate those which have approx 25 or more slips at their facility. For depth, availability and dockage rate information, contact the facility directly. Most marinas monitor VHF channel 16 and a doctor/ nurse or clinic, if not on site, is usually nearby. See **Fig 2.0** and **Boating.**

MARINE PARKS & EXHIBITS

See **Marine research, Paradise Island** and **Wildlife preserves.**

MARINE RESEARCH

The reef-rich seas of The Bahamas have inspired national and international research embracing the gamut of marine-oriented subjects – including dolphins and whales, blue holes, lost civilizations, shipwrecks, shoreline ecosystems, plankton, the Bermuda triangle and underwater habitats.

Much of the marine research carried out in The Bahamas is chronicled in the *Bahamas Journal of Science,* published by Media Publishing in Nassau.

See also **Bahamas National Trust, Nature centres** and **Wildlife preserves.**

Bahamas-based research organizations include:

The Bahamas Environmental Research Centre (BERC): One of two field stations of the College of The Bahamas (COB). Located in Staniard Creek, Andros, the station is dedicated to facilitating education, research and community outreach programmes, which promote sustainable development and an understanding of conservation and ecological issues. Contact Margo Blackwell, Bahamas Environmental Research Centre, c/o Research, Planning and Development, College of The Bahamas, PO Box N-4912, Nassau, tel 302-4307/8 at COB, or (242) 357-2785 at BERC, fax 323-7803, or e-mail margob@batelnet.bs.

The Bahamas Marine Mammal Survey (BMMS): Long-term research programme to support whale and dolphin conservation. Since 1991 BMMS has been documenting the occurrence, distribution and status of marine mammal species in Bahamian waters with a special focus on bottlenose dolphins, beaked whales and sperm whales. The research is funded primarily by a field research grant from Earthwatch and private contributions. The project runs a student internship programme and an environmental camp at Sandy Point, Abaco. Contact Diane Claridge, PO Box AB-20714, Marsh Harbour, Abaco, e-mail bmms@oii.net.

Bimini Biological Field Station: World-class shark research centre devoted to research, education and conservation of shark species, especially lemon sharks, in the wild. Dr Samuel Gruber, professor of marine biology and fisheries at the Univ of Miami's Rosenstiel School of Marine and Atmospheric Science, offers accredited shark awareness and marine biology courses to international high school and college students, and an annual scholarship is also made available to a student in The Bahamas. Contact Dr Samuel Gruber, 9300 SW 99th St, Miami, FL, 33176-2050, USA, tel/fax (305) 274-0628, voice mail (305) 361-4146, e-mail sgruber@rsmas.miami.edu, or visit www.miami.edu/sharklab.

Forfar Field Station: Operated by International Field Studies (IFS), a non-profit scientific and educational organization promoting hands-on learning experiences for high school and college students. Also hosts researchers. Primary focus is marine biology but also caters to interests in geology, botany and ornithology. Forfar Field Station, Blanket Sound, Andros, tel (242) 368-6129, fax (242) 368-6160, or IFS, PO Box 428, 30 Public Sq, Nelsonville, OH, 45764, USA, tel 1-800-962-3805 or (740) 753-9231, fax (740) 753-5100, e-mail office@intlfieldstudies.com, or visit www.intlfieldstudies.com.

Gerace Research Center (formerly Bahamian Field Station): A not-for-profit educational and research institution under The College of The Bahamas with a continuing agreement with the government of The Bahamas. Supports environmental research projects in archaeology, biology, geology and marine sciences. Contact Vincent Voegeli, Executive Director, Gerace Research Center, United Estates, San Salvador, tel (242) 331-2520, fax (242) 331-2524 or GRC c/o Twin Air, 1100 Lee Wagener Blvd, Suite 113, Ft Lauderdale, FL, 33315, USA, or e-mail grcss@juno.com.

Island Expedition: Non-profit research and educational organization dedicated to researching, understanding, documenting and protecting the environment and island community cultures. The School at Sea is a hands-on environmental education programme conducting study excursions throughout The Bahamas and Caribbean for students from all over the world. Contact Dragan or Nicolas Popov, PO Box CB-11934, Nassau, tel/fax 327-8659, e-mail info@islandexpedition.com, or visit www.islandexpedition.com.

Perry Institute for Marine Science (PIMS) – Caribbean Marine Research Center (CMRC): Lee Stocking Island, Exuma. Not for profit organization established in 1970. Internationally recognized for conducting specialized marine studies and educational programmes. Advanced research laboratories, diving facilities and opportunities for experiential learning attract scientists and students from all over the world. Contact PIMS director, c/o Perry Institute for Marine Science, 100 North US Highway 1, Suite 202, Jupiter, FL, 33477, USA, tel (561) 741-0192, fax (561) 741-0193, or e-mail cmrc@cmrc.org.

The Rob Palmer Blue Holes Foundation: A non-profit organization dedicated to scientific and physical exploration and research of Bahamian blue and black holes. Also encourages education in and conservation of these cave systems and their associated habitats. Contact Dr Stephanie Schwabe, 5 Longitude Ln, Charleston, SC, 29401, USA, e-mail steffi@blueholes.org, or visit www.blueholes.org.

See also **Atlantic Undersea Test and Evaluation Center (AUTEC).**

MARRIAGE LICENCES

Marriage licences cost $100 and are obtained in New Providence at the Registrar General's office, R E Bain Bldg, corner of Parliament and Shirley Sts, PO Box N-532, Nassau. No blood test is required.

cont on pg 450

FIG 2.0

MARINAS & CRUISING FACILITIES

Location	Slips	Fuel	Electric	Water/ ice	Shower/ wash/ dry	Groc/ supply	Rest/ bar	Boat/ elect repair	Charter/ boat rental	Motel/ hotel
Abacos										
Abaco Beach Resort & Boat Harbour, Marsh Harbour (242) 367-2736	198	√	110, 220	√	√	x	√	x	√	√
Conch Inn Marina, Marsh Harbour (242) 367-4000	75	√	110, 220	√	√	√	√	x	√	√
Green Turtle Club & Yacht Club, Green Turtle Cay (242) 365-4271	35	√	110, 220	√	√	√	√	x	x	√
Mangoes Marina, Marsh Harbour (242) 367-4255	29	x	110, 220	√	√	x	√	x	x	x
Marsh Harbour Marina, Marsh Harbour (242) 367-2700	67	√	110, 220	√	√	x	√	x	√	x
Spanish Cay Marina (242) 365-0083	80	√	110, 220	√	√	√	√	x	√	√
Treasure Cay Beach Resort & Marina, Treasure Cay (242) 365-8250	150	√	110, 220	√	√	√	√	x	√	√
Walker's Cay Marina, (242) 353-1252	40	√	110, 220	√	√	√	√	√	√	√
Berry Islands										
Chub Cay Club Marina (242) 325-1490	90	√	110, 220	√	√	√	√	x	√	√
Great Harbour Cay Marina (242) 367-8005	67	√	110, 220	√	√	√	√	x	√	x
Bimini										
Bimini Big Game Resort & Marina (242) 347-3391	82	√	110, 220	√	√	x	√	√	√	√
Bimini Blue Water Ltd (242) 347-3166	32	√	110, 220	√	√	x	√	x	√	√
Eleuthera, Harbour Island & Spanish Wells										
Harbour Island Club & Marina, Harbour Island (242) 333-2427	38	√	110, 220	√	√	x	√	x	√	x

Location	Slips	Fuel	Electric	Water/ ice	Shower/ wash/ dry	Groc/ supply	Rest/ bar	Boat/ elect repair	Charter/ boat rental	Motel/ hotel
Spanish Wells Yacht Haven, Spanish Wells (242) 333-4328	40	√	110, 220	√	√	x	√	x	x	√
Valentine's Marina, Harbour Island (242) 333-2142	50	√	110, 220	√	√	x	√	x	√	√
Exumas										
Exuma Docking Service, George Town (242) 336-2578	52	√	110, 220	√	√	x	√	x	x	x
Sampson Cay Club, George Town (242) 355-2034	35	√	110, 220,	√	√	√	√	x	√	√
Grand Bahama										
Lucayan Marina Village, Lucaya (242) 373-8888	130	√	110, 220	√	√	x	√	x	x	√
Old Bahama Bay, West End (242) 346-6500	72	√	110, 220, 440,	√	√	√	√	√	√	√
Port Lucaya Marina, Port Lucaya (242) 373-9090 (to 2)	106	√	110, 220, 440	√	√	√	x	√	x	√
Xanadu Beach Marina, Freeport (242) 352-6782 ext 1212	40	√	110, 220, 440	√	√	x	√	x	x	√
Long Island										
Flying Fish Marina, Clarence Town (242) 337-3430	15	√	110, 220, 440	√	√	√	√	√	x	x
New Providence										
Bayshore Marina, East Bay St (242) 393-8232	192	√	110, 220	√	x	x	x	√	√	x
Brown's Boat Basin, East Bay St (242) 393-3331	70	√	110	√	x	x	x	√	x	x
Harbour Central Marina 671 Bay St (242) 323-2172	32	√	110, 220	√	√	√	x	x	x	x
Lyford Cay Club (private), Lyford Cay (242) 362-4131	74	√	110, 220	√	√	x	√	x	√	√

Location	Slips	Fuel	Electric	Water/ ice	Shower/ wash/ dry	Groc/ supply	Rest/ bar	Boat/ elect repair	Charter/ boat rental	Motel/ hotel
Nassau Harbour Club, East Bay St (242) 393-0771	66	√	110, 220	√	√	√	√	√	√	√
Nassau Yacht Haven, East Bay St (242) 393-8173	150	√	110, 220	√	√	√	√	x	√	x
Paradise Island										
Hurricane Hole Marina (242) 363-3600	67	√	110, 220	√	√	x	√	x	√	x
Marina at Atlantis (242) 363-6068	63	x	110, 220, 440	√	√	x	√	x	x	√

cont from pg 447

Minimum age without parental consent is 18. Minors may be married with both parents' consent if they have reached the age of 15. Under special circumstances, those between the ages of 13-15 may apply to the Supreme Court for permission to marry. Consent forms for minors are available at the Registrar General's office.

Applications for marriage licences and consent forms must be filled out in the presence of a marriage officer (including Family Island administrators), the Registrar General, a magistrate, Justice of the Peace, notary public, registrar of marriages or other person authorized to administer oaths.

Both parties desiring to be married must be in The Bahamas at the time of application and must have resided in The Bahamas at least 24 hours immediately prior to the date of application for a marriage licence.

If either party is not a citizen or resident of The Bahamas, a declaration certifying that he or she is not married must be sworn before a notary public or other person authorized to administer oaths in that country.

Applicants from British Commonwealth countries (except Jamaica) may provide an affidavit of singlehood from a solicitor or commissioner for oaths in their jurisdiction. This declaration must accompany the application. An applicant from any non-Commonwealth country (except Haiti) who has never been married may swear an affidavit of singlehood before a notary public in The Bahamas.

A divorced person is required to provide an original or court-certified copy of the final divorce decree, and a person whose former spouse has died must provide an original or certified copy of the death certificate.

There were 4,654 marriages in The Bahamas in 2003.

MOTOR VEHICLE INSURANCE

All motor vehicles in The Bahamas must be licensed and insured in accordance with The Bahamas Road Traffic Act. Cost of insurance depends on the driver's age, driving experience, traffic convictions, accident record, the vehicle's age, engine size and value, number of drivers, intended use of the vehicle and other criteria.

Minimum coverage required by law is "Road Act" coverage. This covers the insured's legal liability for death and bodily injury to any person other than a passenger in the insured's vehicle. Third party insurance covers legal liability for death, bodily injury (which may include passengers in the insured's vehicle) and property damage. Comprehensive coverage encompasses third party liability, fire, theft and collision damage to the insured's vehicle. Windstorms, hurricanes, flooding and riots are now covered under most comprehensive policies.

Under most policies, only drivers named under the policy are covered to drive. Additional drivers may be added to a policy. Some companies require these drivers to fill out additional driver forms. Whether or not there is a charge depends on the driver's age, experience, and traffic and accident record. In most cases, there is no additional charge for drivers over 25 who have had several years' experience, with a clear driving record.

With the exception of act coverage, no-claims discounts are usually allowed for consecutive claim-free years. The no-claims discount entitlement scale is highest under the comprehensive policy.

Example: A 26-year-old owner of a sedan worth approx $20,000, who has never been insured yet is a driver in good standing, may be issued a comprehensive policy of approx $2,618 (gross). If that individual has been driving with insurance in his name for a minimum of five claim-free years, he would receive the max no-claims discount for a net premium of $916. This example is based on comprehensive coverage where discounts build each claim-free year up to a max discount of 60-65%. This max discount is allowed as long as the insured person maintains a claim-free policy. Discounts vary with different insurance companies.

See also **Driver's licence & vehicle information.**

MUSEUMS

Balcony House Museum, Market St. Named for its overhanging balcony, this 18th-century landmark is perhaps the oldest wooden house of its kind in The Bahamas. The Central Bank of The Bahamas purchased the building in 1985 and restored it to its original state, including period furnishings. Mon-Wed, Fri & Sat 9:30am-4:30pm, Sun 12noon-4pm; closed Thurs. Tel 302-2621.

Nassau Public Library, Museum & Reading Room, Shirley St, a former 18th-century jail, now documents The Bahamas' colourful past in books and a small selection of artefacts and historical documents. Mon-Thurs 10am-8pm, Fri 10am-5pm, Sat 10am-4pm. Tel 322-4907.

Pompey Museum of Slavery & Emancipation at Vendue House, Bay St, a former 18th- and 19th-century slave auction site, houses the history of slavery and emancipation in The Bahamas in photographs, artefacts and replicas. The museum was closed for renovations as a result of the Straw Market fire of Sept 4, 2001. It reopened Jul '04 featuring a renowned exhibition and new research centre. Mon-Wed, Fri & Sat 9:30am-4:30pm; Sun 12noon-4pm; closed Thurs. $5 adults, $3 seniors, $2 students and $1 children under 12. Tel 356-0495.

See also **Art galleries, Bahamas Historical Society** and **Forts.**

MUTUAL FUNDS

See **Investing.**

NATIONAL ANTHEM

See **National symbols.**

NATIONAL INSURANCE

The National Insurance Act, 1972, established a system of national social insurance in The Bahamas. The consummation of this act, the National Insurance Programme, began on Oct 7, 1974. As a result, the Workmen's Compensation Act (covering on-the-job injuries/diseases/death) and the Old Age Pensions Act (providing assistance for senior citizens) were repealed, and their provisions were assimilated into the new programme.

National Insurance is administered by the National Insurance Board of The Bahamas. It provides a wide range of benefits, long and short-term, for qualified insured persons and their dependents. Benefits are in the form of partial, income-replacing payments in times of sickness, invalidity, maternity, retirement, and death.

In the case of injury, disease or death arising out of employment, the programme provides for free medical care and expenses.

Benefits

Payment of benefits to employed persons, began with sickness benefit in Apr 1975, and maternity and funeral benefits in Sept '75. Long-term benefit entitlement began in 1977.

Each benefit has qualifying conditions. For example, to qualify for sickness benefit, the claimant must be incapable of work as prescribed by the National Insurance Act. The claimant must have made at least 40 contributions which must include 13 contributions in the 26 weeks immediately before the week the illness started, 26 contributions in the 52 weeks immediately before the week the illness started, or 26 contributions in the contribution year immediately before the year in which the illness started.

There have been several amendments to the act over the years. Retirement benefit, for example, was initially paid for insured persons 65 years or older upon cessation of employment. Amendments made it possible for insured persons to receive retirement benefit from as early as age 60. Persons who choose to receive earlier benefit are paid a reduced benefit. Persons choosing to claim retirement benefit at age 60 receive 80% of the entitlement. Individuals who are paid the benefit at an early age will not have their rates of payment increased when they reach 65.

Amendments also make it possible for those aged 60 to 69, who receive retirement benefit, to go back to work or continue to work without losing their benefit, if they earn no more than $200 per week. In cases where earnings exceed $200, the benefit is suspended until the individual finally retires from gainful employment.

In the case of persons 70 years and older, a 1999 amendment makes it possible for them to be able to continue to work and receive their retirement benefit, regardless of income.

Assistance: National Insurance also provides a range of assistance payments that parallel the benefits, for needy persons who do not qualify for benefits.

For example, old age non-contributory pension is an assistance payment given to residents 65 years or older who are assessed as being "needy" by a test of resources.

Registration/contributions: From 1974 to '76, only employed persons were required to register and pay contributions. Self-employed persons were brought into the programme in 1976.

For the first 10 years, the insurable wage ceiling (the maximum salary insurable) was $110 per week. This ceiling was raised to $250 per week in 1984, and to $400 in '99. The rate of contributions for employed persons is 8.8% and that is shared by the employer and employee. Contributions for employed persons on wages from $60 to $400 are shared at 5.4% (employer), and 3.4% (employee). Wages of $59 and less are shared 7.1% (employer) and 1.7% employee.

There are two classes of self-employed persons – class A and class B. Class A is not eligible for industrial benefits. Self-employed persons in class A pay contributions at a rate of 6.8%. Self-employed persons in class B are eligible for industrial benefits, and pay contributions at the same rate as employed persons (8.8%). Class B includes:

1. Drivers of taxis or other vehicles, who own them and are licensed to ply them for hire.
2. Licensed fruit, straw or vegetable vendors.
3. Share-fishermen who own and work aboard their own vessels.

Under the National Insurance Act, a previously insured person may, while unemployed, apply to pay into National Insurance as a voluntarily insured person. These contributions accrue towards long-term benefits (retirement, invalidity, etc) but not towards the short-term benefits (sickness, maternity, etc).

Contribution for voluntarily insured persons is 5%, based on the average weekly earnings during the year before the individual ceased to be employed or self-employed.

Pensionable civil servants (persons within the public service, who are eligible for pensions out of the government's consolidated fund), pay contributions based on two wage ceilings. This was made possible by a 1986 provision, which enabled employers to integrate their pension plan with the National Insurance retirement benefit, and to modify their contributions (retirement and other long-term benefits) accordingly. Pensionable civil servants, therefore, pay contributions for their long-term benefits on the ceiling of $110 per week; and for their short-term benefits, on a ceiling of $400 per week.

Survivors' benefit: Paid to the surviving dependents of a deceased insured person who had paid a minimum of 150 contributions into the scheme. This benefit is paid in order of priority, with the widow/widower being the first priority; unmarried dependent children under age 16, or under age 21 if full-time students, the second priority.

Invalidity benefit: Paid to an insured person, age 16-65, who has paid a minimum of 150 contributions and has been diagnosed by the board's medical referee as being permanently incapable of gainful employment.

Sickness and maternity benefits: Pays $53.08-$240 per week (60% of the individual's average weekly insurable wage) for insured persons. Contribution requirements apply. Normally, the sickness benefit is payable for a max of 156 days for a continuous period of illness, but payment may be extended to 240 days in certain circumstances. An amendment to the National Insurance Act raised the rate of maternity benefit to 66.66% of the woman's average insured income. The amendments were enacted in 2004, but this provision had retroactive effect to Jan 1, 2002. Maternity benefit pays $53.08-$266.64 per week. Contribution requirements apply.

In addition to the rate of benefit, the National Insurance (benefit and assistance amendment) regulations, 2004 also allowed for the following:

- A woman can receive maternity benefit in respect of the delivery of a stillborn child after 24 weeks of pregnancy. Previously the pregnancy must have progressed to 28 weeks;
- Maternity benefit will now be assessed daily;
- The maternity benefit period can be broken up to accommodate a woman who returns to work (while a premature child is hospitalized) and then resumes leave (after the child is discharged);
- The maternity benefit period can be extended up to six weeks for a woman who suffers an illness arising out of her confinement;
- The maternity period can be extended by one week for each week that confinement is delayed;
- The unpaid portion of maternity benefit due a deceased woman can be paid to the next-of-kin;
- The maternity grant of $400 for each live birth will be paid to the uninsured wife of a man who satisfies the conditions for the maternity benefit.

Maternity benefit is paid for 13 weeks, starting within six weeks of the expected week of confinement, provided the woman has stopped working.

Funeral benefit: Paid in the form of a $1,500 grant on the death of an insured person to the person paying the funeral expenses. Contribution requirements apply. Funeral benefit is also paid for funeral expenses of an uninsured deceased spouse, based on contributions of the insured husband or wife.

Industrial benefits: Introduced in 1980 to be paid to, or in respect of, employed persons, irrespective of contribution status, and to eligible self-employed persons who suffer injury, disability or death as a result of an accident or a prescribed disease arising out of, or in the course of, employment.

The industrial benefits replaced the provisions of the repealed Workmen's Compensation Act and include: injury benefit, paid for a continuous period or in spells, for up to 240 days from the date of the accident, or the date of development of the prescribed disease; disablement benefit, which is paid according to the degree of disablement the person suffers as a result of the accident or prescribed disease; and death benefit, which is paid to the surviving dependents when death results from the accident or prescribed disease.

Injury benefit ranges from $53.05-$266 per week (66.66% of the person's insurable wage). Payment of disablement benefit is based on the degree of disablement. If it is more than 1% but less than 25%, the benefit is paid in the form of a cash grant at the rate of $100 for each 1% of disablement.

If the degree of disablement is 25% or greater, benefit is paid both as a grant and a pension. This pension is paid for life or a specified period. Death benefit is paid according to the rate of the injury benefit paid or payable.

Adjustment of entitlements: In 1986, a provision was introduced in the Act enabling employers to modify the rates of benefits payable under their own pension schemes. It allows employers to integrate their benefits with those provided under the National Insurance Act and to eliminate overlapping benefits.

Employers wishing to change their occupational pension schemes must first submit proposed modification to the minister responsible for National Insurance, for approval. Employers may modify terms and conditions of the contract of service relating to wage payment during sick, maternity or injury leave, to take into account similar benefits provided under the National Insurance scheme.

Investment

A secondary goal of the National Insurance scheme is to contribute to the socio-economic development of the country. To this end, a large part of the National Insurance Board's (NIB) total investment portfolio, which now exceeds the $1-billion mark, has been made in areas that would achieve this goal. These areas include government registered stock; long-term loans to quasi-governmental corporations to assist in the development of basic infrastructure, especially in the Out Islands; investment in real property, which includes 18 community health centres throughout the country, the NIB's income-producing Freeport office complex in Grand Bahama; Alexander House on Robinson Rd; Claughton House, Shirley and Charlotte Sts; the head office complex on Blue Hill Rd; the Fox Hill complex and the Wulff Rd complex, Nassau.

NIB's investments include a category for social investments, which provides concessional loans through the Bahamas Development Bank (BDB) for entrepreneurial projects in agriculture, fishing and manufacturing.

Administration

The National Insurance scheme is administered by a tripartite board, ordinarily comprising 11 members. Five members are appointed at the discretion of the minister responsible for National Insurance, three are appointed to represent employers and three represent insured persons. A chairman and deputy chairman are appointed by the minister.

NIB headquarters are on Blue Hill Rd, New Providence, with a local office on the ground floor and three regional offices: one in the Wulff Rd complex, one in the Fox Hill complex near the Parade Ground, and one in Alexander House on Robinson Rd. The Board also operates two cashier's windows for payment of contributions in New Providence. These are located on the ground floor of the main post office, East Hill St, and in the post office in Cable Beach.

There are 24 regional offices in the Out Islands, including four offices in Grand Bahama, which provide a full range of services to contributors, claimants and the general public.

The NIB also operates a consumer telephone hotline service Mon-Fri 9am-5pm, through which answers to any National Insurance questions may be obtained. Tel 325-4655/6. A toll-free number, tel (242) 300-1394, serves the Out Islands.

NATIONAL PARKS, RESERVES & PROTECTED AREAS

See **Wildlife preserves.**

NATIONAL SYMBOLS

Coat of arms

By royal warrant dated Dec 7, 1971, The Bahamas was granted a new coat of arms, the description of which, in heraldic terms, is as follows:

"Argent a representation of the Santa Maria on a base barry wavy of four Azure on a Chief Azure a demi Sun Or And for the Crest upon a representation of Our Royal Helmet mantled Azure doubled Argent On a Wreath Or and Azure a Conch Shell proper in front of a Panache of Palm Fronds proper And for Supporters On the dexter a Marlin proper on the Sinister a Flamingo proper; And upon a Compartment Per pale Waves of the Sea and Swampland proper together with the motto: FORWARD, UPWARD, ONWARD, TOGETHER."

The coat of arms was developed from drawings submitted by artist Rev Dr Hervis L Bain, Jr, who also contributed to the design of The Bahamas flag.

Flag

The design of The Bahamas flag is a black equilateral triangle on a background of three equal horizontal stripes of aquamarine, gold and aquamarine. Its design is based on a composite of ideas and suggestions collected from Bahamians in a national competition to design the flag, held two years before independence.

The official symbolism of the flag's colours and design is as follows: Black represents the vigour and force of a united people; the triangle pointing towards the body of the flag represents the enterprise and determination of Bahamians to develop and possess the rich resources of land and sea symbolized by gold and aquamarine respectively; the colours of the flag are symbolic of our bright tropical land of sea and sun.

National anthem

Lift up your head to the rising sun,
Bahamaland;
March on to glory, your bright banners waving high.
See how the world marks the manner of your bearing!
Pledge to excel thro' love and unity.
Pressing onward, march together to a common loftier goal;
Steady sunward, tho' the weather hide the wide and treach'rous shoal.
Lift up your head to the rising sun,
Bahamaland;
'Til the road you've trod lead unto your God,
March on, Bahamaland!

Timothy Gibson, CBE (1903-78)

Pledge of allegiance

I pledge my allegiance to the flag,
And to the Commonwealth of The Bahamas for which it stands,
One people united in love and service

Rev Dr Philip A Rahming, JP

National bird

The national bird is the flamingo, a pink long-legged wader of the genus *Phoenicopterus.* The Bahamas is the site of the world's largest breeding colony of West Indian flamingos, in Inagua.

National fish

The blue marlin, of the genus *Makaira,* is the national fish. It is the sharp-billed aristocrat of Atlantic game fish.

National flower

The yellow elder *(Tecoma stans or Stenolobium stans)*, a tubular-shaped yellow flower with delicate red stripes, is the national flower of The Bahamas.

National tree

The lignum vitae, or tree of life *(Guaiacum sanctum)*, is the national tree. It is the heaviest of all woods with clusters of small blue flowers at the branch tips.

NATURE CENTRES

The Bahamas government is committed to enhancing the country's status as a centre for ecotourism. Various projects have been undertaken to reclaim and restore areas of natural beauty and ecological importance. In New Providence, the Adelaide Creek wetlands, near Adelaide Village, were restored and mangroves and marine life regenerated. Causeways and bridges were built. Since completion of the project, a wide variety of marine wildlife has moved in – including barracuda, shrimp, grey snapper, lobster, bonefish, egrets, ducks and crabs.

Ardastra Gardens, Zoo and Conservation Centre is at the forefront of conservation efforts in The Bahamas. In 1995, a captive breeding programme was set up to prevent the extinction of the Bahama parrot, which is endangered. This 5½-acre exotic garden is home to some 300 mammals, birds and reptiles, many of them endangered species, and houses a large flock of flamingos, The Bahamas' national bird. Visitors may feed lory parrots and watch marching flamingos perform three times daily. Open daily 9am-5pm. Last admission 4:30pm. Admission: adult residents, $6, non-residents, $12; children 4-12, residents $3, non-residents $6; under four, free. Located off West Bay St, one mile west of town, tel 323-5806.

The **Botanical Gardens** contains 18 acres of tropical flora. More than 600 species are featured. Open Mon-Fri 8am-4pm, Sat and Sun 9am-4pm. Adults, $1; children 12 and under, 50¢. Tel 325-0430.

The **Bahamas National Herbarium** was established in 1996. The main branch is housed in the Conservation Unit of the Botanical Gardens with four annex locations, two in New Providence, one in Grand Bahama and one in San Salvador. The collection of more than 7,000 specimens of botanicals comprises more than 129 families collected from all over The Bahamas. The collection is used mainly for research and teaching, but walk-in visitors are welcome at the main branch Mon-Fri 8am-4pm. Tel 356-6475.

See also **Bahamas National Trust, Environment** and **Wildlife preserves.**

NEWSPAPERS

There are three national dailies (Mon-Sat), *The Nassau Guardian, The Tribune* and *The Bahama Journal*. They are printed in Nassau and circulated in Nassau and Freeport with delayed and limited circulation in the Out Islands. All sell for 50¢. *The Tribune* includes *The Miami Herald International Satellite Edition*.

A British-styled tabloid called *The Punch* is on sale every Mon and Thurs for $1.

The Confidential Source, a tabloid, is on sale Mon and Thurs for 50¢.

The Freeport News, published daily (Mon-Sat) in Freeport, sells for 50¢.

Foreign newspapers usually available include: *The Miami Herald* (Sun edition), *The New York Times, The Wall Street Journal* and *USA Today.*

NORTH AMERICAN FREE TRADE AGREEMENT (NAFTA)

The North American Free Trade Agreement (NAFTA) became effective on Jan 1, 1994, as a partnership relaxing – and eventually eliminating – trade barriers between the US, Canada and Mexico. The agreement, which established the world's largest free trade zone, marked the first step in establishment of even broader trade agreements throughout the southern hemisphere.

An unintended consequence of NAFTA was that Caribbean Basin Initiative (CBI) beneficiaries were put at a comparative disadvantage, especially in the textile and apparel sectors. For the past nine years CBI has sought to rectify this through enhancement legislation. On May 18, 2000, then-US President Clinton signed the Trade and Development Act of 2000, which contains CBI enhancement in its Title II, the Caribbean Basin Trade Partnership Act (CBTPA). CBI enhancement will serve as a bridge to the establishment of the Free Trade Area of the Americas, which is on track for completion by 2005.

The new legislation was to expand CBI textile and apparel coverage to grant duty-free and quota-free treatment to apparel using US fabric and yarn. In addition, it was to extend duty-free benefits to knit apparel produced in the Caribbean Basin from regional fabric made with US yarn, knit-to-shape apparel (except socks) and T-shirts (other than underwear), with restrictions. The CBTPA also expands coverage to handloomed, handmade and folklore items, and certain textile luggage.

The legislation extends NAFTA tariff treatment to certain other goods originally excluded from CBI, including canned tuna, footwear, watches and watch parts, and petroleum and derivatives. CBI benefits depend on fulfilment of obligations related to trade, worker rights, market access and narcotics enforcement.

At press time, The Bahamas had expressed no interest in becoming part of NAFTA, nor was it qualified to do so.

See also **Free Trade Area of the Americas (FTAA)** and **Trade agreements.**

ORGANIZATION OF AMERICAN STATES (OAS)

The OAS, the world's oldest regional organization, was formed in 1890 as a forum for hemispheric dialogue. The Bahamas became one of its 35 member states in 1982.

The OAS has a long tradition of defending and maintaining peace in the hemisphere. It is the forum for the developing countries of Latin America and the Caribbean to meet with Canada and the US to consider issues facing hemispheric development. These include:

1. Eradication of poverty and unemployment.
2. Defence of social justice.
3. Incentives for investment and economic growth.
4. Expansion and liberalization of external trade.
5. Alleviation of the external debt burden.

The purpose of the OAS is to:

1. Strengthen the peace and security of the continent.
2. Promote and consolidate representative democracy, with due respect for the principle of non-intervention.
3. Prevent possible causes of difficulties and ensure the peaceful settlement of disputes that may arise among member states.
4. Provide for common action on the part of those states in the event of aggression.
5. Seek the solution of political, juridical and economic problems that may arise among them.
6. Promote, by cooperative action, their economic, social and cultural development.
7. Achieve an effective limitation of conventional weapons so the largest amount of resources can be devoted to the economic and social development of member states.

Contact the Organization of American States (OAS), 42 Queen St, PO Box N-7793, Nassau, tel 326-7746 or 326-0741, fax 325-0196, or e-mail oas.bah@batelnet.bs.

PARADISE ISLAND

This international playground lies across the harbour from Nassau, connected by two one-way bridges. The western toll bridge, which costs $1 per non-commercial vehicle, provides access to the island. Vehicles return to New Providence over the eastern bridge.

Paradise Island offers 15 hotels with 4,101 rooms, numerous restaurants featuring international cuisine, top-calibre entertainment, one of the world's largest casinos, a private 18-hole golf course, medieval cloister and surrounding gardens, marinas, a heliport and world-famous Paradise Beach.

The Atlantis Resort on Paradise Island established The Bahamas as the No 1 destination in the Caribbean region. It represents a $1-billion investment and contains the world's largest man-made marine habitat, housing more than 200 species of fish – including sharks, barracuda and stingrays. The 34-acre waterscape surrounding Atlantis includes 11 swimming areas, water slides, waterfalls, underground grottos, a ¼-mile lazy river ride and a 100-ft underwater acrylic viewing tunnel.

An underground maze shows what Atlantean life may have been like 11,000 years ago, with fierce sea creatures protecting ruins and artefacts. The resort has a full-service spa, sports centre, shops, marina, conference centre, 38 restaurants and lounges and the largest casino in The Bahamas.

In 2004 Kerzner International announced a $1-billion expansion to Atlantis. Work began in June 2004. Phase 3 will include a new 1,500-room hotel, new water-themed attractions and Marina Village, which will feature 22 retail stores and four restaurants. Construction is expected to be completed in 2006.

PASSPORTS

Non-Bahamians

All nationals of foreign countries residing in or visiting The Bahamas must hold valid national passports. Exceptions are for visiting citizens of the US, Canada, the UK and its colonies. US citizens must show proof of citizenship such as a birth certificate or naturalization certificate.

Loss of passport

A national of a foreign country whose passport is lost, damaged or destroyed in The Bahamas should visit the Bahamas-based embassy, consulate or High Commission of their country to receive necessary documentation for repatriation.

If there is no representative embassy, consulate or High Commission, the foreign national should request assistance from the Ministry of Foreign Affairs, East Hill St, Nassau, in procuring a certificate of identity which would enable travel at least to the nearest country in which the relevant embassy, consulate or High Commission is situated.

See **Government section, Resident diplomats & honorary consuls.**

Bahamian nationals

A Bahamas passport or certificate of identity is required by all Bahamians departing The Bahamas. The categories of passports are: diplomatic, red; official, green; and ordinary, dark blue.

Ordinary passports have 32 pages and are issued for a 10-year period at a cost of $30. All passports issued prior to July 15, 1991, are valid until the dates indicated and are renewable for a further period of five years.

Sub-categories of ordinary passports are for children and frequent travellers. The former are issued to persons under 11 and are renewable after five years for a total period not exceeding 10 years. The latter are issued to persons who, for whatever reason, travel on a frequent basis (eg, pilots and business persons). Frequent travellers' passports contain 64 pages, and are valid for a 10-year period at a cost of $60.

Certificates of identity are issued for discretionary periods depending on circumstances, although the usual period is one year. Certificates of identity cost $20 and may be renewed for an annual fee of $4.

Possession of a passport or certificate of identity does not exempt the holder from compliance with immigration regulations in force in any territory, or from the necessity of obtaining a visa or permit when required.

Lost, stolen or destroyed passports or certificates of identity should be immediately reported to the Passport Office, then to the local police and, if abroad, to the nearest Bahamian Mission, Embassy, High Commission or Consulate.

See **Government section, Bahamas diplomatic & consular representatives.**

Application for a passport

Bahamian passports may be issued by the passport office in Freeport, Grand Bahama, and Out Island administrators in Abaco, Eleuthera, Exuma and Andros. Remaining Out Island districts were authorized to issue passports in late 2000. Passports may also be issued by the consular sections of The Bahamas High Commissions in Ottawa, Canada, and London, UK, The Bahamas Embassy in Washington, DC, and The Bahamas Consulates General in New York and Miami, US.

Requirements for a new Bahamas passport or certificate of identity:

1. Proof of citizenship

a. Birth certificate and/or passport. If the birth name is not registered, a baptismal certificate and affidavit signed by two persons who have knowledge of such birth, or such additional evidence as may be requested.
b. Naturalization certificate.
c. Registration certificate.
d. Certificate of citizenship.
e. In the case of a married woman, a marriage certificate.
f. Persons claiming Bahamian citizenship by descent should produce a birth certificate, birth certificates of their parents, their parents' marriage certificate or naturalization documents.
g. Any applicant born in The Bahamas after July 9, 1973, must submit the Bahamian birth certificate of the mother or the Bahamian father's birth certificate together with the parents' marriage certificate, in addition to the documents mentioned in 1(a).

2. Authentication of application

The application must be authenticated and sponsored in Section 5 by a marriage officer, medical practitioner, a counsel and attorney of the Supreme Court, a public officer of or above the rank of senior assistant secretary, a bank officer ranked assistant manager or above, magistrate or Justice of the Peace personally acquainted with the applicant for at least two years. A member of the applicant's immediate family is not an acceptable sponsor.

3. Photographs

Three copies of a recent photograph of the applicant must be included with the application. These must be taken full face without hat or head piece and must not be mounted. The size must not be more than 2½ ins by 2 ins or less than 2 ins by 1½ ins. The person who countersigns the application is also required to endorse the reverse side of one of the photographs with the words: "I certify that this is a true likeness of the applicant (Mr, Mrs, Miss, Ms)" and add his/her signature. All photographs included with an application become the property of The Bahamas government from the time of submission.

4. Additional information

a. A new passport is required by a female who marries and takes her husband's name.
b. A children's passport is required by anyone under 11.
c. All persons under 18 require a parent's or legal guardian's consent for issuance of a passport, except for those under 18 who are married.
d. Either parent can apply, if they are married. The mother applies if the parents are unmarried.
e. A police report is required where a previous passport has been lost, stolen or destroyed.

Contact the Passport Office, Basden Bldg (opp the Police College), Thompson Blvd, PO Box N-792, Nassau, tel 325-2814 (to 7), fax 325-4832. In Freeport, contact the Passport Office, National Insurance Bldg, PO Box F-43536, Freeport, Grand Bahama. Tel (242) 352-5698 or 352-6480; fax (242) 352-5692.

PEOPLE-TO-PEOPLE

This community involvement programme sponsored by the Bahamas Ministry of Tourism is designed to bring visitors and Bahamians together for cultural exchange in New Providence and Paradise Island, Grand Bahama, Abaco, Eleuthera, Exuma, Bimini and San Salvador. Its main objectives are to foster communication and the exchange of ideas and to advance international friendship.

More than 300 People-To-People volunteers in Nassau and 250 in Grand Bahama are available as hosts. These volunteers represent a cross-section of the community and are screened by People-To-People executives.

Ministry of Tourism personnel match volunteers and visitors according to age, interests and occupations. Volunteers arrange to meet their guests at an agreed time and location. As most volunteers work, visits are usually after 5:30pm weekdays or on weekends. Visitors do not live with volunteers.

A highlight of the programme is the tea party at Government House, held the last Fri of each month (Jan-Aug). Approx 120 guests attend and are greeted by the spouse of the Governor General. Dress code is casual (no shorts or T-shirts). Other programmes include:

1. Home-away-from-home programme. Volunteer hosts act as foster parents to foreign students attending Bahamian colleges.
2. Spouses programme. Activities are planned for spouses while delegates are in conventions or on field trips.

Arrangements for participation should be made at least two weeks ahead. Visitors in Nassau may register for People-To-People initiatives at Ministry of Tourism information booths at Nassau International Airport and Rawson Sq, and Ministry of Tourism headquarters at British Colonial Hilton, Bay St, or through social directors or concierges at participating hotels. Overseas, contact Bahamas tourist offices worldwide. See **Tourism, Bahamas Tourism Offices,** or contact the manager, People-To-People, PO Box N-3701, Nassau, The Bahamas, tel (242) 302-2000 or 322-7500, fax (242) 302-2098, e-mail peopletopeople@bahamas.com, or visit www.bahamas.com. In Freeport, contact the coordinator, People-To-People, PO Box F-40251, Grand Bahama, tel (242) 352-8044/5. For Out Island enquiries, contact the Nassau office.

PHARMACIES

These pharmacies fill prescriptions.

The Apothecary 328-0722
or 328-3854
Betandé Drugs......................325-5430
Centreville Pharmacy Ltd........325-4644
or 323-7340
Cole-Thompson
Pharmacies Ltd 322-2062
Doc's Pharmacy 322-3627
Doctors Hospital Pharmacy ..302-4785
Heaven Sent Pharmacy 326-4629
or 322-8046
Lowe's Pharmacy..................393-4813
McCartney's Pharmacy 325-6068
The People's Pharmacy 393-9432
The Prescription Centre
Pharmacy..........................356-6434
Prescription Parlour 356-3973
Sabre Pharmacy 393-1059
Super Mart Pharmacy 323-1305
Super Saver Pharmacy 393-2393
323-8309 or 393-4293
Tom-Mae's Pharmacy 325-5268
Wilmac's Pharmacies Ltd........322-8888
Your Friendly Pharmacy 702-4605

POLICE FORCE

See **Royal Bahamas Police Force.**

POPULATION

A census was taken in 2000. See **Fig. 2.1.** Results record The Bahamas population at 303,611. Provisional projected estimate for 2005 is 324,959.

In 2000, population density (per sq mile) for The Bahamas was 56. For New Providence and Grand Bahama, population density was 2,635 and 89, respectively. The percentage of population under 15 was estimated at 29.4%; 15-59, 62.7%; and 60 and over, 7.9%.

Results of the 2000 census indicate that there were 17.4 births per 1,000 people and 5.3 deaths per 1,000 people in The Bahamas, making the average annual estimated population growth 1.8%.

PORTS OF ENTRY

See **Fig 2.2.**

POSTAL INFORMATION

Post office boxes in New Providence are AP for Airport, CB for Cable Beach, CR for Carmichael Rd, EE for Elizabeth Estates, FH for Fox Hill, GT for Grant's Town, N for Nassau, SB for South Beach, and SS for Shirley St.

FIG 2.1

POPULATION OF THE BAHAMAS OFFICIAL CENSUS, 1980, 1990 & 2000

Island	1980	1990	2000
Abaco	7,271	10,003	13,170
Acklins	618	405	428
Andros	8,307	8,177	7,686
Berry Islands	509	628	709
Bimini	1,411	1,639	1,717
Cat Island	2,215	1,698	1,647
Crooked Island & Long Cay	553	412	350
Eleuthera, Harbour Island & Spanish Wells	10,631	10,584	11,165
Exumas	3,670	3,556	3,571
Grand Bahama	33,102	40,898	46,994
Inagua	924	985	969
Long Island	3,404	2,949	2,992
Mayaguana	464	312	259
New Providence	135,437	172,196	210,832
Ragged Island	164	89	72
Rum Cay & San Salvador	825	518	1,050
Total	**209,505**	**255,049**	**303,611**

Air mail
See **Fig 2.3.**

High speed mail
For a fee of $5, in addition to regular postage, items posted for this service will be delivered to the addressee's postal box at the General Post Office within one hour of posting, within three hours to any other post office in New Providence, and within 24 hours to Freeport. International high speed mail is available to most countries of the world. Items must be handed over the stamp counter for processing. Contact the main post office.

Registration fee
The fee for registration of mail inside The Bahamas is $1; for all other destinations, $1.50. Postage not included. Indemnity for loss of a registered item is $43.80.

Express fee
There is an express (special delivery) fee of $2 to all participating countries. Postage not included.

Parcel post (New Providence)
Weight limit is 22 lbs, size limit 3½ ft in length. No parcel post package may exceed six ft seven ins, combined length and girth. Parcels exceeding this size should be sent by air or sea freight.

Incoming parcels from abroad are charged at $1.50 per item and are subject to customs assessment. Where possible, assessment of duty is included in the notice of arrival sent to the addressee. In other cases, the addressee may be asked to supply invoices or to attend a customs examination. Parcels are collected at parcel post after customs and other charges have been paid.

Air parcel post rates

	up to 2 lbs	over 2 to 5 lbs	over 5 to 11 lbs	over 11 to 22 lbs
Can	$15.40	$20.50	$35.70	$61.10
UK	$21.80	$30.30	$55.70	$98.00
US	$13.20	$16.15	$24.80	$39.30

Surface postal rates

	up to 2 lbs	over 2 to 5 lbs	over 5 to 11 lbs	over 11 to 22 lbs
US	$8.45	$17.10	$30.90	$53.80

FIG 2.2

PORTS OF ENTRY

Major ports	Boats	Land planes	Sea-planes
Abaco			
Grand Cay/Walker's Cay	√	√	√
Green Turtle Cay	√	x	√
Marsh Harbour	√	√	√
Sandy Point (restricted)	√	√	√
Spanish Cay	√	√	x
Treasure Cay	x	√	x
Andros			
Congo Town	√	√	√
Fresh Creek	√	√	√
San Andros	√	√	√
Berry Islands			
Chub Cay	√	√	√
Great Harbour Cay	√	√	√
Bimini			
Alice Town	√	x	√
South Bimini	x	√	x
Cat Cay	√	√	√
Cat Island			
Bennett's Harbour	√	x	x
New Bight	x	√	x
Smith's Bay	√	x	x
Eleuthera			
Cape Eleuthera (restricted)	√	√	√
Governor's Harbour	√	√	√
Harbour Island	√	x	x
North Eleuthera	x	√	x
Rock Sound	√	√	√
Spanish Wells	√	x	x
Exuma			
George Town	√	x	x
Moss Town	√	√	√
Grand Bahama			
Freeport	√	√	√
West End	√	x	√
Inagua			
Matthew Town	√	√	√
Long Island			
Stella Maris	√	√	√
Mayaguana			
Abraham's Bay (restricted)	√	√	x
New Providence			
Nassau	√	√	√
San Salvador			
Cockburn Town	√	√	√

Sufferance wharfs*

Grand Bahama			
Bell Channel (Freeport)	√	x	x
Old Bahama Bay Marina (West End)	√	x	x
South Riding Point (Burma) (Trans-shipment facility terminal)	√	x	x
New Providence			
Arawak Cay	√	x	x
Brown's Boat Basin	√	x	x
Clifton Pier Bahamas Gas & Fuel Dock (restricted)	√	x	x
Coral Harbour (restricted)	√	x	x
East Bay Yacht Basin	√	x	x
Hurricane Hole, Paradise Island (restricted)	√	x	x
John Alfred Dock	√	x	x
Kelly's Dock	√	x	x
Lyford Cay (restricted)	√	x	x
Nassau Harbour Club Marina	√	x	x
Nassau Yacht Haven	√	x	x
Ocean Cay (restricted)	√	x	x
Paradise Island (restricted)	x	x	√
Seaboard Terminal	√	x	x
Union Dock	√	x	x

* *Sufferance wharfs are for use only by operators and their guests.*

Small packets* (up to 4 lbs)
Overseas countries

up to 4 oz .... 50¢
over 4 oz up to 8 oz $1
over 8 oz up to 1 lb $1.75
over 1 lb up to 2 lbs $3
over 2 lbs up to 4 lbs $4.20

* *All countries participate in the small packet service, but some limit the weight to 1 lb.*

Warehouse charge
There is a daily charge of $1 for inter-island or foreign parcels remaining in any post office (including parcel post) in The Bahamas more than 30 days after notice of arrival has been dispatched.

Printed paper rates
Includes books, newspapers, magazines, Christmas and greeting cards.

Inter-island

1 oz or part thereof .... 15¢

All other countries

up to 1 oz .... 25¢
over 1 oz up to 4 oz .... 50¢
over 4 oz up to 8 oz $1
over 8 oz up to 1 lb $1.75
over 1 lb up to 2 lbs $3
over 2 lbs up to 4 lbs $4.20

Postal collection times & hours of service
See **Fig 2.4.**

Surface (regular) mail letters
Mail posted intra-island – within an island for the same island – is 15¢ per oz.

Inter-island

per 1 oz or fraction thereof .... 15¢

All other destinations

up to 1 oz .... 50¢
over 1 oz up to 4 oz $1.10
over 4 oz up to 8 oz $2.20
over 8 oz up to 1 lb $4.30
over 1 lb up to 2 lbs $7.50
over 2 lbs up to 4 lbs $12.25

Postcards

Inter-island .... 15¢
All other destinations .... 35¢

See also **Courier services, Customs** and **Export entry.**

FIG 2.3

AIR MAIL POSTAL RATES

Destination	First class 1 oz	Letters ½ oz	Air letter forms	Post-cards
Inter-island	25¢	–	–	15¢
US (incl Alaska, Hawaii, US Virgin Islands, Puerto Rico), Canada	–	65¢	50¢	50¢
West Indies	–	65¢	50¢	50¢
Central & South America, Bermuda, Falkland Islands, UK, all countries in Europe, islands of the Mediterranean	–	70¢	50¢	50¢
Africa, Asia, Australia, Pacific & Indian Oceans	–	80¢	50¢	50¢

POTTER'S CAY

This tiny cay under the Nassau side of the Paradise Island Eastern Bridge is a colourful, public marketplace for local exotic fruit and vegetables such as sapodilla, sugar apples, guavas and okra and fresh conch and fish.

Café-style sidewalk stalls offer conch salad spiked with lime juice and fiery-hot finger or goat peppers and cooked Bahamian dishes, such as conch fritters, crack' conch, grilled seafood and fried fish. Potter's Cay is open every day 6am-10pm, but some stalls close on Sun. A police station and public telephones are on site.

PROPERTY TAX

Bahamians and non-Bahamians owning real property in The Bahamas must pay property tax. Returns are due on or before Dec 31 each year, and are filed with the chief valuation officer (CVO), PO Box N-13, Nassau, The Bahamas.

Owners are required to file a declaration of real property. The return must be signed by the owner and witnessed by an authorized person, defined as a magistrate, attorney, registered medical practitioner, bank officer, minister of religion, Justice of the Peace or notary public within The Bahamas or similar person outside the Commonwealth. Forms may be obtained from the CVO.

The assessments list is prepared annually before Oct 15. If property subject to assessment has not been assessed, the CVO will assess the property retroactively to a max 10 years at the amount required.

The CVO is required to publish before Oct 15, once in *The Gazette* and once in a daily newspaper published and circulated in The Bahamas, a notice stating:

1. Copies of the assessment lists are available to the public at the Treasury and office of the CVO.
2. Assessment notices for each owner of property liable to tax are available at places specified in the notice.
3. Five days after the notice's publication, a notice of assessment is deemed served on every owner of property subject to tax.
4. A notice of assessment may be sent by mail to any owner of property by the CVO after publication in *The Gazette*.
5. Any other matters which the CVO, with the minister's approval, deems necessary.

Objections to a notice of assessment must be made in writing to the CVO within 30 days of service of the notice, stating grounds for the objection. The CVO may request that the tax levied be paid in whole or in part at the time of objection.

Taxes are due within 60 days of the date on which the assessment notice is deemed to have been served. An owner may choose to pay the tax in quarterly installments. In this case,

FIG 2.4

POSTAL COLLECTION TIMES & HOURS OF SERVICE

Postal collection (from Nassau General Post Office)

Foreign air mail	Days	Hours
US, Central and South America, Asia, Australia and Africa	Mon-Sat	10am & 3pm
Canada, Bermuda, Jamaica, Europe, Haiti and Turks & Caicos	Check with post office for schedules	
Foreign surface mail		
Via the US	Mon & Wed	10am
Via the UK	Fri	10am

Hours of service (Nassau)	Days	Hours
General Post Office, East Hill St	Mon-Fri	8:30am-5pm
Parcel post	Mon-Fri	9am-5pm
Postal Savings Bank	Mon-Fri	9am-5pm
Airport branch	Mon-Fri	9am-5pm
Cable Beach branch	Mon-Fri	9am-5pm
Carmichael Rd branch	Mon-Fri	9am-5pm
Clarence Bain Bldg	Mon-Fri	9am-5pm
Elizabeth Estates branch	Mon-Fri	9am-5pm
Festival Place branch	Mon-Fri	9am-5pm
	Sat	9am-1pm
Fox Hill branch	Mon-Fri	9am-5pm
Grant's Town branch	Mon-Fri	9am-5pm
Shirley St branch	Mon-Fri	9am-5pm
South Beach branch	Mon-Fri	9am-5pm

payment of one or more quarterly instalments must be made within 60 days of the date on which notice of assessment is deemed to have been served.The CVO may postpone the date on which the tax is due in particular cases, by notice in writing.

Taxes are paid to the Public Treasury. Remittance should be in Bahamian or US dollars, as a bank draft or international postal order drawn on a bank in the US or The Bahamas. Personal cheques are not accepted unless bank-certified. Foreign cheques must be bank-certified and drawn on a bank in the US or The Bahamas.

Rate of tax

1. **Owner-occupied property (residential)**
   a. First $250,000 of market value* ....exempt
   b. More than $250,000 and not exceeding $500,000 of market value 3/4%
   c. More than $500,000 of market value 1%
2. **Vacant land owned by non-Bahamians**
   a. First $3,000 of market value $30
   b. More than $3,000 and not exceeding $100,000 of market value 1%
   c. More than $100,000 of market value 1 1/2%
3. **All other properties/commercial**
   a. First $500,000 of market value 1%
   b. More than $500,000 of market value 2%

* *Market value is defined as the amount the property would realize if sold in the open market without any encumbrances or restrictions.*

Penalties

If the return is not filed, the owner is considered guilty of an offence and liable for fines of up to $3,000 upon conviction. Persons knowingly making false statements may be liable upon conviction to a fine of up to $3,000 or six months' imprisonment, or both. If the tax is not paid on or before the last day due, a 10% surcharge is added.

Exemptions

Property owned by Bahamians and located outside of New Providence is exempt from property tax. Property approved as commercial farmland by the Minister of Agriculture, Fisheries and Local Government and the Minister of Finance is eligible for property tax exemptions, along with the following:

1. Unimproved property owned by Bahamians, ie, without physical additions or alterations, or any works benefiting the land which have not increased the market value thereof by $5,000 or more.
2. Public places used exclusively for religious worship; school buildings, their gardens and playing areas, approved by the Ministry of Education.
3. Property owned by foreign governments; property owned by foreign nations used for consular offices or residences of consular officials and employees.
4. Property used exclusively for charitable or public service from which no profit is derived. Property of the Bahamas National Trust.

PROPERTY TRANSACTIONS

In New Providence, real estate agents charge a 10% commission on the sale of undeveloped property. The commission for developed property, whether residential or commercial, is 6%. Agents charge a 10% commission for Out Island property, whether land, home or commercial properties.

The government stamp duty on property conveyances or realty transfers is graded as follows:

From	Up to & including	Stamp duty
$0	$20,000	2%
$20,000.01	$50,000	4%
$50,000.01	$100,000	6%
$100,000.01	$250,000	8%
Over $250,000		10%

In property sales, the vendor and purchaser each pay half of the stamp duty unless otherwise agreed. The fee charged by the lawyer who prepares the conveyance is normally 2½% of the sale price.

Generally, payment of commission, stamp duty and legal fees falls upon the seller. Sometimes property owners list a net sales figure, in which case the agent adds those charges to the price quoted to prospective buyers. Stamp duty on mortgages is payable at a rate of 1% on the amount borrowed.

International Persons Landholding Act, 1993

The Intl Persons Landholding Act made it easier for non-Bahamians and companies under their control to own property.

1. A non-Bahamian or permanent resident who purchases or acquires an interest in a condominium or property to be used by him as a single family dwelling, or for construction of such a dwelling, must apply to the secretary to the Investments Board to register the purchase. Application for Registration Form I must be filed with the Ministry of Financial Services & Investments, along with proof of ownership and payment of stamp duty and real property tax, and a bankers draft/postal money order for $25 made payable to the Public Treasury.
2. Upon receipt of the above, the acquisition is registered and a certificate of registration issued.
3. A permit to acquire property is required if the property is undeveloped land and the purchaser would become the owner of five or more contiguous acres. A permit is also required if the non-Bahamian

intends to acquire land or an interest therein by way of freehold or leasehold, when the acquisition is not in accordance with (1).

4. Non-Bahamians who own homes in The Bahamas may apply to the director of Immigration for an annual home owner's residence card. This card entitles the owner, spouse and any dependent children to enter and remain in The Bahamas for the duration of the validity of the card. This card is intended to facilitate entry into The Bahamas – it does not confer resident status in The Bahamas.

All applications for permits, along with bankers drafts or postal money orders for $25 made payable to the Public Treasury, should be submitted to the Ministry of Financial Services & Investments for consideration by the Investments Board. If approved, the permit will be issued by the secretary to the board. The schedule of fees for the certificate of registration and permit are:

Fee schedule

Application for registration $25
Application for permit....................$25
Upon issue of certificate of registration or issue of permit where:

1. The value* of the property is $50,000 and under..................$50
2. The value of the property is more than $50,000 but less than $101,000 ....$75
3. The value of the property is $101,000 and over $100

Annual home owner's residence card..........................$500

* *Value in relation to a lease is the annual rent reserved times the number of years.*

Certificate of registration or permit (with acquisition documents) must be recorded in the Registrar General's Dept, PO Box N-532, Nassau, The Bahamas, tel (242) 322-3316. Permanent residence may be granted if certain conditions are met. See **Immigration, Permanent residence.**

See also **Exchange control, Immigration** and **Property tax.**

PUBLIC FINANCE

See **Fig 2.5.**

PUBLIC HEALTH

The Bahamas Ministry of Health's National Health and Nutrition Survey, last conducted in 1991, provides a comprehensive assessment of the health of the Bahamian community. Indiscriminate eating, lack of exercise and excessive alcohol consumption have been cited as main causes of diseases such as hypertension, coronary artery disease and diabetes.

Smoking is less of a concern. According to the World Health Organization (WHO), The Bahamas is the most smoke-free nation in the world – just 19% of men and 4% of women smoke.

One out of every four adults (over 15) in The Bahamas can be classified as overweight or obese. The prevalence of high blood pressure is dramatic, with 13% of 15-64 year olds and 38% of the elderly suffering from elevated levels. The ministry's chief priority in preventing and reducing these conditions is promotion of good nutritional habits and regular exercise.

The main health problems affecting adult Bahamians (15-64) are HIV and AIDS, accidental injuries, substance abuse, hypertension, coronary artery disease, including heart attacks and strokes (due to obesity, poor nutrition, undesirable cholesterol levels and high density lipoproteins) and cancer.

The number of persons dying of AIDS decreased between 1997 and the end of 2003. Between 1983 and the end of 2003, 9,764 persons were known to be infected with the virus. See **AIDS/HIV.**

Trends in the incidence of sexually transmitted diseases (other than AIDS) – including gonococcal infections and syphilis – have shown a decrease since the reporting of AIDS first began. However, 2003 figures show a slight increase in the incidence of sexually transmitted infections. There were 44

cont on pg 470

FIG 2.5

PUBLIC FINANCE

Total revenue & expenditure 2002-2005		
Year	**Revenue (B$)**	**Expenditure (B$)**
2002/03 July-June	1,137,047,873 (estimated)	1,034,853,079 (estimated)
2003/04 July-June	1,207,782,879 (estimated)	1,062,292,243 (estimated)
2004/05 July-June	1,323,597,287 (estimated)	1,175,200,807 (estimated)

Revenue of The Bahamas 2002-2005 **Tax Revenue**	**Provisional actual revenue 2002/03 B$**	**Original estimated revenue 2003/04 B$**	**Estimated revenue 2004/05 B$**
Import & export duties	433,243,582	465,000,000	479,122,000
Property tax	37,110,316	44,800,000	62,500,000
Motor vehicle tax	20,556,345	27,749,300	27,747,557
Gaming tax	12,821,236	21,427,400	25,953,952
Tourism tax	82,281,842	90,234,200	88,347,296
Stamp tax	175,226,891	180,500,000	183,659,057
Company fees	21,840,688	19,100,000	24,886,860
Bank & trust co fees	5,673,504	8,000,000	11,500,000
Insurance co fees	11,658,261	12,518,700	11,939,497
Other taxes	1,985,202	1,621,400	1,697,408
Tax revenue sub-total	**802,397,872**	**870,951,000**	**917,353,627**
Non-tax revenue			
Fees & service charges	83,899,460	83,753,500	93,957,339
Revenue from govt property	14,886,298	29,800,000	14,568,169
Interest & dividends	6,634,572	6,900,500	18,101,000
Reimbursement & loan repayment	385,622	650,000	606,500
Services of commercial nature	9,647,187	12,945,000	7,413,365
Non-tax rev sub-total	**115,453,140**	**134,049,000**	**134,646,373**
Total tax & non-tax rev	**917,851,012**	**1,005,000,000**	**1,052,000,000**
Capital revenue			
Capital revenue	1,708	3,000,000	11,000,000
Grants	0	427,000	320,000
Proceeds from borrowings	219,195,153	199,355,879	260,277,287
Capital rev sub-total	**216,196,861**	**202,782,879**	**271,597,287**
Total capital revenue	**216,196,861**	**202,782,879**	**271,597,287**
GRAND TOTAL all revenue	**1,137,047,873**	**1,207,782,879**	**1,323,597,287**

Expenditure of The Bahamas Government 2002-2005 Ministry/dept	Provisional expenditure 2002/03 B$	Approved estimates 2003/04 B$	Proposed estimates 2004/05 B$
Governor General & staff	1,049,919	1,105,757	1,142,139
The Senate	235,667	255,540	255,840
House of Assembly	1,936,852	2,173,824	2,344,584
Dept of the Auditor General	1,551,234	1,943,911	2,022,419
Dept of Public Service	59,103,114	65,672,535	66,017,783
Cabinet Office	3,676,971	4,437,335	4,444,513
Office of the Attorney-General	9,018,478	7,885,894	8,789,378
Judicial Dept	6,389,396	6,924,950	8,376,499
Court of Appeal	1,232,467	1,579,373	1,874,518
Registrar General's Dept	1,878,417	2,082,864	2,225,937
Prisons Dept	12,887,417	14,163,206	15,043,267
Parliamentary Registration	847,269	2,509,432	2,375,098
Ministry of Foreign Affairs & the Public Service	12,058,250	13,726,128	16,135,054
Office of the Prime Minister	1,877,588	1,874,069	3,762,128
Office of the Deputy PM	630,987	721,054	742,321
Bahamas Information Services	678,225	881,144	1,989,874
Government Printing Dept	1,463,071	1,791,662	1,844,962
Dept of Local Government	18,433,842	19,591,662	20,064,337
Dept of Physical Planning	448,829	680,710	677,718
Dept of Lands & Surveys	1,881,168	2,363,273	2,429,665
Ministry of Finance	53,590,631	14,949,854	16,744,372
Treasury Dept	6,422,702	7,036,692	8,428,820
Customs Dept	19,791,305	19,950,197	22,090,251
Dept of Statistics	2,437,091	2,762,491	3,102,616
Magistrates' Courts	4,170,641	4,503,416	5,001,926
Public Debt Servicing – Interest	103,369,104	112,218,243	123,293,634
Public Debt Servicing – Redemption	60,232,764	77,079,879	96,852,058
Ministry of Trade & Industry	3,351,941	3,731,476	4,040,561
Ministry of National Security	608,402	797,269	814,086
Dept of Immigration	11,908,525	12,874,017	14,257,879
Royal Bahamas Police Force	85,645,464	83,912,676	93,231,354
Royal Bahamas Defence Force	28,148,794	29,399,274	33,103,283
Ministry of Works & Utilities	6,162,654	7,113,860	7,355,964
Dept of Public Works	12,973,209	14,579,888	15,624,907
Dept of Education	132,941,112	138,422,231	155,900,466
Bahamas Technical & Vocational Inst	4,279,632	4,673,521	4,737,804
Dept of Archives	2,048,100	2,026,908	2,051,859
Ministry of Education	24,042,049	26,097,838	28,007,032
College of The Bahamas	18,595,024	19,442,785	19,442,785
Ministry of Transport & Aviation	6,372,434	6,730,473	7,636,454
The Simpson Penn Centre for Boys	557,319	732,021	840,646
The Willie Mae Pratt Centre for Girls	514,706	654,177	784,191
Ministry of Social Services & Community Development	2,352,078	2,589,710	2,733,616
Dept of Social Services	21,209,970	22,386,762	23,860,842
Dept of Housing	704,705	1,193,829	1,227,529

Expenditure of The Bahamas Government 2001-2004 (cont)

Ministry/dept	Provisional expenditure 2002/03 B$	Approved estimates 2003/04 B$	Proposed estimates 2004/05 B$
Ministry of Housing & National Insurance	456,582	1,174,751	2,082,297
Ministry of Youth, Sports & Culture	8,493,591	9,515,841	11,716,875
Dept of Labour	2,076,724	2,260,576	2,345,732
Ministry of Financial Services & Investment	1,916,469	3,283,111	3,530,897
Ministry of Labour & Immigration	1,038,815	1,320,232	1,304,517
Post Office Dept	6,790,288	7,487,798	7,834,230
Dept of Civil Aviation	8,636,678	8,706,303	9,172,635
Port Dept	3,560,633	4,050,450	5,281,495
Dept of Road Traffic	3,785,465	4,194,534	5,961,217
Dept of Meteorology	1,697,129	2,045,879	2,368,107
Ministry of Agriculture, Fisheries & Local Government	5,006,129	4,685,518	4,804,810
Dept of Agriculture	5,245,546	6,019,498	6,840,365
Dept of Fisheries	1,765,499	2,083,464	2,280,466
Public Utilities Commission	731,500	428,440	428,440
Ministry of Health	7,941,088	9,652,124	9,911,680
Public Hospitals Authority	112,959,997	108,611,339	118,948,888
Dept of Environmental Health Services	23,119,022	23,084,386	25,929,089
Dept of Public Health	18,985,416	19,323,932	20,143,494
Ministry of Tourism	64,621,718	69,361,429	73,331,093
The Gaming Board	3,109,064	3,778,828	4,261,511
Airport Authority	2,850,000	3,000,000	3,000,000
TOTALS	**1,034,496,870**	**1,062,292,243**	**1,175,200,807**

Totals have been rounded off.

cont from pg 467

reported cases of tuberculosis in 2002, and 38 in 2003. A large percentage of these cases is associated with AIDS.

Malaria is not endemic to The Bahamas, but because of the large number of immigrants from countries where malaria is endemic, there is always a possibility of the disease being introduced. While The Bahamas saw 30 new cases of malaria in 1999, a vigilant treatment programme was successful in controlling the outbreak and in 2003 there were only three reported case of malaria.

Accidents and acts of violence rate high on the list of causes of untimely death in the overall population (25.2% in 2001). This is most significant among men. In 2001, acts of violence represented 28.6% of death among males 15-24 yrs, and 10.4% among males 25-44 yrs.

Alcoholism and cocaine addiction are chronic problems. The number of reported new cases of substance abusers at community counselling and assessment centres was 160 in 2002 and 200 in 2003. The number of new cases of alcohol abusers has declined from 149 in 2002 to 114 cases in 2003.

Current gender-specific estimates, from *The World Health Report, 2003,* a publication of WHO, indicate the average female born in The Bahamas lives to approx 71, while males have a life expectancy of 64.

The publication also estimates the 2003 fertility rate in The Bahamas at 2.33. That is to say, each woman living to the end of her childbearing years will have two children, on average.

Although the rate of teenage pregnancy is declining, it continues to be a concern in the country, with social and health care needs of mothers and babies having to be met at considerable cost to the government.

Abortion is illegal in The Bahamas except in cases where it is necessary for medical or surgical treatment of a pregnant woman. Performing an illegal abortion carries a penalty of 10 years' imprisonment.

Public health services

Public health services are administered by the Dept of Public Health and the Ministry of Health. Health care is delivered through community clinics in New Providence and the Out Islands. Other services are offered through community-based programmes such as school health services, district nursing and disease surveillance.

The Public Hospitals Authority operates Princess Margaret Hospital and Sandilands Rehabilitation Centre in Nassau, and Rand Memorial Hospital in Grand Bahama.

Environmental services are provided by the Dept of Environmental Health, which oversees management, control and conservation of the environment. Its functions are conducted through the health inspectorate division, the environmental monitoring and risk assessment division and the solid waste collection and disposal division.

See also **AIDS/HIV, Doctors, Health care, Hospitals & clinics** and **Social services.**

RADIO STATIONS

See **Broadcasting.**

REAL ESTATE COMPANIES

Following is a selection of companies based in Nassau. Contact the Bahamas Real Estate Assoc, tel 325-4942, fax 322-4649, for information on licensed real estate agents.

Bahamas Realty
Tel 393-8618, fax 393-0326
Brown, Morley & Smith Real Estate
Tel 322-2683, fax 325-8468
C A Christie Real Estate
Tel 325-7960, fax 326-5684
Chris Darville Real Estate
Tel 327-5122, fax 327-4942
Cartwright's Real Estate
Tel/fax 394-3919
Century 21 C Investments Realtors
Tel 323-2121, fax 326-2121
Coldwell Banker Lightbourn Realty
Tel 325-1950, fax 325-2765
Damianos Realty
Tel 322-2305, fax 322-2033
Durrant-Harding Real Estate Co Ltd
Tel 394-4500, fax 394-4501
ERA Dupuch Real Estate
Tel 393-1811, fax 394-1453
Gold Circle Co Ltd
Tel 393-8477, fax 393-4508
Graham Real Estate
Tel 356-5030, fax 326-5005
H G Christie Real Estate Ltd
Tel 322-1041, fax 326-5642
International Management & Investment Services Ltd
Tel 322-2504, fax 322-6949
Islands Ltd
Tel 328-1797, fax 328-3749
Jack Isaacs Real Estate Co
Tel 322-1069, fax 325-7514
Knowles Realty
Tel/fax 327-5237
Levi Gibson & Assoc Real Estate
Tel 322-4654, fax 322-8730
Lyford Cay Home Sales & Rentals
Tel 362-4211, fax 362-4730
Lyford Cay Real Estate Co Ltd
Tel 362-4703/4, fax 362-4513
Maxim Intl Real Estate & Investments Ltd
Tel 328-4684, fax 325-2365
Moir & Ricketts Real Estate
Tel 362-4895, fax 362-4586
Morley Realty Ltd
Tel 394-7070, fax 394-7069
Oris E Symonett Real Estate
Tel 325-8280, fax 325-1739

Paradise Sales & Rentals
Tel 363-6700, fax 363-6787
Paul Ritchie Real Estate
Tel 394-2650, fax 393-4687
Powell's Marketing & Management Services
Tel 328-7238, fax 326-2491
Real Estate Intl
Tel 322-4187, fax 322-6784
Real Estate Sales & Rentals
Tel 322-2680, fax 325-6353
Re/Max Nassau Realty
Tel 394-7777, fax 394-8045
Sterling Hanna Real Estate
Tel/fax 323-6188
W T Lowes & Assoc Ltd
Tel 322-1741, fax 322-7600
World Developers Ltd
Tel 327-8949, fax 327-8948

See also **Freeport/Lucaya information, Real estate companies.**

RELIGION

The Bahamas is a religious country claiming to have the greatest number of churches per capita in the world. Christianity dominates and the church is influential in Bahamian society, including government affairs. Church news and events are prominently positioned in newspapers. The Bible is preached at face value and biblical references and quotations are common in all aspects of daily living. Events and celebrations often include a church service as part of the festivities.

Denominations include Anglican, Assembly of God, Baha'i Faith, Baptist, Brethren, Christian & Missionary Alliance, Christian Science, Church of God of Prophecy, Greek Orthodox, Jehovah's Witnesses, Jewish, Latter-Day Saints (Mormon), Lutheran, Methodist, Muslim/Islamic, Pentecostal, Presbyterian, Roman Catholic, The Salvation Army, Seventh-Day Adventist, and other smaller denominations. In New Providence, the three largest denominations are Baptist (35%), Anglican/Episcopalian (15%) and Roman Catholic (14%). Figures are based on the 2000 census.

ROYAL BAHAMAS DEFENCE FORCE

The Royal Bahamas Defence Force was established in 1980 with the passing of the Defence Act, 1979. Prior to that, since 1976, the Defence Force had worked in cooperation with the now disbanded Marine Division of the Royal Bahamas Police Force, many of whose officers transferred to the Defence Force.

The Defence Force, which comes under the Ministry of National Security, is tasked primarily with defending The Bahamas, assisting in disaster relief, port security and maintaining navigational aids throughout The Bahamas.

Hardware consists of two ocean-going patrol vessels, several coastal patrol vessels and two Dauntless 40-ft patrol craft for harbour and shallow water operations, interceptors and workboats.

The main base is HMBS Coral Harbour, at the southwestern tip of New Providence. A sub-base is located in Matthew Town, Inagua.

The Defence Force consists of about 920 personnel, including officers and marines. Personnel train at some of the finest naval establishments in the world, including Britannia Royal Naval College, England; the US Naval War College, the US Coast Guard Officer Candidate School and the US Coast Guard Academy.

Expansion over the next year calls for enlistment of additional officers and marines, upgrading of hardware and base facilities and modernization of the fleet.

Contact Royal Bahamas Defence Force Headquarters, PO Box N-3733, Nassau, tel 362-2116/7 ext 2017, fax 362-2544; Search & Research, tel 322-2494 or 362-1856, fax 362-1374; Operations tel 362-2821, fax 362-1374; or the Ministry of National Security, PO Box N-3217, Nassau, tel 356-6792, fax 356-6087.

ROYAL BAHAMAS POLICE FORCE

The Bahamas Police Force was formed with 16 men on Mar 1, 1840, under the command of Inspector General John Pinder. Women were allowed to join the

Force in 1964. During the same year, a canine section was established with four dogs. As of Dec 31, 2003, the strength of this semi-military organization was 3,352, including 2,195 officers, 10 local constables, 707 reserves, 62 cadets and 236 civilian support staff.

The prefix "Royal" was conferred in 1966 by Her Majesty Queen Elizabeth II during an official visit.

The world-famous Royal Bahamas Police Force Band began with 12 officers in 1893.

In 1980, the Marine Division was taken over by the Royal Bahamas Defence Force. Other significant changes include the establishment of the Drug Enforcement Unit (DEU), a forensic science laboratory and a community policing section. A computerized records system was introduced in 1990. A fully integrated IBM AS/400 computer enables the Force to link a wide range of incidents and produce data for investigation.

An 800MHz Trunck communications system was introduced to the force in 1997 to afford all government agencies an integrated communication system. In Aug 1999, an automated fingerprint identification system (AFIS) replaced the manual search procedure in New Providence and Grand Bahama.

SCHOOLS

See **Education.**

SECURITIES COMMISSION OF THE BAHAMAS

The Securities Commission of The Bahamas (the Commission) is responsible for regulating the Bahamian securities industry, including market intermediaries, secondary markets and investment funds. Two primary pieces of legislation govern the regulation of these entities. The Securities Industry Act, 1999, established the Commission and governs market intermediaries and secondary markets. The Investment Funds Act, 2003, and its accompanying regulations, govern the activities of investment funds. This act repealed the Mutual Funds Act, 1995.

The functions of the Commission are:

1. formulate principles to regulate and govern mutual funds, securities and capital markets;
2. maintain surveillance over mutual funds, securities and capital markets ensuring orderly, fair and equitable dealings;
3. create and promote conditions to ensure the orderly growth and development of capital markets;
4. advise the Minister of Finance regarding investment funds, securities and capital markets; and
5. educate and protect investors.

The Commission consults with the government to ensure that the development of the capital markets advances on a parallel pattern with the wider financial services industry. The Commission regulates:

1. operations of securities exchanges, securities markets and market participants;
2. contents of prospectuses for the purpose of issuing securities to the public;
3. conduct of securities business and transactions in or from The Bahamas;
4. operation of investment funds, including the role of trustees, custodians and investment fund administrators in relation to investment funds; and
5. fees to be paid in respect of matters arising under or provided for or authorized by this Act.

The Commission authorizes only those firms and individuals satisfying the necessary criteria (including honesty, competence and financial soundness) to engage in regulated activity. In carrying out this function the Commission:

1. licenses or registers firms to carry on regulated activities if they satisfy the conditions;
2. approves individuals occupying control functions in these firms as being fit and proper for the performance of their duties;

3. answers technical questions about whether firms require authorization or individuals require approval for their desired activities;
4. ensures that financial business is not carried on by unauthorized persons; and
5. collects and maintains intelligence information about authorized firms and individuals.

The Securities Industry Act requires that securities exchanges be registered with the Commission and provides for the supervision and regulation of exchanges. Additionally, the Commission may withdraw, add, or vary any powers conferred on an exchange.

The Securities Commission is a member of the International Organization of Securities Commissions (IOSCO) and the Council of Securities Regulators of the Americas (COSRA).

The Commission includes a chairman, a deputy chairman and not more than seven other members appointed by the minister of finance. The current chairman is Calvin B Knowles.

Contact the Securities Commission of The Bahamas, 3rd Floor, Charlotte House, Shirley & Charlotte Sts, PO Box N-8347, Nassau, tel 356-6291/2, fax 356-7530, e-mail info@scb.gov.bs or visit www.scb.gov.bs.

Investment funds

The investments funds industry in The Bahamas is growing rapidly due to speedy registration procedures, low establishment costs, and minimal corporate fees.

The Investment Funds Act, 2003, positions The Bahamas at the cutting edge of investment fund administration. Providing financial services to an international clientele requires a sophisticated legislative approach. In drafting the new Act, the Securities Commission was mindful of the need for flexibility to adequately cater to the evolving needs of the global marketplace and to update the general legislative and supervisory environment.

The new investment funds environment in The Bahamas fulfills the needs of the modern investment fund promoter. These needs include regulatory oversight, high quality local service providers and professional services, modern financial infrastructure, political stability, long term talent pool commitment, favourable location and competitive cost of doing business.

The objective of the new legislation is to ensure that any product falling within the definition of an investment fund under the Act will be required to be regulated.

Two types of funds are regulated under the Act.

Bahamas-based:

- the Professional Fund, available only to accredited or sophisticated investors;
- the SMART Fund, a flexible vehicle designed to accommodate alternative investment structures and products available to the more developed markets;
- the Standard Fund, a retail fund with no minimum subscription levels; and
- Recognized Foreign Fund, which gives recognition to funds regulated in jurisdictions or on exchanges recognized by The Bahamas.

Non-Bahamas based:

- funds incorporated elsewhere which intend to sell their units or shares in or from The Bahamas.

As of Dec 31, 2003 the Securities Commission recorded 713 investment funds with a net asset value of B$129.22 billion.

SHIP REGISTRATION

Since the passing of the Merchant Shipping Act, Chapter 268, The Bahamas has become one of the world's fastest growing ship registry centres. More than 1,400 vessels, including cargo and cruise ships, freighters, tankers and tugboats, are registered here, making The Bahamas ship register the third largest in the world. It is also the premier register for passenger ships.

The Bahamas encourages ship owners of all nationalities to register their ships under the Bahamian flag.

In an effort to register more small cruise ships, luxury yachts and charter boat operators, The Bahamas government has reduced the tariffs and fees for these vessels.

Ships engaged in foreign trade under 12 years of age and over 1,600 net tons are eligible for Bahamian registration. Special permission may be obtained from the minister responsible for ship registration for ships under 1,600 net tons or over 12 years of age to be registered.

Several factors make The Bahamas a prime maritime centre:

1. It is a gateway to North and South America and a major destination for cruise ships.
2. It has one of the largest oil storage, blending and trans-shipment facilities in the western hemisphere and is capable of handling the largest ships in the world.
3. It has modern, state-of-the-art facilities at Nassau and Freeport harbours.
4. It has international banks and trust companies that understand the needs of international businesses such as ship registration.
5. It is a member of the International Maritime Organization (IMO), and adheres to its principal safety conventions.

Contact the Bahamas Maritime Authority, PO Box N-4679, Nassau, The Bahamas, tel (242) 394-3024, fax (242) 394-3014.

See also **Ports of entry.**

Foreign yacht registration

Foreign yachts can operate charters within Bahamian territorial waters under provisions of the Boat Registration (Yachts) Rules 1991. Upon meeting all stipulations of the Port Authority, a Foreign Charter Certificate is issued. Operators face strict penalties for providing false information to the Port Authority. Persons operating charter services are not required to have work permits. No soliciting of clientele is permitted in The Bahamas.

Contact Cyril Roker or Carmen Kellman, Port Department, tel 322-8832.

SHIPPING

Cargo Shipping

Nearly all shipments of cargo coming to The Bahamas from Europe, parts of the Orient and the West Indies are trans-shipped through ports in Florida, mainly by container storage. An exception is the importation of cars shipped directly from Japan. Nassau has direct cargo connections with the US. Shipments between New Providence and the Out Islands may be sent by mailboat. See **Transportation.**

Shipping Agencies

Some shipping agencies which serve Nassau are:

Bahmar Carriers 323-8804
Betty K Agencies, Ltd 322-2142
Crowley Liner Services
(Cavalier Shipping) 328-3035
Ocean Air Bahamas Ltd 394-6874
Pioneer Shipping 325-7889
Seaboard Marine................356-7624/6
Tropical Shipping Co Ltd 322-1012

See also **Ports of Entry.**

SHOPPING

The Bahamas imports most goods from the US. A selection of merchandise from other countries is also available. Most major retailers accept credit cards, including Visa, MasterCard, American Express and Discover Card, and some accept personal cheques from residents with a valid Chekard.

Duty-free shopping

Although subject to a stamp duty, the following items are 100% customs duty free: china, crystal, fine jewellery, leather bags, linens and tablecloths, wine and liquor, perfume, cologne and toilet water, cameras and accessories, cashmere sweaters and watches.

Unlike most duty-free ports, The Bahamas does not require foreign residency. Purchases may be carried from the shop or shipped rather than being collected at departure.

The removal of customs duties refers to those items being imported into The Bahamas. Visitors may still be required to pay duty on goods being brought into their home country after allowed exemptions. See **Customs** for customs exemptions and restrictions and regulations of the US, Canada and the UK.

Sunday shopping

An amendment to the Public Holidays Act in Oct 1995 allowed many shops to open for the first time on Sun. They are:

1. Shops that sell:
   a. Ice, ice cream and other dairy products.
   b. Bread, fresh and frozen marine products, fresh fruit, fresh vegetables, butcher's meat.
   c. Any article required for burial of a dead body, or for illness of any person or animal, or for any other emergency.
   d. Fresh water.
   e. Bahamian straw work, art and handicrafts.
   f. Cooking gas.
   g. Shoes.
   h. Clothes.
2. Any retail shop located in a hotel.
3. Beauty salon or barber shop.
4. Coin operated laundry.
5. Photographic studio.
6. Convenience store or petty shop.
7. Service station.
8. Fast food restaurant.
9. Pharmacy.
10. Any other shop in the city of Nassau or port area may open for business on Sun when a cruise ship is scheduled to be in the port of Nassau or in the port of Freeport. However, these shops are not allowed to be open on Good Friday, Easter Sunday, Labour Day, Independence Day or Christmas Day.

The following shops are prohibited from opening after 10am on Sun, Good Friday, Easter Sunday, Labour Day, Independence Day or Christmas Day:

1. Supermarkets.
2. Wholesale or membership clubs.
3. Shops that sell building supplies, construction materials, electrical fixtures or plumbing fixtures.

See also **Customs, Potter's Cay** and **Straw markets.**

SMALL BUSINESS LOANS

The government loan guarantee programme comprises two pieces of legislation – the Guarantee of Loans (Small Businesses) Act, 1998, and the Guarantee of Loans (Tourism Development) Act, 1998 – intended to support small business development in The Bahamas.

The Guarantee of Loans (Small Businesses) Act, 1998, guarantees up to 80% of an approved loan to a maximum of $250,000. A business is defined as small if it employs 25 persons or fewer, has a gross revenue not exceeding $1 million and the owner participates in the daily management of the business. Loans can be guaranteed to any of the commercial banks or the Bahamas Development Bank.

The loans are available to Bahamian entrepreneurs with sound business proposals who lack the equity or collateral usually required to obtain a loan. The loans must be paid within 10 years of the date on which the first advance was made. The interest rate is fixed at prime plus 2%. Loans are considered for agriculture, fisheries, food processing, handicraft, manufacturing, tourism, public transportation or other service-related small businesses.

The Guarantee of Loans (Tourism Development) Act, guarantees loans for Out Island tourist development projects to establish, refurbish or extend tourist facilities and for projects including restaurants, sport enterprises, bonefish lodges or other related businesses.

The programme will guarantee up to 75% of a loan amount not exceeding $500,000. The maximum loan term is 15 years. The interest rate on loans up to 10 years is prime plus

2% and prime plus 2.5% on loans between 10 and 15 years.

Applicants must be at least 18 and under no liability for a previously approved loan under the programme. Applicants under the programme must have a valid policy of life insurance equal to the value of the loan.

Contact Ministry of Agriculture, Fisheries and Local Government, PO Box N-3028, Nassau, tel 325-7502, fax 322-1767.

SOCIAL SERVICES

The Dept of Social Services is a government agency within the Ministry of Social Services and Community Development. The dept's mission is to respond in a timely, effective, efficient and compassionate manner to the changing social needs of Bahamians.

The dept provides structured programmes for those experiencing problems through 11 divisions: children and family services, child care facilities, senior citizens, community support services, Family Island, Northern Bahamas, school welfare, health social services, disability affairs unit, urban renewal project and rehabilitative/welfare services.

The Dept of Social Services, formerly the Dept of Welfare, was officially established in 1964 with one full-time child care officer. In 1992, all governmental social service agencies were amalgamated. Today, the Dept employs more than 250 persons.

The main office is located on Thompson Blvd in the Clarence A Bain Bldg, with three outreach centres throughout New Providence – VBM Bldg, Horseshoe Dr, and in National Insurance Bldgs on Fox Hill Rd and Wulff Rd. There are also offices and outreach centres in Abaco, Andros, Cat Island, Crooked Island, Eleuthera, Exuma, Grand Bahama, Long Island, Mayaguana and San Salvador. A travelling officer from the New Providence headquarters services the other Out Islands.

Child care facilities division

The child care facilities division was established on Oct 10, 2002 to include all residential care facilities or institutions for children in New Providence and the Out Islands with the exception of Grand Bahama.

This division provides services to Elizabeth Estates Children's Home, Children's Emergency Hostel, the Bilney Lane Children's Home, Colby House and the Early Childhood Development Centre.

The division also assists with technical support, the monitoring of services, training and staff development to ensure that all children who are placed in the care of the Dept of Social Services for any length of time will have the benefit of a nurturing environment under the supervision of trained, caring and empathetic staff.

Children and family services division

The children and family services division seeks to ensure all children in The Bahamas have a physically safe environment with the emotional support and security necessary for healthy growth and development.

Some of its mandates are to investigate reported cases of child neglect, abandonment or abuse, counsel parents and children, remove children from homes when necessary, provide alternative care and furnish court reports.

Urban renewal project

The initial project, the Farm Road Community Project, was started by the Royal Bahamas Police Force in their effort to alleviate crime. The police report identified that there were a number of persons in the area lacking basic household and social services provisions.

Since Sept 2002, a multi-sectorial team comprising representatives from the Dept of Social Services & Community Development, Royal Bahamas Police Force, Environmental Health, Labour, Housing & National Insurance, Works, Youth and Education in conjunction with local churches and key community residents, have implemented a number of initiatives to bring about improvements in the lives of residents in the inner city areas of New Providence.

The project is now managed by a commission headed by Dr David Allen and extends to Long Island, Acklins and Freeport, Grand Bahama.

Senior citizens division
This division seeks to ensure the safety and well-being of senior citizens in The Bahamas by assisting with housing and other miscellaneous services.

Twenty-four hour care is available for senior citizens who are unable to function independently at the Soldier Rd Senior Citizens Group Home and the Mary Ingraham Home. Day care services are also provided through the Senior Citizens' Day Care Centre in Yellow Elder Gardens.

Community support services division
This division ensures that indigent persons have access to basic necessities such as food, shelter and clothing. Outreach centres in New Providence are located in the VBM Bldg, Horseshoe Dr, and in the National Insurance Bldgs on Fox Hill Rd and Wulff Rd.

Family Island division
This division coordinates services to the Out Islands except those in the Northern Bahamas, which are serviced by the Dept of Social Services' local office in Freeport, Grand Bahama.

Services offered in Nassau are provided by a social worker or case-aide and with the assistance of the local public advisory committee under the chairmanship of the district administrator.

Disability affairs unit
Established in 1991, this unit provides a vehicle for disabled people throughout The Bahamas to reach their maximum potential and improve their lives. Programmes include integration, mainstreaming, education, training and economic empowerment.
Tel 326-0451 or 326-0526.

School welfare services
This division is responsible for investigating cases of truancy and all welfare problems related to persistent absenteeism, assisting with school placement and providing financial and material assistance for disadvantaged students. Tel 322-8140, 502-2750/2 or tel/fax 323-7170.

Health social services
The health social services division provides comprehensive physical and social health care through education, intervention, advocacy and networking. These services are fulfilled through medical social services at Princess Margaret Hospital, psychiatric social services at Sandilands Rehabilitation Centre, and the Rand Memorial Hospital, Grand Bahama. Tel 356-0301.

Dept of rehabilitative/welfare services
This dept operates in conjunction with the courts and other agencies to rehabilitate the client and improve his/her environment, develop and provide mechanisms to control inappropriate behaviour and assist him/her in functioning as a law-abiding citizen. The dept also has responsibility for the Willie Mae Pratt Centre for Girls and the Simpson Penn Centre for Boys, juvenile residential facilities. Tel 322-7125, fax 326-3562.

Non-governmental organizations (NGOs)
The Social Services Dept is assisted in various areas by non-profit NGOs. These include:

Abilities Unlimited: Employs the disabled for ceramic manufacturing, furniture repairs, refurbishing and strapping of patio furniture, and stamp collection. Tel 325-2150, fax 326-6080.

Al-Anon (Families and friends of alcoholics): Organization dedicated to the well-being of those with an alcoholic in their life. Weekly meetings. Tel 324-1594, Leslie.

Alcoholics Anonymous: Support through regular meetings for persons with alcohol abuse problems, providing help for recovery and relapse prevention. Tel 322-1685, David Knowles.

Bahamas Assoc for Social Health (BASH): Drug rehab education and prevention facility committed to the alleviation of alcoholism, drug abuse and the illicit drug trade. Tel 356-BASH (2274).

Bahamas Council on Alcoholism: Sidearm of Alcoholics Anonymous that studies aspects of alcoholism in The Bahamas to help reduce the problem. Also provides supervised shelter, food and recreation for persons with alcohol abuse problems. Tel 322-1685.

Bahamas Family Planning Assoc (BFPA). See **Bahamas Family Planning Assoc.**

Bahamas Red Cross Centre for the Deaf: Provides programmes and services for the Bahamian hearing impaired and their families. Tel 323-6767, fax 328-5294. See also **Education, Schools for the handicapped.**

Children's Emergency Hostel: Provides a home for neglected and abandoned children referred by the Dept of Social Services. Tel 361-4124.

Columbus House (Freeport): Residences for teenage girls and boys (until graduation from high school) who have been removed from unsatisfactory situations by the courts. Tel (242) 352-3979 or 352-7852.

The Crisis Centre: Responds to the needs of victims of sexual, physical and psychological abuse. Tel 328-0922 (24 hours), fax 328-7824, e-mail crisiscentre@batelnet.bs, or visit www.crisiscentre.com.

Dean William Granger Memorial Centre: Offers a self-help, drug rehabilitation and outreach programme with emphasis on religious studies, counselling, remedial education, group therapy and physical exercise. Tel 326-7833.

Drug Action Service (Drug/Aids hotline): Provides information and referrals to drug treatment programmes and AIDS-testing. Also administers the Drug-Free Achievers Programme, a group of drug-free youths helping other youths to live positive, drug-free lives, and the I'm Special training programme for primary school teachers and administrators. Tel 322-2308/9, fax 326-7622.

Good Samaritan Senior Citizens Centre: Provides care for seniors through housing assistance and other services. Tel 325-7047.

Grand Bahama Children's Home (Freeport): Home for children from birth-12 yrs who have been neglected or abandoned. Tel (242) 352-7852.

Great Commission Ministries Intl: Emergency shelter and food and clothing distribution centre for the homeless and needy. The commission's **Save The Children Club** is a youth outreach programme for underprivileged and dysfunctional children and adolescents 5-19 yrs. Tel 325-5801.

The Haven: Residential care facility offering men, 18-50 years, with alcohol or drug problems, a year-long, three-phase treatment plan. Tel 393-5923.

Hopedale Centre: Educational and vocational training to students with special needs. Tel 394-4792. See also **Education, Schools for the handicapped.**

Mary Ingraham Care Centre: Group home providing day care for children 1-4 years as well as housing and meals for women 60 years or older who are continent, mobile and independent. Tel 341-0093.

Narcotics Anonymous: Society of men and women who meet regularly to help each other remain drug-free. Tel 322-2308/9, fax 326-7688.

The Nazareth Centre: Home for children who have been neglected, abandoned and abused. Provides programmes to meet the child's social, emotional, health and academic needs. Tel 328-0901.

Persis Rodgers Home for the Aged: Bahamian home where elderly people who are not sick can look after themselves with pride and live in peace and dignity. Tel 325-5092, fax 356-0220.

Ranfurly Home for Children: Provides a home-like atmosphere for children who are alone because of death, sickness or other misfortune, until they can support themselves or are fostered/adopted. Tel 393-3115.

Resources & Education for Autism & Related Challenges (REACH): Provides support and education for individuals with autism and related challenges, as well as support for their families. Volunteers comprise parents, teachers, medical professionals and therapists. Tel 302-1157 or 364-3480, DeCosta Bethel, e-mail dbethel@bahamas.net.bs.

Rosetta House: Encourages personal growth in ex-alcoholics enabling them to develop an awareness of self, learn money management techniques and function more effectively. Tel 322-1685.

Salvation Army Erin Harrison Gilmour School for the Blind & Visually Impaired Children and May & Stanley Smith Resource Centre: Co-ed school for blind and partially sighted students. Tel 394-3197 or 393-2745. See also **Education, Schools for the handicapped.**

Teen Challenge: Housing and outreach programme for troubled males who have life-controlling problems such as drug or alcohol abuse. Tel 341-0613, fax 341-0829, e-mail tchallenge@batelnet.bs.

Training Centre for the Disabled: Provides job placement and special career and industrial training for the disabled. Tel/fax 323-3808.

Young Women's Christian Assoc (YWCA): Aims to develop the body, mind and spirit of young Bahamians through summer camps, sports, educational programmes and housing. Tel 323-3149 or 328-3777.

Youth Against Violence: Organization that provides young men and women with an alternative to gang delinquency through education, counselling, job placement and programmes. Tel 356-6549, fax 326-7269, e-mail yav@batelnet.bs or youthagainstviolence@coralwave.com, or visit www.youthagainstviolence.com.

SPORTS

Sporting activities play a major role in everyday life and culture in The Bahamas. Competitive and leisure sports, plus individual and team sports at the amateur and professional level, are enjoyed by Bahamians and visitors at a variety of venues. See **Fig 2.6.**

Sports venues

Most of The Bahamas' large sports facilities are located at the government-owned Queen Elizabeth Sports Centre in Nassau's Oakes Field area. These are the Thomas A Robinson Track and Field Stadium, Andre Rodgers Baseball Stadium, Churchill Tener-Knowles National Softball Stadium, Little League and Pony League Baseball Diamonds, training track and netball courts.

Additional facilities include the $2.4-million Kendal G L Isaacs Gymnasium, the privately financed and managed National Tennis Centre, the Betty Kelly Kenning National Swim Complex and a cycling track.

Facilities in various stages of planning and construction are a four-court beach volleyball complex, a drag strip (Bahamas Hot Rod Sports Car Assoc), the Bahamas Olympic Assoc Headquarters and a sports heroes memorial park.

Other government-owned sports facilities include Haynes Oval (cricket matches), Southern Recreation Grounds, Blue Hills Sporting Complex, D W Davis Gymnasium, A F Adderley Gymnasium, C I Gibson Gymnasium, R M Bailey Gymnasium, Fort Charlotte (all sports from walking and jogging to soccer), R M Bailey Field, Eastern Parade and Windsor Park (soccer and football), in addition to 54 neighbourhood parks with volleyball/tennis/basketball facilities.

Other privately owned indoor and outdoor facilities exist in New Providence, as well as four 18-hole golf courses – at Cable Beach, South Ocean, Lyford Cay (private), and Paradise Island (private).

cont on pg 485

FIG 2.6

SPORTS INFORMATION

Cruising, snorkelling & fishing	Boat charters	Pleasure cruises
New Providence		
Born Free Charters, 393-4144	$400 half day $800 full day	$600 half day $1,200 full day,
Brown's Charters, 324-2061	$400-$700 half day $800-$1,400 full day snorkelling gear incl	Family-island cruising 2,500 full day food incl
Chubasco Charters, 324-3474	$400-$600 half day $800-$1,200 full day snorkelling gear incl	$400-$600 half day $800-$1,200 full day snorkelling gear incl
Flying Cloud Catamaran Cruises, 363-4430	$400 per hr for a min 3½ hrs	$45 half day $60 all day Sun snorkelling gear incl $45 sunset cruise
Island World Adventures, 363-3333	(call for prices)	$160-175 adults/$120 (3-11) full-day trip to Exuma Cays equipment & lunch incl
Powerboat Adventures, 393-7116	(call for prices)	$175 adults/$99 (2-12) full-day trip to Exuma Cays equipment & lunch incl (Harbour Island trips also)

Diving	Gear rental	Intro scuba	Certification course	Snorkelling
New Providence				
Bahama Divers, 393-5644	√	√	√	√
Custom Aquatics, 362-1492*	√	√	√	√
Dive Dive Dive Ltd, 362-1401	√	√	√	√
Divers Haven, 363-6707	√	√	√	√
Nassau Scuba Centre Ltd, 362-1964	√	√	√	√
Stuart Cove's Aqua Adventures, 362-4171	√	√	√	√
**charters only*				
Freeport/Lucaya				
Caribbean Divers, 373-9111/2	√	√	√	√
Grand Bahama Scuba, 373-6775	√	√	√	√
Sunn Odyssey Divers, 373-4014	√	√	√	√
UNEXSO, 373-1244	√	√	x	√
Xanadu Undersea Adventures, 352-5856	√	√	√	√
Abaco				
Brendal's Dive Shop Intl Ltd, 365-4411	√	√	√	√
Walker's Cay Undersea Adventures, 353-1252	√	√	√	√
Andros				
Small Hope Bay Lodge, 368-2014	√	√	√	√
Bimini				
Bimini Undersea, 347-3089	√	√	x	√

Diving (cont)	Gear rental	Intro scuba	Certification course	Snorkelling
Cat Island				
Cat Island Dive Center, 342-3053	√	√	√	√
Greenwood Beach Resort & Dive Centre, 342-3053	√	√	√	√
Eleuthera				
Ocean Fox Dive, 333-2323	√	√	√	√
Valentine's Dive Centre, 333-2080	√	√	√	√
Exuma				
Exuma Dive Center & Water Sports Ltd, 336-2390	√	√	√	√
Long Island				
Stella Maris Marina Inn, 338-2050/5	√	√	√	√
San Salvador				
Riding Rock Inn, 331-2631	√	√	√	√

Golf	Par	Holes	Length (yds) fr blue tees	Designer
New Providence				
Lyford Cay (private), 362-4271	72	18	6,610	Dick Wilson
Ocean Club Golf Course (private), 363-2000 ext 64561	72	18	7,145	Tom Weiskopf
Radisson Cable Beach Golf Club, 327-1741, 327-1738 or 327-1705	71	18	6,453	Fred Settle
South Ocean Golf Club, 362-4391	72	18	6,707	Joe Lee
Freeport/Lucaya				
Crowne Plaza Resort, 350-7000				
The Emerald	72 men	18	6,679	Jim Fazio
The Ruby	75 wmn	18	6,816	Jim Fazio
Fortune Hills Golf & Country Club, 373-2222	36 men 37 wmn	9	3,458	Joe Lee
Our Lucaya, 373-1066				
Lucayan Course	72	18	6,824	Dick Wilson
The Reef	72	18	6,930	Robert Trent Jones Jr
Abaco				
Treasure Cay Golf Club, 365-8045	72 men 73 wmn	18	6,985	Dick Wilson
Eleuthera				
Cotton Bay Beach & Golf Club, 334-6068	72	18	7,068	Robert Trent Jones
Exuma				
Emerald Bay Golf Course Four Seasons Resort, 336-6800 ext 2600	72	18	6,171	Greg Norman

Horseback riding

New Providence

Happy Trails, 362-1820	Trail rides, $95 per ride, including transportation to and from stable. Accommodates 2-7 people 12 years and older, max weight 200 lbs. Experienced guides. Reservations required.

Freeport/Lucaya

Pinetree Stables, 373-3600	Beach rides $75 for 2 hrs. Horses to suit all levels. Experienced guides, certified coach, max weight 200 lbs. Reservations required. Cash, traveller's cheque, MasterCard or Visa. Closed Mon. No children under 8 years.
Trikk Pony Adventures, 374-4449	Beach and trail rides. Sunset beach ride with dinner and bonfire. No experience necessary.

Squash & Racquetball	Courts	Fee/hr (non-gsts)	Lessons/hr (non-gsts)	Racquet rental
New Providence				
Radisson Cable Beach & Golf Resort, 327-6000	3 squash 3 rktbl	$10 day pass	$50	$5
Freeport/Lucaya				
Grand Bahama Tennis & Squash Club, 373-4567	4 squash intl	$12	–	free

Tennis	Courts	Fee/hr (non-gsts)	Lessons/hr (non-gsts)	Racquet rental
New Providence				
Nassau Beach Hotel, 327-7711 ext 6273 or 327-8410	6 hard	$5-$7	$50 group lessons at reduced rates	$5
National Tennis Centre, Queen Elizabeth Sports Centre, 323-3933	9 hard	$6 adults $1 students	Call for rates	–
Radisson Cable Beach & Golf Resort, 327-6000	5 hard	$10 day pass	$50	$5
Sandals Royal Bahamian, 327-6400	Non-guest couples may purchase a $220 day pass or $198 night pass, which gives access to all facilities.			
South Ocean, 362-4391	1 hard	–	–	–
SuperClubs Breezes, 327-5356	Non-guests may purchase a $60 day pass or $70 night pass, which gives access to all facilities.			
Wyndham Nassau Resort, 327-6200	See Radisson Cable Beach & Golf Resort			

Tennis (cont)	Courts	Fee/hr (non-gsts)	Lessons/hr (non-gsts)	Racquet rental
Paradise Island				
Atlantis, Paradise Island, 363-3000	6 hard 4 clay	–	$70 $40, 30 min	$10 (adults) $5 (children)
One&Only Ocean Club, 363-2501	6 clay	Members & guests only	$70 $40, 30 min	–
Freeport/Lucaya				
Crowne Plaza Tower, 350-7000	3 hard lit	$10 day $12 night	$45 $40	$10
Crowne Plaza Country Club, 350-7000	6 hard 2 lit	$10	$45 $40	$10
Grand Bahama Tennis & Squash Club, 373-4567	Call for information			
Our Lucaya, 373-1333	1 hard 1 artificial grass 1 grass 1 clay	$10 $10 $32 $18	See pro	$5 $5 $5 $5
Xanadu Beach Resort, 352-6782	2 hard	Guests only		
Abaco				
Abaco Beach Resort & Boat Harbour, 367-2158	2 clay	$20	–	–
Bluff House, 365-4247	1 hard	$20	–	Free
Berry Islands, Chub Cay				
Chub Cay Club, 322-5599	1 asph	Free	–	–
Harbour Island				
Coral Sands Hotel, 333-2350 or 333-2320	1 hard plexi-pave	Members or guests only		
Dunmore Beach Club, 333-2200	1 plexi-pave	Guests only		
Pink Sands, 333-2061	3 hard 1 lit	Guests only		
Romora Bay Club, 333-2325	1 hard	$10	–	–
Valentine's Resort & Marina, 333-2142	1 hard	$6	–	–
Long Island				
Stella Maris Marina Inn, 338-2050	2 artificial grass	$20	–	$5

Sports organizations
New Providence organizations registered with the Ministry of Youth, Sports and Cultural Affairs:
Amateur Boxing Assoc of The Bahamas
Anglican Diocese Softball Committee
Bahamas Assoc of Athletic Assocs
Bahamas Amateur Bowlers Federation
Bahamas Amateur Cycling Assoc
Bahamas Amateur Surfing Assoc
Bahamas Assoc of Independent Secondary Schools
Bahamas Assoc for the Physically Disabled
Bahamas Baseball Assoc
Bahamas Basketball Federation
Bahamas Boat Owners Sailing Assoc
Bahamas Bodybuilding Weightlifting & Powerlifting Federation
Bahamas Bridge Assoc
Bahamas Cycling Federation
Bahamas Checkers Assoc
Bahamas Chess Federation
Bahamas Cricket Assoc
Bahamas Darts Assoc
Bahamas Domino Federation
Bahamas Equestrian Assoc
Bahamas Football Assoc
Bahamas Golf Federation
Bahamas Government Departmental Basketball Assoc
Bahamas Government Departmental Softball Assoc
Bahamas Hockey Assoc
Bahamas Hot Rod Sports Car Assoc
Bahamas Judo Academy Budo Kan
Bahamas Karate Federation
Bahamas Lawn Tennis Assoc
Bahamas Martial Arts Federation
Bahamas National Council for Disability
Bahamas National Equestrian Federation
Bahamas Netball Assoc
Bahamas Netball Federation
Bahamas Olympic Assoc
Bahamas Pool Assoc
Bahamas Pool Players Assoc
Bahamas Powerlifting Assoc
Bahamas Professional Golf Assoc
Bahamas Racquetball Federation
Bahamas Rugby Football Union
Bahamas Softball Federation
Bahamas Squash Racquets Assoc
Bahamas Swimming Federation
Bahamas Table Tennis Federation
Bahamas Tae kwon do Federation
Bahamas Tertiary Sports Assoc
Bahamas Track & Field Coaches Assoc
Bahamas Volleyball Federation
Bahamas Youth Sporting Club
Banker Sports Assoc
Baptist Sports Council
Commonwealth American Football League
Commonwealth Bahamas Darts Assoc
Nassau Domino Assoc
Nassau Go-Kart Assoc
Nassau Nastics Gymnastics Club
Nassau Sailing Assoc
Nassau Wholesalers Softball League
New Providence Amateur Basketball Assoc
New Providence Assoc of Umpires & Scorers
New Providence Netball Assoc
New Providence Old Timers Softball Assoc
New Providence Public Primary School Sports Assoc
New Providence Public Secondary Sports Assoc
New Providence Softball Assoc
New Providence Valley 8-Ball Assoc
New Providence Volleyball Assoc
Special Olympics Bahamas

Contact the Sports & Recreation Division, Kendal G L Isaacs Gymnasium, Queen Elizabeth Sports Centre, Oakes Field, tel 356-2850/1.

See also **Hotels.**

STATISTICS

The Dept of Statistics falls within the portfolio of the Ministry of Finance. Its responsibility is to collect, collate and analyze information from all sectors of the country – economic and social, government and private. Collated information is made available to all government depts to facilitate their planning as well as to the private sector. The dept protects the confidentiality of specific information from individual and corporate sources. The two main areas are:

1. Economic statistics relating to imports, exports, prices, income, balance of payments, etc.
2. Social statistics, including population census, migration and vital statistics.

Located in the Clarence A Bain Bldg on Thompson Blvd, the dept produces a number of publications available at the dept's library and at Government Publications, the Old Lighthouse Bldg, Bay St. These include:

All Bahamas Survey of Industry 1989-1992 ....$6
Annual Foreign Trade Statistics $20
Annual Review of Prices $5
Annual Statistical Abstract....$10
The Bahamas in Figures ....annually, $3
Building, Construction Statistics....annually, $3
Census of Insurance Report ....annually, $5
The Census Report 1980:
Vol 1, Demographic and Social Characteristics....$16
Vol 2, Economic Characteristics & Income $20
Vol 3, Migration $20
Vol 4, Fertility $10
Vol 5, Education $16
The Census Report 1990:
Preliminary Results $3
Vol 1, Demographic and Social Characteristics $30
Vol 2, Housing Characteristics $30
Population and Housing $20
The Census Report 2000:
Preliminary Results $3
Population and Housing $20
The Census Report 2000 ....$20
Hotels, Motels and Guest Houses in New Providence and Paradise Island ....annually, $3
Labour Force and Household Income Report ....annually, $7
Labour Market Information Newsletter..$3
Life Table Report 1989-1991 ....$2
National Accounts of The Bahamas $3
Population Projections For The Bahamas 1990-2020....$5
Quarterly Summary of Foreign Trade Statistics $4
Retail Price Index: New Providence; Grand Bahama ....monthly, 50¢
Vital Statistics Report ....annually, $5
Wholesale and Retail Trade Statistics ....annually, $5

Contact the Dept of Statistics, Clarence A Bain Bldg, 1st Floor, Thompson Blvd, Nassau, tel 325-5606 or 502-1067, fax 325-5149.

STRAW MARKETS

Straw markets are located on West Bay St in Cable Beach, and at the BahamaCraft Centre on Paradise Island. The main straw market on Bay St, once the hub of Nassau's native shopping experience, was destroyed by fire on Sept 4, 2001. A temporary location just west of the former site, was being used to house the displaced vendors, until it was damaged by Hurricane Frances on Sept 3, 2004. A new and improved state-of-the-art permanent structure will be constructed and is currently in the design stages. At press time, straw vendors were out of work awaiting repairs to the temporary structure.

Straw markets are also found in many of the Out Islands and at Freeport/Lucaya, Grand Bahama. See **Freeport/Lucaya information, International Bazaar** and **Port Lucaya Marketplace.**

Quality straw work and crafts made in The Bahamas from Bahamian materials are also available at stores throughout New Providence and Paradise Island.

TAX BENEFITS FOR CANADIANS

by Guy Masson, LL L

Despite restrictions imposed by Canadian income tax law on the use of tax havens, there are many circumstances in which The Bahamas retains its attractiveness for Canadians. The islands continue to prove a sound and durable base from which to invest in Canada or the outside world, or from which to conduct offshore operations for the benefit of Canadians.

In fact, increased investment outside Canada, exports by Canadian firms and the growing number of multinational families have increased the scope for The Bahamas as a centre for international activity.

Residence

In Canada, residence remains the foundation of direct taxation for individuals. This benefits Canadians wishing to take advantage of The Bahamas, especially as compared to the US, which taxes on a citizenship basis.

Under the Canadian federal income tax system, individuals resident in Canada are taxed on their world income whereas non-resident individuals are taxed only through the withholding tax regime on certain investment income (discussed later), with respect to income from employment in Canada, a business carried on in Canada and from gains realized on the disposition of taxable Canadian property (also discussed later). They are not taxed with any reference to the fact that they are or are not Canadian citizens. A corporation not resident in Canada is subject to Canadian federal or provincial tax only through the withholding tax regime on certain investment income, on income from its business carried on in Canada and from gains realized on the disposition of taxable Canadian property. Like individuals, resident corporations are taxed on their worldwide income.

Canadian companies incorporated after Apr 26, 1965, are automatically deemed residents of Canada unless they are continued under the laws of another jurisdiction. Corporate continuance is treated as re-incorporation for tax purposes. Consequently, a company's residence for Canadian income tax purposes may be affected by a change in its corporate status.

The Canadian government has enacted an incentive to lure international shipping companies to Canada. If a company deriving all or substantially all (ie, 90%) of its revenue from an international shipping business is incorporated outside of Canada, it can establish its place of central management and control in Canada and yet be deemed a non-resident of Canada. In this way, it avoids Canadian tax on its income.

Canadian withholding tax

The basic Canadian withholding tax is 25%. This applies to investment income, certain pensions, dividends, interest (except on certain long-term obligations, Canadian or provincial government bonds or certain deposits made with a financial institution which carries on an international banking centre business, see following), rent, certain types of royalties, income from a trust and certain other forms of revenue paid by Canadian residents to persons abroad. This tax must be withheld from the gross payment by the payer unless the recipient of the income resides in a country with which Canada has a tax treaty. In that event, the withholding tax may be reduced to 15% or less, depending on the terms of the treaty. The Bahamas and Canada do not have a tax treaty.

Old age security payments under the Canada or Quebec Pension Plans are subject to withholding tax. Non-residents of Canada who are recipients of interest on bonds of the federal or a provincial government or a municipality or which are guaranteed by the federal government will remain immune to this tax – there being no tax of any kind withheld from such income.

Special exemption from withholding tax

Interest paid by a Canadian resident corporation to arm's length non-resident creditors on certain corporate securities is exempt from Canadian withholding tax. The exemption is granted regardless of the currency of the loan or interest. The interest must not be contingent upon the use of, or production from, property in Canada.

Also, interest which depends in whole or in part on revenue, profit, cash flow or other similar criteria, or on dividends paid or payable on shares of a corporation, does not qualify for the exemption. Interestingly, there is no restriction preventing the guarantee of the debt by a non-resident person who is not at arm's length with the borrower. Thus, Bahamians may lend to Canadians against the security of a guarantee by someone outside of Canada not at arm's length with the borrower, upon terms which may exempt the interest paid from Canadian withholding tax (the arrangement must, however, remain in law a guarantee and avoid being characterized as an agency between the guarantor and the lender). The exemption is limited to debts of which the borrower is not obliged to repay more than 25% of the principal amount within five years of the date of issue except in the event of a failure or default, or if terms of the obligation become unlawful or are changed by legislation or by a court. This will not disqualify a security which gives to the borrower a *bona fide* right of prepayment even if it is exercised before the five-year period ends.

Thin capitalization provisions

The "thin capitalization" provisions contained in subsections 18(4), and following, of the Income Tax Act relate to the deductibility of interest paid on money borrowed from abroad by Canadian resident corporations.

Interest payments made to non-residents who hold a substantial interest (ie, 25% of the voting or equity shares) in a Canadian company or which do not deal at arm's length with such a shareholder, are not always entirely deductible in computing income in Canada. They will be disallowed if the ratio of the company's equity capital to the debt due to such non-resident shareholders or non-arm's length persons is less than 1:2.

Bahamas benefits

Despite the restrictive and wide-ranging nature of the Canadian fiscal law, The Bahamas continues to play an important part in Canadian tax planning. In particular, the use of testamentary trusts and certain *inter vivos* trusts can yield rewards. Nevertheless, there is today less emphasis on a search for an absolute tax haven, in which no income tax whatever is imposed. Taxpayers are increasingly searching for jurisdictions which offer low rates of tax and international tax treaties. Treaties may also be used, on expert advice, by Bahamian residents by setting up trusts or corporations in treaty jurisdictions.

Of the few remaining absolute tax havens, there are not many that offer benefits comparable to The Bahamas in terms of flexibility of corporate structure, top quality accounting and legal services, readily available first-class financial and banking services, proximity to major world markets and good docking and harbour facilities.

The modernization and liberalization of the Bahamian company law now provides a flexibility previously unavailable in The Bahamas. The Bahamas can offer a variety of corporate and settlement structures and procedures that are equal to those in any other jurisdiction. A number of Canadians look to The Bahamas to conduct some of their business. Some achieve this by becoming non-residents of Canada and setting up their homes in The Bahamas. Once they do this, they suffer no income tax in Canada, except on income from employment in Canada, the profits from business done there, gains from taxable Canadian property or the 25% withholding tax on certain kinds of investment income derived from Canada.

Capital gains tax on non-residents

Non-resident individuals pay income tax to Canada at applicable personal rates on 50% of the capital gains realized by them on the disposition of "taxable Canadian property." The top marginal rate on capital gains exceeds 24% in most provinces, but is as low as 19.5% in others.

"Taxable Canadian property" is defined in subsection 248(1) of the Income Tax Act and includes Canadian real estate, shares in a Canadian private corporation, and shares in a Canadian public corporation if certain threshold ownership requirements are met.

Certain other types of property are also considered taxable Canadian property. In particular, the definition of taxable Canadian property includes shares of corporations and interests in trusts not resident in Canada which derive their value principally from Canadian real estate or resource properties.

This measure subjects non-residents to Canadian tax on gains from shares of non-resident corporations or interests in non-resident trusts, even where the gain is not attributable to Canadian assets. Liability to Canadian tax could even be triggered by the death of an individual who happens to own shares of a non-resident corporation with Canadian assets. Broadening the tax base in this way is unprecedented. It is advisable to examine how Canadian investments are held to determine the possible impact of this measure.

All non-residents must report dispositions of taxable Canadian property to the Canadian fisc, indicate the name of the person to whom the property is sold and pay an amount on account of Canadian tax or furnish acceptable security (this special requirement is not applicable to the disposition of listed shares in a Canadian public corporation).

Upon payment of a tax instalment, a "certificate" is issued to the non-resident which protects a purchaser of the asset from having to pay some of the tax that might not have been paid by the non-resident.

Becoming a non-resident of Canada

In order to become a non-resident of Canada, an individual must generally give up his home and most attachments within Canada such as employment, provincial medicare coverage, clubs, bank accounts, credit cards and the like, and acquire a residence in another jurisdiction by purchasing a home or renting an apartment in which he lives as his central family headquarters.

Nevertheless, once a former Canadian resident has become a non-resident, he may return to Canada each year for temporary visits without being taxed.

Thus, because The Bahamas imposes no income tax of any kind, a non-resident Canadian citizen may reside there with the advantage of paying to Canada only 25% on certain kinds of investment income derived from Canadian sources and no withholding tax on certain kinds of interest. Royalties and similar payments on or in respect of a copyright related to the production or reproduction of any literary, dramatic, musical or artistic work are exempt from Canadian withholding tax. The Bahamas is, therefore, appealing to Canadian writers, musicians, singers and artists as a place of residence. The same individual, if he wishes to continue his business activities in Canada, may do so as a non-resident and pay tax at the personal graduated rates in Canada on the profit from the business there.

The exit tax

A problem which faces Canadians who consider taking up residence in The Bahamas is the exit tax imposed by Canada upon capital gains deemed to arise from the notional realization of certain capital property at the time they give up Canadian residence.

Until recently, an individual giving up Canadian residence was not required to pay capital gains tax on any property that would fall within the category of "taxable Canadian property" listed previously. This is because, after leaving Canada and becoming a non-resident, he would remain taxable in respect of any capital gain on that property as already stated. The departing individual could, however, elect to realize part or all of any capital gain accrued in respect of these properties upon emigration.

The foregoing exception to the exit tax was eliminated for most types of taxable Canadian property in Oct 1996. This change, like the extension to the definition of taxable Canadian property discussed previously, was unprecedented in the international context and made Canada less attractive as a place for wealthy individuals to reside.

Corporations leaving Canada are also subject to exit rules. In particular, a corporation is treated as having disposed of all of its property at fair market value and to have notionally distributed its net equity. This fictitious distribution is assimilated to a liquidating dividend and subjected to a special tax in lieu of withholding tax.

Succession duty and estate tax advantages

There are no estate and gift taxes in Canada. However, individuals are deemed to dispose of their property at fair market value at the time of their death. Thus, a non-resident individual may be liable to tax on capital gains at the time of his death if he holds taxable Canadian property directly.

Corporate uses of The Bahamas by Canadians

Under Canadian tax law, a foreign company is resident where its seat of management and control is found (subject to restrictions on companies incorporated or continued into Canada set out previously). This is usually held to be the place where the directors meet or from which the day-to-day management instructions emanate or are carried out.

In order to prevent a company from being legally resident in Canada and thereby paying tax at corporate rates ranging from 27-41%, management and control must be exercised, *bona fide* and in fact, outside Canada.

A non-resident company may perform useful functions of an extraterritorial nature such as world advertising, worldwide selling, the financing and organizing of sales abroad, the management and servicing of the facilities needed to maintain the products sold abroad and the operation of ships or certain group insurance activities (except Canadian risk). In each case, it is important to determine whether the income of the Bahamian subsidiary is foreign accrual property income (commonly referred to as FAPI). The FAPI of a "controlled foreign affiliate" of a Canadian resident is attributed to and taxed in the hands of its Canadian resident shareholders on an annual basis.

There have also been cases before the Canadian courts in which attacks made by the Canada Revenue Agency (CRA) on offshore subsidiaries of Canadian corporations have been tested. The income of the subsidiaries has been added, sometimes, to the income of the Canadian parent on the footing that the subsidiary was itself a sham or an instrumentality. Transfer pricing is another line of attack increasingly favoured by CRA. These cases stand on their own facts and need not pose a threat to normal activities carried on *bona fide* in The Bahamas, provided management and control of the Bahamian corporation are not in Canada.

Foreign affiliates

The foreign affiliate rules affect any foreign corporation in which a Canadian resident has a significant interest. A foreign affiliate is defined to include any non-resident corporation in which a Canadian resident holds at least 10% of the shares of any class. A non-resident corporation will also be considered a foreign affiliate of a Canadian resident who holds 1% of the shares of any class where the equity interest of the Canadian resident together with related persons is at least 10%.

When a foreign corporation qualifies as a foreign affiliate, the dividends that pass upstream to a Canadian corporate shareholder are tax free when paid out of "exempt surplus." Exempt surplus is income derived by a company resident and carrying on business in a country with which Canada has a tax treaty.

However, dividends paid by a foreign affiliate from active business profits earned in a non-treaty country are included in full in the income of a Canadian corporate shareholder, subject to the deduction from that income of an amount in respect of taxes paid to the jurisdiction where the profits were earned.

Passive income is treated quite differently from active business income. The concept of FAPI is meant to tax the passive earnings of foreign affiliates controlled by Canadian taxpayers. In many ways it is not unlike its American counterpart, "Subpart F" of the Internal Revenue Code. FAPI is essentially income from property or from a business other than an active business. Each year an appropriate share of the FAPI of a controlled foreign affiliate (and certain trusts), if it exceeds $5,000, is included in the income of Canadian taxpayers controlling the foreign affiliate in the taxation year in which the foreign affiliate's taxation year has terminated.

FAPI does not include interaffiliate dividends, active business income, and certain amounts received from other affiliates. It similarly does not include capital gains from the disposition of "excluded property" (property used principally in an active business and shares of foreign affiliates, most of whose property is used in an active business).

Non-resident trusts

A non-resident of Canada who has not resided in Canada during the 18-month period preceding the end of a taxation year can establish, by will or gift, a Bahamian resident discretionary trust (NRT) for the benefit of Canadian resident family members, which will escape the application of the income attribution rules which have been enacted to govern offshore discretionary trusts. Draft legislation, the latest version of which was released on Oct 30, 2003, proposes significant changes to the Canadian tax treatment of offshore discretionary trusts. This draft legislation gives effect to changes first announced in the Feb 16, 1999, federal budget. Distributions of capital (which can include accumulated income) received by Canadian resident beneficiaries from an NRT funded solely by a non-resident should remain not taxable.

Before, a Canadian resident could also establish an NRT for beneficiaries who did not reside in Canada. Income of such a trust was not subject to Canadian tax provided a person resident in Canada who is related to the settlor was not "beneficially interested" in the trust. The Oct 30, 2003, draft legislation extends the reach of the Canadian fisc in this area by taxing the undistributed income of an NRT to which a Canadian resident has loaned or transferred property irrespective of whether a person related to the settlor is beneficially interested in the trust. The measures apply for taxation years after 2002 and some additional changes are expected.

It is still possible for an NRT established by an immigrant or temporary resident to avoid tax for the first five years of residency in Canada.

The Oct 30, 2003, draft legislation is far reaching and will change the way multinational families transfer, or rather avoid transferring, wealth to Canadian resident family members.

Of course it is important that a trust established outside of Canada not be considered resident in Canada under the normal rules regarding the residency of trusts. This requires that the majority of, if not all, trustees having legal and actual control of the trust assets be non-residents of Canada. Expert professional advice in this area is essential, but use of Bahamian trusts can pay substantial dividends.

International banking centres

Canadian income tax law is reasonably generous toward the income of certain financial institutions from an international banking centre business.

Provided certain conditions are met, these rules exempt from Canadian tax the income of a qualifying financial institution from a business, carried on by it through a branch or office located in Montreal or Vancouver, which consists substantially of accepting deposits from, and making loans to or deposits with, arm's length non-residents and other qualifying institutions.

Qualifying institutions include the Bank of Canada, Canadian banks and subsidiaries of foreign banks that are governed by the Canadian Bank Act, certain other financial institutions and, generally, any entity that accepts deposits transferable by order to a third party, which satisfies certain deposit insurance and other conditions.

Not only is the income from an international banking centre business of such a qualifying institution exempt from Canadian tax but, as already noted, amounts on account of interest on deposits made with such an institution paid or credited to an arm's length non-resident person or partnership are exempt from Canadian withholding tax. Moreover, the amount of interest payable on such deposits may be dependent upon the use of, or production from, property in Canada, or be computed by reference to the revenue, profit or cash flow of any person, the price of a commodity or any similar criterion, or by reference to dividends paid or payable by any corporation.

Accordingly, a Bahamian resident may take advantage of the above rules to earn interest income that is exempt from Canadian tax on a wide variety of financial products and derivative instruments, subject to their availability at qualifying Canadian financial institutions. Moreover, provided certain conditions are satisfied, a Canadian subsidiary of a Bahamian bank (or other foreign bank) may qualify to carry on an international banking centre business from a branch or office in Montreal or Vancouver and, thereby, earn income that will be exempt from Canadian tax. Withholding tax may, however, apply if and when such earnings are repatriated, for example, in the form of dividends paid by the Canadian subsidiary to its non-resident shareholders.

Current attitudes towards tax planning

The Canadian law contains a number of technical provisions that narrow the field of manoeuvre for the taxpayer. Moreover, Section 245 of the Income Tax Act contains a general anti-avoidance rule (GAAR). The GAAR comes into play whenever a taxpayer engages in a transaction or series of transactions that results directly or indirectly in a "tax benefit," (as broadly defined in that provision) unless the transaction does not result in an abuse or misuse of the provisions of the Income Tax Act. Thus, the uses made by Canadians of Bahamian corporations must be limited to commercially defensible activities and should not be employed merely to hide or artificially minimize truly Canadian income. In this whole field, the area of manoeuvre is narrowing and a conservative and realistic approach should be taken.

Guy Masson

is a partner and head of the Montreal Tax Group. His practice is focused on cross-border taxation, corporate tax planning, dispute resolution and general tax advice. In addition to being a frequent speaker at tax conferences, Masson has served and been a member of many tax-based associations, including the International Fiscal Association, the Canadian Tax Foundation, the Quebec Tax and Financial Planning Association (president and chairman – 1989-91), and the Taxation of Capital in Canada Advisory Committee of the Economic Council of Canada. He obtained his law degree from Montreal University in 1978.

TAX BENEFITS FOR EUROPEANS

by Howard M Liebman

It has become increasingly difficult for Europeans to use offshore investment centres, although opportunities still exist for legitimate planning in tax havens such as The Bahamas.

Despite the lifting of European exchange controls, which allowed funds to move more easily out of various European countries, impediments facing Europeans who wish to use offshore centres include the tendency to look for substance over form as well as business purpose, the increasing level of information exchanges and tougher penalties for tax evasion.

Trusts and asset protection

Perhaps the most interesting offshore tool for tax or estate planning is the common law trust, which can take a number of different forms.

Over the past 20 years or so, asset protection trusts (APTs) have gained popularity, mostly as a result of the increase in large damages awarded in the US against doctors, lawyers, financial planners and other advisors. Even though this type of litigation has not impacted Europe to the same extent, the use of trusts to conserve assets against lawsuits is more and more common. See **Investing, Asset Protection Trusts (APT).** When considering a trust for asset protection purposes, the key is to ensure that control over the assets is placed clearly outside of the settlor's hands, and thus out of the jurisdiction of the settlor's country of residence.

This is where the conundrum lies, because many Europeans are concerned about their inability to control assets in such circumstances. Of course, that is at the heart of a trust: one must have "trust," or faith, in both the trust structure and the chosen trustee(s). However, certain methods have been devised to provide settlors with a degree of influence. These include using a protector – usually an attorney or other trusted individual who stands between the trustees and the settlor – or appointing the settlor to a committee of advisors or board of directors of a company which is owned by the trust and which holds all of the settled assets. The second approach is riskier, but still arguably maintains the position that the assets are no longer in the hands of the settlor, even if the latter acts in the capacity of a corporate officer in determining their use or investment.

Certain trust issues are treated differently from country to country. For example, in Belgium, no tax is due on a *don manuel*, or gift of cash. In France, by contrast, a transfer of legal title in property may be regarded as a gift, raising the issue of the level of gift tax to be paid. This, in turn, depends on whether the gift tax is deemed to be due upon transfer to an entirely third party (ie, the trustees) or to closely related parties (such as the beneficiaries). If the trust is revocable, it may be argued that no gift tax is due. In the case of transfers of appreciated property, a capital gains tax may have to be paid, such as in the UK.

If the settlor retains significant powers over the trust, it may be treated as a grantor trust, in which case many jurisdictions will seek to tax the settlor (as the grantor) on the trust's income. Even if the trust passes this test and no tax is due from the grantor/settlor, it is still possible that the beneficiaries will be taxed on any income earned by the trust. In the case of a fully discretionary trust in which the beneficiaries do not receive any income, it may be argued that they cannot be taxed until they receive a taxable economic benefit.

Careful planning on a jurisdiction-by-jurisdiction basis is clearly required in order to minimize the chances of falling into a tax trap.

Fraudulent conveyance laws in various jurisdictions must also be carefully considered. Thus, if an individual is already being sued or is under threat of a suit, transferring assets to an APT may be viewed as an attempt to defraud creditors – even if the suit only begins within a certain period of time (varying between jurisdictions) after the transfer has taken place.

This is one of the first questions a legal advisor is likely to, and in fact should, pose when an individual seeks to establish an APT. No reputable advisor will assist in defrauding creditors.

Assuming no fraud is intended, there should then be no problem in setting up an APT in The Bahamas – as long as the trust is carefully structured and such home country tax issues as gift tax, income tax and inheritance tax are carefully thought through and understood. Nevertheless even properly conceived APTs have been facing increased attacks in court seeking to break through them. Thus, one should never consider an APT as risk-free.

Other uses of trusts

Bahamian trusts may also be used by multinational corporations – especially as part of employee stock ownership plans, which continue to grow in popularity. The latter can be used as an anti-takeover defence, by placing shares of publicly traded companies in "friendly" hands – such as those of employees – under the control of hand-picked trustees. They can also be a means of giving employees a vested interest in the future of the company.

In fact, there are both tax and non-tax reasons for using trusts such as these. Employees can avoid taxation in their home jurisdiction if shares are placed in a trust and are therefore not at their immediate disposal. This, however, depends on the precise terms of the stock ownership plan as well as on the tax laws in the home country.

Even if tax is due, using the vehicle of a trust may still be important for non-tax reasons.

For example, it helps companies to retain the shares under their control until a vesting period has passed, thereby preventing the shares from passing directly into the hands of employees who may leave the company shortly thereafter. Also, if an employee dies, the shares can more readily be sold, rather than transferred to the spouse or family members, which may be preferable from an inheritance point of view, as well as for purposes of maintaining a closer knit shareholder group. A trust may also help on the administrative side, by allowing employee-held stock to be aggregated and more easily dealt with in terms of dividends, voting, notices, etc.

A second popular use of trusts is as part of a fail-safe device in the event of expropriation. These so-called "Phillips trusts" were devised around the time of the Second World War as a means for the shares of a company to be held by trustees for the benefit of the shareholders. In the case of Phillips NV of The Netherlands, the goal was to allow foreign affiliates to continue operating even when the head office was under German control. Otherwise, US law (in particular) would have frozen enemy-controlled assets.

Usually, such trusts hold offshore assets only to shelter them from expropriation in the event of the home country seeking to nationalize the shares of stock of the head office itself. This technique has notably been used for offshore assets of companies located in Latin America.

A third use of offshore trusts relates to in-substance defeasances. This is a technique which involves transferring liabilities to a trust, along with certain assets or income streams sufficient to pay off such liabilities over a period of time. The trust is established as a nongrantor trust, in which liabilities are removed from the balance sheet of the transferor in order to improve its financial position. Peugeot is an example of a major European company which has successfully used this technique, although such off-balance financing techniques have fallen somewhat into disfavour post-Enron.

Offshore holding and trading companies

Given The Bahamas' status as a tax haven, a number of different opportunities may present themselves to European companies and individuals – as long as the laws in the country of residence are taken into account.

An important investment tool is the offshore holding company, which serves both tax and non-tax purposes. Its most obvious use is to shelter income from taxation – a benefit which may be limited by home country legislation.

A Bahamas-based holding company would not be able to take advantage of double taxation conventions to reduce withholding taxes, however, since The Bahamas does not benefit from any such conventions. On the non-tax side, using a holding company allows for centralization of shareholdings, leading to some administrative ease and potential cost savings.

A second commonly used entity in international structuring is the trading company. This can be structured as a commission agent, receiving commissions for assistance in effecting sales of goods or services, or as a buy-sell company that takes title to goods and sells them in its own name as a distributor. Again, anti-abuse provisions in various European and other jurisdictions should be taken into account, most notably the controlled foreign company type of legislation (which continues to spread its wings in Europe), as well as transfer pricing rules.

Although The Bahamas is well-suited for the formation of offshore trading companies, it should be noted that in any international tax structuring of this sort, true substance is more and more imperative.

The mere establishment of a shell company is unlikely to serve its intended purpose, as it may easily be pierced by tax authorities of one or another country looking at the entity and/or transactions it conducts. Substance requires more than merely abiding by corporate formalities. In that regard, the old adage, "You get what you pay for," applies. Setting up an inexpensive entity as a screen will be seen as a sham. Hence, if one wishes to take maximum advantage of The Bahamas, a real company must be formed with substance, business activities and business purpose.

International tax structuring also often entails the use of special purpose vehicles, many of which could be located in The Bahamas. These include captive insurance companies, financing vehicles, licensing companies, and service entities such as headquarter operations. Depending on the circumstances, The Bahamas may be an appropriate jurisdiction for such functions.

Home country legislation

As already noted, individuals and multinationals seeking to use The Bahamas for tax-planning reasons should take into account the impact of anti-abuse legislation throughout Europe. Such legislation may be broken down into four categories:

1. **Controlled foreign company rules,** which treat certain types of "tainted" income (earned by a foreign company and controlled by domestic taxpayers) as a deemed dividend automatically taxable to those taxpayers or shareholders. It usually includes such "passive" income as dividends, interest and royalties as well as related-party sales or services income.

2. **Transfer pricing rules,** which effectively preclude the shifting of profits from a high-tax to a low-tax jurisdiction such as The Bahamas. If a Bahamian entity has substance and can justify earning a certain level of profit commensurate with the functions it performs, it will then be in a position to more convincingly rebut most challenges based on transfer pricing legislation.
3. **Rules tailored to dealings with tax havens.** In certain countries, such as Belgium or Italy, these are effected by means of a formal or informal blacklist, whereas in other countries, they are based on whether tax rates in the offshore jurisdiction are significantly lower than those which the home country would levy on equivalent income. These anti-tax haven rules often preclude deductions for payments made to a tax-haven entity or the applicability of special provisions such as withholding tax exemptions.
4. **Exchange controls,** which (although mostly dismantled in Europe) may still be imposed in the event of currency emergencies, or in cases dealing with tax havens. In some instances, they may even technically remain on the statute books. Or if funds are freely transferrable outside a country, they may still have to be reported as having been transferred. And although some European countries still impose a form of exit tax, such as Denmark, France and Germany, most Europeans can transfer their residence to The Bahamas without much trouble. The English, in particular, are fond of taking up Bahamian residence and thereby avoiding or minimizing their tax liability in the UK.

Summary

Traditionally, Europeans have used European financial jurisdictions such as Switzerland, Luxembourg, Liechtenstein, Gibraltar, the Channel Islands and the Isle of Man. The Bahamas effectively offers a viable alternative when used as part of a proper structure with substance, and after taking into account home country tax constraints.

In this day and age, The Bahamas is not all that distant from Europe and benefits from excellent communications and transportation links. It has a common law system, as do Gibraltar and the Isle of Man, but it is closer to the US. Indeed, for Europeans looking to deal extensively with either North or South America, The Bahamas may be a useful gateway to, or even a turntable of sorts between, those two continents.

For the individual seeking a change of residence, The Bahamas certainly offers a more attractive climate than most European centres. It has stable legal and tax regimes and generally low risk, prime elements for any jurisdiction seeking to establish itself as a favourable tax-planning location.

Howard M Liebman

is a partner in the Brussels office of Jones Day, a US-based law firm of approx 2,200 attorneys in 26 offices in the US, Europe and Asia. Liebman specializes in international tax and corporate structuring, as well as trans-border mergers and acquisitions. In this capacity, he has undertaken the structuring and restructuring of major multinationals and joint ventures, and has led significant cross-disciplinary teams handling all the legal as well as tax aspects of a number of larger European-wide acquisitions. Liebman is a prolific author and speaker, and serves as the EU tax correspondent for *European Taxation* and the Belgian correspondent for the *Tax Management International Forum*. He received his undergraduate degree in International Relations and Economics summa cum laude from Colgate Univ, where he also earned a Masters Degree in International Relations with honours. Liebman graduated cum laude from Harvard Law School and is a member of the District of Columbia and Brussels ("B" list) Bars.

TAX BENEFITS FOR US CITIZENS & COMPANIES

by P Bruce Wright & Arthur J Lynch

A US individual or company can, in some instances, start international operations with relatively small amounts of capital and then expand with tax-free or low-taxed accumulations of earnings instead of net-tax dollars earned in the US. Thus, expansion abroad can be more rapidly accomplished with 100 cent tax-free dollars, instead of 65 cent dollars (which is net after approx 35% US tax).

The tax advantages, or tax deferrals, are available by reason of the foreign taxation provisions of the Internal Revenue Code (IRC) which set forth conditions under which the US will exempt or defer foreign income from US taxation.

To become eligible for US tax advantages, Bahamian business ventures must be operated by a Bahamian company. If a Bahamian or other foreign company (except a passive foreign investment company) is not engaged in a US trade or business, and at least 50% of the voting power and value is owned by non-US persons, US tax laws (insurance companies are an exception) generally do not apply to its foreign income, and only in rare instances will there be any US income tax.

If US persons own 50% or less of the voting power and value of a Bahamian company, and the Bahamian company does not conduct activities in the US which would cause it to be taxable in the US, none of its foreign income will generally be subject to US taxation unless and until dividends are paid to US shareholders, or they sell their shares, or the assets of the company are distributed.

If a Bahamian or other foreign company is more than 50% controlled or more than 50% of its value is owned (directly or indirectly) by US persons who each own at least 10% of the voting power, it is known under US tax laws as a controlled foreign corporation (CFC). US shareholders who own (directly or indirectly) at least 10% of the voting control of a CFC (US 10% shareholders) are taxable each year on their proportionate share of certain kinds of income of the corporation. The kinds of income currently taxable are, generally:

1. Income from the insurance or reinsurance of risks.
2. Passive income such as dividends, rents, interest, gains from the sale of property which itself produced passive income, capital gains from the sale of stocks and securities, gains on commodities and foreign currency transactions, royalties, etc.
3. Sales income where the goods are either purchased from or sold to a related person.
4. Income from services if rendered to a related person.
5. Increases in investments in US property.
6. Aircraft and shipping income (including income from ocean and space activities).
7. Income attributable to international boycotts.
8. Income attributable to the bribery of foreign government officials.
9. Income which is foreign oil or gas related.

Even so, there are many exceptions and exclusions to the above. For example, if such income comprises less than 5% of a Bahamian company's adjusted gross income (and less than $1,000,000), none of the company's income will be taxable by the US.

In most cases, however, every other kind of foreign income is free of

US taxation. In other words, even if the Bahamian company is US-controlled, its US 10% shareholders are not required to include such other foreign earnings in their annual taxable income.

A Bahamian company engaged in a US trade or business will be subject to US corporate taxes on income effectively connected with such trade or business, as well as the "branch profits tax" to the IRC (a 30% tax imposed on earnings of a US branch of a foreign company that are deemed repatriated to the foreign parent company). Therefore, careful planning is required to minimize the effect of this tax.

The types of US CFCs particularly suitable for operations in The Bahamas and having these US tax advantages include, among others, the following:

1. Manufacturing production. Income from the sale of products or goods manufactured or produced in The Bahamas, generally is not subject to US taxation even though purchases and sales involve the parent corporation or other related persons.

The same applies to rental income where such products or goods are leased to an unrelated party instead of sold, provided certain "active-business" tests are met. In addition, rental income from the lease of such products or goods to a related party generally is not subject to US taxation provided that the products or goods are used in The Bahamas. Likewise, income from certain incidental services rendered before a sale or in connection with an effort to sell such products or goods is not currently taxable.

2. Sales of products and goods. If the parent corporation or other related person is not involved in the purchase or sale of products or goods, then income from such sales is not subject to current US taxation, no matter where or by whom the products or goods were manufactured, where the sales are made or where such products or goods are used or consumed.

Even if a related person is involved, the sales income is free of current tax if the products or goods are manufactured, produced, grown or extracted in The Bahamas, or if they are for use, consumption or disposition in The Bahamas.

3. Insurance. A Bahamian insurance company is considered a CFC if more than 25% of the voting power or value of its stock is owned by US 10% shareholders. Income earned by a Bahamian insurance or reinsurance company which is a CFC is taxable only to a US 10% shareholder.

In addition, unless certain exceptions are met, if a Bahamian insurance company is at least 25% US-owned, all US shareholders (even if such shareholders own less than 10%) must include in income their *pro rata* share of the company's related person insurance income (premium or investment income on insurance policies where the person insured, directly or indirectly, is a US shareholder or related person). Related person insurance income also includes income from reinsurance if the ceding company or its insured is a US shareholder in the Bahamian insurer.

A Bahamian insurance company that is a CFC can elect to be treated as a US corporation for all US tax purposes. If this election is made, US shareholders will not be taxed on the company's income until distributed as dividends. The charge for electing is 0.75% of capital and surplus as of Dec 31, 1987, up to a max charge of $1.5 million.

The Bahamas government provides advantages and incentives for insurance companies insuring and reinsuring non-Bahamian risks.

4. Banks and finance companies. Passive income of a Bahamian bank or finance company that is a CFC that is "predominantly engaged in the active conduct of a banking, financing or similar business" (as defined in the IRC) and conducts substantial activity with respect to such business is not subject to current US taxation. Interest earned by a Bahamian bank that is a CFC in connection with export financing for related US persons, with certain exceptions, is not subject to US tax.

5. Service companies. This is a broad category and includes any Bahamian corporation rendering services which are technical, managerial, engineering, architectural, scientific, skilled, industrial, commercial or the like.

Many types of companies in The Bahamas fall into this category. A partial list would include engineering, sales promotion, sales engineering, merchandising, consulting, etc. With reference to such companies, income from such services, rendered outside the US and performed for persons who are not related without substantial assistance of related US persons, is exempt from current US taxation.

Income from services rendered within The Bahamas is also exempt even though such services are rendered for, or on behalf of, a related person. Income from services rendered by a foreign company in The Bahamas before a sale or in connection with an effort to sell products or goods manufactured, produced, grown or extracted by it are also exempt from current US tax even though such income is received from a related person.

6. Leasing and royalties. Rents derived in the active conduct of a trade or business in The Bahamas and received from persons not related are not subject to current US taxation.

Rents are also so exempt even when received from a related person if such rents are for use of property located in The Bahamas, unless the CFC is also a "foreign personal holding company" (FPHC). An FPHC is a foreign corporation that derives at least 60% of its gross income from certain types of passive income, such as rents, royalties, dividends and interest, and more than 50% of the voting power or value of which is owned by, or for, not more than five US citizens or residents.

Royalties, for example – payments in connection with patents, copyrights, inventions, models, designs, secret formulas or processes – are currently exempt from US taxation when derived in the active conduct of a trade or business in The Bahamas and received from persons who are not related, unless the company is an FPHC.

Royalties are also so exempt, even when received from a related person, if such royalties are for the use of property or property rights within The Bahamas, unless the company is an FPHC.

7. Ships and aircraft. Income of a Bahamian company that is a CFC is subject to current US tax when received for the use or hiring or leasing or for services related to the use of any vessel or aircraft in foreign commerce, unless limited to commerce between two points in The Bahamas with respect to an aircraft or vessel registered in The Bahamas.

8. Certain investment income. Dividend and interest income received from a related foreign corporation generally is exempt from current tax if both payer and payee are incorporated in The Bahamas and the payer has a substantial part of its assets used in the business in The Bahamas.

Even if the foreign company is a CFC, the current taxation CFC provisions of the IRC do not apply to US shareholders who own less than 10% of the voting power. However, if more than 50% of total voting power or total value of the shares is owned (directly or indirectly) by five or fewer US persons, and more than 60% of the gross income of the company is interest, dividends and certain other types of passive income, all US shareholders will be taxable on their share of all of the corporation's earnings under the FPHC rules.

Unless the company is more than 50% owned in vote and value by foreign persons, if it is primarily involved in trading in stocks, securities or commodities, the gain recognized on a liquidation or sale of shares will be treated as ordinary income to the extent of the shareholder's *pro rata* share of the earnings of the company.

Passive foreign investment company

A Bahamian company is a PFIC if 75% or more of its gross income is "passive" income (dividends, interest, etc), or 50% or more of its assets are held to produce passive income. Thus, a mutual fund, and even a manufacturing company with large retained earnings invested in securities, could be a PFIC.

US shareholders in a Bahamian PFIC may be subject to additional taxes (plus interest) on certain PFIC distributions or on a sale of PFIC stock. A US shareholder of a PFIC may avoid this result by making one of the following two elections. First, a PFIC shareholder can elect to be taxed currently on his *pro rata* share of PFIC ordinary income and capital gains, which then can be distributed tax free. If a shareholder makes this election, he also can elect to defer the current tax but must pay interest on the deferred taxes. Second, a US shareholder of a PFIC may elect to mark-to-market his stock on an annual basis if such stock is marketable (eg, regularly traded on a national securities exchange registered with the SEC).

Coordination rules prevent the same income being taxed twice in cases where a PFIC also qualifies as a CFC or an FPHC. An important exception is that PFIC rules generally will not apply to *bona fide* insurance companies predominantly engaged in an insurance business and certain banks.

Employment of US citizens abroad

Tax benefits are available to US citizens employed abroad who establish a tax home in a foreign country (ie, the foreign country is the taxpayer's principal place of business) and who meet certain other tests prescribed by the IRC (either a "physical presence" or residency test with respect to the foreign country). Although a US citizen generally is subject to US income tax on his worldwide income, a US citizen employed abroad who satisfies the IRC tests described above may exclude from gross income for any taxable year foreign-source earned income (ie, wages or salary for services performed outside the US) up to $80,000 for taxable years 2002 through '07 and adjusted for inflation for taxable years beginning after 2007. In addition, such individual may either:

1. Exclude from gross income a portion of the housing expenses paid for by his employer, or
2. In the event such expenses are not paid for by his employer, deduct such expenses (subject to certain limitations).

P Bruce Wright

a partner in the firm LeBoeuf, Lamb, Greene & MacRae, LLP, of 125 West 55th St, New York, was employed by the office of the Chief Counsel, Internal Revenue Service, after graduating from law school. During this time he obtained a Masters of Law in Taxes from Georgetown Univ Law Center. Wright was awarded the designation Chartered Property Casualty Underwriter in 1984. He lectures extensively at seminars sponsored by organizations such as the Risk Insurance Management Society and Captive Insurance Co Assoc.

Arthur J Lynch

is a partner in the firm LeBoeuf, Lamb, Greene & MacRae, LLP, of 125 West 55th St, New York. He concentrates in tax law, including matters relating to public and private offerings of securities of offshore insurance companies, domestic and cross-border reorganizations, the formation of captive insurers, the structuring of alternative risk financing arrangements, the structuring of international insurance and reinsurance operations of global insurers, the use of capital market and hedge fund strategies by insurers and other issues related to the convergence of the insurance and capital markets. Lynch has authored articles on Tax Implications of Risk and Alternative Risk Financing.

TELECOMMUNICATIONS

Telecommunications services and facilities in The Bahamas are on par with the US and Canada. A 100% digital switching system allows direct distance dialling to more than 100 countries.

An undersea fibre optic cable system links Grand Bahama, New Providence, Abaco and Eleuthera with the continental US. It is owned and operated by Caribbean Crossings Ltd, a subsidiary of Cable Bahamas Ltd.

The Bahamas Telecommunications Company Ltd (BTC), is a quasi-public corporation owned by the government but operating without subsidy from it. At press time plans to privatize the company were under way.

BTC offers a wide range of services, including telephone, fax, telex, cellular and radio phone networks, private line services, packet switching, satellite service and GSM services.

BTC Marketing, PO Box N-3048, Nassau, tel 302-7827.

Indigo Networks, a subsidiary of Systems Resource Group (SRG), also provides a full range of fixed telephony and mobile data services.

Public Utilities Commission

The Public Utilities Commission (PUC) was established in Mar 2000 to regulate controlled public utilities under the terms of the PUC Act, 1993, as amended in '99.

While it is envisioned that the PUC will eventually regulate electricity and water and sewage services, it now regulates only telecommunications, including the operations of the Bahamas Telecommunications Company (BTC), Internet Service Providers (ISPs), Very Small Aperture Terminals (VSAT), mobile radios, paging systems, SMR Trunking Radio and wireless telephony. PUC also manages the radio frequency spectrum and issues licenses for radio broadcasting stations.

PUC issues licences and determines the conditions of those licences, with the power to revoke or modify them. The Commission determines the prices charged by dominant operators and the conditions under which one operator will interconnect its network with another. It can enforce the conditions of licences and impose sanctions (public censure, fines, revocation of licences) against licensees who infringe the terms of their licences.

Under the terms of the enabling legislation, PUC is an independent office designed to implement government policy. It is funded by means of licence fees and is intended to be independent of subventions from the Public Treasury.

See also **Internet.**

TELEVISION

ZNS TV transmitter power is 50,000 watts ERP on Channel 13, which can be viewed 130 miles from Nassau. Channel 13 operates 10 hours per day Mon-Fri, 17 hours on Sat and 16 hours on Sun.

ZNS TV began test transmission on July 4, 1977, and its official programming commenced July 10. HM Queen Elizabeth II officially opened the station on Oct 20 of that year. In 1983, a facility was installed to receive satellite transmission for re-broadcast.

Channel 13 is autonomous of any external television network, and its programming is chosen by the Broadcasting Corp of The Bahamas to serve the national interest.

Cable Bahamas subscribers view ZNS TV on Channel 11 and 53.

See also **Broadcasting, Cable television** and **Freeport/Lucaya information, Television.**

THEATRE & PERFORMING ARTS

Performing arts groups include the government-funded Bahamas National Youth Choir, National Dance Company of The Bahamas, National Children's Choir and National Youth Orchestra. The National Youth Choir has produced eight compact discs, performed in the US, UK, Canada, France, Finland, Mexico, Russia, China and the Caribbean, and appeared on local and international television. Choir founder and director Cleophas Adderley, an attorney, is the government's former Director of Culture and is currently the Director of Musical Heritage & Research.

Other performing arts groups in The Bahamas include The Bahamas Concert Orchestra, the Bahamas Guild of Artists, Plantation Productions, Nassau Amateur Operatic Society, Nassau Renaissance Singers, Dundas Repertory Company, the Diocesan Chorale, James Catalyn and Friends, Arts International, The Nassau Music Society, The University Players, Track Road Theatre, The Grand Bahama Players and Freeport Players Guild.

The Dundas Centre for the Performing Arts showcases local and international plays, revues, musicals and dance. Performance charges at the 334-seat theatre on Mackey St are usually $10-$20. Performances are staged throughout the year. Tel 393-3728, fax 394-7179.

In July 2001, the National Centre for the Performing Arts opened. With approx 600 seats, the centre can host large-scale performances and international gatherings. Housed in the former Shirley Street Theatre on East Shirley St, the building underwent a $1.2 million renovation prior to the opening. Tel 302-0600, Dept of Culture.

See also **Awards.**

TIME

The Bahamas operates on Eastern Time, which is five hours behind Greenwich Mean Time. This puts our archipelago in the same time zone as the major commercial centres of the eastern US and Canada, such as Miami, Washington, DC, New York, Toronto, and Montreal.

When it is noon in The Bahamas, it is 9am in Los Angeles and Vancouver; 5pm in London; 6pm in Rome, and 2am in Tokyo.

The Bahama islands are on daylight saving time from the first Sun in Apr to the last Sun in Oct.

TIME-SHARING

The Bahamas Vacation Plan and Time-Sharing Act, 1999, was enacted on Jan 12, 2000. It provides increased protection for timeshare purchasers and encourages growth of the industry by offering incentives to developers for construction and renovation of time-sharing projects. The new Act repeals and replaces the Time-Sharing Act, 1984.

The Act provides guidelines for the creation and management of timeshare projects. The Act sets out terms and conditions for licences necessary to construct, manage, improve, market and sell timeshare properties in The Bahamas.

Timeshare facilities must be inspected according to standards outlined in the Act, and must comprise at least 50 units in New Providence, or at least 25 units in the Out Islands to be eligible for incentives. Timeshare units may be purchased for a specific period not exceeding six months per year, for a maximum period of 40 years, or as specified by the Investment Board.

Timeshare projects in New Providence include Club Land'Or, Paradise Harbour Club and Marina, Guanahani Village, Westwind I, Westwind II Club, Royal Holiday, Paradise Island Beach Club, Sandyport Beaches Resort (Portfolio International Vacations), Harborside Resort at Atlantis, and Whispering Winds.

TOURISM

In 2003 there were 4,594,042 foreign arrivals in The Bahamas. This represents an increase of 4.3% from the 2002 figure of 4,405,971, according to the Dept of Research and Statistics at the Ministry of Tourism. Total visitor spending in 2003 was estimated at $1.763 billion, compared to $1.759 billion in 2002. Average room rates rose 5.3% from $155.90 to $164.22. See **Fig 2.8** for visitor arrivals to The Bahamas.

For further information contact the Ministry of Tourism, British Colonial Hilton, Bay St, tel 322-7500 or 302-2000, fax 302-2098, e-mail tourism@batelnet.bs, or visit www.bahamas.com or www.tourismbahamas.org.

See also **Accommodations, Cruise ship incentives, Environment, Gambling** and **Shopping.**

Tourism promotion boards

Three tourism promotion boards promote maximum interest in Nassau, Paradise Island, Grand Bahama and the Out Islands as separate and ideal vacation destinations. The Nassau/Paradise Island/Cable Beach Promotion Board, tel 322-8384; Bahama Out Islands Promotion Board, US toll free 1-800-688-4752 or (305) 931-6612; and Grand Bahama Island Tourism Board, tel (242) 352-8044/5 or 352-8356 or US toll free 1-800-448-3386; work closely with travel partners and vacationers to provide efficient destination-specific information. Travel partners include tour operators, airlines, travel agents, advertising and public relations agencies, cruise lines, hotels and travel media.

Bahamas Tourism Offices

The Ministry of Tourism maintains overseas sales offices that provide information about The Bahamas.

UNITED STATES

Atlanta:
1950 Century Blvd, Suite 4
Atlanta, GA 30345
Tel (404) 636-3911
Fax (404) 636-3191
e-mail cthompson@bahamas.com
or earcher@bahamas.com

Chicago:
8600 W Bryn Mawr Ave, Suite 820
Chicago, IL 60631
Tel (773) 693-1500
fax (773) 693-1114
e-mail vkelly@bahamas.com

Los Angeles:
3450 Wilshire Blvd, Suite 1204
Los Angeles, CA 90010
Tel (213) 385-0033
fax (213) 383-3966
e-mail gjohnson@bahamas.com
Bahamas Film and Television Commission,
3450 Wilshire Blvd, Suite 1204
Los Angeles, CA 90010
Tel (213) 385-0033
or (800) 439-6993
e-mail eglinton@bahamas.com

Miami:
1200 S Pine Island Rd
Suite 750
Plantation, FL 33324
Tel (954) 236-9292
fax (954) 236-0733
e-mail bking@bahamas.com

New York:
150 East 52nd St, 28th Floor North
New York, NY 10022
Tel (212) 758-2777
fax (212) 753-6531
e-mail vbrown@bahamas.com

FIG 2.8

MINISTRY OF TOURISM VISITOR ARRIVALS

Year	Nassau	Grand Bahama & Out Islands	Total
1999	2,284,809	1,363,482	3,648,291
2000	2,685,819	1,518,015	4,203,834
2001	2,711,851	1,470,905	4,182,756
2002	2,583,811	1,822,160	4,405,971
2003	2,635,112	1,958,930	4,594,042

CANADA
Toronto:
121 Bloor St East, Suite 1101
Toronto, Ont M4W 3M5
Tel (416) 968-2999
fax (416) 968-0724
e-mail sjones@bahamas.com

ENGLAND
London:
10 Chesterfield St, London W1J 5JL
Tel (011) 44-0207-355-0800
fax (011) 44-0207-491-9459
e-mail info@bahamas.co.uk
www.bahamas.co.uk

FRANCE
Paris:
113-115 Rue Du Cherche
Midi 75006, Paris
Tel (011) 33-45-26-62-62
fax (011) 33-48-74-06-05
e-mail info@bahamas.tourisme.fr
www.bahama-tourisme.fr

GERMANY
Frankfurt:
Friesstrasse 3, 60388
Frankfurt/Main
Tel (011) 49-69-420-89019
fax (011) 49-69-970-83434
e-mail herzog@herzog-hc.de

ITALY
Milan:
Corso Magenta 54, 20123 Milan
Tel (011) 3902-481-94390
e-mail info@vertex.ws
www.bahamas.it

TRADE AGREEMENTS

See **Caribbean Basin Initiative (CBI), Caribbean Community, CARIBCAN, Cotonou Agreement, Free Trade Area of the Americas (FTAA), North American Free Trade Agreement (NAFTA)** and **World Trade Organization (WTO).**

TRADE UNIONS

There are 55 trade unions registered in New Providence. Contact the Registrar, Dept of Labour, PO Box N-1586, Nassau, tel 502-1000 or 502-1047, fax 356-5585.

See also **Labour relations** and **Freeport/Lucaya information, Trade unions.**

TRANSPORTATION

Taxi rates are government controlled. All taxis are required to have meters in good working condition.

The first quarter-mile is $3 for one or two passengers; each additional quarter-mile is 40¢. Additional passengers after the first two pay $3 per person. Accompanied children under five ride free.

Zone rates, applied to most standard routes on request, are set by government. Taxi waiting charge (except when hired by the hour) is 30¢ per minute.

Car rental prices are competitive with Hertz, Avis, Budget, Dollar and local companies represented. Pick up from a hotel anywhere in New

Providence (including Paradise Island) is free of charge. Prices range from $45 per day ($270 per week) for a compact to $125 per day ($750 per week) for a minivan and include unlimited mileage. Insurance and gas are extra.

Visitors may use their home driver's licences here for three months. Traffic moves on the left side of the road.

Motor scooters are $40-$50 per day, 8am-5pm, including gas. Insurance is $5, and a deposit is required (a credit card can be used as deposit). Hourly rentals are available. It is wise for a novice to practise scooter skills in light traffic before attempting downtown streets. There is a law requiring drivers and riders of motor scooters and motor bikes to wear crash helmets. These helmets are available at no extra charge from the rental companies.

The jitney (bus) provides inexpensive touring and a close view of local life. Fare is $1 in town, more for outlying areas. Transfers and change are not provided. Service is from 6:30am-7pm. Bus stops are marked. However, time schedules may be unpredictable.

A London double decker bus provides complimentary shuttle service hourly between the Olde Towne Mall at Sandyport and Cable Beach hotels daily 10am-10pm.

A complimentary bus shuttle operates between Atlantis hotels at approx 30-min intervals from 6am-12 midnight Sun-Thurs, 6am-2am Fri and Sat. A ferry service operates from the Paradise Island Ferry Terminal across the harbour to Rawson Sq and back at $3 per person one way. This is a daytime service, Mon, Tue, Fri and Sat 9:30am-5:30pm with departures from both sides of the harbour about every 20 mins at peak times.

A horse-drawn surrey ride costs approx $10 per adult for a 25-min tour of Nassau's downtown area. Rates for extended trips should be negotiated with the driver beforehand. The surrey ranks are at Woodes Rogers Walk downtown. Horses are rested 1-3pm May-Oct, 1-2pm Nov-Apr.

Boats

An inexpensive and rewarding way to see the Out Islands is by mailboats which tie up at Potter's Cay under Paradise Island Eastern Bridge. The boats, subsidized by the government as mail carriers, take on freight and passengers as well as the priority mailbags. Costs range from around $60 round trip to Eleuthera to $140 round trip to faraway Inagua. Some mailboats include food with their inter-island transportation service. Check with the dockmaster at Potter's Cay for latest schedules and costs, tel 394-1237 (to 9).

Bahamas Ferries provides regular passenger service between Nassau and North Eleuthera, Spanish Wells and Harbour Island, aboard the *Bo Hengy,* a high-speed catamaran. Bahamas SeaRoad's *Sea Link* and *Sea Wind,* car and passenger ferries, provide regular service from Nassau to Governor's Harbour and Current, Eleuthera; Morgan's Bluff, Driggs Hill and Fresh Creek, Andros; George Town, Exuma; and Sandy Point, Abaco. Tel 323-2166.

See **Air service, Car rental companies, Driver's licence & vehicle information** and **Motor vehicle insurance.**

TRUSTS

See **Investing.**

VACCINATION REQUIREMENTS

Most visitors to The Bahamas do not need special vaccinations before entering the country. However, travellers over age one must provide a yellow fever vaccination certificate if they are coming from infected areas.

Bahamians and Bahamas residents travelling abroad should familiarize themselves with the vaccination requirements of their destination. According to *International Travel and Health**, a publication of the World Health Organization (WHO), no country requires a certificate of vaccination against smallpox and cholera. Bahamians and Bahamas residents travelling to yellow fever or malaria infected countries should consult the Public Health Dept, Ministry of Health, or a doctor regarding vaccinations and other precautionary measures. No vaccinations are required for Bahamians going to the US or Canada.

According to WHO, travellers should be immunized against a certain number of diseases. The organization stresses the distinction between vaccinations required by countries for entry, those recommended for general protection against certain diseases and others which may be advisable in certain circumstances. Travellers are advised to establish a vaccination plan, taking into account their current immune status, destination, duration (especially in malaria infected areas), type of travel and overall state of health.

* *Vaccination requirements and health advice reproduced by permission of* International Travel and Health, *World Health Organization, 1998.*

VETERINARIANS

New Providence

Dr Patrick Balfe,
Eastern Veterinary Clinic ..393-3818
Dr Basil Sands
and Dr Robert Allen,
Central Animal Hospital 325-1288
Dr Peter Bizzell
and Dr Dwight Dorsett,
Palmdale Veterinary Clinic ..325-1354
Dr Dawn Wilson,
Animal Clinic 328-5635
Bahamas Humane
Society 323-5138/325-6742

See also **Bahamas Humane Society.**

VISAS FOR BAHAMIANS

Bahamian passport holders can travel virtually anywhere in the world without fear of detainment. As The Bahamas enjoys diplomatic relations with many countries, visitor entry visas are not necessary on all trips abroad. However, relevant authorities must be contacted to obtain necessary entry permits if one is entering a country to do business or as a student. These would include trips to Canada, the UK and the US. For the US, a visa is required if the possessor of the Bahamian passport is in transit, embarking on a cruise or has not pre-cleared US Immigration in The Bahamas.

Bahamians do not require visas for travel to:

Antigua and Barbuda, Anegada,[2] Anguilla,[3] Aruba,[1] Bangladesh (for a stay of two weeks or less), Barbados, Belize, Bermuda, Bonaire,[1] Botswana, Brazil, Canada, Cayman Islands,[3] Chile, Colombia, Cook Islands (for a stay of less than 31 days), Costa Rica (for a stay of less than 30 days), Curaçao,[1] Cyprus, Dominica, Dominican Republic, Ecuador, Faeroe Islands, Fiji, Finland (for a stay of less than 90 days), Galapagos Islands, Gibraltar, Greenland, Grenada, Guyana, Holy See (Vatican City), Hong Kong, Iceland, Ireland, Israel, Jamaica, Japan, Jost Van Dyke,[2] Kenya, Kiribati (Gilbert Islands), South Korea, Lesotho, Liechtenstein, Malaysia, Maldives, Malta, Mauritius, Mexico, Federated States of Micronesia, Montserrat,[3] Niue, Norfolk Islands, Norway, Peru, St Eustatius,[1] St Kitts & Nevis, St Lucia, St Maarten, St Vincent & the Grenadines, Saba,[1] San Marino, Seychelles, Singapore, Solomon Islands, Swaziland, Sweden, Switzerland, Tanzania, Tortola,[3] Trinidad & Tobago, Turks & Caicos Islands,[3] Tuvalu, Uganda, UK (England, Northern Ireland, Wales, Scotland), Uraguay, US (and its territories), Vanuatu, Virgin Gorda,[2] Zambia, Zimbabwe.

Visas are required for visits to:

Afghanistan, Albania, Algeria, Andorra, Angola, Argentina, Armenia, Australia, Austria, Azerbaijan, Azores, Bahrain, Bangladesh (for a stay of more than two weeks), Belarus, Belgium, Benin, Bhutan, Bolivia, Bosnia and Herzegovina, Brazil (for business),

Brunei, Bulgaria, Burkina Faso, Burundi, Cambodia, Cameroon, Cape Verde, Central African Republic, Ceylon, Chad, China, Federal & Islamic Republic of Comoros, Democratic People's Republic of Congo (Zaire), Republic of Congo, Côte d'Ivoire, Croatia, Cuba, Czech Republic, Denmark, Désirade,[5] Djibouti, Egypt, El Salvador, Equatorial Guinea, Eritrea, Estonia, Ethiopia, Finland, France, French Austral,[4] French Guiana, French Southern & Antarctic Lands (Crozet & Kerguelen), Gabon, The Gambia, Gambier,[4] Republic of Georgia, Germany, Ghana, Greece, Guadeloupe,[5] Guatemala, Guinea, Guinea-Bissau, Haiti, Honduras, Hungary, India, Indonesia, Iran, Iraq, Isle des Saintes,[5] Italy, Jordan, Kazakhstan, North Korea, Kuwait, Kyrgyzstan, Lao People's Democratic Republic, Latvia, Lebanon, Liberia, Lithuania, Luxembourg, Macao, Macedonia, Madagascar, Malawi, Mali, Marie Galante,[5] Marquesas,[4] Marshall Islands, Martinique,[5] Mauritania, Mayotte Islands, Miquelon Islands, Moldova, Monaco, Mongolia, Morocco, Mozambique, Myanmar (formerly Burma), Namibia, Nepal, Netherlands, New Caledonia,[4] New Zealand, Nicaragua, Niger, Nigeria, Oman, Pakistan, Palau, Palestine, Panama, Papua New Guinea, Paraguay, Philippines, Poland, Portugal (incl Azores), Qatar, Reunion, Romania, Russia, Rwanda, St Barthelemy,[5] St Martin,[5] St Pierre, Saudi Arabia, Senegal, Sierra Leone, Slovakia, Slovenia, Society Islands,[4] Somalia, South Africa, Spain, Sri Lanka, Sudan, Suriname, Syria, Tahiti,[4] Taiwan, Tanzania, Thailand, Togo, Tonga, Tuamotu,[4] Turkey, Turkmenistan, Ukraine, United Arab Emirates, Uzbekistan, Venezuela, Vietnam, Wallis & Futuna Islands,[4] Western Samoa, Yemen Arab Republic, Yugoslavia.

[1] Netherlands Antilles [2] British Virgin Islands
[3] British West Indies [4] French Polynesia
[5] French West Indies

Contact the Bahamas-based honorary consul of the country in question, or the Ministry of Foreign Affairs, East Hill St, PO Box N-3746, Nassau, tel 322-7624/5; or the consular section, tel 323-5565 or 323-5578.

See also **Government section, Resident diplomats & consular representatives.**

VOTING

To register in The Bahamas, a voter must:

1. Be a citizen of The Bahamas, by birth or naturalization, and age 18 or older, validated by a birth certificate or passport before first-time voting.
2. Be subject to no legal incapacity (eg, incarcerated in prison or a mental institution).
3. Have been a resident of a constituency for three months before registration. An exception is made for students attending school outside The Bahamas.

To register, apply to the Parliamentary Commissioner's Office, Farrington Rd, Nassau, or to a revising officer, or to an administrator in the Out Islands.

A prospective voter must be registered and must have been ordinarily resident in his constituency for some period during the six months immediately before the day of election. If the voter has moved to a new constituency and has lived there for less than six months, he is entitled to vote in his old constituency if he was registered there.

There are 24 constituencies in New Providence, and 16 in the Out Islands for a total of 40 constituencies. The last general election in The Bahamas was held May 2, 2002.

The next general election is set for 2007. (The Constitution provides for earlier election if the Governor General, on advice of the prime minister, dissolves Parliament and calls for a general election.) In the

Out Islands, local government elections are held every three years. The last local government elections in the Out Islands were held June 27, 2002.

See also **Constitution.**

WAGES

Following is a cross-section of jobs and wage averages per week. Wage scales are for a 40-hour week in Nassau, mid-2004:

Job title	B$
Bricklayer (mason)	300
Carpenter (semi-skilled)	187
Carpenter	315
Caretaker (live-in)	130
Certified public accountant	800
Civil engineer	1,083
Computer programmer	577
Cook (short-order)	300
Electrician	231
Executive secretary	550
Farm labourer	125
Financial controller	1,250
Financial advisor/manager	1,040
Forklift operator	450
Gardener	185
Head chef	769
Heavy equipment mechanic	450
Housemaid/housekeeper	150
Janitor	150
Labourer/handyman	150
Manager (hotel & restaurant)	1,192
Nanny	300
Primary school teacher	446
Portfolio manager	1,250
Project engineer	833
Registered nurse	400
Sales representative	462
Scuba diving instructor	375
Seaman	280
Seamstress	250
Secretary (junior)	300
Senior architect	673
Ship engineer	400
Showgirl	408
Sponge worker	250
Stenographer/secretary	400
Systems analyst	769
Truck driver	300
Vehicle mechanic	300
Waitress/waiter	(+ tips) 100

In 1996, a minimum wage of $4.12 per hour, based on a weekly wage, was introduced for government workers. On July 1, 2000, minimum wage for government workers was increased to $4.45 per hour, or $190 per week. On Jan 21, 2002, a minimum wage of $4 per hour, $30 per day or $150 per week was introduced for all private sector workers.

See also **Cost of living.**

WATER SUPPLY AND RATES

The trans-shipment of potable water began as a result of a decline in water production in New Providence in 1973. Then a responsibility of the Ministry of Works, the island's water supply operated at a limited level until 1976 when the Water and Sewerage Corporation (WSC) was formed. The trans-shipment of potable water from Andros has been instrumental in helping to meet the water usage demand of over 8.2-million imperial gals per day for New Providence.

Today, approx 55 per cent of the water distributed via the WSC facilities is brought by self-propelled tankers. WSC currently charters two vessels, the larger vessel operating with a 22-hour turn-around time delivering approx 3-million imperial gals per day and the smaller vessel operating with 18-hour turn-around time and delivering approx 1.65-million imperial gals per day.

Water consumption in New Providence is measured in imperial gals (277.274 cu in). Water charges are based on the following quarterly rates:

1. A minimum charge (including the first 3,000 gals or part thereof) per meter, per quarter in accordance with **Fig 2.9.**

2. For every 1,000 gals (or part thereof) in excess of 3,000 gals but not exceeding 13,000 gals per meter, per quarter, $12.10 per 1,000 gals ($13.15 non-residential).
3. For every 1,000 gals (or part thereof) in excess of 13,000 gals per meter, per quarter, $18.95 per 1,000 gals ($20.90 non-residential).
4. For every 1,000 gals (or part thereof) in excess of 100,000 gals per meter per quarter, $15.26 per 1,000 gals (residential).
5. For every 1,000 gals (or part thereof) in excess of 400,000 gals per meter per quarter, $15.50 per 1,000 gals (non-residential).

In each case, bills are calculated proportionately for periods other than 13 weeks.

A charge of $8 is made for special meter readings or readings requested by the owner. Reconnection charge after disconnection due to non-payment is $21 when balance due is less than $210, and 10% when balance due is more than $210.

A deposit of $55 is required for dwelling-houses with one water closet or bathroom and $115 for those with two or more. For commercial establishments the deposit is based on estimated water usage per quarter. (See **Fig 2.9** for minimum water charges for residential and non-residential consumers in New Providence.)

Notice of customer's discontinuance of the service should be sent to the Customer Service Section, Water & Sewerage Corp, PO Box N-3905, Nassau, at least seven days before discontinuance.

Water rates (imperial gals) for Abaco, Eleuthera, Exuma and San Salvador are as follows:

1. A minimum charge (incl the first 2,000 gals or part thereof) per meter per quarter in accordance with **Fig 2.9.**
2. For every 1,000 gals (or part thereof) in excess of 2,000 gals, but not exceeding 13,000 gals per meter per quarter, $6 per 1,000 gals ($6.72 non-residential).
3. For every 1,000 gals (or part thereof) in excess of 13,000 gals, but not exceeding 26,000 gals per meter per quarter, $7.40 per 1,000 gals ($8.29 non-residential).
4. For every 1,000 gals (or part thereof) in excess of 26,000 gals per meter per quarter, $8.40 per 1,000 gals ($9.41 non-residential).

Water rates (imperial gals) for the other Out Islands are as follows:

1. A minimum charge (incl the first 2,000 gals or part thereof) per meter per quarter in accordance with **Fig 2.9.**
2. For every 1,000 gals (or part thereof) in excess of 2,000 gals but not exceeding 13,000 gals per meter per quarter, $3.45 per 1,000 gals ($3.86 non-residential).
3. For every 1,000 gals (or part thereof) in excess of 13,000 gals, but not exceeding 26,000 gals per meter per quarter, $4.35 per 1,000 gals ($4.87 non-residential).
4. For every 1,000 gals (or part thereof) in excess of 26,000 gals per meter per quarter, $6 per 1,000 gals ($6.72 non-residential).

Sewer rates for New Providence are determined by the number and rating of fixtures in the home. Each fixture is assigned a unit value (ie a basic kitchen sink is two units) and charges are calculated quarterly on the number of units per premise. Residential rates are $5.44 per unit (downtown) and $2.90 per unit (all other areas). Non-residential rates are $9.18 per unit.

For further information contact the Water & Sewerage Corporation, Thompson Blvd, Oakes Field, tel 302-5600, fax 328-3896 or visit www.wsc.com.bs.

See also **Freeport/Lucaya information, Water rates & supply.**

FIG 2.9

WATER RATES NEW PROVIDENCE

Minimum charge schedule per quarter

Meter size (in inches)	Residential consumer B$	Non-residential consumer B$
½	36.00	60.00
¾	45.00	60.00
1	70.00	91.00
1¼	96.00	124.50
1½	112.00	159.50
2	–	239.00
3	–	297.50
4	–	795.00
6	–	1,390.00
8	–	1,987.00
WATER RATES FAMILY ISLANDS		
½	18.00	25.00
¾	36.00	50.00
1	60.00	83.50
1¼	84.00	116.50
1½	120.00	159.55
2	–	223.00
3	–	371.00
4	–	742.00
6	–	1,298.00
8	–	1,855.00

WATER-SKIING

See **Boating.**

WEATHER

See **Climate** and **Hurricanes.**

WEIGHTS & MEASURES

The Bahamas uses the imperial system for linear, dry and liquid measure. Twelve inches equal a foot; four quarts in a gallon (277.274 cu in). Gas at the pump in The Bahamas is by US gallon (231 cu in).

WILDLIFE PRESERVES

There are 22 national parks, national reserves and protected areas maintained by the Bahamas National Trust (BNT).

The Abacos

Abaco National Park, between Cherokee Sound and Hole in the Wall, encompasses more than 20,500 acres and is a principal habitat for the endangered Bahama parrot and other important wildlife.

Black Sound Cay National Reserve, a small mangrove island in Black

Sound, just off Green Turtle Cay.
Pelican Cays Land and Sea Park, Abaco sister of Exuma Cays Land and Sea Park.
Tilloo Cay National Reserve, between Marsh Harbour and Pelican Cays.

Andros
A naturally functioning giant ecosystem. The first phase of park designation focuses on North Bight, Fresh Creek, Blanket Sound, Young Sound and Staniard Creek.

Conception Island
Conception Island National Park, one of several Bahama islands visited by Christopher Columbus in 1492 and a station for many migrating birds and nesting sea turtles.

Exuma
Exuma Cays Land and Sea Park, approx 40 nautical miles from Nassau, is a 176-sq-mile area notable for yachting, snorkelling, diving, hiking and unique Bahama flora and fauna.
Moriah Harbour Cay, part of the ecosystem between Great and Little Exuma, comprises beaches, sand dunes, mangrove creeks and sea grass beds. Bird life includes gull-billed terns, least terns, nighthawks, ospreys and oystercatchers.

Grand Bahama
Lucayan National Park, the site of the world's longest known underwater cave and cavern system. The park also contains picturesque Gold Rock Beach and a boardwalk through a mangrove wetland, home to many birds.
Peterson Cay National Park, only cay off Grand Bahama's south shore.
Rand Nature Centre, 100-acre site two miles from downtown Freeport, Grand Bahama headquarters for BNT.
Walker's Cay Marine Park, the northernmost island in The Bahamas, is fringed by a barrier reef that hosts tropical fish and marine predators, as well as high concentrations of underwater cathedrals.

Great Inagua
Inagua National Park, site of the world's largest breeding colony of West Indian flamingos. Tours must be arranged through the BNT office in Nassau.
Union Creek National Reserve, seven sq miles of enclosed tidal creek, and an important marine turtle research facility.

Little Inagua
Remote with no fresh water, it is the largest uninhabited island in the Caribbean. The island exists in an undisturbed state with enormous biodiversity.

New Providence
Bonefish Pond National Park, lies on the south-central coast of New Providence. It is an important marine nursery area providing a protective, nutrient-rich habitat for juvenile stocks of fish, crawfish and conch. Encompassing 1,800 acres, Bonefish Pond supports a wide variety of waterfowl and an important variety of native flora.
Harrold and Wilson Ponds, in central New Providence, encompass 250 acres. More than 100 avian species, including the island's highest concentrations of herons, egrets, ibises and cormorants have been identified at this site.
The Primeval Forest, southwest New Providence, is a remarkably undisturbed old growth forest representative of the early evergreen tropical hardwood forests of The Bahamas. This area supports a diverse collection of plant life and features dramatic sinkholes. At press time, The Primeval Forest was closed to the public.
The Retreat, 11 acres in residential Nassau with one of the world's largest private collections of palms. Administrative BNT headquarters.

BNT by-laws
By-laws passed in 1986 govern all land and sea parks and reserves. Some stipulations are:

1. Land and sea parks are designated marine replenishment areas for The Bahamas. Hunting, trapping, netting, capture or removal of any fish, turtle, crawfish, conch or whelk is prohibited.
2. Destruction, injury or removal of any living or dead plant life, beach sand, coral, sea fans or gorgonians is prohibited.
3. Molestation, injury or destruction of any land animal or bird life or the eggs of any animal or bird is prohibited.
4. Permission may be granted for the capture or removal of a designated number of land or sea animals or plants required for valid scientific research.
5. Dumping, burning or discharging of any wastes, oil or rubbish on land or sea is prohibited.
6. No person shall injure, deface or remove any building, structure, sign, ruins or other artefacts.
7. Posting of any sign, placard, advertisement or notice or erecting any structure is prohibited.
8. No person shall display, use, fire, or discharge any explosive, firearm or harpoon gun within the parks, except peace officers or park wardens.
9. Any person charged with an offence against any of these by-laws is liable on summary conviction to a penalty not exceeding $500. Any boat, vessel or aircraft and all equipment, stores, provisions or other effects used for committing an offence may be confiscated.

See also **Bahamas National Trust (BNT).**

WORLD TRADE ORGANIZATION (WTO)

The General Agreement on Tariffs and Trade (GATT) formed the World Trade Organization (WTO) in early 1995 after the Uruguay Round accomplished dramatic dismantling of trade barriers to increase the volume of world trade. The WTO has 146 member countries.

The WTO is the foundation of the multi-lateral trading system and is the only rules-based international organization dealing with the global rules of trade between nations. Decisions are made by consensus and the WTO works to ensure that trade runs smoothly.

On July 17, 2000, The Bahamas was granted "observer status" in the General Council of the WTO. In May 2001, The Bahamas government made a formal request for accession. For more information contact the Ministry of Trade and Industry, tel 328-2700 or visit www.wto.org.

See also **Trade agreements.**

YACHTS

See **Boating** and **Marinas & cruising facilities.**

YWCA

See **Social Services, Non-governmental organizations.**

ZNS

ZNS, the call letters for Radio Bahamas, were assigned in 1936 when the fledgling radio station was recognized and accredited by the American Federal Communications Commission.

The letter Z was assigned to all British stations in the Caribbean and Atlantic islands. The words attached to the call letters are Zephyr (balmy breeze) Nassau Sunshine.

See also **Broadcasting.**

ZOO

See **Nature centres.**

it's just a click away

www.bahamasnet.com

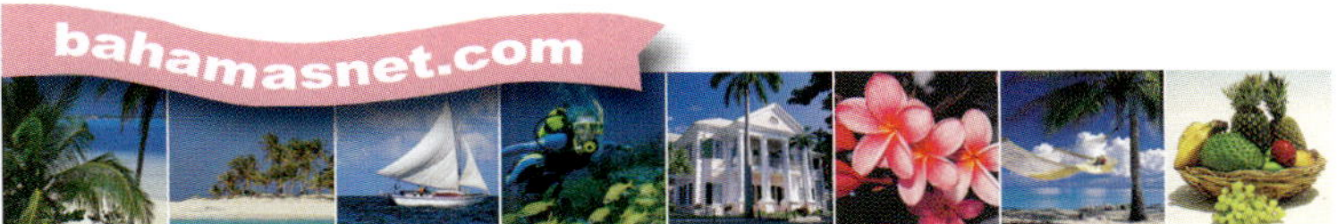

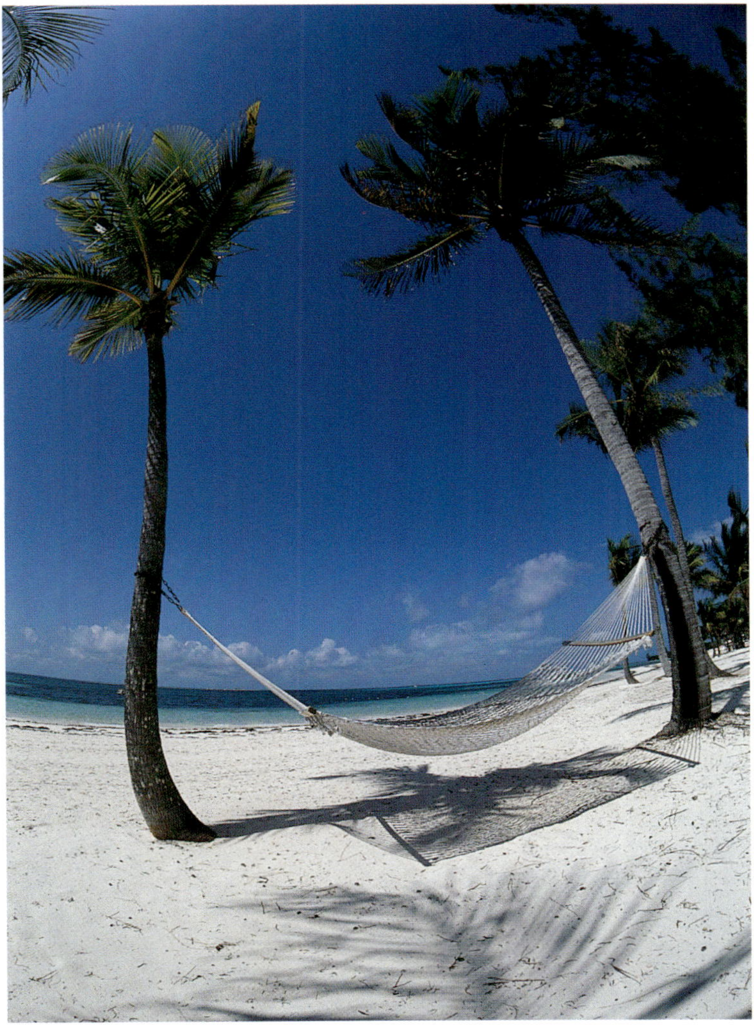

ISLAND PICS/©DUPUCH

Freeport/ Lucaya

Freeport's Doug Silvera

Low-key character with a high-profile life played a major role in the development of Grand Bahama.

BY GORDON LOMER

For a pioneer who has crammed so much useful and exciting activity into his life, Doug Silvera is a surprisingly low-key dynamo. Mind you, he's spent seven and a half decades taking life in stride while making big things happen. He, perhaps more than anyone else, personifies the history of Freeport.

Born in Oracabessa, Jamaica, in October 1928, he grew up in Ocho Rios and attended Cornwall College high school in Montego Bay. He became a fledgling surveyor in 1950, "something like a surveying apprentice but that's not the term," he explains. The following year he was introduced to The Bahamas when he was hired by Consolidated Construction Company, the American firm contracted to build the US missile tracking stations at Gold Rock Creek in Grand Bahama and Governor's Harbour in Eleuthera.

In a speech at an airport seminar, he recalled his initiation to the island on February 14, 1951. "My first visit was a memorable experience. We landed late in the afternoon just before dark, and after spending a couple of hours at Pine Ridge, which was the headquarters for the Abaco Lumber Company, we travelled by Jeep to Gold Rock Creek. It took us four hours then, and we can now make the trip in 30 minutes.

Left, Doug Silvera arrived in Freeport in 1951.

Grand Bahama's airport was once little more than a gravel clearing in the pine forest.

"You have never seen a more miserable ex-Jamaican in your life, for the temperature was 48 degrees and this one had never felt weather colder than 70 degrees. If I thought the weather was my biggest misery, I had not reckoned with travel on the island. Other than a few logging roads and trails, there was absolutely no travel or communication except by plane, boat or foot.

"After spending a miserably cold night in the construction camp, the engineering crew and I started out the next morning in two Abaco dinghies for the settlement of High Rock, approximately seven miles up the coast. A quarter of a mile offshore a sudden gust of wind overturned both boats simultaneously. Everything we owned headed for the bottom except yours truly, who headed for the shore. After the surveying party struggled back to shore, we spent the morning diving in 20 ft of water to recover our luggage and equipment. This was one hell of a way to start life on Grand Bahama. All of my clothing had gotten wet and had shrunk two sizes, including my shoes. I might add here that I only weighed 128 pounds soaking wet, but the grits, grunts and gravy was soon to make this a thing of the past."

A new life begins

Seven months after arriving in The Bahamas Silvera married his fiancée, Patricia Scott, of Montego Bay, at a ceremony in Christ Church Cathedral in Nassau. The couple had three sons, one of whom, Douglas Jr, 51, is a partner with his father in, and runs, the

HARVEY BILT/COURTESY DOUG SILVERA

Awards Presentation, Bahamas 500 winner. From left, Neville Garcia, Bruce Silvera, Darryl Silvera, Doug Silvera Jr, Doug Silvera, Art Waldorf and Carl Kiekhaefer.

COURTESY DOUG SILVERA

Doug Silvera and first granddaughter, Britney Silvera

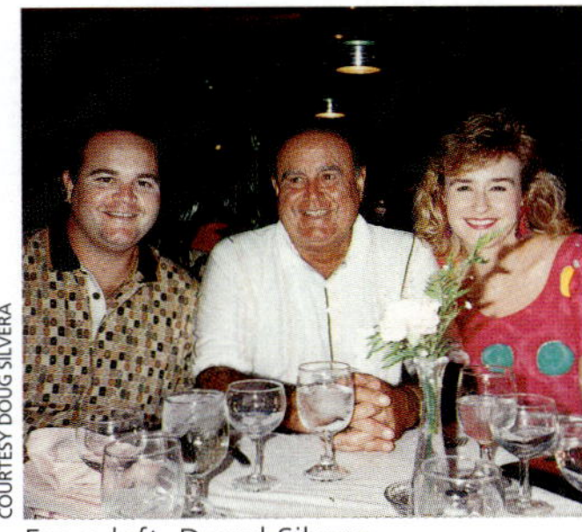
COURTESY DOUG SILVERA

From left, Darryl Silvera, Doug Silvera, Sandye (Darryl's wife)

water sports operation, Reef Tours, at Port Lucaya Marketplace. Bruce, 48, is a mechanical engineering graduate of Tulane University in New Orleans and now runs the day-to-day operation of Freeport Construction with his father. He is also a partner in Marlin Design-Build, custom home contractors in Freeport. The youngest, Darryl Jan, 42, lives and practices law in Dallas, TX. Patricia died in October 2002, after a series of strokes and heart problems.

As the site engineer for Consolidated, Silvera supervised the construction of the airstrip at Gold Rock and the roads from the tracking station to Pelican Point. When Pan-Am Airways took over the operation of the base at Governor's Harbour in Eleuthera, he moved there and recalls building a house for Pan-Am vice president Frank Gledhill. "Those were good times in Eleuthera. I used to go coot hunting with Frank, author

BORCO...the largest oil terminal in the Caribbean
BORCO has 15 million barrels of storage capacity for both crude oil and products. The facility has 73 tanks and six deep-sea berths capable of handling vessels from barges to ULCCs, and can efficiently blend, store, and transship hydrocarbons. The terminal boasts excellent infrastructure, premier geographical location, and a highly professional human resource base.
BORCO...Your Best Dock Stop!!
3005
3006
8035
8033
BORCO
BAHAMAS OIL REFINING
INTERNATIONAL COMPANY LTD.
(242) 352-9811
Fax.: (242) 352-4029
P.O. Box F-42435, Freeport, Grand Bahama
BAHAMAS

BAHAMAS NEWS BUREAU

The Abaco Lumber Company was based at Pine Ridge, Grand Bahama, the centre of activity for the development of Freeport.

Kjeld Helweg-Larsen and Capt Bob Fatt, senior pilot with Pan-Am. I was there from 1953 to 1955, and then went back to Jamaica."

He served as senior mine engineer for Kaiser Bauxite, building roads for the company's three mines. Bauxite is a clay-like rock from which aluminum is made. "That was the best bauxite in the world. We used to blend the bauxite from the three mines and ship it all over the world."

Among the first in Freeport

In the spring of 1956, Silvera had a call from an old Consolidated colleague, Dave Tuck, manager of the Abaco Lumber Company based at Pine Ridge, Grand Bahama. He spoke of the upsurge in building activity as the development of Freeport was being planned, and asked Silvera to come up and be part of it.

Barry Malcolm, longtime friend and now executive director of the Grand Bahama Port Authority (GBPA), wrote in a 1973 edition of *The Bahamian Review:* "He had been to the island before; he knew the people and he knew the operations. Resigning his post at the bauxite mines, he joined the new community as superintendent of construction on June 2, 1956.

"The position placed him squarely at the centre of activity in the development of the young town. Looking back at what really took place, he [Silvera] marvels 'When we started, we operated out of the logging area then known as Pine Ridge. You knew you were involved in

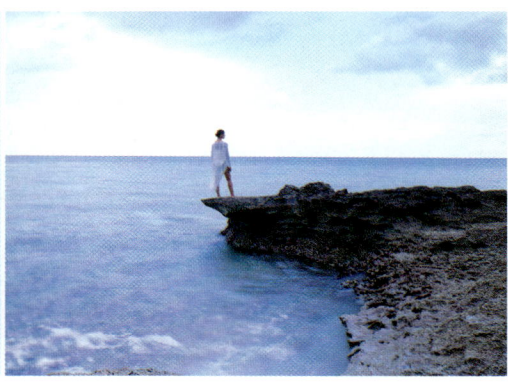

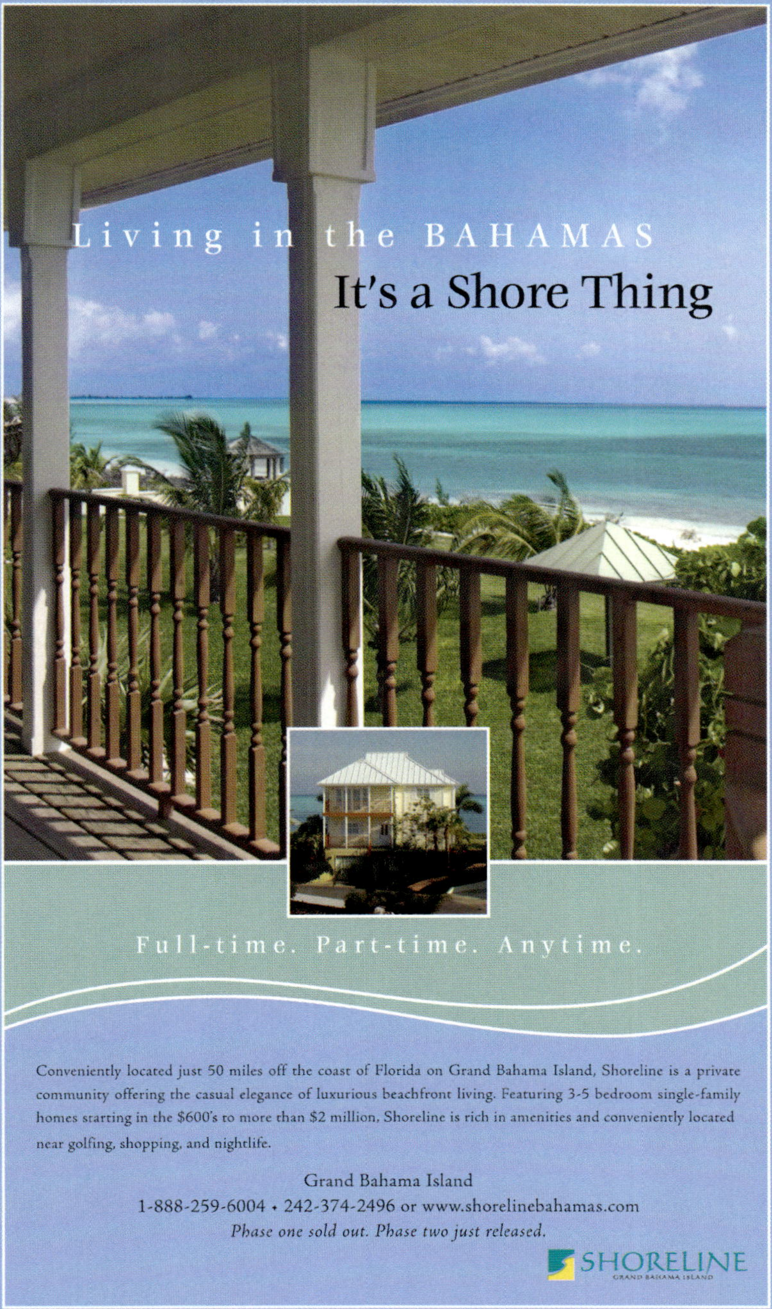
Living in the BAHAMAS
It's a Shore Thing
Full-time. Part-time. Anytime.
Conveniently located just 50 miles off the coast of Florida on Grand Bahama Island, Shoreline is a private community offering the casual elegance of luxurious beachfront living. Featuring 3-5 bedroom single-family homes starting in the $600's to more than $2 million, Shoreline is rich in amenities and conveniently located near golfing, shopping, and nightlife.
Grand Bahama Island
1-888-259-6004 • 242-374-2496 or www.shorelinebahamas.com
Phase one sold out. Phase two just released.
SHORELINE
GRAND BAHAMA ISLAND

"...only Mr [Wallace] Groves had the foresight to see where it was all heading."

COURTESY DOUG SILVERA

Silvera's first home at Gold Rock Creek, 1951

something big, but you didn't really know where it was going. I think only Mr [Wallace] Groves had the foresight to see where it was all heading. As a relatively junior man at the time, I was involved in the day-to-day creation, but not necessarily in the conception.'"

The day-to-day operations included the construction of the first administration building, erecting temporary housing, excavating the harbour, building the first hotel/motel, the Caravel Inn, and the first hospital.

Silvera remembers with precision the first dozen residents of Freeport. "Most of them were surveyors from British Guyana. Ken Yap (who was here with his wife and mother) was in charge of the crew, which included Patrick Yip, Gerry Cheong and Edmond Cheong, Maurice Woon, Stanley Low, myself and my wife. My brother Roy came up from Jamaica to handle equipment maintenance. The commissary was run by Buddy Bush of West Palm Beach, and we all lived in 24 by 24-ft, two bedroom shacks."

Buddy Bush also remembers his stay in Freeport with affection.

COURTESY DOUG SILVERA

One of the first permanent buildings constructed in town, the "Previous" building is now occupied by the Grand Bahama Power Co.

Freeport Oil Company Limited

"Fuelling Growth for People"

Supplying Grand Bahama's petroleum needs since 1967 with:

Gasoline	**Diesel**	**Lubricants**
Propane	**Kerosene**	**Solvents**

Bulk products available at our Queen's Highway office, harbour area.

Retail service station outlets:
Airport Rd • Allied • East Mall • East Sunrise Hwy & East Atlantic Dr
Hawksbill • Queen's Hwy & Yellow Pine St

Freeport Oil Co Ltd
PO Box F-42458
Freeport, Bahamas
Tel (242) 352-8131
Fax (242) 352-2986

COURTESY GRAND BAHAMA PORT AUTHORITY

Before the development of Freeport, Grand Bahama exported lumber to coal mining countries.

Now 75, and living in West Palm Beach, he recalls Silvera building for him what turned out to be the last wooden house constructed with local pine. "They were very good to me. I was single then, and young, and when Wallace Groves was expounding on ideas about building a city I had no idea what he was talking about."

Chief engineer with the GBPA at the time (1955-60) was Jan Porel, who Silvera describes as "a brilliant engineer. He designed the first missile, and the first 15 floors of the Empire State Building. He was an adopted son of J P Morgan, a great teacher and one of the finest people I ever met. His help and effect on me were profound." The relationship must have been mutual. As Bush describes it, "Doug was Jan Porel's right and left arm. Doug Silvera contributed more to the development of Freeport than anyone, dead or alive."

In June 1956 Silvera joined the Port Authority as general superintendent of construction. The same year he bought a Luscombe, single-engine, 65 hp, two-seater, all-metal airplane.

"We only had roads to land on and take off from, until we built a strip where the airport is now. I lived on Settlers Way and used to land on the road in front of my house. I kept the plane in the yard, and I used to fly in Santa Claus every Christmas. By 1957 there were 10 cars on the roads and they forced us off the roads because some stubborn drivers refused to yield the right of way.

"So we built a little 500-ft airstrip, then expanded it to 800 ft and to 1,200 and then 2,000 ft. We flew in a ton of dynamite a day. Then Groves extended it to 5,000 ft and Bahamas Airways started flying

DC3s in and DEVCO (the Grand Bahama Development Company) started flying Viscounts in with casino patrons. Soon it was extended to 8,000 ft and in 1965 we built the major 11,000-ft runway."

Rapid development continues

By 1961 Groves had negotiated a deal with US Steel to build a cement plant. The contractor was Perini Brothers. "One of them was Lou Perini, owner of the Milwaukee Braves at the time, and I still have a baseball signed by all the players, but I don't think it was the 1957 World Series winning team," says Silvera.

Silvera recalls the burgeoning development of the early 1960s with the opening of the Lucayan Beach Hotel, the International Bazaar and El Casino, all built by the GBPA. He became vice president of the GBPA in charge of programming and planning, which was the technical arm of the Port Authority.

"We built the Oceanus South, which later became the Atlantik Beach Hotel and then was imploded a few years ago to make room for Breakers and the casino. We also built Oceanus North, where the Pelican Bay Hotel now stands," recalls Silvera. "Around the same time, Jack Hayward built the tallest building on the island and Ludwig built the Xanadu. Barclays Bank, the Royal Bank of Canada, Scotiabank and CIBC all sprung up through those years.

In the early 1960s the Port Authority, with US partners, formed Freeport Construction Company to meet the growing construction demands on the island. Silvera was named vice-president and general manager, representing the interests of the Port Authority. "Freeport Construction was a separate company owned by the Port Authority. It was a bonded company, and we were number 11. Now there are up to 5,000 bonded licensees."

ETIENNE DUPUCH JR/©DUPUCH

Wallace Groves, left, and Sir Charles Hayward

Silvera remained with the new company until 1964 and moved back to the Port Authority, serving as vice-president of most of its major

ERNIE'S STUDIO

The development of Freeport spawned massive construction projects.

companies, including Freeport Industrial, Freeport Power, Freeport Telephone, Grand Bahama Airport and Freeport Harbour. He retired from the Port Authority in 1974 when the Haywards bought out Wallace Groves. "Jack Hayward was a truly loveable person, a man of his word," says Silvera.

"That year I had a call from Larry B Isette, owner of LBI Ltd. We had worked together digging the cross-island waterways, building Harbour House and Harbour House II and Cove House. We were invited to bid on a 100-mile section of road to be built in Saudi Arabia for a Saudi prince. We estimated we could do it for $20 million. So we said 'Let's bid $50 million,' and they gave us the job. Money didn't mean anything to those people.

A change of scenery

"We built a plant about 15 miles from the Iraq border. We rented 50 Mercedes dump trucks, and were paying $10,000 a month for a four-bedroom house. The first month our materials came in regularly, every week. Then every second week and then only once a month. They were selling our materials to the French and the Germans, after we had paid for them. We built 50 miles of the road and then ran out of materials. That is one strange part of the world. I spent only a year there, one month at a time. One month there and one month back here in Freeport. It was the biggest and probably strangest experience of my life. I'd never been exposed to anything like that. It's so entirely different from anything in The Bahamas."

After Saudi Arabia, Silvera returned to Grand Bahama, bought

COURTESY DOUG SILVERA

Silvera at the controls in his first race in *Quicksilver*.

Freeport Construction and continued to work for the Port Authority. "I thought I would last about five years, and here it is nearly 30 years later and I'm still at it. Next year [2005] is the 50th anniversary of Freeport. It's wonderful to see how something like this started and experience its development first hand. It's a shame the youngsters today don't know the history of Freeport."

New interests in precision and speed

Through all the foregoing and the hectic development of Freeport and Lucaya, Silvera still found time to take up golf in 1963 at West End. "The best advice I got early on, from [Canadian pro] Stan Leonard. I broke six clubs in one round, and Stan told me 'You've got to forget the bad shots.'" He did, improved his game down to a six handicap and won the club championship at the Lucayan Country Club.

Silvera also dabbled in car racing, with professional starts at Sebring in 1968 and in the Daytona 24-hour race in 1969. "I didn't finish either race. In the last one, two cars passed me, one on either side. They couldn't see each other and came together right in front of me and crashed. I pulled over and got out of my car. My legs were shaking so badly. That night I talked to my wife and we both decided to end my race car driving career"

But the competitive urge remained. In the late 1960s Capt Sherman "Red" Crise was promoting powerboat racing in Florida and The Bahamas. He came up with the idea of a Bahamas 500 – a

If I have attained a measure of success, it is because I've received the help of some wonderful people.

500-mile race through Bahamian islands. The first 500, in 1967, started and ended in Freeport and was co-sponsored by the Port Authority and the Ministry of Tourism. It was won by legendary powerboat designer and racer, Don Aronow. Local races were staged in conjunction with the offshore race and Silvera got his start in these smaller races.

"Then Red Crise was bugging me to get into offshore racing and by 1970, when the 4th annual Bahamas 500 came along, it was established as one of the world's toughest offshore races. I decided to give it a try. I had this 32-ft Bertram, called *Quicksilver,* and I put four 140-hp Mercury outboards on the stern," Silvera explains. "I won that race for two reasons. I decided to skip the busy refuelling stop in Nassau and try to run on to Governor's Harbour where I had arranged a fuel stop. That saved me a lot of time, and then the weather was pretty rough and all the big boys broke down. My co-driver was my nephew, Neville Garcia, who came along at the last minute." Silvera completed the race in 10 hours and 14 minutes.

The following year, driving a 36-ft Cigarette, *Starduster,* with twin 700-hp Mercruiser sterndrives, Silvera won again in the record time of 7 hours and 29 minutes, averaging 71.22 miles per hour over the 525-mile course. He eclipsed Don Aronow's time of 8 hours and 24 minutes set in 1969. In 1972 the race was run out of Nassau and Silvera decided to opt out. "I started to run out of money," he explains, "and I didn't have a sponsor. In those days it cost about $100,000 a year to campaign in offshore racing."

Looking back over the era he allows "I learned to drive pretty well. We developed a few things that helped racing, among them a cooling system for sterndrives. The horsepower came up too quickly for sterndrives and we had to figure out a way to keep them from overheating. But the main reason I enjoyed powerboat racing was not in winning races, but because it is one of the few sports where there is a minimum of animosity among competitors. The driving is done with respect and in good spirit. This captivates me."

As Silvera told Barry Malcolm in the 1973 interview: "If I have attained a measure of success, it is because I've received the help of some wonderful people. To make it in life, you have to be given a chance. I got that chance, and I am grateful for it. Beyond that, I've been lucky."

Orlando
West Palm Beach
Ft. Lauderdale
Florida
Grand Bahama
Miami
Abaco
Nassau
New Providence
Eleuthera
Andros
Cat Island
San Salvador
Great Exuma
Long Island
Crooked Island
Long Cay
Mayaguana
Acklins
TURKS & CAICOS ISLANDS
Caicos Islands
Little Inagua
Turk Islands
Great Inagua
Nobody knows the Bahamas, like Bahamasair.
THE ISLANDS OF THE BAHAMAS

COURTESY LADY HENRIETTA ST GEORGE

Lady Henrietta St George

One extraordinary woman has helped to bring happiness to hundreds of needy children.

BY SUZANNE TWISTON-DAVIES

A boy wrote in *The Village Voice,* a quarterly magazine put out by the residents of The Village: "I wanted to spend Christmas with my father and sister, for Christmas to be the best day I ever had. Every Christmas I never get what I want. Sometimes I think my mother forgot about us – I just want her to show me some LOVE!"

This sentiment is typical of many neglected children in The Village, a group of buildings in downtown Freeport used to house and educate disadvantaged youngsters. And this is what Lady Henrietta St George is doing her best to combat. She is a "hands-on" lady, for whom no job is too difficult if it concerns the welfare of children. She has been proving this ever since she came to Freeport in 1980 after her marriage to Edward St George, Executive Chairman of the Grand Bahama Port Authority (GBPA).

Born into a life of privilege as a daughter of the 11th Duke of Grafton, of Thetford, Norfolk, in England, Lady Henrietta was raised with the precept that "we all owed a debt to society, and that work would be our watchword."

Left, Lady Henrietta and son, Henry

COURTESY LADY HENRIETTA ST GEORGE

From left, stepdaughter Caroline, son Henry, husband Edward, daughter Katie, stepdaughter Sarah and Lady Henrietta St George

Lady Henrietta's mother was a nurse during the Second World War, and is now a trustee of the Hospital for Sick Children in Great Ormond Street, London. Lady Henrietta's father spent his working life preserving and saving towns, cathedrals, churches and buildings.

An aristocrat, and married to a rich man, Lady Henrietta could have done nothing but run her home and bring up her children. Instead she has for 25 years given help and hope to more than 1,500 underprivileged children.

The first commitment

Lady Henrietta's cause began to take shape when she was asked to take over a child-care committee which, with minimal funding, was helping children in need. It consisted of just one lady in a small apartment, looking after two needy children. Lady Henrietta asked her husband for help, and he gave her a building on Jobson Avenue.

"I never dreamed when we gave her an old motel in downtown Freeport that, 25 years later, she would be running an entire village for the underprivileged!" says St George. "I have never met a woman more determined in my life. When she wants something done it has to be now, and it has to get finished. I think the work she

COURTESY LADY HENRIETTA ST GEORGE

There were lots of smiling faces at the opening of the new Grand Bahama Children's Home in November 2001.

does here complements all I have tried to do for 30 years, and I hope… I have supported her in all her projects. She considers that the Bahamian children she looks after are part of her extended family; no needy child is ever turned away."

Anglican Archdeacon Keith Cartwright, who has worked frequently with Lady Henrietta, adds: "I have never met someone with such a passion for children. She gives, gives and gives; her heart is overflowing with love. If there is one word used to describe Lady Henrietta, that word is 'extraordinary.'"

The Grand Bahama Children's Home, opened in 1980, at first housed 20 children, then grew as more cases were found. Patrice Panther, known as "Peaches," was one of the first residents, her mother having died when she was six.

"I love Lady Henrietta to death! Without her, I don't know what would have become of me," says Peaches, who attended Grand Bahama Catholic High School (her fees paid by the St Georges, who later helped her get a job at the Grand Bahama Development Company). She became a secretary and is now married.

The project grows

Soon the Children's Home was filled to capacity with nearly 60 children. In 1989, Harmony House was created to house teenage girls who were unable to remain with their families. The Salvation

Lady Henrietta always helps anyone in need, whether it is for their spectacles, the dentist or buying their clothes.

Army provided advice and practical help. In 1992 Columbus House for Teens was started, and has now grown to comprise three homes for boys and two for girls.

The caregivers in these homes are devoted to their charges and there is genuine delight on the faces of the children when they see their benefactor. They throw their arms around Lady Henrietta and show her their recent drawings, or thank her for the special things she does, such as the Easter party she threw at her home in April 2004. One teenager who gives her a hug is almost blind. The St Georges have done much to help her, including taking her to an eye specialist in the US.

One of the first boys in Columbus House was Clifton Francis. "I was a disadvantaged child. I hadn't had a home since I was four, so the place was my home from beginning to end. I was very happy and stayed until I was 17, and then went to the Halfway House (for teenagers who graduate from care)," said Francis. "I had foster-parents, Paulette Russell and her parents, who were so kind to me and took me home on every possible occasion – Easter, Christmas – any time. As to Lady Henrietta, she is a gem! She and Mr St George paid for my college. I was at St Paul's, and won a GBPA scholarship. Lady Henrietta always helps anyone in need, whether it is for their spectacles, the dentist or buying their clothes. Nothing is too much trouble… Now I do evening classes at The College of The Bahamas. I work as a teller at FINCO during the day, but soon I will

COURTESY LADY HENRIETTA ST GEORGE

Lady Henrietta St George with parents, The Duke and Duchess of Grafton, at her 50th birthday

...no child wakes up from a nightmare to find there is no shoulder to cry on.

have my Bachelor of Education degree, and will teach all subjects at primary level. I now go to help out at the Children's Home because I remember what it was like not to have a special friend, and I play games with the kids and help them where I can."

This theme was repeated by Member of Parliament Pleasant Bridgewater at a recent luncheon at the Children's Home, attended by the prime minister and many other dignitaries: "Clothing, food, staff, transportation, education, counselling, entertainment, worship and even job placement are provided. Nothing is left undone in her commitment to our children."

Italia, one of the girls at the Halfway House, was about to leave. "I want to stay," she confides sadly. "This has been my home for a long time." And homes they genuinely are, due to Lady Henrietta. Supervisor Mabel Gibson who has cared for the children for 23 years, says "I can't explain what a mother she is to the children and to the staff, including me, and I am older than she is! She treats us like human beings. I pray that God will give both the St Georges long life. The money they spend on these children is unbelievable."

A gift of love

This group of homes, in pastel colours and in peaceful surroundings, is now called "The Village." There is round-the-clock supervision, and no child wakes up from a nightmare to find there is no shoulder to cry on.

"Henrietta really is a wonderful person," says her friend of 30 years, Nadine Bonsor. "She is a knowing, thinking, giving woman with sensitivity and intelligence. She has discipline and strong religious faith, which is a great prop and source of strength to her. She always has a knack to see what is wrong anywhere. Once we were showing her baby pheasants on our farm in England, and out of the hundreds we looked at, it was she who noticed that one of the birds had a broken leg."

It is this gift for seeing people with the equivalent of a broken leg that has led Lady Henrietta into helping pregnant teenagers. PACE (Providing Access to Continued Education) is a centre for these girls. They are helped through their pregnancies with loving

It is interesting to note that Lady Henrietta's great-great-grandfather founded the original YMCA.

care, and there is an on-site clinic with doctor and nurse, and a nursery for when the babies are born. The Haven is part of the centre that allows them to continue their education and to learn skills such as hairdressing, cooking and sewing. This is a joint venture with the Department of Social Services and the ministries of health and education. Grace House houses four teenage mothers and their babies.

Another building is Genesis Academy, a school for troubled students. It now has a computer centre, donated by the Canadian Rotary Club and the Rotary Club of Freeport.

Lady Henrietta, along with the YMCA, started the Phoenix Project. (It is interesting to note that Lady Henrietta's great-great-grandfather founded the original YMCA.) Partly subsidized by St John's Jubilee Cathedral and Christ the King Anglican Church, the

COURTESY LADY HENRIETTA ST GEORGE

Lady Henrietta and family running along one of Grand Bahama's beaches. From back left, Edward, Lady Henrietta, Henry and Katie

call the

Authority

"25 years ago, I would never have thought I was capable of achieving all these things."

Project provides short-term accommodation, food, job skills, education, training, employment opportunities and spiritual support for young men and women aged 18 to 25 who have gone astray. The Department of Rehabilitative Welfare Services monitors the progress of the participants.

Educational projects

Lady Henrietta spreads her interest widely among the children of Grand Bahama. In 1988, she opened the Discovery Nursery School to provide first-class education for the very young. Proving a great success, this eventually became the Discovery Primary School, opening in 1991 with 140 children. The school was handed over to the Anglican Education Authority in 1993.

These successes are stunning to Lady Henrietta, who says, "25 years ago, I would never have thought I was capable of achieving all these things." Her husband says that living in The Bahamas has enabled her to use her talents far more than she could have done in England. She has also been helped by the Committee of Bahamian Ladies, which was formed in 1980, and continues to this day, plus the government and a team of supervisors, caregivers, house parents, social workers and her "right-hand lady," Geneva Rutherford, former principal of Mary Star of the Sea Catholic School.

Lady Henrietta has also developed an interest in an establishment that was first known as the Catherine Basie School for Exceptional Children. The musician Count Basie lived on Grand Bahama, and he and his wife started this school because their daughter Diana was disabled.

"She [Diana] never attended the school," says Paul Francis, now a prominent broadcaster on radio station Cool 96, who cared for Diana for a long time, "but the parents felt deeply for children with the same predicament. After they died, a concert featuring Ella Fitzgerald and Sarah Vaughan was given on March 11th, 1987, at the Princess Country Club, the proceeds going to the school." But funds ran out, and as the mentally and physically challenged children still had to be cared for, a new building was built across the

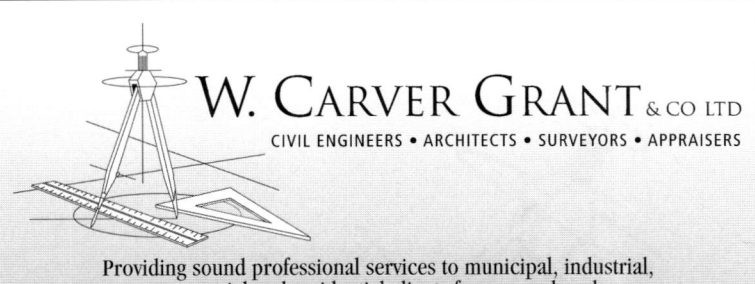

"They must groan every time I go near them, usually for more money."

road, and named the Beacon School. It is supported by the government and cares for 97 children. Lady Henrietta is the patron, as she also is of PACE.

Finding the funding

The costs to run The Village are substantial. The community comprises nine residential houses, two schools and Agape House, a foster home that was opened in 1991. The GBPA gives Lady Henrietta an upkeep budget of $100,000 a year. She finds ways to fund the extras, such as medical fees, additional clothing and upkeep of buildings.

The government helps. "They must groan every time I go near them, usually for more money," she says, "and I work hand-in-hand with them. They pay for Genesis and PACE, and the running of the Columbus Houses. I try not to pay salaries or we really would go broke. But the children must of course have presents as though they belonged to a normal family."

Family is important to Lady Henrietta. "She was marvellous to me when I was a child," says her younger sister, Lady Rose Monson, "and she used to have me to stay in her London flat, which was very exciting. Trained as a kindergarten teacher, she taught in various

COURTESY LADY HENRIETTA ST GEORGE

Discovery Primary School, spring term, 1992

"Your heart is in the right place, and your kindness lifts spirits and makes smiles appear."

schools in England, and managed a play group in a London children's hospital. She then started training as a children's nurse, but this was overtaken by extensive travels in the Far East, followed by her work for a leading children's charity, the 'Save the Children Fund.'" Lady Henrietta's other sister, Lady Virginia Fitzroy, also remembers her generosity. " She had a lovely orange car when she was younger, and used to take terminally ill children out in it from hospital, which must have cheered them up."

When Lady Henrietta is not busy helping people, she finds time to return to England. She loves gardening at her home there and riding her horse around her father's land. When her father was seriously ill for two years, Lady Henrietta spent a lot of time at his bedside. She also loves to spend time with her husband and their two children, Henry and Katie, who are in their early 20s. Katie is already taking a great interest in the children of The Home.

A lasting legacy

A recent letter to *The Freeport News* from the assistant administrator at The Village, Betty Bain, thanks Lady Henrietta on behalf of her staff: "Your heart is in the right place, and your kindness lifts spirits and makes smiles appear." Since 1984 Lady Henrietta has received many Bahamian awards, and was named Citizen of the Year by the Lions Club in 1986.

Lady Henrietta has done an enormous amount for the children of Grand Bahama. Her main wish is that they will never look back and think of themselves as "poor little unloved orphans," or as children from broken homes. Her aim is to stop children falling through the cracks in society, and to make them into useful, contributing adults.

On November 5th, 2003, Lady Henrietta organized a candlelight vigil in memory of five Grand Bahama boys who had been murdered. This was sponsored by the GBPA and Edward St George. Deputy Prime Minister Cynthia "Mother" Pratt, who came over from Nassau for the occasion, remarked, "When God placed Edward St George and Lady Henrietta among us, it was no accident." It certainly has been fortunate for the children of Grand Bahama.

COURTESY ISLE OF CAPRI CASINO

Isle of Capri Casino to help the economy

Delays and disappointment plagued the start, but new numbers spark optimism.

BY GORDON LOMER

When Our Lucaya resort opened in December 2002 merchants and business owners in Freeport and Lucaya breathed a great sigh of relief. The long wait was over and the economy of the island would swing upwards, or so they hoped. It didn't swing, but it did start to creep up. Then merchants and business people waited for the new casino to come on line.

Plagued by delays caused by shifting priorities and a shuffle of potential casino operators, the Isle of Capri Casino opened in December 2003. With plenty of elbow room, the 19,000-sq-ft gaming floor houses 21 table games, including blackjack, Caribbean stud poker, craps, mini-baccarat, American and European roulette and three-card stud. There are also 400 state-of-the-art slot machines, with a vast array of video poker and five-cent video reels. A racing sports book was added in the fall.

For high rollers, the exclusive "Jewel of the Isle" room offers high-limit table games including blackjack, roulette and baccarat. High-limit slot machines handle wagers from $5 to $100. Pai Gow cards are also available. A sitting room for high rollers is serviced by a private kitchen, private bathrooms and plasma television sets.

Left, Bernard Goldstein, chairman and chief executive officer of Isle of Capri Casinos

Isle of Capri owns and operates 18 riverboat, dockside and land-based casinos at 16 locations in five states in the US.

COURTESY ISLE OF CAPRI CASINOS

Isle of Capri Casino at Our Lucaya is one of two casinos outside the US owned and operated by Isle of Capri.

Off the casino is The Cove, an upscale 110-seat restaurant open from 10am to closing. It offers a varied menu, Sunday brunch, live music Friday and Saturday nights and is developing a sophisticated wine list to complement the house wines.

A wealth of international experience

Isle of Capri owns and operates 18 riverboat, dockside and land-based casinos at 16 locations in five states in the US. Casinos include those in Biloxi, where the company's head office is located, Vicksburg, Lula and Natchez, MS; Bossier City and Lake Charles, LA; Black Hawk and Cripple Creek, CO; Bettendorf, Davenport and Marquette, IA; and Kansas City and Boonville, MO. International operations include casinos at Dudley, England, and now Grand Bahama. The company also operates Pompano Park Harness Racing Track in Pompano Beach, FL.

"Our Lucaya offers an exciting fit to the company's tropical branding efforts."

COURTESY ISLE OF CAPRI CASINOS

Timothy Hinkley, president and COO of Isle of Capri Casinos

On opening night, Bernard Goldstein, chairman and chief executive officer of Isle of Capri Casinos, explained: "Following our completion of the Isle of Capri venture into the UK, the Our Lucaya casino furthers the company's presence on an international scale."

Timothy Hinkley, president and chief operating officer, added: "This casino will bring greater opportunities to Isle players through more IsleOne deferred-reward programme benefits with travel to The Bahamas."

The company chose an ideal location for their newest casino. The Westin and Sheraton at Our Lucaya, operated by Starwood Hotels & Resorts Worldwide Inc, includes 14 food and beverage outlets, conference centre, four tennis courts, four oceanside swimming pools, spa and fitness centre, two 18-hole golf courses and the Butch Harmon School of Golf. Restaurants and lounges include Churchill's Chop House, Churchill's Bar, Portobellos, Iries, Lighthouse Pointe Bar, China Grill, Willie Broadleaf plus the cigar-friendly Havana Cay Cigar Bar off the lobby of Manor House.

A slow start

Goldstein, in his operational review of the quarter, observed that "our international operations account for a small percentage of our overall revenues. We are, however, excited about the growth opportunities in the United Kingdom. We believe we are in a strong position to take advantage of the possible liberalization of gaming in the United Kingdom."

First quarter financial results, ending July 25, 2004, showed Isle of Capri Casinos, which is listed on Nasdaq, with a net income of $10.6 million, compared to $13.6 million for the same period in

COURTESY ISLE OF CAPRI CASINOS

Isle of Capri appeals to everyone from serious gamblers to slot machine players.

2003. During the quarter the company had net revenues of $280.9 million, compared to $285.8 million the previous year.

"The ramp-up of this property has been slower than we expected. We continue to focus efforts to better utilize the marketing potential of this property."

Added Hinkley: "We realize the value of a strong marketing effort and we have long used these tools to maximize the growth of our company. This quarter we introduced an aggressive promotions plan, which is starting to turn positive results for the company. We also remain focused on our expansion plan, allowing us to improve our existing product while continuing to provide a consistent and fun experience for our customers."

Aggressive promotional plan

Isle of Capri operates throughout its system the IsleOne Club, whereby players can earn points redeemable for cash, prizes or trips to Grand Bahama. "It's a slot players club," explains London-born Eddie Llambias, manager of the Isle of Capri Casino at Our Lucaya. "Players have cards and they can earn 'isle miles' in any of our casinos. The points or isle miles are then tabulated and we keep track of them. It's a great incentive for players, for instance, in Iowa, to earn a trip to Grand Bahama. They can also cash their points in

COURTESY ISLE OF CAPRI CASINOS

The gaming floor has 21 table games and 400 state-of-the-art slot machines.

on such things as watches or briefcases and that sort of thing. Or they can save their miles up and, depending on the amount, get a trip that includes just the airfare, or one with the full treatment, which would include a luxury suite, meals and the whole ball of wax, so to speak.

"The primary purpose of our being here is to offer the opportunity to reward our loyal customers throughout the United States with a true island destination. It's designed for our high-end regional customers and operates with tiered rewards, depending on the number of miles earned. We feel it is a very powerful impact and helps loyalize (sic) our customers."

Llambias says the casino has been averaging about 2,000 visitors a day in the first quarter. "That's averaging out over seven days. We're pretty happy about the attendance. We've exceeded what we expected to be our market share. The hotel has improved its occupancy, and we're certainly optimistic about the upcoming season." He estimates the casino has contributed up to 14 per cent of the hotel's occupancy.

No stranger to Grand Bahama, Llambias, 40, started out in the casino business in 1983 as a teenager in London. He worked in the mid-1980s as a croupier at the Princess Casino in Freeport. He joined the management team at the International Casino Club in

"The Isle of Capri casino is a long-awaited and welcome new facet of Grand Bahama Island's tourism product."

Gibraltar in 1988 and later moved on to the casinos of the Norwegian Cruise Line.

From 1992 to 2000 he held various positions including casino manager and director of hotel operations with Harrahs Entertainment in Las Vegas, Louisiana, Mississippi and North Carolina. He joined Isle of Capri in 2000 in Bossier City, LA, as senior director of operations, overseeing the hotel, casino, marina, food and beverage and retail operations.

He returned to Grand Bahama in 2003 as vice-president and general manager of the casino, which he describes as an "excellent product. It was well planned, well-built, great architecture and they made extremely good use of wood and marble. It's like a museum with a great feeling and easy upkeep."

Most casino operations stand alone, but Isle of Capri is "part of a macro experience," says Llambias. "Our driving purpose is to provide an amenity to our loyal customers."

Support from government

Minister of Tourism Obie Wilchcombe is excited about the new operation and has earned high respect and admiration from Isle of Capri officials for his ministry's cooperation. "The Minister of Tourism and the people at the Gaming Board have been great to work with and have been very supportive," says Llambias.

COURTESY OBIE WILCHCOMBE

Obie Wilchcombe, Minister of Tourism

The minister's enthusiasm and optimism are triggered in part because the casino employs more than 300 people directly, and the spin-off in economic fortune is showing positive signs.

"The Isle of Capri Casino is a long-awaited and welcome new facet of Grand Bahama Island's tourism product," said Wilchcombe.

"The Bahamas has always relied heavily on the south Florida area for business and, given the ease of access

"The Ministry of Tourism is positioning Grand Bahama Island as an active events-oriented destination."

COURTESY ISLE OF CAPRI CASINOS

A strong marketing campaign is expected to ensure the casino's success.

by air and sea, the casino is playing a major role in Grand Bahama's resurgence as a major offshore recreational destination for that market.

"The Ministry of Tourism is positioning Grand Bahama Island as an active events-oriented destination. While events involve and benefit the entire Grand Bahama community, the Lucaya area, with its concentration of new hotel properties and sophisticated nighttime activities, has been particularly well poised for success. The casino has played a central role in this development.

"The evidence that the formula is working is already in: This year has been a phenomenally successful one for Grand Bahama Island. Arrivals have been up by double digits in months we expected to be flat," said Wilchcombe.

Economic advantages

"We intend to continue on this path and I commend Bernard Goldstein, Isle of Capri's chairman and chief executive officer, for having the foresight to recognize the potential."

The casino is credited with contributing between 15 and 20 per cent to the "newfound spurt" in the economy, according to veteran realtor Lanelle Phillips, district manager for H G Christie Ltd real estate in Grand Bahama. "It is definitely one of the factors driving the economy and sending real estate prices up. We're seeing an entire upward shift in the economy. Canalfront properties in one block at Fortune Bay jumped 50 per cent in four weeks. It created

"I am pleased to see also the added airlift to Grand Bahama from the eastern seaboard, and I hope it will ensure profitability of the casino."

a sort of buying frenzy when these properties went on the market. I can't say the casino had anything to do with that, but it is certainly a factor in the economy."

Neko Grant, businessman and Member of the House of Assembly for the Lucaya constituency of Grand Bahama, sees the casino "automatically improving the economy" with the employment of several hundred people. "I am pleased to see also the added airlift to Grand Bahama from the eastern seaboard, and I hope it will ensure profitability of the casino. I am delighted for the island. It serves as an added attraction, but more importantly, it creates employment."

Not everyone is as enthusiastic. "The Isle of Capri has not had a great effect on the Colombian Emeralds International market," says Kimberley Miller, promotions manager and public relations spokesperson for CEI. "Nevertheless we do plan to open a CEI store on the corner of Retail Street. Hopefully we can catch the business on the actual Our Lucaya property since they are not walking across the street. This will increase our numbers to five CEI stores on the island of Grand Bahama. We are disappointed about the lack of

COURTESY ISLE OF CAPRI CASINOS

Hundreds of slot machines and a vast array of video poker games appeal to low-risk gamblers.

Isle of Capri brings a brand of service and expertise that we need on the island.

COURTESY ISLE OF CAPRI CASINOS

High rollers get special treatment.

traffic but are hopeful that this is just a very slow start and not a reflection of the continued business."

Casino manager Llambias agrees that things were pretty slow at the start. "May to July were slow but satisfactory. August to September is usually pretty slow. It's the hurricane season and it's hot. We expected a slow start, but we're very satisfied with the way things are going We anticipated initial losses, which turned out to be \$1.382 million. We budgeted heavy start-up costs, marketing expenses, setting up airlift routes and working with junket representatives. That's all part of doing business," he says. "But our market share is growing and we've created an awareness. That's important. We have accomplished exactly what we set out to do."

Barry Malcolm, executive director of the Grand Bahama Port Authority feels the casino is "a great addition to the economic family in Grand Bahama and to the tourist product. Isle of Capri brings a brand of service and expertise that we need on the island. We welcome them and hope to see them succeed and grow. It's a good company and we need them."

Malcolm also believes the casino will boost business at Port Lucaya Marketplace across the street. "Given the additional activity the casino creates, the shopkeepers and business people there, who were awaiting the arrival of the casino, can look to a much brighter future. It generates activity for the shops and for the square (Count Basie Square) the centre of most of the action at Port Lucaya Marketplace. It's just one more piece added to the tourism offerings in the Lucaya area."

COURTESY

Big plans for Grand Bahama

The future looks bright, with major projects on the horizon that could transform the island.

BY BERNARD C CLARKE

"Build it and they will come." It's a phrase popular with entrepreneurs who, no doubt, borrowed it from the 1989 hit movie *Field of Dreams.* Is it what American financier Wallace Groves thought when he conceived the idea of Freeport back in the early 1950s? No one will ever truly know. However, from a land of swamp and pine-barren, visionary businessmen excavated canals, paved roads and constructed the beginnings of an industrial area. And the people came. So did the investors.

Groves, who came to The Bahamas in the 1940s, purchased and modernized the Abaco Lumber Company operation. In the mid-1950s, as the company flourished, he started thinking about diversifying his involvement in Grand Bahama. He sold the lumber operation and part of the timber concession for $4 million. "All Nassau thought Groves had to be slightly mad when he approached the government with his plan of creating a new city on Grand Bahama Island," says Peter Barratt in his book, *Grand Bahama: A Rich and Colourful History.*

A few decades later, in 1994, Freeport's deep harbour and location attracted the Hutchison Whampoa Group, one of the largest and

Left, Moon Bahamas is a space-age development proposed for Grand Bahama.

TIM AYLEN/©DUPUCH

Freeport Container Port

most profitable companies in the world. The company invested in Grand Bahama – and in no small way. According to Willie Moss, president of the Grand Bahama Port Authority (GBPA), Hutchison Whampoa has invested $1 billion in the past 10 years. Hutchison Port Holdings owns 50 per cent of Freeport Harbour Company, the Freeport Container Port, the Grand Bahama International Airport Company and the Lucayan Harbour Cruise Facility. The other 50 per cent ownership of these entities is retained by the GBPA.

the Freeport Container Port now handles as many containers in a day as all the Miami ports combined move in a week.

COURTESY HUTCHISON WHAMPOA LTD
Hutchison Whampoa is the largest port operator in the world.

Now, early into the 21st century, Freeport – a winning combination of natural resources, location, modern infrastructure, and investor-friendly tax structure – has worked its way into the world spotlight.

Improvements in infrastructure

In cooperation with Martin Marietta (an aggregate company), Freeport Harbour has been dredged to a depth of 45 ft, and will be lowered to 52 ft, making it the deepest port in the Caribbean region and on the eastern seaboard of the US. The ongoing project has caught the eye of at least one international company. COSCO Group, a Chinese shipping company, is considering investing $90 million to acquire the third dry dock in the port. COSCO would like to make it the world's largest dry dock, capable of berthing the world's largest ocean liner, *Queen Mary 2*.

Located on several major shipping lanes, the Freeport Container Port now handles as many containers in a day as all the Miami ports combined move in a week – and is looking to expand further. The company is analyzing its options as to how to invest another $100 million that would include additional cranes and land.

GORDON LOMER/©DUPUCH
Willie Moss, president of GBPA

The Grand Bahama International Airport Company now boasts one of the longest runways in the world at 11,000 ft. The runway, along with the recently completed new airport terminal, which is built to US Homeland Security standards, makes Freeport's airport a first-class facility. The new terminal can handle up to 800 passengers an hour, compared to 200 at the old terminal. The airport expansion is another incentive for the Lucayan Harbour Cruise Facility to develop Freeport into a location where passengers can begin and

JARVIS DARVILLE/©DUPUCH

Signing of the supplement to the Hawksbill Creek Agreement. Standing, from left, are A G Knox-Johnson, Attorney-General L A W Orr, attorney Stafford L Sands and Warren Levarity. Seated in front are Sir Robert Stapledon, left, and Wallace Groves.

end their cruises as they do in Miami and Fort Lauderdale. Currently the Lucayan Harbour Cruise Facility is only a port of call for cruise ships.

These latest infrastructure improvements have only enhanced the appeal of Freeport, a city originally designed for a population of 250,000, which has so far only grown to about 47,000 residents.

JARVIS DARVILLE/©DUPUCH

Wallace Groves

Birth of a city

Freeport's destiny actually began with the signing of the Hawksbill Creek Agreement which provides financial incentives for firms to set up in Freeport. Signed by the GBPA and the government of The Bahamas on August 4, 1955, the Hawksbill Creek Agreement established Freeport as a 230-sq-mile free-trade zone that emerged from a land grant of 50,000 acres of swamp and scrub.

Within this agreement, firms in Freeport are

The Hawksbill Creek Agreement can save companies that set up in Freeport up to 65 per cent over costs in Nassau.

granted the right to import equipment and materials duty free. Also under the Hawksbill Creek Agreement, businesses pay no taxes on profits, capital gains, inheritance, income, earnings, distributions or gifts. In 1993 the Bahamian government extended the Hawksbill Creek property tax exemptions until 2015 and duty exemptions until 2054. The Hawksbill Creek Agreement can save companies that set up in Freeport up to 65 per cent over costs in Nassau.

In addition to this agreement for Freeport businesses only, The Bahamas is a member of the Caribbean Basin Initiative, CARIBCAN and Lomé IV (to be replaced by the Cotonou Agreement). These agreements allow goods manufactured or processed anywhere in The Bahamas to enter the US, Canada, and the EU duty free.

Polymers International Limited has utilized the many strategic benefits of Freeport since 1997. "We did a site selection study and decided to invest in Freeport for four reasons: financial, because of the tax-free status; logistical, because of the airport and the harbour; efficient infrastructure and utilities; and a skilled work force," says Brian Hess, managing director of Polymers International. Polymers ships the polystyrene produced in Freeport to countries such as Australia, Mexico and China. The company also ships the finished product back to the US duty free thanks to the Caribbean Basin Initiative. Polymers has just expanded its 125,000-sq-ft facility in Freeport to increase production of polystyrene.

Influx of new business

CITIC, a $6-billion electronics group in China, is planning a distribution centre in Freeport. The centre will assemble electronic goods and then export the finished items to the US. CITIC could take advantage of all the benefits that stem from the Hawksbill Creek Agreement and since its primary market is the US, the company could take advantage of the Caribbean Basin Initiative.

Currently three companies, AES Ocean Express LLC, the El Paso Corporation and Tractebel Calypso Pipeline LLC, have plans to use Grand Bahama's location to supply natural gas to Florida via an underwater pipeline. Just 90 miles off the south coast of Florida, Grand Bahama offers both a deep water port and affordable land,

GORDON LOMER/©DUPUCH

Breakers Cay at Our Lucaya

necessities for an economically viable liquefied natural gas (LNG) plant. Tractebel is the farthest along in its plans and is just awaiting final approval from the Bahamian government. According to Dave Clark, site project manager of Tractebel Bahamas LNG Limited, work could begin on the site within two or three weeks of approval.

"Because the pipeline runs along the sea bed outside of the Grand Bahama Port Authority area, we also had to work with The Bahamas government in Nassau. We found both equally enthusiastic and cooperative in the venture," Clark said.

The Tractebel project would create – for three years – a minimum of 325 to 350 construction jobs, peaking at between 900 to 1,000 jobs, one-third of them filled by Bahamians. The finished plant would employ 50 to 60 full-time employees and the goal is to eventually have every position manned by a qualified Bahamian. The construction would inject $180 to $200 million into the economy and, when finished, provide the government with $40 million in revenue annually from the transported gas, Clark said.

He noted that Tractebel's location in the port is a huge benefit as the ships that bring in construction equipment could off-load directly onto the project site, saving considerable transport costs. Another bonus is that ships carrying the LNG would dock right at the re-gasification facility.

The Bahamas will offer its own film production facilities. Work has begun on a $76-million studio.

El Paso is proposing another possible LNG project. The company hopes to have an environmental impact assessment (EIA) completed and approved by early 2005, which would lead to a mid-2008 operational date for the projected $700-million project.

Pieces of the puzzle

The 19,000-sq-ft Isle of Capri Casino at The Westin and Sheraton at Our Lucaya Beach and Golf Resort opened in December, 2003. It is one of two Isle of Capri Casinos outside the US and "offers an exciting fit to the company's tropical branding efforts," said Timothy Hinkley, president and chief operating officer, of Isle of Capri Casinos, Biloxi, MS. For The Bahamas, the casino has created 300 jobs. Harris Chan, managing director of the resort at Our Lucaya called the casino "the final piece of the puzzle to complete the offerings at this resort."

COURTESY ISLE OF CAPRI CASINOS

Timothy Hinkley, president and COO of Isle of Capri Casinos

The sugar-white beaches and the gin-clear waters that complement resorts like Our Lucaya, have attracted film-makers for many years. As far back as the mid-1960s The Bahamas has been featured in movies. *Thunderball,* starring Sean Connery (now a Lyford Cay resident), was partially filmed in The Bahamas. *After the Sunset* with Pierce Brosnan (scheduled for a November 2004 release), was shot in Nassau.

COURTESY CRAIG WOODS

Craig Woods, head of Bahamas Film Commission

Now, instead of film production being a complex bring-in-equipment-shoot-scenes-and-tote-it-all-home exercise, The Bahamas will offer its own film production facilities. Work has begun on a $76-million studio. Bahamas Film Studios at Gold Rock Creek, Grand Bahama, is being built on the site of an

After years of attracting sun-seeking vacationers, Freeport may soon become famous for its Moon.

old American missile tracking base, a relic of the Cold War. The plan calls for a film and television production and post-production facility as well as a music recording studio.

According to Craig Woods, who heads the Bahamas Film Commission, the initial clean-up of the site is complete. "Instead of bulldozing the entire site, workers salvaged what they could to be renovated," he said. Work is ready to begin to renovate structures that were salvageable and start construction of the new facilities. Future phases include a hotel, movie theme park, water park, restaurants and retail stores as well as a historic Bahamian village.

Outer space on earth

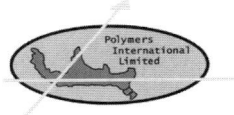

After years of attracting sun-seeking vacationers, Freeport may soon become famous for its Moon. In July 2004 Michael R Henderson and Sandra G Matthews chose Grand Bahama as the site for their

We've come to build the world's largest, most spectacular, most exciting project and the people will come from everywhere."

COURTESY MOON BAHAMAS

Michael R Henderson and Sandra G Matthews

$4.5-billion Moon Resort and Casino now called Moon Bahamas.

"We had to consider air lift capacity, casino license capacity, availability of staff, weather conditions and so it wasn't easy finding the ideal place," Henderson said. While $4.5 billion dollars seems a lot to invest, Moon Bahamas is expected to be financed from the projected $33 billion in revenue generated by vacation, home ownership, and real estate.

"You have a great airport, a wonderful runway and there is great infrastructure here. The Grand Bahama Port Authority is an outstanding company, extremely professional, extremely well-organized and that's very rare. The government is very positive, very business-minded, very keen on tourism… We've come to build the world's largest, most spectacular, most exciting project and the people will come from everywhere." Henderson said.

Henderson's statement is a longer version of Moon's concise business plan: "Build it and they will come." Words sound familiar? Wallace Groves would likely be impressed. So would any of the visionaries who came after him. Freeport continues to build… and the people continue to come.

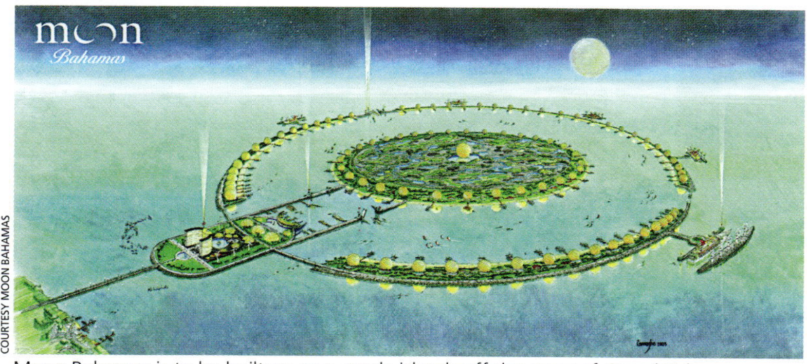

COURTESY MOON BAHAMAS

Moon Bahamas is to be built on man-made islands off the coast of Grand Bahama.

Freeport/Lucaya classified directory

See also Bahamas classified directory, pgs 310-319

ACCOUNTANTS/ACCOUNTING FIRMS
Galanis & Co 231
KPMG 223
PricewaterhouseCoopers 277

AIR CARGO
See **Freight.**

AIRLINES
Bahamasair 533

ANIMAL RESCUE/SHELTER
Grand Bahama Humane Society 553

ARCHITECTS
W Carver Grant & Co Ltd 547

ART SUPPLIES
Lustre Kraft Signs 539

AUDIT & RELATED SERVICES
Galanis & Co....................................231
See **Accountants/Accounting firms.**

AUTOMOBILES – ACCESSORIES, PARTS & REPAIRS
Grand Bahama Millwork 539

BATTERIES – AUTOMOTIVE/HEAVY EQUIPMENT/MARINE
Machinery & Energy Ltd 157

BEEPERS/PAGERS
Bahamas Telecommunications Co (BTC)/BaTelCo 559

BOOKS & MAGAZINES
Bahamas Trailblazer Maps 173
Dupuch Publications 529, 575, 607, 608
Etienne Dupuch Jr Publications Ltd 529, 575, 607, 608
Welcome Bahamas 529

BROADCASTING
See **Communications & broadcasting.**

BUILDING/CONSTRUCTION EQUIPMENT & SUPPLIES
Bahama Rock Ltd 567
Commonwealth Building Supplies Ltd 131
Freeport Aggregate Ltd 543
Grand Bahama Millwork 539
Island Construction Co Ltd 543
Machinery & Energy Ltd 157
See also **Hardware, Heavy equipment rental,** and **Tiles & supplies.**

BUSINESS ADVISORY SERVICES
Galanis & Co....................................231
IBM 233
KPMG 223
PricewaterhouseCoopers 277

BUSINESS SYSTEMS CONSULTING, MANAGEMENT, TROUBLESHOOTING
IBM 233
KPMG 223
PricewaterhouseCoopers 277

CABLE COMPANIES
Cable Bahamas 91

CAR RENTAL COMPANIES
Avis 381

CELLULAR PHONES/SERVICE
Bahamas Telecommunications Co (BTC)/BaTelCo 559

COMMUNICATIONS & BROADCASTING
Bahamas Telecommunications Co (BTC)/BaTelCo 559
Cable Bahamas 91
See also **Books & magazines** and **Internet services.**

COMPANY INCORPORATION & MANAGEMENT
Davis & Co 221
KPMG 223
McKinney, Bancroft & Hughes 229
PricewaterhouseCoopers 277
See also **Law firms.**

COMPUTER SERVICES
IBM 233

CONCRETE PRODUCTS
Grand Bahama Millwork 539

CORPORATE FINANCE, MANAGEMENT & ADVISORY SERVICES
Galanis & Co....................................231
KPMG 223
McKinney, Bancroft & Hughes 229
PricewaterhouseCoopers 277

COURIER SERVICES
DHL 137

CUSTOMS BROKERS
Eastern Freight Forwarders 527
Freeport Transfer Ltd 527

DEVELOPMENT CONSULTANTS & PLANNERS
W Carver Grant & Co Ltd 547

EDUCATION
The College of The Bahamas 115

ELECTRICITY COMPANIES
Grand Bahama Power Co 541

ENERGY SYSTEMS
See **Solar products.**

ENGINEERS/CONSULTANTS
W Carver Grant & Co Ltd 547

ENGRAVING
Lustre Kraft Signs 539

FREIGHT
Bahamasair 533
DHL 1
Eastern Freight Forwarders 527
Freeport Transfer Ltd 527

FURNITURE
Island Bedding & Furniture 537

GAS STATIONS
Freeport Oil Co Ltd (FOCOL) 525

GENERATORS
Machinery & Energy Ltd 157

HARDWARE
Commonwealth Building Supplies Ltd 131
Grand Bahama Millwork 539

HEAVY EQUIPMENT RENTAL
Freeport Transfer Ltd 527
Machinery & Energy Ltd 157

HOTELS
Old Bahama Bay 522

HOUSEWARES
Grand Bahama Millwork 539

IMPORT & EXPORT SERVICES
DHL 137
Eastern Freight Forwarders 527
Freeport Transfer Ltd 527
See also **Freight, Movers, Shipping companies** and **Trucking.**

INFORMATION TECHNOLOGY SERVICES
Galanis & Co....................................231
IBM 233
Integrated Business Solutions Ltd 231
KPMG 223

INSURANCE
DMG Intl Marine Service Agency 155
The National Insurance Board 135
WAM Co Ltd 155

INTERNET SERVICES
Bahamas Telecommunications Co (BTC)/BaTelCo 559
Cable Bahamas 91
CoralWave 91

INTRODUCING BROKER
Petra Securities Ltd 547

INVESTMENT ADVISORY/ASSET MANAGEMENT SERVICES
Galanis & Co 231
KPMG 223
Petra Securities Ltd 547
PricewaterhouseCoopers 277

INVESTMENT OPPORTUNITIES
The Grand Bahama Port Authority 544-545
See also **Insurance, Investment advisory/asset management services** and **Real estate – appraisals, developement, rentals and sales.**

LAW FIRMS
Davis & Co 221
McKinney, Bancroft & Hughes 229
Moss & Associates 537

MANAGEMENT CONSULTING
Galanis & Co 231
KPMG 223
PricewaterhouseCoopers 277

MARINAS/MARINE SERVICES
DMG Intl Marine Service Agency 155
Lucayan Marina Village 42
Old Bahama Bay 522
WAM Co Ltd 155

MATTRESS MANUFACTURER
Island Bedding & Furniture 537

MEDIA
See **Books & magazines** and **Communications & broadcasting.**

MOVERS
Freeport Transfer Ltd 527
See also **Freight, Import & export services, Shipping companies** and **Trucking.**

NETWORK PLANNING
IBM 233

OFFICE EQUIPMENT, FURNITURE & SUPPLIES
Bahamas Telecommunications Co (BTC)/BaTelCo 559
IBM 233

OIL COMPANIES/PETROLEUM PRODUCTS
Bahamas Oil Refining Co Intl Ltd (BORCO) 520
Freeport Oil Co Ltd (FOCOL) 525

PAINT SUPPLIES
Grand Bahama Millwork 539

POLYSTYRENE MANUFACTURERS
Polymers Intl Ltd 570

PRINTING
Lustre Kraft Signs 539

PROPERTY DEVELOPMENT & MANAGEMENT
W Carver Grant & Co Ltd 547

REAL ESTATE – APPRAISALS, DEVELOPMENTS, RENTALS & SALES
Damianos Realty 301
H G Christie Ltd 303
Lucayan Marina Village 42
Old Bahama Bay 522
Shoreline Properties 523
W Carver Grant & Co Ltd 547

RUBBER STAMPS
Lustre Kraft Signs 539

SALVAGE, TOWING & RESCUE SERVICES
DMG Intl Marine Service Agency 155
WAM Co Ltd 155

SCHOOLS
See **Education.**

SHIP SERVICES/CHANDLERS
DMG Intl Marine Service Agency 155
WAM Co Ltd 155

SHIPS' AGENTS
Freeport Transfer Ltd 527

SHIPPING COMPANIES
DHL 137
Eastern Freight Forwarders 527
Freeport Transfer Ltd 527
See also **Freight** and **Courier services.**

SIGNS – ALL TYPES
Lustre Kraft Signs 539

STORAGE & WAREHOUSING
Eastern Freight Forwarders 527
Freeport Transfer Ltd 527

SURVEYORS – LAND & MARINE
DMG Intl Marine Service Agency........155
W Carver Grant & Co Ltd 547
WAM Co Ltd......................................155

TELECOMMUNICATIONS
Bahamas Telecommunications
Co (BTC)/BaTelCo 559

TILES & SUPPLIES
Commonwealth Building Supplies Ltd 131

TOOLS – BUILDING/CONSTRUCTION
Commonwealth Building Supplies Ltd 131

TRANS-SHIPMENT FACILITIES & SERVICES
Bahamas Oil Refining Co
Intl Ltd (BORCO) 520
Freeport Transfer Ltd 527

TRAVEL
Bahamasair 533

TRUCKING
Eastern Freight Forwarders 527
Freeport Transfer Ltd 527

WATER FILTER SYSTEMS
Brita Water Filter Systems 127

YACHT SERVICE & REPAIRS
See **Marinas/marine services; Salvage, towing & rescue services; Ship services/chandlers** and **Surveyors – land & marine.**

Grand Bahama
N

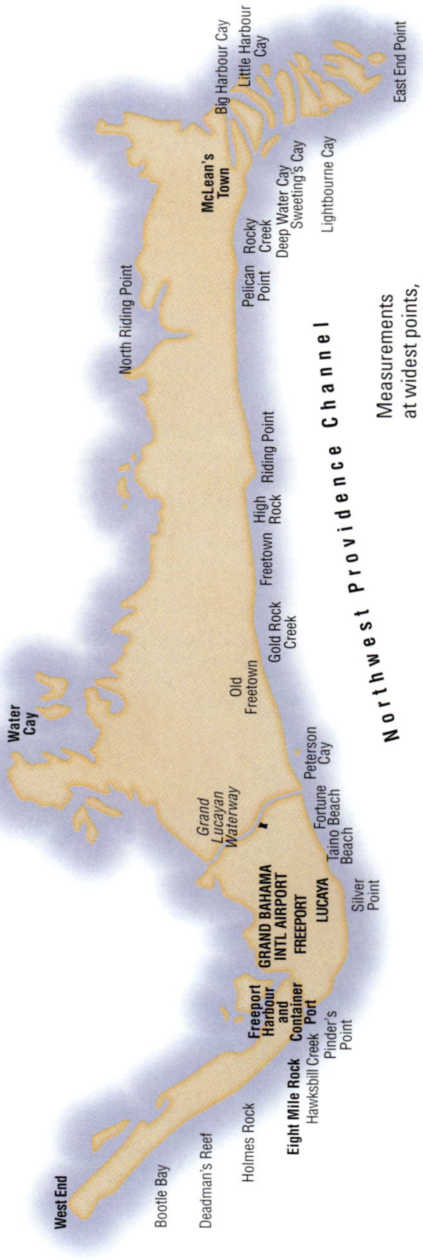
West End
Bootle Bay
Deadman's Reef
Holmes Rock
Eight Mile Rock
Hawksbill Creek
Pinder's Point
Freeport Harbour and Container Port
GRAND BAHAMA INTL AIRPORT
FREEPORT
LUCAYA
Silver Point
Taino Beach
Fortune Beach
Grand Lucayan Waterway
Peterson Cay
Water Cay
Old Freetown
Gold Rock Creek
Freetown
High Rock
Riding Point
North Riding Point
Pelican Point
Rocky Creek
Deep Water Cay
Sweeting's Cay
Lightbourne Cay
McLean's Town
Big Harbour Cay
Little Harbour Cay
East End Point
Northwest Providence Channel
Measurements at widest points, 80 x 16 miles

Freeport/ Lucaya Information

Blue page index, this section

Accommodations
Accounting firms
Agriculture
Air service
Ambulance/air ambulance services
Animals
Architectural firms
Bahamas National Trust
Banking
Birds
Boating
Building contractors & engineers
Building costs & permits
Business licensing
Cable television
Car rental companies
Casinos
Chamber of Commerce
Churches
Cinemas
Climate
Clinics
Community organizations & service clubs
Cost of living
Courier services
Cruising
Cultural activities
Customs
Defence Force
Dentists
Departure tax
Diving & snorkelling
Divorce
Doctors
Driver's licence & vehicle information
Education
Electricity
Emergency numbers
Employers' organizations
Encouragement acts
Engineers
Entertainment
Exchange control
Export entry
Fire brigade
Fishing
Freight services
Gambling
Geography
Golf courses
Government offices
Grand Bahama Humane Society
Gun permits
Harbour control
Hawksbill Creek Agreement
Health/medical services
History
Hospitals & clinics
Hotels
Housing
Immigration
Import entry
Industry
International Bazaar
Internet
Judicial system
Junkanoo
Law firms
Libraries
Marinas & cruising facilities
Marriage licences
National Insurance
Nature centres
Newspapers
Passports
People-To-People
Police certificates
Population
Port Lucaya Marketplace
Postal information
Property transactions
Radio stations
Real estate companies
Religion
Schools
Service clubs
Shipping
Shopping
Snorkelling
Sports venues
Straw markets
Supermarkets
Tax incentives
Telecommunications
Television
Theatre & dramatic arts
Tourism
Trade unions
Transportation
Veterinarians
Wages
Water supply & rates
Weather

The 233-sq-mile Grand Bahama Port Authority (GBPA) area of Freeport/Lucaya is governed by the terms of the Hawksbill Creek Agreement between The Bahamas government and businesses licensed by the GBPA. For this reason, certain headings are specific to Freeport/Lucaya only. As the rest of Grand Bahama is governed on the same terms as New Providence and other Bahama islands, see **Bahamas information** for general information not specific to Freeport/Lucaya or Grand Bahama.

ACCOMMODATIONS

Accommodations for visitors range from luxury beachfront properties to apartment complexes booked through local real estate agencies. Apartments usually include television hook-up, maid service, coin-operated washers/dryers, swimming pools and beach access.

Rates at small hotels start at $80 per day in summer, double or single occupancy, and $100 in winter. Daily maid service, plus energy charge of $12-$14 per person per day, is sometimes included in the rate.

Rates at medium-sized hotels are approx $145 per day in summer, double occupancy, and $160 in winter, plus maid service and energy charges. Rates at luxury hotels are approx $159 in summer and $189 in winter, plus service charges.

Government tax of 12% per room per night is charged in all hotels.

See also **Bahamas information, Hotels** and this section, **Cost of living.**

ACCOUNTING FIRMS

Cates & Co 351-4025
*Deloitte & Touche 373-3015
*Galanis & Co 352-5564
*KPMG 352-9384
*Michael Hepburn & Co 352-7354
*Pannell Kerr Forster 352-2912
*PricewaterhouseCoopers 352-8471
Worrell Russell & Co 373-7105

*Nassau office also

AGRICULTURE

The Dept of Agriculture has resident agricultural officers responsible for the development and management of the agricultural sector and enforcement of agricultural laws.

Grand Bahama has a thriving agricultural sector, including operations from five to 100 acres, which supply local and export markets. Products range from honey, chicken and eggs to ornamentals, native fruits, vegetables and livestock.

See also **Bahamas information, Agriculture.**

AIR SERVICE

Grand Bahama International Airport is a full-service, US port-of-entry airport that provides pre-clearance to all passengers destined for the US. The airport has an 11,000-ft runway with the capacity to land the largest aircraft built today.

A $30-million airport renovation, including a new 128,000-sq-ft terminal and pre-clearance facility, has been completed. The project more than doubles the capacity of the original airport and is designed to process more than 800 passengers per hour. The terminal was constructed by a joint venture of Bahamian companies – Reef Construction and Cavalier Construction. The airport security standards meet all of the US port-of-entry security requirements.

The new building is customer-oriented with shops, restaurants and modern operation systems that include new baggage-handling systems, security systems and flight information displays. The new terminal was opened in June 2004. The Airport Company is now jointly owned by the GBPA and Hutchison Port Holdings.

Airlines serving Grand Bahama include:

AirTran Airways
Flights daily to **Atlanta** and **Baltimore.**

American Eagle
Flights daily to **Miami.**

Bahamasair
Regular daily flights to **Nassau** and **Ft Lauderdale.**

Continental Connection
Flights daily to **Miami, West Palm Beach, Ft Lauderdale** and **Orlando.**

Continental Express
Daily flights to **Newark.**

Delta Connection
Twice daily flights to **Atlanta.**

Eurofly
Fri flights from **Milan, Italy** between May and Nov.

Falcon Air
Seasonal flights to **Boston, Cincinnati, Cleveland, Hartford, Houston, Raleigh/Durham** and **Richmond.**

Flamingo Airways
Flights to **Moore's Island** and **Sandy Point, Walker's Cay** and **Great Harbour Cay.** Also flights to the **Caribbean,** and ambulance flights.

Laker Airways
Flights to **Ft Lauderdale** Fri and Sun.

Major's Air Services
Daily flights to **Bimini** and **Marsh Harbour.** Fri and Sun flights to **Andros** and **Governor's Harbour.**

US Airways
Daily flights to **Charlotte** and **Philadelphia.** Flights to La Guardia airport, **New York,** with non-stop service on Saturdays only.

See also **Bahamas information, Air service** and **Airports.**

AMBULANCE/AIR AMBULANCE SERVICES

Air ambulances

Advanced Air
Ambulance (AAA)....1-800-633-3590
Aero-Medical Group/
Air Evacuation 1-800-854-2569
Air Ambulance Professionals Inc
(Ft Lauderdale)........1-800-752-4195
Air Ambulance Services 351-3211
Medical Air Services Assoc Intl
(for members)..................351-5122
or 362-1606

Ground ambulance

Rand Memorial Hospital....352-2689
or 352-6735

See also **Bahamas information, Ambulance/air ambulance services** and this section, **Emergency numbers** and **Hospitals & clinics.**

ANIMALS

See **Bahamas information, Animals** and this section, **Grand Bahama Humane Society** and **Nature centres.**

ARCHITECTURAL FIRMS

Architects & Engineers 373-6938
Architects Inc........................352-4835
Architectural Group 352-1570
Bruce Lafleur & Assoc 352-2101
Charles J Moss & Assoc 352-5204
Griffiths & Assoc 352-2101
Hiram H Lockhart & Assoc......373-1257
L V Evans & Assoc..................351-5644
or 352-3558
W Carver Grant & Co...........352-4333

BAHAMAS NATIONAL TRUST (BNT)

The Bahamas National Trust (BNT) administers three national parks in Grand Bahama – the BNT Rand Nature Centre, Lucayan National Park and Peterson Cay National Park.

See also **Bahamas information, Bahamas National Trust** and this section, **Nature centres.**

BANKING

There are five clearing banks in Freeport/Lucaya: Bank of The Bahamas Intl, Commonwealth Bank Ltd, FirstCaribbean International Bank, Bank of Nova Scotia and RBC Royal Bank of Canada. All offer 24-hour banking with automated teller machines.

Other banks that offer commercial banking services are: RBC Finco and the British American Bank (a subsidiary of Fidelity Merchant Bank & Trust Intl Ltd).

The Bahamas Development Bank (BDB) assists in the establishment and financing of local business.

Commercial banks (authorized dealers) may issue and approve certain foreign currency payments without Exchange Control permission.

Banking hours are Mon-Thurs 9:30am-3pm and Fri 9:30am-4:30pm. Commonwealth Bank is open at 9am-3:30pm (9:30am-4:30pm on Fri).

See also **Bahamas information, Bahamas Development Bank, Banking, Banks, Exchange control** and **Import entry.**

BIRDS

Seventeen species of birds are endemic to Grand Bahama. There has been an influx of red-winged blackbirds on the island. Colourful painted buntings and indigo buntings visit occasionally. One of the rarest birds in the world, the yellow and black Kirtland's warbler, was sighted in Nov 1995 by an ornithological group visiting Lucayan National Park, and two more were later seen in the same area. These birds only winter in The Bahamas. Once rare visitors to The Bahamas, purple gallinules, the northern parula and olive-capped warblers are also being seen more often. Snow geese have also been travelling from the Arctic Circle to winter in Grand Bahama.

Bridled terns nest on Peterson Cay and Key West quail doves have been seen in Lucayan National Park. Flocks of cedar waxwings have been spotted passing through Fortune Cay. New residents are whippoorwills, singing their name up to 1,000 times at night.

See also **Nature centres.**

BOATING

Marinas, boat dealers and repairers, charter agencies and fishing guides exist throughout Freeport/Lucaya and at West End.

Owners of pleasure vessels visiting The Bahamas pay a fee of $150 for boats up to 35 ft and $300 for larger boats. This cruising permit allows the boat to stay in the country for one year, after which the owner must apply for renewal in writing. If approved for a two-year extension, a $500 fee must be paid. After three continuous years, the boat must leave or duty must be paid. With a cruising permit, owners may import spare parts (by sea only) free of duty, paying only 7% stamp tax.

Volunteers from the Bahamas Air Sea Rescue Assoc (BASRA) keep a 24-hour watch for boaters in Bahamian waters in collaboration with the US Coast Guard.

The Grand Lucayan Waterway is 6½ ft at Mean Low Water at North Shore. Boaters from Freeport/Lucaya seeking a direct route to Abaco must clear the 26-ft Casuarina Bridge.

See also **Harbour control** and **Marinas & cruising facilities.**

BUILDING CONTRACTORS & ENGINEERS

Albacore Construction Co . . 352-5159
Arawak Construction & Truss Co Ltd 352-6569
B & H Construction Co 352-8688
Broncestone Construction Co Ltd 352-3914
Canon Construction Co . . . 351-4047
Cavalier Construction Co . . .352-5099
City Services Ltd 351-5800
Diesel Engineers Ltd 351-7040
Edwards Construction Co . . 352-4001
FES Construction 352-5425

Freeport Construction Co Ltd . 352-8137
Glenerik Intl Ltd 352-8186
Good Holdings Construction
Co Ltd 352-7305
Grand Bahama
Construction Co Ltd 351-8711
H & F Babak Construction
Co Ltd 351-4667
H & S Construction 352-4431
Industrial/Mechanical
Engineering Ltd 352-3622
Island Construction Ltd 352-7435
Island Electric Ltd 352-7664
Island Projects Ltd 352-6700
Jubilee Construction Co Ltd . 351-8761
Knowles Construction
Co Ltd 352-3527
L & R Construction Ltd 352-7592
McAce Technical
Construction Co 352-2682
Marlin Design Build Ltd 352-9200
Maximise Construction 351-7450
Mechanical Engineering Ltd . 352-5562
Meco 373-6938
Nervée Engineering Ltd/Arthur
Jones & Assoc 351-2061
Outten Construction 352-9785/6
Pinnacle Investment
Construction Ltd 351-2001
Qualfast Construction Co . . 352-3587
Reef Construction Ltd 352-6387
SRA Construction 352-5127
Triple L Construction
Co Ltd 351-8045
United Caribbean Construction
(Bah) Ltd 352-5530
Virmar Construction Co . . . 352-4967
W Carver Grant
(consulting engineers) . . . 352-4333
W G & S Construction Ltd . . 352-3832
Waugh Construction
(Bah) Ltd 352-9378

BUILDING COSTS & PERMITS

All major building work needs prior approval of the Ministry of Public Works. Permit fees vary according to type of building and inspections are made at prescribed stages. Regulations on building within the Grand Bahama Port Authority (GBPA) area are similar to those in Nassau.

Building permit applications are available at the building dept, GBPA, East Atlantic Dr, PO Box F-42666, tel 352-6611 ext 2053. Guidance pamphlets are at the same address or from full-service real estate companies.

BUSINESS LICENSING

All businesses operating in the Freeport area must be licensed by the Grand Bahama Port Authority Ltd (GBPA).

Licensees, whether individual, limited company or other corporate entity, are eligible for all tax benefits granted under the Hawksbill Creek Agreement as part of Bahamian law.

Customs concessions continue until 2054. The GBPA levies an annual licence fee for businesses operating in the port area. This fee varies according to size and type of business, with the lower limit being $10 for a non-profit organization. A non-refundable deposit of $250 is charged as a processing fee in respect of all GBPA business licence applications. The fee is spent not only on maintaining the area around the licensee's business, but contributes to the annual GBPA Group of Companies' spending on landscaping, road repairs, garbage collection, etc.

To apply for a licence:

1. A detailed description of the nature of business, including facilities, equipment and staff, must be submitted to the GBPA on a licence proposal form.
2. The project is analyzed by the GBPA using information on the form together with a detailed reference check, financial affidavit and business competence report.
3. Upon approval by the licensing committee of the GBPA and subsequent notation by the government of The Bahamas, a letter of intent is issued to the licensee outlining terms and conditions of the business and indicating duration of the licence and initial fee payable to the GBPA.

4. Upon acceptance of these terms by the licensee, the formal licence agreement dictating finalized terms and location of the business is drawn up. Any subsequent changes or additions require an amendment to the licence.

Contact GBPA, Licensing Dept, PO Box F-42666, tel 352-6711.

See also **Customs** and **Hawksbill Creek Agreement.** Outside the GBPA area, see **Bahamas information, Business licence fee.**

CABLE TELEVISION

See **Bahamas information, Cable television** and this section, **Television.**

CAR RENTAL COMPANIES

Car rentals vary from $45 daily for a sub-compact to $190 for a luxury car, plus $15.95 for insurance. The weekly rental rate is $390-$900. Most companies give unlimited mileage. Collision damage waiver at $15.95 daily is optional.

Avis ....352-7666 (airport)
or 373-1102
Bahama Buggies 352-8750
Brad's Car Rental ....352-7930 (airport)
Dollar ....352-9325 (airport)
Hertz ....352-9250 (airport)
Thrifty 352-9308
VIP Bahamas Rent-a-car..........351-3860

CASINOS

See **Entertainment** and **Gambling.**

CHAMBER OF COMMERCE

The Grand Bahama Chamber of Commerce, affiliated with the Bahamas Chamber of Commerce in Nassau, has 160 members. President is Gwen Newbold. Contact the Chamber of Commerce, Pioneer's Way, PO Box F-40808, tel 352-8329, fax 352-3280 or e-mail gbchamber@batelnet.bs.

CHURCHES

See **Religion.**

CINEMAS

RND Cinemas (five screens) ..351-3456
or 351-9190

CLIMATE

Because of its northerly location, Grand Bahama has winter temperatures slightly below those of New Providence, although the weather tends to be similar throughout the rest of the year.

Grand Bahama temperatures traditionally are at their lowest in Feb, with a daily max of about 76°F. In the summer the daily max is usually in the 80s. Humidity can be high, although tempered by prevailing breezes. Wind speeds are below 10 knots most of the year but can reach 25 knots in winter.

Grand Bahama has a May-Oct rainy season and rainfall is especially heavy in Sept. The Bahamas can be affected by hurricanes or tropical storms June-Nov, the greatest risk being Aug-Oct.

See also **Bahamas information, Climate.**

CLINICS

See **Hospitals & clinics.**

COMMUNITY ORGANIZATIONS & SERVICE CLUBS

Alcoholics Anonymous..........352-6267
American Women's Club
of Grand Bahama
(Joyce Harrison) 373-3694
Bahamas Air Sea Rescue Assoc
(BASRA)............................352-2628
(24-hour pager) 352-6222
(pin 8339 and 8440)
Bahamas National Trust 352-5438
Bahamian Women's Club
(Annalise Miller)................373-3454
Canadian Men's Club
(Mike Pilgrim) 373-4564
Canadian Women's Club
(Lynne Donney) 351-7138
Child Abuse Hotline.............351-7763
The Crisis Centre........352-HELP (4357)

Freeport Garden Club (Judy Zuber)......................374-2772
Freeport Toastmasters (Kalesa Gibbs) 352-6735
Grand Bahama Chamber of Commerce 352-8329
Grand Bahama Children's Home 352-7852
Grand Bahama Red Cross Centre.............352-7163
Human Rights Assoc (Fred Smith)......................352-7458
Kiwanis Club of Freeport (Karen Brennan)................373-5766
Narcotics Anonymous ....351-3413 (or call YMCA)
Northern Bahamas Council for the Disabled................352-7720
Operation Hope (Drug Abuse Hotline) 352-3002
Pilot Club of Freeport (Rose Carson) 352-8256
Rotary Club of Freeport (Christopher Gouthro) 351-5050
Rotary Club of Lucaya (Michelle Thompson) 351-5216
Sunrise Rotary Club (Alarie Turner) 350-8046
Susan J Wallace Community Centre..............................352-2092
YMCA 352-7074
Yellow Elder 2828 (Jacquie Gray) 373-8728
Zonta Club Freeport/Lucaya 373-8906

See also **Grand Bahama Humane Society.**

COST OF LIVING

Food costs in Freeport are generally slightly higher than in Nassau because of its lower population. As Grand Bahama imports 90% of all consumer goods from the US, its cost of living is directly tied to the US Consumer Price Index.

Most rented homes and apartments are furnished and have facilities for washers and dryers. Most apartment complexes have pools; duplexes generally do not.

Rents vary widely depending on amenities. There are two rental scales in Freeport: employees of Grand Bahama Port Authority licensees may rent "bonded" (no duty paid) apartments at the lower end of the scale. Visitors must rent duty-paid apartments, which sometimes include maid service, linen and cutlery, etc, at the higher end of the scale.

Efficiencies generally rent from $450-$550 per month. One-bdrm apt, $400-$850; two-bdrm apt, $550-$1,650; three-bdrm apt, $750-$2,000, or more for bonded accommodation. A good three-bdrm house with garage and pool rents for $2,500 upwards, depending on location and amenities.

Building costs vary according to location and finish. A house with above-average finishes costs $120-$150 per sq ft to build. Office and industrial construction cost from $80 per sq ft, and steel-framed warehouses from $30-$40 per sq ft to build.

See also **Housing.**

COURIER SERVICES

There are several courier services based in Freeport, including UPS (GWS), tel 352-3636; DHL, tel 352-6415; FedEx, tel 352-3402/3; Mail Drop, tel 351-7663; Arising Courier Services, tel 351-4005 and Dash Delivery Service, tel 351-2768. It costs $10 to send a package weighing up to two lbs to Nassau, $26.75 to Miami or New York.

See also **Postal information.**

CRUISING

See **Bahamas information, Marinas & cruising facilities** and this section, **Boating** and **Marinas & cruising facilities.**

CULTURAL ACTIVITIES

The Freeport Players' Guild (Ivy Elden, tel 373-3718) and the Grand Bahama Players (Patrice Johnson, tel 557-6997 or 352-9851) stage several plays throughout the year at the 450-seat Regency Theatre.

CUSTOMS

All persons entering Freeport/Lucaya, including Grand Bahama Port Authority licensees, must adhere to customs regulations as set out in **Bahamas information, Customs.**

Licensees, however, have been granted certain duty exemptions on import and export of goods until the year 2054 under the Hawksbill Creek Agreement, which allows certain "supplies and manufacturing supplies" to be imported or purchased without payment of duty.

1. Supplies are defined as all materials, supplies and things of every kind and description; equipment, building materials and supplies; factory plant and apparatus; replacement parts, spare parts, machine and hand tools; contractor's plant; vehicles to be used for the business purposes of a licensee only; vessels; petroleum products and nuclear fission products other than consumable stores.
2. Manufacturing supplies are defined as all materials, supplies and things, whether raw, partly processed or processed, or any combination thereof of every kind and description, other than consumable stores, imported for the purpose of any manufacturing, industrial or other business, undertaking or enterprise within the Freeport area.
3. Consumable stores are defined as any article imported for personal use or made available after its importation for personal use either by sale or gift. Also, any article imported into the Freeport area and subsequently exported from the Port Area to any other part of The Bahamas, and any article assembled, processed or manufactured within the Freeport area and subsequently exported to any other part of The Bahamas, except pine lumber products or pine timber processed within the Freeport area.

The provisions of the Hawksbill Creek Agreement also permit licensees to erect or purchase one private residence, duty free, for the personal use and occupation of:

1. A licensee and his family.
2. A bona fide employee of a licensee and that employee's family.

Duty-free contents of the residence include cooking range or stove, dishwasher, refrigerator, vacuum cleaner, washing machine and dryer, non-portable TV sets, non-portable stereos, all permanent fixtures in the house, curtains, lamps and lampshades, carpets and pictures.

Conditions for obtaining customs exemptions

The Hawksbill Creek Agreement places full responsibility upon each licensee to ensure duty-free materials are used only for the prescribed purposes within the Freeport area, since it is the use of goods exclusively in the licensee's business that generates the duty exemptions conferred by the Agreement. Consequently, the licensee must either own the goods himself or be in such a close relationship with the true owner (eg, as hirer or fully responsible agent for an absent owner) as to be able to exercise full and effective control of the subsequent use of the goods.

The Agreement states there are only three instances when a licensee may claim duty-free privileges for his goods:

1. When the goods are imported into the Freeport area.
2. When the goods are taken out of a customs-bonded warehouse in The Bahamas.
3. When the goods are purchased in The Bahamas, duty having been paid and the licensee is claiming a refund of such duty.

When a licensee wishes to claim customs duty exemption on any goods at these points, he must first enter the goods on a Conditionally Free Entry form. On this form, the licensee declares that the goods are intended to be used solely as supplies or manufacturing supplies within the Freeport area. It is a criminal offence to make a false declaration.

In addition to this declaration, the value of the imported goods, and the rates of duty to which they would be liable, must be declared. Where applicable, evidence of freight and insurance should be attached. Original invoices, copy bills of lading and packing lists should be submitted with the entry. To facilitate the calculation of varying rates of duty and to ensure importers obtain any refund to which they are entitled, original invoices must in all cases show unit prices.

Licensee's bond
Licensees are required to enter a legally binding bond to pay double duty to the government on any goods admitted duty free which are subsequently used or applied to any purpose other than those permitted under the Hawksbill Creek Agreement.

Customs authorities may require licensees to provide a surety for the bond. Although the bond is a continuing obligation, the licensee is released from it on specific goods when satisfactory evidence can be produced that:

1. He has paid the proper duty.
2. The goods no longer exist (he must produce a destruction certificate).
3. The goods have been exported to foreign parts from The Bahamas either in their original state or in a different state resulting from manufacturing, processing or assembly in the Freeport area.
4. The goods have been transferred to the bond of another licensee.

Further information on Freeport customs regulations can be found in the *Guide to Customs Duties Exemptions and Procedures in Freeport, Grand Bahama Island, under the Hawksbill Creek Agreement*, published jointly by the Ministry of Finance and the Grand Bahama Port Authority (GBPA).

See also **Hawksbill Creek Agreement.**

DEFENCE FORCE

See **Bahamas information, Royal Bahamas Defence Force.**

DENTISTS

Dr Catherine Adderley, Hawksbill Clinic 352-3888
Dr Larry Bain, Insurance Management Bldg 352-8492
Dr Karen Bastian, The New Sunrise Medical Centre – Hospital Complex 373-3333
Dr Desirée Clarke, Tree Root Plaza 351-2112
Dr Carl Hensel, The New Sunrise Medical Centre 373-3333
Dr Kendal Major (periodontist c/o Dr Bain), first Fri and Sat of the month 352-8492
Dr Kenworth Newbold (c/o Dr Bain), two days per month 352-8492
Dr Leatendore Percentie, The New Sunrise Medical Centre – Hospital Complex 373-3333
Dr Hayward E Romer Bloneva Bldg, suite 9 . . . .352-4082 (emergency) 352-7507
Dr Barry Russell, Bahamas Orthodontic Centre 352-5756
Dr Woodley Thompson (orthodontist c/o Dr Romer), two days per month 352-4082
Dr James Washington (oral and maxillo-facial), Lucayan Medical East 373-7400

Freeport Dental Centre (an affiliate of Dent-Plan Ltd). This centre uses the Health Maintenance Organization (HMO) concept as a means of providing Bahamians with affordable dental care.

Contributions are received by salary deduction. The centre has the only Panarex scanner in Freeport. Three dentists are available. Pioneer's Professional Bldg, Pioneer's Way. Tel 352-4552.

DEPARTURE TAX

Air

A $15 departure tax must be paid by every traveller six yrs and over upon leaving The Bahamas. It is included in the cost of the airline ticket. An additional $5 security fee must be paid in cash by each traveller departing Grand Bahama International Airport. It is collected at check-in.

Sea

Departure tax for ship passengers is built into the fare. The fee is $15 per passenger on ships remaining in The Bahamas for more than a day. For one-day excursion passengers it is $13. Children under six are exempt.

There is also a $7 ticket tax on the price of each airline or cruise ship ticket purchased in The Bahamas (except for domestic flights). This is included in the price of the ticket and should not be confused with the departure tax.

DIVING & SNORKELLING

Grand Bahama is a first-class diving and snorkelling destination with thriving, healthy reefs, blue holes, wrecks and caves.

A number of full-service diving operations throughout Freeport/Lucaya offer instruction at all levels; guided tours (shark, wreck, reef and night dives); underwater videos and diving equipment sales, rental and repair.

Dive and snorkelling companies

Caribbean Divers 373-9111
Grand Bahama Scuba 373-9791
Paradise Cove 349-2677
Paradise Watersports 373-4001
Pat & Diane (*Fantasia*) 373-8681
Sunn Odyssey Divers' Club....373-4014
Superior Watersports 373-7863
UNEXSO 373-1244
Xanadu Undersea Adventures ..352-3811

See also **Bahamas information, Sports.**

DIVORCE

See **Bahamas information, Divorce.**

DOCTORS

Medical officers

Eight Mile Rock,
Dr K Gutam 348-2227/8
Freeport, see **Hospitals & clinics.**
Hawksbill, Dr N Sawyer 352-7722
High Rock, Dr M Khan 353-5600
Sweeting's Cay and
Grand Cay, Dr M Khan 353-2178
West End, Dr M Nayak 346-6463

DRIVER'S LICENCE & VEHICLE INFORMATION

Driver's and motor vehicle licences are obtained from the Road Traffic Dept, National Insurance Bldg, Freeport. Cars must be inspected for roadworthiness at Workers House, Settler's Way. All new driver's licences carry the driver's photograph.

EDUCATION

Following is a selection of schools. For a complete list contact the Ministry of Education, PO Box F-42595, tel 352-9688, fax 352-4060.

Preschool & Kindergarten

Freeport Nursery School and Play Group (Calvary Academy), Kinglake Ln. Three terms. Six qualified teachers, 110 children. Day care 7:30am-6pm, $35-$40 per week. Nursery, 2½-3½ yrs, $360 per term. Children's group, 3½-6 yrs, $410 per term; grade 1, $425 per term; grades 2-3, $450 per term; grades 4-6, $475 per term; 8:45am-2:30pm. After-school care, $60 per term, 2:30-5:30pm. Operated by Calvary Temple. Acting principal, Rev Joyce Cameron, PO Box F-41576, tel 352-5490.

St John's Kindergarten, Ponce de Leon Dr and Coral Rd. Four teachers, 50 children 2-5 yrs. $100 per month. Principal, Laverne Cooper, PO Box F-40176, tel 352-2276.

Primary

Discovery Primary School, Beach Way Dr. Anglican prep school (with kindergarten) for Freeport High School. 24 teachers, one aide, 223 pupils. Three terms, $980 per term, including insurance and computer fee. Pre-school from 3 yrs. Principal, Samuel Bethel, PO Box F-40667, tel 373-4391.

Mary Star of the Sea School, Sunrise Hwy. Roman Catholic. Kindergarten-grade 6, 500 pupils, 40 lay teachers, one aide. Three terms, $635 per term plus $75 per year registration. Headmaster, Kenneth Sampson, PO Box F-42418, tel 373-3456.

St Vincent de Paul, Hunter's. Roman Catholic. Kindergarten-grade 6, 109 pupils, 10 teachers, 8:30am-3pm. Registration $25, tuition $495 per term, books $42 (rental), insurance $15; computer fee $10. Uniforms. Headmistress, Dorothy Lewis, PO Box F-42517, tel 353-7727.

Primary & Secondary

Grand Bahama Academy of Seventh-Day Adventists, Sancombe Dr and Torcross Rd, Grasmere. Kindergarten-grade 7, with new grades being added as the school expands. 265 students, 12 teachers. Kindergarten, $522; grades 1-6, $599 a term. Books $180-$300 according to grade. Registration $65. Uniforms. Principal, Haydn Hanna, PO Box F-44399, tel 373-4794.

Lucaya International School, Chesapeake Rd. Non-profit, non-denominational, independent. 163 pupils 2½-18 yrs, 14 teachers, six part-time. Fees $3,211-$10,165 per year, registration $150, development fund $1,500, except pre-school students (one-time fee). International curriculum includes International Baccalaureate, International Certificate of Secondary Education and BGCSE. The school prepares children for the educational systems to which they may later move. The faculty is fully qualified and many hold advanced degrees. Library, computer lab, auditorium and speciality rooms for science, music, arts/crafts and academic support. Director, Anthony Baron, PO Box F-44066, tel 373-4004.

St Paul's Methodist College, Clive Ave. Administered by the Methodist Church in the Caribbean and the Americas board of trustees. 380 pupils 3-16 yrs, 30 teachers. Infant dept, reception, kindergarten, $605 per term; junior dept, grades 1-6, $682 per term; junior and senior high, grades 7-12, $775 per term; 10% discount for children other than oldest in school from one family. Registration $20, seat deposit $50. Uniforms same as Queen's College, Nassau. SAT, Advance Placement and BGCSE. Principal, Lin Glinton, PO Box F-40897, tel 352-6225.

Sunland Lutheran School, Gambier Dr. 560 pupils, nursery-grade 12, 37 teachers. Nursery (3 yrs) and kindergarten (4 yrs), $750; grades 1-6, $800. Grades 7-12 $850. Registration $100. Includes textbooks up to and including grade 9. Headmistress, Myrton King; vice-principal, Sheila Robinson. PO Box F-42469, tel 373-3700/1.

Tabernacle Baptist Christian Academy, Settler's Way. Pre-school-grade 12. 550 pupils, 32 teachers. Fees per term: kindergarten, $475; grades 1-6, $420; grades 7-9, $575; grades 10-12, $600. Principal, Norris Bain, PO Box F-42705, tel 352-9556.

Secondary

Freeport High School, East Sunrise Hwy. Administered by the Anglican Diocese of The Bahamas. 465 pupils 11-19 yrs, 37 teachers. Tuition $1,000 per term, 5% deduction per term for second child. Non-refundable seat fee of $50. Books cost an additional $200-$300. Insurance, $20 per year. Computer fee, $75 per year. BGCSE, Pitman and American College Board exams. Uniforms. Principal, Samuel Bethell, PO Box F-40667, tel 373-3579.

Grand Bahama Catholic High School, East Settler's Way. Roman Catholic. 415 pupils, grades 7-12, 36 teachers. Three terms. BJC, BGCSE, PSAT, Pitman, RSA, SAT, ACT exams. $810 per term. Uniforms. Principal, Daisy McPhee, PO Box F-42635, tel 352-2544.

Jack Hayward High School, Pioneer's Loop. Public school. Annual maintenance fee of $20. 1,359 pupils, 100 teachers. Principal, Hubert Marshall, PO Box F-41314, tel 373-8750.

St Georges' High School, Sunset Hwy. Public school. Small fee for technical courses. 1,494 pupils, 86 teachers. Uniforms. Principal, Mary Cooper, PO Box F-40787, tel 352-7373.

Tertiary education

Bahamas Technical and Vocational Institute, GB Trade School Bldg (next to College of The Bahamas), West Settler's Way. One-year programmes from Sept-July. Classes in carpentry, electrical installation, electronics, office administration, plumbing and welding, auto mechanics, cosmetology, computer operations and air conditioning and refrigeration. Day classes in cosmetology and office technology. There are nine full-time programmes. Registration fee $100 (Bahamians), $150 (non-Bahamians), books and tools not included. Tuition free. Short general interest courses on demand, fee $200, subject to change. Approx 200 students. Coordinator, Fred Delancy, PO Box F-40477, tel 352-2190.

College of The Bahamas (COB), GB Trade School Bldg, West Settler's Way. Eight full-time lecturers and 15 part-time. Programmes include business administration, associate's degree in accounting, computer data processing, bachelor's degree in accounting, diploma in education and preschool teacher's certificate. The former Bahamas Hotel Training College was amalgamated into COB as the School of Hospitality and Tourism Studies in Aug 2000. Evening classes include fashion design, electrical installation, plumbing, vehicle maintenance, conversational Spanish, French and Creole. Books cost approx $500 per semester, lab fees $5-$100, security deposit $100 refundable on graduation, insurance $20, orientation fee $50. Fees are $100 per credit and $150 per credit for bachelor's degrees for Bahamians, double for non-Bahamians. Assistant vice-president, Dr Coralie Kelly, PO Box F-42766, tel 352-9761.

Success Training College, East Mall Dr. Diploma and associate's degree programmes in business administration, accounting, banking and finance, computer information systems, office automation science, computer systems management, internet systems management, network systems administration, medical assisting and early childhood education. The college also offers more than 50 comprehensive certificate courses. Administrator, Eric Stewart. Tel 351-2673.

Special education

Beacon School for Special Education, Frobisher Dr. School for exceptional children. Dedicated to the memory of Diana, Princess of Wales, this school has been rebuilt with equal funding from Lady Henrietta St George and the govt. 13 teachers, 96 pupils, non-residential. Principal, Cheryl Woods, PO Box F-40032, tel 352-8445.

ELECTRICITY

Electricity is generated by Grand Bahama Power Co Ltd at the Peel St generating plant. Grand Bahama Power is jointly owned by ICD Utilities and Mirant Corp. Facilities consist of a 27,000 kW diesel plant, two gas turbines totalling 35,000 kW and a 75,000 kW steam plant. Total installed generating capacity is 141,500 kW.

Total net MWh generated by Freeport Power Co

Year	MWh
1999	336,724
2000	338,281
2001	353,846
2002	370,424
2003	382,198

Total average active meters

Year	Meters
1999	16,553
2000	17,014
2001	17,521
2002	18,000
2003	18,300

Supply voltage and frequency

3 phase, 4 wire, 208/120 volts, 60 cycles
3 phase, 4 wire, 240/120 volts, 60 cycles
1 phase, 3 wire, 240/120 volts, 60 cycles
1 phase, 3 wire, 208/120 volts, 60 cycles
3 phase, 4 wire, 480/277 volts, 60 cycles

Voltage and frequency depend on location.

Tariffs
Principal rates are:

1. **Residential (monthly)**
   First 350 kWh, 13.64¢/kWh
   Next 450 kWh, 15.83¢/kWh
   Additional kWh, 18.55¢/kWh
   Min charge, $10/month
2. **Temporary service (TS)**
   All kWh, 18.55¢/kWh
   Min charge, $10/month
   Meter rental, $10/month
3. **Commercial service (CS)**
   First 20,000 kWh, 14.28¢/kWh
   Next 80,000 kWh, 13.26¢/kWh
   Additional kWh, 12.24¢/kWh
   First 5 kilovolt amperes (kVA) or less, $33
   Additional kVA, $6.60/kVA/month
   Min charge, same as demand charge
4. **GS Large (GSL)**
   First 100,000 kWh, 12.24¢/kWh
   Next 400,000 kWh, 11.22¢/kWh
   Next 800,000 kWh, 10.20¢/kWh
   Additional kWh, 8.16¢/kWh
   First 1,000 kVA or less, $6,600/month
   Additional kVA, $6.60/kVA/month
   Min charge, same as demand charge
5. **Reconnection for non-payment** $30

Grand Bahama Power provides electricity services to all of Grand Bahama and to the offshore communities of Deep Water Cay and Sweeting's Cay.

EMERGENCY NUMBERS

Ambulance 352-2689
Bahamas Air Sea Rescue Assoc
(BASRA)............................352-2628
or pager 352-6222
(pin 8339 and 8440)
Fire brigade....................................911
Police 911
Rand Memorial Hospital 352-6735
Grand Bahama Island
Tourism Board................352-8044/5
or 352-6512

Embassies (in Nassau)
British High
Commission ....(242) 325-7471 (to 3)
Canadian
Consulate ....(242) 393-2123/4
US Embassy ....(242) 322-1181/3

Credit card companies
American Express
Cards 1-800-327-1267
Traveller's Cheques ..1-800-221-7282
Barclay Card (Freeport) 352-8391
Discover Card
(collect) ....(801) 902-3100
MasterCard (collect) ....(314) 542-7111
Visa............................1-800-847-2911
Suncard...............................352-4428

See also **Ambulance/air ambulance services.**

EMPLOYERS' ORGANIZATIONS

Employers' interests are generally looked after by the Grand Bahama Chamber of Commerce, although there is also a Grand Bahama Hotel Assoc and Freeport Hotel Restaurant Employers' Assoc.

See also **Chamber of Commerce.**

ENCOURAGEMENT ACTS

As well as absence of taxes, other incentives for investors to do business in The Bahamas include the Caribbean Basin Initiative (CBI), CARIBCAN, Lomé/ Cotonou Agreement, Industries Encouragement Act, Hotels Encouragement Act and the Agricultural Manufactories Act. See **Bahamas information, Agriculture.** For information on initiatives, see relevant headings in **Bahamas information.**

Licensees of the 233-sq-mile Grand Bahama Port Authority (GBPA) area gain a bonus over the rest of The Bahamas: until Aug 2054 at the earliest, they do not pay excise or import duties on materials or equipment used by their businesses. Nor, until Aug 2015, will businesses under the Liquor Licences Act, the Shop Licences Act or the Road Traffic Act pay a business licence fee. Also until Aug 2015, non-Bahamian owners of Freeport/Lucaya property are exempt from paying real property tax.

See also **Customs** and **Hawksbill Creek Agreement.**

ENGINEERS

See **Building contractors & engineers.**

ENTERTAINMENT

The Royal Oasis Casino has slot machines open from 8:30am and gaming tables from 10am until the early hours. It has a floor show twice nightly and first-class dining.

A new 19,000-sq-ft casino, the Isle of Capri, opened in Dec 2003, with 400 slot machines and 21 table games as part of the Our Lucaya Resort. The casino offers live music Sat and Sun nights.

There are several nightclubs and discos on the island, as well as nightly live entertainment at Count Basie Sq, Port Lucaya Marketplace.

See also **Gambling.**

EXCHANGE CONTROL

Regulations apply as in Nassau. The Central Bank's Exchange Control office is on the first floor of the Regent Centre West. PO Box F-41666, tel 352-5963.

See **Bahamas information, Exchange control.**

EXPORT ENTRY

An export entry form is required for all goods exported by ship or air freight. It is advisable to export goods through a freight service that will supply forms and deal with Customs.

Ordinary parcels such as clothing and gifts sent through the post office at Explorer's Way do not incur the $10 stamp tax and do not require an export entry form, but must have a post office-issued label giving weight and value of contents.

Customs brokers

Expert Customs Brokers 352-7494
Freeport Transfer 352-7821
General Brokers and Agents 352-7891
Lucaya Shipping & Trading Co Ltd 352-3581
Professional Brokers Agency Co Ltd 351-3839
Swann's Shipping 352-7705
Tanja Customs Clearance Centre 352-4268
Taylor & Taylor Ltd 352-7250
United Shipping Co Ltd 352-9315
Wide World Forwarding........352-3636

See also **Bahamas information, Export entry** and **Customs.**

FIRE BRIGADE

The Grand Bahama Fire Brigade has four large fire trucks and is manned by 40 firefighters. To report a fire call 911. For permission to start a controlled bonfire, tel 352-8441.

FISHING

Gamefish found in Grand Bahama waters include sailfish, blue marlin, white marlin, tuna, dolphin, kingfish and wahoo.

Bonefishing is popular and is available at Pelican Bay at Lucaya, Deepwater Cay and North Riding Point Clubs, and at McLean's Town, Water Cay and West End.

Commercial fishing

In 2003, commercial fishermen in Grand Bahama caught 2,059,628 lbs of fish valued at $14,630,275. The largest catches were crawfish tails, 1,137,600 lbs; conch, 258,981 lbs; Nassau grouper, 161,696 lbs; and snapper, 184,142 lbs.

For fishing regulations, see **Bahamas information, Fishing.**

FREIGHT SERVICES

Freight may be shipped to and from Freeport/Lucaya by sea or air. Scheduled airlines provide regular freight service and Convair cargo service, which flies Tues-Fri, is operated by Wide World Forwarding.

From Miami to Nassau and Freeport there is a minimum charge of $45 per 100 lbs or less. However, in order to encourage the Grand Bahama export market, Wide World Forwarding charges $30 for the same weight, adding 36¢ per lb. The minimum charge is $45 up to 1,000 lbs and 34¢ per lb for 1,001 lbs and over. Ocean freight rate for a 20-ft container is $900 plus insurance and for a 40-ft container, $1,400 plus insurance.

Five shipping lines provide freight service between Freeport and Florida. Crowley American and Savoy Shipping sail three times a week from Port Everglades; Seaboard Marine sails four times a week from Miami to Freeport; and Tropical Shipping, four times a week from Riviera Beach. Bahmar arrives twice a week via Nassau. Major container companies serving Grand Bahama are Maersk/Sealand, CMA, Navieras/NPR, Cagema and Mediterranean Shipping Co.

A container shipped to England takes two to three weeks to deliver. Cost of shipping depends on the commodity and weight.

Freeport Harbour's entrance channel is 500 ft wide and 51 ft deep and can accommodate the largest container ships in the world.

See also **Shipping agents.**

GAMBLING

Casino gambling is legal in The Bahamas for non-residents 18 and older.

There are two casinos in Freeport/ Lucaya. The Royal Oasis Casino, owned by Driftwood Bahamas Ltd, offers a full-service Las Vegas-style Sports Book, slot machines and table games. The Our Lucaya Resort opened its 19,000-sq-ft Isle of Capri Casino in 2003, with 400 slot machines, 21 table games and a racing sports book.

See also **Entertainment.**

GEOGRAPHY

Grand Bahama covers an area of 530 sq miles. The highest point is 68 ft.

See also **Bahamas information, Geography.**

GOLF COURSES

There are four 18-hole championship golf courses operating in Freeport/ Lucaya: Emerald and Ruby golf courses at the Crowne Plaza Golf Resort & Casino and Our Lucaya's Lucayan and Reef courses.

Fortune Hills Golf & Country Club operates a nine-hole course. Numerous local, inter-island and international tournaments are held throughout the year.

Water World Enterprises Ltd offers two professionally designed miniature golf courses.

See **Bahamas information, Sports** and this section, **Sports venues.**

GOVERNMENT OFFICES

Administrator's Office
Caraway Bldg, West Atlantic Dr
PO Box F-40001
Tel 352-6332, fax 352-9027

Bahamas Customs Dept
National Insurance Bldg
PO Box F-42484
Tel 352-7361, fax 352-7365

Bahamas Development Bank
(govt offices)
Bank of The Bahamas Bldg
PO Box F-42573
Tel 352-9025, fax 352-4166

Bahamas Information Services
BTC Bldg, The Mall
PO Box F-40001
Tel 352-8525, fax 352-8520

Bahamas Investment Authority
BTC Bldg, The Mall
PO Box F-40001
Tel 352-8525, fax 352-8520

Bahamas Mortgage Corp
The Mall Dr
PO Box F-42605
Tel 352-7513/4, fax 352-6478

Bahamas Telecommunications Co
BTC Bldg, The Mall
PO Box F-42483
Tel 350-1000 or 352-6731, fax 352-4708

The Central Bank of The Bahamas
Exchange Control Dept
Regent Centre West, Suites B & C
PO Box F-42521
Tel 352-5963, fax 352-5397

City of Freeport Council
Pioneer's Professional Plaza
PO Box F-42067
Tel 351-2303, fax 351-2309

College of The Bahamas
West Settler's Way
PO Box F-42766
Tel 352-9761, fax 352-6167

Ministry of Agriculture and Fisheries
West Mall Dr
PO Box F-40006
Tel 352-2144, fax 352-4935 or 351-5049

Dept of the Auditor General
National Insurance Bldg
PO Box F-40182
Tel 352-2355, fax 351-6159

Ministry of Finance & Planning
Bain Bldg, West Atlantic Dr
Tel 351-4374, fax 352-5937

Ministry of Labour and Immigration
Churchill Bldg
PO Box F-40062
Tel 352-9338, fax 352-5275

Dept of Rehabilitative Welfare Services
Probation Division
Insurance Management Bldg
PO Box F-40997
Tel 351-7357, fax 351-6216

Dept of Statistics
Regent Centre North
PO Box F-42561
Tel 352-7196, fax 352-6120

Gaming Board
British American Bldg, Queen's Hwy
PO Box F-42313
Tel 352-9007, fax 352-6507

Grand Bahama Island Tourism Board
International Bazaar (above China Temple)
PO Box F-40251
Tel 352-8044, fax 352-2714

Ministry of Health
Rand Memorial Hospital
PO Box F-40071
Tel 352-6735 (to 9), fax 352-6791

Social Development Dept
National Insurance Bldg
PO Box F-40997
Tel 352-9851, fax 352-7960

Ministry of Trade and Industry
Consumer Welfare Protection Division
National Insurance Bldg
PO Box F-43328
Tel 352-3414, fax 351-5507

Ministry of Transport – Road Traffic Dept
National Insurance Bldg
PO Box F-40338
Tel 352-7204/5, fax 352-4874

Ministry of Works and Utilities
National Insurance Bldg
PO Box F-40530
Tel 352-2478, fax 352-9160

National Insurance Board
National Insurance Bldg
PO Box F-42618
Tel 352-7222/3, fax 352-6143

Office of the Attorney-General
Regent Centre North, Suites 2 & 3
PO Box F-42218
Tel 351-5785, fax 352-7896

Office of The Prime Minister
BTC Bldg, The Mall
PO Box F-60137
Tel 352-8525/6, fax 352-8520

Passport Office
National Insurance Bldg
PO Box F-43536
Tel 352-5698, fax 352-5672

Police Dept
International Bldg, The Mall
PO Box F-40082
Tel 352-8280 or 352-8352, fax 352-2587

Port Dept
(Registration of motor boats, tugs, etc)
National Insurance Bldg
PO Box F-42044
Tel 352-9163, fax 351-4538

Post Office Dept
Explorer's Way
PO Box F-40000
Tel 352-9371, fax 352-6170

Public Works
National Insurance Bldg
PO Box F-40530
Tel 352-2478, fax 352-9160

Registrar General's Dept
Regent Centre, 16/17
PO Box F-42602
Tel 352-4934, fax 352-4060

Supreme & Magistrates Courts
Garnet Levarity Justice Centre
PO Box F-40174
Tel 352-6806, fax 352-2533

Treasury Dept
National Insurance Bldg
PO Box F-42485
Tel 352-2351, fax 352-2145

See also **Government section.**

GRAND BAHAMA HUMANE SOCIETY

Just off Queen's Hwy on Cedar St, this organization is operated by volunteers, three paid staff members, and two part-time kennel staff. Strays are given necessary medication and housed in kennels – 16 for dogs and 10 for cats. A fenced area can accommodate more dogs and cats. Unclaimed animals are put up for adoption and about 10% find homes. Hours are Mon-Fri 9am-1pm, Sat 9am-12 noon. Tel 352-2477.

See also **Bahamas information, Animals** and **Bahamas Humane Society.**

GUN PERMITS

Applications for gun licences should be made to the Criminal Investigation Department (CID), Peel St, tel 352-9774. A shotgun licence costs $50 and a rifle licence is $100. A separate application must be made for each gun. Gun licences must be renewed annually. Replacement of a lost licence costs $5.

See also **Bahamas information, Gun permits.**

HARBOUR CONTROL

Freeport Harbour Control gives clearance to all ships leaving and entering Freeport Harbour. Permission must be obtained from Freeport Harbour Control (open 24 hours) by all vessels wishing to enter or leave Freeport Harbour and those wishing to move from one berth to another. Operators of small fishing boats and small pleasure craft should contact Harbour Control before departing the harbour so their whereabouts can be ascertained if overdue. Tel 352-9651.

Harbour Control's VHF radio frequencies are channels 14 and 16. AM radio ship-to-ship frequencies are 2182, 2638 and 2670 kHz.

The international emergency frequency, 2182 kHz, is controlled by Bahamas Telecommunications Co (BTC). For commercial traffic, AM frequency 2198 kHz should be used. Single sideband frequencies are 3300.0, 4139.5, 5057.0, 8100.0.

MariSat (the Marine Satellite System) enables the placing of overseas telephone and telex calls to ships at sea throughout the world via Atlantic or Pacific satellites. Dial "0" for the marine operator, who will book calls via a MariSat operator. No collect or credit card charges are accepted. Freeport residents may use an improved VHF-FM radio telephone service to contact ships at sea through the Nassau marine operator.

See also **Boating** and **Marinas & cruising facilities.**

HAWKSBILL CREEK AGREEMENT

The Hawksbill Creek Agreement, essentially a contract between The Bahamas government and Freeport businesses licensed by the Grand Bahama Port Authority (GBPA), was the foundation stone of Freeport/Lucaya. Under the 1955 pact, the government granted the GBPA 50,000 acres of unused Crown land to be developed as an international port and industrial centre. Later, the Port Authority obtained additional land from the Crown and from private sources for a total holding of 149,000 acres, or 233 sq miles.

To encourage business development on this land, the government granted further concessions to the Port Authority and its licensees to apply only to the Freeport area. Principal concessions were:

1. Freedom from taxation – there was a contractual guarantee that, at least until 1990, there would be no personal income taxes, no corporate profit taxes, no capital gains taxes or levies on capital appreciation and no personal or real property or inventory taxes. A two-year extension was granted, then a one-year extension. From Aug 4, 1993, the exemptions – which include real property tax for non-Bahamian owners of Freeport/Lucaya property – were extended 22 years to 2015 "notwithstanding anything to the contrary in any other law." See also **Bahamas information, Property tax.** Persons or companies carrying on business in the Port Area under the Road Traffic Act, Liquor Licences Act or Shop Licences Act are exempt from the Bahamian business licence fee until Aug 4, 2015.
2. Freedom from customs duties – at least until Aug 2054 no excise or import duties will be levied on equipment or materials used by licensees. Only goods for personal use or consumption are dutiable.

Persons interested in starting a business in Freeport/Lucaya should acquaint themselves with the Hawksbill Creek Agreement and other encouragement acts. See also **Encouragement acts.**

The port area covers about one-third of the island, and should be checked with a map by drivers of bonded cars, which cannot be driven outside the area without incurring penalties, eg, Eight Mile Rock is outside the area.

See also **Customs** and **History.**

HEALTH/MEDICAL SERVICES

See **Ambulance/air ambulance services, Dentists, Doctors** and **Hospitals & clinics.**

HISTORY

Remains and artefacts found in Grand Bahama provide evidence that Lucayan tribes lived here until the time of the Spanish conquerors. The island was probably deserted for some time thereafter.

During the late 18th century a few settlements grew up as people drifted over from other islands. West End had spurts of activity (due to its proximity to the Florida coast) as a haven for gun-runners during the Civil War and rum-runners during Prohibition.

Three big finds of treasure from sunken galleons have been made off the Grand Bahama coast since 1964, including the salvaging of the *Nuestra Señora de las Maravillas.*

It is only in the last 50 years that the island has been fully developed. The population of about 4,000 in the 1950s had risen to 46,954 by 2000, due entirely to the advent of American-born Wallace Groves and his Abaco Lumber Co. While cutting the island's crop of Caribbean pine, Groves devised a plan for making a huge free port and industrial centre in the midst of the scrub and swamp around Hawksbill Creek.

Groves started the Grand Bahama Port Authority (GBPA) with a grant of 50,000 acres of land, which was eventually increased to 149,000 acres, from the Bahamian government. In return, the GBPA built houses, churches, schools and roads under the terms of the Hawksbill Creek Agreement. A deep-water harbour was dredged for oil tankers and an oil refinery (which now stores and trans-ships oil) was erected. An airport, hotels and casinos were also added. By 1966 there were 214 miles of paved roads, hundreds of buildings and areas set apart for shops and light and heavy industry. Hotels, golf courses, beaches and marinas were soon to make it a tourist haven.

In 1993 Southern Electric Intl (now Mirant Corp), from Georgia, became a 50/50 partner with the Freeport Power Co, resulting in the provision of electric power to the outlying parts of the island. Mirant Corp presently owns 55% of what is now Grand Bahama Power Co.

In 1995 the largest container company in the world, Hutchison Port Holdings Ltd, became an equal partner with the GBPA. A contract was signed to build a massive container trans-shipment port, which opened up enormous potential for Freeport. The container port is now run by Hutchison Port Holdings. In 2000 another subsidiary, Hutchison Lucaya Ltd, completed construction of a giant hotel complex in Lucaya, now managed by Westin and Sheraton.

A new state-of-the-art airport was completed in 2004.

See also **Bahamas information, History** and this section, **Hawksbill Creek Agreement.**

HOSPITALS & CLINICS

Rand Memorial Hospital, East Atlantic Dr. Govt-owned, community-type hospital. Departments: medical, intensive care, surgery, gynaecology and obstetrics, paediatrics, psychiatry, pathology, clinical laboratories, physiotherapy, orthopaedics, EKG and radiology. General practice clinics are available. Ophthalmology services are provided at Davies House, Nansen Ave, and Eight Mile Rock Clinic. Mammography services are provided at Davies House. The hospital is scheduled for a $35-$40 million redevelopment. Administrator, Grand Bahama Health Services, Sharon Williams. Tel 352-6735.

The New Sunrise Medical Centre – Hospital Complex, East Sunrise Hwy, is the oldest private medical facility on the island. The Centre has seen extensive renovations and expansion over the past five years. It supports a team of physicians, surgeons, dentists, and other allied health care professionals offering an array of medical, surgical, paediatric, ophthalmologic, urologic obstetric and gynaecologic, as well as pharmacy, laboratory, imaging and nursing services. The Centre has an upgraded 17-bed facility with 10 in-patient beds, four equipped for critical care, a seven-bed recovery room and two operating theatres. The Centre has x-ray, ultrasonography, fluoroscopy, CT and MRI scanning. The Centre is a private 24-hour medical facility. The rest of the centre is open 8:30am-9:30pm daily. Administrator, Michelle Major. Tel 373-3333 (to 6), fax 373-3342.

Lucayan Medical Centre West, Adventurers Way. Multi-speciality ambulatory care clinic including diagnostic and ambulatory surgery facilities. Care is provided by 15 physicians specializing in family medicine, internal medicine, obstetrics and gynaecology, kidney diseases, ophthalmology, paediatrics, podiatry, ENT surgery, urology and orthopaedic surgery. The Centre has the only renal dialysis unit on the island. Audiology and speech therapy specialists are available. Diagnostic facilities include X-ray and ultrasonography, laboratory and electrocardiography. Full-service pharmacy 8:30am-5:30pm. Financial Controller, Jasmine Davis. Tel 352-7288, fax 352-3644.

Lucayan Medical Centre East, East Sunrise Hwy. Multi-speciality ambulatory care clinic with five physicians providing care in general/family medicine, internal medicine, general surgery, cardiology and psychiatry. Dental unit offers care in dentistry and oral-maxillo facial surgery. Full-service pharmacy, X-ray and laboratory services. Financial Controller, Jasmine Davis. Tel 373-7400, fax 373-7367.

Government clinics
Govt clinics are served by doctors and nurses who provide medical services at minimal fees. Eight government community clinics provide primary care services to residents under the supervision of assigned district medical officers. These clinics, managed by Grand Bahama Health Services, are located at Eight Mile Rock, Hawksbill, West End, High Rock, McLean's Town, Grand Cay and Sweeting's Cay. The Clinics provide dental services by appointment. There are two government dentists in Grand Bahama and a visiting dental surgeon.

Private care
Family Wellness Centre, West Atlantic Dr. Dr Gerald Raftopoulos, Dr Kevin Bethel, Suzanne Pipes (acupuncturist), Dr Foster Walton (chiropractor). Tel 373-2454.
GB Family Medical Centre, Seventeen Centre. Dr Michael Darville and Dr Ian Archer. Tel 351-9282.
Health Enhancement Centre, 16C Kipling Bldg. Obstetrics and gynaecology. Dr Havard Cooper. Tel 352-4444.
Immuno-Augmentative Cancer Clinic (IAT), East Atlantic Dr. Cancer patients treated on out-patient basis. Three medical doctors. Tel 352-7455.
LEAS Nursing Agency. Private registered nurses and midwives for special care and general nursing, also available for overseas travel. Joan McKay, tel 373-5497 or Anna Cooper, tel 352-7146 or 373-3230.
Northern Bahamas Paediatrics, Ste 6, Lucayan Plaza, Coral Rd. Dr G Bartlett, Dr W Pratt. Tel 373-3631.
Quantum Physicians Plus, Quantum House, Atlantic & Poinciana Dr. Dr Eric Brown (dermatologist). Tel 351-4400.
St Jude's Medical Centre, 11B Coral Rd. Dr Paul Ward (gynaecologist), Dr Wilfred Ferguson (paediatrician), Dr Charles Johnson (ENT specialist), Dr Timothy Barrat (psychiatrist). Tel 373-2544.
Seahorse Family Health Centre, New Sunrise Medical Centre. Dr Renee Lockhart. Tel 373-9174.

HOTELS

See **Bahamas information, Hotels** and this section, **Accommodations.**

HOUSING

The Bahamas government promotes the development of low-cost housing in Freeport through a guaranteed mortgage financing programme granting purchasers long-term financing (up to 30 years) at below-market interest rates to encourage low-income families to purchase homes. RBC Finco, British American Bank, Bahamas Mortgage Corp and Commonwealth Bank participate in this programme. Independent developers have built low-cost housing using the government's guaranteed mortgage financing programme.

Middle-cost housing as well as upscale real estate developments are available.

See also **Cost of living.**

IMMIGRATION

To apply for immigration status specifically in Freeport/Lucaya contact the Dept of Immigration, Churchill Bldg, PO Box F-40062, tel 352-9338. Inquiries may also be made at the Grand Bahama Port Authority, tel 352-6611, PO Box F-42666, or any reliable real estate company, about the possibilities of permanent residency for serious investors. The procedure for applying for a work permit is the same as in Nassau. Freeport applications are dealt with regularly when the Immigration Board meets in Freeport.

See **Bahamas information, Immigration.**

IMPORT ENTRY

Regulations apply as in Nassau. The Central Bank's Exchange Control Office in Freeport is on the first floor of Regent Centre West, PO Box F-42521, Freeport, Grand Bahama, tel 352-5963.

See **Bahamas information, Import entry.**

INDUSTRY

Several large industries have been established in Freeport, attracted by tax advantages, a first-class infrastructure and availability of certain natural resources.

Bahama Rock quarries and crushes limestone for export to the US, Caribbean, and (in small quantities) various Bahamian islands. It also processes material used in stack emission control for power plants, and lime used in chemical, industrial and agricultural applications. Employs 45.

The first Freeport industry was established in 1958, a bunkering terminal that was absorbed in the late '60s by the **Bahamas Oil Refining Co (BORCO).** The huge oil refinery ceased processing crude oil in 1985 as a result of deteriorating refining economics in the Caribbean. BORCO concentrates currently on continuing terminal operations – trans-shipping, storing and blending of oil and bunkering of ships. Total oil imports for 2003 were 72,524,050 barrels; exports were 69,614,146 barrels. BORCO has 107 employees, 34 support staff and approx 33 contractors per day.

Bradford Grand Bahama Ltd is a subsidiary of Bradford Marine Inc in Ft Lauderdale, the world's largest covered yacht repair facility. Bradford GB repairs yachts, pleasure cruisers, commercial boats and fishing vessels. Mechanical and electrical repairs, metal fabrication, piping and plumbing, bottom painting, carpentry and fibreglass work are provided, as well as finish painting. Dry docking is available through a 150-ton lift and a 1,200-ton floating dry dock. Wet dockage is available for vessels up to 315 ft. Employs 70.

Fragrance of The Bahamas at the International Bazaar affords visitors the opportunity to see how perfumes are made, packaged and prepared for the Bahamian market. There is a showroom on site.

Freepoint Tug & Towing Services Ltd provides towage service to all of Grand Bahama, particularly South Riding Point and the Lucayan Harbour. It also offers towage, salvage, ship management and brokerage to The Bahamas and the Caribbean and employs 46.

Freeport Container Port, operated by Hutchison Port Holdings (HPH), offers 3,000 ft of berthing, seven Super Post Panamax quay cranes, 30 straddle carriers and 225 reefer points. There is a short approach of one mile from pilot station to berth. The approach depth is 52 ft and the alongside depth is 51 ft. The Port has an annual capacity of more than 950,000 20-ft containers.

Grand Bahama Brewing Co Ltd began operation in 1996 and sells four different brews under the Hammerhead and Lucayan labels – Lucayan Light, Lucayan Lager and Hammerhead Amber Ale and Stout. There are six full-time and eight part-time Bahamian employees and a salesperson on the premises at Logwood Rd. It is owned by Canadian bio-physicist Greg Langstaff. Some 4,000 cases are produced per month. The brewery has a potential capacity of 5,000 cases. Some of the ale is exported to Nassau.

Grand Bahama Food Ltd Wholesale Division serves a customer base throughout Grand Bahama, as well as several large wholesalers and hotels in Nassau. It maintains an inventory of approx 3,000 different product lines, including fresh produce, paper and plastic products, chemicals and cleaning supplies, fresh and frozen meats, fish and seafood.

Grand Bahama Shipyard, a $100-million world-class ship-repair facility in Freeport Harbour, owned mainly by the GBPA, has two floating docks and two wet-dock positions. Its floating dock can lift ships weighing up to 150,000 tons. Many large ships (including the world's largest cruise ship) have already taken advantage of this yard, which provides a complete repair and renovation service for cruise and cargo ships, tankers and container vessels.

Hemisphere Container Repair Ltd (HCR) stores, maintains and repairs ocean cargo equipment for container ships and is a dealer for both Carrier and Thermo King. HCR has two established companies in Wilmington and Charlotte, NC, serving steamship lines. Situated on two acres near the Freeport Container Port, it employs 10 Bahamians.

Lucayan Harbour, a joint venture of HPH and GBPA on 1,630 acres, with minimum depth alongside of 32 ft, can accommodate six cruise ships and five ro-ro vessels. A $10.9-million upgrade to the cruise ship terminal provides state-of-the-art facilities plus a 25,000-sq-ft landscaped retail village.

Polymers Intl Ltd manufactures expandable polystyrene, a plastic used in the manufacture of disposable food service containers. Expandable polystyrene produced in The Bahamas is exported to various international destinations including the UK, Australia, Argentina and the US.

South Riding Point Holding Ltd (SRPHL) is an $80-million crude oil storage and trans-shipment terminal with 5.25-million-barrel storage capacity. With deep berths and pilotage available, SRPHL provides service to the largest crude oil tankers in the world. The terminal is close to the Gulf of Mexico and the US eastern seaboard, and near the routes to and from the Panama Canal.

Todhunter-Mitchell Distillers produces approx 100,000 cases of rum and other liquors per year.

See also **Agriculture.**

INTERNATIONAL BAZAAR

One of Freeport's attractions is the International Bazaar, a large shopping complex featuring more than 80 businesses and offering the merchandise and cuisine of 36 countries.

Completed in 1967, the 10-acre Bazaar was designed by a motion picture special effects expert. Visitors are greeted at the entrance by a torii gate, the Japanese symbol of welcome. Also represented in the Bazaar are Spain, South America, the Caribbean, France, Greece, China, Denmark, Norway, Sweden, England and the Middle East. There is colourful entertainment and a straw market.

Open Mon-Sat, 9:30/10am-6pm. Some stores open Sun 10am-5pm.

See also **Shopping.**

INTERNET

See **Bahamas information, Internet.**

JUDICIAL SYSTEM

Freeport has two supreme courts and three magistrates' courts. A fourth magistrates' court is at Eight Mile Rock. There are two permanent judges.

See also **Bahamas information, Judicial system.**

JUNKANOO

A Junkanoo parade is held on New Year's Day from 5-11pm at the International Bazaar. This event is staged by the Grand Bahama Junkanoo Committee. Groups compete for prizes amounting to several thousand dollars.

See also **Bahamas information, Junkanoo.**

LAW FIRMS

Alexiou, Knowles & Co
Tel 351-7371/7, fax 351-7505
Ayse Rengin Dengizer Johnson & Co
Tel 351-9103/9277, fax 351-8714
Bain, Gomez & Co
Tel 352-5971, fax 352-6075
Bridgewater & Co
Tel 351-5101, fax 351-8007
Cafferata & Co
Tel 351-4086, fax 351-3506
Callenders & Co
Tel 352-7458, fax 352-4000
Cash, Fountain
Tel 352-7774, fax 351-5988
Chancery Law Assoc
Tel 351-6367, fax 356-6108
Davis & Co
Tel 352-8311, fax 352-4458
Dupuch & Turnquest
Tel 352-8134, fax 352-5687
Godfrey Pinder
Tel 351-3311, fax 352-3433
Graham Thompson & Co
Tel 351-7474, fax 351-7752
Higgs & Johnson
Tel 351-5515, fax 351-4955
James Roosevelt Thompson
Tel 352-7451, fax 352-7453
Kevin M Russell & Co
Tel 373-9740, fax 374-2780
Lockhart & Munroe
Tel 352-2253, fax 352-2258
Malcolm E Adderley & Co
Tel 352-5622, fax 352-8757
Maurice O Glinton & Co
Tel 352-4484, fax 352-4526
McDonald & Co
Tel 352-4545, fax 352-7649
McKinney, Bancroft & Hughes
Tel 352-7425/6, fax 352-7214
Norris R Carroll & Co
Tel 352-8635, fax 352-3162
Nottage, Miller & Co
Tel 352-4222, fax 352-4232
Rawle Maynard
Tel 352-4222, fax 352-4232
Ryan & Co
Tel 351-3583, fax 351-2878
Simeon Brown & Co
Tel 352-2316, fax 352-5605
Stephanie J Saunders & Co
Tel 351-3331/4370, fax 351-5626
Stephen Wilchcombe & Co
Tel 352-7696, fax 352-3437
Tynes & Tynes
Tel 352-4761, fax 352-6209
V Alfred Gray & Co
Tel 352-7043, fax 352-4010
Vernon Darville
Tel 352-3008, fax 352-2524
Veronica Grant
Tel 351-3911, fax 351-4927
Wallace Whitfield & Co
Tel 352-8156, fax 352-8159
Wells-Carmona, Gottlieb & Co
Tel 352-7291, fax 351-4524

See also **Bahamas information, Law firms.**

LIBRARIES

The **Sir Charles Hayward Library** in the grounds of the Rand Memorial Hospital was opened by James Henry Rand in 1962. The lending library is operated by a volunteer group under a salaried librarian.

Subscription fees are $15 per year. The library is open Mon-Fri 10am-5pm, Sat 10am-2pm (closed on holidays). Librarian, Elaine Talma. Tel 352-7048. The **Sir Charles Hayward Children's Library** was established in 1994. Subscription fees are $10 per year. Librarian, Josephine Zonicle. Tel 352-3524. The **Grand Bahama Public Youth Library** is in the Syntex Operation Outreach Teen Centre. Tel 352-2092.

MARINAS & CRUISING FACILITIES

Year-round boating weather and excellent full-service marinas make Freeport/Lucaya a popular venue with the yachting crowd. Marinas include: **Lucayan Marina Village.** A full-service marina with slips for 125 vessels of varying size up to 200 ft in a private gated community with 24-hour security. Telephone and television hook-up available. Pool complex with waterside bar serving food and drinks. Complimentary water shuttle to Port Lucaya Marketplace and Pelican Bay

Hotel. Fuelling dock open 24 hours. Ice, bait and other essentials available at the fuel dock.

Port Lucaya Marina. A full-service marina with slips accommodating more than 100 vessels up to 170 ft. Telephone and cable TV hook-ups available at minimum charges. The marina specializes in yacht services, including boat-cleaning inside and out, caretaking in owner's absence, complimentary shopping service and transportation to the airport. A modern refuelling operation and holding tank pump-out facility is open 7am-12 midnight. The marina is adjacent to Our Lucaya Beach & Golf Resort, and marina guests have access to Our Lucaya facilities. The marina hosts two legs of the Bahamas Wahoo Championship and the Bacardi Rum Billfish Tournament.

See also **Bahamas information, Boating** and **Marinas & Cruising Facilities** and this section, **Boating, Harbour control** and **Telecommunications.**

MARRIAGE LICENCES

Marriage licences may be obtained from the Registrar General's Office, 16/17 Regent Centre, Freeport, at a cost of $100. Tel 352-4934.

See also **Bahamas information, Marriage licences.**

NATIONAL INSURANCE

There are four National Insurance offices in Grand Bahama – one in Freeport on The Mall, PO Box F-42618, tel 352-7222; one at Eight Mile Rock, tel 348-1014; one at West End, tel 346-6033; and one at High Rock, tel 353-4180.

See also **Bahamas information, National Insurance.**

NATURE CENTRES

The **Bahamas National Trust (BNT) Rand Nature Centre,** East Settler's Way. A 100-acre pineland preserve with a wide variety of bird species, including a captive native Bahama parrot and reptiles such as the Bahama boa. The pine forest trails highlight native plants and their medicinal and cultural uses. Guided bird tours are available by arrangement. Open Mon-Fri 9am-4pm. Admission $5, children 5-12 yrs $3. Tel 352-5438.

Garden of the Groves, Midshipman Rd and Magellan Dr. A tropical theme park featuring 12 acres of waterfalls, lakes, indigenous plant life, macaws, ducks, cockatoos, alligators, iguanas and a petting zoo with pygmy goats and pot-bellied pigs. Scenic trails and well-manicured lawns. There is a snack bar and mini straw market. Open seven days 9am-4pm. Admission $9.95 adults, $6.95 children 3-10. Residents $6 adults, $3.50 children 3-10. Guided tours $12.95 (call ahead). Tel 373-5668 or 373-1456.

Lucayan National Park, 42 acres, is managed by BNT through a volunteer committee. Nature trails and boardwalks lead to a variety of ecosystems, including pinelands, hardwood hammocks and coppices, mangrove swamps and sand dunes. Two large caves, part of one of the longest underwater cavern systems in the world, Ben's Cave and Burial Mound Cave, are habitats for rare underwater crustaceans and migratory bats in summer. Swimming is prohibited and diving requires a special permit. There is a beach, creek, orchids in spring, rare Ming trees and an array of birds. The park is open 9am-4pm daily. Admission $3, children under 12 yrs free. Tickets are available at Rand Nature Centre or at the park. Tel 352-5438.

Peterson Cay National Park, also managed by BNT, is a small island one mile off the south coast of Grand Bahama. For those with access to a boat, active coral reefs surrounding the cay are excellent for snorkelling and/or diving, and there is a multitude of gulls and crabs. Fishing is prohibited. Tel 352-5438. See also **Birds.**

See also **Bahamas information, Bahamas National Trust** and **Wildlife preserves.**

NEWSPAPERS

One daily newspaper, *The Freeport News,* is published in Freeport and printed every morning, Mon-Sat, except holidays, 50¢. Also available are two Nassau morning newspapers, *The Tribune* and *The Nassau Guardian*. Both sell for 50¢.

Some New York and Miami papers are available the same day of publication and some a day later at increased cost due to air freight charges. Magazines from abroad also cost more for the same reason.

PASSPORTS

Bahamian residents of Grand Bahama may obtain or renew passports at the Passport Office, National Insurance Bldg, PO Box F-43536, Freeport, Grand Bahama. Tel 352-5698 or 352-6480.

See also **Bahamas information, Passports.**

PEOPLE-TO-PEOPLE

Visitors who would like to spend time with Bahamians and learn more about their host country should complete an application form from their local tourism office or write directly to the Coordinator, People-To-People, PO Box F-40251, Freeport, Grand Bahama, tel 352-8044/5.

See also **Bahamas information, People-To-People.**

POLICE CERTIFICATES

Police certificates documenting an individual's past police record are often required in The Bahamas, eg, by prospective employers and in applications for immigration status.

The certificates may be obtained from the Criminal Investigation Dept (CID), 2nd floor, Kipling Bldg, at a cost of $2.50. Waiting period is 48 hours. Office hours are 9am-1pm and 2-3:30pm. Tel 352-8109.

POPULATION

According to the official 2000 census, Grand Bahama's population was 46,954. In 1990 it was 41,035. In 1980 it was 33,102.

See also **Bahamas information, Population.**

PORT LUCAYA MARKETPLACE

This gaily painted 7½-acre waterside village is popular with visitors as well as Bahamian shoppers. There are more than 60 stores, 22 restaurants and bars and a large straw market stocked with gift items, souvenirs, T-shirts and all types of straw hats, bags and baskets. There are also steel bands, strolling guitarists and firework displays at various times.

See also **Entertainment** and **Shopping.**

POSTAL INFORMATION

The main post office, Explorer's Way, provides the same service as the Nassau post office. Branch offices are located in West End, Eight Mile Rock, Smith's Point, High Rock, McLean's Town and Sweeting's Cay. Postal rates are the same as Nassau's.

See also **Courier services** and **Bahamas information, Postal information.**

PROPERTY TRANSACTIONS

The government of The Bahamas charges a stamp duty (equivalent to a transfer tax) on all property conveyances and mortgages.

The government stamp duty on property conveyances or realty transfers is graded as follows:

From	Up to & including	Stamp duty
$0	$20,000	2%
$20,000.01	$50,000	4%
$50,000.01	$100,000	6%
$100,000.01	$250,000	8%
Over $250,000		10%

Stamp duty on mortgages is payable by the borrower at a rate of 1%. Attorneys' fees are subject to negotiation. The Bahamas Bar has recommended a minimum scale fee for conveyancing and mortgage transactions at the rate of 2.5% of the consideration plus out-of-pocket expenses. The minimum fee is $750 plus out-of-pocket expenses.

Commissions charged by real estate agents vary according to the type of property and should be agreed in writing between the seller, who normally pays the commission, and his agent.

In Freeport much of the vacant land is owned by international investors, and unlike Nassau, the majority of transactions still involve foreigners, either as buyers or sellers, or both. When there is a glut of undeveloped land on the market many sellers offer high incentive commissions for quick cash sales. As a guideline the following commission scales* apply:

Sale of undeveloped land 10%
(but not less than $500)
Residential property 6-10%
Commercial property....................10%

** Scales are under continual review.*

See also **Bahamas information, Property transactions.**

RADIO STATIONS

ZNS-3, Radio Bahamas' northern service, is one of three stations operated by the Broadcasting Corp of The Bahamas. Based in Freeport, ZNS-3 covers Grand Bahama, Abaco and Bimini, with local programming and advertising as well as national programming originating in the Nassau studio. It transmits on a frequency of 810 AM with 10,000 watts.

100 JAMZ, the first private radio station in The Bahamas, transmits from Nassau on a frequency of 100.3 FM with 5,000 watts. Its programme of island and urban music is also received in Grand Bahama.

Cool 96, Grand Bahama's first private radio station, started in 1995, broadcasts on FM 96. Format is Bahamian, popular and classical music, and local advertising. The BBC World News is broadcast at 9am and 6pm, and The Caribbean News at 1pm.

Mix 102.1, the island's newest radio station began in 2003 programming urban, Bahamian and Caribbean music, local daily news and weekly shows. It transmits on a frequency of 102.1 FM at 10,000 watts.

See also **Bahamas information, Broadcasting.**

REAL ESTATE COMPANIES

Following is a list of full-service companies in Grand Bahama:

Bahamas Realty 351-2703
Churchill & Jones Real Estate ..352-7305
Damianos Realty 351-9081
First Atlantic Realty 352-7071
H G Christie..........................351-8501
James Sarles Realty 351-9081
Levi Gibson & Assoc..............352-9727
Garo Realty & Investments Ltd 352-7281
Robert Hall & Assoc 351-6609
Modform..............................352-4663
Morley Realty Ltd..................351-8888
Mosko Realty Ltd 351-6445
J Stuart Robertson 352-7201
Real Estate Exchange 373-1430
Tennant & Cooper Ltd........352-7841/2
Thompson Real Estate Ltd 373-9050
Woodcraft Realty..................352-5908

RELIGION

Many denominations are established in Freeport/Lucaya:

Anglican/Episcopal: Pro-Cathedral of Christ the King, tel 351-5202; Church of the Ascension, tel 352-6245; Church of the Good Shepherd, tel 353-7661; and St Jude's (Smith's Point), tel 373-3009.

Assemblies of Brethren: Freeport Gospel Chapel, tel 373-5600.

Assemblies of God: Calvary Temple, tel 352-7578.

Baptist: First Baptist, tel 352-9224; Emmanuel Missionary Baptist, tel 352-6461; Upper Zion Baptist, tel 353-7771; St John's Native Baptist Cathedral, tel 352-5013; and Fellowship Union Baptist, tel 373-4011.

Calvary Bible Church: Independent, tel 373-4975 or 373-8217.

Christian Science Society: tel 373-2044.
Church of God of Prophecy: Community at Heart Tabernacle, tel 373-3464.
Church of Jesus Christ of Latter-Day Saints: tel 351-3730.
Freeport Hebrew Congregation: Luis De Torres Synagogue, tel 373-2008.
Jehovah's Witness: Kingdom Halls – Freeport West, tel 351-6711; Grand Bahama, tel 373-6821.
Lutheran: Our Saviour Lutheran Church, tel 373-3500.
Methodist: St Paul's, tel 373-5752.
Presbyterian: Lucaya Presbyterian Kirk, tel 351-3575.
Roman Catholic: Mary Star of The Sea, tel 373-3300; and St Vincent de Paul, tel 353-7986.
Salvation Army: tel 352-4863.
Seventh Day Adventist: tel 373-3349.

SCHOOLS

See **Education.**

SERVICE CLUBS

See **Community organizations & service clubs.**

SHIPPING

Cruise Ships

Many cruise ships call regularly at Lucayan Harbour. US Navy, Royal Canadian Navy and US Coast Guard ships also come into port.

Shipping Agents

BORCO Agency Services........352-9744
or 352-3581
Lucaya Shipping & Trading Co 352-3581/2
Professional Brokers Agency 351-3839
Seaboard Marine 352-9766
Swann's Shipping..................352-7705
Tanja Enterprises Ltd 352-2328
Tropical Shipping 352-6428
United Shipping Co Ltd 352-9315
Wide World Forwarding........352-3636

SHOPPING

Main shopping areas for clothes, leather goods, jewellery and perfume are the Port Lucaya Marketplace, Lucaya, and the International Bazaar. In downtown Freeport are Churchill Square, the West Mall Shopping Centre, Seventeen Shopping Mall and Regent Centre.

See also **International Bazaar** and **Port Lucaya Marketplace** and **Bahamas information, Shopping.**

SNORKELLING

See **Diving & snorkelling.**

SPORTS VENUES

Fortune Hills Golf & Country Club 373-2222
Freeport Rugby Club 373-2952
Grand Bahama Tennis & Squash Club..................373-4567
Hawksbill Yacht Club 373-1144
Lucayan Cricket Club 373-1460
Our Lucaya
Lucayan golf course (Butch Harmon School of Golf) 373-1066
Reef golf course................373-2002
Pinetree Stables 373-3600
Crowne Plaza Golf Resort & Casino
Emerald & Ruby golf courses 350-7000
YMCA 352-7074

Most hotels have tennis courts.

See **Bahamas information, Sports** and this section, **Diving & snorkelling.**

STRAW MARKETS

See **International Bazaar** and **Port Lucaya Marketplace.**

SUPERMARKETS

Winn Dixie, downtown Freeport, Mon-Sat 7am-9pm; Sun 7-10am.
Winn Dixie, Seahorse Plaza, Lucaya, Mon-Sat 7am-9pm; Sun 7-10am.
Solomon's Wholesale Club, Cedar St, Freeport, Mon-Sat 8am-8pm.

TAX INCENTIVES

The Bahamas is a world-class tax haven, and Freeport in particular has further advantages to offer.

See **Encouragement acts** and **Bahamas information, Tax benefits for Canadians, Tax benefits for Europeans, Tax benefits for US citizens and companies** and **Trade agreements.**

TELECOMMUNICATIONS

All telephone service facilities are provided by Bahamas Telecommunications Co (BTC), with direct distance dialling available to most countries.

Freeport residents can use an improved VHF-FM radio telephone service to contact ships at sea through the Nassau marine operator reached by dialling "0." Contact Bahamas Telecommunications Co, PO Box F-42483, Freeport, Grand Bahama, tel 352-9352.

See also **Bahamas information, Telecommunications.**

TELEVISION

Cable television has been available in Grand Bahama for more than 30 years, initially supplied by Grand Bahama CATV Ltd.

The Broadcasting Corp introduced local programmes to the CATV cable system in Freeport in 1990. The Bahamian channel ZNS is received on channel 13, and operates Mon-Fri 6:30-11pm.

In 1995 Cable Bahamas, owned by Canadian-based Cable 2000 Inc and Bahamian interests, acquired Grand Bahama CATV Ltd and rebuilt the system to supply approx 40 channels of basic television and up to 60 channels of premium television.

See also **Bahamas information, Cable television** and **ZNS.**

THEATRE & DRAMATIC ARTS

See **Cultural activities.**

TOURISM

See **Fig 1.0** for Grand Bahama tourism figures.

The Grand Bahama Island Tourism Board (GBITB) is located above the China Temple in the International Bazaar, PO Box F-40251, tel 352-8044/5.

The office provides visitors with information, coordinates Junkanoo and People-To-People events, monitors standards in hotels and restaurants and subsidizes College of The Bahamas' School of Hospitality and Tourism Studies.

TRADE UNIONS

Bahamas Hotel Catering & Allied Workers' Union
Tel 352-9804/5
Bahamas Public Service Union
Tel 352-7810
Bahamas Union of Teachers
Tel 352-8854
Commonwealth Group of Unions
Tel 352-9361
Freeport Flight Services and Allied Workers' Union
Tel 352-8881
Grand Bahama Construction Refinery Maintenance & Allied Workers' Union
Tel 352-2476
Grand Bahama Port Authority Workers' Union
Tel 352-6611
Grand Bahama Public Bus Union
Tel 352-6666
Grand Bahama Taxi Union
Tel 352-7101 or 352-7858

TRANSPORTATION

Taxi rates are set by government and are the same as Nassau; metered $3 for the first quarter mile and 40¢ for each additional quarter mile. For two passengers, approx fare from the airport to Lucaya is $19; to The Royal Oasis and the downtown area, $11. The fare from the harbour area to The Royal Oasis is $15; to Our Lucaya, $24; to the airport, $16. For more than two passengers, there is an additional charge of $3 per person.

FIG 1.0

MINISTRY OF TOURISM VISITOR ARRIVALS, GRAND BAHAMA

Year	Air arrivals	Sea arrivals	Total
1999	247,898	421,059	668,957
2000	283,653	392,445	676,098
2001	286,528	347,104	633,632
2002	301,830	333,809	635,639
2003	294,057	336,814	630,871

Adult bus fare is $1 from downtown to Lucaya; $1.25 from Hawksbill to downtown; $1.50 from Eight Mile Rock to downtown. Bicycles rent for $20 per day with a $50 deposit. Motor scooters are from $40 daily, with a $100 deposit (or more) for a two-seater. Half a tank of gasoline is supplied by the agency and there is no mileage charge. Insurance is usually included. A valid driver's licence is required. By law, drivers and passengers must wear helmets, supplied free by the agency.

See also **Ambulance/air ambulance services, Air service** and **Car rental companies.**

VETERINARIANS

Freeport Animal Clinic
Dr Alan Bater....................352-6521
Caribbean Veterinary Health and Healing Centre
Dr Owen G Hanna 351-2103
Dr Valentino Grant ....351-3647 (dogs) or 351-2287 (cats) or 352-2287 (evenings)

WAGES

Uniforms and meals for housemaids are at the employer's discretion. Gardeners are generally paid $49 a day or more. Cocktail waitresses earn about $100 per week basic pay and bartenders about $170, plus tips. Uniforms and meals are usually supplied by the employer.

	Average weekly wage
Top executive secretary	$700
Stenographer/secretary	$340-$360
Head cook or chef	$400
Short-order cook	$300
Receptionist	$300
Executive housekeeper	$650
Janitor	$280
Security guard	$300
Farm helper	$250
Housemaid (40-hour week)	$165
Truck driver	$300
Fork lift operator	$400-$450

See also **Bahamas information, Wages.**

WATER SUPPLY & RATES

The Grand Bahama Utility Co supplies water to Freeport and several other communities in Grand Bahama. Total developed well field capacity is nine million gal per day from four well fields. Average daily water consumption is about 7.5 million gal.

Monthly water rates for residential, commercial and industrial consumers in Freeport is $3.537 per thousand for the first 10,000 US gal; $4.182 per thousand for the next 10,000 gal; and $4.994 per thousand for usage in excess of 20,000 gal. Minimum monthly billing is $10.40.

See also **Bahamas information, Water rates.**

WEATHER

See **Climate.**

Government

LINDA M HUBER/©DUPUCH

How Government Works

Governor General

The Governor General is the queen's representative in The Bahamas. In 1973 The Bahamas became fully independent, but as a former British colony retained Queen Elizabeth II as its head of state. The Governor General, who is appointed and serves at Her Majesty's pleasure, signs bills into law after they are passed by the House of Assembly and the Senate, opens Parliament, and gives the annual Speech from the Throne, as prepared by the prime minister. Like the queen, the Governor General never presents any personal views or opinions.

Executive branch

The executive branch consists of a Cabinet of at least nine members, including the prime minister and the Attorney-General. The prime minister and the Minister of Finance must be members of the House of Assembly. Cabinet ministers are appointed from the House of Assembly, and up to three ministers can be appointed from among the senators.

Legislative branch

The bicameral, or two-house, legislative branch consists of the senate and the lower House of Assembly. They are physically located in Parliament Square in downtown Nassau – the House in the western building and the senate in the centre building. The supreme court building is located behind the senate.

The House of Assembly, dating to 1729, is the most powerful segment of government. It makes the laws of The Bahamas and consists of at least 38 elected representatives of the people. There are currently 40 members. They serve five-year terms, unless the House is dissolved before that time by the prime minister.

The senate has 16 members, nine appointed by the Governor General on the advice of the prime minister, four on the advice of the Leader of the Opposition and three on the advice of the prime minister after consultation with the Leader of the Opposition. This arrangement provides for the Opposition to have no less than four members in the Senate and to claim up to three more based on its numerical strength in the House of Assembly.

A law begins as a bill introduced to the House of Assembly. It is read three times, debated, and if passed, is sent to the senate. The bill is read three times in the senate, debated and if passed, sent to the Governor General. Upon his or her signature the bill becomes a law.

The House of Assembly corresponds to Britain's House of Commons and observes many of the same traditions.

Judiciary

An independent judiciary is provided for under the constitution, along with the right of appeal to Her Majesty's Privy Council in England. Judges are appointed by the Governor General. Judiciary departments are comprised of the Court of Appeal, the highest tribunal in the country, the supreme court, magistrates' courts and Her Majesty's Privy Council.

Governor General

HE Dame Ivy Dumont, DCMG

Governor General, Government House, Nassau

Governor General since Jan 2002. Former Minister of Education and Youth, Minister of Health and Environment, government leader in the senate. Educator. Born Oct 2, 1930, Rose's, Long Island, to Alphonso Turnquest and Elizabeth Turnquest (née Darville). Educated: Nova Univ and Univ of Miami, FL. Past president (founding member) Women's Aglow International (Bahamas); past vice-president Bahamas Humane Society; and past secretary (founding member) Bahamas Union of Teachers. Married to Reginald Deane Dumont. Two children. Denomination: Brethren. Interests: dressmaking, public speaking and horticulture.

Governors General from Independence, July 10, 1973

1973 Sir John Warburton Paul, GCMG, OBE, MC; appointed July 10, 1973; retired July 31, 1973.

1973 Sir Milo Butler, appointed Aug 1, 1973; retired Jan 22, 1979.

1976 Sir Gerald Cash, GCMG, GCVO, OBE, JP; acting Governor General, Sept 2, 1976-Sept 23, 1979.

1979 Sir Gerald Cash, GCMG, GCVO, OBE, JP; appointed Governor General, Sept 24, 1979; retired June 25, 1988.

1988 Sir Henry Milton Taylor, Kt, JP; acting Governor General, June 26, 1988-Feb 28, 1991.

1991 Sir Henry Milton Taylor, Kt, JP; appointed Governor General, Mar 1, 1991; retired Jan 1, 1992.

1992 Sir Clifford Darling, Kt, JP; appointed Jan 2, 1992; retired Jan 2, 1995.

1995 Sir Orville A Turnquest, GCMG, QC, JP; appointed Jan 3, 1995, retired Nov 13, 2001.

2001 Dame Ivy Dumont, DCMG, DPA; acting Governor General Nov 13, 2001-Dec 31, 2001.

2002 Dame Ivy Dumont DCMG; appointed Jan 1, 2002.

Cabinet Ministers & Portfolios

THE RT HON PERRY G CHRISTIE, MP

Prime Minister and Minister of Finance,
Sir Cecil Wallace Whitfield Centre, Cable Beach, Nassau

The Cabinet Office
Coordination of ministries, government and parliamentary business; disaster preparedness; Official Gazette; Hansard. Tel 322-3220, fax 328-8294.

Office of the Prime Minister
Constitutional Review Commission; relations with the Grand Bahama Port Authority; relations with the Public Utilities Commission. Tel 327-5826/9, fax 327-5806/7.

Government Printing Dept
Government publications; printing and stationery.

Dept of Lands and Surveys
Lands and Surveys; acquisition of lands.

Ministry of Finance
Economic development and planning; government finance and borrowing; Central Bank of The Bahamas; Bahamas Development Bank; Bank of The Bahamas; Banks and Trust Companies; Post Office Savings Bank; auctions; treasure trove; spirits and beer; privatization of BaTelCo; cable television; relations with the Bahamas Agricultural and Industrial Corporation (BAIC). Tel 327-1530, fax 327-1618.

Customs Dept
Revenue.

Treasury Dept
Budget and budgetary control; privatization of BaTelCo; cable television.

Securities Exchange
Securities; relations with the Securities Commission; licensing of shops and businesses; development of electronic commerce.

Dept of Statistics
National statistics; retail price index.

Pratt

Roberts

Peet

THE HON CYNTHIA A PRATT, MP

Deputy Prime Minister and Minister of National Security

Churchill Bldg, Bay St, Nassau

Office of the Deputy Prime Minister
Tel 356-6792, fax 356-6087.

Ministry of National Security
Public safety; flags and coats of arms; cinemas and films.

Royal Bahamas Police Force
Police.

Royal Bahamas Defence Force
Defence.

Prisons Dept
Prisons; prisoners; prerogative of mercy.

Parliamentary Registration Dept
Parliamentary registration; elections.

THE HON BRADLEY B ROBERTS, MP

Minister of Works and Utilities

Ministry of Works Bldg, John F Kennedy Dr, Nassau

Ministry of Works and Utilities
Public infrastructure; drainage; explosives and volatile substances; private roads and subdivisions; Paradise Island Bridge Authority; local improvement associations; relations with the Bahamas Telecommunications Company; Montagu Beach and foreshore; relations with the Water and Sewerage Corporation; relations with the Bahamas Electricity Corporation; relations with Bahamasair. Tel 322-4830/1.

Dept of Public Works
Construction of government buildings, roads, docks, bridges and cemeteries; maintenance and upkeep of government buildings, roads, docks, bridges and cemeteries.

Dept of Physical Planning
Physical planning and land use; town and country planning.

THE HON VINCENT A PEET, MP

Minister of Labour and Immigration

Post Office Bldg, East Hill St, Nassau

Ministry of Labour and Immigration
Manpower and employment; employment agencies; trade unions; trade disputes; wages councils; labour education; inspection and safety; workmen's compensation; relations with the Industrial Tribunal. Tel 323-7814, 323-7547 or 322-3348.

Dept of Labour
Labour relations.

Dept of Immigration
Immigration; emigration; nationality; citizenship; work and residency permits.

Wilchcombe

Mitchell

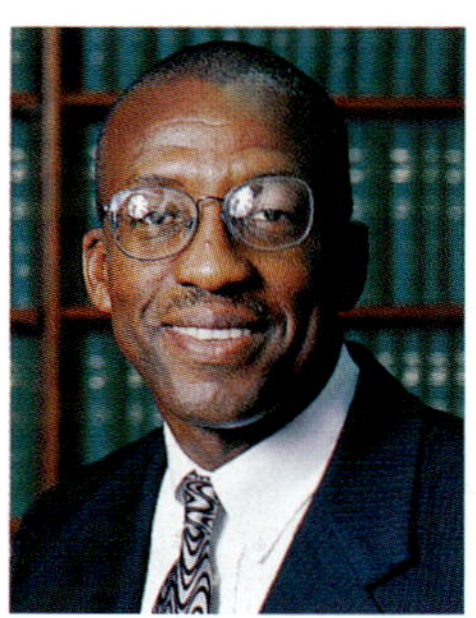
Sears

THE HON OBEDIAH H WILCHCOMBE, MP

Minister of Tourism

British Colonial Hilton, Bay St, Nassau

Ministry of Tourism

Promotion and development of tourism; tourism product improvement; relations with Nassau Tourism and Development Association; tourism publicity and advertisement; relations with promotion boards; Welcome Centre, Prince George Dock; radio and television broadcast; relations with the Broadcasting Corporation of The Bahamas; relations with the Gaming Board; lotteries and gaming. Tel 322-7500, fax 302-2098.

Bahamas Information Services

Bahamas Information Services.

THE HON FREDERICK A MITCHELL, MP

Minister of Foreign Affairs and the Public Service

Ministry of Foreign Affairs, East Hill St, Nassau

Ministry of Foreign Affairs

Foreign affairs; foreign missions; protocol matters; extradition; treaty succession; coordination of applications for technical assistance; law of the sea; CARICOM affairs; passports; visas. Tel 322-7624/5.

Dept of Public Service

Public service union; pensions and gratuities; office accommodation; organization and methods. Tel 502-7200.

THE HON ALFRED M SEARS, MP

Attorney-General and Minister of Education

Ministry of Education, Thompson Blvd, Nassau

Office of the Attorney-General

Tel 322-1142.

Dept of Legal Affairs

Legal advisor to the government; mutual legal affairs; international legal cooperation; law reform and revision; legal education; coroners; Justices of the Peace; notaries public.

Dept of Public Prosecutions

Criminal proceedings; legal aid.

Judicial Dept

Administration of justice; law courts; law reports; enquiries

Ministry of Education

Education; scholarships; distance learning; relations with the College of The Bahamas; relations with the University of the West Indies; relations with church-operated and other private schools; public libraries and reading centres; Bahamas Hotel Training College; Bahamas Technical and Vocational Institute; apprenticeship; industrial arts and crafts training; Technical Cadet Corp. Tel 502-2703/4.

Dept of Education

Primary, secondary and tertiary education; pre-schools; relations with school boards.

Dept of Archives

Archives, old public records and antiquities.

Miller

Gray

Wisdom

THE HON LESLIE O MILLER, MP

Minister of Trade and Industry

Manx Corporate Centre, West Bay St, Nassau

Ministry of Trade and Industry
Trade; small business development; development of handicraft industry; straw and crafts markets; industry and manufacturing; industries encouragement; Down Home Fish Fry; mining, geological surveys, fuel, oils and petrochemicals; Lomé convention; NAFTA; EU/ACP; World Trade Organization; FTAA. Tel 328-2700-4.

Consumer Welfare
Consumer welfare; consumer protection, consumer education; weights and measures; hire purchase; standards.

THE HON V ALFRED GRAY, MP

Minister of Agriculture, Fisheries and Local Government

Levy Bldg, East Bay St, Nassau

Ministry of Agriculture, Fisheries and Local Government
Family Island affairs; relations with local government authorities. Tel (242) 325-7502.

Dept of Agriculture
Agriculture; food production; agricultural marketing; horticulture; quality control of food and beverage; Potter's Cay dock; protection of wild animals and birds; protection of plants; veterinary services and animal diseases; public markets; slaughter houses; agricultural lands.

Dept of Fisheries
Fisheries; natural history specimens; reefs and blue holes.

Dept of Cooperatives
Cooperatives; credit unions.

THE HON NEVILLE W WISDOM, MP

Minister of Youth, Sports and Culture

Thompson Blvd, Nassau

Ministry of Youth, Sports and Culture
Youth development; athletic and sporting development. Tel 502-0600/5.

Dept of Sports
Recreational programmes; relations with sporting organizations; sports promotion; Bahama Games; CARIFTA Games.

Dept of Culture
Cultural development; relations with cultural organizations; cultural exchange programmes; Junkanoo; development of playgrounds and community parks; promotion of arts, music and the performing arts; museums; historical sites including forts; relations with the Antiquities, Monuments and Museums Corporation.

Griffin

Martin

Gibson

THE HON MELANIE S GRIFFIN, MP

Minister of Social Services and Community Development

Frederick House, Frederick St, Nassau

Ministry of Social Services and Community Development
Tel 356-0765, fax 323-3883.

Dept of Social Services
Social services; public assistance; social welfare; old age pension; indigent and aged persons; care facilities; child protection; self help; disabled persons.

Dept of Rehabilitative Services
Rehabilitative services; the Simpson Penn Centre for Boys; the Willie Mae Pratt Centre for Girls; community development.

Bureau of Women's Affairs
Women's affairs.

THE HON GLENYS M E HANNA MARTIN, MP

Minister of Transport and Aviation

Gold Circle House, East Bay St, Nassau

Ministry of Transport and Aviation
Tel 394-0445 or 394-0451/3.

Dept of Road Traffic
Ground transportation; road traffic management; motor vehicles; drays and surreys.

Post Office Dept
Postal service.

Port Dept
Maritime affairs; relations with Bahamas Maritime Authority; merchant ship registration; inter-island passenger, freight and mail service; lighthouses; wrecks; ports and harbours; abutments; boat registration; shipping and navigation.

Dept of Civil Aviation
Aviation; air transport licensing; Nassau Flight Services; relations with the Airport Authority.

Dept of Meteorology
Meteorology.

THE HON ALLYSON MAYNARD GIBSON, MP

Minister of Financial Services and Investments

Goodman's Bay Corporate Centre, Cable Beach, Nassau

Ministry of Financial Services and Investments
Promotion of financial services industry; promotion of investment; relations with the Hotel Corporation of The Bahamas; relations with the financial services industry; promotion of the electronic commerce industry; insurance (excluding National Insurance); mutual funds; Bahamas Investment Authority (BIA); hotels encouragement.
Tel 356-5960, fax 356-5990.

Gibson

Bethel

Smith

Registrar General's Dept
Registration of documents; companies; business names; registration of commission merchants; copyrights, patents and trademarks.

THE HON D SHANE GIBSON, MP

Minister of Housing and National Insurance
Claughton House, Shirley & Charlotte Sts, Nassau

Ministry of Housing and National Insurance
Tel 322-6005/6, fax 322-6091.

Dept of Housing
Housing; urban renewal and improvement; expansion of new single-family home construction; expansion of new public multi-family unit construction; relations with the Housing Commission; relations with the Bahamas Mortgage Corporation; National Insurance; relations with the National Insurance Board.

SEN THE HON DR MARCUS C BETHEL

Minister of Health
Poinciana Hill House, Meeting St, Nassau

Ministry of Health
Relations with the National Health Insurance Commission. Tel 502-4700.

Dept of Public Health
Public health; public health education; vaccination; quarantine; port health; medical, nursing and health services; regulation of manufacturing of drugs and pharmaceuticals; dangerous drugs; Public Analyst Laboratories; relations with the Public Hospitals Authority; relations with the Hospital Facilities Board; relations with the Health Care Professionals Board.

Dept of Environmental Health Services
Environmental control; solid waste collection and disposal; poisons; vector control; Environment, Science and Technology Commission; beautification and maintenance of roadsides, sidewalks, road verges, parks and beaches.

SEN THE HON JAMES H SMITH

Minister of State for Finance
Ministry of Finance, Sir Cecil Wallace Whitfield Centre, Cable Beach, Nassau

See **the Rt Hon Perry G Christie, MP, Ministry of Finance, for portfolio.**

Senators

GOVERNMENT

SEN THE HON SHARON R WILSON

President of the senate. Attorney, Sharon Wilson & Co. Born Sept 25, 1948, Nassau, to Valerie Lockhart Handy. Educated: Florida Memorial College (BA), Univ of Miami (MA), FL. Former: chief magistrate of The Commonwealth of The Bahamas; stipendiary and circuit magistrate; former English Dept head, St John's College and Jordan Prince Williams High School; past president, the Nassau Chapter of The Links Inc. Member: Bahamas Bar Assoc; Board of Trustees, Florida Memorial College, FL. Director: Grand Bahama Port Authority. Honoured by Pan Hellenic Council, Zeta Phi Beta and Delta Sigma Theta sororities for contribution to the field of law in The Bahamas. Married to Franklyn R Wilson. Three children. Denomination: Anglican. Interests: reading and cooking.

SEN THE HON REV DR C B MOSS

Vice-president of the senate. Financial and business consultant, real estate development. Founder and pastor, Mt Olive Baptist Church. Born Feb 27, 1946, Acklins, to Ethelbert Talbot Moss and the late Rev Celeta Darling Moss. Educated: College of The Bahamas, Nassau; Lindsay Hopkins Inst, Univ of Miami, FL; Bahamas Baptist Bible Inst, Nassau; Trinity Seminary, IL. Honorary doctorate in divinity from Richmond Virginia Theological Seminary. Ordained Jan 1981. Former general manager, Commonwealth Bank; former managing director, Workers Bank; former president, Bahamas Christian Council, Bahamas Red Cross Society, Scouts Assoc of The Bahamas, Rotary Club of West Nassau. Chairman, Crusaders Junkanoo Council, Coalition to Save Clifton Cay; president, Bain Town Advancement Assoc. Married to Francisca Marie Moss (née Johnson). Five children, six grandchildren. Denomination: Baptist. Interests: reading, historical documentaries and writing.

SEN THE HON DR MARCUS BETHEL

Government leader in the senate. Minister of Health. Served as Opposition leader in the senate 1997-2002. Physician. Born July 7, 1947, Nassau, to Jane Bethel and the late Marcus Bethel. Educated: McGill Univ, Montreal (BSc and MD); internship, Toronto General Hospital, Toronto; residency, Internal Medicine, Mayo Clinic and Graduate School, Rochester, MN. Medical director/administrator/consultant internist, Lucayan Medical Centre, Freeport. Former president, Grand Bahama Medical and Dental Assoc; medical adviser, Grand Bahama Diabetic Assoc 1987-97; member, board of directors, Commonwealth Bank 1999-2001. Awarded the Distinguished Physician Award of the Medical Assoc of The Bahamas 1991; the Seashell Award for Health and Environment, 1998; the Silver Jubilee Award in Medicine, 1998. Married to Chantal Bethel (née Victor). Three sons. Denomination: Anglican. Interests: travelling, reading and boating.

SEN THE HON JAMES SMITH, JP

Minister of State in the Ministry of Finance. Born Oct 26, 1947, Nassau, to Bertram James Smith and Rosalie B Smith, both deceased. Educated: Univ of Windsor (BA), Ontario; Univ of Alberta

(MA), Alberta; Ryerson Polytechnical College, Toronto. Former Ambassador for Trade, Office of the Prime Minister 1997-2002; former Governor, Central Bank of The Bahamas; former Permanent Secretary and Secretary for Revenue, Ministry of Finance 1984-86; former chairman, the Bahamas Maritime Authority, the Paradise Island Bridge Authority, the Bahamas Development Bank and the Negotiating Group on Services in the Free Trade Area of the Americas (FTAA); former director, the Bahamas Stock Exchange. Named to the Queen's Honours List, Commander of the Most Excellent Order of the British Empire (CBE) 2000. Widower. Three children. Denomination: Anglican. Interests: golf, jogging and reading.

SEN THE HON PHILIP C GALANIS

Chartered accountant. Managing partner, Galanis & Co. Born Aug 23, 1954, Nassau, to Clifford and Zoe Galanis. Educated: St John's Univ (BA cum laude), Collegeville, MN; Rutgers Univ, NJ. Former president, Bahamas Institute of Chartered Accountants 1988-92; and Institute of Chartered Accountants of the Caribbean 1995-97; former member of the senate 1992-97; former board member, St Augustine's College and Financial Advisory Services Board; former Member of Parliament for Englerston 1997-2002. Married to Tonya Galanis (née Bastian). Three children. Denomination: Roman Catholic. Interests: golf, boating, fishing, walking and reading.

SEN THE HON DAMIAN A L GOMEZ

Barrister-at-law. Partner, Deal & Gomez. Born Aug 17, 1962, New Providence, to the Most Rev Drexel W Gomez and Carol Gomez (née Chandler). Educated: Univ of the West Indies; Cave Hill Campus, Barbados; Univ of Bristol, England; Holburn Law Tutors, England. Called to the Bar of England and Wales 1988 and to the Bahamas Bar 1989. Member, Lincoln's Inn 1987; former executive member, Bahamas Bar Council 1995-97; former examiner, Bahamas Bar Assoc 1992-98. Shadow Attorney-General 1997 to 2000; former Senator 1997-99; chairman of the PLP Young Liberals Committee 1997. Married to Camille D Gomez. Four children. Denomination: Anglican. Interests: reading, watching movies and listening to jazz music.

SEN THE HON MICHELLE M PINDLING-SANDS

Attorney. Partner, Graham, Thompson & Co. Born Nov 21, 1962, Nassau, to Lady Pindling (née Marguerite McKenzie) and the late Sir Lynden Pindling, former Prime Minister of The Commonwealth of The Bahamas. Educated: London School of Economics & Political Science, Council of Legal Education, London. Admitted to the Bar of England and Wales and the Bahamas Bar 1986; member, the Honourable Society of the Middle Temple; the Bahamas Bar Assoc; chairman, Sir Lynden Pindling Foundation. Married to Robert D L Sands. Two children. Denomination: Anglican. Interests: politics, travelling and dancing.

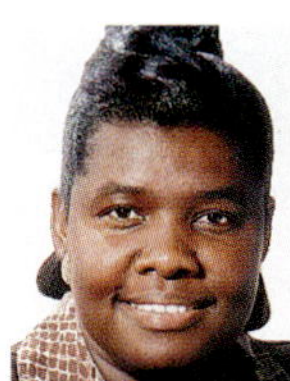

SEN THE HON YVETTE NATASHA TURNQUEST, JP

CEO, Chain Reaction Jewellers. Born Jun 1, 1964, Nassau, to Norma Duncombe and the late Solomon

George Forbes. Educated: C I Gibson School and R M Bailey High School, Nassau; Stewart's Intl School for Jewelers, West Palm Beach, FL; Jewelry Technology, Santa Fe, NM and Vail, CO; BTVI, Nassau. Vice-president, Glass Bottom Ferry Assoc 1998-99. Married to Peter Simeon Turnquest. Two children. Denomination: Baptist. Interests: boating, reading and art. Residence: Mount Vernon.

SEN THE HON TRAVER RICARDO WHYLLY

Special consultant to the prime minister. Born Dec 18, 1958, Nassau, to Theresa Albury-Fairweather and Jeffrey James Whylly. Educated: Morehouse College (BA), Atlanta, GA. President, Morehouse College Alumni, Nassau, Bahamas chapter. Founding member and first national chairman, Progressive Young Liberals 1980-84; coordinator, Farm Road PLP Branch; president and CEO, Outstanding Students in Bahamian High Schools Awards Programme; district deputy, grand regional director of education and executive assistant to the president of the Bahamas State Assoc of Elks. Denomination: Methodist. Interests: reading, coordinating special events, international relations and writing.

SEN THE HON CYPRIANNA V McWEENEY

Homemaker. Born Jul 5, 1952, Nassau, to Winifred Dorsette Munnings and the late Frederick Munnings, OBE. Educated: the Bahamas Technical Institute, Nassau. Former Manager of Promotions, Bahamas Ministry of Tourism; former Miss Bahamas, radio actress, casting director and Bahamas location scout for the print and electronic media. Has been involved with the School for the Deaf, the Bahamas Assoc for the Mentally Retarded, the Woman Exhibition, the Dundas Centre for the Performing Arts and the movement for the preservation of Clifton Cay. Chairperson, the Sir Lynden Pindling Foundation Ball Committee. Married to Sean McWeeney. Three children. Denomination: Baptist. Interests: gardening, swimming and reading – particularly literature on African diaspora.

SEN THE HON PAULETTE E ZONICLE

Sales manager, Colina Insurance. Former broadcaster. Born Jan 27, 1961, Nassau, to Althea Winfred Knowles and the late Mervin James Adderley. Educated: College of The Bahamas School of Entrepreneurship, Nassau; Lambert College (BA), Jackson, TN; Horizon Computer School, Nassau; Journalist Around the World managerial training, People's Republic of China. Producer and host of local programmes at the Broadcasting Corporation of The Bahamas (ZNS) 1996-97; senior producer and manager of local television programmes 1997-98; asst director and manager, news dept 1998-2000. Member, Mount Tabor Full Gospel Baptist Church. Married to Charles Anthony Zonicle. One child. Denomination: Full Gospel Baptist. Interests: reading, cooking, meeting people and travelling.

SEN CALEB E OUTTEN

CEO, Caribbean Lighthouse Intl. Born Sept 14, 1973, Freeport, Grand Bahama, to Rev Hilton and Cecelia

Outten. Educated: Hawksbill High School, Grand Bahama; Lake Community College, Lake City, FL and Valdosta State University, Valdosta, GA. Founder/president, People United to Make Progress (PUMP); president, Grand Bahama Small Business Association; community activist and motivator of youth. Single. Denomination: Nazarene. Residence: Freeport, Grand Bahama.

OPPOSITION

SEN THE HON O A T (TOMMY) TURNQUEST

Opposition leader. Leader of the FNM. Banker. Born Nov 16, 1959, Nassau, to HE Sir Orville A Turnquest, GCMG, QC, LLB, former Governor General, and Lady Turnquest (née Edith Thompson). Educated: Malvern College, England; Univ of Western Ontario (BA, Hons), London, ON, Canada; Fellow, Institute of Canadian Bankers. Married to the former Shawn Carey of Nassau. Three children. Denomination: Anglican. Interests: tennis and boating.

SEN THE HON GLADYS JOHNSON-SANDS

Insurance executive. Managing director & partner, Bahamas Insurance Services. Born Oct 27, 1956, Nassau, to Oscar N Johnson and the late Sylvia Ethlyn Roberts-Johnson. Educated: Ontario Ladies College and Univ of Toronto, ON, Canada. Immediate past president, FNM Women's Assoc. Married to Reginald A Sands. Two children. Denomination: Baptist. Interests: fishing, reading and writing.

SEN THE HON TANYA C McCARTNEY

Attorney. Born Mar 30, 1971, Nassau, to Ellen Rosemary McCartney and Alphonso Robert Elliott. Educated: St John's College and The College of The Bahamas, Nassau; Univ of Reading (LLB Hons); London School of Economics and Political Science, Univ of London (LLM), England; Intl Law Institute, Georgetown Univ, Washington, DC. Admitted to the Bahamas Bar and the Bar of England and Wales 1995. Legal Counsel and Compliance Officer, Union Bancaire Privée (Bahamas) Limited; former assistant counsel, Office of Attorney-General; former lecturer, The College of The Bahamas and the Institute of Business & Commerce. Member: Lincoln's Inn. Sunday school teacher and vestry member, St Barnabas Anglican Church. Single. Denomination: Anglican. Interests: reading, travelling and writing.

SEN THE HON DESMOND BANNISTER

Attorney. Senior partner, The Law Partnership. Born Oct 28, 1958, Andros, to Horatio David and Joyce Nell Bannister. Educated: Grinnell College (BA), Grinnell, IA; Univ of West Indies (LLB), Barbados; Norman Manley Law School, Jamaica. Called to the Bahamas Bar and the Barbados Bar 1988. Former crown counsel, office of the Attorney-General 1988-91; former acting stipendiary and circuit magistrate; former part-time lecturer, the Bahamas Bar, the Bahamas Institute of Bankers and The College of The Bahamas. President, the Bahamas Amateur Athletic Assoc (BAAA). Married to Donna Bannister (née Charlow). Two children. Non-denominational. Interests: sports, reading, travelling and meeting people.

House of Assembly

SPEAKER: James Oswald Ingraham (see pg 630)
DEPUTY SPEAKER: Anthony D E Moss (see pg 630)
NOTE: There are currently 40 seats in the House of Assembly, 28 are held by the Progressive Liberal Party (PLP), eight by the Free National Movement (FNM), the official Opposition, and four by independent members of the House. Cabinet ministers devote full time to government. Occupations for Cabinet ministers are for background information only.

NEW PROVIDENCE

ADELAIDE

MICHAEL B HALKITIS CFA, MP (PLP)

Parliamentary Secretary, Ministry of Finance. Financial Analyst. Born Feb 1, 1969, Nassau, to Inez Brown. Educated: Old Bight All Age School, Cat Island; Yellow Elder Primary School, Nassau; St Augustine's College, College of The Bahamas, Nassau; Univ of Western Ontario (BA), London, Ontario. Married to the former Dr Tracy Roberts. One child. Denomination: Church of God. Interests: politics, sports, gardening, cooking and reading. Residence: Coral Lakes Drive, PO Box CR-56107, Nassau.

BAIN AND GRANTS TOWN

THE HON BRADLEY BERNARD ROBERTS, MP (PLP)

Minister of Works and Utilities. Immediate past chairman of PLP. Businessman. Born Dec 25, 1943, Nassau, to Merle Roberts (née Albury) and the late R A Cyril (Tony) Roberts III. Educated: St Augustine's College, the Eastern Senior School, Government High School Evening Inst, Nassau. Former director, Sunshine Holdings Ltd; Burns House Ltd; Commonwealth Brewery Ltd; Arawak Homes Ltd; Associated Bahamian Distillers and Brewers (1979) Ltd; Eleuthera Properties Ltd; Bethel, Robertson & Co. President, Inflight Kitchens Ltd; House of Music Ltd. Vice-chairman, General Bahamian Companies Ltd. Vice-president & director, Freeport Oil Ltd. Former chairman, Bahamas Electricity Corp, New Providence Port Authority, Housing Commission, Bahamas Gaming Board; former vice-chairman, Water and Sewerage Corp and General Bahamian Companies Ltd; and vice-president and director of Freeport Oil Ltd; former director, Development Corp, now BAIC; member, Rotary Club of West Nassau and Royal Eagle Lodge. Married to the former Hartlyn M Mackey of Eleuthera. Three children, five grandchildren. Denomination: Roman Catholic. Interests: music and travelling. Residence: Skyline Heights, PO Box N-8208, Nassau.

BAMBOO TOWN

TENNYSON ROSCOE WELLS, LLB, MP (IND)

Barrister-at-law. Partner, Wells & Wells (inactive). Businessman. Born Dec 30, 1946, Deadman's Cay, Long Island, to Cleveland and Emma Wells (née Cartwright). Former Attorney-General and Minister of Justice. Educated: St John's College, Nassau; St Mary's Univ, Halifax, NS, Canada; Univ of London, England. Married to the former Stephanie Ann Thompson of Nassau. Three children. Denomination: Anglican. Interests: reading and swimming. Residence: Blue Hill Estates, PO Box N-9665, Nassau.

BLUE HILLS

THE HON LESLIE O MILLER, MP (PLP)

Minister of Trade and Industry. Businessman. CEO, president and director, Sunburst Paints & Litec Coatings Ltd. Born Mar 24, 1948, Nassau, to Leroy and Sybil Miller (née Lockhart), both deceased. Educated: Palmetto Senior High School, Miami, FL; Univ of Texas, El Paso (BA). Former chairman, the Town Planning Committee 1991-92; the Bahamas Electricity Corp 1989-91; New Providence Port Authority 1987-89. Former asst vice-president of planning, General Bahamian Companies Ltd; vice-president of planning, AC Butler/HBW Finance Ltd. Founding president, The Bahamas Light Industries Development Council. Former Olympic athlete and British Commonwealth games record holder, Miami Herald Track and Field Athlete of the Year, and captain of the US All-American track and field team. Married to the former Helen Pratt. Five children, two grandchildren. Denomination: Brethren. Residence: Winton Estates, PO Box EE-16796, Nassau.

CARMICHAEL

JOHN G F CAREY, MP (PLP)

Parliamentary Secretary, Ministry of Works and Utilities. Born Aug 31, 1971, Nassau, to Dr John and Shezarah Carey (née Baksh). Educated: Bahamas Academy elementary and secondary schools, Nassau; Walla Walla College, WA (BSE in Mechanical Engineering). Former safety, health & environment coordinator, project engineer, area manager for New Providence, Texaco Bahamas Ltd; former columnist, *The Nassau Guardian*. Member: Bahamas Society of Engineers. Married to Khichala McDonald-Carey. One child. Denomination: Seventh Day Adventist. Interests: travelling, golf, badminton, public speaking, writing and surfing the Internet. Residence: Mt Vernon, PO Box FH-14157, Nassau.

DELAPORTE

THE HON NEVILLE W WISDOM, MP (PLP)

Minister of Youth, Sports and Culture. Owner/operator, Florarama. Born Aug 11, 1950, Nassau, to Walter and Dorothy Wisdom (née Roberts), both deceased. Educated: St Anne's School, Queen's College, Nassau; Mankato State Univ, Mankato, MN. Former PLP senator 1987-92; former deputy chairman, Water & Sewerage Corp, Sports Advisory Council. President and head coach, Bain Town Flyers Track & Field Club. Chairman, Hillcrest Academy School; director of education, Christian & Missionary Alliance Church. Recipient, Dr Eme Achara Humanitarian Award. Married to the former Manita Gilbert. One child. Denomination: Christian & Missionary Alliance. Interests: athletics and golf. Residence: Cable Beach, PO Box N-1828, Nassau.

ELIZABETH

MALCOLM E ADDERLEY JR, MP (PLP)

Attorney, Malcolm E Adderley & Co. Born Dec 18, 1945, Nassau, to Malcolm C Adderley Sr and Elaine Maude Adderley (née Major), both deceased. Educated: St Augustine's College, Nassau; Univ of Oklahoma (BBA), OK; Univ of the West Indies (LLB), Barbados; Norman Manley Law School, (CLE) Jamaica. Admitted to the Bahamas Bar 1975. Chairman House Select Committee on Banking. Founding member of The Bahamas Association of Certified Officials, Development Foundation of The Bahamas, Bahamas

Law Guild and Law Society, Univ of the West Indies. Council member, the Bahamas Amateur Athletic Assoc; former secretary-general, the Bahamas Brewery & Distillers Workers Union; first acting president, the Bahamas Industrial Tribunal 1997-99; acting Supreme Court Judge 1999-2000. Married to the former Daphne T Williams. Five children. Denomination: Anglican. Interests: sports, farming, gardening, travelling and reading. Residence: Colony Village East, PO Box N-1342, Nassau.

ENGLERSTON

THE HON GLENYS M E HANNA MARTIN, MP (PLP)
Minister of Transport and Aviation. Attorney, Arthur D Hanna & Co (inactive). Born Oct 27, 1958, Nassau, to The Hon Arthur Dion and Beryl Hanna (née Church). Educated: St Anne's School, Queen's College, Nassau; Padworth College, Reading, England; York Univ (BA, Specialized Hons), Toronto, Canada; Univ of Buckingham (LLB, Hons); Inner Temple, England. Former executive officer, Ministry of Education. Called to Bar of England and Wales and the Bahamas Bar 1988. Elected president of the New Providence Women's Branch of the PLP 1998-2001. Married to Leon A Martin. Three children. Denomination: Anglican. Interests: reading, walking, yoga, creative writing and poetry. Residence: Hanna Road, Fox Hill, PO Box N-4877, Nassau.

FARM ROAD

THE RT HON PERRY GLADSTONE CHRISTIE, LLB, MP (PLP)
Prime Minister and Minister of Finance. Attorney. Born Aug 21, 1943, Nassau, to Gladstone and Naomi Christie (née Allen), both deceased. Educated: Eastern Senior School, Nassau; Univ Tutorial College; Birmingham Univ (Hons); Inner Temple, London, England. Senator 1974-77; Representative for the Centreville constituency 1977-2002; Minister of Health and National Insurance 1977-82; Minister of Tourism 1982-84; Minister of Agriculture, Trade and Industry 1990-92. Co-deputy leader of the Progressive Liberal Party 1992-97. Founding member of the Valley Boys Junkanoo Group and the Pioneers' Sporting Club. Married to the former Bernadette Joan Hanna of Nassau. Three children. Denomination: Anglican. Residence: Cable Beach, PO Box N-7940, Nassau.

FORT CHARLOTTE

THE HON ALFRED M SEARS, MP (PLP)
Attorney-General and Minister of Education. Attorney. Born Jan 13, 1953, Nassau, to Winifred Sears (née Wilkinson). Educated: St Augustine's College, Nassau; Columbia Univ (BA, MIA, MPhil), New York Law School, New York; Norman Manley Law School, Jamaica. Former executive director, Assoc of Caribbean Studies, Univ of New York 1984-86; former honourable secretary, the Bahamas Bar Assoc 1997-99. Member: the Bahamas, District of Columbia, Jamaican, New Jersey State and New York State bars; CUNY Assoc of Caribbean Studies; American Assoc of University Professors; African Heritage Assoc. Board member, Fort Charlotte Community Development Centre; advisory board member, Caribbean Theatre of the Performing Arts and Caribbean Culture and Arts Foundation, New York. Married to the former Marion Bethel. Three children. Denomination: Roman Catholic. Residence: New Providence, PO Box N-3645, Nassau.

FOX HILL

THE HON FREDERICK A MITCHELL JR, JP, MPA, LLB, BA, MP (PLP)

Minister of Foreign Affairs and the Public Service. Counsel and attorney. Born Oct 5, 1953, Nassau, to Frederick A Mitchell Sr and Lilla Angelina Mitchell (née Forde), both deceased. Educated: St Augustine's College, Nassau; Antioch College, OH, and John F Kennedy School of Government, Harvard Univ, MPA; Univ of Buckingham (LLB, Hons), England. Admitted to the Bar of England and Wales, and to the Bahamas Bar 1986. Former senator 1992-97; Opposition senator 1997-2002; chairman, Senate Select Committee on Culture 1992-97; founding member of the Bahamas Committee on Southern Africa. Former chairman, Harvard's John F Kennedy School of Government Alumni Assoc; former director, international mutual fund Zweig Dimenna. Denomination: Anglican. Residence: Eastern Rd, PO Box N-3928, Nassau.

GARDEN HILLS

VERONICA OWENS, MP (PLP)

Parliamentary Secretary, Ministry of Education. Founder/ CEO, Intellect; founder/editor-in-chief, *Creative Education* magazine; partner/co-host, Let's Talk radio talk show. Born August 3, 1956, Nassau, to Catherine Wilson (née Conyers) and the late Alphonso Harcourt Wilson. Educated: A F Adderley Senior High School; Prairie View A&M Univ (BA), Prairie View, TX; Barclays College, Sacramento, CA. Former director/marketing manager, Total Care Ltd, CA 1980-86; owner/instructor, Friend's Daycare & Pre-school, CA 1988-90; founder, Faithway Christian Academy. Member: Alpha Kappa Alpha Sorority Inc. Three children. Denomination: Baptist. Interests: reading and travelling. Residence: Fox Hill, PO Box N-8530, Nassau.

GOLDEN GATES

THE HON DAVID SHANE GIBSON, MP (PLP)

Minister of Housing and National Insurance. Born Sep 7, 1961, Nassau, to Eric "King Eric" Gibson and Gerlene Gibson (née Ferguson). Educated: R M Bailey High School, College of The Bahamas, Nassau; St Augustine's College, Raleigh, NC; DeVry Inst of Technology, Toronto, Canada; Intl Law Inst, Washington, DC; Trade Union Education Inst, Univ of the West Indies, Jamaica; British Industrial Tribunal, London, UK; Communications Intl, Switzerland and Canada. Former: treasurer, The Bahamas Communications & Public Officers Union (BCPOU); administrator and trustee, BCPOU Pension Plan; president, BCPOU; director, BCPOU Medical Plan, chairman, Bahamas Golf Federation; manager, national golf team. Married to the former Jacqueline Elaine Williams. Four children. Denomination: Baptist. Interests: golf, jogging, softball and music. Residence: Lake Cunningham, PO Box N-275, Nassau.

HOLY CROSS

SIDNEY STUBBS, MP (PLP)

President, SMS Consultancy; chairman, Sentosa Group. Born Nov 1, 1960, Lovely Bay, Acklins, to Bishop Teuton C Stubbs, MBE and Helena Stubbs (née Stuart). Educated: Norfolk State Univ (BA, Hons), Norfolk, VA; Univ of Cambridge, Cambridge, England (MPhil); The Hague Academy of Intl Law, The Netherlands. Former: investigative reporter, Broadcasting Corp of The Bahamas; foreign service officer, Legal Treaty & Political Dept, Ministry of Foreign Affairs. Worked in the Political Dept, United Nations, NY; the Legal & Co-financing Dept, World Bank Intl Monetary Fund, Washington DC; US Iranian Claims Tribunal, The Netherlands; Intl Law

Commission, Geneva, Switzerland. Single. Denomination: Roman Catholic. Interests: reading, travelling and meeting people. Residence: Eastern Rd, PO Box N-1629, Nassau.

KENNEDY

KENYATTA MBOYA GIBSON, MP (PLP)

Attorney and Justice of the Peace, K M Gibson & Co. Born Dec 15, 1968, Nassau, to Clara Gibson (née Edgecombe) and the late James F Gibson. Educated: St Anne's Anglican High School, Nassau; College of The Bahamas, Nassau; Univ of Windsor, Canada; Univ of Buckingham (LLB), England. Called to the Bar of England and Wales and the Bahamas Bar in 1994. Chairman, Gaming Board for The Commonwealth of The Bahamas. Member, executive steering committee of the International Association of Gaming Regulators; alumnus, Toastmasters; columnist. Single. Two children. Denomination: Anglican. Interests: studying history and global political science, squash and travelling. Residence: Lyford Cay, PO Box CB-13908, Nassau.

MARATHON

RON O'NEAL PINDER, MP (PLP)

Parliamentary Secretary, Ministry of Health and Environment. Born Dec 31, 1973, Nassau to Oswald and Melrose Pinder (née Bowe). Educated: C I Gibson Secondary School, Nassau; St Augustine's College, NC; Robertson School of Government and Regent School of Education, Regent Univ, VA. Professional qualifications in military science, political strategy and communication, education administration and curriculum design. Member: Omega Psi Phi Fraternity, Phi Eta Sigma Honour Society. Former lecturer at Atlantic College and Theological Seminary; former investments officer, Bahamas Investment Authority; former vice-principal, Faith Temple Christian Academy. Non-denominational. Interests: travelling, reading, music, art and design. Residence: Claridge Dale Gardens, PO Box CB-11272, Nassau.

MONTAGU

BRENT SYMONETTE, MP (FNM)

Businessman, attorney and real estate broker. Born Dec 2, 1954, Nassau, to Sir Roland Symonette and Lady Symonette (née Margaret Thurlow), both deceased. Educated: St Andrews School, Nassau; Leys School, Cambridge and Brunel Univ, London, England. Member of the senate 1987-1997. Former: Minister of Tourism; Attorney-General; chairman, the Hotel Corporation; chairman, the Airport Authority. Responsible for Mount Vernon, Royal Valley & Vista Marina (West) developments. Married to the former Robin MacTaggart. Three children. Residence: East Bay St, PO Box N-3709, Nassau.

MOUNT MORIAH

HE KEOD M SMITH, MP (PLP)

Ambassador for the Environment. Attorney, Commercial Law Advocates, Nassau. Born Oct 15, 1964 to David Samuel Smith Sr and Eddlene Thelma Smith (née Bonaby). Educated: Government High School and College of The Bahamas, Nassau; Loras College (BA), Dubuque, IA; Cardiff Law School, Univ of Wales, UK. Called to the Bahamas Bar 1997. National vice-chairman, PLP 2000-01. Chairman, Bahamas Environment Science & Technology (BEST) Commission; director, Youth Empowerment & Skills Training (YEAST); council member, Bahamas

National Trust; initiator/leader, Save Clifton Cay Campaign; treasurer, National Heroes Committee. Married to the former Monique Roker. Three children. Interests: cooking, hiking and debating. Residence: Perpall Tract, PO Box N-10707, Nassau.

PINEWOOD

THE HON ALLYSON MAYNARD GIBSON, MP (PLP)

Minister of Financial Services and Investments. Born Jan 11, 1957, Nassau, to the Hon Sir Clement Maynard and Lady Maynard (née Zoe Cumberbatch). Educated: Barry Univ (BSc, Hons), Miami, FL; London School of Economics & Political Science [LLB (Hons), LLM], Council of Legal Education, The Honourable Society of the Inner Temple, London, England. Former senior partner, Gibson & Co. Admitted to the Bar of England and Wales and the Bahamas Bar 1980. Member: the Links Inc, Nassau chapter (charter secretary and past-president); The Anglican Church Women; director, the Intl Women's Forum. President, the IWF Leadership Foundation; founding vice-president, Tiny Tots Day Care Centre; founding director, Yellow Elder Community Library Assoc and the Senior Citizen's Centre; founding director, Bahamas Financial Services Board 1998-2000. Activist for women's and children's rights. Married to Maxwell E Gibson. Two children. Denomination: Anglican. Residence: Cable Beach, PO Box CB-13442, Nassau.

ST CECILIA

THE HON CYNTHIA "MOTHER" PRATT, MP (PLP)

Deputy Prime Minister and Minister of National Security. Retired nurse, educator and coach. Born Nov 5, 1945, Nassau, to Herman and Rose Moxey (née Johnson), both deceased. Educated: Western Junior and Senior Schools, A F Adderley, C C Sweeting and Aquinas College evening institutions, Princess Margaret School of Nursing, Nassau; St Augustine's College, Raleigh, NC (BSc, summa cum laude). Honorary doctorate in humane letters and Hall of Fame inductee, St Augustine's College, Raleigh, NC. Former: Whip, PLP; part-time lecturer and assistant director of student activities at The College of The Bahamas. Ordained Minister of Christian Missionary Alliance. Affiliate, Zonta-Living Legend 2002; adviser, Teen Challenge Bahamas; founder, Coconut Grove and St Cecilia's Community Clubs. An all-round athlete and coach, Mother Pratt has represented The Bahamas internationally in softball, basketball and volleyball. Recipient of the Women of Great Esteem Award and the Award of Excellence by QKingdom Ministries Inc for her contributions to the advancement of world peace and community service. Married to Joseph Pratt. Five children. Interests: working with underprivileged people, coordinating sports events, coaching and meeting people. Residence: Coconut Grove, PO Box N-1572, Nassau.

ST MARGARET

PIERRE VALIANT LAUNCELOT DUPUCH, BA, BSc, JP, MP (IND)

Born Apr 23, 1938, Nassau, to Lady Dupuch (née Marie Plouse) and the late Sir Etienne Dupuch. Educated: St Augustine's College, Nassau; De La Salle High School, Canada; St John's Univ, MN, and Carnegie Mellon Univ, PA. Former Minister of Consumer Welfare and Aviation. Former Minister of Agriculture and Fisheries. Founder and first president of the Bahamas National Equestrian Federation. Former member of East Nassau Rotary. First elected to House of Assembly in 1982 and in '92 received 80 per cent of the popular vote. Elected four consecutive terms for the constituency of Shirlea 1982-2002. Married to the former Susan Thompson of Kent, England. Five children. Denomination: Roman Catholic. Interests: horses, fishing and boating. Residence: Camperdown Heights, PO Box N-4555, Nassau.

ST THOMAS MORE

FRANK E SMITH, CPA, CA, MP (PLP)

Government Whip. Chartered Accountant, Frank E Smith & Co. Born Oct 24, 1966, Nassau, to Richard F Smith and Elease Smith (née Pratt). Educated: St Augustine's College, College of The Bahamas, Success Training College, Sojourner-Douglass College, Nassau; St Francis Xavier Univ, Saint Mary's Univ, NS, Canada. Member: National General Council, Bahamas Institute of Chartered Accountants (BICA), American Institute of Certified Public Accountants (AICPA), Illinois CPA Society, St Thomas More Catholic community. Married to the former Sharlyn R Wilson. Denomination: Roman Catholic. Interests: swimming, jogging and martial arts. Residence: Eastern Road, PO Box SS-5583, Nassau.

SOUTH BEACH

AGATHA MARCELLE, MP (PLP)

Parliamentary Secretary, Ministry of Tourism. Human resources/training specialist. President, Transformation Strategies Associated and Corporate Wellness Centre; executive director, Bahamas Quality Council; motivational speaker; industrial relations arbitrator. Born Mar 8, 1950, Cat Island, to James and Menerva Rolle (née McDonald). Educated: Government High School, Nassau; McMaster Univ, ON, Canada; Univ of Miami, Zoë College, FL. Co-organizer, Bahamas Human Resource Development Association (BHRDA); member, American Society for Training and Development (ASTD), Society for Human Resource Management (SHRM). Former lecturer at the College of The Bahamas, Bahamas Hotel Training College, Bahamahost, Mayflower Management Institute, Price Waterhouse, Intl Correspondence School. One child. Denomination: Anglican. Interests: reading, travelling and people development. Residence: Bahamia West, PO Box N-8586, Nassau.

YAMACRAW

THE HON MELANIE S GRIFFIN, MP (PLP)

Minister of Social Services and Community Development. Born August 10, 1956, Nassau, to Telator Strachan (née Moxey). Educated: St Augustine's College, Government High School, College of The Bahamas (AA), Bahamas Baptist Institute, Nassau. Founding member of the College of The Bahamas Union of Students (COBUS). Former senator 1999-2002; national vice-chairman, PLP. Member of Judaea Baptist Church, serving as minister of music, chairman of trustee board and director of tabernacle choir. Board member, Bahamas Baptist Community College. Advocate for child and family welfare. Married to Leon Griffin. One child. Denomination: Baptist. Interests: singing, reading and gardening. Residence: Winton Meadows III, PO Box, N-3206, Nassau.

FAMILY ISLANDS

NORTH ABACO

HUBERT A INGRAHAM, PC, MP (FNM)

Attorney. Former Prime Minister, 1992-2002. Born Aug 4, 1947, Pine Ridge, Grand Bahama, to Isabella Laroda (née Cornish) and Jerome Ingraham, both deceased. Educated: Southern Senior School, Government High School Evening Institute, Nassau. Called to the Bahamas Bar 1973. First elected to the House of Assembly in 1977. Former Minister of Housing and National Insurance 1982-1984. Leader of the FNM 1990-2002. Former chairman, Bahamas Mortgage Corp. Married to the former Delores Velma Miller of Long Island. Six children. Denomination: Baptist. Interests: reading, swimming and fishing. Residence: Croton Ave, PO Box CB-11233, Nassau.

SOUTH ABACO

ROBERT PERCIVAL SWEETING JR, MP (FNM)

Businessman. Owner, Rich's Boat Rentals. Born Feb 4, 1945, Nassau, to Robert Percival and Venie Sweeting. Educated: Man-O-War All Age School, Abaco. Member: Abaco Concerned Citizens Committee; Abaco Chamber of Commerce. Married to the former Margaret Russell of Hope Town, Abaco. Three children, seven grandchildren. Denomination: Brethren. Interests: softball and sailing. Residence: Marsh Harbour, PO Box AB-20012, Abaco.

NORTH ANDROS AND BERRY ISLANDS

THE HON VINCENT A PEET, MP (PLP)

Minister of Labour and Immigration. Born Oct 25, 1953, Stafford Creek, Andros, to Arthur Peet and the late Letis Neely. Educated: Queen's College, Nassau; Univ of the West Indies (LLB Hons), Barbados and Jamaica; Norman Manley Law School, Jamaica. Called to the Bahamas Bar 1981. Former: crown counsel, Office of the Attorney-General 1981-84; chairman of PLP, Real Property Tax Tribunal, Housing Commission 1987-89; Town Planning Committee 1989-90; Minister of Consumer Affairs 1990-92. Two children. Denomination: Methodist. Interests: sports, reading and music. Residence: The Grove, West Bay St, PO Box N-3008, Nassau.

SOUTH ANDROS

RUBON WHITNEY BASTIAN, MP (IND)

Businessman. Co-founder, Success Training College. Born Dec 2, 1956, Mangrove Cay, Andros, to Melva Bastian (née Bain) and the late Rev Abraham E Bastian. Former teacher and fisherman; former hotel operator, Mangrovian Manor, Mangrove Cay Beach Resort. Educated: Mangrove Cay All Age School, Andros; College of The Bahamas, Nassau. Denomination: Baptist. Interests: sailing and fishing. Residence: Port New Providence, PO Box EE-17459 Nassau.

CAT ISLAND, RUM CAY AND SAN SALVADOR

PHILIP E "BRAVE" DAVIS, MP (PLP)

Attorney. Senior partner, Davis & Co. Past-president, Bahamas Bar Assoc. Born Jun 7, 1951, Nassau, to Brave Edward and Dorothy Davis (née Smith). Educated: Old Bight All-age School, Eastern Junior and Senior Schools, St John's College, Nassau. Called to the Bahamas Bar 1975. PLP MP for Cat Island constituency 1992-97. Member: Council of Legal Education; Academic Committee, Norman Manley Law School. Former president, Toastmasters International, Sea Bees Swim Club.

Former vice-president, Bar Council, Bahamas Swim Federation. Married to the former Ann-Marie Austin. Six children. Denomination: Anglican. Interests: baseball, softball, swimming and jogging. Residence: Westridge, PO Box N-7940, Nassau.

NORTH ELEUTHERA

ALVIN A SMITH, MP (FNM)

Leader of the Opposition in the House of Assembly. Educator. Born Sept 23, 1951, Hatchet Bay, Eleuthera, to Bernice Smith (née Johnson) and the late Alfred Smith. Educated: Hatchet Bay All-Age School; San Salvador Teachers' Training College; Univ of Miami, Miami, FL (BSc). Former principal, Exuma All-Age School 1973-76. Former Parliamentary Secretary, Ministry of Education. Former executive member and trustee, Bahamas Union of Teachers. Former executive chairman, Bahamas Agricultural & Industrial Corp; vice-president, Bahamas Senate; and Deputy Speaker of the House of Assembly. Founding member, Staniel Cay Exuma Development Assoc. Married to the former Arnette Pinder. Two children. Denomination: Methodist. Interests: fishing, softball and gardening. Residence: South Beach, PO Box SB-52060, Nassau.

SOUTH ELEUTHERA

THE HON JAMES OSWALD INGRAHAM, JP, MP (PLP)

Speaker of the House. Businessman. Owner/operator, Ingraham's Furniture Supply, Ingraham's Beach Inn, and Rock Sound Hardware and Building Supply. Born June 24, 1937, Tarpum Bay, Eleuthera, to Samuel and Marion Ingraham, both deceased. Educated: Tarpum Bay Primary School and the Univ of Indiana. Elder and preacher at Ebenezer Gospel Chapel, Tarpum Bay; president and former chairman, the Eleuthera branch of Gideons International. Former chairman of the United Missions Dept of the Assemblies of Brethren in The Bahamas. Married to the former Emily Marie Culmer of Savannah Sound, Eleuthera. Six children. Denomination: Brethren. Interests: farming, fishing and reading. Residence: Queen's Highway, PO Box 7, Tarpum Bay, Eleuthera.

EXUMA

ANTHONY DONALD EDWARD MOSS, MP (PLP)

Deputy Speaker of the House. Insurance agent. Sales Director, Bahama Sound. Born Nov 20, 1958 to Irene Moss (née Charlton) and the late Leamon Moss. Educated: George Town Public School, Exuma; St Augustine's College, Nassau. Former member, Local Government Town Committee, George Town, Exuma. Former commissioner, Exuma Basketball Assoc. Former executive, Exuma Softball Assoc. Married to the former Sheila Bethel of George Town, Exuma. Seven children. Denomination: Baptist. Interests: softball and sailing. Residence: 18 Bahama Sound, PO Box EX-29008, Exuma.

EIGHT MILE ROCK, GRAND BAHAMA (GB)

LINDY H RUSSELL, MP (FNM)

Life Underwriter. Former Parliamentary Secretary, Office of the Prime Minister. Born Jan 4, 1954, Eight Mile Rock, Grand Bahama, to Harris Russell Sr and Gennevie Russell (née Smith), both deceased. Educated: Freeport Anglican

High School. Former airline agent with Delta and manager with Air Florida and Gull Air. Elected Eight Mile Rock East township local government member, chairman and chief council, West Grand Bahama district, June 1996. FNM MP since 1997. Married to the former Nell Lavern Wildgoose of Eight Mile Rock. Two children. Denomination: Baptist. Interests: baseball, water sports and basketball. Residence: Bartlett Hill, PO Box F-40557, Eight Mile Rock.

HIGH ROCK, GB

KENNETH RUSSELL, JP, MP (FNM)

Managing partner, Trinity Builders, Grand Bahama. Owner, Best Home Designs. Former Minister of Public Works. Born Oct 22, 1953, Bailey Town, Bimini, to Olsworth and Eunice Russell (née Lightbourne). Educated: Hawksbill High School, Grand Bahama; C R Walker Technical College, Bahamas Teachers College, Nassau; Nova Southeastern Univ, Fort Lauderdale, FL. First elected to House of Assembly Mar 1997. Married to Georgina Russell (née Bridgewater). Four children. Denomination: Church of God. Interests: powerboat and car racing, motorcycle riding, drawing and painting. Residence: Harlow Rd, Lucaya, PO Box F-42950, Freeport.

LUCAYA, GB

NEKO C GRANT, JP, MP (FNM)

Business executive, group corporate manager, Burns House Ltd. First elected to Parliament in Aug 1992. Born Mar 1, 1950, West End, Grand Bahama, to Reva L Grant. Educated: St John's College, Nassau; La Salle Extension Univ (Business Management), Chicago, IL. Diamond Distinguished past president of Kiwanis International; past and honorary president of the Bahamas Softball Federation. Past president, West End Offshore Power Boat Assoc and Kiwanis Club of Lucaya. Chairman, Grand Bahama Housing Commission 1992-97; Bahamas Mortgage Corp 2000-02. Inducted into the Intl Softball Hall of Fame Aug 1997. Married to the former Barbara Evans of George Town, Exuma. Two children. Denomination: Baptist. Interests: softball, fishing. Constituency office: East Sunrise Shopping Centre, PO Box F-44200, Freeport.

MARCO CITY, GB

PLEASANT M M BRIDGEWATER, MP (PLP)

Vice-chairman of the PLP. Attorney, Bridgewater & Co. Born Sept 26, 1960, Freeport, Grand Bahama, to Prince Albert Bridgewater and Coramae McIntosh-Bridgewater. Educated: R M Bailey Sr High School, Nassau; Freeport Anglican High School, Freeport; College of The Bahamas, Nassau. Called to the Bahamas Bar 1992. Former senator. First female Grand Bahamian senator and elected Member of Parliament. Represented The Bahamas (opposition PLP) in 1993 at the 39th Commonwealth Parliamentary Conference in Cypress. Sunday school teacher/superintendent, Boss of the Year (2000/2001) for Grand Bahama. Advisor to Christian Youth Movement, St Nicholas Anglican Church. Panelist since 1999 on Cool 96 radio talk show On Common Ground. Host of ZNS radio talk show The Law and You. Member, the Bahamas Red Cross Society. Former member Ministry of Education Scholarship Advisory Council, former member of the National Youth Advisory Council; BORCO Scholarship Board, BaTelCo Board of Directors, Local Board of

Works; Quincentennial Committee, GB. Denomination: Anglican. Interests: reading, exercising and working with young people. Residence: Bevans Town, PO Box F-41572, Grand Bahama.

PINERIDGE, GB

ANN PERCENTIE, MP (PLP)

Parliamentary Secretary, Office of the Prime Minister, Freeport, Grand Bahama. Paralegal. Born August 8, 1953, Harbour Island, Eleuthera, to Herman and Elmara Percentie (née Nixon), both deceased. Educated: Harbour Island All-Age School; Robinson Road High School, Nassau; Freeport High Institute and Grand Bahama Business Academy, Freeport; Univ of London (external). Former director and wardrobe coordinator, Elite Modelling Agency, Freeport. Model of the year 1983-84. Two children. Denomination: Church of God. Interests: community involvement, modelling, travelling and reading. Residence: 54 Coconut Rd, Freeport, PO Box F-43280, Grand Bahama.

WEST END, GB AND BIMINI

THE HON OBEDIAH H WILCHCOMBE, MP (PLP)

Minister of Tourism. Journalist. Former chairman of the Progressive Liberal Party. Former Opposition senator 1994-2002. Born Nov 4, 1958, Freeport, Grand Bahama, to Mary Wilchcombe and the late Jackson Wilchcombe. Educated: Mary Star of the Sea, Freeport; Queen's College, Nassau; Univ of the West Indies, Kingston, Jamaica. President, Commonwealth American Football League, Grand Bahama Basketball Assoc and Grand Bahama Junkanoo Committee and chairman of the Caribbean Tourism Organization.

LONG ISLAND & RAGGED ISLAND

LAWRENCE CARTWRIGHT, MP (IND)

Farmer/fisherman. Retired high school principal. Born Jan 19, 1948, Gray's, Long Island, to Delbert C Cartwright and Emma L Cartwright (née Wells). Educated: Buckley's Public School, Long Island; Bahamas Teachers' College, Nassau; Univ of the West Indies, Nassau Campus; International Correspondence Schools. Principal: Salt Pond Public School 1968-1975, Glinton's All-Age School 1981-86 and N G M Major High School 1986-99, Long Island. Member: Long Island Junkanoo Committee, church catechist, Justice of the Peace. Married to Theresa Ann Cartwright. Three children. Denomination: Anglican. Interests: fishing, reading and sports. Residence: Gray's, PO Box DC-30677, Long Island.

MICAL (MAYAGUANA, INAGUA, CROOKED ISLAND, ACKLINS & LONG CAY)

THE HON VERGENEAS ALFRED V GRAY, MP (PLP)

Minister of Agriculture, Fisheries and Local Government. Attorney-at-law. Born Aug 5, 1951, Hardhill, Acklins, to Charles W Gray and Vera Darling (née Collie). Educated: St Anne's High School, Nassau; Univ of Pennsylvania (BSc). Former PLP MP for Carmichael constituency 1987-92. Family Island Commissioner for Mayaguana, Acklins/Crooked Island, Andros, Exuma and Grand Bahama 1974-1981. Called to the Bahamas Bar 1985. Deacon, Annex Baptist Church, Nassau. Member: Rotary Club of West Nassau, Toastmasters 3569. Married to Bessley E Williamson-Gray. Five children. Denomination: Baptist. Interests: flying, reading and fishing. Residence: Winton Heights, PO Box N-9777, Nassau.

Parliamentarians' Salaries

	Salary	Duty allowance
Prime Minister	$86,000	$25,000
Deputy Prime Minister	$76,000	$15,000
Attorney-General	$66,000	$5,000
Cabinet Ministers with portfolio	$66,000	$5,000
Minister of State	$66,000	$5,000
Speaker of the House	$62,000	$3,000
Deputy Speaker	$32,000	–
Parliamentary Secretaries	$45,000	$3,000
Leader of the Opposition	$50,000	–
House of Assembly members	$28,000	–
Government Whip	–	$11,550
Government Deputy Whip	–	$6,000
Opposition Whip	–	$11,250
President of the Senate	$17,500	–
Vice-President of the Senate	$15,000	–
Leader of the Senate	$15,000	–
Senators	$12,500	–

Cabinet Ministers hold full-time positions. Senators and House members meet regularly but not on a full-time basis, and customarily hold positions in a profession or business.

House of Assembly members (MPs) who hold other positions in government are paid these salaries in addition to the MP salary. In the case of MPs holding more than one Cabinet position, only one Cabinet salary is received in addition to the MP salary. Additionally, MPs receive a constituency office allowance of $18,000 per year.

A subsistence allowance for international travel is based on official destination, length of stay, etc. A claim is submitted afterwards. Out Island representatives receive a constituency allowance for travel to and from their constituencies.

Parliamentary Secretaries

Office of the Prime Minister, Freeport, Grand Bahama
Ann Percentie, MP

Ministry of Finance
Michael Halkitis, MP

Ministry of Tourism
Agatha Marcelle, MP

Ministry of Health
Ron Pinder, MP

Ministry of Education
Veronica Owens, MP

Ministry of Works and Utilities
John Carey, MP

Permanent Secretaries

Secretary to the Cabinet
Wendell G Major, CMG

Financial Secretary
Ruth Millar, CMG

Office of the Prime Minister
Ronald Thompson

Office of the Deputy Prime Minister and Ministry of National Security
Mark Wilson

Ministry of Tourism
Colin Higgs

Ministry of Foreign Affairs
Dr Patricia Rodgers

Cabinet Office
(vacant at press time)

Ministry of Education
Creswell Sturrup

Ministry of Health
Elma Garraway

Ministry of Trade and Industry
Helen Ebong

Ministry of Works and Utilities
Anita Hilton-Bernard

Ministry of Labour and Immigration
Thelma Ferguson-Beneby

Ministry of Social Services and Community Development
Barbara Burrows

Ministry of Transport and Aviation
Archie Nairn

Office of the Attorney-General
Jacqueline Murray

Ministry of Agriculture, Fisheries and Local Government
Camille Johnson

Dept of Public Service
Irene Stubbs

Ministry of Financial Services and Investments
Sheila Carey

Ministry of Housing and National Insurance
Leila Greene

Ministry of Youth, Sports and Culture
Harrison Thompson

Commission Chairpersons

Legal and Judicial Service Commission ....Chief Justice Sir Burton Hall
Police Service Commission ....Rev Dr Charles W Saunders, CBE
Public Disclosure Commission ....H C Walkine
Public Service Commission ....M Teresa Butler
Public Utilities Commission ....Peter Bethel, CMG

Public Service Officials

Dept of Agriculture
Valerie Outten, Director
Simeon Pinder, Deputy Director
Melanie Williams, Agriculture Officer (Freeport)

Audit Dept
Terrance Bastian, Auditor-General
Carolyn Patton, Deputy Auditor-General (Freeport)

Dept of Archives
Dr D Gail Saunders, Director

Bahamas Agricultural & Industrial Corp
Michael Halkitis, MP, Executive Chairman

Bahamas Development Bank
K Neville Adderley, Chairman of the Board
George Rodgers, Managing Director
Anthony Woodside, Deputy Managing Director
George Miller, Manager, Credit Cycle (Family Islands)
Justin A Sturrup, Manager (Freeport)

Bahamas Electricity Corp (BEC)
Kevin Basden, General Manager

Bahamas Gaming Board
B K Bonamy, Secretary
Georgette Dorsett, Assistant Manager

Bahamas Hotel Corp
Deepak Bhatnager, Financial Controller/ Acting Chief Executive Officer

Bahamas Information Services
Christopher Symmonett, Executive Director

Bahamas Investment Authority
Basil Albury, Director of Investments

Bahamas Mortgage Corp
Jerome Godfrey, Managing Director
Joycelyn Varence, Deputy Managing Director
Dennis Lightbourne, Manager and Senior Loans Officer (Freeport)

Bahamas Technical and Vocational Institute (BTVI)
Dr Celestine Williams, Director

Bahamas Telecommunications Co (BTC)
Michael Symonette, President

Bahamasair
Paul Major, General Manager

Broadcasting Corp of The Bahamas
Anthony Foster, General Manager

Central Bank of The Bahamas
Julian Francis, CBE, Governor

Civil Aviation Dept
Cyril Saunders, Acting Director

College of The Bahamas
Dr Leon Higgs, President

Dept of Cooperatives
Nathaniel Adderley, Director

Customs Dept
John Rolle, Comptroller

Royal Bahamas Defence Force
Commodore Davy Rolle, Commander

Dept of Environmental Health Services
Mellany McKenzie, Director

Fire Dept
ASP Alexander Roberts, Director

Dept of Fisheries
Michael Braynen, Director

Government House
Steve Pennerman, Acting Comptroller

Government Printing Dept
Clifton Johnson, Acting Chief Superintendent

Governor General's Office
Cynthia Gibbs, Secretary to the Governor General

House of Assembly
Edward Ellis, Editor of the Hansard
Maurice Tynes, Chief Clerk

Dept of Housing
Christopher Russell, Acting Chief Housing Officer
Quentin Glover, Office Manager (Freeport)

Immigration Dept
Vernon E L Burrows, Director

Industrial (Arbitration) Tribunal
Patrenda Russell, Acting Secretary
Elkenny Lockhart, Assistant Secretary (Freeport)

Judicial Dept
Sir Burton Hall, Chief Justice
Estelle Gray-Evans, Registrar
Donna Newton, Deputy Registrar
Indira Demeritte-Francis, Deputy Registrar of the Court of Appeal
Ernie Wallace, Deputy Registrar
Stephana Strachan, Acting Deputy Registrar (Freeport)
Tabitha Cumberbatch, Assistant Registrar

Court of Appeal Justices: Dame Joan Sawyer (President), Maurice Churaman, Loris Milton Ganpatsingh, Mustapha Ibrahim (non-resident), Emmanuel Osadebay

Supreme Court Justices: Sir Burton Hall (Chief Justice), Ricardo Marques (Sr Justice), Hartman Longley, Anita Allen, Austin Davis, John Lyons, QC, Hugh Small, Jeanne Thompson, Jon Isaacs, Faizool Mohamad, Stephen Isaacs (Freeport)

Stipendiary and Circuit Magistrates: Vera Watkins (Chief Magistrate), Franklyn Williams (Deputy Chief Magistrate, Freeport), Cheryl Albury, Helen Amorales-Jones (Freeport), Guillamina Archer, Carolita Bethell, William Campbell, Susan Charles-Sylvester, Debbye Ferguson, Roger Gomez, Subusola Lawanson-Swain (Freeport), Marilyn Meeres, Carol Misiewicz, Linda Virgill, Kathleen Hassan, Crawford McKee (Abaco), Jeanine Weech-Gomez (Acting, Night Court), Andrew Thompson (Acting, Night Court), James Moxey (Acting, Night Court)

Dept of Labour
Harcourt Brown, Acting Director
Tyrone Gibson, Assistant Director (Freeport)

Dept of Lands & Surveys
Tex Turnquest, Director

Legal Affairs Dept
Rhonda Bain, Director

Maritime Affairs
John Mervyn Jones, Director (London)
Christine Abrigo, Senior Deputy Director (New York),
Erma Rahming-Mackey, Assistant Director, Nassau

Meteorological Dept
Arthur Rolle, Acting Director

Ministry of Education
Iris Pinder, Director

Ministry of Finance
Ruth Millar, CMG, Financial Secretary
Edgar Hall, Deputy Director of Budget
Ehurd Cunningham, Secretary for Revenue
Gaynell Bullard, Controller, Data Processing Unit

Ministry of Foreign Affairs
Andrew McKinney, Acting Chief of Protocol

Ministry of Health
Dr M Dahl-Regis, Chief Medical Officer
Mary Johnson, Director of Nursing
Herbert Brown, Hospital Administrator, Princess Margaret Hospital
Catherine Weech, Hospital Administrator, Sandilands Rehabilitation Centre

Ministry of Tourism
Vincent Vanderpool-Wallace, Director-General

Ministry of Youth, Sports and Culture
Autherine Turnquest, Acting Director of Youth
Martin Lundy, Director of Sports
Dr Nicolette Bethel-Burrows, Director of Culture

National Insurance Board
Lennox McCartney, Director

Parliamentary Registration Department
Errol Bethel, Parliamentary Commissioner

Passport Office
Clifford Scavella, Chief Passport Officer

Dept of Physical Planning
Michael Major, Director

Royal Bahamas Police Force
Paul Farquharson, Police Commissioner

Port Dept
Capt Anthony J Allens, Port Controller
Collimae Ferguson, Deputy Controller
Benjamin Ferguson, Deputy Controller (Freeport)

Post Office
Godfrey Clarke, Postmaster-General

Prisons Dept
Edwin Culmer, Acting Superintendent

Public Hospitals Authority
Ruth Millar, CMG, Chairman
Nathaniel Beneby, Deputy Chairman
Herbert Brown, Managing Director
Hannah Gray, Deputy Managing Director

Dept of Public Works
Colin Marshall, Acting Director
Roland Bevans, Engineering Assistant (Freeport)

Registrar General's Dept
Sterling Quant, Registrar General

Dept of Rehabilitative Welfare Services
Sharon Farquharson, Director

Road Traffic Dept
Brensil Rolle, Controller

Simpson Penn Centre for Boys
Wrensworth Butler, Acting Superintendent

Social Services Dept
Mellany Zonicle, Acting Director
Lillian Quant-Forbes, Assistant Director (Freeport)
Paula Marshall, Assistant Director (Freeport)

Statistics Dept
Charles Stuart, Director
Clara Lowe, Officer in Charge (Freeport)

Treasury Dept
Eugenia Cartwright, Treasurer

Water & Sewerage Corp (WSC)
Godfrey Sherman, Acting General Manager

Willie Mae Pratt Centre for Girls
Betty Farquharson, Acting Superintendent

Government Offices

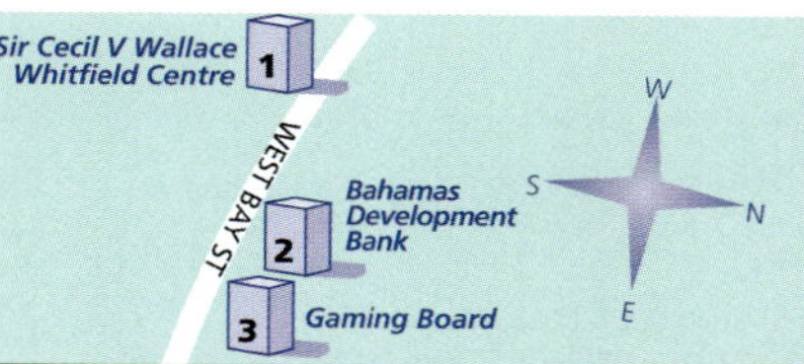

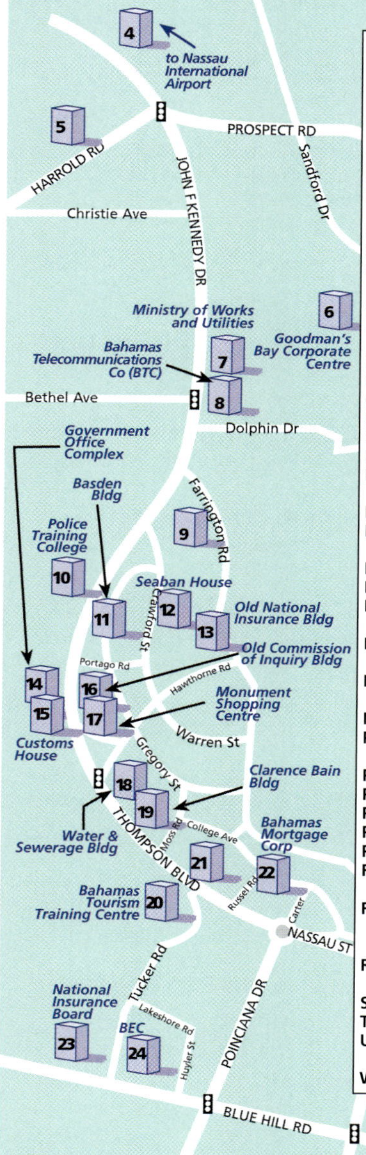

Bahamas Customs ***(Bldg 15),*** Thompson Blvd
Bahamas Development Bank ***(Bldg 2),*** West Bay St
Bahamas Electricity Corp (BEC) ***(Bldg 24),*** Tucker Rd
Bahamas Information Services ***(Bldg 3),*** West Bay St
Bahamas Industrial Tribunal ***(Bldg 17),*** Thompson Blvd
Bahamas Investment Authority ***(Bldg 6),*** West Bay St
Bahamas Mortgage Corp ***(Bldg 22),*** Russel Rd
Bahamas Telecommunications Co (BTC) ***(Bldg 8),*** John F Kennedy Dr
Central Detective Unit ***(Bldg 16),*** Thompson Blvd
Civil Aviation, Dept of ***(Bldg 12),*** Crawford St
College of The Bahamas School of Hospitality & Tourism Studies ***(Bldg 20),*** Thompson Blvd
Criminal Records Office ***(Bldg 16),*** Thompson Blvd
Environmental Health, Dept of ***(Bldg 9),*** Farrington Rd
Fingerprinting Dept, ***(Bldg 16),*** Thompson Blvd
Gaming Board ***(Bldg 3),*** West Bay St
Gun Licensing Dept, ***(Bldg 16),*** Thompson Blvd
Housing, Dept of ***(Bldg 11),*** Thompson Blvd
Meteorology, Dept of ***(Bldg 4),*** Nassau Intl Airport
Ministry of Education ***(Bldg 14),*** Thompson Blvd
Ministry of Education Testing and Evaluation Unit ***(Bldg 5),*** Harrold Rd
Ministry of Finance ***(Bldg 1),*** West Bay St
Ministry of Financial Services and Investments ***(Bldg 6),*** West Bay St
Ministry of Health ***(Bldg 25),*** Meeting St
Ministry of Labour ***(Bldg 19),*** Thompson Blvd
Ministry of Works and Utilities ***(Bldg 7),*** John F Kennedy Dr
Ministry of Youth, Sports and Culture ***(Bldg 14),*** Thompson Blvd
Nassau International Airport ***(Bldg 4),*** John F Kennedy Dr
National Insurance Board ***(Bldg 23),*** Blue Hill Rd
Parliamentary Commissioner's Office ***(Bldg 13),*** Farrington Rd
Passport Office ***(Bldg 11),*** Thompson Blvd
Police Training College ***(Bldg 10),*** Thompson Blvd
Post Office ***(Bldg 19),*** Thompson Blvd
Prime Minister, Office of the ***(Bldg 1),*** West Bay St
Public Service, Dept of ***(Bldg 25),*** Meeting St
Rehabilitative/Welfare Services, Dept of ***(Bldg 21),*** Thompson Blvd
Road Traffic Dept ***(Bldg 19),*** Thompson Blvd
Vehicle Inspection & Licensing Centre
Drivers Licenses
Roads, Parks and Grounds Beautification (Admin offices) ***(Bldg 5),*** Harrold Rd
Statistics, Dept of ***(Bldg 19),*** Thompson Blvd
Town Planning ***(Bldg 7),*** John F Kennedy Dr
University of the West Indies ***(Bldg 20),*** Thompson Blvd
Water and Sewerage Corp ***(Bldg 18),*** Thompson Blvd

MEETING ST
25
Poinciana Hill House

GOVERNMENT OFFICES

Archives, Dept of ***(Bldg 31),*** Mackey St
Attorney-General's Office ***(Bldg 14),*** East Hill St
Auditor General ***(Bldg 9),*** Frederick St
Bahamas Agricultural and Industrial Corp (BAIC) ***(Bldg 30),*** East Bay St
Bahamas Environment Science and Technology (BEST) Commission ***(Bldg 4),*** off Marlborough St
Broadcasting Corp of The Bahamas: Radio Bahamas, ZNS TV ***(Bldg 27),*** Third Ter East
Business Licensing and Valuation Dept ***(Bldg 10),*** Frederick St
Cabinet Office ***(Bldg 22),*** Bay St
Central Bank of The Bahamas, The ***(Bldg 8),*** Frederick St
Central Police Station ***(Bldg 23),*** Bank Ln & East St
Chief Justice, Offices of ***(Bldg 21),*** Bank Ln
Court of Appeal ***(Bldg 11),*** Charlotte St
Deputy Prime Minister, Office of ***(Bldg 22),*** Woodes Rogers Walk
Fisheries, Dept of ***(Bldg 32),*** East Bay St
Government House ***(Bldg 7),*** (office and residence of Governor General), West Hill St
Government Publications ***(Bldg 24),*** Bay St
Hotel Corp of The Bahamas ***(Bldg 6),*** Bay & Marlborough Sts
House of Assembly ***(Bldg 18),*** Bay & Parliament Sts
Immigration, Dept of ***(Bldg 28),*** Mount Royal Ave
Lands & Surveys, Dept of ***(Bldg 29),*** East Bay St
Local Government, Dept of ***(Bldg 30),*** East Bay St
Ministry of Agriculture, Fisheries and Local Government ***(Bldg 30),*** East Bay St
Ministry of Foreign Affairs and the Public Service ***(Bldg 13),*** East Hill St
Ministry of Housing and National Insurance ***(Bldg 11),*** Charlotte St
Ministry of Labour and Immigration ***(Bldg 14),*** East Hill St
Ministry of Social Services and Community Development ***(Bldg 10),*** Frederick St
Ministry of Tourism ***(Bldg 5),*** Bay St
Ministry of Trade & Industry ***(Bldg 2),*** West Bay St
Ministry of Transport and Aviation ***(Bldg 33),*** East Bay St
Nursing Council of The Bahamas ***(Bldg 3),*** Delancy St
Police and Fire Brigade Headquarters ***(Bldg 15),*** East St
Police Marine (Harbour Control) ***(Bldg 24),*** Bay St
Port and Marine Dept ***(Bldg 20),*** Woodes Rogers Walk
Post Office, General ***(Bldg 14),*** East Hill St
Prince George Dock ***(20),*** Woodes Rogers Walk
Princess Margaret Hospital ***(Bldg 25),*** Shirley St
Produce Exchange ***(Bldg 34),*** Potter's Cay Dock
Registrar General's Office ***(Bldg 12),*** Parliament St
Senate, The ***(Bldg 17),*** Parliament Sq
Speaker of the House, Offices of ***(Bldg 21),*** Parliament Sq
Supreme Court, The ***(Bldg 16),*** Bank Ln
Supreme Court Bailiff, Offices of ***(Bldg 21),*** Bank Ln/Parliament Sq
Tourist Information Centre ***(Bldg 19),*** Rawson Sq
Vehicle Inspection & Licensing Centre ***(Bldg 1),*** West Bay St

Resident Diplomatic & Consular Representatives

EMBASSY OF THE PEOPLE'S REPUBLIC OF CHINA
#3 Orchard Terrace, Village Rd, PO Box SS-6389, Nassau. Tel (242) 393-1415, fax (242) 393-0733
HE Dongcun Jiao, Ambassador
Boheng Ni, First Secretary (Deputy Chief of the Mission)
Zhenguang Song, First Secretary
Dayu Chen, Second Secretary
Xiang Wang, Attaché
Yu Zhang, Attaché

EMBASSY OF THE UNITED STATES OF AMERICA
Mosmar Building, Queen St, PO Box N-8197, Nassau. Tel (242) 322-1181
John D Rood, Ambassador
Robert M Witajewski, Deputy Chief of Mission
Kay Crawford, First Secretary and Consul (Management)
Abdelnour Zaiback, First Secretary and Consul
Michael Taylor, Second Secretary (Chief, Political-Economic Section and Public Affairs Officer)
Myrna Ortiz-Kerr, Third Secretary (Narcotics Affairs)
John Kane, Attaché (Regional Security Officer)
Ronnie Fontenot, Attaché (Information Management Officer)
Thomas H Hill, Attaché (Narcotics)
LCDR Zane Thomas, Naval Liaison Officer
LCDR Terrence M Johns, Coast Guard Liaison Officer
LaFonda Sutton-Burke, Interim Port Director (Customs and Border Protection/Nassau)
Frederick Waters, Port Director (Customs and Border Protection/Freeport)

BRITISH HIGH COMMISSION
Ansbacher House (3rd Floor), East St, PO Box N-7516, Nassau. Tel (242) 325-7471 (to 3), fax (242) 323-3871
HE Roderick Gemmell OBE, High Commissioner
Steve Firstbrook, Deputy High Commissioner
Col Charles LeBrun, Defence Adviser (resident in Kingston, Jamaica)

EMBASSY OF THE REPUBLIC OF HAITI
Sears House, Shirley St, PO Box N-3046, Nassau. Tel (242) 326-0325, fax (242) 322-7712, e-mail haitianembassy@batelnet.bs
HE Louis Harold Joseph, Ambassador (Resident Dean of the Diplomatic Corps)
Greny B Antoine, Counsellor (Consular Affairs)
Spana David, Second Secretary

THE CONSULATE GENERAL OF THE REPUBLIC OF CUBA
Cash Fountain Bldg, Shirley & Armstrong Sts, Nassau. Tel (242) 356-3473, fax (242) 356-3472, e-mail cubahcons@coralwave.com
Felix Wilson, Consul General
Homero Saker, Consul

EUROPEAN UNION DELEGATION OF THE EUROPEAN COMMISSION
Frederick House (2nd Floor), Frederick St, PO Box N-3246, Nassau. Tel (242) 325-5850, fax (242) 323-3819, e-mail eucom@coralwave.com
Gerd Jarchow, Ambassador, Head of Delegation (resident in Jamaica)
Nicola Cole, Secretary

Bahamas Diplomatic & Consular Representatives

ANTIGUA AND BARBUDA

His Excellency (HE) A Leonard Archer, OBE
High Commissioner (non-resident)
Address: The High Commission for The Commonwealth of The Bahamas to Antigua and Barbuda, c/o The Ministry of Foreign Affairs, PO Box N-3746, Nassau, The Bahamas.
Tel (242) 322-7624/5, fax (242) 328-8212, e-mail mfabahamas@batelnet.bs.

REPUBLIC OF ARGENTINA

Vacant at press time
Ambassador (non-resident)
Address: The Embassy of The Commonwealth of The Bahamas to the Republic of Argentina, c/o The Ministry of Foreign Affairs, PO Box N-3746, Nassau, The Bahamas.
Tel (242) 322-7624/5, fax (242) 328-8212, e-mail mfabahamas@batelnet.bs.

BARBADOS

HE A Leonard Archer, OBE
High Commissioner (non-resident)
See Antigua and Barbuda

BELGIUM

HE Basil G O'Brien, CMG
Ambassador (non-resident)
See United Kingdom

BELIZE

HE A Leonard Archer, OBE
High Commissioner (non-resident)
See Antigua and Barbuda

FEDERATIVE REPUBLIC OF BRAZIL

Vacant at press time
Ambassador (non-resident)
See Argentina

CANADA

HE Philip Smith
High Commissioner
Address: The High Commission for The Commonwealth of The Bahamas, Metropolitan Life Centre, 50 O'Connor St, Ste 1313, Ottawa, ON, K1P 6L2, Canada.
Tel (613) 232-1724, fax (613) 232-0097, e-mail ottawa.mission@bahighco.com.
Diplomatic Staff: Jack Thompson, Deputy High Commissioner; Kerry Bonamy, Second Secretary/Vice Consul

REPUBLIC OF CHILE

Vacant at press time
Ambassador (non-resident)
See Argentina

REPUBLIC OF COLOMBIA

HE Joshua Sears
Ambassador Designate (non-resident)
See United States

REPUBLIC OF COSTA RICA

Vacant at press time
Ambassador (non-resident)
See Panama

REPUBLIC OF CUBA

Vacant at press time
Ambassador (non-resident)
Address: The Embassy of The Commonwealth of The Bahamas to the Republic of Cuba, c/o The Ministry of Foreign Affairs, PO Box N-3746, Nassau, The Bahamas. Tel (242) 322-7624/5, fax (242) 328-8212, e-mail mfabahamas@batelnet.bs.

DOMINICA

HE A Leonard Archer, OBE
High Commissioner (non-resident)
See Antigua and Barbuda

COMMISSION OF THE EUROPEAN UNION
HE Basil G O'Brien, CMG
Ambassador/Permanent Representative
Address: c/o The High Commission of The Commonwealth of The Bahamas, 10 Chesterfield St, London, W1X 8AH England. Tel (011) 44-207-408-4488, fax (011) 44-207-499-9937, e-mail bahamas.hicom.lon@cableinet.co.uk.
Diplomatic Staff: Julie Campbell, First Secretary; Charmaine Williams, Second Secretary/Vice Consul

FRANCE
HE Basil G O'Brien, CMG
Ambassador (non-resident)
See United Kingdom

FEDERAL REPUBLIC OF GERMANY
HE Basil G O'Brien, CMG
Ambassador (non-resident)
See United Kingdom

GRENADA
HE A Leonard Archer, OBE
High Commissioner (non-resident)
See Antigua and Barbuda

REPUBLIC OF GUATEMALA
Vacant at press time
Ambassador (non-resident)
See Republic of Panama

THE COOPERATIVE REPUBLIC OF GUYANA
HE A Leonard Archer, OBE
High Commissioner (non-resident)
See Antigua and Barbuda

THE REPUBLIC OF HAITI

HE Dr Eugene Newry
Ambassador
Address: The Embassy of The Commonwealth of The Bahamas, 12 Rue Goulard, Place Boyer Pétion-Ville, Port-au-Prince, Haiti. Tel (011) 509-256-4407 or 509-257-8782, fax (011) 509-256-5729, e-mail bahamasembassy@hainet.net.
Diplomatic Staff: Anthony Williams, Second Secretary; Michelle Williams, Second Secretary/Attaché

REPUBLIC OF HONDURAS
Vacant at press time
Ambassador (non-resident)
See Republic of Panama

HONG KONG

Freddie Tucker
Consul General (acting) **Address:** Consulate General of The Commonwealth of The Bahamas, Ste 704-705 A Sino Plaza 7F, 255-257 Gloucester Rd, Causeway Bay, Hong Kong, Republic of China, Tel (852) 2147-0202, fax (852) 2893-3917.

ITALY
HE Basil G O'Brien, CMG
Ambassador (non-resident)
See United Kingdom

JAMAICA
HE A Leonard Archer, OBE
High Commissioner (non-resident)
See Antigua and Barbuda

JAPAN

HE Sir Sidney Poitier, KBE
Ambassador (non-resident)
Address: The Embassy of The Commonwealth of The Bahamas to Japan, c/o The Ministry of Foreign Affairs, PO Box N-3746, Nassau, The Bahamas. Tel (242) 322-7624/5, fax (242) 328-8212, e-mail mfabahamas@batelnet.bs.

KINGDOM OF LESOTHO
HE Philip Smith
High Commissioner Designate (non-resident)
See Canada

MALAYSIA
HE Joshua Sears
High Commissioner Designate (non-resident)
See United States

MEXICO
HE Joshua Sears
Ambassador (non-resident)
See United States

REPUBLIC OF NICARAGUA
Vacant at press time
Ambassador Designate (non-resident)
See Republic of Panama

ORGANIZATION OF AMERICAN STATES (OAS)
HE Joshua Sears
Permanent Representative
Address: c/o The Embassy of The Commonwealth of The Bahamas, 2220 Massachusetts Ave, NW, Washington, DC 20008. Tel (202) 319-2660/7, fax (202) 319-2668, e-mail bahemb@aol.doc.
Alternate representatives: Eugene Torchon-Newry, First Secretary/Consul; Monique Vanderpool, Second Secretary/Vice Consul; Betty Greenslade, Second Secretary/Vice Consul; Chanelle Brown, Third Secretary/Vice Consul

REPUBLIC OF PANAMA
Vacant at press time
Ambassador (non-resident)
Address: The Embassy of The Commonwealth of The Bahamas to the Republic of Panama, c/o The Ministry of Foreign Affairs, PO Box N-3746, Nassau, The Bahamas.
Tel (242) 322-7624/5, fax (242) 328-8212, e-mail mfabahamas@batelnet.bs.

ST KITTS AND NEVIS
HE A Leonard Archer, OBE
High Commissioner (non-resident)
See Antigua and Barbuda

ST VINCENT AND THE GRENADINES
HE A Leonard Archer, OBE
High Commissioner (non-resident)
See Antigua and Barbuda

SURINAME
HE A Leonard Archer, OBE
High Commissioner (non-resident)
See Antigua and Barbuda

THE REPUBLIC OF TRINIDAD AND TOBAGO
HE A Leonard Archer, OBE
High Commissioner (non-resident)
See Antigua and Barbuda

UNITED KINGDOM

HE Basil G O'Brien, CMG
High Commissioner
Address: The High Commission of The Commonwealth of The Bahamas, 10 Chesterfield St, Mayfair, London, W1J 5JL England. Tel (011) 44-207-408-4488, fax (011) 44-207-499-9937, e-mail bahamas.hicom.lon@cableinet.co.uk.
Diplomatic Staff: Charmaine Williams, Second Secretary/Vice Consul; Judith Francis, Attaché (Maritime); Julie Campbell, First Secretary/Consul

INTERNATIONAL MARITIME ORGANIZATION
HE Basil G O'Brien, CMG
Permanent Representative
Address: c/o The High Commission of The Commonwealth of The Bahamas, 10 Chesterfield St, London W1X 8AH, England. Tel (011) 44-207-408-4488, fax (011) 44-207-499-9937, e-mail bahamas.hicom.lon@cableinet.co.uk.
Permanent Representative: Basil O'Brien, CMG
Alternate Representatives: J Mervyn Jones, Director; Capt Douglas Bell, Deputy Director

UNITED STATES OF AMERICA

HE Joshua Sears
Ambassador
Address: The Embassy of The Commonwealth of The Bahamas, 2220 Massachusetts Ave, NW, Washington, DC 20008. Tel (202) 319-2660/7, fax (202) 319-2668, e-mail bahemb@aol.doc.
Diplomatic Staff: Eugene Torchon-Newry, First Secretary/Consul; Monique Vanderpool, Second Secretary/Vice Consul; Betty Greenslade, Second Secretary/Vice Consul; Chanelle Brown, Third Secretary/Vice Consul

UNITED NATIONS

HE Dr Paulette Bethel
Ambassador/ Permanent Representative
Address: The Permanent Mission of The Commonwealth of The Bahamas to the United Nations, 231 East 46th St, New York, NY 10017. Tel (212) 421-6925/6, fax (212) 759-2135, e-mail bshun@undp.org.
Diplomatic Staff: Rhoda Jackson, Minister Counsellor; Tiska Fraser, First Secretary; Frank Davis, First Secretary; Nicole Archer, Second Secretary

THE ORIENTAL REPUBLIC OF URUGUAY

Vacant at press time
Ambassador (non-resident)
See Argentina

REPUBLIC OF ZAMBIA

HE Philip Smith
High Commissioner Designate (non-resident)
See Canada

REPUBLIC OF ZIMBABWE

HE Philip Smith
High Commissioner Designate (non-resident)
Address: The Embassy of The Commonwealth of The Bahamas to the Republic of Zimbabwe, c/o The Ministry of Foreign Affairs, PO Box N-3746, Nassau, The Bahamas.
Tel (242) 322-7624/5, fax (242) 328-8212, e-mail mfabahamas@batelnet.bs.
See Canada

MIAMI

Alma Adams
Consul General
Address: The Consulate General of The Commonwealth of The Bahamas, Suite 818, Ingraham Building, 25 SE 2nd Ave, Miami, FL 33131.
Tel (305) 373-6295, fax (305) 373-6312.
Consular Staff: Sandra Carey, Consul; Nestor Sands, Vice Consul

NEW YORK

E Edison Bethel
Consul General
Address: The Consulate General of The Commonwealth of The Bahamas, 231 East 46th St, New York, NY 10017.
Tel (212) 421-6420, fax (212) 688-5926, e-mail mailbox@bahamasconsulate-ny.com.
Consular Staff: Renee Pinder, Vice Consul; Christine Abrigo, Consul (Maritime Affairs)

BAHAMAS ENVIRONMENT, SCIENCE & TECHNOLOGY COMMISSION (BEST)

HE Keod M Smith, MP
Ambassador for the Environment
Address: Ministry of Agriculture and Fisheries, Nassau Court, off Marlborough St. PO Box N-3028, Nassau, The Bahamas.
Tel (242) 322-4546, 322-2576, 356-3067 or 328-7454, fax (242) 326-3509.

UNITED NATIONS FOOD & AGRICULTURE ORGANIZATION (FAO)

HE Godfrey Eneas
Ambassador/ Permanent Representative
Address: Ministry of Foreign Affairs, East Hill Street, PO Box N-3746, Nassau, The Bahamas.
Tel (242) 393-2102, 356-2555, fax (242) 393-1168, e-mail eneasag@batelnet.bs.

International Organizations' Representatives

In the Commonwealth of The Bahamas

ORGANIZATION OF AMERICAN STATES
Office of the General Secretariat, 42 Queen St, PO Box N-7793, Nassau
Tel (242) 326-7746 or 326-0741, fax (242) 325-0196. E-mail oas.bah@batelnet.bs

PAN-AMERICAN HEALTH ORGANIZATION (PAHO)/ WORLD HEALTH ORGANIZATION (WHO)
Union Court Bldg, Elizabeth Ave, 2nd Floor, PO Box N-4833, Nassau
Tel (242) 326-7390, fax (242) 325-0121
Lynda Campbell, Representative. E-mail e-mail@bah.paho.org

INTER-AMERICAN DEVELOPMENT BANK
IDB House, East Bay St, PO Box N-3743, Nassau
Tel (242) 393-7159, fax (242) 393-8430
Richard Herring, Representative

INTER-AMERICAN INSTITUTE FOR COOPERATION ON AGRICULTURE
Centreville Professional Plaza, 8th Terrace and Collins Ave, Ste 5
PO Box SS-6205, Nassau
Tel (242) 325-8800/2, fax (242) 325-8803
Errol Berkeley, Representative. E-mail iica@batelnet.bs

Decorations, Degrees, Honours

AS Associate in Science
BA Bachelor of Arts
BD Bachelor of Divinity
BEd Bachelor of Education
BEM British Empire Medal
BSc Bachelor of Science
CBE Commander of the Order of the British Empire
CCFP Certificate of the Canadian Family Physician
CMG Companion of the Order of St Michael and St George
CA Chartered Accountant
CPA Chartered Public Accountant
ChB Bachelor of Surgery
DCMG Dame Commander of the Order of St Michael and St George
DHL Doctor of Humane Letters
FRCOG Fellow of the Royal College of Obstetricians and Gynaecologists
GCMG Knight or Dame Grand Cross of the Order of St Michael and St George
HE His Excellency
JP Justice of the Peace
KBE Knight Commander of the Order of the British Empire
KCMG Knight Commander of the Order of St Michael and St George
Kt Knight
LVO Lieutenant of Royal Victorian Order
LLB Bachelor of Laws
LLD Doctor of Laws
MBA Master of Business Administration
MBE Member of the British Empire
MD Doctor of Medicine
MIA Master of International Affairs
MP Member of Parliament
MPA Master of Public Administration
MPhil Master of Philosophy
MSW Master of Social Work
MSc Master of Science
MB BS Bachelor of Medicine and Bachelor of Science
MB ChB Bachelor of Medicine and Bachelor of Surgery
OBE Officer of the Order of the British Empire
PC Privy Council
PhD Doctor of Philosophy
QC Queen's Counsel

Honorary Consuls & Representatives

In the Commonwealth of The Bahamas

HONORARY CONSULS UNLESS INDICATED OTHERWISE.

S Anders Wiberg, LLB, Dean of Honorary Consular Corps **(see Sweden)**
Ralph D Seligman, QC, Vice-Dean of Honorary Consular Corps **(see Israel)**
Dorothy Baker, Secretary to Honorary Consular Corps
Tel (242) 362-6424

AUSTRIA
Heinz R Kloihofer, PO Box FH-14591, Nassau. Tel (242) 363-2520 (w) or 457-3328 (cell), e-mail heinz008@hotmail.com.

BARBADOS
Carlton I Jones, PO Box N-8759, Nassau. Tel (242) 325-5591 (w) or 327-5697 (h), fax (242) 322-6353.

BELGIUM
Hervé Kelekom, PO Box CB-11090, Nassau. Tel (242) 362-4218 (w) or 362-4218 (h), fax (242) 362-4050.

BRAZIL
Pedro G Wassitsch, PO Box N-4893, Nassau. Tel (242) 325-4462 (w) or 327-0946 (h), fax (242) 325-4458.

CANADA
Robert Nihon, tel (242) 393-2123, fax (242) 324-3691.
Monique Brooks, Honorary Vice-Consul, PO Box SS-6371, Nassau. Tel (242) 393-2123/4, fax (242) 393-1305.
Robert G Farrell, Counsellor (Commercial), PO Box 1500, Kingston, 10, Jamaica. Tel (876) 926-1500 (to 4), fax (876) 511-3491.

CHILE
Carmen Massoni, PO Box N-4949, Nassau. Tel (242) 325-1950 (w) or 324-1928 (h), fax (242) 325-2765.

COSTA RICA
Robert S Jagger, Honorary Consul General, PO Box CB-11297, Nassau. Tel (242) 327-3796 (w) or 327-6246 (h), fax (242) 327-3416.

DENMARK
Berlin W Key, PO Box N-4005, Nassau. Tel (242) 322-1340 (w) or 324-2727 (h), fax (242) 323-8779.

DOMINICAN REPUBLIC
Paul McWeeney, PO Box N-7771, Nassau. Tel (242) 326-2560 (w) or 393-1597 (h), fax 325-2762.

FRANCE
Thierry Boeuf, PO Box CB-12830, Nassau. Tel (242) 356-7651 (w), 327-8060 (h), fax (242) 356-7653.

GERMANY
Herman-Josef Hermanns, PO Box N-1724, Nassau. Tel (242) 394-6161 (w) or 327-0557 (h), fax (242) 394-6262.

GREECE
Gus Constantakis, PO Box N-7682, Nassau. Tel/fax (242) 323-3523 (w), tel 362-5065 (h), fax (242) 323-3523.

ICELAND
Clement T Maynard III, PO Box CB-10957, Nassau. Tel (242) 323-1234 (w) or 362-4740 (h), fax (242) 326-3779.

INDONESIA
Dr Davidson L Hepburn, PO Box EE-16616, Nassau. Tel (242) 322-3759 (w) or 364-4407 (h), fax (242) 328-1229.

ISRAEL
Ralph D Seligman, QC, Honorary Consul General (Vice Dean of Honorary Consular Corps), PO Box N-7776, Nassau. Tel (242) 322-2670, fax (242) 323-8914.

ITALY
Paolo Garzaroli, Honorary Vice Consul, PO Box N-10246, Nassau. Tel (242) 322-2796 (w) or 324-2267 (h), fax (242) 326-6110.

JAMAICA
Patrick Hanlan, PO Box N-3451, Nassau. Tel/fax (242) 394-8538.

JAPAN
Basil L Sands, Honorary Consul General, PO Box N-8335, Nassau. Tel (242) 322-8560/1 (w) or 393-0391 (h), fax (242) 326-7524.

REPUBLIC OF KOREA
Maxwell E Gibson, PO Box N-623, Nassau. Tel (242) 326-4745 (w) or 327-8408 (h), fax (242) 328-4211.

MEXICO
Barbara Fox, Honorary Vice-Consul, PO Box SS-19463, Nassau. Tel (242) 362-5040 (w), 364-8288 (h), fax (242) 362-5045.

THE NETHERLANDS
Peter Newton Andrews, PO Box N-44, Nassau. Tel (242) 361-6398, fax (242) 361-6842.

NICARAGUA
Dr K J A Rodgers, PO Box N-386, Nassau. Tel (242) 323-7997 or 356-6486 (w) or 363-2585 (h), fax (242) 325-1647.

NORWAY
Berlin W Key, PO Box N-4005, Nassau. Tel (242) 322-1340 (w) or 324-2727 (h), fax (242) 323-8779.

PANAMA
David McGrath, Honorary Consul General, PO Box N-7776, Nassau. Tel/fax (242) 362-4429, fax (242) 362-4886, e-mail dcm@coralwave.com.

PERU
Stephen Jenkins Melvin, PO Box N-3247, Nassau. Tel (242) 322-8571/9, fax (242) 328-7727.

PORTUGAL
Robert Arnold, PO Box N-7776, Nassau. Tel (242) 362-4449, fax (242) 362-5140.
Manuela Camacho-Major, Honorary Vice-Consul, PO Box SS-19407, Nassau. Tel (242) 324-6150, fax (242) 364-5427.

SPAIN
Francisco Carrera-Justiz, PO Box N-4880, Nassau. Tel (242) 362-3108 (w) or 362-4350 (h), fax (242) 362-1859.

SURINAME
Fritz G H Stubbs, PO Box N-4637, Nassau. Tel (242) 325-0005 or 323-4967, fax (242) 356-5005, e-mail orangecreek@coralwave.com.

SWEDEN
S Anders Wiberg, LLB, Honorary Consul General (Dean of Honorary Consular Corps), PO Box CB-11000, Nassau. Tel (242) 327-7944, fax (242) 327-7782.

SWITZERLAND
Beat Wernli, PO Box CB-10976, Nassau. Tel (242) 502-2200 (w), fax (242) 502-2300.

UGANDA
John Thompson Dorrance III, PO Box N-7776, Nassau. Tel (242) 362-4887 or 362-4151, fax (242) 362-5013.

URUGUAY
Analia Whitehead, PO Box SS-6208, Nassau. Tel (242) 328-5165 (w) or 324-3347 (h), fax (242) 325-9127.

Bahamas Honorary Consuls Abroad

BARBADOS
Selwyn Smith, 102 Husband Heights, St James, Barbados, WI. Tel (246) 424-5082, fax (246) 424-0556, e-mail sims@sunbeach.net.

BELGIUM
Albert Jean Niels, 76/78 Quae aux Breques, 1000 Brussels, Belgium.Tel 32 2 512-9348, fax 32 2 512-9292, e-mail aj.neils@online.be.

CANADA
Gordon Feeney, 270 The Kingsway, PO Box 74569, Toronto, ON, M9A 3T0, Canada. Tel/fax (416) 233-6776 (w), e-mail gord.feeney@sympatico.ca.

CHILE
Magdalena Klein de Schmalzle, Camino Los Trapenses 4188 La Dehesa, Santiago, Chile. Tel 562-241-7117, fax 562-241-7118, e-mail bahamas@rdc.cl.

DOMINICAN REPUBLIC
Hernando Perez Montas, Cesar Nicolas Penson 116, Edificio TPA, Santo Domingo, Dominican Republic. Tel (809) 688-3787, fax (809) 682-0237 or 011-33-142-86-04-00, e-mail c.actuariales@verizon.net.do.

FRANCE
Claude Le Gris, 5 Rue de Beaune, 75007 Paris, France. Tel 011-33-142-86-03-60, or 011-33-142-86-04-00, fax 011-33-147-03-39-27.

GERMANY
Hartwig Piepenbrock,Flottenstrasse 14-20, 13407 Berlin, Germany. Tel 49-30-409-004107, fax 49-30-409-004105, e-mail bahamas@piepenbrock.de

ISRAEL
Talia Glantz, 10 Paamoni St, Tel-Aviv 62918, Israel. Tel 972-05-0277014 (w) or 972-03-6058902 (h), fax 972-03-5465604, e-mail glantz@tascm.health.gov.ii

ITALY, MILAN
Michaelangela Vismara, Vertex Srl, Corso Magenta 54, 20123 Milano, Italy. Tel 39-02-481-94390, fax 39-02-469-3248, e-mail mvismara@vertex.ws

ITALY, ROME
Pasquale Intonti, Via Giolia, n 200, 00186 Rome, Italy. Tel 39-06-687-8086, Tel/fax 39-06-687-8276, e-mail i.c.studium@flashnet.it.

JAPAN
Shoichi Yamada, GTR Campbell (Japan) Co Ltd/Seizan Shipping Co Ltd, Rm#63 Kyodo Shin-Aoyama Bldg, 5-9-15 Minami-Aoyama Minato-Ku, Tokyo, Japan 107-0062. Tel 813-5464-1868, fax 813-3797-9177.

MONACO
Count Niccolo Caissottidi Chiusano, L´estoril 1/A1, 31 Avenue Princesse Grace, MC98000, Monaco Principality. Tel 377-9330-5150, fax 377-9330-5177.

PANAMA
Facundo I Bacardi, Edif Vista Bella, Jose G Duque #20, La Cresta, Panama, Republic of Panama Apdo Postal 6-1054, El Dorado, Panama. Tel 011-507-223-4911, fax 011-507-269-0193, e-mail conshonbahamaspty@surinvest.net

PARAGUAY
Anipal Raul Casal, Mcal Estigarribia 2130-PB A, Asuncion, Paraguay. Tel 595-21-228-270, fax 595-21-228-271, e-mail plinchi@hotmail.com

SWEDEN
Gustaf Wachtmeister, Valhallavagen 27, SE 181 35 Lidingö, Stockholm, Sweden. Tel 46-8-767-4388, fax 46-8-767-6291, e-mail gustaf.wachtmeister@telia.com.

SWITZERLAND
Katherine Helena Klainguti-Kemp, Bahnofplatz 9, Postfach 6075, CH-8023 Zurich, Switzerland. Tel 011-411-226-4042, fax 011-441-222-4043, e-mail klainguti@bluewin.ch

TURKEY
Kemal Yardimci, Aydintepe Mahallesi, Tersaneler Caddesi 50, Sokak #7, Tuzzla 34947, Istanbul, Turkey. Tel 90-216-493-8000, fax 90-216-493-8080, e-mail omer@yardimci.gen.tr or moliva@turk.net

The Queen's New Years Honours – 2004

COURTESY EXPRESS NEWSPAPERS

The Most Distinguished Order of St Michael and St George (CMG)

Companion

William Wilton Cartwright – outstanding contribution to building the concept of the ideals of nationhood

Pastor Frederick Edward Allen – outstanding spiritual leadership and example as a minister of religion over many years

Bishop Samuel Greene – steadfast dedication to the spiritual upliftment of The Bahamas

The Most Excellent Order of the British Empire (OBE)

Civil Division – Officer

Judy Virginia Cornell Munroe – for being a trailblazer in Bahamian entrepreneurship

George Washington McKinney – pioneering role in business and philanthropic activism

Rupert Winer Roberts – pioneering role in the economic development of The Bahamas

Pauline Davis-Thompson – outstanding role as a symbol of national potential and persistence to the youth of The Bahamas

The Most Excellent Order of the British Empire (OBE)

Civil Division – Member

Maureen Duvalier – contribution as a veteran singer and entertainer

Mable Alean Isaacs Bostwick – contribution as a civic and community leader

Leroy Stephen Hanna – outstanding service as a musician and union leader

Eric Preston Gibson – outstanding contribution as an entertainer and sportsman

Edgar Joseph Outten – outstanding service as a nation builder and contributor to the economic development of Grand Bahama and community outreach programmes

Calvin Neilly – outstanding service as a political and social activist and businessman

Enoch Pedro Roberts II – outstanding contribution to the development of pharmacology in The Bahamas

The British Empire Medal (BEM)

Civil Division

Ethelyn Bernice Michael – for service as a nation builder and contributor to community and social outreach programmes

Evangelist Alma Oleta Trotman – for service as a nation builder and contributor to religious, community and social outreach programmes

Rev George Alexander Emmanuel – for service as a nation builder and contributor to religious, community and social outreach programmes

Leonard John Dames – for service as a nation builder and contributor to community and social outreach programmes

Mabel Viola Colton – for service as a nation builder and contributor to community and social outreach programmes

Capt Frederick Chapin Morgan – for service as a nation builder and contributor to community and social outreach programmes

Rev Lawrence Laing – for service as a nation builder and contributor to religious, community and social outreach programmes

Granville Alphaeus Coleby – for service as a nation builder and contributor to community and social outreach programmes

Eloise Eleanor Colebrook – for service as a nation builder and contributor to community and social outreach programmes

Queen's Police Medal (QPM)

Ellison Edroy Greenslade – for exemplary courage and gallantry for outstanding leadership as a law enforcement officer

Douglas Oden Hames Hanna – for exemplary courage and gallantry for outstanding leadership as a law enforcement officer

TRIBUNE/FELIPÉ MAJOR

The year in review

Bahamas diary of events, August 2003 to July 2004

BY GORDON LOMER

Trends and events that shaped life in The Bahamas over the past year included crime and the missing youngsters of Grand Bahama, seizures of illegal drugs in the battle to stop drug trafficking through the country, the continuing influx and repatriation of illegal Haitian immigrants and Bahamian success in international sports.

August

1 Scotland Yard joins local police, FBI, Florida police agencies and US National Centre for Missing Children in hunt for four Grand Bahama boys who have disappeared.

2 Four die and 25 are injured as mail boat *Sea Hauler,* on its way with 200 passengers to Cat Island reunion, collides with 178-ft freighter *United Star* in Exuma Sound.

4 Bahamas Maritime Authority inspector Capt Glen Bain chairs a committee to probe boat collision that PM Perry Christie terms "a national disaster."

5 Long jumper Jackie Edwards wins Bahamas first medal, a silver, with 21-ft jump at XIV Pan Am Games in Santo Domingo, Dominican Republic.

5 Police seize 1,100 pounds of cocaine worth about $70 million in nine duffel bags hidden among Colombian coffee beans in container at Freeport Container Port.

6 Motorcycle passenger Jiselle Glinton, 16, is shot in the chest and killed by police reservist. Commissioner names team to investigate incident.

7 Transport Minister Glenys Hanna-Martin announces a public inquiry, known as a Wreck Commission, into weekend boat collision that killed four and injured 25.

7 Bahamian Laverne Eve wins silver medal in javelin at XIV Pan Am Games in Santo Domingo. She won Pan Am medals in 1995 in Argentina and 1999 in Canada.

7 Police seize another $10 million worth of cocaine at Freeport Container Port. Both seizures (Aug 5 and 7) were from Colombia bound for Antwerp, Belgium.

Left, Tonique Williams-Darling poses with her gold medal at the 2004 Olympics in Athens, Greece.

11 Former MP, international and Olympic sailor, Basil Kelly, with business interests in Kelly's Freeport Hardware, Millionaire Jet Centre and 100JAMZ radio, dies at 73.

11 Prominent insurance and business executive, Fane Solomon, whose trademark home was the lighthouse on Eastern Rd, dies at 85.

12 Garth Rolle, 28, is sentenced to 20 years in prison for killing his son, Ackiem, 4, in July 2002. Rolle led police to the body three months after the boy disappeared.

15 Most Rev Patrick Pinder, described by Archbishop Lawrence Burke as a "local son of the soil," is ordained as first Bahamian Roman Catholic Bishop.

20 Junkanoo artist Eric "Cardico" Rolle, 53, of Rupert Dean Lane, is gunned down in front of his house in the nation's 30th homicide of the year.

HANS DODTHAGEN/©DUPUCH

The *Sea Hauler*

25 Triple jumper Leevan Sands wins bronze medal, Bahamas first (and only) at 9th IAAF World Outdoor Athletics Championships in Paris, France.

29 An American visitor, Jason Mellon, 21, of New Jersey, dies when his jet ski and a 30-ft powerboat collide off Cable Beach during a severe rainstorm.

29 Dr Jackson Logan Burnside, a dentist for 43 years, and father of artist Stan Burnside and architect/artist Jackson Burnside III, dies at 89.

31 Philanthropist Harry Clare Moore, an active force in the Lyford Cay Club and its scholarship foundations and full-time resident since 1985, dies at 89.

September

3 A US Federal Court awards $1.8 million to Latina Walker, of Charlotte, NC, whose daughter, Tosha, 27, died in a parasailing accident off Paradise Island in Aug 1999.

10 Ground is broken for the $600-million Phase 3 expansion of Atlantis, Paradise Island, which Sol Kerzner says "will rival Disney." Plans include a 1,200-room hotel at Pirate's Cove and a golf course on Athol Island.

12 Rev Joseph Perna, outspoken Pennsylvanian priest, dies at 72. Father Joe served in the Bahamas Catholic diocese since his ordination in 1968.

18 A Peruvian housemaid, Maura Pelacun Salome, 46, and friend, Maria Quispe, 40, die as a gas blast levels the $3-million Lyford Cay home of attorney Colin Callender.

19 Kerzner International buys Club Med property on Paradise Island for $40 million.

28 Bahamas recaptures title from Venezuela in 31st Central American and Caribbean Bodybuilding and Fitness Championships. Bahamian super heavyweight Joel Stubbs wins his division and overall title.

HANS DODTHAGEN/©DUPUCH

Club Med, Paradise Island

28 A fifth Grand Bahama boy, Desmond Rolle, 14, of Williams Town, disappears. In May three boys went missing within 18 days, and another disappeared July 30.

29 Billed as "one of the biggest deals in Bahamian business history," luxury retailer Solomon's Mines Ltd is bought by liquor company Burns House.

October

1 Grand Bahama police question several Bahamians and detain one in the first breakthrough in connection with the disappearance of five young boys since May.
10 Police charge four minors, aged 11 to 15, with manslaughter in the disappearance of Jake Grant, 12, the first of the five Grand Bahama boys to go missing.
21 A teen feud in the Kemp Road area ends in the stabbing death of Jeffrey Clerveau 14, and the arrest of a 17-year-old in Nassau's 37th murder of the year.
24 A 17-year-old is formally charged with the murder of Clerveau, 14, and remanded without bail until Oct 29 for preliminary hearing.
26 Grand Bahama police discover skeletal remains believed to be of the four remaining missing young boys, and confirm they have a 35-year-old suspect in custody.
26 Three girls are severely burned and two teenagers escape after a dormitory fire damages Williemae Pratt Centre for Girls in Fox Hill.
27 Anastacia Alexandria, 15, one of three burn victims from Fox Hill girl's centre fire, dies in Princess Margaret Hospital.
29 Cordell Farrington, 35, of Freeport, is charged with five murders, including four of the missing boys, and one in the death of Jamaal Robins, 22, of Freeport.
30 The body of a man with stab wounds is found on a beach at Yamacraw. The year's 43rd murder is identified as Christopher Woodside, 34.

November

3 Anglican Archbishop Drexel Gomez says priests who participated in consecration of openly gay Bishop Gene Robinson in New Hampshire are not welcome in his diocese.
3 Deshawn Basset Ingraham, 13, becomes the second victim from girl's centre fire to die. Police are still seeking two escapees, ages 14 and 15.
5 Col Oakley Bidwell, former president of the Nassau Chamber of Commerce and head of the Bahamas News Bureau, dies in Canada. He was in his early 90s.
6 A fault in a BEC line between Clifton Pier and Big Pond blacks out New Providence for 10 hours, snarls traffic, closes most schools, shops and businesses.
6 Captain Philip Farrington, legendary flier and pilot of the first scheduled Bahamas Out Island flight, dies in Nassau at age 82.
7 Former Supreme Court Justice, Maxwell James Thompson, OBE, dies at 93.
8 Two teenagers who escaped from Williemae Pratt Centre for Girls Oct 26 are found separately and two men in their 20s are charged with harbouring fugitives.
11 A fleet of 15 state-of-the-art Korean fishing boats arrives in Freeport, enters duty-free, and subsequently moves to North Andros, igniting major controversy.
16 Industrial unrest and "sick-outs" at Bahamasair suspend all flights and close down airline's operations at Nassau International Airport.
17 While Bahamasair remains grounded, 200 disgruntled housekeeping workers at Atlantis stage walkout, blocking entrance to Royal Towers on Paradise Island.
21 Nassau's *The Tribune,* founded Nov 21, 1903, celebrates its 100th birthday with a special 100-page centenary edition.
26 Bahamas Agricultural and Industrial Corp (BAIC) chairman Sidney Stubbs resigns, blaming a "media feeding frenzy" over Korean fishing boats controversy.
28 Twenty-six people are injured in morning traffic when a jitney swerves to miss another car and rolls over in Fox Hill. Six are hospitalized.
29 The decomposed body of a woman, hands and feet bound, is found in an unfinished building in downtown Freeport.

December

1 Grand Bahama's all-inclusive Viva Club Fortuna Beach Resort is rebranded as Viva Wyndham Resorts under a 10-year strategic alliance agreement.
3 The decomposed body of a bound woman, found Nov 29 in Freeport, is identified as Jewell Vonchelle Wallace-Mott, 34, a mother of four, missing since Nov 9.
8 Three men are charged in Freeport following seizure on the Lucayan Waterway Dec 5 of half a ton of cocaine worth $16 million. Bail is set at $100,000 each.
10 Bahamian-based businessmen Craig Symonette, Frank Crothers, Juan Bacardi and partners buy 70 per cent of a premium South African wine estate for $34.6 million.
15 PM Perry Christie opens 183-room Four Seasons Resort at Emerald Bay, Exuma, while Tourism Minister Obie Wilchcombe opens Isle of Capri Casino at Our Lucaya.

23 Hotel union and management talks stall but Christmas strike is averted at major hotels with talks to resume after holiday.
26 Valley Boys win Boxing Day Junkanoo title.
28 President Thabo Mbeki of South Africa begins a five-day state visit to The Bahamas, to include state dinner at Atlantis, visit to RAF cemetery, trip to Grand Bahama, state reception at Government House and New Year's Junkanoo parade.
29 Atlantis, the British Colonial and Radisson hotels are hit by crippling "go-slow" union activities.

TIM AYLEN/VISION PHOTOGRAPHY

From left, Prime Minister Perry Christie, Governor General HE Dame Ivy Dumont and South African President Thabo Mbeki

January, 2004

1 Valley Boys repeat by winning New Year's Junkanoo by six points over Saxon Superstars, inciting violent outbursts among participants and spectators.
5 Politician Jimmy Shepherd, one of the "Dissident Eight" who broke from the PLP to form the Free PLP, later the Free National Movement dies at his Fox Hill home at 85.
6 Saxon Superstars are declared winners after National Junkanoo Committee overturns, for first time in Junkanoo history, New Year's parade award to Valley Boys.
8 Police launch search for 40-year-old kidnapper after Khatrell Dorsett, 14, is found shackled to a tree near Nassau airport. She had been missing for five days.
16 The new $9.2-million state-of-the-art police complex opens in Freeport and is named after the late Police Commissioner Gerald Bartlett.
24 Welder Wendell "Sarge" Maxxam, 33, of Eight Mile Rock, is killed and co-worker, Ramon Neely, 35, is injured in two explosions at the Grand Bahama Shipyard.
30 Veteran entertainer Ronnie Butler receives Cacique's Lifetime Achievement Award and Bimini bonefish guide and boat builder Ansil Saunders wins Minister's Award.

February

8 Mark Merklein with two singles wins and Merklein and Bjorn Monroe in doubles lead Bahamas to 3-2 Americas Zone II Davis Cup victory over host Puerto Rico.
10 New Providence and Paradise Island are blacked out after an apparent sabotage of four high-tension power poles amid strained BEC union and management talks.
11 Valley Boys are New Year's Junkanoo champions after independent committee overturns National Junkanoo Committee's Jan 6 ruling favouring Saxon Superstars.
12 BEC offers $25,000 reward for information leading to apprehension of people responsible for "deliberate acts of sabotage" in Feb 10 blackout.
12 Prime Minister Christie officially opens the Isle of Capri Casino at Our Lucaya in Grand Bahama.
15 Prime Minister Perry Christie is named to the Privy Council, with the lifetime title of Rt Hon. It is the highest honour the queen can bestow after a peerage, and ranks above a knighthood.
17 Most Rev Patrick Pinder becomes the first Bahamian Catholic Archbishop of Nassau, succeeding Archbishop Lawrence Burke, who returns to his native Jamaica after 23 years in The Bahamas.
20 Abaco senator and former MP Edison Key resigns from the senate and the Progressive Liberal Party ending a PLP career spanning more than 30 years.

23 Bahamas embassy staff in Port-au-Prince is recalled and advisory against travel issued in wake of Cape Haitian takeover and increasing rebel violence in Haiti

25 Renowned Bahamian artist, Brent Malone, considered the founding father of modern art in The Bahamas, dies of an apparent heart attack. He was 63.

27 Cordell Farrington, 35, pleads not guilty at preliminary hearing into murders of four Grand Bahama boys and one 22-year-old Freeport resident.

ROLAND ROSE/©DUPUCH

Brent Malone

March

6 Playboy A&P heir Huntington Hartford, 93, who bought Hog Island from Swedish industrialist Axel Wenner-Gren and renamed it Paradise Island, returns to visit.

7 Dominic Demeritte is first Bahamian male sprinter to win gold in the 200m at the 10th IAAF World Championships in Budapest in national record 20.66 secs. Tonique Williams-Darling wins bronze in women's 400m at same event.

13 Nassau's smallest hotel, Pink House on Paradise Island, which dates back to the roaring 1920s and '30s, is sold to Atlantis by owner Minnie Winn, and closed.

JARVIS DARVILLE

Huntington Hartford

14 A billion-dollar proposal by group headed by Lyford Cay businessman Dikran Izmirlian to rebuild Cable Beach fizzles for alleged government "foot dragging."

14 A Spanish hotel chain, RIU Hotels & Resorts, buys the Sheraton Grand on Paradise Island for 30 million Euros ($36.58 million) with plans to refurbish by Dec 2004.

31 St Francis Xavier Cathedral's new $6-million, 1,400-seat church is officially dedicated by outgoing Archbishop Lawrence Burke.

April

9 Track and field star Aymara Albury wins discus gold medal for under-20 girls at 2004 Carifta track and field championships in Bermuda.

10 Albury wins second gold medal with 48-ft, 9-in shot put in Bermuda. Michelle Cumberbatch wins Bahamas' only other gold in under-17 girls 300-metre hurdles.

10 The bound, gagged and weighted body of Jermaine Thompson, 30, of Murphy Town, Abaco, is retrieved from a blue hole near Marsh Harbour.

11 Former UBP chairman and senator, labour law expert and Chamber of Commerce president, Reginald Lobosky, dies after extended illness. He was 71.

17 Francoise Newry, wife of Bahamian Ambassador to Haiti, Dr Eugene Newry, is shot and slightly wounded while shopping in Port-au-Prince, Haiti.

20 Cordell Farrington, 36, is charged in supreme court with the previous summer's murders of four Freeport boys and one man. Each case is to be tried separately.

21 Basil Johnson, WWII RAF flying hero, who flew 50 missions over Germany and won the Distinguished Flying Medal (DFM) on April 21,1944, dies at 84. He was the father of *Punch* publisher Ivan Johnson.

May

2 Mark Knowles and Daniel Nestor win season's second doubles title at the Open SEAT Godo in Barcelona.

2 Bahamas' other touring pro Mark Merklein and American James Blake upset second seeded Julian Knowle and Nenad Zimonjic to win BMW Open in Munich.

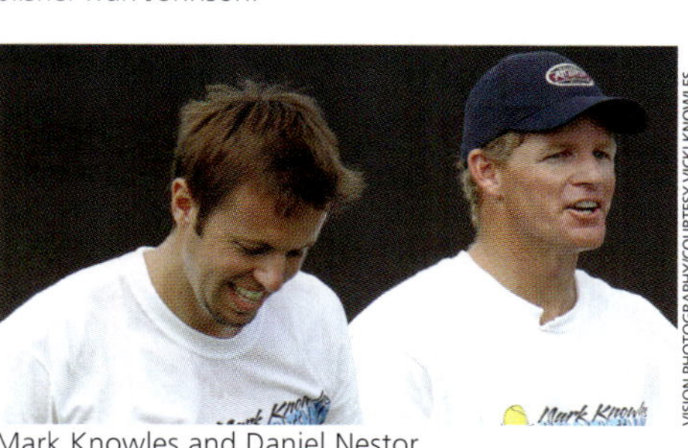

VISION PHOTOGRAPHY/COURTESY VICKI KNOWLES

Mark Knowles and Daniel Nestor

3 Kerzner unveils billion-dollar Atlantis expansion including a 1,500-room hotel, world-class water theme park, Marina Village with 22 shops and four restaurants and a huge convention centre with Caribbean's largest ballroom.

4 Archbishop Patrick Pinder is installed as the first Bahamian head of the Roman Catholic Church in The Bahamas, succeeding Archbishop Lawrence Burke.

10 President Bush names realtor John D Rood new US Ambassador to The Bahamas succeeding controversial Richard Blankenship.

26 Five Bahamians and a Puerto Rican are arrested in two boats 10 miles off Dania, FL, and charged with conspiracy to smuggle $100 million in cocaine into US.

27 Three Americans, including the pilot, die and two are injured as a five-seater Cessna 172 crashes near Marsh Harbour airport en route to Man O' War Cay.

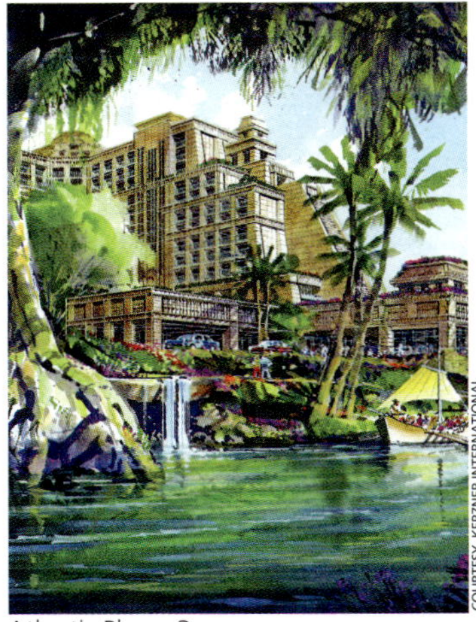
COURTESY KERZNER INTERNATIONAL

Atlantis Phase 3

June

8 Gasoline prices, climbing in recent weeks, shoot up 26 cents a gallon at Nassau gas stations, now averaging about $3.50 a gallon and 20 cents more in the Out Islands.

9 A scaled-down compromise agreement for the Bimini Bay development is signed by PM Perry Christie and developer Gerardo Capo.

11 Quarter miler Tonique Williams-Darling runs world's fastest 400 meters in 2004 with 49.79 sec win at IAAF Bislett Games in Oslo, Norway.

15 Court of Appeal orders new trial for Neil Brown, 27, convicted in December, 2002, of May, 2000, shotgun murder of Anglican Archdeacon William Thompson.

15 A US Appeals Court in Miami upholds a $1.8-million wrongful damages award against the Sheraton Grand hotel for the 1999 parasailing death of a woman in The Bahamas.

16 The Securities Commission of The Bahamas approves the offering by Kerzner Intl Ltd for the issue of one million of the company's shares to the Bahamian public, the largest IPO offering ever held in The Bahamas.

19 Highly-regarded veteran journalist Chris Symmonett, director of Bahamas Information Services and former *Nassau Guardian* editor, dies of cancer at 62.

23 Supreme Court rules Samuel "Ninety" Knowles cannot be held for extradition to US, after President Bush referred to him as a "foreign narcotics kingpin."

23 US Attorney-General John Ashcroft says major Colombia/Jamaica/Bahamas/US cocaine trafficking network is smashed with arrest of 15 Bahamians in New Providence, Eleuthera and Bimini and 21 Colombians including drug czar Elias Cobos-Munoz.

23 Kenneth Kimes admits in California court murdering banker Sayed Ahmed in Sept, 1996, and disposing anchor-weighted body in the ocean off Nassau.

23 Family and police in New Providence search for nine-year-old Devon Arthur Knowles Jr, known as DJ, who disappeared on his way to a basketball court.

27 The partly clothed body of DJ Knowles is found in a bushy area behind St George's Park, near his home in New Providence.

29 Appeals Court justices dismiss the appeal of Suisse Security Bank and Trust, setting the stage for a possible hearing by the Privy Council on the first case challenging the right of the Central Bank governor to revoke a bank's licence.

29 Charles Shepherd, 27, is killed in a drive-by shooting in Pinewood Gardens. Shepherd lived two doors away from DJ Knowles. Police say the two murders are not related.

July

2 Tonique Williams-Darling sets a new national record in the women's 400 metres at the MGK Vis Golden Gala in Rome, Italy.

3 Bahamian tennis player Mark Knowles and his Canadian doubles partner Daniel Nestor are shut down in the semi-finals at Wimbledon.

5 Capt Anthony Allens, Port Controller, announces that 21 of the 22 Bahamian ports have met the July 1 deadline for compliance with the new International Ship and Port Facility Security Code.

8 A supreme court jury finds Sergio Penn, 19, guilty of manslaughter in the Aug 2002 killing of Canadian tourist Marcia Rose McKenzie in Abaco. Penn is sentenced to 16 years in prison.

11 Members of the Save The Bahamas Campaign stage a 500-person demonstration in Rawson Square to protest the arrival scheduled for July 16 of a gay cruise backed by American actress/comedian Rosie O'Donnell.

14 Upgrading of Nassau International Airport begins. A $35-million contract was signed in May for the upgrade, which Prime Minister Christie describes as "the most significant project in the history of the independent Bahamas."

16 More than 200 angry Bahamians demonstrate with placards in Rawson Square protesting the arrival of the *Norwegian Dawn,* carrying gay passengers and their families. Members of the Bahamian gay rights group Rainbow Alliance are on hand to welcome the visitors.

16 PRK Holdings, owner of South Ocean Golf and Beach Resort in New Providence, announces the immediate closure of the resort to begin a 15-month renovation.

23 Tonique Williams-Darling sets a new national record in the women's 400 metres at the Golden League track and field meet in France. She held the previous record.

27 Ministry of Health suspends stem cell research and treatment at the IAT Clinic in Grand Bahama "in the interest of the public's health and safety" after it is revealed that the clinic did not obtain permits for the research.

30 Michael Henderson, chairman of RJH Holdings, announces the selection of The Bahamas as the proposed location for the $4.5-billion Moon Bahamas project, the world's largest resort. The massive development would be located off Grand Bahama's north coast and is expected to be completed by 2010.

Significant happenings in The Bahamas up to press time

Tonique Williams-Darling won a gold medal in the women's 400-metre final at the 2004 Olympic Games in Athens, Greece. Williams-Darling became the first Bahamian to win gold in an individual track event. Debbie Ferguson won a bronze in the women's 200-metre final.

Hurricanes Frances and Jeanne lashed The Bahamas in Sept 2004, causing considerable damage. San Salvador, Cat Island, Abaco, Eleuthera and Grand Bahama saw the worst of the storms which caused massive flooding, toppled trees and ripped roofs off buildings.

Tennis duo Bahamian Mark Knowles and Canadian Daniel Nestor won the Grand Slam title in doubles at the US Open in New York, NY.

Advertisers in this book

See also classified directories, pgs 310-319; pgs 572-575

NEW PROVIDENCE & PARADISE ISLAND

Accuvest Fund Services Ltd 271
Accuvest Ltd 271
Ansbacher (Bah) Ltd 201
The Architectural Studio 227
Arner Bank & Trust (Bah) Ltd 237
ATC Trustees (Bah) Ltd 265
Atlantic Asset Mgmt Ltd (AAM) 253
Avis 381
Bahamas Electricity Corp (BEC) 251
Bahamas Financial Services Board (BFSB) 197
Bahamas First General Insurance Co Ltd............................217
Bahamas Food Services 169
Bahamas Handbook 121
Bahamas Incorporation Services Ltd 253
Bahamas Marine Construction 293
Bahamas Ministry of Financial Services & Investments 215
Bahamas Ministry of Tourism 32
Bahamas Multi-Media Ltd 113, 513
Bahamas Post Office Philatelic Bureau 99
Bahamas Realty 285
Bahamas Telecommunications Co (BTC)/BaTelCo 109
Bahamas Trailblazer Maps 173, 211, 608
Bahamasair 533
bahamasnet.com 113, 513
Banca del Gottardo 256
Bank deGroof Group 245
Bank of The Bahamas Intl 254
The Bank of Nova Scotia Trust Co (Bah) Ltd 237
Banque Privée Edmond de Rothschild Ltd 207
Banque SCS Alliance (Nas) Ltd 249
BDO Mann Judd 229
Bearbull Intl Ltd 245
Berkeley (Bah) Ltd 241
Brita Water Filter Systems 127
Britannia Consulting Group 225
British Colonial Hilton 95
BSI Overseas (Bah) Ltd 205
Budget 93
Butterfield Bank 263
Cable Bahamas 91
Cardinal Intl 209
caribbean.com 38, 319
Caribbean Crossings 219
The Central Bank of The Bahamas......105
Centre for Entrepreneurship 97
Cole Insurance 249
The College of The Bahamas 97, 115
Commonwealth Building Supplies Ltd 131
CoralWave 91
Credit Suisse (Bah) Ltd 203
Crystal Palace Casino 101
Custom Computers Ltd 239
Damianos Realty 301
Dartley Bank & Trust Ltd 279
Davis & Co 221
Department of Environmental Health Services 125
Derivatives Portfolio Mgmt (Bah) Ltd (DPM) 267
DHL 137
DMG Intl Marine Services Agency 155
Dining & Entertainment Guide ..211, 608
Dupuch Publications 173, 211, 318, 529, 575, 607, 608
Ernst & Young 269
Etienne Dupuch Jr Publications Ltd ..38, 173, 211, 318, 319, 529, 575, 607, 608
Executive Printers of The Bahamas, Ltd 123
Experta Trust Co (Bah) Ltd..................275
Ferrier Lullin Bank & Trust (Bah) Ltd 199
Fitzgerald & Fitzgerald 241
Fox Hill Nursery 149
FTP Corporate Services Ltd 241

Galanis & Co 231
Geriatric Hospital................................133
Harlsbury Chambers 275
H G Christie Ltd 303
Holowesko & Co 137
IBM 233
Integrated Business Solutions Ltd 231
Island Industries (Bah) Ltd 169
JBR Building Supplies Ltd 149
Jerome E Pyfrom & Co 253
John Bull 23-25
J P Morgan Trust Co (Bah) Ltd 279
Kendolyn V Cartwright-Robinson 318
KPMG 223
Lampkin & Co 165
The Landfall Centre 281
Lombard Odier Darier Hentsch
Private Bank & Trust Ltd 193
Lowes Realty 303
Lyford Cay Sales and Rentals 301
Machinery & Energy Ltd 157
Magnetic Resonance Therapy
(Bah) Ltd 119
Maxil Communications 219
McKinney, Bancroft & Hughes 229
Micronet Business Technology 273
Miriam J Curling & Co 173
Montaque Securities Intl 267
Mosko's Furniture 293
Mosko's Group of Building Cos 293
Mosko's United Construction 293
Munroe's Landscaping 227
Nassau Beach Hotel 101
The Nassau Guardian 117
The National Insurance Board 135
New Oriental Cleaners 315
NMC Leasing 271
NP Building Supplies 293
NUCA Insurance Agency 147
Pictet Bank & Trust Ltd 195
PricewaterhouseCoopers 277
Princess Margaret Hospital 133
The Private Trust Corp Ltd 273
Public Hospitals Authority 133
RBC Dominion Securities
(Global) Ltd .... Back cover
RBC Finco ....Back cover
RBC Royal Bank of Canada ....17, Back cover
RBC Royal Bank of Canada
Global Private Banking 17
RBC Royal Bank of Canada
Trust Co (Bah) Ltd ....17, Back cover
Sandilands Rehabilitation Centre 133
Satellite Bahamas 173
Scotia Private Banking Services 237
Scotiabank (Bah) Ltd 237
Scotiatrust 237
Securities Commission
of The Bahamas 243
Sentinel Bank & Trust 265
Sigma Management Bahamas 269
Sovereign Bahamas Ltd 223
Strategic Marketing Corporate
Services...271
The Nassau Guardian 117
Tops Lumber & Plumbing 149
Tropical Brokerage Services Ltd 165
UBS (Bah) Ltd 191
United European Bank & Trust
(Nas) Ltd (UEB) 231
Veritas Consultants Ltd 95
WAM Co Ltd 155
Water and Sewerage Corp 153
Welcome Bahamas 211, 529, 608
What-to-do 211, 608
Wongs' Rubber Stamp
& Printing Co Ltd 119
Wyndham Nassau Resort
& Crystal Palace Casino 101

GRAND BAHAMA

Avis 381
Bahamas Multi-Media Ltd 113, 513
Bahamas Oil Refining Co
Intl Ltd (BORCO) 520
Bahamas Telecommunications
Co (BTC)/BaTelCo 559
Bahamas Trailblazer Maps 173, 608
Bahamasair 533
Bahamasnet 113, 513
bahamasnet.com 113, 513
Brita Water Filter Systems 127
Cable Bahamas 91
The College of The Bahamas 115
Commonwealth Bldg Supplies Ltd 131
CoralWave 91
Damianos Realty 301
Davis & Co 22
DHL 137
DMG Intl Marine Services Agency 153
Dupuch Publications ..155, 529, 607, 608
Eastern Freight Forwarders 527
Etienne Dupuch Jr
Publications Ltd 529, 607, 608
Freeport Oil Co Ltd (FOCOL) 525
Freeport Transfer Ltd 527

Galanis & Co 231
Grand Bahama Humane Society 553
Grand Bahama Millwork 539
The Grand Bahama
Port Authority 544-545
Grand Bahama Power Co 541
H G Christie Ltd 303
IBM 233
Integrated Business Solutions Ltd 231
Island Bedding & Furniture 537
KPMG 223
Lucayan Marina Village 42
Lustre Kraft Signs 539
Machinery & Energy Ltd 157
McKinney, Bancroft & Hughes 229
Moss & Associates 537
The National Insurance Board 135
Old Bahama Bay 522
Petra Securities Ltd 547
Polymers Intl Ltd 570
PricewaterhouseCoopers 277
Rand Memorial Hospital 133
Shoreline Properties 523
W Carver Grant & Co Ltd 547
Welcome Bahamas 529, 608
What-to-do Freeport 575, 608
WAM Co Ltd 155

ABACO
Bahamas Realty 285
Bahamasair 533
The College of The Bahamas 123
Damianos Realty 301
DHL 137
H G Christie Ltd 303
John Bull 23-25
The National Insurance Board 135
Treasure Cay Hotel Resort & Marina ..155

ACKLINS
Bahamasair 533
The National Insurance Board 135

ANDROS
Bahamasair 533
DHL 137
H G Christie Ltd 303
The National Insurance Board 135

BIMINI
The National Insurance Board 135

CAT ISLAND
Bahamasair 533
H G Christie Ltd 303
The National Insurance Board 135

CROOKED ISLAND
Bahamasair 533
H G Christie Ltd 303
The National Insurance Board 135

ELEUTHERA
Bahamas Realty 285
Bahamasair 533
Damianos Realty 301
DHL 137
H G Christie Ltd 303
John Bull 23-25
The National Insurance Board 135

EXUMA
Bahamas Realty 285
Bahamasair 533
The College of The Bahamas 115
DHL 137
H G Christie Ltd 303
Halsbury Chambers 275
John Bull 23-25
The National Insurance Board 135

INAGUA
Bahamasair 533
The National Insurance Board 135

LONG ISLAND
Bahamas Realty 285
Bahamasair 533
DHL 137
H G Christie Ltd 303
The National Insurance Board 135

MAYAGUANA
Bahamasair 533
The National Insurance Board 135

SAN SALVADOR
Bahamasair 533
The National Insurance Board 135

Index

A

A Baker and Sons, 90
Abaco Club resort, 292
Abaco Independence Movement (AIM), 180-183
Abaco Island Roots Festival, 224
Abaco Lumber Company, 517, 521, 563
Abaco separatist movement, 176, 178
Abrigo, Christine, 636, 644
Academy Awards, 55-57
Adams, Alma, 644
Adderley, Cleophas, 180-181, 502
Adderley, K Neville, 635
Adderley, Malcolm E Jr, 623
Adderley, Nathaniel, 635
AES Ocean Express LLC, 567
After the Sunset, 220, 569
Agape House, 548
Agriculture, 156, 324-325, 331, 338, 347, 391, 405, 435, 454, 466, 476-477, 579, 593
Ahmed, Sayed, 656
AIDS, 326-327, 358-359, 467, 470, 479
AIDS Foundation, 326
AIDS Secretariat, 326, 358
Aircraft Owners and Pilots Association, 216
Airports, 218, 288, 291-292, 328-329, 439
Alba, Jessica, 222
Albury, Aymara, 655
Albury, Basil, 635
Albury, Charles Eugene, 134
Albury, Cheryl, 636
Albury, Jack, 185
Alday, Sarah Elizabeth Sears, 129
Allen, Anita, 636
Allen, Pastor Frederick Edward, 649
Allens, Capt Anthony J, 637
American Civil War, 122, 412
American Legion, 107
American Negro Theater, 55, 77
Amorales-Jones, Helen, 636
Andrews, Peter Newton, 647
Annual Airventure convention, 216
Antiquities, Monuments and Museums Corp (AMMC), 98, 100, 331-332, 405
Apartheid, 198
Arawak Cay, 85, 222, 332, 463
Archer, HE A Leonard, 641-643
Archer, Guillamina, 636
Architectural firms, 332, 580
Ardastra Gardens, Zoo and Conservation Centre, 94, 226, 456
Arison, Ted, 112
Armbrister, Anthony, 145
Armbrister, Cyril Edward, 145, 156
Armbrister, John Jr, 144
Armbrister, Tony, 141
Armbrister, Hon William E, 144
Arnold, Robert, 647
Aronow, Don, 532
Arthur's Town, 50, 52-53, 59, 295, 327
Ashcroft, John, 656
Asset Protection Trust, 493
Association of International Banks and Trust Companies (AIBT), 262, 266, 440
Atlantic Undersea Test & Evaluation Centre (AUTEC), 334, 407
Atlantik Beach Hotel, 528
Atlantis, 71, 189-190, 192, 194, 198, 200, 204, 206, 208, 210, 283-284, 286-287, 305, 383, 394, 407, 413-414, 419, 450, 457-458, 484, 652-656
Atlas Development Company, 183

B

Bacardi, Facundo, 648
Bacardi, Juan, 653
Bahama Rock, 598
Bahama Star, 111-112
Bahamahost, 335
Bahamas 500, 519, 531-532
Bahamas Agricultural & Industrial Corp (BAIC), 335-336, 653
Bahamas Air Sea Rescue Assoc (BASRA), 336, 358, 392, 581, 583, 590
Bahamas Airways, 526
Bahamas Billfish Championship, 232
Bahamas Business Outlook, 116
Bahamas Defence Force, **see Royal Bahamas Defence Force**
Bahamas Development Bank (BDB), 336-337, 441, 454, 476, 581, 592
Bahamas Development Board, 88
Bahamas Diplomatic & Consular Representatives, 458
Bahamas Environment, Science and Technology Commission (BEST), 296, 395-396
Bahamas Family Planning Assoc, 337, 411
Bahamas Film Studios, 569
Bahamas Financial Services Board (BFSB), 238, 264, 266, 337, 441
Bahamas Heritage Festival, 222
Bahamas Historical Society, 337, 359
Bahamas Humane Society, 338, 359, 506
Bahamas International Film Festival, 220, 222
Bahamas International Securities Exchange (BISX), 338, 413
Bahamas Investment Authority (BIA), 338-339, 431, 438, 440, 592
Bahamas Ironmongery, 92
Bahamas Maritime Authority (BMA), 258-259, 435, 475, 651

Bahamas National Herbarium, 456
Bahamas National Trust (BNT), 126, 132, 224, 226, 339, 346-347, 359, 396, 400, 405, 466, 510-511, 580, 583, 601
Bahamas National Youth Choir, 502
Bahamas Oil Refining Co, 598
Bahamas Red Cross, 339-340, 359, 391, 479
Bahamas Ship Owners Association, 259
Bahamas Sport Fishing and Conservation Association, 232
Bahamas Telecommunications Co (BTC), 410, 501, 594, 605
Bahamas Waste Management, 288
BAIC, **see Bahamas Agricultural and Industrial Corp**
Bain, Betty, 549
Bain, Rhonda, 636
Baker, Dorothy, 646
Balamena II, 167, 172
Balance of payments, 340-341, 485
Balmoral Hotel, 68
Balniel, Lord, 180
Banks and Trust Companies Regulation Act, 340, 342, 351-352, 361, 438
Bannister, Sen The Hon Desmond, 621
Barratt, Peter, 563
Barry, Bishop Colman J, 154
Bartlett, Gerald, 297, 654
Basden, Kevin, 635
BASRA, **see Bahamas Air See Rescue Assoc**
Bastian, Rubon Whitney, 629
Bastian, Terrance, 635
BayParl Building, 126, 136
Beacon School, 548, 589
Beckford, Tyson, 222
Belafonte, Harry, 54-55, 77
Bell, Ronald, 180
Ben Warry's Pub, 127
Beneby, Nathaniel, 637
Benjamin, Samuel Henry, 70
Bennett, Sir Frederick, 180
Benton, Kenneth, 162
Berlin, Irving, 73-74
Bermuda Triangle, 161, 446
Bernadino, Count, 96
Bethel, E Edison, 644
Bethel, Errol, 637
Bethel, Sen the Hon Dr Marcus C, 617-618
Bethel, Nalini, 214
Bethel, Dr Paulette, 644
Bethel, Peter, 634
Bethel-Burrows, Dr Nicolette, 637
Bethell, Carolita, 636
Bevans, Roland, 637
BFSB, **see Bahamas Financial Services Board**
Bhatnager, Deepak, 635
Bidwell, Col Oakley, 653
Big Bamboo, 98
Big Red Boat, 111
Bimini Bay, 294, 656
Bimini Big Game Fishing Club, 294, 422
Bimini Native Fishing Tournament, 224
Birds, 346-347, 403, 456, 511, 581, 601
Bishop, James, 159
Bjork, 81
Blackbeard, 96, 98, 141
Blacklist(ing), 413, 496
Blackwell, Chris, 78-79
Blake, Blind, 76, 96
Blake, James, 655
Blankenship, Richard, 656
Blue Moon, 167-168
Boat registration, 348, 475
Boeuf, Thierry, 646
Bonamy, B K, 635
Bonefish, 399-400, 402, 456, 654
Bonefishing, 156, 226, 591
Bonsor, Nadine, 542
Boomerang, 166
Bootleggers, 87
Bostwick, Mable Alean Isaacs, 649
Botanical Gardens, 456
Bott, Jack, 68, 70
Bott, Rubin, 68-70
Bowe, R J, 63
Braynen, Michael, 635
Brick Store, 92
Bridgewater, Pleasant M M, 542, 631
British High Commission, 590
British Loyalists, 143
Broadcasting, 349, 501-502, 603, 605
Brolin, Josh, 222
Brook, Kelly, 222
Brooks, Monique, 646
Brosnan, Pierce, 220, 569
Brown, Carl, 111
Brown, Harcourt, 636
Brown, Herbert, 637
Brown, James, 96
Brown, Sir Joseph, 92
Brown, Neil, 656
BTC, **see Bahamas Telecommunications Co**
Buffett, Jimmy, 73, 81
Building permits, 350
Bullard, Gaynell, 636
Burke, Archbishop Lawrence, 652, 654-656
Burma Road riots, 86
Burns House Ltd, 94, 652
Burnside, Dr Jackson Logan, 652
Burnside, Jackson III, 88, 652
Burnside, Stan, 652
Burrows, Barbara, 634
Burrows, Vernon E L, 636
Bush, Buddy, 524
Business licence fee, 351-353, 363, 590, 595
Business licensing, 582
Business name registration, 352, 363
Butch Harmon School of Golf, 554, 604
Butler, M Teresa, 634
Butler, Sir Milo, 89, 288, 611
Butler, Ronnie, 96, 98, 654
Butler, Wrensworth, 637

C

Cable television, 352, 605
Cacique Awards, 334

Café Martinique, 284
Calstar Properties, 284
Calypso Island, 76
Camacho-Major, Manuela, 647
Campbell, George T R, 258
Campbell, Julie, 642-643
Campbell, William, 636
Cannes Film Festival, 222
Capo, Geraldo, 294
Captive insurance, 343, 353, 436-438, 441, 495, 500
Carey, John, 633
Carey, Sandra, 644
Carey, Sheila, 634
Caribbean Basin Initiative (CBI), 353-354, 372, 440, 456-457, 567, 590
Caribbean Community & Common Market (CARICOM), 354
CARIBCAN, 355, 440, 504, 567, 590
Carmichael, Hoagy, 76
Carnival Cruise Lines, 112, 118
Carnival Miracle, 103
Carrera-Justiz, Francisco, 647
Cartwright, Eugenia, 637
Cartwright, Archdeacon Keith, 538
Cartwright, Lawrence, 632
Cartwright, William Wilton, 649
Cash, Sir Gerald, 611
Castaway Cay, 114, 226, 329, 383
Cat and Fiddle, 96
Cat Island, 49-54, 59, 67, 77, 141-157, 222, 295, 329, 414, 416, 423, 426, 651, 657
Cat Island Rake and Scrape Festival, 222
Catherine Basie School for Exceptional Children, 546
Catt, Arthur, 141
Cayce, Edgar, 204
CBI, **see Caribbean Basin Initiative**
Cenotaph, 121
Censorship, 355
Central Andros Crabfest, 224
Central Bank, **see The Central Bank of The Bahamas**
Chan, Harris, 569
Charles Towne, 86, 411
Charles-Sylvester, Susan, 636
Cheadle, Don, 220
Cheong, Edmond, 524
Cheong, Gerry, 524
Chevron, 118, 259
Chickcharnie, 151, 403
Chihuly, Dale, 204, 206, 208
Chiusano, Count Niccolo Caissottidi, 648
Christ the King Anglican Church, 543, 603
Christie, The Rt Hon Prime Minister Perry, 85, 202, 228, 289, 291, 294-295, 414, 612, 624, 654
Christie, Peter, 167, 172
Churaman, Maurice, 636
Church of the Lord Jesus Christ of the Apostolic Faith, 228
Churches, 143, 151, 393-394, 472, 477, 536, 596
Churton, Bishop Henry, 150
Cinemas, 356, 393, 583
Citizenship, 357-358, 363-364, 426, 428, 431, 459, 487
Clapton, Eric, 79
Clark, Dave, 568
Clarke, Godfrey, 637
Cleare, Gregory P, 238
Cleveland, Grover, 124
Cleveland, Lewis, 124
Clifton Pier, 110, 391, 445, 463, 653
Clifton Plantation, 289
Clipper Shipping Company, 259
Club Med, 210, 295, 424, 652
Cobos-Munoz, Elias, 656
Cohen, David, 196
Cole, Nat King, 96
Colebrook, Eloise Eleanor, 649
Coleby, Granville Alphaeus, 649
Colin "Mad Mitch" Mitchell, 183-184
College of The Bahamas, 385, 389, 391, 414, 416, 443, 446-447, 469, 589, 593, 605
Colton, Mabel Viola, 649
Columbus House, 479, 540
Columbus, Christopher, 61-62, 103, 142, 411, 511
Commercial fishing, 383, 400-401, 591
Company formation, 276, 343, 360
Compass Point Studios, 76, 78-81
Compleat Angler Hotel, 74
Conception Island, 511
Conch, 332, 401-403, 464, 511-512, 591
Conchman Triathlon, 230
Conner, Dennis, 166-167, 171
Connery, Micheline Roquebrune, 76
Connery, Sean, 73, 75, 569
Conover, Harvey, 160
Conover-Mast Publishing Company, 161
Consolidated Construction Company, 517
Constantakis, Gus, 646
Constitution, 182, 357, 363-364, 412-413, 507
Consumer protection, 364
Cooke, Sam, 96
Copyright laws, 365
Cost of living, 365, 584
Cotonou Agreement, 366, 440, 567, 590, **see also Lomé IV**
Coumantaros, George, 166
Council for a Free Abaco, 181, 183
Courageous, 162, 170
Courier services, 367, 584
Cox, Sheila, 224, 226
Crash Test Dummies, 80
Craton, Michael, 64, 66, 68, 148, 175
Crawfish, 369, 401-403, 406, 435, 511-512, 591
Crime, 367, 398, 477, **see also Drugs**
Criminal Investigation Department (CID), 594, 602
Crise, Capt Sherman "Red," 531-532
Crothers, Frank, 653
Cruise ships, 103, 108, 110, 116, 368, 407, 474-475, 566, 599, 604

Crystal Gate, 206, 208
Culmer, Edwin, 637
Cumberbatch, Michelle, 655
Cumberbatch, Tabitha, 636
Cunard, 259
Cunningham, Ehurd, 636

D

Dahl-Regis, Dr M, 637
Dames, Leonard John, 649
Dangerous Drugs Act, 342, 382
DANSA Awards, 334-335
Darling, Sir Clifford, 611
Davidson, Bill, 151
Davis, Austin, 636
Davis, Philip E "Brave," 629
Davis, Sammy Jr, 53
Davis-Thompson, Pauline, 649
Day, Adrian, 182
Days of our Youth, 55, 77
Dee, Ruby, 54
Defence Force, **see Royal Bahamas Defence Force**
Delamore, Richie, 96
Demeritte, Dominic, 655
Demeritte-Francis, Indira, 636
Dennis Conner Sports, Inc, 171
Dentists, 374, 415, 586, 596-597
Department of Archives, 64, 104
Departure tax, 374-375, 586-587
Deveaux, Andrew, 87, 412
Diamonds Are Forever, 76
Diocesan Building, 88-89
Dion, Celine, 73, 79-80
DiPace, Juan Pable, 222
Dire Straits, 79
Dirty Dick's, 98
Discovery Day, 414
Discovery Nursery School, 546
Discovery Primary School, 546, 548, 587
Disney Cruise Line, 118, 226, 383
Disney Magic, 114, 226
Disney Wonder, 114, 116, 118, 226, 368
Divorce, 375, 450
Dixon, Aaron, 128
Dockendale House, 259
Dockendale Shipping Co Ltd, 258-259
Doctors, 375, 587, 597
Doctors Hospital, 65, 328, 366, 392, 415, 460
Doctors Hospital Health System, 65, 328, 415
Dodge, Steve, 179-180, 184
Dolphins, 403, 446
Don't Stop The Carnival, 81
Dorrance, John Thompson III, 647
Dorsett, Georgette, 635
Driver's licence & vehicle information, 378, 587
Drugs, 342, 348, 359, 368, 382, 651
Dry dock, 565, 598
Duke of Windsor, 67, 87, 126, 408, 412
Dumont, HE Dame Ivy, DCMG, 611
Duncome, Robert, 128
Dupuch, Pierre Valiant Launcelot, 627
Duvalier, Maureen, 649

E

Earthwatch, 446
East of Eden, 74
Ebong, Helen, 634
E-commerce, 337
Economy, 286, 356, 367, 382-384, 398, 406, 434-435, 440, 446, 551, 558, 560, 568
EDAW Inc, 100
Education, 384-391, 446, 587-589
Edwards, Jackie, 651
El Paso Corporation, 567
Elangeni, 194
Electricity, 391-393, 501, 589-590
Eleuthera Pineapple Festival, 224
Ellis, Edward, 636
Ellis, Franklyn, 96, **see also Count Bernadino**
Ellis, Bishop Neil, 230
Emancipation Day, 414
Emerald Bay, 291, 295-296, 383, 424, 653
Emmanuel, Rev George Alexander, 649
Encouragement acts, 590, 595
Eneas, HE Godfrey, 644
Environment, 224, 226, 296, 395-396, 447, 471
Eugene Dupuch Law School, 389-390
Eve, Joseph, 122
Eve, Laverne, 651
Eves development, 286
Exchange Control, 210, 340, 396-398, 591, 598
Exempted Limited Partnership, 363
Export entry, 370, 398, 406, 591
Extradition, 368, 398, 656
Exuma Cays Land & Sea Park, 339, 347, 400, 403, 511
Exxon, 118, 259

F

Farquharson, Betty, 637
Farquharson, Paul, 637
Farquharson, Sharon, 637
Farrah, Damite, 53
Farrell, Robert G, 646
Farrington, Cordell, 653, 655
Farrington, Sidney, 126
Father Jerome, 141, 146, 151-152, 154, **see also Hawes, John**
Fatt, Capt Bob, 521
Feeney, Gordon, 648
Ferguson, Benjamin, 637
Ferguson, Collimae, 637
Ferguson, Debbye, 636
Ferguson-Beneby, Thelma, 634
Fernandes, Leslie J, 258
Fernandez Bay, 141-142, 146, 416, 423
Fienburg Department Store, 70
Film Commission, 220, 222, 569-570
Financial Action Task Force, 413
Financial Intelligence Unit, 343
Financial Transactions Reporting Act, 343
Finnish Finnpulp, 111

Finnistere, 161, 171
Fintel, Francis, 145
Fire brigade, 86, 399, 590-591
Fire services, 398-399
Firstbrook, Steve, 640
Fishing laws, 400
Fitzroy, Lady Virginia, 549
Five Days Ablaze, 228
Flagler, Henry Morrison, 104, 124
Flora & fauna, 403, 405
Fly fishing, 232-233
Fly-ins, 216, 218
FNM, **see Free National Movement**
Fontenot, Ronnie, 640
Forsyth, Elgin, 151
Fort Charlotte, 332, 405, 412, 480
Fort Fincastle, 405, 412
Fort Montagu, 405, 412
Fort Montagu Beach Hotel, 104, 106
Fort Nassau, 405, 411-412
Foster, Anthony, 635
Foundations Act, 261, 266, 278
Fox, Barbara, 647
Foyil Asset Management, 240
Foyil, Dorian, 236
Fragrance of The Bahamas, 598
Frampton, Peter, 81
Francis, Judith, 643
Francis, Julian, 635
Frank, Moses, 62-64, 70
Franklin Group, 238
Franklin Templeton Group, 238
Franklin, Aretha, 96
Free National Movement (FNM), 67, 179-181, 262, 270, 413-414, 654
Free Trade Area of the Americas (FTAA), 356, 406, 456
Freedom Proposals, 183
Freeport Construction, 519, 528, 531, 582
Freeport Container Port, 100, 413, 564-565, 596, 598-599, 651
Freeport Harbour, 530, 564-565, 592, 594, 599
Freeport Jewish Congregation, 69-70
Friedman, Dion, 244
Friemark and Hoffer, 68
Friends of Abaco, 184
From Russia with Love, 75
FTAA, **see Free Trade Area of the Americas**
Fun Ships, 112

G

Galanis, Sen The Hon Philip C, 619
Gambling, 194, 394, 406, 592
Ganpatsingh, Loris Milton, 636
Garcia, Francisco, 161
Garcia, Neville, 519, 532
Garden of Remembrance, 121
Garden of the Groves, 226, 601
Garfunkel, Joe, 63-64, 70
Garraway, Elma, 634
Garzaroli, Paolo, 647
Gates, Erika, 226
GDP, **see Gross Domestic Product**
Gee, Anthony, 71
Genesis Academy, 543
Geography, 407, 592
George, Edward St, 535, 549
Gibbs, Cynthia, 636
Gibson, The Hon Allyson Maynard, 198, 255, 261, 264, 266, 268, 270, 274, 276, 616, 627
Gibson, Eric Preston, 649
Gibson, Kenyatta Mboya, 626
Gibson, Maxwell E, 627, 647
Gibson, The Hon Shane, 296, 617, 625
Gibson, Tyrone, 636
Ginn Development Company, 296
Glantz, Talia, 648
Gledhill, Frank, 519
Global warming, 403
Glover, Quentin, 636
GNP, **see Gross National Product**
Godfrey, Jerome, 635
Gold Digger, 159, 172
Gold Rock Creek (Enterprises Ltd), 296-297, 435, 569
Goldstein, Bernard, 551, 554, 558
Gomez, Sen The Hon Damian A L, 619
Gomez, Archbishop Drexel, 653
Gomez, Roger, 636
Governor General's Cup, 162, 170
Governor's Harbour Resort and Marina Ltd, 295
Grafton, Duchess of, 540
Grafton, Duke of, 535, 540
Grand Bahama Airport Company, 564-565
Grand Bahama Brewing Co Ltd, 598
Grand Bahama Chamber of Commerce, 583-584, 590
Grand Bahama Children's Home, 479, 538, 584
Grand Bahama Development Co (DEVCO), 296, 524, 528
Grand Bahama Humane Society, 580, 594
Grand Bahama International Airport, 564-565, 579, 586
Grand Bahama Port Authority (GBPA), 71, 116, 296-297, 521, 526, 528, 535, 548-549, 561, 564-565, 568, 571, 579-580, 582-586, 590, 595-597, 599, 605
Grand Bahama Power Ltd, 589
Grand Bahama Shipyard, 116, 599, 654
Grand Lucayan Waterway, 581
Grant, Neko C, 560, 631
Gray, Hannah, 637
Gray, The Hon Vergeneas Alfred V, 615, 632
Graycliff, 246, 417, 446
Gray-Evans, Estelle, 636
Green Cay Asset Management, 244, 248
Green Shutters, 126, 128
Greene, Leila, 634
Greene, Bishop Samuel, 649
Greenslade, Ellison Edroy, 649
Grey, Zane, 73, 75, 412

Griffin, The Hon Melanie S, 616, 628
Gris, Claude Le, 648
Gross Domestic Product (GDP), 342, 383-384, 435
Gross National Product (GNP), 384
Grouper, 400, 402-403, 591
Groves, Wallace, 524, 526, 528, 530, 563, 566, 571, 595-596
Guava, 404
Guess Who's Coming to Dinner, 57
Gun permits, 409, 594

H

Hailey, Arthur, 73, 75
Halkitis, Michael B, 622, 633, 635
Hall, Chief Justice Sir Burton, 634, 636
Hall, Chuck, 180-181, 183-185
Hall, Edgar, 636
Hanlan, Patrick, 647
Hanna, Douglas Oden Hames, 649
Hanna, Leroy Stephen, 649
Hansen, Acting Bishop Bonaventure, 152
Harborside at Atlantis, 284, 287, 419, 503
Harbour control, 410, 594
Harmony House, 538
Harrelson, Woody, 220
Harris, Richard, 77
Harry Potter and the Chamber of Secrets, 77
Harry Potter and the Sorcerer's Stone, 77
Hartford, Huntington II, 202, 204, 655
Hassan, Kathleen, 636
Hawes, John, 146, 151, **see also Father Jerome**
Hawksbill Creek Agreement, 412, 566-567, 579, 582, 585-586, 595-596
Hayek, Selma, 220
Hayward, Sir Charles, 528, 600
Hayward, Jack, 528, 530, 588
Health care, 288, 384, 411, 414-415, 471, 478, 596
Heart and Soul, 76
Hedge funds, 235-236, 238, 240, 242, 248, 250, 252
Heliport, 328, 457
Helweg-Larsen, Kjeld, 521
Hemingway, Ernest, 73-74, 412
Henderson, Michael R, 297, 570-571
Hepburn, Dr Davidson L, 57, 59, 647
Hepburn, Katherine, 56
Heritage Tourism Unit, 222
Hermanns, Herman-Josef, 646
Herring, Richard, 645
Higgs, Colin, 634
Higgs, Dr Leon, 635
Hillier, Phillip, 134
Hilton-Bernard, Anita, 634
Hinkley, Timothy, 554-555, 569
Hinn, Pastor Benny, 230
Historical Nassau Renovation Committee, 88
HIV, **see AIDS**
Hoffer & Sons, 69
Hoffer, Harold, 61-62, 68, 70
Hoffer, Norman, 68-69
Hoffer, Steven, 70
HofferSport, 68
Hog Island, 202, 655
Holidays, 414, 476
Holland-America, 259
Holmes Company Ltd, 295
Holmes, Abraham Turton, 134
Holmes, Dr Francis, 134
Holowesko Global Fund, 238, 240, 244
Holowesko, Mark, 236, 238
Home Furniture Company, 64, 70
Homer, Winslow, 76
Hope, Bob, 74
Horizontal markets, 214
Hospers, Dr John, 181, 183
Hotel and Steam Service Act, 104, 412
Hotel Colonial, 68, 104, 106
Hotelier of the World, 189
Hotels encouragement, 416, 440, 590
Hotels Magazine, 189
Humane Society, **see Bahamas Humane Society** and **Grand Bahama Humane Society**
Hunting, 512, 519
Hurricane Floyd, 325, 413
Hurricane Frances, 325, 414, 426, 486, 657
Hurricane Jeanne, 325, 414, 426, 657
Hurricane Michelle, 426
Hurst, Geoffrey, 69-71
Hutchison Whampoa, 563-565
Hutchison Port Holdings (HPH), 383, 563, 580, 596, 598

I

IAT Clinic, 597, 657
IBC, **see International Business Company**
Ibrahim, Mustapha, 636
Iglesias, Julio, 73, 79
Imagination, 114, 151
I Married a Best-Seller, 75
Immigration, 426-431, 467, 593, 597-598, 602
In the Heat of the Night, 57
Inagua National Park, 346-347, 395, 511
Independence Golf Series, 230
Indofoods, 248, 250
Industrial Tribunal, 431, 434, 443
Industries encouragement, 398, 434-435, 440-441, 590
Inflation, 383-384, 500
Ingraham, Hubert A, 628
Ingraham, The Hon James Oswald, 630
Internal Revenue Service, 252, 413, 500
International Bazaar, 528, 599, 604
International Business Company (IBC), 342-343, 352, 362-363, 413, 438
International Maritime Organization (IMO), 112, 118, 475
International Monetary Fund (IMF), 383
International Persons Landholding Act, 466
International Ship and Port Facility Security Code, 657
International Star Class Yacht Racing Association, 164

Into the Blue, 222
Intonti, Pasquale, 648
Investment Funds Act, 242, 250, 473-474
Isaacs, Edward, 67
Isaacs, Janeen, 67
Isaacs, Jon, 636
Isaacs, Sir Kendal G L, 67
Isaacs, Stephen, 636
Isette, Larry B, 530
Island hopping, 291
Island Records, 78
Islanders in the Stream, 64, 148
Islands in the Stream, 74
Isle of Capri Casino, 406-407, 413-414, 551-561, 569, 591-592, 653-654
Izmirlian, Dikran, 284, 655

J

J P Sands' food store, 92
Jacaranda, 126-127
Jagger, Mick, 78
Jagger, Robert S, 646
Jakes, Bishop T D, 230
Jaws, 220
Jewish community, 61-62, 69, 71
John, Elton, 198
Johns, LCDR Terrence M, 640
Johnson, Basil, 655
Johnson, Camille, 634
Johnson, Clifton, 636
Johnson, Howard, 63
Johnson, Mary, 637
Johnson-Sands, Sen The Hon Gladys, 621
Jones, Carlton I, 646
Jones, Grace, 79
Jones, John Mervyn, 636
Jones, Quincy, 53
Judicial system, 441, 599
Junkanoo Club, 98
Junkanoo, 89, 394, 442, 446, 599, 605, 652, 654

K

Kaiser Bauxite, 521
Kayak Nature Tours, 226
Kelekom, Hervé, 646
Kelly, Basil, 652
Kelly's Hardware, 92, 652
Kerzner International, 71, 190, 198, 208, 210, 283, 328, 383, 406, 413-414, 458, 652, 656
Kerzner Unauthorized, 190
Kerzner, Butch, 198, 210, 283
Kerzner, Sol, 71, 189-190, 192, 194, 196, 198, 200, 202, 204, 206, 208, 210, 283, 652
Key, Berlin W, 646-647
Kiekhaefer, Carl, 519
Kimes, Kenneth, 656
King, Brigitte, 214, 216
Kinski, Lynn, 185
Klainguti-Kemp, Katherine Helena, 648
Klein de Schmalzle, Magdalena, 648
Kloihofer, Heinz R, 646
Know Your Customer, 244, 252, 268
Knowles, Devon Arthur, 656
Knowles, Sir Durward, 108, 110, 163
Knowles, Mark, 655, 657
Kravitz, Lenny, 73, 80-81
Kravitz, Syl, 80
Ku Klux Klan, 54
KYC, **see Know Your Customer**

L

Lagan Holdings International, 288
Laing, Rev Lawrence, 649
Lauth, Eddie III, 295
Law, Andrew, 262
Lawrence, John, 162-164, 166-168, 276, 278
Le Saint Geran, 194
Leonard, Stan, 531
Levy, Austin, 66-67
Lewis, Eloise, 96
Libraries, 110, 352, 443, 600
Liddell, Oliver, 167-168
Lightbourn, Mike, 180
Lightbourne, Dennis, 635
Lilies of the Field, 49, 55, 57
Lindroth, Orjan, 100, 289
Lingier, Kristof, 167, 172
Liquor Laws, 444
Literacy, 385
Lizzie Carry Basket on de Head, 76
Llambias, Eddie, 555-557, 561
Lobosky, Reginald, 655
Lockhart, Elkenny, 636
Lofthouse, Harold, 92
Lomé IV, 366, 567, **see also Cotonou Agreement**
Longley, Hartman, 636
Lost City, 200
Lotteries, 444-445
Low, Stanley, 524
Lowe, Clara, 637
Lucayan Beach Hotel, 528
Lucayan Harbour Cruise Facility, 564-566
Lucayan National Park, 226, 347, 511, 580-581, 601
Luis De Torres Synagogue, 61, 71, 604, **see also De Torres, Luis**
Lundy, Martin, 637
Lyons, John, 636

M

Mackey, George, 100
Mademoiselle, 94
Maersk Line, 118, 259, 592
Magistrate's Court 13, 126, 132
Magna Carta Court, 126, 128-130, 132
Mailboats, 445, 505
Major, Michael, 637
Major, Paul, 635
Major, Wendell G, 634
Makaroff, Vadim, 160, 170
Malcolm House, 134
Malcolm, Barry, 521, 532, 561

Malcolm, Harcourt, 134
Malcolm, Sir Osmond, 134
Malone, Brent, 414, 655
Mandela, Nelson, 198
Manning, Terry and Sherrie, 79
Manufacturing, 336, 351, 389, 435, 440-441, 445-446, 454, 476, 498, 585-586
Marcelle, Agatha, 628, 633
Mardi Gras, 108, 112, 442
Marina Village, 208, 283-284, 458, 656
Marine Protected Areas, 395
Marine research, 446-447
Marley, Bob, 78
Marques, Ricardo, 636
Marquis, John, 177
Marriage licence, 450
Marshall, Colin, 637
Marshall, Paula, 637
Martin, The Hon Glenys M E Hanna, 289, 616, 624, 651
Martin Marietta, 565
Mary Carter Paint Co, 204
Massoni, Carmen, 286, 646
Matthews, Sandra G, 570-571
Maynard, Clement T III, 646
Mbeki, Thabo, 198, 654
McCartney, Lennox, 637
McCartney, Sen The Hon Tanya C, 621
McDonald, Ross, 255, 257
McGrath, David, 647
McKee, Crawford, 636
McKenzie, Mellany, 635
McKinney, Andrew, 637
McKinney, George Washington, 649
McNeely, Terrence, 53
McWeeney, Sen The Hon Cyprianna V, 620
McWeeney, Paul, 646
McWeeney, Sean, 262, 264
Meeres, Marilyn, 636
Meeres, Paul, 96
Mellon, Jason, 652
Melvin, Stephen Jenkins, 647
Merchant Shipping Act, 118, 474
Merklein, Mark, 654-655
Merv Griffin's Resorts International, 204
Miami to Nassau Ocean Cup, 159, 161, 166
Miami to Nassau Ocean Race, 159-160, 162, 166, 233
Miami Yacht Club, 162-163
Michael, Ethelyn Bernice, 649
Mike's Shoe Store, 92
Millar, Ruth, 634, 636-637
Millennium Dome, 190
Miller, Earl, 232
Miller, George, 635
Miller, Kimberley, 560
Miller, The Hon Leslie O, 615, 623
Miller, William, 126
Mills, Frank, 80
Misiewicz, Carol, 636
Mitchell, Carleton, 166
Mitchell, The Hon Frederick A, 614, 625
Mohamad, Faizool, 636
Mohegan Sun Casino, 210
Moncur, Eris, 144
Money laundering, 252, 342-343
Monroe, Bjorn, 654
Monson, Lady Rose, 548
Montana Holdings Ltd, 297
Montas, Hernando Perez, 648
Moon Bahamas, 297, 563, 571, 657
Moore House, 129, 132
Moore, Ernest Kingsbury, 129
Moore, Harry Clare, 652
Moore, Maria, 129
Moore, Walter K Jr, 129-130
Morgan, Capt Frederick Chapin, 649
Morgan, Henry, 141
Morgan, J P, 526
Morissette, Alanis, 80
Mosbacher, Bus, 166
Moseley, Edwin Charles, 103
Moss, Anthony Donald Edward, 630
Moss, Sen The Hon Rev Dr C B, 618
Moss, Willie, 116, 296, 564-565
Motor vehicle insurance, 450
Mount Alvernia, 146
Moxey, James, 636
Munargo, 107-108
Munnings, Freddie Jr, 76, 96
Munroe, Judy Virginia Cornell, 649
Munroe, Pastor Miles, 230
Munson Line, 107-108
Munson, Allen, 68
Munson, Walter D, 107
Murray, Jacqueline, 634
Musgrove, R N, 92
Music Box Dancer, 80
Mutual Funds Act, 250, 473
Mutual fund(s), 235-257, 338, 342-343, 473, 500
My Father, the Hero, 220, 412
Myers's Rum, 70

N

Nairn, Archie, 634
Nassau Guardian, ***see The Nassau Guardian***
Nassau International Airport, 288-289, 328, 370, 372, 406, 460, 653, 657
Nassau Jewish Congregation, 67, 70
Nassau Public Library, 122, 126, 443, 451
Nassau Shop, 92
Nassau Tourism and Development Board, 100
Nassau Yacht Club, 162-163
Nassau's Historic Buildings, 98, 103
National Anthem, 455
National Art Gallery, 334, 413
National Baptist Conventions, 228
National Centre for the Performing Arts, 502
National debt, 384
National Insurance, 297, 451-454, 470, 601
National Investment Policy, 339, 439
National park(s), 346-347, 395, 405, 510-511, 580-581, 601
National symbols, 455

Navigator of the Seas, 116
Neilly, Calvin, 649
Nestor, Daniel, 655, 657
New Colonial Hotel, 68
Newry, HE Dr Eugene, 642
Newspapers, 332, 365, 456, 463, 472, 602
Newton, Donna, 636
Niche market, 214, 216, 226, 228
Niels, Albert Jean, 648
Nihon, Robert, 646
Nixon, Richard, 183
No Way Out, 56, 78
Nobel Prize for Literature, 74
North American Free Trade Agreement (NAFTA), 456-457
Norwegian Cruise Line, 112, 118, 557
Norwegian Dawn, 114, 657
No-take zones, 400

O

Oakes, Lady, 126
Oakes, Nancy Von-Hoyningen Huene, 126
Oakes, Shirley Butler, 128
Oakes, Shirley, 126
Oakes, Sir Harry, 126
OAS, **see Organization of American States**
Obeah, 146, 148, 150-151, 154
O'Brien, HE Basil G, 641-643
Oceanic, 108, 110-111, 118, 346
Oceanus North, 528
Oceanus South, 528
Oceanwatch, 396
OECD, **see Organization for Economic Cooperation and Development**
Old Bahama Bay, 296, 306, 420, 449, 463
Old Fort Bay, 287, 289, 302, 405
Oliver, Mike, 176, 183-184
Olympic Games, 163, 413-414, 657
Onderdont, Lorraine, 68
O'Neil, Paul, 210
One&Only Ocean Club, 324, 333-334
Optique Shoppe, 126, 132, 134
Organization for Economic Cooperation and Development (OECD), 257
Organization of American States (OAS), 457
Osadebay, Emmanuel, 636
Out Island Regatta, 52-53, 224
Outten, Sen Caleb E, 620
Outten, Edgar Joseph, 649
Outten, Valerie, 635
Owens, Veronica, 625, 633

P

Palace Hotel, 192
Panther, Patrice, 538
Parliament Buildings, 89
Parliament Hotel, 126, 134, 136
Parliament Street, 121, 124, 126, 136
Passports, 426-427, 458, 602
Patton, Carolyn, 635
Paul, Sir John Warburton, 611
Peet, The Hon Vincent A, 613, 629
Pennerman, Steve, 636
People-To-People, 459-460, 602, 605
Percentie, Ann, 632-633
Perini Brothers, 528
Perini, Lou, 528
Permanent residence, 358, 426, 428, 430-431, 467
Perna, Rev Joseph, 652
Perpetuities Act, 272
Perry Institute, 447
Peterson Cay National Park, 347, 511, 580, 601
Phillips, Hank, 184
Phillips, Lanelle, 558
Piepenbrock, Hartwig, 648
Pinder, Iris, 636
Pinder, Hon John, 127
Pinder, Most Rev Patrick, 652, 654
Pinder, Ron O'Neal, 288, 626, 633
Pinder, Simeon, 635
Pindling, Prime Minister Lynden, 175-177, 289, 412-413
Pindling-Sands, Sen The Hon Michelle M, 619
Pirie, Lockwood, 166
PLP, **see Progressive Liberal Party**
Poitier, Evelyn, 50
Poitier, Reginald, 50
Poitier, HE Sir Sidney, 49-59, 77, 642
Police certificates, 602
Police force, **see Royal Bahamas Police Force**
Polymers International, 567
Pompey Museum of Slavery and Emancipation, 89, 332
Porel, Jan, 526
Port Lucaya Marina, 232, 449, 601
Port Lucaya Marketplace, 306, 561, 591, 600, 602, 604
Ports of entry, 328, 370, 372, 427, 460, 462
Potter's Cay, 98, 325, 405, 464, 505
Powles, Liston Diston, 150
Pratt, Deputy Prime Minister Cynthia A "Mother," 292, 297, 413, 549, 613
Preston, Billy, 81
Prince George Dock, 98, 289, 368, 407
Princess Margaret Hospital (PMH), 288, 328, 365, 385, 391, 414, 416, 471, 478
Pritchard, Asa H, 92
PRK Holdings, 657
Proceeds of Crime Act, 252, 342-343, 382
Progressive Liberal Party (PLP), 176, 179, 181, 412-413, 654
Prohibition, 87, 92, 412, 595
Property tax, 425, 464, 466, 468, 567, 590, 595
Property transactions, 466, 602
Prudden, Harry, 134
Public finance, 467-468
Public Market, 90
Purpose trusts, 272

Q

Qualified Jurisdiction, 413
Quant, Sterling, 637
Quant-Forbes, Lillian, 637

Quarterly Economic Review, 286
Queen Elizabeth, 108, 413, 421, 473, 480, 483, 485, 501
Queen Mary 2, 565
Queen Victoria, 89, 121
Queen's Counsel, 409, 442

R

Radio stations, 349, 603, **see also Broadcasting**
Rahming-Mackey, Erma, 636
Rainbow Alliance, 657
Rake 'n scrape, 394
Rand Memorial Hospital, 414, 416, 471, 478, 580, 590, 593, 596, 600
Rand, Ayn, 183
Rassin Hospital, 65
Rassin, Dr Meyer, 65
Re-Earth, 396
Registrar General's Department, 270
Religious tourism, 228
Revonoc II, 161
RIU Hotels & Resorts, 284, 655
RJH Holdings, 297, 657
Roberts, ASP Alexander, 635
Roberts, Brad, 80
Roberts, The Hon Bradley Bernard, 294, 622
Roberts, E Dawson, 130
Roberts, Enoch Pedro II , 649
Roberts, Rupert Winer, 649
Rodgers, George, 635
Rodgers, Dr K J A, 647
Rodgers, Dr Patricia, 634
Rodney Bain Building, 126, 128-129
Rogers, David, 128
Rogers, Woodes, 86, 408, 411, 505
Roker, Roxie, 80
Rolle, Arthur, 636
Rolle, Brensil, 637
Rolle, Commodore Davy, 635
Rolle, Garth, 652
Rolle, Greg, 216, 218
Rolle, John, 635
Rolle, Raymond, 157
Rolling Stones, 78
Rood, John D, 414, 640, 656
Rosenberg, Wilf, 196, 198
Royal Bahamas Defence Force, 469, 472-473
Royal Bahamas Police Force, 178, 367-368, 398, 469, 472, 477
Royal Bahamas Police Force Band, 473
Royal Nassau Sailing Club, 80, 172
Royal Victoria Hotel, 68, 90, 103-104, 106, 122, 124, 126, 412
Rubin's, 69-70
Rum-runners, 87, 595
Russell, Christopher, 636
Russell, Kenneth, 631
Russell, Lindy H, 630
Russell, Patrenda, 636
Russell, T Seighbert, 103
Russell, Wade, 288
Rutherford, Geneva, 546

S

Saadi, Anthony Baker, 90
Sadkin, Alex, 79
Salem Baptist Church, 132
Samaritan Ministry, 327, 360
Sandals Royal Bahamian, 383, 418, 483
Sandilands Psychiatric Hospital, 415
Sandilands Rehabilitation Centre, 288, 414-415, 471, 478
Sands, Basil L, 647
Sands, Leevan, 652
Sands, Sir Stafford, 94, 130, 213
Saunders, Ansil, 654
Saunders, Rev Dr Charles W, 634
Saunders, Cyril, 635
Saunders, Dr D Gail, 64, 66, 68, 104, 132, 148, 333-334, 635
Savary, Peter de, 292
Save The Bahamas Campaign, 657
Sawyer, Dame Joan, 636
Saxon Superstars, 654
Scavella, Clifford, 637
Schoonmaker, Ding, 164
Scott, Bon, 80
Scott, Patricia, 518
Sea Hauler, 651-652
Sears, The Hon Alfred M, 58-59, 614, 624
Sears, HE Joshua, 641-643
Secessionists, 175
Securities and Exchange Control (SEC), 242, 244, 248, 500
Securities Board Act, 250
Securities Commission, 236, 242, 248, 250, 338, 473-474, 656
Securities Industry Act, 250, 361, 413, 473-474
Seligman, Ralph D, 65-66, 442, 646-647
Separatists, 175, 179
Seymour, Antoinette, 148
Seymour, Keith Sr, 236
Shakira, 80
Shedden, Roscow, 150
Shepherd, Jimmy, 414, 654
Sheraton Grand Resort, 324, 419
Sherman, Godfrey, 637
Shimkus, Joanna, 56
Ship registration, 441, 474-475
Ship registry, 258, 435, 474
Siebels, Jane, 236, 244
Silence of The Lambs, 220
Silvera, Bruce, 519
Silvera, Darryl, 519
Silvera, Doug, 517, 519, 526
Silvera, Doug Jr, 519
Simmons, Sir Oliver, 68
Simms, Alice, 76, 96
Simon, Carly, 78
Simpson, Wallace, 88
Sinatra, Frank, 96, 198
Skala, Lilia, 55
Small, Hugh, 636
Smith, Alvin A, 630

Smith, Frank E, 628
Smith, Sen the Hon James H, 255, 617-618
Smith, HE Keod M, 626, 644
Smith, HE Philip, 641-642, 644
Smith, Prescott, 232
Smith, Selwyn, 648
Smithsonian Folklife Festival, 222
Snorkelling, 247, 324, 481-482, 511, 587, 601
Society of Trust and Estate Practitioners (STEP), 262, 278
Solomon Bros Ltd, 94
Solomon Group of Companies, 94
Solomon, Fane, 94, 652
Solomon, Norman, 85, 94, 100
Southern Sun Hotels, 194
Sponging, 333
Sports venues, 480, 604
SS Miami, 104, 106
SS Morton, 124
SS Nassau, 108
St Augustine's Monastery, 151
St Francis of Assisi, 141, 151
St George, Edward, 535, 549
St George, Lady Henrietta, 535-536, 540, 549, 589
St Matthew's Cemetery, 70, 333
Staniel Cay, 218, 330, 392, 416
Starwood Hotels & Resorts Worldwide Inc, 554
Stat Care Medical & Emergency Centre, 392, 415
Steinbeck, John, 73-74, 412
Stevens, Olin, 160
Stock exchange, 250
Strachan, Stephana, 636
Straw market, 90, 451, 486, 599, 601-602
Stuart, Charles, 637
Stubbs, Fritz G H, 647
Stubbs, Irene, 634
Stubbs, Joel, 652
Stubbs, Sidney, 625, 653
Sturrup, Creswell, 634
Sturrup, Justin A, 635
Suisse Security Bank and Trust, 656
Sun City, 194, 196, 198, 200
Sun International Hotels Ltd, 190, 413
Sundance Film Festival, 222
Sutton-Burke, LaFonda, 640
Swain, Subusola Lawanson, 636
Sweeting, Robert Percival Jr, 629
Symmonett, Christopher (Chris), 635, 656
Symonette, Bobby, 161, 171
Symonette, Brent, 626
Symonette, Craig, 653
Symonette, George, 76
Symonette, Michael, 635
Symonette, Sir Roland, 159, 161, 175, 181, 412
Synagogue, 61-62, 71, 604

T

Tariff Act, 370, 435, 440
Tax benefits, 276, 486, 493, 497, 500, 582
Tax haven, 488, 495, 605
Taylor, Berkley "Peanuts," 76, 96, 98
Taylor, Sir Henry Milton, 611
Taylor, Michael, 640
Teekay Shipping, 118, 259
Telecommunications, 157, 350, 354, 407, 410, 413, 438, 501, 605
Temple of the Moon, 206, 208
Temple of the Sun, 206, 208
Templeton funds, 236, 238
Templeton, Sir John, 236, 238
Texaco, 259
The Central Bank of The Bahamas, 274, 283, 286, 333, 340-342, 344, 362, 382-384, 396-398, 431, 438, 440, 451, 591, 593, 598, 656
The Dissident Eight, 179, 654
The Grapes of Wrath, 74
The Hermitage, 152
The Nassau Guardian, 64, 103-104, 111, 134, 164, 179, 456, 602, 656
The Old Man and the Sea, 74
The Pink Pearl, 150
The Retreat, 132, 339, 511
The Strand, 86
The Tribune, 106, 110, 177, 185, 349, 456, 602, 653
The Village, 535, 542, 548-549
Thompson, Andrew, 636
Thompson, Harrison, 634
Thompson, Jack, 641
Thompson, Jeanne, 636
Thompson, Leonard, 179-180
Thompson, Linda, 228, 230
Thompson, Maxwell James, 653
Thompson, Ronald, 634
Thompson, Archdeacon William, 656
Thunderball, 75, 246, 412, 569
Tiamo Nature Resort, 226
Timeshare, 208, 210, 287, 297, 414, 441, 502-503
Time-sharing, 502
Tinker, Dr Keith, 98, 100, 332
Todhunter-Mitchell, 599
Torode, Graham, 296
Torres, Luis De, 61-62, 71, 604
Tourism Encouragement Act, 213
Toussaint, Andre, 76
Tracey, Spencer, 56
Tractebel Calypso Pipeline LLC, 567
Tractebel, 567-568
Trade unions, 504, 605
Trotman, Evangelist Alma Oleta, 649
Trustee Act, 264, 439
Tucker, Freddie, 642
Turner, Robert Edward (Ted) III, 162, 166, 170
Turnquest, Autherine, 637
Turnquest, Sen The Hon O A T (Tommy), 621
Turnquest, Sir Orville A, 611, 621
Turnquest, Sen The Hon Yvette Natasha, 619
Turnquest, Tex, 636
Twain, Shania, 73, 79
Tynes, Maurice, 636

UV

UNESCO, 49, 57-59, 385, 396
UNEXSO, 481, 587
United Bahamian Party (UBP), 94, 175, 178-179, 181, 346, 655
United Star, 651
University of the Witwatersrand, 192
Upon These Rocks, 154
Ups and Downs in a West Indian Diocese, 150
US Civil War, 87
US Libertarian party, 181, 183
US War of Independence, 87, 143
Valentine's Resort & Marina, 328, 424, 484
Valley Boys, 442, 654
Valluri, Kamanna, 258-259
Value-added tax, 373
Vamarie, 159-160, 170
Vanderpool-Wallace, Vincent, 637
Varence, Joycelyn, 635
Vehicle inspection, 380
Vendue House, 89, 129, 451
Vertical market, 214
Veterinarians, 338, 506, 606
Villa Doyle, 334, 413
Virgill, Linda, 636
Vismara, Michaelangela, 648
Voodoo, 148

W

Wachtmeister, Gustaf, 648
Wahoo Championship Series, 232
Waldorf, Art, 519
Walker, Paul, 222
Walkine, H C, 634
Wallace, Ernie, 636
Wallace-Whitfield, Cecil, 179
War of Independence, 87, 143-144
Warren, Wendy, 242, 264, 274, 276, 337
Warry, Charles Bennett, 127
Wassitsch, Pedro G, 646
Water-skiing, 247, 348
Watkins, Errington Washington, 177-181, 185
Watkins, Vera, 636
Watson, Clint, 230
Weech, Catherine, 637
Weech-Gomez, Jeanine, 636
Wendy's restaurants, 94
Wenner-Gren, Axel, 202, 655
WerBell, Mitchell Livingston III,183-184, 185
Wernli, Beat, 647
Whales, 403, 446
Whitehead, Analia, 647
WHO, **see World Health Organization**
Whylly, Sen The Hon Traver Ricardo, 620
Wiberg, S Anders, 646-647
Wilchcombe, The Hon Obediah H, 164, 291, 557, 614, 632, 653
Wild horses, 403
Wildlife Preserves, 510
William's Shoe Store, 70, 92
Williams, Anthony, 642
Williams, Dr Celestine, 635
Williams, Charmaine, 642-643
Williams, Franklyn, 636
Williams, Melanie, 635
Williams, Michelle, 642
Williams-Darling, Tonique, 414, 651, 655-657
Williemae Pratt Centre for Girls, 653
Wilson, Mark, 634
Wilson, Sen The Hon Sharon R, 618
Windermere Corporate Management, 276
Windsor, Duke of, 67, 87, 126, 408, 412
Wisdom, The Hon Neville W, 615, 623
Woodes Rodgers Wharf, 87
Woods, Craig, 218, 220, 569-570
Woods, Yvonne, 222
Woodside, Anthony, 635
Woodside, Christopher, 653
Woon, Maurice, 524
Work permit, 358, 380, 427-431, 598
World Health Organization (WHO), 467, 470, 505-506
World Heritage Site, 289
World Trade Organization (WTO), 406, 512
Wouk, Herman, 81
Wreck Commission, 651
Wrinkle, Jean, 136
Wrinkle, Skip, 136
Wrinkle, Steve, 136
WTO, **see World Trade Organization**

XYZ

Yachtsman's Guide to The Bahamas, 142
Yamada, Shoichi, 648
Yanowitz, William, 70
Yap, Ken, 524
Yardimci, Kemal, 648
Yarmouth Castle, 111-112
Yip, Patrick, 524
YMCA, 543, 584, 604
You Only Live Twice, 76
Yule, Alyson I, 278
YWCA, 360, 480
Zane, Billy, 222
Zhang, Yu, 640
ZNS, 501-502, 512, 605
Zonicle, Mellany, 637
Zonicle, Sen The Hon Paulette E, 620

TO ORDER DIRECT FROM THE BAHAMAS

Please rush me the
NEW
2006
edition of
BAHAMAS *handbook*
as soon as it is available

SOFTBACK EDITION

	US$*
USA	68.95
CANADA	74.95
OTHER COUNTRIES	77.95

*Price includes $35.95 per book and courier charges (2-3 day delivery).
Contact publisher for bulk rates.

Name ____________________
Street ____________________ City ____________________
State or Province ____________________ Zip/Postal code ____________________
Country ____________________ Tel # (____) ____________________
E-mail ____________________ Fax # (____) ____________________

Payment in US$ must be enclosed *(money order or bank draft only)*
Bahamas Handbook, PO Box N-7513, 51 Hawthorne Rd, Nassau, The Bahamas,
tel: (242) 323-5665, fax: (242) 323-5728, e-mail: handbook@dupuch.com

1.

TO ORDER DIRECT FROM THE BAHAMAS

Please rush me the
NEW
2006
edition of
BAHAMAS *handbook*
as soon as it is available

SOFTBACK EDITION

	US$*
USA	68.95
CANADA	74.95
OTHER COUNTRIES	77.95

*Price includes $35.95 per book and courier charges (2-3 day delivery).
Contact publisher for bulk rates.

Name ____________________
Street ____________________ City ____________________
State or Province ____________________ Zip/Postal code ____________________
Country ____________________ Tel # (____) ____________________
E-mail ____________________ Fax # (____) ____________________

Payment in US$ must be enclosed *(money order or bank draft only)*
Bahamas Handbook, PO Box N-7513, 51 Hawthorne Rd, Nassau, The Bahamas,
tel: (242) 323-5665, fax: (242) 323-5728, e-mail: handbook@dupuch.com

2.

WORLDWIDE CREDIT CARD ORDERS

Please contact:

Taylor & Francis Inc
10650 Toebben Dr
Independence, KY 41051, USA

Tel (859) 525-2230
Fax (859) 647-5027
Toll-free 1-800-634-7064
Toll-free Fax 1-800-248-4724

Please reference code: BH 06

FOR INFORMATION AND ORDERS WITHIN THE BAHAMAS

Please contact:

Etienne Dupuch Jr Publications
PO Box N-7513, 51 Hawthorne Rd
Nassau, The Bahamas
Tel (242) 323-5665
Fax (242) 323-5728

Visit us online:
www.bahamashandbook.com
E-mail: handbook@dupuch.com